AMERICA

DETAIL OF ENGRAVING BASED ON
THE CHASM OF THE COLORADO
BY THOMAS MORAN

AMERICA

A NARRATIVE HISTORY

SIXTH EDITION
VOLUME II

GEORGE BROWN TINDALL
DAVID E. SHI

W · W · NORTON & COMPANY · NEW YORK · LONDON

FOR BRUCE AND SUSAN
AND FOR BLAIR

FOR
JASON AND JESSICA

Copyright © 2004, 1999, 1996, 1992, 1988, 1984 by W. W. Norton & Company, Inc.

Printed in the United States of America

Composition by TechBooks
Manufacturing by Courier Westford, Inc.
Book design by Antonina Krass
Editor: Steve Forman
Manuscript editor: Jan Hoeper
Project editor: Lory A. Frenkel
Production manager: JoAnn Simony
Editorial assistant: Sarah England
Cartographer: CARTO-GRAPHICS/Alice Thiede and William Thiede,
with relief maps from Mountain High Maps®, Digital Wisdom, Inc.

Acknowledgments and copyrights continue on page A101,
which serves as a continuation of the copyright page.

The Library of Congress has cataloged the one-volume edition as follows:

Tindall, George Brown.
    America : a narrative history / George Brown Tindall,
David Emory Shi.—6th ed.
        p.   cm.
    Includes bibliographical references and index.
    ISBN 0-393-97812-5
    1. United States—History.   I. Shi, David E. II.   Title.
E178.1 .T55 2003   2003051038
973—dc21

ISBN 0-393-92427-0 (pbk.)

W. W. Norton & Company, Inc., 500 Fifth Avenue, New York, N.Y. 10110
www.wwnorton.com
W. W. Norton & Company Ltd., Castle House, 75/76 Wells Street, London W1T 3QT

1 2 3 4 5 6 7 8 9 0

*W. W. Norton & Company has been independent since its founding in
1923, when William Warder Norton and Mary D. Herter Norton first published lectures delivered at the People's Institute, the adult education division of New York City's Cooper Union. The Nortons soon expanded their
program beyond the Institute, publishing books by celebrated academics
from America and abroad. By mid-century, the two major pillars of Norton's
publishing program—trade books and college texts—were firmly established. In the 1950s, the Norton family transferred control of the company
to its employees, and today—with a staff of four hundred and a comparable
number of trade, college, and professional titles published each year—
W. W. Norton & Company stands as the largest and oldest publishing
house owned wholly by its employees.*

CONTENTS

*P*ART SIX / **MODERN AMERICA**

$\mathcal{P}$ART SEVEN / **THE AMERICAN AGE**

MAPS

PREFACE

Just as history is never complete, neither is a historical textbook. We have learned much from the responses of readers and instructors to the first five editions of *America: A Narrative History.* Perhaps the most important and reassuring lesson is that our original intention has proved valid: to provide a compelling narrative history of the American experience, a narrative animated by human characters, informed by analysis and social texture, and guided by the unfolding of events. Readers have also endorsed the book's distinctive size and format. *America* is designed to be read and to carry a moderate price.

As in previous revisions of *America,* we have adopted an overarching theme that informs many of the new sections we introduce throughout the Sixth Edition. In previous editions we have traced such broad-ranging themes as immigration, the frontier and the West, and popular culture. In each case we blend our discussions of the selected theme into the narrative, where they reside through succeeding editions.

The Sixth Edition of *America* highlights the social, political, cultural, and economic history of work in American life. Frederick Douglass, the former slave who became a leading abolitionist, declared in 1853 that Americans are not valued "for what they are; they are valued for what they can do." Work, of course, is a central aspect of human endeavor; it forms an indelible part of our lives. Labor structures our days and transforms the world we live in. It helps shape our identities and define our possibilities. Through almost four centuries of American history, workers have built, sustained, and transformed the economy. Their everyday lives have helped shape American society and culture. Their needs and aspirations have fueled American politics at every level and have been mediated by the courts. The history of work takes in all dimensions of American history.

The Sixth Edition of *America* includes new material reflecting this expansive sense of the history of work in the United States. Here are some of the highlights:

- Chapter 3 includes a new discussion of shipbuilding in colonial New England that explores maritime work and its significance in the colonial economy
- Chapter 9 explores how the emerging factory system changed the nature of work for many laborers
- Chapter 12 includes an expanded discussion of early labor organization and the rise of professions
- Chapter 14 includes a section on the Spanish missions in California and their use of Indian labor
- Chapter 15 offers a new discussion of slave women and their work
- Chapter 20 has been revised and includes an expanded discussion of the rise of big business after the Civil War, a new section on child labor and its regulation, and a profile of the colorful labor organizer Mother Jones
- Chapter 26 features new sections on women workers and Margaret Sanger's efforts to educate them on the issue of birth control
- Chapter 27 includes a section on the dramatic strike at the Loray textile mills in Gastonia, North Carolina, in 1929
- Later chapters include new discussions of the rise of high-tech industry and how the expanding service sector has compensated for dwindling manufacturing jobs, with widespread effects on work and society.

Beyond these explorations of work in American history, we have introduced other new discussions throughout the Sixth Edition. We have revised the book to reflect the best of recent scholarship and we feel confident that the text provides students an excellent introduction to the current state of scholarship in American history.

We are pleased that even with the addition of rich new material throughout, we have managed to reduce the length of *America* by almost 10 percent in the Sixth Edition. This was not achieved by crash diet, but by the authorial equivalent to regular exercise: the careful pruning of detail throughout the book. We trust that the result retains all the character and color that students and instructors have prized in the book, but in a trimmer form.

To enhance the pedagogical features of the text, we have included a **Glossary** in this new edition. It provides a handy reference for checking basic events, concepts, legal decisions, and so on. The Glossary was researched and drafted by Brenda Eagles with the assistance of Charles Eagles.

A new item to supplement this edition is *The Norton Map Workbook in American History.* It includes a range of work-maps covering the core of American history from the colonial period to the present. Questions for each map reinforce students' skills in geography and probe their knowledge of historical events.

We have also revised the outstanding ancillary package that supplements the text. *For the Record: A Documentary History of America,* Second Edition, by David E. Shi and Holly A. Mayer (Duquesne University), is a rich resource with over 300 primary source readings from diaries, journals, newspaper articles, speeches, government documents, and novels. It also has four special chapters on interpreting illustrations and photographs as historical documents. The *Study Guide,* by Charles Eagles (University of Mississippi), is another valuable resource. This edition contains chapter outlines, learning objectives, timelines, expanded vocabulary exercises, and many new short-answer and essay questions. *America: A Narrative History* Online Tutor, prepared by Tom Pearcy (Slippery Rock University), is an online collection of tools for review and research. It includes chapter summaries, review questions and quizzes, interactive map exercises, timelines, and research modules, many new to this edition. *Norton Presentation Maker* is a CD-ROM slide and text resource that includes images from the text, four-color maps, additional images from the Library of Congress archives, and audio files of significant historical speeches. Finally, the *Instructor's Manual and Test Bank,* by Mark Goldman (Tallahassee Community College) includes a test bank of short-answer and essay questions, as well as detailed chapter outlines, lecture suggestions, and bibliographies.

In preparing the Sixth Edition, we have benefited from the insights and suggestions of many people. Some of these insights have come from student readers of the text and we encourage such feedback. Among the scholars and survey instructors who offered us their comments and suggestions are: James C. Cobb (University of Georgia), Kara Miles Turner (Virginia State University), Vernon Burton (University of Illinois), Blanche Brick, Cathy Lively, Harley Haussman and others at the Bryan campus of Blinn College, Charles Eagles (University of Mississippi), Timothy Gilfoyle (Loyola University), James M. Russell (University of Tennessee, Chattanooga), Matthew Plowman (Waldorf College), and Rand Burnette (MacMurray College). Our special thanks go to Tom Pearcy (Slippery Rock University) for all of his work on the timelines. Once again, we thank our friends at W. W. Norton, especially Steve Forman, Steve Hoge, Sarah England, Neil Hoos, Kate Barry, Lory Frenkel, JoAnn Simony, Karl Bakeman, and Matt Arnold, for their care and attention along the way.

—George B. Tindall
—David E. Shi

18 ✧ RECONSTRUCTION:
NORTH AND SOUTH

CHAPTER ORGANIZER

This chapter focuses on:

- the different approaches to Reconstruction.

- congressional efforts to reshape southern society.

- the role of African Americans in the early postwar years.

- national politics in the 1870s.

*I*n the spring of 1865 the cruel war was over. At a frightful cost of 620,000 lives and the destruction of the southern economy and much of its landscape, American nationalism had emerged triumphant, and nearly 4 million slaves had seized their freedom. Ratification of the Thirteenth Amendment in December 1865 abolished slavery throughout the Union. But peace had come only on the battlefields. "Cannon conquer," recognized a northern editor, "but they do not necessarily convert." Now the North faced the task of re-uniting the nation, coming to terms with the abolition of slavery, and "reconstructing" a ravaged and resentful South.

THE WAR'S AFTERMATH

In the war's aftermath, important questions faced the victors in the North: Should the Confederate leaders be tried for treason? How should new governments be formed? How and at whose expense was the South's economy to be rebuilt? Should debts incurred by Confederate state governments be honored? Who should pay to rebuild the South's railroads and public buildings, dredge the clogged southern harbors, and restore damaged levees? What was to be done with the freed slaves? Were they to be given land? social equality? education? voting rights? Such complex questions required sober reflection and careful planning, but policy makers did not have the luxury of time or the benefits of consensus.

DEVELOPMENT IN THE NORTH   To some Americans the Civil War had been more truly a social revolution than the War of Independence, for it reduced the once-dominant power of the South's planter elite in national politics and elevated the power of the northern "captains of industry." Government became more friendly to business leaders and unfriendly to those who would probe into their activities. The wartime Republican Congress had delivered on the major platform promises of 1860, which had cemented the allegiance of northeastern businessmen and western farmers to the party of free labor.

In the absence of southern members, Congress during the war had centralized national power and enacted the Republican economic agenda. It passed the Morrill Tariff, which doubled the average level of import duties. The National Banking Act created a uniform system of banking and bank-note currency, and helped to finance the war. Congress also passed legislation guaranteeing that the first transcontinental railroad would run along a north-central route from Omaha, Nebraska, to Sacramento, California, and it donated public lands and public bonds to ensure its financing. In the Homestead Act of 1862, moreover, Congress voted free homesteads of 160 acres to settlers. They only had to occupy the land for five years to gain title. The Morrill Land Grant Act of the same year conveyed to each state 30,000 acres of federal land per member of Congress from the state. The sale of some of the land provided funds to create colleges of "agriculture and mechanic arts." Such measures helped stimulate the North's economy in the years after the Civil War.

DEVASTATION IN THE SOUTH   The postwar South, where most of the fighting had occurred, offered a sharp contrast to the victorious North. Along the path of General William T. Sherman's army, one observer reported in 1866, the countryside "looked for many miles like a broad black streak of ruin and desolation." Columbia, South Carolina, said another witness, was "a wilderness of ruins," Charleston a place of "vacant houses, of widowed women, of rotting wharves, of deserted warehouses, of weed-wild gardens, of miles of grass-grown streets, of acres of pitiful and voiceless barrenness." In 1866 fully one-fifth of Mississippi's state revenues went to purchase artificial limbs for returning Confederate soldiers. The border states of Missouri and Kentucky had experienced a guerrilla war that lapsed into postwar anarchy as marauding bands of bushwhackers turned into outlaws. The most notorious were the James boys, Frank and Jesse.

Throughout the South, property values had collapsed. Confederate bonds and paper money were worthless; most railroads were damaged or destroyed. Cotton that had escaped destruction was seized by federal troops. Emancipation of the slaves wiped out perhaps $4 billion invested in human flesh and left the labor system in disarray. The great age of expansion in the cotton market was over. Not until 1879 would

The "burned district" of Richmond, Virginia, April 1865.

the cotton crop again equal the record harvest of 1860; tobacco production did not regain its prewar level until 1880; the sugar crop of Louisiana not until 1893; and the old rice industry of the Tidewater and the hemp industry of the Kentucky Blue Grass never regained their prewar status.

A TRANSFORMED SOUTH   The defeat of the Confederacy transformed much of southern society. The freeing of slaves, the destruction of property, and the free fall in land values left many planters destitute and homeless. Amanda Worthington, a planter's wife from Mississippi, saw her whole world destroyed. In the fall of 1865, she assessed the damage: "None of us can realize that we are no longer wealthy—yet thanks to the yankees, the cause of all unhappiness, such is the case."

Genteel southerners found themselves forced to rebuild lives and families without the help of slaves. Women accustomed to relying on slaves for their every need were unprepared for the tasks at hand. "I did the washing for six weeks," one tired woman wrote, "[and] came near ruining myself for life as I was too delicately raised for such hard work." Those who still had some money after the war often recruited former slaves to work as domestic servants. Now, however, they had to pay for their services.

After the Civil War many former Confederates were so embittered by defeat that they abandoned their native region rather than submit to "Yankee rule." Some migrated to Canada, Europe, Mexico, South America, and Asia. Others preferred the western territories and states. Still others moved north, settling in northern and midwestern cities on the assumption that educational and economic opportunities would be better among the victors.

Those who remained in the South found old social roles reversed. One Confederate army captain reported that on his father's plantation "Our negroes are living in great comfort. They were delighted to see me with overflowing affection. They waited on me as before, gave me breakfast, splendid dinners, etc. But they firmly and respectfully informed me: 'We own this land now. Put it out of your head that it will ever be yours again.'"

Union troops that fanned out across the defeated South were cursed and spat upon. A Virginia woman expressed a spirited defiance common among her circle of friends: "Every day, every hour, that I live increases my hatred and detestation, and loathing of that race. They [Yankees] disgrace our common humanity. As a people I consider them vastly inferior to the better classes of our slaves." Fervent southern nationalists, both men and women, planted in their children a similar hatred of Yankees and a defiance of northern rule. One mother said that she trained her children to "fear God, love the South, and live to avenge her."

LEGALLY FREE, SOCIALLY BOUND In the former Confederate states, the newly freed slaves suffered most of all. According to the black abolitionist Frederick Douglass, the former slave remained dependent: "He had neither money, property, nor friends. He was free from the old plantation, but he had nothing but the dusty road under his feet. . . . He was turned loose, naked, hungry, and destitute to the open sky."

A few northerners argued that what the ex-slaves needed most was their own land. But even dedicated abolitionists shrank from proposals to confiscate white-owned land and distribute it to the freed slaves. Citizenship and legal rights were one thing, wholesale confiscation of property and land redistribution quite another. Discussions of land distribution, however, fueled false rumors that freed slaves would get

According to a former Confederate general, recently freed blacks had "nothing but freedom."

"forty acres and a mule," a slogan that swept the South at the end of the war. Instead of land or material help, the freed slaves more often got advice and moral platitudes.

THE FREEDMEN'S BUREAU   On March 3, 1865, Congress set up within the War Department the Bureau of Refugees, Freedmen, and Abandoned Lands, to provide "such issues of provisions, clothing, and fuel" as might be needed to relieve "destitute and suffering refugees and freedmen and their wives and children." Agents of the Freedmen's Bureau were entrusted with negotiating labor contracts (something new for both blacks and planters), providing medical care, and setting up schools, often in cooperation with northern agencies such as the American Missionary Association and the Freedmen's Aid Society. The bureau had its own courts to deal with labor disputes and land titles, and its agents were further authorized to supervise trials involving blacks in other courts.

White intransigence and the failure to grasp the intensity of racial prejudice increasingly thwarted the efforts of Freedmen's Bureau agents to protect and assist the former slaves. Congress was not willing

The Freedmen's Bureau set up schools such as this throughout the former Confederate states.

to strengthen the powers of the Freedmen's Bureau to reflect such problems. Beyond temporary relief measures, no program of Reconstruction ever incorporated much more than constitutional and legal rights for freedmen. These were important in themselves, of course, but the extent to which even these should go was very uncertain, to be settled more by the course of events than by any clear-cut commitment to social and economic equality.

THE BATTLE OVER RECONSTRUCTION

The problem of reconstructing the South politically centered on deciding what governments would constitute authority in the defeated states. This problem arose first in the state of Virginia at the very beginning of the Civil War, when the thirty-five western counties of Virginia refused to go along with secession. In 1861 a loyal state government of Virginia was proclaimed at Wheeling, and this government in turn formed a new state called West Virginia, admitted to the Union in 1863. As Union forces advanced into the South, Lincoln in 1862 named military governors for Tennessee, Arkansas, and Louisiana. By the end of the following year he had formulated a plan for regular governments in those states and any others that might be liberated from Confederate rule.

LINCOLN'S PLAN AND CONGRESS'S RESPONSE   Acting under his pardon power, President Lincoln issued in late 1863 a Proclamation of Amnesty and Reconstruction, under which any rebel state could form a Union government whenever a number equal to 10 percent of those who had voted in 1860 took an oath of allegiance to the Constitution and the Union and had received a presidential pardon. Participants also had to swear support for laws and proclamations dealing with emancipation. Certain groups, however, were excluded from the pardon: civil and diplomatic officers of the Confederacy; senior officers of the Confederate army and navy; judges, congressmen, and military officers of the United States who had left their federal posts to aid the rebellion; and those accused of failure to treat captured black soldiers and their officers as prisoners of war.

Under this plan, governments loyal to the Union appeared in Tennessee, Arkansas, and Louisiana, but Congress recognized them neither by representation nor in counting the electoral votes of 1864. In the absence of any specific provisions for Reconstruction in the Constitution, politicians disagreed as to where authority properly rested. Lincoln claimed the right to direct Reconstruction under the clause that set forth the presidential pardon power, and also under the constitutional obligation of the United States to guarantee each state a republican form of government. Republican congressmen, however, argued that this obligation implied that Congress, not the president, should supervise Reconstruction.

A few conservative and most moderate Republicans supported Lincoln's program of immediate restoration. The small but influential group of Radical Republicans, however, favored a sweeping transformation of southern society based on granting freedmen full-fledged citizenship. The Radicals hoped to reconstruct southern society so as to mirror the North's emphasis on small-scale capitalism. This meant thwarting the efforts of the old planter class to reestablish a caste system and keep the freed blacks in a state of peonage.

The Radicals were talented, earnest men who insisted that Congress control the Reconstruction program. To this end, they helped pass in 1864 the Wade-Davis Bill, sponsored by Senator Benjamin Wade of Ohio and Representative Henry Winter Davis of Maryland. In contrast to Lincoln's 10 percent plan, the Wade-Davis Bill required that a majority of white male citizens declare their allegiance and that only those who could take an "ironclad" oath (required of federal officials since 1862) attesting to their *past* loyalty could vote or serve in the state constitutional conventions. The conventions, moreover, would have to abolish slavery, exclude from political rights high-ranking civil and military officers of the Confederacy, and repudiate debts incurred during the conflict.

Passed during the closing day of the session, the Wade-Davis Bill never became law. Lincoln exercised a pocket veto. That is, he simply refused to sign it, but he issued an artful statement that he would accept any state back into the Union that preferred to present itself under the congressional plan. In retaliation, furious Republicans penned the Wade-Davis Manifesto, which accused the president, among other sins, of usurping power and attempting to use readmitted states to ensure his reelection.

Lincoln offered his last view of Reconstruction in his final public address, on April 11, 1865. Speaking from the White House balcony, he pronounced that the Confederate states had never left the Union. These states were simply "out of their proper practical relation with the Union," and the object was to get them "into their proper practical relation." At a cabinet meeting, Lincoln proposed to get new southern state governments in operation before Congress met in December. He described the Radical Republicans as possessing feelings of hate and vindictiveness with which he did not sympathize and could not participate. He wanted "no persecution, no bloody work," no radical restructuring of southern social and economic life.

THE ASSASSINATION OF LINCOLN On the evening of April 14, Lincoln went to Ford's Theater and his rendezvous with death. With his trusted bodyguard called away to Richmond and with the policeman assigned to his box away from his post watching the play, Lincoln was helpless as John Wilkes Booth slipped into the presidential box. Booth, a crazed actor and Confederate zealot, blocked the door to the box and fired his derringer point-blank at the president's head. He then stabbed Lincoln's aide and jumped from the box onto the stage, crying *"Sic semper tyrannis"* (Thus always to tyrants), the motto of Virginia.

The funeral procession for President Lincoln.

The president died nine hours after he had been shot. Accomplices of Booth had also targeted Vice-President Andrew Johnson and Secretary of State William Seward. Seward and four others, including his son, were victims of severe but not fatal stab wounds. Johnson escaped injury, however, because his would-be assassin got cold feet and wound up tipsy in the barroom of Johnson's hotel.

The nation extracted a full measure of vengeance from the conspirators. Booth was pursued into Virginia and shot in a burning barn. His last words were: "Tell Mother I die for my country. I thought I did for the best." Three of Booth's collaborators were convicted by a military court and hanged, along with the woman at whose boardinghouse they had plotted. Three others got life sentences, including a Maryland doctor who set the leg Booth had broken when he jumped to the stage. President Johnson eventually pardoned them all, except one who died in prison. Apart from those cases, however, there was only one other execution in the aftermath of war: Confederate Henry Wirz, who commanded the infamous prison at Andersonville, Georgia, where Union prisoners were probably more the victims of war conditions than of deliberate cruelty.

JOHNSON'S PLAN   Lincoln's death suddenly elevated to the White House Andrew Johnson of Tennessee, a man whose state was still in legal limbo and whose party affiliation was unclear. He was a War Democrat (pro-Union) who had been put on the Union ticket in 1864 as a gesture of unity. Of humble origins like Lincoln, Johnson had moved as a youth from his birthplace in Raleigh, North Carolina, to Greeneville, Tennessee, where he became proprietor of a tailor shop. Self-educated with the help of his wife, he had made himself into an effective orator of the rough-and-tumble school, served as mayor, congressman, governor, and senator, then as military governor of Tennessee before he became vice-president. In the process he had become an advocate of the small farmers against the privileges of the large planters—"a bloated, corrupted aristocracy." He also shared the racial attitudes of most white yeomen. "Damn the negroes," he exclaimed to a friend during the war, "I am fighting those traitorous aristocrats, their masters."

Some of the Radicals at first thought Johnson, unlike Lincoln, to be one of them. Johnson had, for example, once asserted that treason "must be made infamous and traitors must be impoverished." Senator Benjamin Wade loved such language. "Johnson, we have faith in you," he promised.

"By the gods, there will be no trouble now in running this government." But Wade would soon find Johnson to be as unsympathetic as Lincoln, if for different reasons.

Johnson's loyalty to the Union sprang from a strict adherence to the Constitution and a fervent belief in limited government. Given to dogmatic abstractions that were alien to Lincoln's temperament, he nevertheless arrived by a different route at similar objectives. The states should be quickly brought back into their proper relation to the Union because

Andrew Johnson.

the states and the Union were indestructible. And like many other whites, he found it hard to accept the growing Radical sentiment to provide the vote to blacks. In 1865 Johnson declared that "there is no such thing as reconstruction. Those States have not gone out of the Union. Therefore reconstruction is unnecessary."

Johnson's plan to restore the Union thus closely resembled Lincoln's. A new Proclamation of Amnesty (May 1865) added to those Lincoln had excluded from pardon everybody with taxable property worth more than $20,000. These wealthy planters, bankers, and merchants were the people Johnson believed had led the South into secession. But those in the excluded groups might make special applications for pardon directly to the president, and before the year was out Johnson had issued some 13,000 such pardons.

Johnson followed up his amnesty proclamation with his own plan for readmitting the former Confederate states. In each state a native Unionist became provisional governor with authority to call a convention of men elected by loyal voters. Lincoln's 10 percent requirement was omitted. Johnson called upon the state conventions to invalidate the secession ordinances, abolish slavery, and repudiate all debts incurred to aid the Confederacy. Each state, moreover, was to ratify the Thirteenth Amendment. Lincoln had privately advised the governor of Louisiana to consider giving the vote to some blacks, "the very intelligent and those who have fought gallantly in our ranks." In his final public address he had also endorsed a limited black suffrage. Johnson repeated Lincoln's advice. He reminded the provisional governor of Mississippi, for example, that the state conventions might "with perfect safety" extend suffrage to blacks with education or with military service so as to "disarm the adversary"—the adversary being "radicals who are wild upon Negro franchise."

The state conventions for the most part met Johnson's requirements. But Carl Schurz, a prominent Missouri politician, found during his visit to the South "an *utter absence of national feeling* . . . and a desire to preserve slavery . . . as much and as long as possible." Southern whites had accepted the situation because they thought so little had changed after all. Emboldened by Johnson's indulgence, they ignored his counsels of expediency. Suggestions of black suffrage were scarcely raised in the state conventions and promptly squelched when they were.

SOUTHERN INTRANSIGENCE   When Congress met in December 1865, for the first time since the end of the war, it faced the fact that new state governments were functioning in the postwar South, and they were remarkably like the old ones. Southern voters had acted with extreme disregard for northern feelings. Among the new legislative members presenting themselves were Georgia's Alexander H. Stephens, ex-vice-president of the Confederacy, now claiming a seat in the Senate, four Confederate generals, eight colonels, and six cabinet members. The Congress forthwith denied seats to all members from the eleven former Confederate states. It was too much to expect, after four bloody years, that the Unionists in Congress would welcome ex-Confederates like prodigal sons.

Furthermore, the new southern state legislatures, in passing repressive "Black Codes" restricting the freedom of blacks, demonstrated that they intended to preserve slavery as nearly as possible. As one white southerner stressed, "the ex-slave was not a free man; he was a free Negro," and the Black Codes were intended to highlight the distinction.

The details of the Black Codes varied from state to state, but some provisions were common. Existing marriages, including common-law marriages, were recognized (although interracial marriages were prohibited), and testimony of blacks was accepted in legal cases involving blacks—and in six states, in all cases. Blacks could own property.

They could sue and be sued in the courts. On the other hand, blacks could not own farm lands in Mississippi or city lots in South Carolina; they were required to buy special licenses to practice certain trades in Mississippi; and in some states they could not carry firearms without a license. Blacks were required to enter into annual labor contracts. Dependent children were subject to compulsory apprenticeship and corporal punishment by masters. Unemployed (vagrant) blacks were punished with severe fines, and, if unable to pay, they were forced to labor in the fields for those who paid the courts for this source of cheap labor. To many people it indeed seemed that slavery was on the way back in another guise. The new Mississippi penal code virtually said so: "All penal and criminal laws now in force describing the mode of punishment of crimes and misdemeanors committed by slaves, free negroes, or mulattoes are hereby reenacted, and decreed to be in full force."

Faced with such blatant evidence of southern intransigence, moderate Republicans in the Congress drifted toward Radical views. Having

Slavery Is Dead (?) *Thomas Nast's cartoon suggests that, in 1866, slavery was only legally dead.*

excluded the "reconstructed" southern members, the new Congress set up a Joint Committee on Reconstruction, with nine members from the House and six from the Senate, to gather evidence of southern efforts to thwart Reconstruction. Initiative on the committee fell to determined Radical Republicans who knew what they wanted: Ben Wade of Ohio, George W. Julian of Indiana—and most conspicuously of all, Thaddeus Stevens of Pennsylvania and Charles Sumner of Massachusetts.

THE RADICAL REPUBLICANS   Most Radical Republicans had been connected with the antislavery cause for decades. In addition, few could escape the bitterness bred by the long and bloody war or remain unaware of the partisan advantage that would come to the Republican party from black suffrage. The Republicans needed black votes to maintain their control of Congress and the White House. Also they needed to disenfranchise former Confederates to keep them from helping elect Democrats who would restore the old southern ruling class to power. In public, however, the Radical Republicans rarely disclosed such partisan self-interest. Instead they asserted that the Republicans, the party of Union and freedom, could best guarantee the fruits of victory and that extending voting rights to blacks would be the best way to promote their welfare.

The growing conflict of opinion over Reconstruction policy brought about an inversion in constitutional reasoning. Secessionists—and Andrew Johnson—were now arguing that the Rebel states had in fact remained in the Union, and some Radical Republicans were contriving arguments that they had left the Union after all. Thaddeus Stevens argued that the Confederate states were now conquered provinces, subject to the absolute will of the victors, and that the "whole fabric of southern society must be changed." Charles Sumner maintained that the southern states, by their pretended acts of secession,

Senator Charles Sumner, a leading Radical Republican.

had reverted to the status of unorganized territories subject to the will of Congress. But few ever took such ideas seriously. Republicans converged instead on the "forfeited-rights theory," later embodied in the report of the Joint Committee on Reconstruction. This held that the states as entities continued to exist, but by the acts of secession and war, they had forfeited "all civil and political rights under the constitution." And Congress, not the president, was the proper authority to determine how such rights might be restored.

JOHNSON'S BATTLE WITH CONGRESS   A long year of political battling remained, however, before this idea triumphed. By the end of 1865, the Radical Republicans' views had gained a majority in Congress, if one not yet large enough to override presidential vetoes. But the critical year 1866 saw the gradual waning of Andrew Johnson's power and influence; much of this was self-induced. Johnson first challenged Congress in 1866, when he vetoed a bill to extend the life of the Freedmen's Bureau. The measure, he said, assumed that wartime conditions still existed, whereas the country had returned "to a state of peace and industry." Because it was no longer valid as a war measure, the bill violated the Constitution in several ways, he declared. It made the federal government responsible for the care of indigents. It was passed by a Congress in which eleven states were denied seats. And it used vague language in defining the "civil rights and immunities" of blacks. For the time being, Johnson's prestige remained sufficiently intact that the Senate upheld his veto.

Three days after the veto, however, Johnson undermined his already weakening authority with a fiery assault on Radical Republican leaders during an impromptu speech. From that point forward, moderate Republicans backed away from a president who had opened himself to counterattack. The Radical Republicans took the offensive. Johnson was "an alien enemy of a foreign state," Stevens declared. Sumner called him "an insolent drunken brute"—and Johnson was open to the charge because of an incident at his vice-presidential inauguration in 1865. Weakened by illness at the time, he had taken a belt of brandy to get him through the ceremony and, under the influence of fever and alcohol, had become incoherent.

In mid-March 1866 the Radical-led Congress passed the Civil Rights Act. A response to the Black Codes created by unrepentant southern state legislatures, this bill declared that "all persons born in the United States and not subject to any foreign power, excluding Indians not taxed," were citizens entitled to "full and equal benefit of all laws." The grant of citizenship to native-born blacks, Johnson fumed, went beyond anything formerly held to be within the scope of federal power. It would, moreover, "foment discord among the races." Johnson vetoed the bill, but this time, on April 9, 1866, Congress overrode the presidential veto. On July 16 it enacted a revised Freedmen's Bureau Bill, again overriding a veto. From that point on, Johnson steadily lost both public and political support.

THE FOURTEENTH AMENDMENT   To remove all doubt about the constitutionality of the new Civil Rights Act, the Joint Committee recommended a new constitutional amendment, which passed Congress on June 16, 1866, and was ratified by the states on July 28, 1868. The Fourteenth Amendment, however, went far beyond the Civil Rights Act.

The amendment reaffirmed state and federal citizenship for persons born or naturalized in the United States, and it forbade any *state* (the word "state" was important in later litigation) to abridge the "privileges and immunities" of citizens, to deprive any *person* (again an important term) of life, liberty, or property without "due process of law," or to deny any person "the equal protection of the laws." The last three of these clauses have been the subject of many lawsuits resulting in applications not widely, if at all, foreseen at the time. The "due-process clause" has come to mean that state as well as federal power is subject to the Bill of Rights, and it has been used to protect corporations, as legal "persons,"

A cartoon depicting Andrew Johnson as a "cruel uncle" leading two children, "civil rights" and "the freedmen's bureau," into the "veto wood."

from "unreasonable" regulation by the states. Other provisions of the amendment had less far-reaching effects. One section specified that the debt of the United States "shall not be questioned" by the former Confederate states and declared "illegal and void" all debts contracted in aid of the rebellion. Another section specified the power of Congress to pass laws enforcing the amendment.

Johnson's home state was among the first to ratify the Fourteenth Amendment. In Tennessee, which had harbored probably more Unionists than any other Confederate state, the government had fallen under Radical Republican control. The state's governor, in reporting the results to the secretary of the Senate, added: "Give my respects to the dead dog of the White House." His words afford a fair sample of the growing acrimony on both sides of the Reconstruction debates. In May and July, race riots in Memphis and New Orleans added fuel to the flames. Both incidents involved indiscriminate massacres of blacks by local police and white mobs. The carnage, Radical Republicans argued, was the natural fruit of Johnson's policy. "Witness Memphis, witness New Orleans," Senator Charles Sumner cried. "Who can doubt that the President is the author of these tragedies?"

RECONSTRUCTING THE SOUTH

THE TRIUMPH OF CONGRESSIONAL RECONSTRUCTION As 1866 drew to an end, the congressional elections promised to be a referendum on the growing split between Andrew Johnson and the Radical Republicans. Johnson sought to influence voters with a speaking tour of the Midwest, a "swing around the circle," which turned into an undignified shouting contest between Andrew Johnson and his critics. In Cleveland he described the Radical Republicans as "factious, domineering, tyrannical" men, and he foolishly exchanged hot-tempered insults with a heckler. At another stop, while Johnson was speaking from an observation car, the engineer mistakenly pulled the train out of the station, making the president appear quite the fool. Such incidents tended to confirm his image as a "ludicrous boor" and "drunken imbecile," which Radical Republican papers projected. In the congressional elections, the Republicans won over a two-thirds majority in each house, a comfortable margin with which to override any presidential vetoes.

The Congress in fact enacted a new program even before new members took office. Two acts passed in 1867 extended the suffrage to African Americans in the District of Columbia and the territories. Another law provided that the new Congress would convene on March 4 instead of the following December, depriving Johnson of a breathing spell. On March 2, 1867, two days before the old Congress expired, it passed three basic laws promoting congressional Reconstruction over Johnson's vetoes: the Military Reconstruction Act, the Command of the Army Act (an amendment to an army appropriation), and the Tenure of Office Act.

The first of the three acts prescribed new conditions under which the formation of southern state governments should begin all over again. The other two sought to block any effort by the president to obstruct the process. The Command of the Army Act required that all orders from the commander-in-chief go through the headquarters of the general of the army, then Ulysses S. Grant. The Radical Republicans trusted Grant, who was already leaning their way. The Tenure of Office Act required the consent of the Senate for the president to remove any officeholder whose appointment the Senate had to confirm in the first place. The purpose of at least some congressmen was to retain Secretary of War Edwin M. Stanton, the one Radical Republican sympathizer in Johnson's cabinet. But an ambiguity crept into the wording of the act. Cabinet officers, it said, should serve during the term of the president who appointed them—and Lincoln had appointed Stanton, although, to be sure, Johnson was serving out Lincoln's term.

The Military Reconstruction Act was hailed or denounced as the triumphant victory of "Radical" Reconstruction. The act declared that "no legal state governments or adequate protection for life and property now exists in the rebel States. . . ." One state, Tennessee, which had ratified the Fourteenth Amendment, was exempted from the application of the new act. The other ten states were divided into five military districts, and the commanding officer of each was authorized to keep order and protect the "rights of persons and property." To that end he might use military tribunals in place of civil courts. The Johnson governments remained intact for the time being, but new constitutions were to be framed "in conformity with the Constitution of the United States," in conventions elected by male citizens twenty-one and older "of whatever race, color, or previous condition." Each state constitution had to provide the same universal male suffrage. Then, once the constitution was ratified by a majority of voters and accepted by Congress, other criteria had to be met. The state legislature had to ratify the Fourteenth Amendment, and once the amendment became part of the Constitution, any given state would be entitled to representation in Congress. Persons excluded from officeholding by the proposed amendment were also excluded from participation in the process.

Johnson reluctantly appointed military commanders under the act, but the situation remained uncertain for a time. Some people expected the Supreme Court to strike down the act, and no machinery existed at the time for the new elections. Congress quickly remedied that on March 23, 1867, with the Second Reconstruction Act, which directed the army commanders to register all adult males who swore they were qualified. A Third Reconstruction Act, passed on July 19, directed registrars to go beyond the loyalty oath and determine each person's eligibility to take it, and also authorized district commanders to remove and replace officeholders of any existing "so-called state" or division thereof. Before the end of 1867 new elections had been held in all the states but Texas.

Having clipped the president's wings, the Republican Congress moved a year later to safeguard its program from possible interference by the Supreme Court. On March 27, 1868, Congress simply removed the power of the Supreme Court to review cases arising under the Military Reconstruction Act, which Congress clearly had the right to do under its power to define the Court's appellate jurisdiction. The Court accepted this curtailment of its authority on the same day it affirmed the principle of an "indestructible union" in *Texas v. White* (1868). In that case it also asserted the right of Congress to reframe state governments, thus endorsing the Radical Republican point of view.

THE IMPEACHMENT AND TRIAL OF JOHNSON   By 1868, Radical Republicans were convinced that not only did the power of the Supreme Court and the president need to be curtailed, but Johnson himself had to be removed from office. Horace Greeley, the prominent editor of the *New York Tribune,* called Johnson "an aching tooth in the national jaw, a screeching infant in a crowded lecture room. There can be no peace or comfort till he is out."

Johnson, though hostile to the congressional Reconstruction program, had gone through the motions required of him. He continued, however, to pardon former Confederates and transferred several of the district military commanders who had displayed Radical sympathies. Johnson was revealing himself to be a man of limited ability and narrow vision. He lacked Lincoln's resilience and pragmatism. In the process of promoting his lenient southern strategy, Johnson allowed his temper to get the better of his judgment. He castigated the Radical Republicans as "a gang of cormorants and bloodsuckers who have been fattening upon the country." During 1867, newspapers reported that the differences between Johnson and the Republicans were irreconcilable.

The Republicans unsuccessfully tried to impeach Johnson early in 1867, alleging a variety of flimsy charges, none of which represented an indictable crime. The head of the Secret Service, for example, shared rumors about an alleged presidential affair with a woman seeking pardons for former Confederates. Johnson was also accused of public drunkenness, and one congressman even tried to implicate him in the assassination of Lincoln. After listening to the hodgepodge of charges, a House member from Iowa concluded: "While the President has been guilty of many great follies and wickedness," it is better to "submit to two years of misrule . . . than subject the country, its institutions and its credits to the shock of an impeachment." But the impasse between the congressional leadership and the president continued.

At last, Johnson himself provided the occasion for impeachment when he deliberately violated the Tenure of Office Act in order to test its constitutionality. Secretary of War Edwin Stanton had become a thorn in the president's side, refusing to resign despite his disagreements with Johnson's Reconstruction policy. On August 12, 1867, during a congressional recess, Johnson suspended Stanton and named General Grant in his place. When the Senate refused to confirm Johnson's action, however, Grant returned the office to Stanton.

The Radical Republicans now saw their chance to remove the president, and they were quite explicit about their political purposes. As Charles Sumner declared, "Impeachment is a political proceeding before a political body with a political purpose." The debate in the House was clamorous and vicious. One congressman said Johnson had dragged the robes of his office through the "filth of treason." Another denounced the president as "an ungrateful, despicable, besotted traitorous man—an incubus." Still another called Johnson's advisers "the worst men that ever crawled like filthy reptiles at the footstool of

House of Representatives managers of the impeachment proceedings and trial of Andrew Johnson. Among them were Benjamin Butler (R-Mass., seated left) and Thaddeus Stevens (R-Pa., seated with cane).

power." On February 24, 1868, the Republican-dominated House passed eleven articles of impeachment by a party-line vote of 126 to 47.

Of the eleven articles of impeachment, eight focused on the charge that Johnson had unlawfully removed Stanton and had failed to give the Senate the name of a successor. Article 9 accused the president of issuing orders in violation of the Command of the Army Act. The last two articles in effect charged him with criticizing Congress by "inflammatory and scandalous harangues." Article 11 also accused Johnson of "unlawfully devising and contriving" to violate the Reconstruction Acts, contrary to his obligation to execute the laws. At the very least, it stated, Johnson had tried to obstruct Congress's will while observing the letter of the law.

The Senate trial began on March 5, 1868, and continued until May 26, with Chief Justice Salmon P. Chase presiding. It was a great spectacle before a packed gallery. Witnesses were called, speeches made, and rules of order debated. Johnson wanted to plead his case in person, but his attorneys refused, fearing that his short temper might erupt and hurt his cause. The president thereupon worked behind the scenes to win over undecided Republican senators, offering them a variety of political incentives.

As the weeks passed, the trial grew tedious. Senators slept during the proceedings, spectators passed out in the unventilated room, and poor acoustics prompted repeated cries of "We can't hear." Debate eventually focused on Stanton's removal, the most substantive impeachment charge. Johnson's lawyers argued that Lincoln, not Johnson, had appointed Stanton, so the Tenure of Office Act did not apply to him. At the same time, they claimed (correctly, as it turned out) that the law was unconstitutional.

As the five-week trial ended and the voting began in May 1868, the Senate Republicans could afford only six defections from their ranks to ensure the two-thirds majority needed to convict. In the end, seven moderate Republicans and all twelve Democrats voted to acquit. The final tally was 35–19 for conviction, one vote short of the two-thirds needed for removal from office. The renegade Republicans offered two primary reasons for their controversial votes: they feared damage to the separation of powers among the branches of government if Johnson were removed, and they were assured by Johnson's attorneys that he would stop obstructing congressional policy in the South.

In a moment of high drama, the deciding vote was cast by Edmund Ross, a first-term Kansas Republican who in the days leading up to the verdict was "hunted like a fox" by both sides. He insisted that his decision was an act of courage based on principled constitutional scruples: "If the president must step down upon insufficient proofs and from partisan considerations, the office of president would be degraded" and "ever after subordinated to the legislative will."

Historians have since discovered that Ross was not so principled: he demanded several political favors from Johnson in exchange for his vote. Whatever his motives, Ross's defection infuriated those promoting impeachment. One of his constituents fired off a bitter telegram: "Kansas repudiates you as she does all perjurers and skunks."

Although the Senate failed to remove Johnson, the trial crippled his already weak presidency. During the remaining ten months of his term, he initiated no other clashes with Congress. In 1868 Johnson sought the Democratic presidential nomination but lost to New York governor Horatio Seymour, who then lost to Republican Ulysses Grant in the general election. A bitter Johnson refused to attend Grant's inauguration. His final act as president was to issue a pardon to former Confederate president Jefferson Davis. In 1874, after failed bids for the Senate and the House, Johnson won a measure of vindication with election to the Senate, the only former president ever to do so, but he died a few months later. He was buried with a copy of the Constitution tucked under his head.

As for the impeachment trial, only two weeks after it ended, a Boston newspaper reported that people were amazed at how quickly "the whole subject of impeachment seems to have been thrown into the background and dwarfed in importance" by other events. Moreover, impeachment of Johnson was in the end a great political mistake, for the failure to remove the president damaged Radical Republican morale and support. Nevertheless, the Radical cause did gain something. To blunt the opposition, Johnson agreed not to obstruct the process of Reconstruction, and thereafter Radical Reconstruction began in earnest.

REPUBLICAN RULE IN THE SOUTH In June 1868 Congress agreed that seven southern states had met the conditions for readmission, all but Virginia, Mississippi, and Texas. Congress rescinded Georgia's admission, however, when the state legislature expelled twenty-eight black members and seated former Confederate leaders. The federal military commander in Georgia then forced the legislature to reseat the black members and remove the Confederates, and the state was compelled to ratify the Fifteenth Amendment before being admitted in July 1870. Mississippi, Texas, and Virginia had returned earlier in 1870, under the added requirement that they too ratify the Fifteenth Amendment. This amendment, submitted to the states in 1869, ratified in 1870, forbade the states to deny any person the vote on grounds of race, color, or previous condition of servitude.

Long before the new governments were established, Republican groups began to spring up in the South, chiefly sponsored by the Union League, founded at Philadelphia in 1862 to promote support for the Union. Emissaries of the League enrolled African Americans and loyal whites, initiated them into the secrets and rituals of the order, and instructed them "in their rights and duties." Their recruiting efforts were so successful that in 1867, on the eve of South Carolina's choice of convention delegates, the League reported eighty-eight chapters, which claimed to have enrolled almost every adult black male in the state.

THE RECONSTRUCTED SOUTH

THE FREED SLAVES   To focus solely on what white Republicans did to reconstruct the defeated South creates the false impression that the freed slaves were simply pawns in the hands of others. In fact, however, southern blacks were active agents in affecting the course of Reconstruction. It was not an easy road, though. Many former Confederates continued to harbor deeply ingrained racial prejudices. They adopted a militant stance against federally imposed changes in southern society. During the era of Reconstruction, whites used terror, intimidation, and violence to suppress black efforts to gain social and economic equality. In July 1866, for instance, a black woman in Clinch County, Georgia, was arrested and given sixty-five lashes for "using abusive language" during an encounter with a white woman. A month later another black woman suffered the same punishment. The Civil War had brought freedom to the slaves, but it did not bring protection against exploitation or abuse. Many former slaves found themselves liberated but destitute after the fighting ended. The mere promise of freedom, however, raised their hopes about achieving a biracial democracy, equal justice, and economic opportunity. "Most anyone ought to know that a man is better off free than as a slave, even if he did not have anything," said the Reverend E. P. Holmes, a black Georgia preacher and former domestic servant. "I would rather be free and have my liberty."

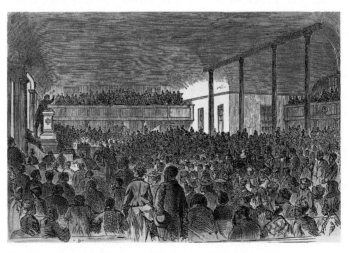

The First African Church at Richmond, Virginia, 1874.

Participation in the Union army or navy gave many freedmen a training ground in leadership. Black military veterans would form the core of the first generation of African-American political leaders in the postwar South. Military service provided many former slaves with the first opportunities to learn to read and write. Army life also alerted them to new opportunities for advancement and respectability. "No negro who has ever been a soldier," reported a northern official after visiting a black unit, "can again be imposed upon; they have learnt what it is to be free and they will infuse their feelings into others." Fighting for the Union cause also instilled a fervent sense of nationalism. A Virginia freedman explained that the United States was "now *our* country—made emphatically so by the blood of our brethren."

Former slaves established independent black churches after the war, churches that would serve as the foundation of African-American community life. In war-ravaged Charleston, South Carolina, the first new building to appear after the war was a black church on Calhoun Street; by 1866 ten more had been built. Blacks preferred the Baptist denomination, in part because of the decentralized structure that allowed each congregation to worship in its own way. By 1890 there were over 1.3 million black Baptists in the South, nearly three times as many as any other black denomination. For many former slaves, churches were the first institutions they owned and controlled. In addition to forming viable new congregations, freed blacks organized thousands of fraternal, benevolent, and mutual-aid societies, clubs, lodges, and associations. Memphis, for example, had over two hundred such organizations; Richmond boasted twice that number.

The freed slaves, both women and men, also hastened to reestablish and reaffirm families. Marriages that had been prohibited during slavery were now legitimized through the assistance of the Freedmen's Bureau. By 1870 a preponderant majority of former slaves lived in two-parent households. One white editor in Georgia, lamenting the difficulty of finding black women to serve as house servants, reported that "every negro woman wants to set up house keeping" for herself and her family. To do so they often had little choice but to become tenant farmers, gaining access to land in exchange for a share of their crop. With little money or technical training, freed slaves faced the prospect of becoming wage laborers. Yet in order to retain as much autonomy as possible over their productive energies and those of their children on both a daily and seasonal basis, many husbands and wives chose sharecropping. This enabled mothers and wives to devote more of their time to domestic needs while still contributing to family income.

Black communities in the postwar South also sought to establish schools. The antebellum planter elite had denied education to blacks because they feared that literate slaves would organize uprisings. After the war the white elite worried that education programs would encourage both poor whites and blacks to leave the South in search of better social and economic opportunities. Economic leaders wanted to protect the competitive advantage afforded by the region's low-wage labor market. "They didn't want us to learn nothin'," one former slave recalled. "The only thing we had to learn was how to work." White opposition to education for blacks made it all the more important to African Americans. South Carolina's Mary Jane McLeod Bethune, the fifteenth child of former slaves and one of the first children in the household born after the Civil War, reveled in the opportunity to gain an education: "The whole world opened to me when I learned to read." She walked five miles to school as a child, earned a scholarship to college, and went on to become the first black woman to found a school that became a four-year college, Bethune-Cookman, in Daytona Beach, Florida.

The general resistance among the former slaveholding class to new education initiatives forced the freed slaves to rely on northern assistance or to take their own initiative. A Mississippi Freedmen's Bureau agent noted in 1865 that when he told a gathering of some 3,000 former slaves that they "were to have the advantages of schools and education, their joy knew no bounds. They fairly jumped and shouted in gladness." Black churches and individuals helped raise the money and often built the schools and paid the teachers. Soldiers who had acquired some reading and writing skills often served as the first teachers, and the students included adults as well as children. A Florida teacher reported that a sixty-year-old former slave woman in her class was so excited by literacy that she "spells her lesson all the evening, then she dreams about it, and wakes up thinking about it."

BLACKS IN SOUTHERN POLITICS   In the postwar South, the new role of African Americans in politics caused the most controversy, then and afterward. If largely illiterate and inexperienced in the rudiments of politics, they were little different from millions of propertyless whites

Black Suffrage. *The Fifteenth Amendment was passed in 1870 and guaranteed the rights of citizens, including the right to vote, regardless of race, color, or previous condition of servitude, on the federal level. But former slaves had been registering to vote and voting in large numbers in state elections since 1867, as shown here.*

enfranchised in the age of Jackson or immigrants taken to the polls by political bosses in New York and other cities after the war. Some freedmen frankly confessed their disadvantages. Beverly Nash, a black delegate in the South Carolina convention of 1868, told his colleagues: "I believe, my friends and fellow-citizens, we are not prepared for this suffrage. But we can learn. Give a man tools and let him commence to use them, and in time he will learn a trade. So it is with voting."

Several hundred black delegates participated in the statewide political conventions. Most had been selected by local political meetings or by churches, fraternal societies, Union Leagues, and black army units from the North, although a few simply appointed themselves. "Some bring credentials," explained a North Carolina black leader, "others had as much as they could to bring themselves, having to escape from their homes stealthily at night" to avoid white assaults. The African-American delegates "ranged all colors and apparently all conditions," but free mulattoes from the cities played the most prominent roles. At Louisiana's

Republican state convention, for instance, nineteen of the twenty black delegates had been born free.

By 1867, however, former slaves began to gain political influence and vote in large numbers, and this revealed emerging tensions within the black community. Some southern blacks resented the presence of northern brethren who moved south after the war, while others complained that few ex-slaves were represented in black leadership positions. Northern blacks and the southern free black elite, most of whom were urban dwellers, tended to oppose efforts to confiscate and redistribute land to the rural freedmen, and many insisted that political equality did not mean social equality. As an Alabama black leader stressed, "We do not ask that the ignorant and degraded shall be put on a social equality with the refined and intelligent." In general, however, unity rather than dissension prevailed, and blacks focused on common concerns such as full equality under the law.

Brought suddenly into politics in times that tried the most skilled of statesmen, many African Americans served with distinction. Nonetheless, the derisive label "black Reconstruction" used by later critics exaggerates black political influence, which was limited mainly to voting, and overlooks the political clout of the large numbers of white Republicans, especially in the mountain areas of the upper South, who also favored the Radical plan for Reconstruction. Only one of the new state conventions, South Carolina's, had a black majority, 76 to 41. Louisiana's was evenly divided racially, and in only two other conventions were more than 20 percent of the members black: Florida's, with 40 percent, and Virginia's, with 24 percent. The Texas convention was only 10 percent black, and North Carolina's 11 percent—but that did not stop a white newspaper from calling it a body consisting of "baboons, monkeys, mules . . . and other jackasses."

In the new state governments, any African-American participation was a novelty. Although some 600 blacks—most of them former slaves—served as state legislators, no black man was ever elected governor, and only a few served as judges. In Louisiana, however, Pinckney Pinchback, a northern black and former Union soldier, won the office of lieutenant-governor and served as acting governor when the white governor was indicted for corruption. Several blacks were elected lieutenant-governors, state treasurers, or secretaries of state. There were two black senators in Congress, Hiram Revels and Blanche K. Bruce,

A lithograph depicting five of the major black political figures of the Reconstruction period: Hiram Revels (top left) and Blanche K. Bruce (center) served in the U.S. Senate; Joseph H. Rainey (bottom left), John R. Lynch (bottom right), and James T. Rapier (top right) in the House of Representatives.

both Mississippi natives who had been educated in the North, and fourteen black members of the House during Reconstruction.

CARPETBAGGERS AND SCALAWAGS   The top positions in southern state governments went for the most part to white Republicans, whom the opposition whites soon labeled "carpetbaggers" and "scalawags," depending on their place of birth. The northern opportunists who allegedly rushed South with all their belongings in carpetbags to grab the political spoils were more often than not Union veterans who had arrived as early as 1865 or 1866, drawn South by the hope of economic opportunity and by other attractions that many of them had seen in Union service. Many other so-called carpetbaggers were teachers, social workers, or preachers animated by a missionary impulse.

The "scalawags," or native white Republicans, were even more reviled and misrepresented. A Nashville editor called them the "merest trash that could be collected in a civilized community, of no personal credit or social responsibility." Most "scalawags" had opposed secession, forming a Unionist majority in many mountain counties as far south as Georgia and Alabama, and especially in the hills of eastern Tennessee. Among the "scalawags" were several distinguished figures, including former Confederate general James A. Longstreet, who decided after Appomattox that the Old South must change its ways. He became a successful cotton broker in New Orleans, joined the Republican party, and supported the Radical Reconstruction program. Other "scalawags" were former Whigs attracted by the Republican party's economic program of industrial and commercial expansion.

THE RADICAL REPUBLICAN RECORD   Former Confederates also resented the new state constitutions because of their provisions allowing for black suffrage and civil rights. Yet most remained in effect for some years after the end of Radical Republican control, and later constitutions incorporated many of their features. Conspicuous among Radical innovations were such steps toward greater democracy as requiring universal manhood suffrage, reapportioning legislatures more nearly according to population, and making more state offices elective.

Given the hostile circumstances under which the Radical governments operated, their achievements are remarkable. For the first time in most of the South, they constructed an extensive railroad network and established state school systems, however inadequate and ill-supported at first. Some 600,000 black pupils were in southern schools by 1877. State governments under the Radicals also gave more attention than ever before to poor relief and to orphanages, asylums, and institutions for the deaf and blind of both races. Public roads, bridges, and buildings were repaired or rebuilt. Blacks achieved new rights and opportunities that would never again be taken away, at least in principle: equality before the law and the rights to own property, carry on business, enter professions, attend schools, and learn to read and write.

Yet several of these Republican regimes also engaged in corrupt practices. Bids for contracts were accepted at absurd prices, and public officials took their cut. Public money and public credit were often voted to privately owned corporations, notably railroads, under conditions that invited influence peddling. Corruption was not invented by the Radical

Republican regimes, nor did it die with them. Louisiana's "carpetbag" governor recognized as much: "Why," he said, "down here everybody is demoralized. Corruption is the fashion." In three years Louisiana's government printing bill ran to $1.5 million, about half of which went to a newspaper belonging to the young governor, who left office with a tidy nest egg and settled down to a long life as a planter. At about the same time, Mississippi's Democratic state treasurer embezzled over $315,000.

WHITE TERROR   In general, however, southern whites were hostile to Republican regimes less because of their corruption than because of their inclusion of blacks. Most white southerners remained so conditioned by the social prejudices embedded in slavery that they were unable to conceive of blacks as citizens. In some places hostility to the new biracial regimes turned violent. In Grayson County, Texas, three whites murdered three freed slaves because they felt the need to "thin the niggers out and drive them to their holes."

The prototype of terrorist groups was the Ku Klux Klan (KKK), first organized in 1866 by some young men of Pulaski, Tennessee, as a social club with the costumes, secret ritual, and mumbo-jumbo common to fraternal groups. At first a group of pranksters, they soon turned to intimidation of blacks and white Republicans, and the KKK and its imitators, like Louisiana's Knights of the White Camellia, spread

This Thomas Nast cartoon chides the Ku Klux Klan and the White League for promoting conditions "worse than slavery" for southern blacks after the Civil War.

rapidly across the South in answer to the Republican party's Union League. Klansmen rode about the countryside hiding under masks and robes, spreading horrendous rumors, issuing threats, harassing African Americans, and occasionally wreaking violence and destruction.

Klansmen focused their terror on prominent Republicans, black and white. In Mississippi they killed a black Republican leader in front of his family. Three white "scalawag" Republicans were murdered in Georgia in 1870. That same year an armed mob of whites assaulted a Republican political rally in Alabama, killing four blacks and wounding fifty-four. In South Carolina the Klan was especially active. Virtually the entire white male population of York County joined the Klan, and they were responsible for eleven murders and hundreds of whippings. In 1871 some 500 masked men laid siege to the Union County jail and eventually lynched eight black prisoners. Although most Klansmen were poor farmers and tradesmen, middle-class whites—planters, merchants, bankers, lawyers, doctors, even ministers—also joined the group and participated in its brutalities.

Congress struck back with three Enforcement Acts (1870–1871) to protect black voters. The first of these measures levied penalties on persons who interfered with any citizen's right to vote. A second placed the election of congressmen under surveillance by federal election supervisors and marshals. The third (the Ku Klux Klan Act) outlawed the characteristic activities of the Klan—forming conspiracies, wearing disguises, resisting officers, and intimidating officials—and authorized the president to suspend habeas corpus where necessary to suppress "armed combinations." In 1871, the federal government singled out nine counties in upcountry South Carolina as an example, suspended habeas corpus, and pursued mass prosecutions. In general, however, the federal Enforcement Acts suffered from weak and inconsistent execution. President Grant vacillated between clamping down on the Klan and capitulating to racial intimidation. The strong tradition of states' rights and local autonomy in the South resisted federal force.

CONSERVATIVE RESURGENCE The Klan's impact on politics varied from state to state. In the upper South it played only a modest role in facilitating a Democratic resurgence. But in the Deep South, Klan violence and intimidation had more substantial effects. In Georgia, for instance, Republicans virtually quit campaigning and voting. In overwhelmingly black Yazoo County, Mississippi, vengeful whites used violence to reverse the political balance of power. In the 1873 elections the Republicans cast 2,449 votes and the Democrats 638; two years later the Democrats polled 4,049 votes, the Republicans 7. Throughout the South the activities of the Klan weakened black and Republican morale, and in the North they encouraged a growing weariness with the whole southern question. "The plain truth is," noted the *New York Herald*, "the North has got tired of the Negro."

The erosion of northern interest in civil rights resulted from more than weariness, however. Western expansion, Indian wars, new economic opportunities, and political controversy over the tariff and the currency distracted attention from southern outrages against Republican rule and black rights. In addition, after a business panic that occurred in 1873 and the ensuing depression, desperate economic circumstances in the North and South created new racial tensions that helped undermine already inconsistent federal efforts to promote racial justice in the former Confederacy. Republican control in the South gradually loosened as "Conservative" parties—Democrats used that name to mollify former Whigs—mobilized the white vote. Old prewar political leaders reemerged to promote the antebellum Democratic goals of limited government, states' rights, and free trade. They politicized the race issue to excite the white electorate and intimidate black voters. The Republicans in the South had no effective response. They became increasingly an organization limited to blacks and federal officials. Many scalawags and carpetbaggers drifted away from the Radical Republican ranks under pressure from their white neighbors. Few of them had joined the Republicans out of concern for black rights in the first place. And where persuasion failed to work, Democrats were willing to use chicanery. As one enthusiastic Democrat boasted, "the white and black Republicans may outvote us, but we can outcount them."

Republican political control collapsed in Virginia and Tennessee as early as 1869, in Georgia and North Carolina in 1870, although North Carolina had a Republican governor until 1876. Reconstruction lasted longest in the Deep South states with the largest black population, where whites abandoned Klan masks for barefaced intimidation in paramilitary groups such as the Mississippi Rifle Club and the South Carolina Red Shirts. By 1876 Radical Republican regimes survived only

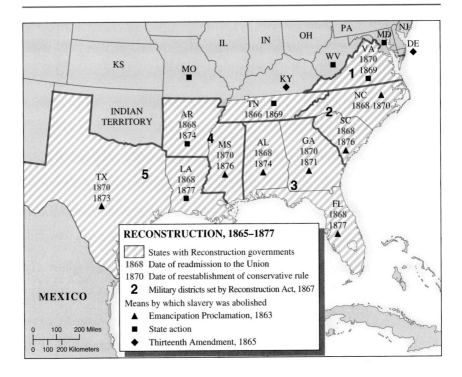

RECONSTRUCTION, 1865–1877

States with Reconstruction governments
1868 Date of readmission to the Union
1870 Date of reestablishment of conservative rule
2 Military districts set by Reconstruction Act, 1867
Means by which slavery was abolished
▲ Emancipation Proclamation, 1863
■ State action
◆ Thirteenth Amendment, 1865

in Louisiana, South Carolina, and Florida, and these all collapsed after the elections of that year. Later the last carpetbag governor of South Carolina explained that "the uneducated negro was too weak, no matter what his numbers, to cope with the whites."

THE GRANT YEARS

THE ELECTION OF 1868   Ulysses S. Grant, who presided during the collapse of Republican rule in the South, brought to the White House little political experience. But in 1868 the rank-and-file northern voter could be expected to support "the Lion of Vicksburg" because of his record as a war leader. Both parties wooed him, but his falling-out with President Johnson pushed him toward the Republicans and built trust in him among the Radicals. They were, as Thaddeus Stevens said, ready to "let him into the church."

The Republican platform of 1868 endorsed the Reconstruction policy of Congress, congratulating the country on the "assured success" of the program. One plank cautiously defended black suffrage as a necessity in the South, but a matter each northern state should settle for itself. Another urged payment of the national debt "in the utmost good faith to all creditors," which meant in gold. More important than the platform were the great expectations of a soldier-president and his slogan: "Let us have peace."

The Democrats took opposite positions on both Reconstruction and the debt. The Republican Congress, the platform charged, instead of restoring the Union had "so far as in its power, dissolved it, and subjected ten states, in the time of profound peace, to military

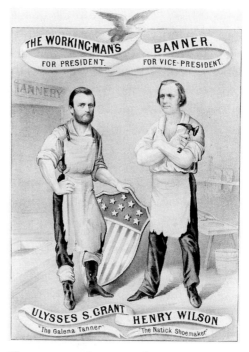

This campaign banner makes reference to the working-class origins of Ulysses S. Grant and his vice-presidential candidate Henry Wilson by depicting Grant as a tanner and Wilson as a shoemaker.

despotism and Negro supremacy." As to the public debt, the party endorsed Representative George H. Pendleton's "Ohio idea" that, since most war bonds had been bought with depreciated greenbacks, they should be paid off in greenbacks. With no conspicuously available candidate in sight, the convention turned to Horatio Seymour, war governor of New York and chairman of the convention. His friends had to hustle him out of the hall to prevent his withdrawal. The Democrats made a closer race of it than showed up in the electoral vote. Eight states, including New York and New Jersey, went for Seymour. While Grant swept the electoral college by 214 to 80, his popular majority was only 307,000 out of a total of over 5.7 million votes. More than 500,000 black voters accounted for Grant's margin of victory.

Grant had proven himself a great leader in the war, but in the White House he seemed blind to the political forces and influence peddlers around him. He was awestruck by men of wealth and unaccountably loyal to some who betrayed his trust. His conception of the presidency was "Whiggish." The chief executive carried out the laws; in the formulation of policy he passively followed the lead of Congress. This approach endeared him at first to Republican party leaders, but it left him at last ineffective and left others disillusioned with his leadership.

At the outset Grant consulted nobody on his cabinet appointments. Some of his choices indulged personal whims; others simply displayed bad judgment. In some cases appointees learned of their nomination from the newspapers. As time went by Grant betrayed a fatal gift for losing men of talent and integrity from his cabinet. Secretary of State Hamilton Fish of New York turned out to be a happy exception; he guided foreign policy throughout the Grant presidency.

THE GOVERNMENT DEBT   Financial issues dominated the political agenda during Grant's presidency. After the war, the Treasury had assumed that the $432 million worth of greenbacks issued during the conflict would be retired from circulation and that the nation would revert to a "hard-money" currency—gold coins. Many agrarian and debtor groups resisted any contraction of the money supply resulting from the elimination of greenbacks, believing that it would mean lower prices for their crops and would make it harder for them to repay long-term debts. They were joined by a large number of Radical Republicans who thought a combination of high tariffs and inflation would generate more rapid economic growth. As Senator John Sherman explained, "I prefer gold to paper money. But there is no other resort. We must have money or a fractured government." In 1868 congressional supporters of such a "soft-money" policy halted the retirement of greenbacks. There matters stood when Grant took office.

The "sound" or hard-money advocates, mostly bankers and merchants, claimed that Grant's election was a mandate to save the country from the Democrats' "Ohio idea" of using greenbacks to repay government bonds. Quite influential in Republican circles, the "sound-money" advocates also had the benefit of a deeply ingrained popular assumption that hard money was morally preferable to paper currency. Grant agreed, and in his inaugural address he endorsed payment of the national debt in gold as a point of national honor. On March 18, 1869, the Public Credit Act endorsing that principle became the first act of

Congress that he signed. Under the Refunding Act of 1870, the Treasury was able to replace 6 percent Civil War bonds with a new bond issue promising purchasers a 4 to 5 percent return in gold.

SCANDALS The complexities of the "money question" exasperated Grant, but that was the least of his worries, for his administration soon fell into a cesspool of scandal. In the summer of 1869, two financial buccaneers, the crafty Jay Gould and the flamboyant Jim Fisk, connived with the president's brother-in-law to corner the nation's gold market. That is, they would create a public craze for gold by purchasing massive quantities of the yellow metal and convincing traders and the general public that the price would keep climbing. As more buyers joined the frenzy, the value of gold would soar. The only danger to the scheme was if the federal Treasury sold large amounts of gold. Gould concocted an argument that the government should refrain from selling gold on the market because the resulting rise in gold prices would raise temporarily depressed farm prices. Grant apparently smelled a rat from the start, but he was seen in public with the speculators. As the rumor spread on Wall Street that the president had bought the argument, gold rose from $132 to $163 an ounce. When Grant finally persuaded his brother-in-law to pull out of the deal, Gould began quietly selling out. Finally, on "Black Friday," September 24, 1869, Grant ordered the Treasury to sell a large quantity of gold, and the bubble burst. Fisk got out by repudiating his agreements and hiring thugs to intimidate his creditors. "Nothing is lost save honor," he said.

The plot to corner the gold market was only the first of several scandals that rocked the Grant administration. During the campaign of 1872 the public first learned about the financial crookery of the Crédit Mobilier, a construction company composed of the directors of the Union Pacific Railroad that had milked the Union Pacific for exorbitant fees in order to line the pockets of the insiders who controlled both firms. Union Pacific shareholders were left holding the bag. The schemers bought political support by giving congressmen stock in the enterprise. This chicanery had transpired before Grant's election in 1868, but it now touched a number of prominent Republicans. The beneficiaries had included Speaker of the House Schuyler Colfax, later vice-president, and Representative James A. Garfield, later president. Of thirteen members of Congress involved, only two were censured.

Even more odious disclosures soon followed, and some involved the president's cabinet. The secretary of war, it turned out, had accepted bribes from merchants who traded with Indians at army posts in the West. He was impeached, but he resigned in time to elude a Senate trial. Post-office contracts, it was revealed, went to carriers who offered the highest kickbacks. The secretary of the treasury had awarded a political friend a commission of 50 percent for the collection of overdue taxes. In St. Louis a "Whiskey Ring" bribed tax collectors to bilk the government of millions in revenue. Grant's private secretary was enmeshed in that scheme, taking large sums of money and other valuables in return for inside information. There is no evidence that Grant himself was ever involved in, or that he personally profited from, any of the fraud, but his poor choice of associates and his gullibility earned him widespread censure.

REFORM AND THE ELECTION OF 1872   Long before Grant's first term ended, a reaction against Radical Reconstruction and against incompetence and corruption in the administration had incited mutiny

The People's Handwriting on the Wall. *An 1872 engraving comments on the corruption engulfing Grant.*

within the Republican ranks. The Liberal Republicans favored free trade, gold to redeem greenbacks, a stable currency, ending federal Reconstruction efforts in the South, restoring the rights of former Confederates, and civil service reform. Open revolt broke out first in Missouri where Carl Schurz, a German immigrant and war hero, led a group of Liberal Republicans that elected a governor with Democratic help in 1870 and sent Schurz to the Senate. In 1872 the Liberal Republicans held their own national convention at Cincinnati that produced a compromise platform condemning the Republicans' Reconstruction policy and favoring civil service reform, but remained silent on the protective tariff. The delegates embraced an anomalous presidential candidate: Horace Greeley, editor of the *New York Tribune,* a longtime champion of just about every reform available. His image as a visionary eccentric was complemented by his record of hostility to Democrats, whose support the Liberals needed. The Democrats nevertheless swallowed the pill and gave their nomination to Greeley as the only hope of beating Grant.

The result was a foregone conclusion. Republican regulars duly endorsed Radical Reconstruction and the protective tariff. Grant still had seven carpetbag states in his pocket, generous contributions from business and banking interests, and the stalwart support of the Radical Republicans. Above all, he still evoked the imperishable glory of Appomattox. Greeley, despite an exhausting tour of the country—still unusual for a presidential candidate—carried only six southern and border states and none in the North. Grant won by 3,597,132 votes to Greeley's 2,834,125 votes, and by an electoral college vote of 286 to 66.

PANIC AND REDEMPTION Economic distress followed close upon the public scandals besetting the Grant administration. Such developments explain why northerners lost interest in Reconstruction. Contraction of the money supply resulting from the withdrawal of greenbacks and investments in new railroads had made investors cautious and helped precipitate a financial crisis. During 1873 the market for railroad bonds turned sour as some twenty-five railroads defaulted on their interest payments. The investment-banking firm of Jay Cooke and Company, unable to sell the bonds of the Northern Pacific Railroad, financed them with short-term deposits in hope that a European market would develop. But in 1873 the opposite happened when a panic in

Vienna forced many financiers to unload American stocks and bonds. Caught short, Cooke and Company went bankrupt on September 18, 1873. The ensuing stampede of investors to exchange securities for cash forced the stock market to close for ten days. The Panic of 1873 set off a depression that lasted for six years, the longest and most severe that Americans had yet suffered, marked by widespread bankruptcies, unemployment, and a drastic slowdown in railroad building.

Hard times and political scandals hurt Republicans in the midterm elections of 1874. The Democrats won control of the House of Representatives and gained seats in the Senate. The new Democratic House immediately launched inquiries into the scandals and unearthed further evidence of corruption in high places. The financial panic, meanwhile, focused attention once more on greenback currency.

Since greenbacks were valued less than gold, they had become the chief circulating medium. Most people spent greenbacks first and held their gold or used it to settle foreign accounts, which drained much gold out of the country. The postwar reduction of greenbacks in circulation from $432 million to $356 million had made for tight money. To relieve the currency shortage and stimulate business, the Treasury reissued $26 million in greenbacks that had been previously withdrawn.

For a time the advocates of paper money were riding high. But in 1874 Grant vetoed a bill to issue more greenbacks. Then, in his annual message he called for the gradual resumption of specie payments—that is, the redemption of greenbacks in gold. This would make greenbacks "good as gold" and raise their value to a par with the gold dollar. Congress obliged by passing the Resumption Act of 1875. The payment in gold to people who turned in their paper money began on January 1, 1879, after the Treasury had built a gold reserve for that purpose and reduced the value of greenbacks in circulation. This act infuriated those promoting an inflationary monetary policy and provoked the formation of the National Greenback party, which elected fourteen congressmen in 1878. The much-debated and very complex "money question" was destined to remain one of the most divisive issues in American politics.

THE COMPROMISE OF 1877 Grant, despite the controversies swirling around him, wanted to run again in 1876, but many Republicans were not enthusiastic about Grant being the first three-term president.

James G. Blaine of Maine, former Speaker of the House, emerged as the Republican front-runner, but he too bore the taint of scandal. Letters in the possession of James Mulligan of Boston linked Blaine to some dubious railroad dealings, and these "Mulligan letters" found their way into print.

The Republican convention therefore eliminated Blaine and several other hopefuls in favor of Ohio's favorite son, Rutherford B. Hayes. Three times elected governor of Ohio, most recently as an advocate of hard money, Hayes had also made a name as a civil service reformer. But his chief virtue was that he offended neither Radicals nor reformers. As Henry Adams put it, he was "a third rate nonentity, whose only recommendation is that he is obnoxious to no one."

The Democratic convention was abnormally harmonious from the start. The nomination went on the second ballot to Samuel J. Tilden, a millionaire corporation lawyer and reform governor of New York who had directed a campaign to overthrow the notorious Tweed Ring controlling New York City politics and the Canal Ring in Albany, which had bilked the state of millions.

The 1876 campaign generated no burning issues. Both candidates favored the trend toward white conservative rule in the South. During one of the most corrupt elections ever, both candidates also favored civil service reform. In the absence of strong differences, Democrats aired the Republicans' dirty linen. In response, Republicans waved the "bloody shirt," which is to say that they engaged in verbal assaults on former Confederates and the spirit of rebellion, linking the Democratic party with secession and with the outrages committed against black and white Republicans in the South. As one Republican speaker insisted, "Every man that tried to destroy this nation was a Democrat. . . . The man that assassinated Abraham Lincoln was a Democrat. . . . Soldiers, every scar you have on your heroic bodies was given you by a Democrat!"

Early election returns pointed to a Tilden victory. He enjoyed a 300,000 edge in the popular vote and had 184 electoral votes, just one short of a majority. Hayes had 165 electoral votes, but the Republicans also claimed nineteen doubtful votes from Florida, Louisiana, and South Carolina. The Democrats laid a counterclaim to one electoral vote from Oregon. But the Republicans had clearly carried Oregon. In the South the outcome was less certain, and given the fraud and intimidation perpetrated on both sides, nobody will ever know what might have happened if, to use a slogan of the day, "a free ballot and a fair count" had prevailed.

In all three of the disputed southern states, rival canvassing boards sent in different returns. In Florida, Republicans conceded the state election, but in Louisiana and South Carolina rival state governments also appeared. The Constitution offered no guidance in this unprecedented situation. Even if Congress were empowered to sort things out, the Democratic House and the Republican Senate proved unable to reach an agreement.

Finally, on January 29, 1877, the two houses decided to set up a special Electoral Commission that would investigate and report its findings. It had fifteen members, five each from the House, the Senate, and the Supreme Court. Members were so chosen as to have seven from each major party, with Justice David Davis of Illinois as the swing man. Davis, though appointed to the Court by Lincoln, was no party regular and was in fact thought to be leaning toward the Democrats. Thus, the panel appeared to be stacked in favor of Tilden.

But as it turned out, the panel got restacked the other way. Shortsighted Democrats in the Illinois legislature teamed up with minority Greenbackers to name Davis their senator. Davis accepted, no doubt with a sense of relief. From the remaining justices, all Republicans, the panel chose Joseph P. Bradley to fill the vacancy. The decision on each state went by a vote of 8 to 7, along party lines, in favor of Hayes. After much bluster and threat of filibuster by Democrats, the House voted on March 2 to accept the report and declare Hayes elected by an electoral vote of 185 to 184.

Critical to this outcome was the defection of southern Democrats who, seeing the way the wind was blowing with the composition of the Electoral Commission, had made several informal agreements with the Republicans. On February 26, 1877, prominent Ohio Republicans (including James A. Garfield) and powerful southern Democrats struck a bargain at the Wormley House, a Washington hotel. The Republicans promised that, if elected, Hayes would withdraw the last federal troops from Louisiana and South Carolina, letting the Republican governments there collapse. In return, the Democrats promised to withdraw their opposition to Hayes, to accept in good faith the Reconstruction amendments (including civil rights for blacks), and to refrain from partisan reprisals against Republicans in the South.

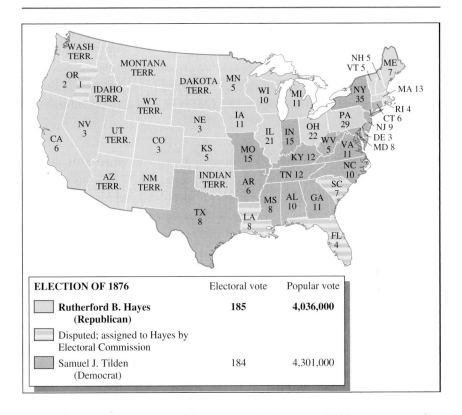

ELECTION OF 1876	Electoral vote	Popular vote
Rutherford B. Hayes (Republican)	**185**	**4,036,000**
Disputed; assigned to Hayes by Electoral Commission		
Samuel J. Tilden (Democrat)	184	4,301,000

Southern Democrats could now justify deserting Tilden because this so-called Compromise of 1877 brought a final "redemption" from the "Radicals" and a return to "home rule," which actually meant rule by white Democrats. Other, more informal promises, less noticed by the public, bolstered the Wormley House agreement. Hayes's friends pledged more support for Mississippi levees and other internal improvements, including a federal subsidy for a transcontinental railroad along a southern route. Southerners extracted a further promise that Hayes would name a white southerner as postmaster-general, the cabinet position with the most patronage jobs at hand. In return, southerners would let Republicans make Garfield Speaker of the new House. Such a deal illustrates the relative weakness of the presidency compared to Congress during the post–Civil War era.

THE END OF RECONSTRUCTION In 1877 President Hayes withdrew federal troops from Louisiana and South Carolina, and the Republican governments there collapsed soon thereafter—along with much of Hayes's claim to legitimacy. Hayes chose a Tennessean and former Confederate as postmaster-general. But after southern Democrats failed to permit the choice of James Garfield as House Speaker, Hayes expressed doubt about any further subsidy for railroad building, and none was voted. Most of the other "Wormley House" promises were either renounced or forgotten.

As to southern promises regarding the civil rights of blacks, only a few Democratic leaders, such as the new governors of South Carolina and Louisiana, remembered them for long. Over the next three decades, protection of black civil rights crumbled under the pressure of white rule in the South and the force of Supreme Court decisions narrowing the application of the Reconstruction amendments. Radical Reconstruction never offered more than an uncertain commitment to black civil rights and social equality. Yet it left an enduring legacy, the Thirteenth, Fourteenth, and Fifteenth Amendments—not dead but dormant, waiting to be awakened. If Reconstruction did not provide social equality or substantial economic opportunities for blacks, it did create the foundation for future advances. It was a revolution, sighed North Carolina governor Jonathan Worth, and "nobody can anticipate the action of revolutions."

MAKING CONNECTIONS

- The political, economic, and racial policies of the conservatives who overthrew the Republican governments in the southern states are described in Chapter 19.

- Several of the political scandals mentioned in this chapter were related to the railroads, a topic discussed in greater detail in Chapter 20.

- This chapter ended with the election of Rutherford B. Hayes; for a discussion of Hayes's administration, see Chapter 22.

FURTHER READING

The most comprehensive treatment of Reconstruction is Eric Foner's *Reconstruction: America's Unfinished Revolution, 1863–1877* (1988). For a study of Andrew Johnson, see Hans L. Trefousse's *Andrew Johnson: A Biography* (1989).

Scholars have been fairly sympathetic to the aims and motives of the Radical Republicans. See, for instance, Herman Belz's *Reconstructing the Union* (1969) and Richard Nelson Current's *Those Terrible Carpetbaggers: A Reinterpretation* (1988). The ideology of the Radicals is explored in Michael Les Benedict's *A Compromise of Principle: Congressional Republicans and Reconstruction, 1863–1869* (1974).

The intransigence of southern white attitudes is examined in Michael Perman's *Reunion without Compromise* (1973) and Dan T. Carter's *When the War Was Over: The Failure of Self-Reconstruction in the South, 1865–1867* (1985). Allen W. Trelease's *White Terror* (1971) covers the various organizations that practiced vigilante tactics, chiefly the Ku Klux Klan. The difficulties former slaves had in adjusting to the new labor system are documented in James L. Roark's *Masters without Slaves* (1977). Books on southern politics during Reconstruction include Michael Perman's *The Road to Redemption* (1984), Terry L. Seip's *The South Returns to Congress* (1983), and Mark W. Summer's *Railroads, Reconstruction, and the Gospel of Prosperity* (1984).

Numerous works study the freed blacks' experience in the South. Start with Leon F. Litwack's *Been in the Storm So Long* (1979). Joel Williamson's *After Slavery* (1965) argues that South Carolina blacks took an active role in pursuing their political and economic rights. The Freedmen's Bureau is explored in William S. McFeely's *Yankee Stepfather: General O.O. Howard and the Freedmen* (1968). The situation of freed slave women, which was often quite different than that of freed slave men, is discussed in Jacqueline Jones's *Labor of Love, Labor of Sorrow: Black Women, Work, and the Family from Slavery to Present* (1985).

The land confiscation issue is discussed in Eric Foner's *Politics and Ideology in the Age of the Civil War* (1980), and Janet S. Hermann's *The Pursuit of a Dream* (1981), covers the Davis Bend experiment in Mississippi.

The politics of corruption outside the South is depicted in William S. McFeely's *Grant: A Biography* (1981). The political maneuvers of the election of 1876 and the resultant crisis and compromise are explained in C. Vann Woodward's *Reunion and Reaction* (1951) and William Gillette's *Retreat from Reconstruction, 1869–1879* (1979).

PART FIVE

GROWING
PAINS

The northern victory in 1865 restored the Union and in the process helped to accelerate America's transformation into a modern nation-state. A distinctly national consciousness began to displace the sectional emphases of the antebellum era. During and after the Civil War, the Republican-led Congress pushed through legislation to foster industrial and commercial development and western expansion. In the process, the United States abandoned the Jeffersonian dream of a decentralized agrarian republic and began to forge a dynamic new industrial outlook generated by an increasingly national and even international market.

After 1865, many Americans turned their attention to the unfinished business of settling a continent and completing an urban-industrial revolution begun before the war. Huge new national corporations based upon mass production and mass marketing began to dominate the economy. As the prominent sociologist William Graham Sumner remarked, the process of industrial development "controls us all because we are all in it. It creates the conditions of our own existence, sets the limits of our social activity, and regulates the bonds of our social relations."

The industrial revolution was not only an urban phenomenon; it transformed rural life as well. Those who got in the way of the new emphasis on large-scale, highly mechanized commercial agriculture and ranching were brusquely pushed aside. Farm folk, as one New Englander stressed, "must understand farming as a business; if they do not it will go hard with them." The friction between new market forces and traditional folkways generated political revolts and social unrest during the last quarter of the nineteenth century. Fault lines appeared throughout the social order, and they unleashed tremors that exerted what one writer called "a seismic shock, a cyclonic violence" upon the body politic.

The clash between tradition and modernity peaked during the decade of the 1890s, one of the most strife-ridden in American history. A deep depression, agrarian unrest, and labor violence provoked fears of a class war. This turbulent situation transformed the presidential election campaign of 1896 into a clash between two rival visions of America's future. The Republican candidate, William McKinley, campaigned on behalf of modern urban-industrial values. By contrast, William Jennings Bryan, the nominee of both the Democratic and Populist parties, was an eloquent defender of America's rural past. McKinley's victory proved to be a watershed in American political and social history. By 1900 the United States would emerge as one of the world's greatest industrial powers, and it would thereafter assume a new leadership role in world affairs.

19 ⌒ NEW FRONTIERS:

SOUTH AND WEST

CHAPTER ORGANIZER

This chapter focuses on:

• the economic and political policies of the states in the post-
Reconstruction South.

• race relations in the New South.

• the experiences of farmers, miners, and cowboys.

• late-nineteenth-century Indian policy.

fter the Civil War, the West and the South provided enticing opportunities for American inventiveness and entrepreneurship to flourish. Before 1860, most people had
viewed the region between the Mississippi River and California as a bar-
ren landscape unfit for human habitation or cultivation, an uninviting
land suitable only for Indians and animals. Half of the state of Texas, for
instance, was still not settled at the end of the Civil War. After 1865,
however, the federal government encouraged western settlement and
economic exploitation. The construction of transcontinental railroads,
the military conquest of the Indians, and a liberal land distribution policy

combined to help lure thousands of pioneers and expectant capitalists westward. Charles Goodnight, a Texas cattleman, recalled that "we were adventurers in a great land as fresh and full of the zest of darers."

Although the first great wave of railroad building occurred in the 1850s, the most spectacular growth took place during the quarter century after the Civil War. From about 35,000 miles of track in 1865, the network grew to nearly 200,000 miles by 1897. The transcontinental rail lines led the way, and they helped populate the plains and the Far West. Of course, such a railroad network was very expensive, and the long-term debt required to finance it would become a major cause of the Panic of 1893 and the ensuing depression.

In the postwar South, rail lines were rebuilt and supplemented with new branch lines. The defeated Confederacy offered capitalists a fertile new ground for investment and industrial development. Proponents of a "New South" after 1865 argued that the region must abandon its single-minded preoccupation with agriculture and pursue industrial and commercial development. As a result, the South as well as the West experienced dramatic social and economic changes during the last third of the nineteenth century. By 1900, these new "frontiers" had been transformed in ways that few could have predicted, and fourteen new states were created out of the western territories.

THE NEW SOUTH

A FRESH VISION   Amid the pains of defeat and the ruins of war many southerners looked back wistfully to the plantation life that had dominated their region before the firing on Fort Sumter. A few prominent leaders, however, insisted that the postwar South must liberate itself from such nostalgia and create a modern society of small farms, thriving industries, and bustling cities. The major prophet of this "New South" was Henry W. Grady, editor of the *Atlanta Constitution*.

During the 1880s, Grady set forth the vision that inspired a generation of southerners: "The Old South," he said, "rested everything on slavery and agriculture, unconscious that these could neither give nor maintain healthy growth." The New South, on the other hand, "presents a perfect democracy" of small farms and diversifying industries. The postwar South, he believed, held the promise of being a real democracy, no longer run by the planter aristocracy and no longer dependent on slave labor.

Grady's compelling vision of a New South attracted many supporters. In the aftermath of the Civil War, these men preached with evangelical fervor the gospel of industrial development. The Confederacy, they reasoned, had lost the war because it had relied too much on King Cotton. In the future the South must follow the North's example and industrialize. From that central belief flowed certain corollaries: that a more diversified and efficient agriculture would be a foundation for economic growth, that more widespread education, especially vocational training, would promote material success, and that sectional peace and racial harmony would provide a stable environment for economic growth.

ECONOMIC GROWTH   The chief accomplishment of the New South movement was an expansion of the area's textile production that began in the 1880s and overtook its older New England competitors by the 1920s. From 1880 to 1900, the number of cotton mills in the South grew from 161 to 400, the number of mill workers (among whom women and children outnumbered the men) increased fivefold, and the consumption of cotton went up eightfold.

Tobacco growth also increased significantly. One key to the rise of the tobacco industry was the Duke family of Durham, North Carolina. At the end of the Civil War, the story goes, old Washington Duke had only fifty cents obtained from a Yankee soldier for a souvenir Confederate five-dollar bill. He took a barnful of tobacco and, with the help of his three sons, beat it out with hickory sticks, stuffed it in bags, hitched up two mules to his wagon, and set out across the state, selling tobacco as he went. By 1872 the Dukes had a factory producing 125,000 pounds of tobacco annually, and Washington Duke prepared to settle down and enjoy success.

His son Buck (James Buchanan Duke), however, wanted even greater success. He recognized that the tobacco industry was "half smoke and half ballyhoo," so he poured large sums into advertising schemes. Duke also undersold competitors in their own markets and cornered the supply of ingredients. Eventually his competitors agreed to join forces, and in 1890 Duke brought most of them into the American Tobacco Company, which controlled nine-tenths of the nation's cigarette production and, by 1904, about three-fourths of all tobacco production. In 1911 the

General Ulysses S. Grant and General Robert E. Lee share this 1889 album cover The Heroes of the Civil War, *issued by W. Duke Sons & Co. to promote their cigarettes.*

Supreme Court ruled that the company was in violation of the Sherman Anti-Trust Act and ordered it broken up, but by then Duke had found new worlds to conquer in hydroelectric power and aluminum.

Systematic use of other natural resources helped revitalize the area along the Appalachian Mountain chain from West Virginia to Alabama. Coal production in the South (including West Virginia) grew from 5 million tons in 1875 to 49 million tons by 1900. At the southern end of the mountains, Birmingham, Alabama, sprang up during the 1870s in the shadow of Red Mountain, so named for its iron ore, and boosters soon tagged the city the "Pittsburgh of the South."

Industrial growth spawned a need for housing, and after 1870 lumbering became a thriving industry in the South. Lumber camps sprouted across the mountains and flatlands. By the turn of the century, their product, mainly southern pine, had outdistanced textiles in value. Tree cutting seemed to know no bounds, despite the resulting ecological devastation. In time the lumber industry would be saved only by the warm climate, which fostered quick renewal of forests, and the rise of scientific forestry.

The South still had far to go to achieve the "diversified industry" that Henry Grady envisioned in the mid-1880s, but a profusion of other products poured from southern plants: phosphate fertilizers from coastal South Carolina and Florida; oysters, vegetables, and fruits from widespread canneries; ships, including battleships, from the Newport News Shipbuilding and Drydock Company; leather products; liquors and beverages; and clay, glass, and stone products.

AGRICULTURE, OLD AND NEW   At the turn of the century, however, most of the South remained undeveloped, at least by northeastern standards. Despite the optimistic rhetoric of New South spokesmen, the typical southerner was less apt to be tending a loom or forge than, as the saying went, facing the eastern end of a westbound mule. King Cotton survived the Civil War and expanded over new acreage even as its export markets leveled off. Louisiana cane sugar, probably the most war-devastated of all crops, flourished again by the 1890s.

In the old rice belt of coastal South Carolina and elsewhere, vegetable farming flourished with the advent of the railroads and refrigerator cars. But the majority of southern farmers were not flourishing. A prolonged

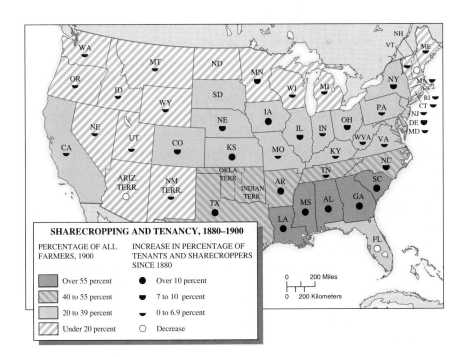

SHARECROPPING AND TENANCY, 1880–1900

deflation in crop prices affected the entire Western world during the last third of the nineteenth century. Sagging prices made it more difficult than ever to own land. Sharecropping and tenancy grew increasingly prevalent. By 1890 most southern farms were worked by people who did not own the land. Tenancy rates in the Deep South belied Henry Grady's dream of a southern democracy of small landowners: South Carolina, 61 percent; Georgia, 60 percent; Alabama, 58 percent; Mississippi, 62 percent; and Louisiana, 58 percent.

How did sharecropping and tenancy work? Sharecroppers, who had nothing to offer the landowner but their labor, worked the land in return for supplies and a share of the crop, generally about half. Tenant farmers, hardly better off, might have their own mule, plow, and line of credit with the country store. They were entitled to claim a larger share, commonly three-fourths of the cash crop and two-thirds of the subsistence crop, which was mainly corn. The system was horribly inefficient, for the tenant lacked incentive to care for the land, and the owner had little chance to supervise the work. In addition, the system bred a morbid suspicion on both sides. The folklore of the rural South overflowed with stories of tenants who remained stubbornly shiftless and landlords who kept books with crooked pencils.

The postwar South suffered from an acute shortage of capital. So people had to devise ways to operate without cash. One way to do this was through the crop-lien system: country merchants furnished supplies to small farmers in return for liens (or mortgages) on their crops. Such credit offered a way out of dependency for some farmers, but to most it offered only a hopeless cycle of perennial debt. The merchant, who assumed great risks, generally charged interest that ranged, according to one publication, "from 24 percent to grand larceny." The merchant, like the planter (often the same man), required his farmer clients to grow a cash crop that could be readily sold at harvest time. So for all the wind and ink expended by promoters of a "New South" based on diversified agriculture, the routines of tenancy and sharecropping geared the marketing, supply, and credit systems to a staple crop, usually cotton. The stagnation of rural life thus held millions, white and black, in bondage to privation and ignorance.

THE BOURBON REDEEMERS   In post–Civil War politics, habits of deference and elitism still prevailed. "Every community," one Union officer noted in postwar South Carolina, "had its great man, or its little great man, around whom his fellow citizens gather when they want information, and to whose monologues they listen with a respect akin to humility." After Reconstruction, southern politics was dominated by small groups of such men, collectively known as Redeemers or Bourbons. The supporters of these postwar leaders referred to them as Redeemers because they supposedly "redeemed," or saved, the South from Yankee domination as well as the straitjacket of a purely rural economy. The Redeemers included a rising class of entrepreneurs who were eager to promote a more diversified economy based on industrial development and railroad expansion. The opponents of the "Redeemers" labeled them "Bourbons" in an effort to depict them not as progressives but as reactionaries. Like the French royal family which, Napoleon said, forgot nothing and learned nothing in the ordeal of revolution, Bourbons of the postwar South were said to have forgotten nothing and learned nothing in the ordeal of the Civil War.

These Bourbons of the New South perfected a political alliance with northern conservatives and an economic alliance with northern capitalists. They generally pursued a government fiscal policy of retrenchment and frugality, except for the tax exemptions and other favors they offered to business. The Bourbons slashed state government expenditures, including the public school systems started during Reconstruction. In 1871 the southern Atlantic states were spending $10.27 per pupil; by 1880 the figure was down to $6.00, and in 1890 it stood at $7.63. In 1882 there were 3,183 schools in South Carolina but only 3,413 teachers. Illiteracy rates in the South at the time ran at about 12 percent of the native white population and 50 percent of the black population.

The urge to reduce state expenditures created in the penal system one of the darkest blots on the Bourbon record: convict leasing. The wartime destruction of prisons and the poverty of state treasuries combined with the demand for cheap labor for the railroads, mines, and lumber and turpentine camps to make the leasing of convict labor a way for southern states to avoid expenses and generate revenues. The burden of detaining criminals grew after the war because freed slaves, who had been subject to the discipline of masters, were now subject to the criminal law. Convict leasing, in the absence of state supervision, allowed inefficiency, neglect, and disregard for human life to proliferate. White political and economic leaders often used a racial argument to rationalize the leasing of convicts, most of whom were black. An "inferior" and "shiftless" race, they claimed, required the regimen of such coercion to elevate it above its idle and undisciplined ways.

The Bourbons reduced not only state expenditures but also the public debt, and by a simple means—they repudiated a vast amount of debt issued by the post–Civil War Reconstruction governments. The corruption and extravagance of Radical rule were commonly advanced as justification for the process, but repudiation did not stop with Reconstruction debts. Altogether nine states repudiated more than half of what they owed to bondholders and creditors.

Despite their penny-pinching ways, these frugal Bourbon regimes, so ardently devoted to free enterprise, did respond to the demand for commissions to regulate the rates charged by railroads for commercial transport. They also established boards of agriculture and public health, agricultural experiment stations, agricultural and mechanical colleges, teacher-training schools and women's colleges, and even state colleges for African Americans.

Nor can any simplistic interpretation encompass the variety of Bourbon leaders. The Democratic party of the time was a mongrel coalition that threw Unionists, secessionists, businessmen, small farmers, hillbillies, planters, and even some Republicans together in alliance against the Reconstruction Radicals. Democrats therefore, even those who bore the Bourbon label, often marched to different drummers. And once they gained control, Bourbon regimes never achieved complete unity in philosophy or government.

Perhaps the ultimate paradox of the Bourbons' rule was that these paragons of white supremacy tolerated a lingering black voice in politics and showed no haste about raising the barriers of racial separation. In the 1880s southern politics remained open and democratic with 64 percent of the eligible voters, blacks and whites, participating in elections. Blacks sat in the state legislatures of South Carolina until 1900 and of Georgia until 1908; some of these black representatives were Democrats. The South sent black congressmen to Washington in every election until 1900 except one, though they always represented gerrymandered districts into which most of the state's black voters had been placed. Under the Bourbons the disenfranchisement of black voters remained inconsistent, a local matter brought about mainly by fraud and intimidation, but it occurred often enough to ensure white control of the southern states.

A like flexibility applied to other areas of race relations. The color line was drawn less strictly after the Civil War than it would be in the twentieth century. In some places, to be sure, racial segregation appeared before the end of Reconstruction, especially in schools, churches, hotels and rooming houses, and private social relations. In places of public accommodation such as trains, depots, theaters, and soda fountains, however, discrimination was more sporadic.

The ultimate achievement of the New South prophets and their allies, the Bourbons, was that they reconciled tradition with innovation. Their relative moderation in racial policy, at least before the 1890s, allowed them to embrace just enough of the new to disarm adversaries and keep control. By promoting the growth of industry, the Bourbons led the South into a new economic era, but without sacrificing a mythic reverence for the Old South. Bourbon rule left a permanent mark on the South. As the historian C. Vann Woodward has noted, "it was not the Radicals nor the Confederates but the Redeemers who laid the lasting foundations in matters of race, politics, economics and institutions for the modern South."

DISENFRANCHISING BLACKS   During the 1890s, the attitudes that permitted such moderation in race relations evaporated. A violent "negrophobia" swept across the South and much of the nation at the end of the century. One reason was that many whites resented signs of black success and social influence. An Alabama newspaper editor declared that "our blood boils when the educated Negro asserts himself politically. We regard each assertion as an unfriendly encroachment upon our native superior rights, and a dare-devil menace to our control of the affairs of the state."

Education did bring enlightenment—as it was supposed to do. In 1889, the student newspaper at all-black Fisk University in Nashville predicted a profound change in race relations at the end of the century. It stressed that a new generation of young black adults born since the end of the Civil War and educated in schools and colleges were determined to gain true equality. They were more assertive and less patient than their parents. "We are not the Negro from whom the chains of slavery fell a quarter century ago, most assuredly not," the editor announced. A growing number of young white adults, however, were equally determined to keep "Negroes in their place."

The Effects of Radical and Bourbon Rule in the South. *This 1880 cartoon shows the South staggering under the oppressive weight of military Reconstruction* (left) *and flourishing under the "Let 'Em Alone Policy" of Hayes and the Bourbons* (right).

The result of such renewed racism was a distressing surge in racial violence and repression during the last decade of the nineteenth century and first two decades of the twentieth. Organized efforts at harassment, violence, intimidation, and segregation aimed to reestablish the authority and imagined superiority of the white race. By the end of the nineteenth century, the so-called New South had come to resemble the Old South. Ruling whites ruthlessly imposed their will over all areas of black life and codified the principles of racial subjugation and segregation by preventing blacks from voting and by enacting "Jim Crow" laws mandating public segregation of the races. This was not the logical culmination of the Civil War and emancipation but rather the result of a calculated campaign by white elites and thugs to limit African-American political, economic, and social life.

The political dynamics of the 1890s exacerbated racial tensions. The rise of populism, a farm-based protest movement that spawned a third political party in the 1890s, divided the white vote to such an extent that in some places the black vote became the balance of power. Some populists courted black votes and brought blacks prominently into their leadership councils. In response, the Bourbons revived the race issue, which they exploited with seasoned finesse, all the while controlling for their ticket a good part of the black vote in plantation areas. Nevertheless the Bourbons soon reversed themselves and began arguing in the 1890s that the black vote should be eliminated completely from southern elections. The affluent and well-educated Democrats in southern counties with large black populations led the way in promoting disenfranchisement. They wanted to eliminate the voting of poor whites as well as blacks. It was imperative, said the governor of Louisiana in 1894, that "the mass of ignorance, vice and venality without any proprietary interest in the State" be denied the vote. Some farm leaders hoped that disenfranchisement of blacks would make it possible for whites to divide politically without raising the specter of "Negro domination." But since the Fifteenth Amendment made it impossible simply to deny blacks the right to vote, disenfranchisement was accomplished indirectly through devices such as poll taxes (or head taxes) and literacy tests.

Mississippi led the way to near-total disenfranchisement of blacks and many poor whites as well. The state called a constitutional convention in 1890 to change the suffrage provisions of the old Radical constitution of 1868. The Mississippi plan set the pattern that seven more states would follow over the next twenty years. First, a residence requirement—two years in the state, one year in the election district—struck at those black tenant farmers who were in the habit of moving yearly in search of better opportunities. Second, voters were disqualified if convicted of certain crimes. Third, all taxes, including a poll tax, had to be paid before a person could vote. This proviso fell most heavily on poor whites and blacks. Fourth and finally, all voters had to be literate. The alternative, designed as a loophole for whites otherwise disqualified, was an "understanding" clause. The voter, if unable to read the Constitution, could qualify by being able to "understand" it—to the satisfaction of the registrar. Not surprisingly, registrars declared far more blacks ineligible than whites.

In other states, variations on the Mississippi plan added a few flourishes. In 1895 South Carolina tacked on the proviso that owning property assessed at $300 would qualify an illiterate voter. In 1898 Louisiana invented the "grandfather clause," which allowed illiterates to vote if their fathers or grandfathers had been eligible to vote on January 1, 1867, when blacks were still excluded. Black educator Booker T. Washington sent the convention a sarcastic telegram expressing hope that "no one clothed with state authority will be tempted to perjure and degrade himself by putting one interpretation upon it for the white man and another for the black man." By 1910 Georgia, North Carolina, Virginia, Alabama, and Oklahoma had adopted the grandfather clause. Every southern state, moreover, adopted a statewide Democratic primary between 1896 and 1915, which became the only meaningful election outside isolated areas of Republican strength. With minor exceptions, the Democratic primaries excluded black voters altogether. The effectiveness of these measures can be seen in a few sample figures. Louisiana in 1896 had 130,000 black voters registered. By 1900 the number was only 5,320. Alabama in 1900 had 121,159 literate black males over twenty-one, according to the census; only 3,742, however, were registered to vote.

SEGREGATION SPREADS   What came to be called "Jim Crow" segregation followed disenfranchisement and in some states came first. The symbolic first target was the railway train. In 1885, the novelist George Washington Cable noted that in South Carolina blacks "ride in first class [rail] cars as a right" and "their presence excites no comment." From 1875 to 1883 in fact, any racial segregation violated a federal Civil Rights Act, which forbade discrimination in places of public accommodation. But in 1883 the Supreme Court ruled on seven civil rights cases involving discrimination against blacks by corporations or individuals. The Court held, with only one dissent, that the force of federal law could not extend to individual action because the Fourteenth Amendment, which provided that "no State" could deny citizens the equal protection of the laws, stood as a prohibition only against *state* action.

This left as an open question the validity of state laws *requiring* separate racial facilities under the rubric of "separate but equal," a slogan popular with the New South prophets. In 1881 Tennessee had required railroads in the state to maintain separate first-class rail cars for blacks and whites. In 1888 Mississippi went a step further by requiring passengers, under penalty of law, to occupy the car set aside for their race. When Louisiana followed suit in 1890, dissidents challenged the law in the case of *Plessy* v. *Ferguson,* which the Supreme Court decided in 1896.

The test case originated in New Orleans when Homer Plessy, an octoroon (a person having one-eighth black ancestry), refused to leave a white railroad car when told to do so. He was convicted, and the case rose on appeal to the Supreme Court. The Court ruled that segregation laws "have been generally, if not universally recognized as within the competency of state legislatures in the exercise of their police power."

Very soon the principle of racial segregation extended into every area of southern life, including street railways, hotels, restaurants, hospitals, recreations, sports, and employment. If an activity was overlooked by the laws, it was not overlooked in custom and practice. In 1900 the editor of the *Richmond Times* expressed the prevailing view: "It is necessary that this principle be applied in every relation of Southern life. God Almighty drew the color line and it cannot be obliterated. The negro must stay on his side of the line and the white man must stay on his side, and the sooner both races recognize this fact and accept it, the better it will be for both."

Violence accompanied the "Jim Crow" laws. From 1890 to 1899, lynchings in the United States averaged 188 per year, 82 percent of which occurred in the South; from 1900 to 1909 they averaged 93 per year, 92 percent in the South. Whites constituted 32 percent of the victims during the first period, only 11 percent in the latter. A young Episcopal priest in Montgomery said that extremists had proceeded "from an undiscriminating attack upon the Negro's ballot to a like attack upon his schools, his labor, his life."

By the end of the nineteenth century, legalized racial discrimination—segregation of public facilities, political disenfranchisement, and vigilante justice punctuated by brutal public lynchings and race riots—had elevated government-sanctioned bigotry to an official way of life in the South. South Carolina senator Benjamin Tillman declared in 1892 that blacks "must remain subordinate or be exterminated."

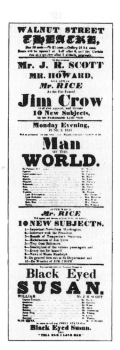

"Jim Crow," a stock character in old minstrel shows, became a synonym for racial segregation in the twentieth century.

How did blacks respond to the resurgence of racism and statutory segregation? Some left the South in search of equality and opportunity, but the vast majority stayed in their native region. The few who resisted—even in self-defense—were ruthlessly suppressed. In the face of overwhelming force and prejudicial justice, most blacks accommodated themselves to the realities of white supremacy and segregation. "Had to walk a quiet life," explained James Plunkett, a Virginia black. "The least little thing you would do, they [whites] would kill ya." Survival in the South required blacks to wear a mask of deference and discretion. The black novelist Richard Wright remembered how in his native Mississippi the "sustained expectation of violence" at the hands of whites induced a "paralysis of will and impulse" in him.

Yet accommodation did not mean total submission. Excluded from the dominant white world, and eager to avoid confrontations, black southerners after the 1890s increasingly turned inward and constructed their own culture and nurtured their own pride. A young white visitor to Mississippi in 1910 noticed that nearly every black person he met had "two distinct social selves, the one he reveals to his own people, the other he assumes among the whites."

Black churches continued to provide a hub for black communities. Outside the family, churches provided the primary locus of community life. Often the only public buildings available for blacks, churches were used not only for worship but also for activities that had nothing to do with religion: social gatherings, club meetings, political activities. For men especially, churches offered leadership roles and political status. Being a deacon was one of the most prestigious roles a black man could achieve. As in many white churches, men stood in the pulpit and governed church affairs, and women pretty much did everything else. Churches fostered racial pride and personal dignity and enabled blacks of all classes to interact and to exercise roles denied them in the larger society. Religious life provided great comfort to people worn down by the daily hardships and abuses associated with segregation.

One irony of segregation is that it opened up new economic opportunities for blacks. A new class of black entrepreneurs emerged to provide services—insurance, banking, barbering, funerals, hair salons—to the black community in the segregated South. At the same time, blacks formed their own social and fraternal clubs and organizations, all of which helped bolster black pride and provide fellowship and opportunities for service. For example, the Odd Fellows, the largest of the black male fraternal orders, had over 400,000 members in 1904.

Middle-class black women formed a network of thousands of racial-uplift organizations across the South and around the nation. The women's clubs were engines of social service in their communities. They cared for the aged and infirm, the orphaned and abandoned. They created homes for single mothers and provided nurseries for working mothers. They sponsored health clinics for black families and classes in home economics for women. In 1896 the leaders of women's clubs from around the country converged to form the National Association of Colored Women to combat racism and segregation. The organization's first president, Mary Church Terrell, told the members that they had an obligation to serve the "lowly, the illiterate, and even the vicious to whom we are bound by the ties of race and sex, and put forth every effort to uplift and reclaim them." Female activists declared that black men were not providing sufficient leadership in dealing with the race problem; an editorial in *Woman's Era* called for "timid men and ignorant men" to step aside.

IDA B. WELLS   One of the most outspoken black activists was Ida B. Wells. Born into slavery in 1862 in Mississippi, she attended a school staffed by white missionaries. In 1878, an epidemic of yellow fever killed both of her parents as well as an infant brother. At age sixteen Wells assumed responsibility for her five younger siblings and secured a job as a country schoolteacher. About 1880, in search of greater economic security and opportunity, Wells moved to nearby Memphis, then fast-emerging as a commercial hub and cultural center. In Memphis Wells taught in segregated country and city schools and soon gained entrance into the social life of the city's striving black middle class.

Ida B. Wells.

In 1883 Wells confronted the reality and power of white supremacy. After being denied a seat in a railroad car because she was black, she became the first African American to file suit against such discrimination. The circuit court decided in her favor and fined the railroad, but the Tennessee supreme court overturned the ruling. Wells thereafter discovered her "first and [it] might be said, my only love"—journalism—and, through it, a weapon with which to wage her lifelong crusade for justice. Writing under the pen name "Iola," she became a prominent editor of *Free Speech,* a black newspaper in Memphis.

In 1892, when three of her friends were lynched by a white mob, Wells launched a lifelong crusade against lynching. She called on Memphis blacks to "leave a town which will neither protect our lives and property, nor give us a fair trial in the courts, when accused by white persons." Angry whites destroyed the newspaper offices and threatened to lynch Wells. Having become "an exile from home for hinting at the truth," she moved to New York and continued to use her fiery journalistic talent to criticize "Jim Crow" laws and demand that blacks have their voting rights restored.

In 1895 Wells married Ferdinand Lee Barnett, a lawyer and editor of the *Chicago Conservator.* While raising four children in Chicago, Wells sustained her commitment to help end racial and gender discrimination. She played a pivotal role in the development of black women's clubs. Wells also continued to educate the nation about the pervasiveness of lynching in the South. She declared that "a Winchester rifle should have a place of honor in every black home, and it should be used for that protection which the law refuses to give." Only by armed self-defense, she concluded, could the lynching of blacks be stopped.

Such incendiary rhetoric prompted calls from moderate black leaders for Wells to soften her message, but she steadfastly refused. In the spring of 1898, the lynching of a black postmaster in South Carolina so incensed Wells that she went to Washington, D.C., and spent five weeks fruitlessly trying to convince the federal government to intervene. Later, in 1909, she would help found the National Association for the Advancement of Colored People (NAACP) and would also work to promote women's suffrage. In promoting full equality, Wells often found herself in direct opposition to the accommodationist views of black leader Booker T. Washington.

WASHINGTON AND DU BOIS   Booker T. Washington, born in Virginia of a slave mother and a white father, had fought extreme adversity to get an education at Hampton Institute, one of the postwar missionary schools, and then to build at Tuskegee, Alabama, a leading college for African Americans. Washington argued that blacks should first establish an economic base for their advancement. They should focus "upon the everyday practical things of life, upon something that is needed to be done, and something which they will be permitted to do in the community in which they reside." In his famous speech at the Atlanta Cotton States and International Exposition in 1895, which propelled him to fame, Washington advised fellow blacks: "Cast down your bucket where you are—cast it down in making friends . . . of the people of all races by whom we are surrounded. Cast it down in agriculture, mechanics, in commerce, in domestic service, and in the professions." He conspicuously omitted politics and offered an oblique endorsement of segregation: "In all things that are purely social we can be as separate as the five fingers, yet one as the hand in all things essential to mutual progress."

Some people bitterly criticized Washington, then and since, for making a bad bargain: the sacrifice of broad education and of civil rights for the dubious acceptance of white conservatives and economic opportunities. W. E. B. Du Bois led blacks in this criticism of Washington. A native of Massachusetts, Du Bois first experienced southern racial practices as an undergraduate at Fisk University in Nashville. Later he earned a Ph.D. in history from Harvard and briefly attended the University of Berlin. In addition to an active career in racial protest, he left a distinguished record as a scholar and author. Trim and dapper in appearance, sporting a goatee, cane, and gloves, Du Bois possessed a combative spirit. Not long after he began his teaching

Booker T. Washington.

W. E. B. Du Bois.

career at Atlanta University in 1897, he began to assault Washington's accommodationist philosophy of black progress and put forward his own program of "ceaseless agitation."

Washington, Du Bois argued, preached "a gospel of Work and Money to such an extent as . . . to overshadow the higher aims of life." The education of blacks, he maintained, should not be merely vocational but should nurture leaders willing to challenge segregation and discrimination through political action. He believed in work, "but work is not necessarily education. Education is the development of power and ideal." He demanded that disenfranchisement and legalized segregation cease and that the laws of the land be enforced. And he provided the formula for attaining such goals: "By voting where we may vote, by persistent, unceasing agitation, by hammering at the truth, by sacrifice and work." Du Bois minced no words in criticizing Washington's philosophy: he called Washington's 1895 speech "the Atlanta Compromise" and said that he refused "to surrender the leadership of this race to cowards."

THE NEW WEST

Like the South, the West is a region wrapped in myths. The lands west of the Mississippi River contain remarkable geographic extremes— majestic mountains, roaring rivers, searing deserts, and dense forests. For vast reaches of western America the great epics of Civil War and Reconstruction were remote events hardly touching the lives of the Indians, Mexicans, Asians, trappers, miners, and Mormons scattered through the plains and mountains. There the march of Manifest Destiny continued on its inexorable course, propelled by a lust for land and a passion for profits. On one level, the settlement of the West beyond the Mississippi River constitutes a colorful drama of determined pioneers and two-fisted gunslingers overcoming all obstacles to secure their visions of freedom and opportunity amid the region's awesome vastness. The post–Civil War West offered the promise of democratic individualism, economic opportunity, and personal freedom that had long before come to define the American Dream. But on another level, the colonization of the Far West was a tragedy of shortsighted greed and irresponsible behavior, a story of reckless exploitation that scarred the land, decimated its wildlife, and nearly exterminated the culture of Native Americans. Both images of the process of western settlement are accurate in some respects.

In the second tier of trans-Mississippi states—Iowa, Kansas, Nebraska—and in western Minnesota, the last frontier of farmers began spreading across the Great Plains after mid-century. From California the miners' frontier spread east through the mountains at one new strike after another. From Texas the nomadic cowboys migrated northward into the plains and across the Rockies into the Great Basin. Now there were two frontiers of settlement, east and west, and even a third to the south; in another generation there would be none.

As they moved west, the settlers encountered a different climate and landscape. The Great Plains were arid, and the scarcity of water and timber rendered useless or impossible the familiar trappings of the pioneer: the axe, the log cabin, the rail fence, and the accustomed methods of tilling the soil. For a long time the region had been called the Great American Desert, a barrier to cross on the way to the Pacific, unfit for human habitation and therefore, to white Americans, the perfect refuge for Indians. But that pattern changed in the last half of the nineteenth century as a result of new finds of gold, silver, and other minerals, completion of transcontinental railroads, destruction of the buffalo, the collapse of Indian resistance, the rise of the range-cattle industry, and the dawning realization that the arid region need not be a sterile desert. With the use of what water was available, techniques of dry farming and irrigation could make the land fruitful after all.

THE MIGRATORY STREAM   During the second half of the nineteenth century, an unrelenting stream of migrants flowed into the largely Indian and Hispanic West. Millions of Anglo-Americans, African Americans, Mexicans, and European and Chinese immigrants transformed the patterns of western society and culture. Most of the settlers were relatively prosperous white, native-born farming families. Because of the expense of transportation, land, and supplies, the very poor could not afford to relocate. Three-quarters of the western migrants were men.

The largest number of foreign immigrants came from northern Europe and Canada. In the northern plains, Germans, Scandinavians, and Irish were especially numerous. Not surprisingly, these foreign settlers tended to cluster together according to ethnic and kinship ties. Norwegians and Swedes, for example, often gravitated toward others from the same home province or parish to form cohesive rural communities. In the new state of Nebraska in 1870, a quarter of the 123,000 residents were foreign-born. In North Dakota in 1890, 45 percent of the residents were immigrants. Compared to European immigrants, those from China and Mexico were much less numerous but nonetheless significant. More than 200,000 Chinese arrived in California between 1876 and 1890.

In the aftermath of the collapse of Radical Republican rule in the South, thousands of blacks began migrating west from Kentucky, Tennessee, Louisiana, Arkansas, Mississippi, and Texas. Some 6,000 southern blacks arrived in Kansas in 1879 alone, and as many as 20,000 may have come the following year. They came to be known as "Exodusters," making their "exodus" out of the South in search of a haven from racism and poverty.

Nicodemus, Kansas: a colony founded by southern blacks in the 1860s.

The foremost promoter of black migration to the West was Benjamin "Pap" Singleton. Born a slave in Tennessee in 1809, he escaped and settled in Detroit, where he operated a boardinghouse that became a refuge for other runaway slaves. After the Civil War, he returned to Tennessee, convinced that God was calling him to rescue his black brethren. He decided that the brightest future for African Americans lay not in sharecropping or tenant farming but in farm ownership. When Singleton learned that land in Kansas could be had for $1.25 an acre, he led the first party of 200 colonists to Kansas in 1878, bought 7,500 acres that was formerly an Indian reservation, and established the Dunlop community.

Over the next several years, thousands of African Americans followed Singleton into Kansas, leading many southern leaders to worry about the loss of laborers from the Old South. In 1879 white Mississippians closed access to the river and threatened to sink all boats carrying black colonists to the West. An army officer reported to President Rutherford B. Hayes that "every river landing is blockaded by white enemies of the colored exodus; some of whom are mounted and armed, as if we are at war."

The black exodus to Kansas and the Oklahoma Territory died out by the early 1880s. Many of the settlers encountered terrible hardships. They were unprepared for the living conditions on the Plains. Their homesteads were not large enough to be self-sufficient, and most of the black farmers were forced to supplement their income by hiring themselves out to white ranchers in the area. Drought, grasshoppers, prairie fires, and dust storms led to crop failures. The sudden influx of so many people taxed resources and patience. Although sympathizers formed the Kansas Freedmen's Relief Association and collected thousands of dollars for food and clothing, they could not keep up with the needs of the swelling tide of migrants. Many of the black pioneers soon abandoned their land and moved to the few cities in the state. Life on the frontier was not the "promised land" that people had been led to expect. Nonetheless, by 1890, some 520,000 blacks lived west of the Mississippi River. As many as 25 percent of the cowboys who participated in the Texas cattle drives were African Americans.

In 1866 Congress passed legislation establishing two "colored" cavalry units and dispatched them to the western frontier. Nicknamed "Buffalo Soldiers" by the Indians, they were mostly Civil War veterans from Louisiana and Kentucky. They built and maintained forts, mapped vast areas of the Southwest, strung hundreds of miles of telegraph lines, protected railroad construction crews, subdued hostile Indians, and captured outlaws and rustlers. Eighteen of the "Buffalo Soldiers" won Congressional Medals of Honor for their service in the West.

MINING THE WEST   Miners were also ethnically diverse. Every race and nationality was represented in the mining communities. The California miners of 1849 (Forty-niners) set the typical pattern in which the sudden, disorderly rush of prospectors to the new find was quickly followed by the arrival of the camp followers—a motley crew of peddlers, saloonkeepers, prostitutes, cardsharps, hustlers, and assorted desperadoes, out to mine the miners. If the new field panned out, the forces of respectability and more subtle forms of exploitation slowly worked their way in. Lawlessness gave way to vigilante rule and, finally, to a stable community.

As mining became more dependent on capital, the day of the individual prospector began to wane. The Forty-niners sifted the gold out of the dirt and gravel through "placer" mining or "panning," or by diverting a stream through a "sluice box" or "long tom." But once the rich diggings tailed off, efficient mining required shafts sunk into the ground or crushing mills built to extract the precious metal locked in quartz. The wild rush then gave way to organized enterprise. The miners either moved on, settled down to work for the corporate mines, or took up farming in the vicinity.

Deadwood, Dakota Territory, a gold rush town photographed in 1876 before the Dakotas became states.

The drama of the 1849 gold rush was reenacted time and again in the following three decades. Though the California fever had passed by 1851, and no big strikes were made for seven years, new finds in Colorado and Nevada revived hopes for riches. Along the South Platte River, not far from Pike's Peak in Colorado, a prospecting party found gold in 1858, and stories of success there brought perhaps 100,000 "Fifty-niners" into the country by 1859, only to find that the rumors had been greatly exaggerated. Wagons that headed west with the legend "Pike's Peak or Bust!" on their sides were soon rumbling back with the sardonic message "Busted, by gosh." Still, a few mines were successful, some new arrivals took up farming to exploit high prices for farm products in Denver and other mining centers, and the census of 1860 showed 35,000 people still in the region. New discoveries kept occurring: near Central City in 1859, at Leadville in the 1870s, and the last important strikes in the West, again gold and silver, at Cripple Creek in 1891–1894. During these years, farming and grazing had given the economy a stable base, and Colorado had become the "Centennial State" in 1876.

While the early miners were crowding around Pike's Peak, the Comstock Lode was discovered near Gold Hill, Nevada. H. T. P. Comstock, a Canadian-born fur trapper, had drifted to the Carson River diggings opened in 1856. He talked his way into a share in a new discovery made by two other prospectors in 1859 and gave it his own name. The lode produced gold and silver. Within twenty years the Comstock Lode alone had yielded more than $300 million from shafts that reached hundreds of feet into the mountainside. In 1861 Nevada became a territory, and in 1864 the state of Nevada was admitted in time to give its three electoral votes to Lincoln.

The growing demand for orderly government in the West led to the hasty creation of new territories and eventually the admission of a host of new states. After Colorado was admitted in 1876, however, there was a long hiatus because of the party divisions in Congress. Democrats were reluctant to create states out of territories that were heavily Republican. After the sweeping Republican victory of 1888, however, Congress admitted the Dakotas, Montana, and Washington in 1889, and Idaho and Wyoming in 1890, completing a tier of states from coast to coast. Utah entered in 1896 (after the Mormons abandoned the practice of polygamy), Oklahoma in 1907, and in 1912 Arizona and New Mexico finally rounded out the forty-eight contiguous states.

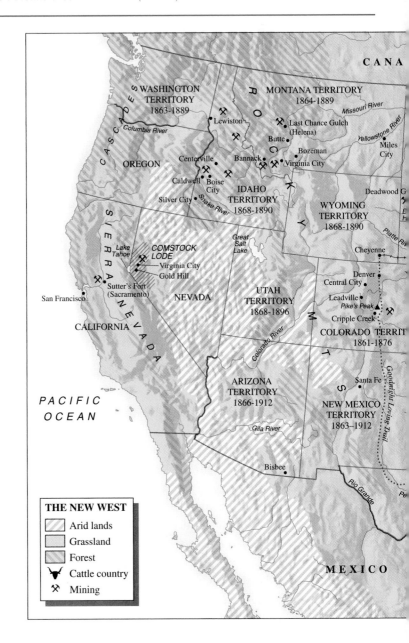

THE NEW WEST
- Arid lands
- Grassland
- Forest
- Cattle country
- Mining

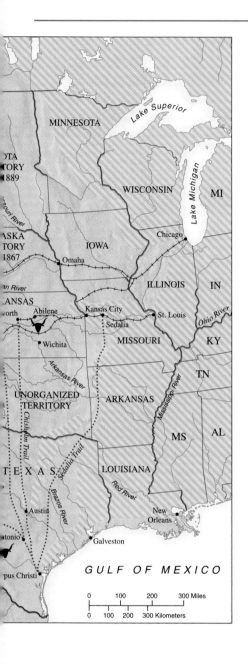

THE INDIAN WARS As the frontier pressed in from east and west, Indians were forced into what was supposed to be their last refuge. Perhaps 250,000 Indians in the Great Plains and mountain regions lived mainly off the buffalo herds, which provided food and, from their hides, clothing and shelter. In 1851 the chiefs of the principal Plains tribes had gathered at Fort Laramie in Wyoming Territory, where they agreed to accept more or less definite tribal borders and to leave the emigrants unmolested on their trails. The treaty worked for a while, with wagon trains passing safely through Indian lands and the army building roads and forts without resistance from the Indians. Fighting resumed, however, as the emigrants began to encroach upon Indian lands on the Plains rather than merely passing through them.

From the early 1860s until the late 1870s, the frontier raged with Indian wars, and intermittent outbreaks continued through the 1880s. In Colorado, where Cheyenne and Arapaho chiefs were coerced into accepting a treaty forcing them westward, protesting warriors began sporadic raids on the trails and mining camps. In 1864 the territorial governor persuaded most of the warring Indians to gather at Fort Lyon on Sand Creek, where they were promised protection. Despite this promise, Col. J. M. Chivington's untrained militia fell upon an Indian camp flying the American flag and a white flag of truce, slaughtering 200 peaceful Indians—men, women, and children—in what one general called the "foulest and most unjustifiable crime in the annals of America."

With other scattered battles erupting, a congressional committee began to gather evidence in 1865 on the grisly Indian wars and massacres. Its 1867 *Report on the Condition of the Indian Tribes* led to an act to establish an Indian Peace Commission charged with ending the Sioux War and removing the causes of Indian wars in general. Congress decided this was best accomplished at the expense of the Indians, by persuading them to take up life on out-of-the-way reservations. Yet the persistent encroachment on Indian hunting grounds continued.

In 1867 a conference at Medicine Creek Lodge, Kansas, ended with the Kiowa, Comanche, Arapaho, and Cheyenne reluctantly accepting lands in western Oklahoma. The following spring, the Sioux agreed to settle within the Black Hills reservation in Dakota Territory. But Indian resistance in the southern Plains continued until the Red River War of 1874–1875. General Philip Sheridan scattered the Indians and finally brought them to terms in the spring of 1875.

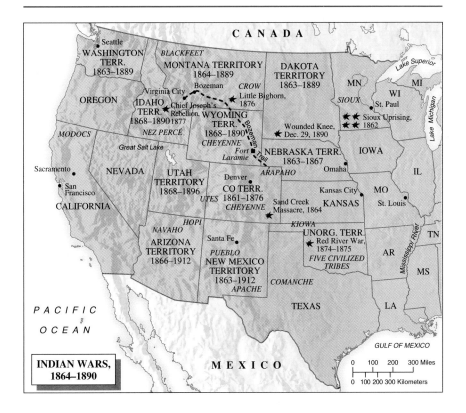

INDIAN WARS,
1864–1890

By then, trouble was brewing again in the north. In 1874 Lieutenant-Colonel George A. Custer, a reckless, glory-seeking officer who graduated last in his class at West Point but who then distinguished himself as a cavalry officer during the Civil War, led an exploring expedition into the Black Hills, accompanied by gold seekers. Miners were soon filtering into the Sioux hunting grounds despite promises that the army would keep them out. The army had done little to protect the Indian lands, but when ordered to move against wandering bands of Sioux hunting on the range according to their treaty rights, the army moved vigorously.

What became the Great Sioux War was the largest military event since the end of the Civil War and one of the largest campaigns against Indians in American history. The war lasted fifteen months, and entailed fifteen battles in a vast area of present-day Wyoming, Montana, South Dakota, and Nebraska. In 1876, after several indecisive encounters, Custer found the main encampment of Sioux and their Northern Cheyenne allies on the Little Bighorn River. Separated from the main

The Battle of Little Bighorn in a painting by an Oglala Sioux, Amos Bad Heart Bull, 1876.

body of his men, Custer's detachment of 210 soldiers was surrounded by 2,500 warriors and annihilated.

Instead of following up their victory, the Indians celebrated and renewed their hunting. The army regained the offensive and compelled the Sioux to give up their hunting grounds and gold fields in return for payments. Forced onto reservations situated on the least valuable lands in the region, the Indians soon found themselves struggling to subsist under harsh conditions. Many of them died of starvation or disease. When a peace commission imposed a settlement, Chief Spotted Tail said: "Tell your people that since the Great Father promised that we should never be removed, we have been moved five times. . . . I think you had better put the Indians on wheels and you can run them about wherever you wish."

In the Rocky Mountains and westward the same story of hopeless resistance was repeated. The Blackfoot and Crow had to leave their homes in Montana. In a war along the California-Oregon boundary, the Modocs held out for six months in 1871–1872 before they were overwhelmed. In 1879 the Utes were forced to give up their vast territories in western Colorado after a brief battle. In Idaho the peaceful Nez Percés finally refused to surrender lands along the Salmon River. Chief Joseph tried to avoid war, but when some unruly warriors started a fight, he directed a masterful campaign against overwhelming odds, one of the most spectacular feats in the history of Indian warfare. After a retreat of 1,500 miles, through mountains and plains, across the Yellowstone region and through the Bitterroot Mountains of Montana, he was finally caught thirty miles short of the Canadian border, and exiled to Oklahoma.

The heroic Joseph maintained strict discipline among his followers, countenanced

Chief Joseph of the Nez Percé tribe.

no scalpings or outrages against civilians, paid for supplies that he could have confiscated, and kept his dignity to the end. His eloquent speech of surrender was an epitaph to the warrior's last stand against the march of empire: "I am tired of fighting. Our chiefs are killed. . . . The old men are all dead. . . . I want to have time to look for my children, and see how many of them I can find. . . . Hear me, my chiefs! I am tired. My heart is sick and sad. From where the sun now stands I will fight no more forever."

A generation of Indian wars virtually ended in 1886 with the capture of Geronimo, a chief of the Chiricahua Apaches, who had fought white settlers in the Southwest for fifteen years. But there would be one tragic epilogue. Late in 1888 Wovoka (or "Jack Wilson"), a Paiute in western Nevada, fell ill and in a delirium imagined he had visited the spirit world where he learned of a deliverer coming to rescue the Indians and restore their lands. To hasten the day, he said, they had to take up a ceremonial dance at each new moon. The Ghost Dance craze fed upon old legends of a coming Messiah and spread rapidly. In 1890 the Sioux took it up with such fervor that it alarmed white authorities. On December 29, 1890, a bloodbath occurred at Wounded Knee, South Dakota. An accidental rifle discharge led nervous soldiers to fire into a group of Indians who had come to surrender. Nearly 200 Indians and 25 soldiers died in the "Battle of

Wounded Knee." The Indian wars had ended with characteristic brutality.

Over the long run the collapse of Indian resistance resulted as much from the killing off of the buffalo herds on which they subsisted as from direct suppression. White hunters felled buffaloes for sport, sometimes firing from train windows merely for the pleasure of seeing them die. By the mid-1880s the herds were nearly extinct.

INDIAN POLICY The slaughter of Indians and buffalo provoked widespread criticism. Politicians and religious leaders spoke out against mistreatment of Indians. In his annual message of 1877 President Hayes echoed the protest: "Many, if not most, of our Indian wars have had their origin in broken promises and acts of injustice on our part." In the 1880s Helen Hunt Jackson, a novelist and poet, focused attention on the Indian cause in *A Century of Dishonor* (1881). Indian policy gradually became more benevolent, but this did little to ease the plight of the Indians and actually helped to destroy the remnants of their cultures. The reservation policy inaugurated by the Peace Commission in 1867 did little more than extend a practice that dated from colonial Virginia. Partly humanitarian in motive, this policy also saved money: it cost less to house and feed Indians on reservations than it did to fight them.

Well-intentioned reformers sought to "Americanize" the Indians by dealing with them as individuals rather than as tribes. The fruition of reform efforts came in the Dawes Severalty Act of 1887. Sponsored by Senator Henry M. Dawes of Massachusetts, the act permitted the president to divide the lands of any tribe and grant 160 acres to each head of family and lesser amounts to others. To protect the Indian's property, the government held it in trust for twenty-five years, after which the owner won full title and became a citizen. Under the Burke Act of 1906, Indians who took up life apart from their tribes became citizens immediately. Members of the tribes granted land titles were subject to state and federal laws like all other persons. In 1901 citizenship was extended to the Five Civilized Tribes of Oklahoma, and in 1924 to all Indians.

But the more it changed, the more Indian policy remained the same. Despite the best of intentions, the Dawes Act created opportunities for more plundering of Indian land, and it disrupted what remained of the traditional cultures. The Dawes Act broke up reservations and often led to the loss of Indian lands to whites. Those lands not distributed to Indian families were sold, while others were lost to land sharks because of the Indians' inexperience with private ownership, or simply their weakness in the face of fraud. Between 1887 and 1934, they lost an estimated 86 million of their 130 million acres. Most of what remained was unsuited to agriculture.

American policy toward the Indians after the Civil War first paralleled and then differed from the way southern state governments treated blacks in this era. During the last quarter of the nineteenth century, white government officials sought to separate both Indians and blacks from the social mainstream while at the same time exploiting their labor or expropriating their lands. Through the Dawes Act, however, the federal government tried to force Indians to adopt white ways of life. In the segregated South, the white leadership sought to separate African Americans from white culture. In both cases, racial prejudice governed social policy. And such policies only served to alienate and degrade blacks and Indians.

CATTLE AND COWBOYS   While the West was being taken from the Indians, cattle entered the grasslands where the buffalo had roamed. The cowboy enjoyed his brief heyday, fading then into the folklore of the Wild West. From colonial times, especially in the South, cattle raising had been a common enterprise just beyond the fringe of settlement. In many cases the early slaves took care of the livestock. Later, in the West, African-American cowboys were a common sight.

Much of the romance of the open-range cattle industry derived from its Mexican roots. The Texas longhorns and the cowboys' horses had in large part descended from stock brought over by the Spaniards, and many of the industry's trappings had been worked out in Mexico first: the cowboy's saddle, chaps (*chaparejos*) to protect the legs, spurs, and lariat.

For many years wild cattle competed with the buffalo in the Spanish borderlands. Natural selection and contact with "Anglo" scrub cattle produced the Texas longhorns: lean and rangy, they were noted more for speed and endurance than for providing a choice steak. They had little value, moreover, because the largest markets for beef were too far away. At the end of the Civil War, as many as 5 million cattle roamed the grasslands of Texas, still neglected—but not for long. In the upper Mississippi River Valley, where herds had been depleted by the war, cattle were in great demand, and the Texas cattle could be had just for the effort of rounding them up.

So the cattle drives began anew after the Civil War, but on a scale far greater than before. In 1866 a large Texas herd set out for Sedalia, Missouri, the western terminus of the Missouri-Pacific Railroad. But that route proved unsuitable because it was subject to raids by postwar bushwhackers (bandits), obstructed by woodlands, and opposed by Arkansas and Missouri farmers. New opportunities arose as railroads pushed farther west where cattle could be driven through relatively vacant lands.

Joseph G. McCoy, an Illinois livestock dealer, recognized the possibilities for moving the cattle trade west. He turned Abilene into the first successful Kansas cowtown. Located on the Kansas-Pacific Railroad at the northern end of a trail laid out through Indian Territory by the part-Cherokee Jesse Chisholm, Abilene was a "small, dead place, consisting of about one dozen log huts" when McCoy arrived in early 1867.

McCoy bought up 250 acres for a stockyard, laid plans for a barn, an office building, livestock scales, a hotel, and a bank—and sent an agent into Indian Territory to cultivate owners of herds bound north. Over the next few years Abilene developed into a flourishing town. But, as the

Cowboys herd cattle near the Cimarron River in Colorado, 1898.

railroads moved west, so did the cowtowns and the trails: Ellsworth, Wichita, Caldwell, and Dodge City, all in Kansas; and farther north Ogallala, Nebraska; Cheyenne, Wyoming; and Miles City, Montana.

During the twenty years after the Civil War, some 40,000 cowboys roamed the Great Plains. They were young—the average age was twenty-four—and from diverse backgrounds. Thirty percent of them were either Mexican or African American, and hundreds were Indians. Many others were Civil War veterans from North and South, and still others were immigrants from Europe. The life of a cowboy, for the most part, was rarely as exciting as movies and television shows have depicted. Being a ranch hand involved grueling, dirty wage labor interspersed with drudgery and boredom, often amid terrible weather conditions.

The cattle industry spurred rapid growth in the region. The population of Kansas rose from 107,000 in 1860 to 365,000 ten years later and reached almost a million by 1880. Nebraska witnessed similar increases. During the 1860s, the cattle would be delivered to rail depots, loaded onto freight cars, and shipped east. By the time they arrived in New York or Massachusetts, some would be dead or dying and all would have lost significant weight. The secret to higher profits for the cattle industry was to devise a way to slaughter the cattle in the Midwest and ship the dressed carcasses east and west. That required refrigeration to keep the meat from spoiling. In 1869 G. H. Hammond, a Chicago meat packer, shipped the first refrigerated beef in an air-cooled car from Chicago to Boston. Eight years later, Gustavus Swift developed a more efficient system of mechanical refrigeration, an innovation that earned him a fortune and provided a major stimulus to the growth of the cattle industry.

The flush times of the cowtown soon passed, and the long cattle drives played out too, because they were economically unsound. The dangers of the trail, the wear and tear on men and cattle, the charges levied on drives across Indian Territory, and the advance of farms across the trails combined to persuade cattlemen that they could best function near the railroads. As railroads spread out into Texas and the Plains, the cattle business spread with them over the High Plains as far as Montana and on into Canada.

In the absence of laws governing the open range, the cattle ranchers at first worked out a code of action largely dictated by circumstances. As cattle often wandered onto other people's claims, cowboys would "ride the line" to keep the cattle off the adjoining ranch. In the spring, they would "round up" the mixed herds and sort out ownership by identifying the distinctive ranch symbol "branded" or burned into the cattle.

All this changed in 1873 when Joseph Glidden, an Illinois farmer, invented the first effective barbed wire, which ranchers used to fence off their claims at relatively low cost. Skeptical cattlemen discovered that their meanest longhorns shied away from the fence, which was purported to be light as air, cheaper than dirt, and "bull strong and hog tight." Ranchers rushed to buy the new wire fencing, and soon the open range was no more.

The greatest boom in the range-cattle trade came in the early 1880s, when eastern and European investors began to pour money into the "Beef Bonanza." Cattle growing, like mining, entered a season of wild speculation, and then evolved from a romantic adventure into a big business dominated by giant enterprises.

END OF THE OPEN RANGE A combination of factors conspired to end the open range. Farmers kept crowding in and laying out homesteads on the open range, waging "barbed-wire wars" with ranchers by either cutting the ranchers' fences or policing their own. The boundless range was beginning to be overstocked with cattle by 1883, and expenses mounted as stock breeders formed associations to keep intruders

Judge Roy Bean's courthouse and saloon, Langtry, Texas, 1900.

out of overstocked ranges, to establish and protect land titles, to deal with railroads and buyers, to fight prairie fires, and to cope with rustlers and predatory beasts. The rise of sheep herding by 1880 caused still another conflict with the cattle ranchers. A final blow to the open-range industry came with two unusually severe winters in 1886 and 1887, followed by ten long years of drought.

Those who survived the hazards of the range did so by establishing legal title and fencing in the lands, restricting the herds to a reasonable size, and providing shelter and hay against the rigors of winter. Moreover, as the long cattle drives ended with the advent of more rail lines and refrigerated cars, the cowboy settled into a more sedentary existence. Within merely two decades, 1866–1886, the era of the cowboy had come and gone.

RANGE WARS   Conflicting claims over land and water rights ignited violent disputes between ranchers and farmers. Ranchers often tried to drive off neighboring farmers, and farmers in turn tried to sabotage the cattle barons, cutting their fences and spooking their herds. The cattle ranchers also clashed with sheepherders over access to grasslands. A strain of ethnic and religious prejudice heightened the tension between ranchers and herders. In the Southwest, shepherds were usually Mexican Americans; in Idaho and Nevada they were Basques or Mormons. Many Anglo-American cattle ranchers and cowboys viewed these ethnic and religious groups as un-American and inferior. This attitude helped them rationalize the use of violence against the sheepherders. Warfare gradually faded, however, as the sheep for the most part found refuge in the high pastures of the mountains, leaving the grasslands of the Plains to the cattle ranchers.

There also developed a perennial tension over grassland use between large and small cattle ranchers. The large ranchers fenced in huge tracts of public lands, leaving the smaller ranchers with too little pasture. To survive, the smaller ranchers cut the fences. In central Texas this practice sparked the Fence-Cutters' War of 1883–1884. Several ranchers were killed and dozens wounded before the state ended the conflict by passing legislation outlawing fence cutting.

FARMERS AND THE LAND   Among the legendary figures of the West, the sodbusters projected an unromantic image in contrast to the cowboys, cavalry, and Indians. Farming has always been a hard life, and it was made more so on the Great Plains by the unforgiving environment and mercurial weather. After 1865, on paper at least, the federal land laws offered favorable terms to the farmer. Under the Homestead Act of 1862 a settler could either realize the old dream of free land simply by staking out a claim and living on it for five years, or by buying the land at $1.25 an acre after six months. But such land legislation was predicated upon the tradition of farming the fertile lands east of the Mississippi River, and the laws were never adjusted to the fact that much of the prairie land was suited only for cattle. Cattle ranchers were forced to obtain land by gradual acquisition from homesteaders or land-grant railroads.

The unchangeable fact of aridity, rather than new land laws, shaped institutions in the New West. Where farming was impossible the ranchers simply established dominance by control of the water, regardless of the laws. Belated legislative efforts to develop irrigable lands finally achieved a major success when the Newlands Reclamation Act (after the aptly named Senator Francis G. Newlands of Nevada) of 1901 set up the Bureau of Reclamation. The proceeds of public land sales in sixteen states created a fund for irrigation works, and the Reclamation Bureau set about building such major projects as Boulder (later Hoover) Dam on the Nevada-Arizona line, Roosevelt Dam in Arizona, and Elephant Butte Dam and Arrowrock Dam in New Mexico.

The lands of the New West, as on previous frontiers, passed to their ultimate owners more often from private hands than directly from the government. Many of the 274 million acres claimed under the Homestead Act passed quickly to ranchers or speculators, and thence to settlers. The land-grant railroads got some 200 million acres of the public domain in the twenty years from 1851 to 1871, and sold much of this land to build population centers and traffic along the lines. The New West of ranchers and farmers was in fact largely the product of the railroads.

The first arrivals on the sodhouse frontier faced a grim struggle against danger, adversity, and monotony. Though land was relatively cheap, horses, livestock, wagons, wells, fencing, seed, and fertilizer were not. Freight rates and interest rates on loans seemed criminally high. As in the South, declining crop prices produced chronic indebtedness that led strapped western farmers to embrace virtually any plan to inflate the money supply. The virgin land itself, although fertile, resisted planting; the heavy sod broke many a plow. Since wood was almost nonexistent on the prairies, pioneer families used buffalo chips (dried dung) for fuel.

Farmers and their families also fought a constant battle with the elements: tornadoes, hailstorms, droughts, prairie fires, blizzards, and pests. Swarms of locusts would cloud the horizon, occasionally covering the ground six inches deep. A Wichita newspaper reported in 1878 that the grasshoppers devoured "everything green, stripping the foliage off the bark and from the tender twigs of the fruit trees, destroying every plant that is good for food or pleasant to the eyes, that man has planted."

As the railroads arrived bearing lumber from the East, farmers could leave their dugouts and sodhouses (homes roofed with sod) to build more comfortable frame houses. New machinery helped open fresh opportunities for farmers. In 1868 James Oliver of Indiana made a successful chilled-iron plow. The "sodbuster" greatly eased the task of breaking the tough grass roots of the Plains. Improvements and new inventions in threshing machines, hay mowers, planters, manure spreaders, cream separators, and other devices lightened the burden of farm labor but added to the capital outlay for the farmer.

In Minnesota, the Dakotas, and central California, the gigantic "bonanza farms" with machinery for mass production became the marvels of the age. On one farm in North Dakota, 13,000 acres of wheat made a single field. Another bonanza farm employed over a thousand migrant workers to tend 34,000 acres.

To get a start on a family homestead required a minimum capital investment of $1,000. While the overall value of farm lands and farm products increased in the late nineteenth century, the small farmers did not keep up with the march of progress. Their numbers grew but decreased in proportion to the population at large. Wheat, like cotton in the antebellum period, provided the great export crop that spurred economic growth. For a variety of reasons, however, few small farmers prospered. By the decade of the 1890s they were in open revolt against the "system" of corrupt processors and greedy bankers who they believed conspired against them.

PIONEER WOMEN The West remained a largely male society throughout the nineteenth century. In Texas, for example, the ratio of men to women in 1890 was 110 to 1. Women continued to face traditional legal barriers and social prejudice. A wife could not sell property

A woman and her family in front of their sodhouse. The difficult life on the prairie led to more egalitarian marriages.

without her husband's approval. In Texas women could not sue except for divorce, nor could they serve on juries, act as lawyers, or witness a will.

But the fight for survival in the trans-Mississippi West made men and women more equal partners than were their eastern counterparts. Many women who lost their mates to the deadly toil of sodbusting thereafter assumed complete responsibility for their farms. In general, women on the prairie became more independent than those living domestic lives back East. One woman declared that she insisted on leaving out the phrasing about "obeying" her husband from their marriage vows. "I had served my time of tutelage to my parents as all children are supposed to. I was a woman now and capable of being the other half of the head of the family." Similar examples of independence abound. Explained one Kansas woman: "The outstanding fact is that the environment was such as to bring out and develop the dominant qualities of individual character. Kansas women of that day learned at an early age to depend on themselves—to do whatever work there was to be done, and to face danger when it must be faced, as calmly as they were able."

"THE FRONTIER HAS GONE" American life reached an important juncture at the end of the nineteenth century. After the 1890 population count, the superintendent of the census noted that he could no longer locate a continuous frontier line beyond which population thinned out to fewer than two per square mile. This fact inspired the historian Frederick Jackson Turner to develop his influential frontier thesis, first outlined in his paper "The Significance of the Frontier in American History," delivered to the American Historical Association in 1893. "The existence of an area of free land," Turner wrote, "its continuous recession, and the advance of American settlement westward, explain American development." The frontier had shaped the national character in fundamental ways. It was

> to the frontier [that] the American intellect owes its striking characteristics. That coarseness and strength combined with acuteness and acquisitiveness; that practical, inventive turn of mind, quick to find expedients; that masterful grasp of material things, lacking in the artistic but powerful to effect great ends; that restless, nervous energy; that dominant individualism, working for good and for evil, and withal that buoyancy and exuberance which comes with freedom—these are traits of the frontier, or traits called out elsewhere because of the existence of the frontier.

In 1893, Turner concluded, "four centuries from the discovery of America, at the end of a hundred years under the Constitution, the frontier has gone and with its going has closed the first period of American history."

Turner's "frontier thesis" guided several generations of scholars and students in their understanding of the distinctive characteristics of American history. His view of the frontier as the westward-moving source of America's democratic politics, open society, unfettered economy, and rugged individualism, far removed from the corruptions of urban life, gripped the popular imagination as well. But it left much out of the story. The frontier experience Turner described exaggerated the homogenizing effect of the frontier environment and virtually ignored the role of women, blacks, Indians, Mormons, Hispanics, and Asians in shaping the diverse human geography of the western United States. Turner also implied that the West would be fundamentally different after 1890 because the frontier experience was essentially over. But in many respects that region has retained the qualities associated with the rush for land, gold, timber, and water rights during the post–Civil War decades. The mining frontier, as one historian has recently written, "set a mood that has never disappeared from the West: the attitude of extractive industry—get in, get rich, get out."

MAKING CONNECTIONS

- The problems of southern and western farmers described in this chapter will set the stage for the rise of the Populists as discussed in Chapter 22.

- This is a crucial period in the evolution of race relations in the South, bridging the antebellum period and the twentieth century.

- This chapter closed with the observation that, as of 1890, according to the superintendent of the census and the historian Frederick Jackson Turner, "the frontier has gone." Where would Americans now look to fulfill their expansionist urges?

FURTHER READING

The classic study of the emergence of the New South remains C. Vann Woodward's *Origins of the New South, 1877–1913* (1951). A more recent treatment of southern society after the end of Reconstruction is Edward L. Ayers's *Southern Crossing: A History of the American South, 1877–1906* (1995). A good survey of industrialization in the South is James C. Cobb's *Industrialization and Southern Society, 1877–1984* (1984).

C. Vann Woodword's *The Strange Career of Jim Crow* (3rd ed., 1974) remains the standard on southern race relations. Some of Woodward's points are challenged in Howard N. Rabinowitz's *Race Relations in the Urban South, 1865–1890* (1978). Leon Litwack's *Trouble in Mind: Black Southerners in the Age of Jim Crow* (1998) treats the rise of legal segregation. J. Morgan Kousser's *The Shaping of Southern Politics:*

Suffrage Restriction and Establishment of the One-Party South, 1880–1910 (1974) handles disenfranchisement. An award-winning study of white women and the race issue is Glenda Gilmore's *Gender and Jim Crow: Women and the Politics of White Supremacy in North Carolina, 1896–1920* (1996).

For stimulating reinterpretations of the frontier and the development of the West, see William Cronon's *Nature's Metropolis: Chicago and the Great West* (1991), Patricia Nelson Limerick's *The Legacy of Conquest: The Unbroken Past of the American West* (1987), Richard White's *"It's Your Misfortune and None of My Own": A New History of the American West* (1991), and Walter Nugent's *Into the West: The Story of Its People* (1999).

The role of blacks in western settlement is the focus of William L. Katz's *The Black West* (1996) and Nell Painter's *Exodusters: Black Migration to Kansas after Reconstruction* (1992). The best account of the conflicts between Indians and whites is Robert Utley's *The Indian Frontier of the American West, 1846–1890* (1984). For a presentation of the Native American side of the story, see Peter Nabokov and Vine Deloria's *Native American Testimony: A Chronicle of Indian-White Relations from Prophecy to the Present, 1492–1992* (1992).

20 ⟡ BIG BUSINESS AND ORGANIZED LABOR

CHAPTER ORGANIZER

This chapter focuses on:

- factors that fueled the growth of the post–Civil War economy.

- the methods and achievements of major entrepreneurs.

- the rise of large labor unions.

merica's rise as an industrial and agricultural giant in the late nineteenth century is a fact of towering visibility. Between 1869 and 1899, the nation's population nearly tripled, farm production more than doubled, and the value of manufactures grew sixfold. Within three generations after the Civil War, the nation that had long been a predominantly rural society burst forth as the world's preeminent economic power. The United States became a highly structured, increasingly centralized, urban-industrial society buffeted by the imperatives of mass production, mass consumption, and time-clock efficiency. Bigness became the prevailing standard of corporate life, and social tensions worsened with the rising scale of business enterprise.

THE RISE OF BIG BUSINESS

The industrial revolution created huge corporations that came to dominate the economy—as well as political and social life—during the late nineteenth century. An older economy dependent upon small business and craftspeople could not satisfy the rapidly growing national market. Entrepreneurs who recognized this fact focused their attention on developing systems of mass production and distribution. As the volume of these businesses grew, the owners sought to integrate all the processes of production and distribution into single companies, thus producing even larger firms. Others joined forces with their competitors in an effort to dominate entire industries. This process of industrial combination and concentration, whether the result of natural economic forces or human machinations, transformed the nation's economy and social order. It also provoked widespread dissent and the emergence of an organized labor movement.

Many factors converged to help launch the dramatic business growth after the Civil War. A nationwide shortage of labor served as a powerful incentive to inventors and business owners to develop and install more efficient, high-speed, labor-saving machinery. Technological innovations not only created new products but also brought about improved machinery and equipment that spurred dramatic advances in productivity. As production volume increased, the larger businesses and industries expanded into multiple states and in the process they came to prefer standardized machinery and parts available nationwide. A group of shrewd, determined, and energetic entrepreneurs took advantage of fertile business opportunities to create huge enterprises. Federal and state government leaders after the Civil War actively encouraged the growth of business by imposing high tariffs on foreign manufacturers and by providing land and cash to finance railroads and other internal improvements.

The American agricultural sector, by 1870 the world's leader, fueled the rest of the economy by providing wheat and corn to be milled into flour and meal. With the advent of the cattle industry, the processes of slaughtering and packing meat themselves became major industries. So the farm sector directly stimulated the industrial sector of the economy. A national, government-subsidized network of railroads connecting the East and West coasts played a crucial role in the development of related industries and in the evolution of a national market for goods and services. Industry in the United States also benefited from an abundance of inexpensive power sources—water, wood, coal, oil, and electricity—compared to other nations of the world.

THE SECOND INDUSTRIAL REVOLUTION The industrial revolution "controls us all," said Yale sociologist William Graham Sumner, "because we are all in it." Sumner and other Americans living during the second half of the nineteenth century experienced what economic historians have termed the second industrial revolution. The first industrial revolution began in Britain during the late eighteenth century. It was propelled by the convergence of three new technologies—the coal-powered steam engine; textile machines for spinning thread and weaving cloth; and blast furnaces to produce iron.

The second industrial revolution began in the mid–nineteenth century and was centered in the United States and Germany. It was sparked by an array of innovations and inventions in the production of metals, machinery, chemicals, and foodstuffs. While the first industrial revolution helped accelerate the growth of the early American economy, the second transformed the economy and society into its modern urban-industrial form.

The Hand of Man, *photogravure by Alfred Stieglitz, 1902.*

The second industrial revolution involved three related developments. The first of these was the creation of an interconnected national transportation and communication network that in turn facilitated the emergence of a national and even international market for American goods and services. Contributing to this development were the completion of the national telegraph and railroad system, the emergence of steamships, and the laying of the undersea telegraph cable spanning the Atlantic Ocean and connecting the United States with Europe.

During the 1880s, a second major breakthrough—the use of electric power—accelerated the pace of change. Electricity created dramatic advances in the power and efficiency of industrial machinery. It also spurred urban growth through the addition of electric trolleys and subways, and it greatly enhanced the production of steel and chemicals.

The third major aspect of the second industrial revolution was the systematic application of scientific research to industrial processes. Laboratories sprouted across the country, and scientists and engineers discovered dramatic new ways to improve industrial processes. Researchers, for example, figured out how to refine kerosene and gasoline from crude oil. They also developed improved techniques for refining steel from iron and spawned new products—telephones, typewriters, adding machines, sewing machines, cameras, elevators, and farm machinery—and lowered consumer prices. These advances in turn expanded the scope and scale of industrial organizations. Capital-intensive industries such as steel and oil, and processed food and tobacco, took advantage of new technologies to gain economies of scale that emphasized maximum production and national as well as international marketing and distribution.

BUILDING THE TRANSCONTINENTAL RAILROADS   Railroads were the first big business, the first magnet for the great financial markets, and the first industry to develop a large-scale management bureaucracy. The railroads opened the western half of the nation, connected raw materials to factories and retailers, and in so doing created a national market. At the same time, they were themselves gigantic markets for iron, steel, lumber, and other capital goods.

The renewal of railroad building after the Civil War filled out the rail network east of the Mississippi River. Gradually, southern tracks were rebuilt and a spiderweb of new trunk lines was added in the North. But the most spectacular exploits were the monumental transcontinental lines built through granite mountains, over roaring rivers and deep canyons, and across desolate plains. Running through sparsely settled lands, the railroads promised little quick return on investment, but they served the national purpose of binding the country together and so received generous government support.

Before the Civil War, sectional differences over the choice of routes held up the start of a transcontinental line. Secession and the departure of southern congressmen finally permitted passage of the Pacific Railway Bill, which Abraham Lincoln signed into law in 1862. The act authorized a line along a north-central route, to be built by the Union Pacific Railroad westward from Omaha and the Central Pacific Railroad eastward from Sacramento.

Both railroads began construction during the war, but most of the work was done after 1865, as the companies raced to build most of the line and thereby get most of the federal subsidy, paid per mile of track. The Union Pacific pushed across the plains at a rapid pace, avoiding the Rocky Mountains by going through Evans Pass in Wyoming. Construction of the rail line and bridges was hasty and much of it so flimsy

The celebration after the last spike was driven at Promontory, Utah, on May 10, 1869, completing the first transcontinental railroad.

that it had to be redone later, but the Union Pacific pushed on to its celebrated rendezvous with the Central Pacific in 1869. Driven more by the lure of quick profits than national interest, railroad developers from both companies cut corners and bribed politicians in an effort to get the track laid on time.

The Union Pacific work crews, comprised of ex-soldiers, blacks, and Irish immigrants as laborers, had to cope with bad roads, water shortages, extreme weather, and Indian marauders. The Central Pacific crews were mainly Chinese workers lured first by the California gold rush and then by railroad jobs. Thousands of Chinese men migrated to America, raising their numbers in the United States from 7,500 in 1850 to 105,000 in 1880. Most of these "coolie" laborers were single males intent upon accumulating money and then returning to their homeland, where they could then afford to marry and buy a parcel of land. Their temporary status and dream of a good life back in China apparently made them more willing than American laborers to endure the dangerous working conditions, blatant racism, and low pay of railroad work. Many Chinese laborers died on the job.

All sorts of issues delayed the effort to finish the transcontinental line. Iron prices spiked. Broken treaties prompted Indian raids. Blizzards shut down work for weeks. Fifty-seven miles east of Sacramento, the construction crews encountered the towering Sierras, but they were eventually able to cut through to more level country in Nevada. The Union Pacific had built 1,086 miles compared with the Central Pacific's 689 when the race ended on the salt plains of Utah at Promontory. There, on May 10, 1869, California governor Leland Stanford drove a gold spike that symbolized the railroad's completion.

The next transcontinental railroad linked the Atchison, Topeka and Santa Fe Railroad with the Southern Pacific Railroad at Needles in southern California. The Santa Fe completed its line to San Diego by 1884. Meanwhile the Southern Pacific, which had absorbed the Central Pacific, continued on by way of Yuma to El Paso in 1882, where it made connections to St. Louis and New Orleans. To the north, the Northern Pacific had connected Lake Superior with Portland by 1883, and ten years later the Great Northern, which had slowly and carefully been building westward from St. Paul, Minnesota, thrust its way to Tacoma, Washington. Thus, before the turn of the century five major

TRANSCONTINENTAL RAILROAD LINES, 1880s

trunk lines existed, supplemented by connections that afforded other transcontinental routes.

FINANCING THE RAILROADS   The railroads were built by private companies that raised money for construction primarily by selling railroad bonds to American and foreign investors. Until 1850 constitutional scruples had constrained federal aid for internal improvements, although many states had subsidized railroads within their borders. But in 1850 Stephen Douglas secured from Congress a grant of public lands to subsidize two north-south railroads connecting Chicago and Mobile. Over the next twenty years, federal land grants, mainly to transcontinentals, totaled 129 million acres. In addition to land, the railroads received massive financial aid from federal, state, and local governments. Altogether the railroads received about $707 million in cash and $335 million in land.

In the long run, the federal government recovered much if not all of its investment in transcontinentals and accomplished the purpose of linking the country together. As farms, ranches, and towns sprouted around the rail lines, the value of the alternate sections of government land on either side of the tracks skyrocketed. The railroads also benefited the public by hauling government freight, military personnel and equipment, and the mails at half fare or for free. Moreover, by helping to accelerate the creation of a national market, the railroads spurred economic growth and thereby increased government revenues.

The shady financial practices of the railroad men earned them the label of "robber barons," an epithet soon extended to other "captains of industry" as well. They were shrewd, determined, often dishonest men, driven more by greed than glory. The building of both the Union Pacific and the Central Pacific—as well as other transcontinentals—induced shameless profiteering through construction companies controlled by insiders, which overcharged the railroad companies. The Crédit Mobilier Company, according to congressional investigators, paid off congressmen and charged the Union Pacific $94 million for construction that cost at most $44 million.

Eastern rail lines engaged in similar acts of financial buccaneering. The prince of the railroad "robber barons" was Jay Gould, a secretive trickster who mastered the fine art of buying rundown railroads, making cosmetic improvements, and selling out at a profit, meanwhile using corporate funds for personal speculation and judicious bribes. Ousted by a reform group after having looted New York's Erie Railroad, Gould moved on to richer spoils in western railroads. Nearly every enterprise he touched was either compromised or ruined, while Gould was building a fortune that amounted to $100 million upon his death at age fifty-six.

Few railroad fortunes were built in those freewheeling times by purely honest methods, but compared to opportunists such as Gould, most railroad owners were saints. They at least took some

Jay Gould, prince of the railroad buccaneers.

"Commodore" Cornelius Vanderbilt consolidated control of the vast New York Central Railroad in the 1860s.

interest in the welfare of their companies, if not always in that of the public. Cornelius Vanderbilt, called "Commodore" by virtue of his early exploits in steamboating, stands out among the railroad barons. Already rich before the Civil War, he decided to give up the hazards of wartime shipping in favor of land transport. Under his direction, the first of the major eastern railroad consolidations took form.

Vanderbilt merged separate trunk lines connecting Albany and Buffalo into a single powerful rail network led by the New York Central. This accomplished, he forged connections to New York City and then tried to corner the stock of his chief competitor, the Erie Railroad. But the directors of that line beat him there by the simple expedient of printing new Erie stock faster than he could buy it. In 1873, however, he bought the Lake Shore and Michigan Southern Railroad, which gave his lines connections into the lucrative Chicago market. After the Commodore's death in 1877, his son William Henry extended the Vanderbilt railroads to include more than 13,000 miles in the Northeast. The consolidation trend was nationwide: about two-thirds of the nation's railroad mileage fell under the control of only seven major groups by 1900. This colossal national rail network was a major factor in stimulating the growth of the economy.

MANUFACTURING AND INVENTIONS   The story of manufacturing after the Civil War shows much the same pattern of expansion and merger in both old and new industries. The Patent Office, which had recorded only 276 inventions during its first decade of existence, the 1790s, registered almost 235,000 in the decade of the 1890s. New processes in steel-making and oil refining enabled those industries to flourish. The refrigerator car made it possible for the beef, mutton, and pork of the New West to reach a national market, giving rise to great packinghouse enterprises. Corrugated rollers that could crack the hard spicy wheat of the Great Plains provided impetus to the flour milling that centered in Minneapolis under the control of the Pillsburys and others.

The list of innovations after the Civil War can be extended indefinitely: barbed wire, farm implements, George Westinghouse's air brake for trains (1868), steam turbines, gas distribution and electrical devices, Christopher Sholes's typewriter (1867), J. W. McGaffey's vacuum cleaner (1869), and countless others. Before the end of the century, the internal-combustion engine and the motion picture, each the work of many hands, were laying the foundations for new industries that would emerge in the twentieth century.

These technological advances altered the daily lives of ordinary people far more than did activities in the political and intellectual realms. In no field was this more true than in the applications of electricity to power and communications. Few if any inventions of the times could rival the importance of the telephone, which Alexander Graham Bell patented in 1876.

To promote the new device the inventor and his supporters formed the National Bell Telephone Company. Its stiffest competition came from Western Union, which, after turning down a chance to buy Bell's "toy," employed Thomas Edison to develop an improved version. Edison's telephone became the prototype of the modern instrument, with its separate transmitter and receiver. But Bell had a prior claim on the basic principle, and Western Union, rather than risk a legal defeat, sold its rights and properties for a tidy sum, clearing the way for the creation of a monopoly. In 1885 the Bell interests organized the American Telephone and Telegraph Company. By 1899 it was a huge holding company in control of forty-nine licensed subsidiaries and itself an operating company for long-distance lines.

In the rise of electrical industries, the name of Thomas Edison stands above that of other inventors. He started his career at an early age, selling papers and candies on trains, soon learned telegraphy, and began making improvements in that and other areas. He invented the phonograph in 1877 and the first successful incandescent light bulb in 1879. Altogether he created or perfected hundreds of new devices and processes, including the storage battery, dictaphone, mimeograph, electric motor, electric transmission, and the motion picture. Edison thus demonstrated the significance of "research and development" activities to American business.

Alexander Graham Bell being observed by businessmen at the New York end of the first long-distance call to Chicago, 1893.

In 1882, with the backing of J. P. Morgan, the Edison Electric Illuminating Company began to supply current to eighty-five customers in New York City, beginning the great electric utility industry. A number of companies making light bulbs merged into the Edison General Electric Company in 1888. Financially secure, Edison retired from business to devote himself full time once again to invention.

The use of direct current limited Edison's lighting system to a radius of about two miles. To cover more distance required an alternating current, which could be transmitted at high voltage and then stepped down by transformers. George Westinghouse, inventor of the air brake, developed the first alternating-current system in 1886 and manufactured the equipment through the Westinghouse Electric Company. Edison resisted the new method as too risky, but the Westinghouse system won the "Battle of the Currents," and the Edison companies had to switch over. After the invention of the alternating-current motor by a Croatian immigrant named Nikola Tesla, Westinghouse acquired and improved the motor. This invention enabled factories to locate wherever they wished; they no longer had to cluster around waterfalls and coal supplies for their energy.

ENTREPRENEURS

Edison and Westinghouse were rare examples of inventors with the luck and foresight to get rich from the industries they created. The great captains of commerce were more often pure entrepreneurs rather than inventors, men skilled mainly in organizing and promoting big business. Several post–Civil War entrepreneurs stand out both for their achievements and for their special contributions: John D. Rockefeller and Andrew Carnegie, for their innovations in organization; J. Pierpont Morgan, for his development of investment banking; and Richard Sears and Alvah Roebuck, pioneers of mail-order retailing.

ROCKEFELLER AND THE OIL TRUST Born in New York State, the son of a flamboyant con man and a devout Baptist mother, Rockefeller moved as a youth to Cleveland. Soon thereafter, his father abandoned his family and started a new life under an assumed name with a second wife. Raised by his mother, John Rockefeller developed a passion for systematic organization and self-discipline. He was obsessed with precision, order, and tidiness. And early on, he decided to bring order and rationality to the chaotic oil industry.

Cleveland's railroad and ship connections made it a strategic location for servicing the oil fields of western Pennsylvania. The first oil well was struck in 1859 in Titusville, Pennsylvania, and led to the Pennsylvania oil rush of the 1860s. As oil could be refined into kerosene, which could be used in lighting, heating, and cooking, the economic importance of the oil rush soon came to outweigh that of the California

Wooden derricks crowd the John Benninghoff farm on Oil Creek, Pennsylvania, in the 1860s.

gold rush of just ten years before. Well before the end of the Civil War, derricks checkered the area, and refineries sprang up in Pittsburgh and Cleveland. Of the two cities, Cleveland had the edge in transportation, and Rockefeller focused his energies there.

Young Rockefeller recognized the potential profits in refining oil and backed a refinery in Cleveland started by his friend Samuel Andrews. He then formed a partnership with Andrews, and in 1867 added H. M. Flagler to create the firm of Rockefeller, Andrews, and Flagler. In 1870 Rockefeller incorporated his various interests as the Standard Oil Company of Ohio.

Although Rockefeller was the largest refiner, he wanted all of the business. So he decided to weed out the competition, which he perceived as flooding the market with too much refined oil, bringing down prices and reducing profits. Rockefeller approached his Cleveland competitors and offered to buy them out at his own price. Those who resisted were forced out. In less than six weeks, Rockefeller took over twenty-two of his twenty-six competitors. By 1879 Standard Oil controlled 90 to 95 percent of the oil refining in the country.

Much of Rockefeller's success was based on his determination to "pay nobody a profit." Instead of depending on the products or services of other firms, known as "middlemen," Standard Oil undertook to make its own barrels, cans, staves, and whatever else it needed. In economic terms this is called vertical integration. The company also kept large amounts of cash reserves to make it independent of banks in case of a crisis. In line with this policy, Rockefeller set out also to control his transportation needs. With Standard Oil owning most of the pipelines leading to railroads, plus the tank cars and the oil-storage facilities, it was able to dissuade the railroads from servicing eastern competitors. Those rivals who insisted on holding out then faced a giant marketing organization capable of driving them to the wall with price wars.

Eventually, in order to consolidate scattered business interests under more efficient control, Rockefeller and his advisers resorted to a new legal device: the trust. Long established in law to enable one or more people to manage property belonging to others, such as children or the mentally incompetent, the trust now was used for another purpose—centralized control of business. Since Standard Oil of Ohio was not permitted to hold property out of state, it began in 1872 to place

John D. Rockefeller, whose Standard Oil Company dominated the oil business.

properties or companies acquired elsewhere in trust, usually with the company secretary. This was impractical, however, since the death of the trustee would endanger the trust. To solve this problem, in 1882 Rockefeller organized the Standard Oil Trust. All thirty-seven stockholders in various Standard Oil enterprises would convey their stock to nine trustees, receiving "trust certificates" in return. The nine trustees would thus be empowered to give central direction to all the Standard companies.

The original plan, never fully carried out, was to organize a Standard Oil Company in each state in which the trust did business. But the trust device, widely copied in the 1880s, proved legally vulnerable to prosecution under state laws against monopoly or restraint of trade. In 1892 the supreme court of Ohio ordered the Standard Oil Trust dissolved. For a while the company managed to unify control by the simple device of interlocking directorates, through which the board of directors of one company was made identical or nearly so to the boards of the others. Gradually, however, Rockefeller took to the idea of the holding company: a company that controlled other companies by holding all or at least a majority of their stock. He was convinced that big business was a natural result of capitalism at work. "It is too late," he declared in 1899, "to argue about the advantages of industrial combinations. They are a necessity." That same year Rockefeller brought his empire under the direction of the Standard Oil Company of New Jersey, a holding company. Though less vulnerable to prosecution under state law, some holding companies proved vulnerable to the Sherman Anti-Trust Act of 1890 (see Chapter 22).

Rockefeller not only made a fortune, he also gave much of it away, mostly to support education and medicine. A man of simple tastes, who opposed the use of tobacco and alcohol and believed his fortune was a public trust awarded by God, he became the world's leading philanthropist. He donated more than $500 million during his ninety-eight-year life. "I have always regarded it as a religious duty," Rockefeller said late in life, "to get all I could honorably and to give all I could."

CARNEGIE AND THE STEEL INDUSTRY Andrew Carnegie, like Rockefeller, experienced an untypical rise from poverty to riches. Born in Scotland, he migrated in 1848 with his family to Allegheny, Pennsylvania. Then thirteen, he started out as a bobbin boy in a textile mill at wages of $1.20 per week. At fourteen he was earning $2.50 per week as a telegraph messenger. In 1853 he became personal secretary and telegrapher to Thomas Scott, then district superintendent of the Pennsylvania Railroad and later its president. When Scott moved up, Carnegie took his place as superintendent. During the Civil War, when Scott became assistant secretary of war in charge of transportation, Carnegie went with him, developed a military telegraph system, and personally helped evacuate the wounded from Bull Run.

Carnegie kept on moving—from telegraphy to railroading to bridge building and then to iron-and steel-making and investments. In 1873

Andrew Carnegie.

Carnegie resolved to concentrate on steel. Steel was the miracle material of the post–Civil War era, not because it was new, but because it suddenly was cheap. Until the mid–nineteenth century, the only way to make steel was from wrought iron—itself expensive—and in small quantities. Then in 1856 Sir Henry Bessemer invented what became known as the Bessemer converter, a process by which steel could be produced directly and quickly from pig iron (crude iron made in a blast furnace). As the volume of steel rose, its price dropped, and its use soared. In 1860 the United States produced only 13,000 tons of steel. By 1880 production had reached 1.4 million tons.

Carnegie was never a technical expert on steel. He was a promoter, salesman, and organizer with a gift for finding and using men of expert ability. He always insisted on up-to-date machinery and equipment, and he used times of recession to expand cheaply. Carnegie retained a large part of his annual profits during good times to tide the business over during lean years. Amid business depressions, when construction costs were low and competitors were forced to the wall, Carnegie used his surplus capital to buy them out and expand. He also preached to his employees a philosophy of constant innovation in order to reduce operating costs.

Carnegie stood out from other business titans as a thinker who fashioned and publicized a philosophy for big business, a conservative rationale that became deeply implanted in the conventional wisdom of some Americans. He believed that, however harsh their methods at times, he and other captains of industry were on the whole public benefactors. In his best-remembered essay, "The Gospel of Wealth," published in 1889, he argued that in the evolution of society the contrast between the

Carnegie plant at Homestead, Pennsylvania.

millionaire and the laborer measures the distance society has come. "Not evil, but good, has come to the race from the accumulation of wealth by those who have the ability and energy that produces it." The process had been costly in many ways, but the law of competition was "best for the trade, because it insures the survival of the fittest in every department."

When he retired at age sixty-five, Carnegie devoted himself to dispensing his fortune for the public good, out of a sincere desire to promote social welfare and to further world peace. He called this being a "distributor" of wealth (he disliked the term "philanthropy"). He gave money to universities, libraries, hospitals, parks, halls for meetings and concerts, swimming pools, and church buildings.

J. P. MORGAN, THE FINANCIER   J. Pierpont Morgan was born to wealth and increased it enormously through his bold innovations. His father was a partner in a London banking house, which he later came to direct. Young Pierpont attended boarding school in Switzerland and university in Germany. After a brief apprenticeship, he was sent in 1857 to work in a New York firm representing his father's interests, and in 1860 set himself up as its New York agent under the name of J. Pierpont Morgan and Company. This firm, under various names, channeled European capital into America and grew into a financial power in its own right.

J. Pierpont Morgan. *A famous portrait by the photographer Edward Steichen, done in 1903.*

Morgan was an investment banker, which meant that he would buy corporate stocks and bonds wholesale and then sell them at a profit. The growth of large corporations put Morgan's and other investment firms in an increasingly strategic position in the economy. Since the investment

A lavish dinner celebrated the merger of the Carnegie and Morgan interests into U.S. Steel in 1901. These executives are seated at a table that is shaped like a huge rail.

business depended on the general good health of client companies, investment bankers became involved in the operation of their clients' firms, demanding seats on the boards of directors and helping to shape their fiscal dealings. By these means bankers could influence company policies. But this often resulted in heavy emphasis on fiscal matters to the detriment of technical innovation.

Morgan early realized that railroads were the key to the times, and he acquired and reorganized one line after another. By the 1890s, he alone controlled one-sixth of the nation's railway system. To Morgan, an imperious, domineering man, the stability brought by his operations helped the economy and the public. Like Rockefeller, he regarded competition as chaotic and inefficient. Morgan's crowning triumph was consolidation of the steel industry, to which he was led by his interests in railroading. After a rapid series of mergers in the iron and steel industry, he bought out Andrew Carnegie's huge steel and iron holdings in 1901. Carnegie demanded $500 million. In rapid succession, Morgan added other steel interests and the Rockefeller holdings in both Minnesota's Mesabi ore range and a Great Lakes ore fleet. Altogether the new United States Steel Corporation, a holding company for these varied interests, was capitalized at $1.4 billion, a total that was heavily "watered" (valued well above the company's actual assets) but was soon made solid by large profits. The new business behemoth was a marvel of the new century, the first billion-dollar corporation, the climactic event in that age of consolidation.

SEARS AND ROEBUCK American inventors helped manufacturers after the Civil War produce a vast number of new products, but the most important challenge was how to extend the reach of national commerce to the millions of people who lived on isolated farms and in small towns. In the aftermath of the Civil War, a traveling salesman from Chicago named Aaron Montgomery Ward decided that he could reach more people by mail than on foot and in the process could eliminate the "middlemen" whose services increased the retail price of goods. Beginning in the early 1870s, the Montgomery Ward Company began selling goods at a 40 percent discount through mail-order catalogs.

Sears, Roebuck, and Company, catalog cover, 1897. Sears's extensive mail-order service and discounted prices allowed its many products to reach people in both cities and backcountry.

By the end of the century, a new retailer came to dominate the mail-order industry: Sears, Roebuck and Company, founded by two young midwestern entrepreneurs, Richard Sears and Alvah Roebuck, who began offering a cornucopia of goods by mail in the early 1890s. The Sears, Roebuck and Company catalog in 1897 was 786 pages long. It included groceries, drugs, tools, bells, furniture, ice boxes, stoves and household utensils, musical instruments, farm implements, boots and shoes, clothes, books, and sporting goods. The company's ability to buy goods in high volumes from wholesalers enabled it to sell items at prices below those offered in rural general stores. By 1907, Sears, Roebuck and Company had become one of the largest business enterprises in the nation.

The Sears catalog helped create a truly national market and in the process transformed the lives of millions of people. With the advent of free rural mail delivery in 1898 and the widespread distribution of Sears catalogs, families on farms and in small towns and villages could purchase by mail the products that heretofore were either prohibitively expensive or available only to city dwellers. By the turn of the century, 6 million Sears catalogs were distributed each year, and the catalog had become the single most widely read book in the nation except for the Bible.

LABOR CONDITIONS AND ORGANIZATION

SOCIAL TRENDS   Accompanying the spread of huge industrial combinations during the so-called Gilded Age was a rising standard of living for most people. If the rich were still getting richer, a lot of other people were at least better off, and the pre–Civil War trend toward even higher concentrations of wealth slacked off. This, of course, is far from saying that disparities in the distribution of wealth had disappeared. One set of estimates reveals that in both 1860 and 1900 the richest 2 percent of American families owned more than a third of the nation's physical wealth, while the top 10 percent owned almost three-fourths. All the nation's physical assets were in the hands of half its families. Studies of social mobility in towns across the country show, however, that while the rise from rags to riches was rare, "upward mobility both from blue-collar to white-collar callings and from low-ranked to high-ranked manual jobs was quite common."

The continuing demand for unskilled or semiskilled workers, meanwhile, attracted new groups entering the workforce at the bottom: immigrants above all, but also growing numbers of women and children. Because of a long-term decline in prices and the cost of living, real wages and earnings in manufacturing went up about 50 percent between 1860 and 1890, and another 37 percent from 1890 to 1914. By modern-day standards, however, working conditions were dreary indeed. At the turn of the century, the average hourly wage in manufacturing was 21.6¢, and average annual earnings were $490. The average workweek was fifty-nine hours, or nearly six ten-hour days, but that was only an average. Most steelworkers put in a twelve-hour day, and as late as the 1920s, a great many worked a seven-day, or eighty-four-hour, week.

Although wage levels were rising overall, working and living conditions remained precarious. In the crowded tenements and immigrant neighborhoods in major cities, the death rates ran substantially higher than in the countryside. Factories often maintained poor health and safety conditions. In 1913, for instance, there were some 25,000 factory fatalities and 700,000 job-related injuries that required at least four weeks' disability. America was the only industrial nation in the world that had no workmen's compensation program to provide support for workers injured on the job. And American industry had the highest accident rate in the world. In this new industrial world, ever-larger numbers of people were dependent on the machinery and factories of owners whom they seldom if ever saw. In the simpler world of small shops, workers and employers could enter into close personal relationships; the larger corporation, on the other hand, was likely governed by a bureaucracy in which ownership was separate from management. Much of the social history of the modern world in fact turns on the transition from a world of personal relationships to one of impersonal and contractual relationships.

CHILD LABOR A growing number of these wage laborers were children—boys and girls who worked full-time for meager wages amid unhealthy conditions. Of course, young people had always worked in America. Farms required everyone to pitch in. After the Civil War, however, millions of children took up work outside the home, operating machines, digging coal, stitching clothes, shucking oysters, peeling shrimp, canning food, blowing glass, and tending looms in textile mills. Parents desperate for income felt they had no choice but to put their children to work. In 1870 there were 750,000 children between the ages of ten and fifteen employed in hazardous conditions in industry, agriculture, and the so-called street trades. By 1880 the number had risen to 1,118,000, meaning that one out of every six children in the nation was working full-time. And by 1900 there were almost 2 million child laborers in the United States. In southern cotton mills, where few blacks were hired, one-fourth of the employees were below the age of fifteen, with half of these children below age twelve. Children as young

These young boys did the dangerous work of mine helpers in West Virginia, c. 1900.

as eight were laboring alongside adults, twelve hours a day, six days a week. This meant they received little or no education and had little time for play or parental supervision.

Factories, mills, mines, and canneries were dangerous places, especially for children. Few machines had guardrails or safety devices, and few factories or mills had ventilating fans or fire escapes. During the nineteenth century, employers were much more concerned about maintaining production than preventing accidents or ensuring a healthy workplace. Throughout Appalachia, thousands of soot-smeared boys worked deep in the coal mines. In New England and the South, thousands of young girls worked in dusty textile mills, walking up and down the aisles all day, brushing away lint from the clacking machines and retying broken threads. Foremen kept the children awake by dousing them with water. Children suffered three times as many on-the-job accidents as adult workers, and respiratory diseases were common in the unventilated buildings. A child working in a textile mill was only half as likely to reach the age of twenty as a child outside the mill. Although some states passed laws limiting the number of hours children could work and establishing minimum age requirements, they were rarely enforced and often ignored. By 1881 only seven states, mostly in New England, had laws requiring children to be at least twelve before they worked for wages. Yet the only proof required by employers in such states was a statement from parents. Working-class and immigrant parents were often so desperate for income that they forged work permits for their children or taught them to lie about their age to keep their jobs.

In 1903 a New York social reformer named Marie Van Vorst traveled south, disguised herself, and took a job in a South Carolina textile mill to see what conditions were like. Her account was shocking. She described a one-armed teenage boy in ragged clothes who worked from 5:45 A.M. to 6:45 P.M. six days a week. He earned fifty cents a day. "It keeps me in existence," he explained. Van Vorst saw numerous girls as young as seven working as bobbin girls near the spinning looms. Both their employers and their parents had taught the children to lie about their age. The child workers, few of whom could read or write, were given twenty minutes to eat pitiful meals on the mill floor, often falling asleep with their mouths full, only to be brusquely awakened by supervisors starting the next shift. "The children," Van Vorst reported, "all seemed malnourished, their stomachs distended and swollen, their bones nearly through their skin."

DISORGANIZED PROTEST   In these circumstances it was very difficult for workers to organize unions. Civic leaders respected property rights more than the rights of labor. Many businessmen believed that a "labor supply" was simply another commodity to be procured at the lowest possible price.

Among workers recently removed from an agrarian world, the idea of labor unions was slow to take hold. Immigrant workers came from many cultures. They spoke different languages and harbored ethnic animosities. Many, if not most, saw their jobs as transient, the first rung on the ladder to success. They hoped to move on to a homestead, or to return with their earnings to the old farms of their European homelands. With or without unions, though, workers often staged impromptu strikes in response to wage cuts and other grievances. But such action often led to violence, and three incidents of the 1870s colored much of the public's view of labor unions thereafter.

The decade's early years saw a reign of terror in the eastern Pennsylvania coal fields, attributed to an Irish group called the Molly Maguires. They took their name from an Irish patriot who had directed violent resistance against the British. The group was incited by the dangerous working conditions in the mines and the owners' brutal efforts to suppress union activity. Convinced of the justness of their cause, the Molly Maguires used intimidation, beatings, and killings to right perceived wrongs against Irish workers. Later investigations have shown that agents of the mine operators themselves stirred up some of the trouble. The terrorism reached its peak in 1874–1875, and mine owners hired Pinkerton detectives to stop the movement. One of the agents who infiltrated the Mollies produced enough evidence to indict the leaders. At trials in 1876 twenty-four of the Molly Maguires were convicted; ten were hanged. The trials also resulted in a wage reduction in the mines and the final destruction of the Miners' National Association, a weak union the Mollies had dominated.

THE RAILROAD STRIKE OF 1877 Far more significant, because more widespread, was the Great Railroad Strike of 1877, the first major interstate strike in American history. After the Panic of 1873 and the ensuing depression, the major rail lines in the East had cut wages. In 1877 they made another 10 percent cut, which provoked most of the railroad workers at Martinsburg, West Virginia, to walk off the job and block the tracks. Without organized direction, however, their picketing groups degenerated into a mob that burned and plundered railroad property.

Walkouts and sympathy demonstrations spread spontaneously from Maryland to San Francisco. The strike engulfed hundreds of cities and towns, leaving in its wake over a hundred people killed and millions of dollars in property destroyed. Federal troops finally quelled the violence. The greatest outbreak began at Pittsburgh, when the Pennsylvania Railroad put on "double-headers" (long trains pulled by two locomotives) in order to reduce crews. Public sympathy for the strikers was so great at first that local militiamen, called out to suppress them, instead joined the workers. Militiamen called in from Philadelphia managed to disperse one crowd at the cost of twenty-six lives, but then found themselves besieged in the railroad's roundhouse, where they disbanded and shot their way out.

The looting, rioting, and burning went on for another day until the frenzy wore itself out. A reporter described the scene as "the most horrible ever witnessed, except in the carnage of war. There were fifty miles of hot rails, ten tracks side by side, with as many miles of ties turned into glowing coals and tons on tons of iron car skeletons and wheels almost at white heat." Public opinion, sympathetic at first, tended to blame the workers for the looting and violence. Eventually the strikers, lacking organized bargaining power, had no choice but to drift back to work. Everywhere the strikes failed.

For many people, the railroad strike raised the specter of a worker-based social revolution like the Paris Commune of 1871, in which disgruntled mobs chanted "Bread or Blood." As a Pittsburgh newspaper warned, "This may be the beginning of a great civil war in this country between labor and capital." Equally disturbing to those in positions of corporate and political power was the presence of many women among the protesters. A Baltimore journalist noted that the "singular part of the disturbances is the very active part taken by the women, who are the wives and mothers of the [railroad] firemen." From the point of view of organized labor, however, the Great Railroad Strike demonstrated potential union strength and the need for tighter organization.

THE "SAND LOT" INCIDENT In California the railroad strike indirectly gave rise to a working-class political movement. At San Francisco's "Sand Lot," a meeting to express sympathy for the strikers ended with attacks on some passing Chinese. Within a few days, sporadic anti-Chinese riots led to a mob attack on Chinatown. The depression of the 1870s had hit the West Coast especially hard, and the Chinese were handy scapegoats for frustrated white laborers who felt the Asians had taken their jobs.

Soon an Irish immigrant, Dennis Kearney, organized the "Workingmen's Party of California." Its platform called for an end to further Chinese immigration. A gifted agitator, himself only recently naturalized, Kearney harangued the "sand lotters" about the "foreign peril" and assaulted the rich railroad barons for exploiting the poor—sometimes at gatherings beside their mansions on Nob Hill. In 1878 his new party won a hefty number of seats in a state constitutional convention, but managed to incorporate in the state's basic law little more than ineffective attempts to regulate the railroads. The workingmen's movement peaked in 1879 when it elected many members of the new legislature and the mayor of San Francisco. Kearney lacked the gift for building a durable movement, but as his party went to pieces, his anti-Chinese theme became a national issue. In 1882 Congress voted to prohibit Chinese immigration for ten years.

TOWARD PERMANENT UNIONS   Meanwhile, efforts to build a national labor union movement had begun to bear fruit. Earlier efforts, in the 1830s and 1840s, had largely been dominated by reformers with schemes that ranged from free homesteads to utopian socialism. But the 1850s had seen the beginning of "job-conscious" unions in selected skilled trades. By 1860 there were about twenty such craft unions. During the Civil War, because of the demand for labor, such unions grew in strength and numbers.

Yet there was no overall federation of these groups, until 1866, when the first National Labor Union (NLU) convened in Baltimore. The NLU was composed of congresses of delegates from labor and reform groups more interested in political and social reform, however, than in bargaining with employers. The groups espoused such ideas as the eight-hour workday, workers' cooperatives, greenbackism (the printing of paper money to inflate the currency and thereby relieve debtors), and equal rights for women and blacks. After the head of the union died suddenly, its support fell away quickly, and by 1872 the NLU had disbanded. The National Labor Union was not a total failure, however. It was influential in persuading Congress to enact an eight-hour workday for federal employees and to repeal the 1864 Contract Labor Law, which had been passed during the Civil War to encourage the importation of labor by allowing employers to pay for the laborers' passage to America. Employers had taken advantage of the Contract Labor Law to recruit foreign laborers who were willing to work for lower wages than their American counterparts.

THE KNIGHTS OF LABOR   Before the National Labor Union collapsed, another labor group of national standing had emerged: the Noble and Holy Order of the Knights of Labor. The name evoked the aura of medieval guilds. The founder of the Knights of Labor, Uriah S. Stephens, a Philadelphia tailor, was a habitual "joiner" involved with several secret orders, including the Masons. His early training for the Baptist ministry also affected his outlook. Secrecy, he felt, along with a semireligious ritual, would protect members against retaliation by employers and at the same time create a sense of solidarity.

The Knights of Labor, started in 1869, grew slowly, but during the years of depression, as other unions collapsed, it spread more rapidly. In 1878 its first General Assembly established a national organization. Its preamble and platform endorsed the reforms advanced by previous workingmen's groups, including bureaus of labor statistics, mechanics' lien laws (to ensure payment of salaries), elimination of convict-labor competition, the eight-hour day, and paper currency. One plank in the platform, far ahead of the times, called for equal pay for equal work by both men and women.

Throughout its existence the Knights of Labor emphasized reform measures and preferred boycotts to strikes as a way to put pressure on employers. The Knights allowed as members all who had ever worked for wages except lawyers, doctors, bankers, and those who sold liquor. Theoretically it was one big union of all workers, skilled and unskilled, regardless of race, color, creed, or sex.

In 1879 Stephens was succeeded as head of the Knights of Labor by Terence V. Powderly, the thirty-year-old mayor of Scranton, Pennsylvania. Born of Irish immigrant parents, Powderly had started working for a railroad at age sixteen. In many ways he was unsuited to his new job as head of the Knights of Labor. He was physically frail, sensitive to criticism, and indecisive at critical moments. He was temperamentally opposed to strikes, and when they did occur, he did not always back up the local groups involved. Yet the Knights owed their greatest growth to strikes that occurred under his leadership.

Members of the Knights of Labor.

In the 1880s the Knights increased from about 100,000 members to more than 700,000. In 1886, however, the Knights peaked and then went into rapid decline after a railroad strike failed.

ANARCHISM   The tensions between labor and management during the late nineteenth century in both the United States and Europe helped generate the doctrine of anarchism. The anarchists believed that government, any government, was in itself an abusive device used by the rich and powerful to oppress and exploit the working poor. Anarchists dreamed of the eventual disappearance of government altogether, and many of them believed that the transition to this stateless society could be hurried along by promoting revolutionary action among the masses. One favored tactic was the use of dramatic acts of violence against representatives of the government. Many European anarchists emigrated to the United States during the last quarter of the nineteenth century, and they brought with them this belief in the impact of "propaganda of the deed."

THE HAYMARKET AFFAIR   Labor-related violence increased during the 1880s. The Haymarket Affair grew indirectly out of agitation for the eight-hour workday. In 1884 Knights of Labor organizers set May 1, 1886, as the deadline for the institution of the eight-hour workday in all trades. Chicago became the center of the movement, and on May 3 the International Harvester plant became the site of an unfortunate clash between strikers and policemen in which one striker was killed.

Leaders of a minuscule anarchist movement in Chicago scheduled an open meeting the following night at Haymarket Square to protest the killing. After listening to long speeches promoting socialism and anarchism, the crowd was beginning to break up when a group of policemen arrived and called upon the meeting to disperse. At that point somebody threw a bomb at the police, killing one and wounding others. The police then fired into the crowd. In a trial marked by prejudice and hysteria, seven anarchist leaders were sentenced to death despite the lack of any evidence linking them to the bomb-thrower, whose identity was never established. Of these, two were reprieved, one committed suicide in prison, but four were hanged. All but one of the group were German-speaking, but that one held a membership card in the Knights of Labor.

The violent incident at Haymarket Square provoked widespread revulsion against the Knights and labor groups in general. Despite his best efforts, Terence Powderly could never dissociate in the public mind the Knights from the anarchists. He clung to leadership until 1893, but after that the union evaporated. By the turn of the century it was but a memory. A number of problems accounted for the Knights' decline besides fears of their supposed radicalism: a leadership devoted more to reform than to the nuts and bolts of organization, the failure of the Knights' cooperative enterprises, and a preoccupation with politics that led the Knights to sponsor labor candidates in hundreds of local elections.

The Knights nevertheless attained some lasting achievements, among them the creation of the federal Bureau of Labor Statistics in 1884 as well as several state labor bureaus; the Foran Act of 1885, which, though weakly enforced, penalized employers who imported contract labor (an arrangement similar to the indentured servitude of colonial times in which workers were committed to a term of labor in exchange for transportation to America); and a national law enacted in 1880 for the arbitration of labor disputes. The Knights by example also spread the idea of unionism and initiated a new type of union organization: the industrial union, an industrywide union of the skilled and unskilled.

GOMPERS AND THE AFL   The craft unions opposed such industrial unionism. They organized workers who shared special skills, such as typographers or cigarmakers. Leaders of the crafts feared that joining with the unskilled laborers would mean a loss of their separate craft identities and a loss of the bargaining power held by skilled workers.

In 1886 delegates from twenty craft unions organized the American Federation of Labor (AFL). Its structure differed from the Knights of Labor in that it was a federation of national organizations, each of which retained a large degree of autonomy and exercised greater leverage against management.

Samuel Gompers served as president of the AFL from its start until his death in 1924, with only one year's interruption. Born in London of Dutch-Jewish ancestry, Gompers came to the United States as a teenager, joined the Cigarmakers Union in 1864, and became president of his New York local in 1877. Unlike Terence Powderly and the Knights of Labor, Gompers focused on concrete economic gains, avoiding involvement with utopian ideas or politics. "We have no ultimate ends," Gompers told a Senate hearing. "We are going on from day to day. We are fighting only for immediate objects—objects that can be realized in a few years."

Gompers hired organizers to spread unionism and worked as a diplomat to prevent overlapping unions and to settle jurisdictional disputes. The AFL represented workers in matters of national legislation and acted as a sounding board for their cause. On occasion it exercised its power to request from members dues for the support of strikes. Gompers was temperamentally more fitted than Powderly for the rough-and-tumble world of unionism. He had a thick hide, liked to talk and drink with workers in the back room, and willingly used the strike to achieve favorable trade agreements, including provisos for

Samuel Gompers, head of the American Federation of Labor, striking an assertive pose.

union recognition in the form of closed shops (which could hire only union members) or union-preference shops (which could hire others only if no union members were available).

The AFL at first grew slowly, but by 1890 it had surpassed the Knights of Labor in membership. By the turn of the century, it claimed 500,000 members in affiliated unions; in 1914, on the eve of World War I, it had 2 million; and in 1920, it reached a peak of 4 million. But even then it embraced less than 15 percent of the nation's nonagricultural workers. All unions, including the unaffiliated railroad brotherhoods, accounted for little more than 18 percent of these workers. Organized labor's strongholds were in transportation and the building trades. Most of the larger manufacturing industries, including steel, textiles, tobacco, and packinghouses, remained almost untouched. Gompers never frowned on industrial unions, and several became important affiliates of the AFL: the United Mine Workers, the International Ladies' Garment Workers, and the Amalgamated Clothing Workers. But the AFL had its greatest success in organizing skilled workers.

Cigar box label celebrating union workers, c. 1898.

THE HOMESTEAD STRIKE   Two violent incidents in the 1890s stalled the emerging industrial union movement and set it back for the next forty years—the Homestead Steel Strike of 1892 and the Pullman Strike of 1894. The Amalgamated Association of Iron and Steel Workers, founded in 1876, had by 1891 a membership of more than 24,000 and was probably the largest craft union at that time. But it excluded the unskilled and had failed to organize the larger steel plants. The Homestead Works at Pittsburgh was an important exception. There the union had enjoyed friendly relations with Andrew Carnegie's company until H. C. Frick became its president in 1889. A showdown was delayed, however, until 1892, when the union contract came up for renewal. Carnegie, who had expressed sympathy for unions in the past, had gone to Scotland and left matters in the hands of Frick. Carnegie, however, knew what was afoot: a cost-cutting reduction in the number of workers through the use of labor-saving devices, and a deliberate attempt to smash the union.

As negotiations dragged on, the company announced it would treat workers as individuals unless an agreement was reached by June 29. A strike, or more properly a lockout of unionists, began on that date. In no mood to negotiate, Frick built a twelve-foot fence around the entire plant and hired 300 union-busting Pinkerton detectives to protect what was soon dubbed Fort Frick. On the morning of July 6, 1892, when the Pinkertons floated up the Monongahela River on barges, unionists were waiting behind breastworks on shore. Who fired the first shot remains unknown, but a battle broke out in which six workers and three Pinkertons died. In the end the Pinkertons surrendered and were marched away, subjected to taunts from crowds in the street. Six days later the state militia appeared at the plant to protect the strikebreakers hired by Frick to restore production. The strike dragged on until November, but by then the union was dead at Homestead. Its cause was not helped when a deranged anarchist, a Lithuanian immigrant, shot and stabbed Frick. Much of the local sympathy for the strikers evaporated.

THE PULLMAN STRIKE   The Pullman Strike of 1894 was perhaps the most notable walkout in American history. It paralyzed the economies of twenty-seven states and territories making up the western half of the nation. It involved a dispute at the "model" town of Pullman, Illinois, which housed workers of the Pullman Palace Car Company. The town's idyllic appearance, however, was deceptive. Employees were required to live there, pay rents and utility costs higher than those in nearby towns, and buy goods from company stores. During the Depression of 1893, George Pullman laid off 3,000 of 5,800 employees, and cut wages 25 to 40 percent, but not his rents and other charges. When Pullman fired three members of a workers' grievance committee, a strike began on May 11, 1894.

During this tense period, Pullman workers had been joining the American Railway Union, founded the previous year by Eugene V. Debs. The tall, gangly Debs was a man of towering influence and charismatic appeal. A child of working-class immigrants, he quit school in 1869 at age fourteen and began working for an Indiana railroad. There, he would later write, "I learned of the hardships of the rail in snow, sleet, and hail, of the ceaseless danger that lurks along the iron highway, the uncertainty of employment, scant wages and altogether trying lot of the workingman, so that from my very boyhood I was made to feel the wrongs of labor." He felt these wrongs so deeply that he eagerly accepted an invitation to start a local of the railroad brotherhood, a craft union of skilled workers.

By the early 1890s Debs had become a tireless spokesman for labor radicalism, and he launched a crusade to organize *all* railway workers—

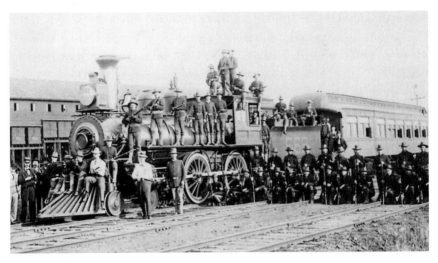

Troops guarding the railroads during the Pullman Strike, 1894.

skilled or unskilled—into the American Railway Union. Soon he was in charge of a powerful new labor organization, and he quickly turned his attention to the Pullman controversy.

In June 1894, after Pullman refused Debs's plea for arbitration, the union workers stopped handling Pullman cars and by the end of July had tied up most of the railroads in the Midwest. Railroad executives then brought strikebreakers from Canada and elsewhere, instructing them to connect mail cars to Pullman cars so that interference with Pullman cars also meant interference with the mails. The U.S. attorney-general, a former railroad attorney himself, swore in 3,400 special deputies to keep the trains running. When clashes occurred between these deputies and some of the strikers, angry workers ignored Debs's plea for an orderly boycott. They assaulted employees and destroyed property.

Finally, on July 3, 1894, President Grover Cleveland sent federal troops into the Chicago area, where the strike was centered. The Illinois governor insisted that the state could keep order, but Cleveland claimed authority and a duty to ensure delivery of the mails. Meanwhile, the attorney-general won an injunction forbidding any interference with the mails or any combination to restrain interstate commerce; the principle was that a strike or boycott violated the Sherman Anti-Trust Act. On July 13 the union called off the strike and on the same day the district court cited Debs for violating the injunction and sentenced him to six months in jail. The Supreme Court upheld the decree in the case of *In re Debs* (1895) on broad grounds of national sovereignty: "The strong arm of the national government may be put forth to brush away all obstructions to the freedom of interstate commerce or the transportation of the mails." Debs served his term, during which time he read deeply in socialist literature, and he emerged to devote the rest of his life to that cause.

MOTHER JONES One of the most colorful and beloved labor agitators at the end of the nineteenth century was a remarkable woman known simply as Mother Jones. White-haired, pink-cheeked, and dressed in matronly black dresses and hats, she was a tireless champion of the working poor and a rabble-rouser who skillfully used fiery rhetoric to excite crowds and attract media attention. She led marches, dodged bullets, served jail terms, and confronted business titans and police with disarming courage. In 1913 a district attorney called her the "most dangerous woman in America."

Born in Cork, Ireland, in 1837, Mary Harris was the second of five children in a poor, Catholic family. At mid-century they fled the Irish potato famine and settled in Toronto, where Mary learned to sew, attended school, and became certified to teach. In 1861 she moved to Memphis and began teaching. There, as the Civil War was erupting, she met and married George Jones, an iron molder and staunch union member. They had four children and were quite content until disaster struck.

In 1867 a yellow fever epidemic devastated Memphis, killing Mary Jones's husband and four children. The grief-stricken thirty-year-old widow moved to Chicago and took up dressmaking, only to see her shop, home, and belongings destroyed in the great fire of 1871. Having lost her family and her finances, angry at the social inequality and injustices all around her, Mary Jones drifted into the labor movement and soon emerged as its most

Mother Jones.

passionate advocate. Chicago was then the seedbed of American labor radicalism, and the union culture nurtured in Mary Jones a lifelong dedication to the cause of workers and their families. "Those were the days of sacrifice for the cause of labor," she recalled. "Those were the days when we had no [meeting] halls, when there were no high salaried officers. . . . Those were the days of the martyrs and the saints."

The gritty woman who had lost her family now declared herself to be the "mother" to the fledgling American labor movement. She joined the Knights of Labor as an organizer and public speaker. In 1886, however, she resigned from the Knights because in her view it had failed to support the Chicago anarchists convicted of assaulting police officers during the Haymarket incident. Thereafter, she became an ardent speaker for the United Mine Workers (UMW), various other unions, and the Socialist party. For the next thirty years, she crisscrossed the nation, recruiting union members, supporting strikers (her "boys"), raising funds, walking picket lines, defying court injunctions, berating politicians, and spending time in jail.

Wherever Mother Jones went, she promoted higher wages, shorter hours, safer conditions, and restrictions on child labor. Coal miners, said the UMW president, "have had no more staunch supporter, no more able defender than the one we all love to call Mother." During a miners' strike in West Virginia, Jones was arrested, convicted of "conspiracy that resulted in murder," and sentenced to twenty years in prison. The outcry over her plight helped spur a Senate committee to investigate conditions in the coal mines. The governor set her free.

Mother Jones was especially determined to end the exploitation of children in the workplace. In 1903 she organized a highly publicized, weeklong march of child workers from Pennsylvania to the New York home of President Theodore Roosevelt. The children were physically stunted and mutilated, most of them missing fingers or hands from machinery accidents, walking evidence of the abusive conditions of their labor. President Roosevelt refused to see the ragtag children, but, as Mother Jones explained, "our march had done its work. We had drawn the attention of the nation to the crime of child labor." Soon the Pennsylvania state legislature raised the legal working age to fourteen.

Mother Jones lost most of the strikes she participated in, but over the course of her long life she saw average wages increase, working conditions improve, and child labor diminish. Her own commitment to the cause of social justice never wavered. At age eighty-three, she was arrested after joining a miners' strike in Colorado and jailed in solitary confinement. Not content to sit idly while there was work to be done, she wrote a letter describing her plight. It was smuggled out of the jail and published in newspapers around the country. In the letter, Jones expressed her characteristic tenacity: "I will stand firm. To be in prison is no disgrace." At her funeral in 1930, one of the speakers urged people to remember her famous rallying cry: "Pray for the dead and fight like hell for the living."

SOCIALISM AND THE UNIONS   The major American unions, for the most part, never allied themselves with the socialists, as many European labor movements did. But socialist ideas had been circulating in the country at least since the 1820s. Marxism, one strain of socialism, was imported mainly by German immigrants. Karl Marx's International Workingmen's Association, the First International, founded in 1864, inspired a few affiliates in the United States. In 1872, at Marx's urging, the headquarters was moved from London to New York. In 1877 followers of Marx in America organized the Socialist Labor party, a group so filled with immigrants that German was its official language in the first years.

The movement gained little notice before the rise of Daniel DeLeon in the 1890s. As editor of its paper, *The People,* he became the dominant figure in the Socialist party. A native of the Dutch West Indies, DeLeon had studied law and lectured for some years at Columbia University. He proposed to organize industrial unions with a socialist purpose, and to build a political party that would abolish the state once it gained power, after which the unions of the Socialist Trade and Labor Alliance would become the units of control. DeLeon preached revolution at the ballot box, not by violence.

Eugene Debs was more successful than DeLeon at building a socialist movement in America. To many, DeLeon seemed doctrinaire and inflexible. In 1897 Debs announced that he was a socialist and organized the Social Democratic party from the remnants of the American Railway Union. He got over 4,000 votes as its candidate for president in 1900. In 1901 his followers joined a number of secessionists from DeLeon's party to set up the Socialist Party of America. In 1904 Debs polled over 400,000 votes as the party's candidate for president and more than doubled that to almost 900,000 votes in 1912, or 6 percent of the popular vote. In 1910 Milwaukee elected a socialist mayor and congressman.

Eugene V. Debs, founder of the American Railway Union and later candidate for president as head of the Socialist Party of America.

By 1912 the Socialist party seemed well on the way to becoming a permanent fixture in American politics. Thirty-three cities had socialist mayors. The party sponsored five English daily newspapers, eight foreign-language dailies, and a number of weeklies and monthlies. Its support was not confined to urban workers and intellectuals. In the Southwest the party built a sizable grassroots following among farmers and tenants. Oklahoma, for instance, in 1910 had more paid-up party members than any other state except New York, and in 1912 gave 16.5 percent of its popular vote to Debs, a greater proportion than any other state ever gave. But the Socialist party reached its peak in 1912. During World War I, it was wracked by disagreements over America's participation in the war, and it was split thereafter by desertions to the new Communist party.

THE WOBBLIES   During the years of Socialist party growth, there emerged a parallel effort to revive industrial unionism, led by the Industrial Workers of the World (IWW). The chief base for this group was the Western Federation of Miners, organized at Butte, Montana, in 1893. Over the next decade the Western Federation was the storm center of violent confrontation with unyielding bosses who mobilized private armies against it in Colorado, Idaho, and elsewhere. In 1905 the founding convention of the

IWW drew a variety of people who opposed the AFL's philosophy. Eugene Debs participated, although many of his comrades preferred to work within the AFL. DeLeon seized this chance to strike back at craft unionism. He argued that the IWW "must be founded on the class struggle" and "the irrepressible conflict between the capitalist class and the working class."

But the IWW waged class war better than it articulated class ideology. Like the Knights of Labor, it was designed to be "One Big Union," including all workers, skilled or unskilled. Its roots were in the mining and lumber camps of the West, where unstable conditions of employment created a large number of nomadic workers, to whom neither the AFL's pragmatic approach nor the socialists' political appeal held much attraction. The revolutionary goal of the Wobblies, as they came to be called, was an idea labeled syndicalism by its French supporters: the ultimate destruction of the state and its replacement by one big union. But just how it would govern remained vague.

Like other radical groups, the IWW was split by sectarian disputes. Because of policy disagreements, all the major founders withdrew, first the Western Federation of Miners, then Debs, then DeLeon. William D. "Big Bill" Haywood of the Western Federation remained, however, and as its leader held the group together. Haywood was an imposing figure. Well over six feet tall, handsome and muscular, he commanded the attention and respect of his listeners. This hardrock miner, union organizer, and socialist from Salt Lake City despised the AFL and its conservative labor philosophy. He called Samuel Gompers "a squat specimen of humanity" who was "conceited, petulant, and vindictive." Instead of following Gompers's advice to organize only skilled workers, Haywood promoted the concept of one all-inclusive union whose credo would be the promotion of a socialism "with its working clothes on."

Haywood and the Wobblies, however, were reaching out to the fringe elements that had the least power and influence, chiefly the migratory workers of the West and the ethnic groups of the East. Always ambivalent about diluting their revolutionary principles, they scorned the usual labor agreements, even when they participated in them. Consequently, they engaged in spectacular battles with employers but scored few victories. The largest was a textile strike at Lawrence, Massachusetts, in 1912, that garnered wage raises, overtime pay, and other benefits. But the next year a strike of silk workers at Paterson, New Jersey, ended in disaster, and the IWW entered a rapid decline.

The fading of the Wobblies was accelerated by the hysterical opposition they aroused. Branded as anarchists, bums, and criminals, the IWW was effectively destroyed during World War I, when most of its leaders were jailed for conspiracy because of their militant opposition to the war. Big Bill Haywood fled to the Soviet Union, where he married a Russian woman, died in 1928, and was honored by burial in the Kremlin wall. The Wobblies left behind a rich folklore of nomadic working men and a gallery of heroic agitators such as Elizabeth Gurley Flynn, a dark-haired Irish woman who at age eighteen chained herself to a lamppost to impede her arrest during a strike. The movement also bequeathed martyrs such as the Swedish singer and labor organizer Joe Hill, framed (so the faithful assumed) for murder and executed by a Utah firing squad. His last words were written to Haywood: "Goodbye, Bill. I die like a true blue rebel. Don't waste any time mourning. Organize." The intensity of conviction and devotion to a cause shown by Hill, Flynn, and others ensured that the IWW's ideal of a classless society did not die.

MAKING CONNECTIONS

- The Darwinian ideas implicit in the attitudes of many leading entrepreneurs, especially Andrew Carnegie, are described in greater detail in the next chapter.

- In response to the growth of the railroads, reformers in the 1880s and 1890s began to push for regulation, a trend explored in Chapter 22.

- The economic and industrial growth described in this chapter was an important factor in America's "new imperialism" in the late nineteenth century, as shown in Chapter 23.

- The socialist approach to reform was a significant influence on the Progressive movement, covered in Chapter 24.

FURTHER READING

For a masterly synthesis of post–Civil War industrial development, see Walter Licht's *Industrializing America: The Nineteenth Century* (1995). On the growth of railroads see Albro Martin's *Railroads Triumphant: The Growth, Rejection, and Rebirth of a Vital American Force* (1992). Walter Licht's *Working for the Railroad: The Organization of Work in the Nineteenth Century* (1983) treats the life of the railroad workers.

On entrepreneurship in the iron and steel sector, see Thomas J. Misa's *A Nation of Steel: The Making of Modern America, 1865–1925* (1995). The best biographies of the leading business tycoons are Ron Chernow's *Titan: The Life of John D. Rockefeller, Sr.* (1998) and Jean Strouse's *Morgan, American Financier* (1999). Nathan Rosenberg's *Technology and American Economic Growth* (1972) documents the growth of invention during the period.

Much of the scholarship on labor stresses the traditional values and the culture of work that people brought to the factory. Herbert G. Gutman's *Work, Culture, and Society in Industrializing America* (1976) best introduces these themes. The best survey remains David Montgomery's *The Fall of the House of Labor: The Workplace, the State and American Labor Activism, 1865–1925* (1987).

For the role of women in the changing workplace, see Alice Kessler-Harris's *Out to Work* (1983) and Susan E. Kennedy's *If All We Did Was to Weep at Home: A History of White Working-Class Women in America* (1979).

As for the labor unions, Gerald N. Grob's *Workers and Utopias* (1961) examines the difference in outlook between the Knights of Labor and the American Federation of Labor. For the Knights, see Leon Fink's *Workingmen's Democracy* (1983). Also useful is Susan Levine's *Labor's True Woman* (1984), on the role of women in the Knights. On Mother Jones, see Elliot Gorn's *Mother Jones: The Most Dangerous Woman in America* (2002). To trace the rise of socialism among organized workers, see Nick Salvatore's *Eugene V. Debs: Citizen and Socialist* (1982). Strikes are discussed in Paul Avrich's *The Haymarket Tragedy* (1984) and Paul Krause's *The Battle for Homestead, 1880–1892: Politics, Culture, and Steel* (1992).

21 ∽ THE EMERGENCE
OF URBAN AMERICA

CHAPTER ORGANIZER

This chapter focuses on:

- immigration and the growth of the modern city.

- the rise of powerful reform movements.

- the impact of Darwinian thought on the social sciences.

- literary and philosophical trends of the late nineteenth century.

*D*uring the second half of the nineteenth century, the United States experienced an urban transformation unparalleled in world history. As factories, mines, and mills sprouted across the landscape, cities grew up around them. The late nineteenth century, declared an economist in 1899, was "not only the age of cities, but *the* age of great cities." Between 1860 and 1910, the urban population grew from 6 million to 44 million. By 1920, more than half of the population lived in urban areas.

The rise of big cities during the nineteenth century created a distinctive urban culture. People from different ethnic and religious backgrounds and representing every walk of life poured into the high-rise apartment buildings and ramshackle tenements springing up in every major city. They came in search of jobs, wealth, and new opportunities. Rising wages and the availability of new consumer goods in the dazzling new downtown department stores improved the material standard of living for millions—while widening the gap between the poor and the affluent. Broadened access to public education and to public health services improved literacy and lowered infant mortality rates. Breakthroughs in medical science eventually brought cures for tuberculosis, typhoid, and diphtheria—although these infectious diseases remained the century's leading killers.

The rise of metropolitan America also created an array of new social problems. Corporations became so powerful that some of their owners decided that they were above the law. When someone warned Cornelius Vanderbilt, the railroad tycoon, that he might be violating the law, he is alleged to have replied, "Law? What do I care about the law. Hain't I got the power?" Rapid urban development also produced widespread poverty and political corruption. How to feed, clothe, shelter, and educate the new arrivals taxed the imagination—and patience—of urban leaders. Further complicating efforts to improve the quality of life in the nation's cities was the pattern of increasing residential segregation according to racial and ethnic background and social class.

AMERICA'S MOVE TO TOWN

The prospect of good jobs and social excitement in the cities lured workers by the millions from the countryside and overseas. City people and folks who worked in factories rather than on farms became distinctively urban in demeanor and outlook. The contrasts between farm and city life grew more vivid with each passing year.

EXPLOSIVE URBAN GROWTH   The frontier was a societal safety valve, historian Frederick Jackson Turner said in his influential thesis on American development. Its cheap lands afforded a release for the population pressures mounting in the cities. If there was such a thing as a safety valve in his own time, however, he had it exactly backward. The flow of population toward the city was greater than toward the West.

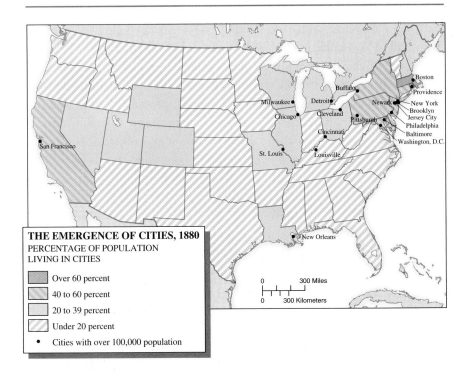

THE EMERGENCE OF CITIES, 1880
PERCENTAGE OF POPULATION
LIVING IN CITIES

Over 60 percent
40 to 60 percent
20 to 39 percent
Under 20 percent
• Cities with over 100,000 population

Much of the westward movement in fact was itself an urban movement, spawning new towns near the mining digs or at the railheads.
On the Pacific coast a greater portion of the population was urbanized
than anywhere else; its major concentrations were around San Francisco Bay at first, and then in Los Angeles, which became a boom town
after the arrival of the Southern Pacific and Santa Fe Railroads in the
1880s. Seattle grew quickly, first as the terminus of three transcontinental railroad lines, and by the end of the century as the staging area
for the Yukon gold rush. Minneapolis, St. Paul, Omaha, Kansas City,
and Denver were no longer the mere villages they had been in 1860.
The South, too, produced new cities: Durham, North Carolina, and
Birmingham, Alabama, which were centers of tobacco and iron manufactures, and Houston, Texas, which handled cotton and cattle, and
later oil.

While the Far West had the greatest proportion of urban population,
the Northeast had far greater numbers of people in its teeming cities.
These city dwellers were increasingly landless, and homeless—an urban
proletariat with nothing but their labor to sell. By 1900 more than 90

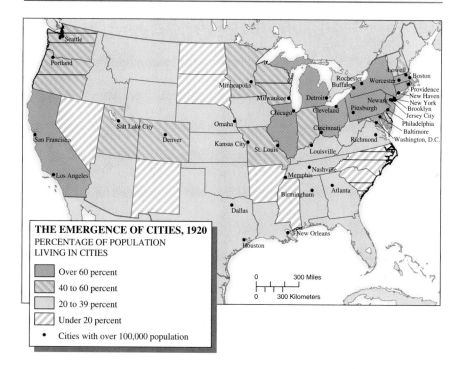

THE EMERGENCE OF CITIES, 1920
PERCENTAGE OF POPULATION
LIVING IN CITIES

Over 60 percent
40 to 60 percent
20 to 39 percent
Under 20 percent
• Cities with over 100,000 population

percent of the residents in New York's Manhattan lived in rented homes or tenements (congested apartment buildings).

Several technological innovations combined to enable cities to expand vertically to accommodate their huge populations. In the 1870s heating innovations, such as steam circulating through radiators, enabled the construction of large apartment buildings, since landlords no longer had to provide fireplaces to heat every room. In 1889 the Otis Elevator Company installed the first electric elevator, which made possible the erection of taller buildings. Before the 1860s, few structures had gone higher than three or four stories. And during the 1880s, engineers developed cast-iron and steel-frame construction techniques. Because such materials were stronger than brick, developers could erect high-rise buildings.

Cities also expanded horizontally after the introduction of important transportation innovations. Before the 1890s, the chief power sources of urban transport were either animals or steam. Horse- and mule-drawn streetcars had appeared in antebellum cities, but they were slow and cumbersome, and cleaning up after the animals added to the cost.

In 1873 San Francisco became the first city to use cable cars that clamped onto a moving underground cable driven by a central power source. Some cities used steam-powered trains on elevated tracks, but by the 1890s electric trolleys were preferred. Mass transit received an added boost when subways were built in Boston, New York City, and Philadelphia.

The spread of mass transit allowed large numbers of people to become commuters, and a growing middle class (working folk often could not afford even the nickel fare) retreated to quieter tree-lined "streetcar suburbs" whence they could travel into the central city for business or entertainment. The pattern of urban growth often became a sprawl, since it took place usually without plan, in the interest of a fast buck, and without thought to the need for parks and public services.

The use of horse-drawn railways, cable cars, and electric trolleys helped transform the social characters of cities. Until the implementation of such new transportation systems, people of all classes lived and worked together in the central city. After the Civil War, however, the emergence of suburbs began to segregate people according to their

A horse-drawn streetcar moving along rails, New York City.

economic standing. The more affluent moved outside the city, leaving behind the working folk, many of whom were immigrants or African Americans. The poorer districts in the city became more congested and crime-ridden as the population grew, fueled by waves of newcomers from abroad.

ALLURE AND PROBLEMS OF THE CITY The wonder of the cities—their glittering new electric lights, their streetcars, telephones, vaudeville shows and other amusements, newspapers and magazines, and a thousand other attractions—cast a magnetic lure on the youth of the farms. The new cities threw into stark contrast the frustration of unending toil and the isolation and loneliness of country life. In times of rural depression, thousands left for the cities in search of opportunity and personal freedom. The exodus from the countryside was especially evident in the East, where the census documented the shift in population from country to city, and stories began to appear of entire regions where buildings were abandoned and going to ruin, and where the wilderness was reclaiming farms that had been wrested from it during the previous 250 years.

Yet those who moved to the city often traded one set of problems for another. Workers in the big cities often had no choice other than to live in crowded apartments, most of which were poorly designed. In 1900 Manhattan's 42,700 tenements housed almost 1.6 million people, an average of 37 residents per building. Before the day of high-rise apartments, this represented an extremely high density, and such unregulated urban growth created immense problems of health and morale.

As the number of new arrivals mushroomed during the last quarter of the nineteenth century, cities became so cramped and land so scarce that designers were forced to build upward. In New York City this resulted in the "dumbbell" tenement house. These structures, usually six to eight stories tall and jammed tightly against one another, derived their name from the fact that housing codes required a two-foot wide air shaft between buildings, giving the structure the appearance of a dumbbell when viewed from overhead. Twenty-four to thirty-two families would cram into each building. Some city blocks housed almost 4,000 people. The tiny air shaft provided little ventilation; instead, it proved to be a fire hazard, fueling and conveying flames from building to building.

The early tenements were poorly heated and had toilets outside in the yard or alley for communal use. By the end of the century, they would feature two toilets on each floor. Shoehorned into such quarters, families had no privacy, free space, or sunshine; children had few places to play except in the city streets; infectious diseases and noxious odors were rampant. Not surprisingly, the mortality rate for the urban poor was much higher than that of the general population. In one poor Chicago district at the end of the century, three out of five babies died before their first birthday.

CITY POLITICS   The sheer size of the cities helped create a new form of politics. Since individuals could hardly provide for themselves necessary services such as transit, paving, water, sewers, street lighting and cleaning, and fire and police protection, they came increasingly to rely on city government support. Because local government was often fragmented and beset by parochial rivalries, a need grew for a central organization to coordinate city-wide issues such as public transportation, sanitation, and utilities. Urban political machines developed, consisting of local committeemen, district captains and leaders, and culminating in a political boss. While these political bosses engaged in patronage favors and graft, buying and selling votes, taking kickbacks and payoff money, they also provided needed services. They distributed food, coal, and money to the poor; found jobs for those who were out of work; sponsored English-language classes for immigrants; organized sports teams, social clubs, and neighborhood gatherings; fixed problems at city hall; and generally helped newcomers adjust to their new life. As one ward boss in Boston said: "There's got to be in every ward somebody that any bloke can come to—no matter what he's done—and get help. Help, you understand, none of your law and justice, but help." In return, the political professionals felt entitled to some reward for having done the grubby work of the local organization.

THE NEW IMMIGRATION

The industrial revolution brought to American shores waves of new immigrants from every part of the globe. By the end of the century, nearly 30 percent of the residents of major cities were foreign-born.

These newcomers provided much-needed labor, but their arrival created ugly racial and ethnic tensions.

AMERICA'S PULL   In steadily rising numbers European immigrants moved from the great agricultural areas of eastern and southern Europe directly to the foremost cities of America. They wanted to live with others of like language, customs, and religion. Many of them settled in cities because they lacked the means to go west and take up farms. Though cities of the South and West (excepting the Far West) drew their populations mainly from the native-born of their regions, American cities as a whole drew more residents from abroad. During the peak decade of immigration, 1900–1910, 41 percent of the urban newcomers arrived from abroad.

Ethnic neighborhoods in American cities preserved familiar folkways and shielded newcomers from the shocks of a strange culture. In 1890 four out of five New Yorkers were foreign-born, a higher proportion than any other city in the world. New York had twice as many Irish as Dublin, as many Germans as Hamburg, and half as many Italians as

Steerage Deck of the S.S. *Pennland,* 1893. *These immigrants are about to arrive at New York's Ellis Island.*

Naples. In 1893 Chicago claimed the largest Bohemian (Czech) community in the world, and by 1910 the size of its Polish population ranked behind only Warsaw and Lodz.

This nation of immigrants continued to draw new inhabitants for much the same reasons as always, and from much the same strata of society. Immigrants took flight from famine or the grinding lack of opportunity in their native lands. They fled racial, religious, and political persecution and compulsory military service. Yet more immigrants probably were pulled by America's promise than were pushed out by conditions at home. American industries, seeking cheap labor, sent recruiting agents abroad. Railroads, eager to sell land and build up the traffic on their lines, put out tempting propaganda in a medley of languages. Many of the western and southern states set up official bureaus and agents to attract immigrants. Under the Contract Labor Law of 1864, the federal government itself encouraged immigration by helping to pay the immigrant's passage through a lien on his or her wages. The law was repealed in 1868, but not until 1885 did the government forbid companies to import contract labor, which put immigrant workers under the control of their employers.

After the Civil War the tide of immigration rose from just under 3 million in the 1870s to more than 5 million in the 1880s, then fell to a little over 3.5 million in the depression decade of the 1890s, and rose to its highwater mark of nearly 9 million in the first decade of the new century. The numbers declined to 6 million in the 1910s and 4 million in the 1920s, after which official restrictions cut the flow of immigration down to a negligible level.

A NEW WAVE   During the 1880s, corporate America's continuing search for cheap labor combined with renewed persecutions in eastern Europe to bring a noticeable change in the source of immigration to the United States. Before 1880 immigrants were mainly of Teutonic and Celtic origin, hailing from northern and western Europe. By the 1870s, however, that began to change. The proportion of Slavic and Jewish peoples from southern and eastern Europe rose sharply. After 1890 these groups made up a majority of the newcomers, and by the first decade of the new century they formed 70 percent of the immigrants to this country. Among these new immigrants were Italians, Hungarians, Czechs, Slovaks, Poles, Serbs, Croats, Slovenes, Russians,

Romanians, and Greeks—all people of markedly different cultures and languages from those of western Europe, and most followers of different religions, including Judaism and Catholicism.

ELLIS ISLAND   As the number of immigrants passing through the Port of New York soared during the late nineteenth century, the state-run Castle Garden receiving center overflowed with corruption. Moneychangers cheated new arrivals, railroad agents overcharged them for tickets, and baggage handlers engaged in blackmail. With reports of these abuses filling the newspapers, Congress ordered an investigation of Castle Garden, which resulted in the closure of the facility in 1890. Thereafter the federal government's new Bureau of Immigration took over the business of admitting newcomers to New York City.

To launch this effort, Congress funded the construction of a new reception center on a tiny island off the New Jersey coast, a mile south of Manhattan near the Statue of Liberty. In 1892 Ellis Island opened its doors to the "huddled masses" of the world. In 1907, the reception center's busiest year, more than a million new arrivals filtered through the receiving center, an average of about 5,000 per day; in one day alone immigration officials processed some 11,750 arrivals. These were the

Immigrants waiting in the Registry Room for further inspections.

immigrants who arrived crammed into the steerage compartments deep in the ships' hulls. Those refugees who could afford first- and second-class cabins did not have to visit Ellis Island; they were examined on board ship, and most of them simply walked down the gangway onto the docks in lower Manhattan.

Ellis Island was not a comforting place. Its bureaucratic purpose was to process immigrants, not welcome them. An army of inspectors, doctors, and nurses questioned and examined the newcomers. Inspectors asked twenty-nine probing questions, including: Have you money, relatives, or a job in the United States? Are you a polygamist? An anarchist? Doctors and nurses poked and prodded, searching for any sign of debilitating handicap or infectious disease. All the while, the immigrant worried: "Will they let me in?" Although some who were sick or lame were detained for days or weeks, the vast majority of immigrants received stamps of approval and were on their way after three or four hours. Only 2 percent of the newcomers were denied entry altogether, usually because they were criminals, anarchists, or carriers of some "loathsome or dangerous contagious disease," such as tuberculosis or trachoma, a contagious eye disease resulting in blindness. These luckless folk were then returned to their places of origin, with the steamship companies picking up the tab.

Among the arrivals at Ellis Island were many youngsters who would distinguish themselves in their new country: songwriter Irving Berlin (Russia), football legend Knute Rockne (Norway), Supreme Court justice Felix Frankfurter (Austria), singer Al Jolson (Lithuania), and comedian Bob Hope (England). But many others found America's opportunities harder to grasp. An old Italian saying expresses the disillusionment that was felt by many: "I came to America because I heard the streets were paved with gold. When I got here, I found out three things: First, the streets weren't paved with gold; second, they weren't paved at all; and third, I was expected to pave them."

MAKING THEIR WAY Once on American soil in Manhattan or New Jersey, the immigrants felt exhilaration, exhaustion, and usually a desperate need for work. Many were greeted by family and friends who had come over before, others by representatives of the many immigrant aid societies or by hiring agents offering jobs in mines, mills, and sweatshops. Since most knew little if any English and nothing about American employment practices, the immigrants were easy subjects for exploitation. In exchange for providing arrivals with a bit of whiskey and a job, obliging hiring agents claimed a healthy percentage of their wages. Among Italians and Greeks these agents were known as *padrones,* and they came to dominate the labor market in New York. Other contractors provided train tickets for immigrants to travel inland to jobs in cities such as Buffalo, Pittsburgh, Cleveland, Chicago, Milwaukee, Cincinnati, and St. Louis.

Eager to retain a sense of community and to use skills they brought with them, the members of ethnic groups tended to cluster in particular vocations. Poles, Hungarians, Slovaks, Bohemians, and Italians used to the pick and shovel flocked to coal mines, just as the Irish, Cornish, and Welsh had done at mid-century; Slavs and Poles comfortable with muscle work gravitated to the steel mills; Greeks preferred working in textile mills; Russian and Polish Jews peopled the sewing trades and pushcart markets of New York. A few determined peasants uprooted from their agricultural heritage made their way west and were able to find work on farms or even a parcel of land for themselves.

Most of the immigrants, however, settled in the teeming cities. Strangers in a new land, they naturally gravitated to neighborhoods populated by their own kind. These immigrant enclaves—nicknamed Little Italy, Little Hungary, Chinatown, and so on—served as crucial transitional communities between the newcomers' Old World past and their New World future. By 1920 Chicago had some seventeen separate Little Italy colonies scattered across the city representing various home provinces. In such kinship communities the immigrants could practice their religions and native customs, converse in their

Mulberry Street, Little Italy. New York City, 1906. Immigrants established their own enclaves where old-world traditions could be carried on within their new American homes.

native tongue, and fill an aching loneliness. But they paid a price for such community solidarity. When the "new immigrants" moved into an area, older residents typically moved out, taking with them whatever social prestige and political influence they had achieved. The quality of living conditions quickly deteriorated as housing and sanitation codes went unenforced.

THE NATIVIST RESPONSE   Many native-born Americans saw the new immigration as a threat to their way of life and their jobs. "Immigrants work for almost nothing," groused one American laborer. Others felt that the new immigrants threatened traditional American culture and values. A Stanford University professor called them "illiterate, docile, lacking in self-reliance and initiative, and not possessing the Anglo-Teutonic conceptions of law, order, and government." Cultural differences confirmed in the minds of nativists the assumption that the Nordic peoples of the old immigration were superior to the Slavic and Latin peoples of the new immigration. Many of the new immigrants were illiterate, and more appeared so because they could not speak English. Some resorted to crime in order to survive in the new land, encouraging suspicions that criminals were being quietly helped out of Europe just as they had once been transported from England to the colonies.

Religious prejudice, mainly anti-Catholic and anti-Semitic sentiments, also underlay hostility toward the latest newcomers. During the 1880s nativist prejudices spawned groups devoted to stopping the immigrant flow. The most successful of these nativist groups, the American Protective Association (APA), operated mainly in Protestant strongholds of the upper Mississippi River Valley. Its organizer harbored paranoid fantasies of Catholic conspiracies, and was especially anxious to keep the public schools free from Jesuit control. The association grew slowly from its start in 1887 until 1893, when leaders took advantage of a severe depression to draw large numbers of the frustrated to its ranks. The APA promoted restricted immigration, more stringent naturalization requirements, refusal to employ aliens or Catholics, and the teaching of the "American" language in the schools.

IMMIGRATION RESTRICTION   The movement to restrict immigration had mixed success beyond the exclusion of certain individuals deemed undesirable. In 1891 Representative Henry Cabot Lodge of

Massachusetts took up the cause of excluding illiterate foreigners—a measure that would have affected much of the new immigration even though the language did not have to be English. Bills embodying the restriction were vetoed by three presidents on the ground that they penalized people for lack of opportunity: Grover Cleveland in 1897, William W. Taft in 1913, and Woodrow Wilson in 1915 and 1917. The last time, however, Congress overrode the veto.

Proponents of immigration restriction during the late nineteenth century did succeed in excluding the Chinese, who were victims of everything the European immigrants suffered, plus color prejudice as well. By 1880 there were some 75,000 Chinese in California, about one-ninth of the state's population. Their nemesis was himself an immigrant (from Ireland), Dennis Kearney, leader of the Workingmen's party. Many white workers resented the Chinese for accepting lower wages, but their greatest sin, the editor of the *New York Nation* opined, was perpetuating "those disgusting habits of thrift, industry, and self-denial."

In 1882 President Chester Arthur signed the Chinese Exclusion Act. It shut the door to Chinese immigrants for ten years. The legislation

Anti-Chinese protest, California, 1880. Widespread prejudice and racism against the Chinese finally resulted in a ban on Chinese immigration with the 1882 passage of the Chinese Exclusion Act.

received overwhelming support. One congressman explained that because the "industrial army of Asiatic laborers" was increasing the tension between workers and management in the American economy, "the gate must be closed." The Chinese Exclusion Act was periodically renewed before being extended indefinitely in 1902. Not until 1943 were such barriers finally removed.

The West Coast counterpart to Ellis Island was the Immigration Station on rugged Angel Island, six miles offshore from San Francisco. Opened in 1910, it served as a processing center for tens of thousands of Asian immigrants, most of them Chinese. Although the Chinese Exclusion Act had sharply reduced the flow of Chinese immigrants, it did not stop the influx completely. Those arrivals who could claim a Chinese-American parent were allowed to enter, as were certain officials, teachers, merchants, and students. The powerful prejudice the Chinese immigrants encountered helps explain why over 30 percent of the arrivals at Angel Island were denied entry. Those who appealed such denials were housed in prison-like barracks for weeks or months. One of the detainees scratched a poignant poem on a wall:

> This place is called an island of immortals,
> When, in fact, this mountainous wilderness is a prison.
> Once you see the open net, why throw yourself in?
> It is only because of empty pockets. I can do nothing else.

POPULAR CULTURE

The influx of people into large towns and cities created new patterns of recreation and leisure. Whereas people in rural areas were tied into the rituals of the harvest season and intimately connected to their neighbors and extended families, most middle-class urban whites were mobile and lived in nuclear families (made up of only parents and children), and their affluence enabled them to enjoy greater leisure time and rising discretionary income.

Middle- and upper-class urban families spent much of their leisure time together at home, usually in the parlor, singing around the piano, reading novels, or playing cards, dominoes, backgammon, chess, and checkers. A new invention called the "stereopticon" was all the rage. It was a hand-held device that placed several photographs or paintings at facing angles to one another. When viewed through binocular glasses, it gave the appearance of three-dimensional views.

Where social and economic conditions remained the same as in earlier periods, popular culture also remained much the same. For example, most blacks continued to live in rural areas and operated within extended family networks that included cousins, aunts, uncles, and other relatives who provided assistance and emotional support. Popular culture in rural areas included many traditional forms of entertainment, centered on the family and the planting and harvesting of crops, or the arrival of an itinerant evangelist intent upon conducting a revival or camp meeting.

In the towns and cities, however, people were not as dependent upon traveling ministers or harvest rituals and festivities, and popular culture took on new or greatly expanded dimensions that endowed life with a more cosmopolitan quality. For example, traveling circuses brought entertainment to large cities and small towns. The midwestern writer Hamlin Garland recalled how the circus came to rural hamlets "trailing clouds of glorified dust and filling our minds with the color of romance. . . . It brought to our ears the latest band pieces and taught us the popular songs. It furnished us with jokes. It relieved our dullness. It gave us something to talk about."

In the congested metropolitan areas, politics became as much a form of public entertainment as it was a process of providing civic representation and public services. People flocked to hear visiting candidates give speeches in cavernous halls, outdoor plazas, or from railway cars. Membership in a political party in cities such as New York, Philadelphia, Boston, and Chicago was akin to belonging to a social club. In addition, labor unions also included activities that were more social than economic in nature, and members often visited the union hall as much to socialize as to discuss working conditions. The sheer numbers of people congregated in cities also helped generate a market for new forms of mass entertainment such as traveling Wild West shows, vaudeville shows, and spectator sports.

WILD WEST SHOWS   One of the touring extravaganzas that enjoyed incredible popularity during the last quarter of the nineteenth century was "Buffalo Bill's Wild West" traveling show. William "Buffalo Bill"

Cody was a rugged frontiersman and sharpshooter. Born in Iowa and raised in Kansas, he became a rider for the Pony Express in 1860 and later served as a Union scout during the Civil War. After the war, he operated a hotel and a freight business, then became a renowned buffalo hunter, providing meat for the crews building railroads. His ability earned him the nickname Buffalo Bill.

Cody's exploits attracted the attention of writer Ned Buntline, who wrote a series of popular novels that brought international celebrity to Buffalo Bill. Always alert to financial opportunity and ever eager to exaggerate his own accomplishments, Cody took advantage of his popularity to organize a stage show. By 1883 he had broadened its scope into a traveling spectacle that included live elk and buffalo, hundreds of horses, genuine cowboys, authentic Indians, rope tricks, shooting exhibitions, cowgirl Annie Oakley, and Cody himself as the star attraction.

Indians were prominently featured in the show. One advertisement promised "a horde of war-painted Arapahoes, Cheyenne, and Sioux Indians." Their role in the show was to stage attacks on wagon trains and stagecoaches, as well as to reenact the battle between Indians and soldiers in General George Custer's last stand at the Little

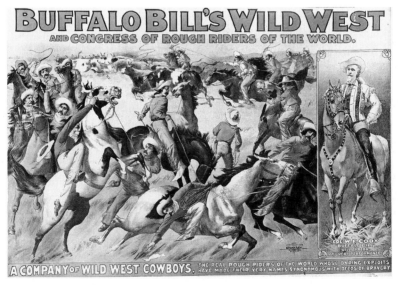

Buffalo Bill's Wild West Show. Although the shows included genuine cowboys and authentic Indians, they romanticized the Amerian West.

Bighorn. The Indians were always portrayed as the aggressors, and the whites as the victims. These images of murderous Indians attacking helpless whites set in motion the mythic depiction of the West that later became the staple of television and movie Westerns. When Buffalo Bill died in 1917, his shows died with him, but he bequeathed to Americans a new form of entertainment that has since taken deep root: the rodeo.

VAUDEVILLE Growing family incomes and innovations in urban transportation—cable cars, subways, electric streetcars and streetlights—enabled more people to take advantage of urban cultural life. Attendance at theaters, operas, and dance halls soared. Those interested in serious music could attend concerts by symphony orchestras appearing in every major city by the end of the nineteenth century.

But by far the most popular—and diverse—form of theatrical entertainment in the late nineteenth century was known as vaudeville. The term derives from a French word meaning a play accompanied by music. It emerged in the United States in saloons whose owners wanted to attract more customers by offering free shows.

Vaudeville "variety" shows featured comedians, singers, musicians, blackface minstrels, farcical plays, animal acts, jugglers, gymnasts, dancers, mimes, and magicians. Because variety shows were held in seedy beer halls and because the entertainers often included vulgar material, they quickly developed a bad reputation. To combat such an image so as to encourage families to attend, promoters of variety shows built elegant new theaters, banned alcoholic beverages, upgraded the performers, hired policemen and bouncers to handle "rowdies," and began to use the more elegant French word "vaudeville" to describe the genre.

Vaudeville houses sprouted in cities across the United States in the 1870s and 1880s. They quickly became popular gathering places for all social classes and types—men, women, and children—all of whom were expected to behave according to middle-class standards of gentility and decorum when attending performances. Raucous cheering, booing, and tobacco spitting were prohibited.

The diverse vaudeville shows included something to please every taste and, as such, reflected the heterogeneity of city life. To commemorate the opening of a palatial new Boston theater in 1894, an actress read a dedicatory poem in which she announced that "All are equals here." The vaudeville house was the people's theater; it knew "no favorites, no class." She promised the spectators that the producers would "ever seek the new" in providing entertainers who epitomized "the spice of life, Variety," with its motto, "ever to please—and never to offend."

OUTDOOR RECREATION   The congestion and diseases associated with city life led many people to participate in forms of outdoor recreation intended to restore their vitality and improve their health. A movement to create urban parks flourished after the construction of New York's Central Park in 1858. Its designer, Frederick Law Olmsted, viewed city parks as much more than recreational centers; he sought to create oases of culture that would promote social stability and cohesion. He was convinced that Central Park would exercise "a distinctly harmonizing and refining influence upon the most unfortunate and lawless classes of the city—an influence favorable to courtesy, self-control, and temperance." Olmsted went on to design parks for Boston, Brooklyn, Chicago, Philadelphia, and San Francisco.

Although originally intended as places where people could walk and commune with nature, the parks soon offered more vigorous forms of exercise and recreation—for men and women. During most of the nineteenth century, prevailing social attitudes scoffed at the notion of proper young women participating in even the lightest athletic endeavors. Women were deemed too delicate for such behavior. Before the Civil War, women essentially had only one exercise option: pedestrianism, the formal title for outdoor walking. After the war, however, the growing number of women enrolled in colleges began to participate in physical education, and they in turn demanded access to more vigorous sports.

Croquet and tennis courts were among the first additions to city parks because they took up little space and required little maintenance. Because croquet could be played by both sexes, it combined the virtues of sport with the opportunities of courtship. Croquet as a public sport suffered a setback in the 1890s, however, when Boston clergymen lambasted the drinking, gambling, and licentious behavior associated with it.

Lawn tennis was invented by an Englishman in 1873 and arrived in the United States a year later. By 1885 Central Park had thirty courts.

Tandem tricycle. In spite of the danger and discomfort of early bicycles, "wheeling" became a popular form of recreation and mode of transportation.

Lawn tennis was originally viewed as a leisurely sport best suited for women. The Harvard student newspaper declared in 1878 that the sport was "well enough for a lazy or *weak* man, but men who have rowed or taken part in a nobler sport should blush to be seen playing Lawn Tennis."

Even more popular than croquet or tennis was cycling or "wheeling." In the 1870s, bicycles began to be manufactured in the United States, and by the end of the century, a "bicycle craze" had swept the country. The first bicycles were called "high-wheelers" or "boneshakers" because the front wheel was huge, as much as five feet high, while the rear wheel was tiny, no more than a foot in diameter. The high-wheelers were hard to ride, uncomfortable, and dangerous, as they had no brakes. During the 1880s, an Englishman named J. K. Starley produced the first "safety bicycle." These bicycles had wheels of equal size and axles with ball bearings, which made them easier and safer to ride than high-wheelers. By 1890, bicycles had air-filled rubber tires and brakes. Millions of middle-class Americans (who could afford the new invention) discovered a new mobility and freedom through the bicycle, which had few of the drawbacks of horses. Bicycles went where pointed, did not need to be fed, and did not leave droppings in the road.

Bicycles were especially popular with women who chafed at the restricting conventions of Victorianism. The new vehicles offered exercise, freedom, and access to the countryside. Female cyclists were able to discard their cumbersome corsets and full dresses in favor of bloomers and split skirts. Critics feared that the bicycle mania was encouraging young women to grow independent and shun conventional domestic responsibilities. Some guardians of morality believed that cycling was also sexually provocative. In 1899 the Reverend W. W. Reynolds expressed outrage because a "large number of female bicyclists wear shorter dresses than the laws of morality and decency permit, thereby inviting the improper conversations and remarks of the depraved and immoral."

The working poor in the cities could not afford to acquire a bicycle or join a croquet club. Nor did they have as much free time as the affluent. They toiled long hours, six days a week, and at the end of their long days and on Sundays they eagerly sought recreation and fellowship on street

Steeplechase Park, Coney Island, New York. This amusement park attracted working-class patrons who could afford the inexpensive rides.

corners or on the front stoops of their apartment buildings. Organ grinders and musicians would perform on the sidewalks among the food vendors. Many ethnic groups, especially the Germans and the Irish, formed male singing, drinking, or gymnastic clubs. Working folk also attended bare-knuckle boxing matches or baseball games, and on Sundays would gather for picnics. By the end of the century, large-scale amusement parks such as New York's Coney Island provided entertainment for the entire family. Yet many inner-city youth could not afford the trolley fare to visit a suburban amusement park, so the crowded streets and dangerous alleys became their playgrounds.

SALOON CULTURE The most popular places for working-class Americans to spend their free time were saloons and dance halls. The saloon was the poor man's social club during the late nineteenth century. The term, derived from the French word *salon*, meaning a large, decorated social room, seemed more stylish than "tavern," which faded from use after 1870. By the end of the nineteenth century, there were more saloons in the United States than there were grocery stores and meat markets. New York City alone had 10,000 saloons in 1900, or one for every 500 residents. Chicago had one saloon for every 335 people; Houston, one for every 300; and San Francisco, one for every 215. Often sponsored by beer brewers and frequented by local politicians, saloons offered free lunch to encourage patrons to visit and buy five-cent beer or fifteen-cent whiskey.

Saloons, however, provided much more than food and drink; they were in effect public homes, offering haven and fellowship to people who often worked ten hours a day, six days a week. Saloons were especially popular among male immigrants seeking friends and companionship in a new land. The saloons served as busy hubs of social life and were often aligned with local political machines. In New York City in the 1880s, most of the primary elections and local political caucuses were conducted in saloons.

Men went to saloons to learn about possible jobs, engage in labor union activities, cash paychecks, mail letters, read newspapers, and gossip about neighborhood affairs. Because saloons were heated and open long hours, and offered public restrooms, they also served as places of refuge for poor people whose own slum tenements or cramped lodging houses were not as accommodating. Many saloons included

Men gather at a neighborhood saloon in New York City, 1895.

gymnasiums. Patrons could play handball, chess, billiards, darts, cards, or dice. They could also bet on sporting events. Group singing was an especially popular activity among saloongoers.

Saloons were defiantly male enclaves. Although women or children occasionally entered saloons through a special side door in order to carry home a pail of beer (called "rushing the growler") or to drink at a back-room party, the main bar at the front of the saloon was all male. Some saloons provided "snugs"—small separate rooms for female patrons.

Saloons aroused intense criticism. Anti-liquor societies such as the Women's Christian Temperance Union and Anti-Saloon League charged that saloons contributed to alcoholism, divorce, crime, and absenteeism from work. The reformers demanded that saloons be closed down. Yet drunkenness in saloons was the exception rather than the rule. To be sure, most patrons of working-class saloons had little money to waste, but recent studies have revealed that the average amount of money spent on liquor was no more than 5 percent of a man's annual income. Saloons were the primary locus of the workingman's leisure time and political activity. As a journalist observed, "The saloon is, in short, the social and intellectual center of the neighborhood."

WORKING WOMEN AND LEISURE   In contrast to the male public culture centered in saloons, the leisure activities of working-class women, many of them immigrants, were more limited at the end of the nineteenth century. Married women were so encumbered by housework and maternal responsibilities that they had little free time. As a social worker noted, "The men have the saloons, political clubs, trade-unions or [fraternal] lodges for their recreation . . . while the mothers have almost no recreation, only a dreary round of work, day after day, with occasionally doorstep gossip to vary the monotony of their lives." Married working-class women could not afford domestic help or sitters for their children, so they usually had to combine entertainment with their work. They often used the streets as their public space. Washing clothes, supervising children, or shopping at the local market provided opportunities for fellowship with other women.

Among the women who worked outside the home the most common activity was domestic service. Adolescent Irish and German immigrant girls, especially, tended to work as maids, cooks, or nurses in upperclass households. In the large cities, girls and women also were concentrated in the needle trades, working as dressmakers, tailors, and milliners (hatmakers). Rolling tobacco into cigars was also a common source of wage labor for city women. By the early twentieth century, the maturation of the American economy created new job opportunities for women. The "white-collar" sector of the economy grew dramatically. Banks, insurance companies, and retail stores needed clerks, typists, receptionists, secretaries, and telephone operators. By 1900 the "saleslady" had become a fixture of department stores. Work in retail became second only to domestic service as the most common occupation for single women.

Single women had more opportunities for leisure and recreation than did working mothers. As the average workday gradually declined from twelve hours in the 1880s to nine or ten hours in 1914, people had more free time. In the cities, young factory hands, domestic servants, office workers, and retail clerks eagerly sought access to the world of urban pleasure. City amusements enticed women away from their congested and drab tenements. They flocked to dance halls, theaters, amusement parks, and picnic grounds. On hot summer days many working-class folk went to public beaches. For young workingwomen in and around New York City, for example, an excursion to Coney Island was a special treat. Not only could they swim but they could also experience the beach's sideshow attractions, vaudeville shows, dance pavilions, restaurants, and boardwalk. By 1900 as many as a half million people converged on Coney Island on Saturdays and Sundays. With the advent of movie theaters during the second decade of the twentieth century, the cinema became the most popular form of entertainment for women.

Young single women participated in such urban amusements for a variety of reasons: escape, pleasure, adventure, comradeship, and autonomy. As a promotional flyer for a movie theater promised, "If you are tired of life, go to the movies. If you are sick of troubles rife, go to the picture show. You will forget your unpaid bills, rheumatism and other ills, if you stow your pills and go to the picture show." Urban recreational and entertainment activities also allowed opportunities for romance and sexual relationships. Not surprisingly, young women eager for such recreation encountered far more obstacles than did men. Just as reformers sought to shut down saloons, parental and societal concerns tried to restrict the freedom of young single women to engage in such "cheap amusements." Daughters of immigrants confronted "Old World" notions of leisure and pleasure that conflicted with modern American culture. Yet many young women followed their own wishes, and in so doing, they helped carve out their own social sphere.

SPECTATOR SPORTS   In the last quarter of the nineteenth century, horse racing and prizefighting remained popular, but team sports also began to attract legions of fans. New spectator sports such as college football and basketball and professional baseball gained mass popularity, reflecting the growing urbanization of American life. People could gather easily for sporting events in the large cities. And news of the games could be conveyed quickly by newspapers and specialized sporting magazines relying upon telegraph reports. Saloons also posted the scores. Athletic rivalries between distant cities were made possible by the network of railroads spanning the continent and facilitating team travel. Spectator sports became urban extravaganzas, unifying the diverse ethnic groups in the large cities and attracting people with the leisure time and cash to spend (or bet) on watching others perform.

Football emerged as a modified form of soccer and rugby. The College of New Jersey (Princeton) and Rutgers played the first college football game in 1869. By the end of the century, scores of colleges and high schools had started football teams, and some college games attracted more than 50,000 spectators.

Basketball was invented in 1891 when Dr. James Naismith, a physical education instructor, nailed two peach baskets to the walls of the YMCA training school in Springfield, Massachusetts. Naismith wanted to create an indoor winter game that could be played between the fall football and spring baseball seasons. The baskets were ten feet high because that was the height of the balcony at each end of the gym to which the baskets were attached. The first game had nine men on a side, and they used a soccer ball. Basketball quickly grew in popularity among both boys and girls. Vassar and Smith Colleges added the sport in 1892. In 1893, Vanderbilt became the first college to field a men's team.

Baseball laid claim to being America's national pastime at mid-century. Contrary to popular opinion, Abner Doubleday did not invent the game. Instead, Alexander Cartwright, a New York bank clerk and sportsman, is recognized as the father of organized baseball. In 1845 he gathered a group of merchants, stockbrokers, and physicians to form the Knickerbocker Base Ball Club of New York. They began playing a bat-and-ball game on a field at the corner of Twenty-seventh Street and Fourth Avenue in Manhattan. Soon they moved to a field in Hoboken, New Jersey. After their games they would gather at a nearby hotel bar. There they drafted a list of rules that included setting the bases ninety feet apart and allocating nine players to a side.

The first professional baseball team was the Cincinnati Red Stockings, which made its appearance in 1869. Seven years later, seven other teams joined the Red Stockings in creating the National League. Reporters began to cover the games, and sports sections appeared in every newspaper. In 1901 the American League was organized, and two years later the first World Series was held.

Baseball became the "national pastime" and the most democratic sport in America. People from all social classes (mostly men) attended the games, and ethnic immigrants were among the most faithful fans. The *St. Louis Post-Dispatch* reported in 1883 that "a glance at the audience on any fine day at the ball park will reveal . . . telegraph operators,

Professional baseball game, 1887. The excitement of rooting for the home team united all classes as they watched the athletes who graced the playing field.

printers who work at night, travelling men [salesmen] . . . men of leisure . . . men of capital, bank clerks who get away [from work] at 3 P.M., real estate men . . . barkeepers . . . hotel clerks, actors and employees of the theater, policemen and firemen on their day off . . . butchers and bakers." Cheering for a city baseball team gave rootless people a common loyalty and a sense of belonging.

Only white players were allowed in the major leagues. African Americans played on "minor league" teams or in all-black "Negro leagues." In 1867 the National Association of Base Ball Players excluded black clubs from membership. The National League followed suit when it was organized nine years later. In 1887 black players were banned from minor league teams as well. That same year, the Cuban Giants, an exhibition team made up of black players, traveled the country. A few major league white teams agreed to play them. An African-American-owned newspaper announced in early 1888 that the Cuban Giants "have defeated the New Yorks, 4 games out of 5, and are now virtually champions of the world." But it added, "the St. Louis Browns, Detroits and Chicagos, afflicted by Negrophobia and unable to bear the odium of being beaten by colored men, refused to accept their challenge."

By the end of the nineteenth century, sports of all kinds had become a major cultural phenomenon in the United States. A writer in *Harper's Weekly* announced in 1895 that "ball matches, football games, tennis tournaments, bicycle races, [and] regattas, have become part of our national life." They "are watched with eagerness and discussed with enthusiasm and understanding by all manner of people, from the day-laborer to the millionaire." One reporter in the 1890s referred to the "athletic craze" that was sweeping the American imagination. Moreover, it was in 1892 that a Frenchman, Pierre de Coubertin, called for the revival of the ancient Olympic games, and the first modern olympiad was held four years later.

EDUCATION AND THE PROFESSIONS

THE SPREAD OF PUBLIC EDUCATION   The spread of public education, spurred partly by the determination to "Americanize" immigrant children, helped quicken the emergence of a new urban America. The growing importance of public education is evident in statistics compiled by the national commissioner of education, whose office was created in 1867. In 1870 there were 7 million pupils in public schools; by 1920 the number had risen to 22 million. The percentage of school-age children in attendance went from 57 to 78 during these years. City schools quickly became schools of several rooms and separate grades with a teacher for each. In rural areas one-room schools lingered on into the twentieth century, when good roads made it possible to bus children to "consolidated schools." Despite these signs of progress, educational leaders all too often had to struggle against a pattern of political appointments, corruption, and incompetence in the public schools.

The spread of secondary schools accounted for much of the increased enrollment in public schools. In antebellum America private academies prepared those who intended to enter college. At the beginning of the Civil War there were only about 100 public high schools in the whole country, but their number grew rapidly to about 800 in 1880 and 6,000 at the turn of the century. Their curricula at first copied the academies' emphasis on higher mathematics and classical languages, but the public schools gradually accommodated their programs to those not going on to college, devising vocational training in such arts as bookkeeping, typing, drafting, and the use of tools.

VOCATIONAL TRAINING Vocational training was most intensely promoted after the Civil War by missionary schools for African Americans such as Hampton Institute in Virginia, which trained Booker T. Washington, founder of Tuskegee Institute in Alabama. Congress had supported vocational training at the college level for many years. The Morrill Act of 1862 granted each state 30,000 acres per representative and senator, the income from which was to be applied to teaching agriculture and the mechanic arts in what came to be known as the "land-grant colleges." Among these new institutions were Clemson University, Pennsylvania State University, and Iowa State University. In 1890 a Second Morrill Act provided federal grants to these colleges.

HIGHER EDUCATION American colleges at this time, whether church schools or state "universities," sought to instill discipline, morality, and a curriculum stressing mathematics and the classics (and in church schools, theology), along with ethics and rhetoric. History,

Students in a current-events class at the Hampton Institute, 1899.

modern languages and literature, and some science were tolerated, although laboratory work was usually limited to a professor's demonstration to the class.

Nevertheless, the demand for higher learning led to an increase in the college student population from 52,000 in 1870 to 157,000 in 1890 and to 600,000 in 1920. During the same years the number of institutions rose from 563 to 998 and then to 1,041, and the number of faculty from 5,553 to 15,809 to 48,615. To accommodate the diverse needs of these growing numbers, colleges moved away from rigidly prescribed courses toward an elective system. In 1866 Washington College in Virginia, under its president, Robert E. Lee, adopted electives, and after 1869 Harvard College did so under its young president Charles W. Eliot. The new approach allowed students to favor their strong points and colleges to expand their scope. But as Senator Henry Cabot Lodge complained, it also allowed students to "escape without learning anything at all by a judicious selection of unrelated subjects taken up only because they were easy or because the burden imposed by those who taught them was light."

Women's access to higher education improved markedly in the late nineteenth century. Before the Civil War, a few male colleges had admitted women, and most state universities in the West were open to women from the start. But colleges in the South and East fell in line very slowly. Vassar, opened in 1865, was the first women's college to teach by the same standards as the best of the men's colleges, though it had to maintain a Preparatory Department for twenty-three years to upgrade poorly prepared entrants. In the 1870s, two more excellent women's schools appeared in Massachusetts: Wellesley and Smith, the latter being the first to set the same admission requirements as men's colleges. The older women's colleges quickly moved to upgrade their standards in the same way. By the end of the century, women made up more than a third of all college students.

The dominant new trend in American higher education after the Civil War was the rise of the graduate school. The versatile professors of the antebellum era had a knowledge more broad than deep. They engaged in little research, nor were they expected to advance the frontiers of knowledge. But gradually more and more Americans experienced a different system at the German universities, where training was more systematic and focused. After the Civil War, the German system be-

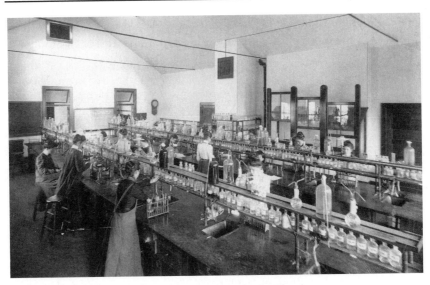

Students in the chemistry lab at Mount Holyoke College, 1900.

came the basis for the modern American university. Yale awarded its first Ph.D. in 1861 and Harvard its first in 1872.

The Johns Hopkins University, opened in Baltimore in 1876, set a new precedent by making graduate work its chief concern. The graduate students gathered in seminar rooms or laboratories, where under the guidance of an experienced scholar they learned a craft, much as journeymen had in the medieval guilds. The crowning achievement, signifying admission to full membership in the craft, was a masterpiece—in this case the Ph.D. dissertation, which was expected to make an original contribution to knowledge.

In the early 1890s two more major universities were founded to spread the gospel of Germanic education. The first, established by railroad magnate Leland Stanford (and named after his son), opened at Palo Alto, California, in 1891, and the following year the University of Chicago, endowed by oil baron John D. Rockefeller, began operation. Other established institutions, including Columbia, Cornell, Michigan, and Wisconsin, also set up graduate schools. By 1900 American universities annually conferred hundreds of doctorates. The Ph.D. was fast becoming the ticket of admission to the guild of professors.

THE RISE OF PROFESSIONALISM   The Ph.D. revolution was but one aspect of a growing emphasis on professionalism, with its imposition of standards, licensing of practitioners, and accreditation of professional schools. The number of professional schools grew rapidly in fields such as theology, law, medicine, dentistry, pharmacy, and veterinary medicine. While these fields accounted for 60 postgraduate schools in 1850, there were 146 in 1875 and 283 in 1900. Growth in numbers brought pressures for higher standards. At Harvard in 1870 one could qualify for a medical degree by attending two lecture courses for four months, proving three years of medical experience, and passing a simple examination. Harvard president Charles Eliot then insisted on requiring three years of class attendance, together with laboratory and clinical work. In 1870 the Harvard Law School developed a rough equivalent to the laboratory by introducing the "case method," which required students to dig out the rules for themselves.

The requirement for advanced schooling in the professions accompanied a movement for licensing practitioners in certain fields. The first state licensing law for dentistry, for instance, came in 1868, for pharmacy in 1874, for veterinary medicine in 1886, for accounting in 1896, and for architecture in 1897. By 1894 twenty-one states held standard examinations for doctors, and fourteen others recognized only graduates from accredited medical schools. Licensing benefited the public by certifying competence in a given field, but it also benefited members of the profession by controlling the number of practitioners and thereby limiting competition.

Learned and professional associations began to proliferate after the Civil War in response to the growing specialization of the professions. Earlier societies, such as the American Association for the Advancement of Science (1848), which had seemed specialized enough, made way for still more specialized groups such as the American Chemical Society (1876) and the National Statistical Association (1888). By 1888 the profession of medicine alone had over a dozen specialty associations, from opthamology to dentistry to pediatrics. Modern-language scholars organized in 1883, American historians in 1884, economists in 1885, political scientists in 1889, folklorists in 1888, and all sponsored meetings and journals to keep members in touch with developments in the field.

THEORIES OF SOCIAL CHANGE

Every field of thought in the post–Civil War years felt the impact of Charles Darwin's *On the Origin of Species* (1859), which argued that existing species, including humanity itself, had evolved through a long process of "natural selection" from less complex forms of life. Those species that adapted to survival by reason of quickness, shrewdness, or other advantages reproduced their kind, while others fell by the wayside.

The idea of species evolution shocked people of conventional religious views by contradicting a literal interpretation of the biblical creation stories. Heated arguments arose among scientists and clergymen. Some of the faithful rejected Darwin's doctrine, while others found their faith severely shaken not only by evolutionary theory but also by the urging of professional scholars to apply the critical standards of scholarship to the Bible itself, and by the study of comparative religion, which found parallels to biblical stories and doctrines in other faiths. Most of the faithful, however, came to reconcile science and religion. They viewed evolution as the Divine Will, as one of the secondary causes through which God worked.

SOCIAL DARWINISM   Though Darwin's theory of evolution applied only to biological phenomena, other thinkers drew broader inferences from it. The temptation to apply evolutionary theory to the social (human) world proved irresistible. Darwin's fellow Englishman Herbert Spencer became the first major prophet of Social Darwinism and an important influence on American thought. Spencer argued that human society and institutions, like organisms, passed through the process of natural selection, which resulted, in Spencer's chilling phrase, in the "survival of the fittest." For Spencer, social evolution implied progress, ending "only in

Charles Darwin.

the establishment of the greatest perfection and the most complete happiness."

If, as Spencer believed, society naturally evolved for the better, then governmental interference with the process of social evolution was a serious mistake. This view used biological laws to justify the working of the free market. Social Darwinism implied a governmental policy of hands-off; it decried the regulation of business, the graduated income tax, sanitation and housing regulations, and even protection against medical quacks. Such interventions, Spencer charged, would help the "unfit" survive and thereby impede progress. The only acceptable charity was voluntary, and even that was of dubious value. Spencer warned that "fostering the good-for-nothing at the expense of the good, is an extreme cruelty."

For Spencer and his many American supporters, successful businessmen and corporations were the engines of social progress. If small businesses were crowded out by trusts and monopolies, that too was part of the evolutionary process. John D. Rockefeller told his Baptist Sunday school class that the "growth of a large business is merely a survival of the fittest. . . . This is not an evil tendency in business. It is merely the working-out of a law of nature and a law of God."

The ideas of Darwin and Spencer spread quickly in America. *Popular Science Monthly,* founded in 1872, became the chief medium for popularizing Darwinism. That same year Darwin's chief academic disciple, William Graham Sumner, took up the new chair of political and social science at Yale and preached the gospel of natural selection under titles such as "What Social Classes Owe to Each Other" and "The Absurd Effort to Make the World Over." Sumner's most lasting contribution, made in his book *Folkways* (1907), was to argue that forms of societal organization such as democracy or aristocracy were set by the working of tradition, or the customs of a community, and not by reason or natural laws. The implication here too was that it would be a mistake for government to interfere with established customs in the name of ideals of equality or natural rights.

REFORM DARWINISM Efforts to use Darwinism to promote "rugged individualism" did not go without challenge. Reform found its major philosopher in an obscure Washington civil servant, Lester Frank Ward, who had fought his way up from poverty and never lost

Lester Frank Ward, proponent of Reform Darwinism.

his empathy for the underdog. Ward's book *Dynamic Sociology* (1883) singled out one product of evolution that Darwin and Spencer had neglected: the human brain. People, unlike animals, had minds that could shape social evolution. Far from being the helpless pawn of evolution, Ward argued, humanity could control the process of evolution. The competition extolled by Sumner was in fact highly wasteful, as was the natural competitive process: plant or cattle breeding, for instance, could actually improve on the results of natural selection.

Ward's Reform Darwinism challenged Sumner's conservative Social Darwinism, holding that cooperation, not competition, would better promote progress. According to Ward, Sumner's "irrational distrust of government" might have been justified in an earlier day of autocracy, but no longer under a representative system. Government could become the agency of progress by striving to reach two main goals: to ameliorate poverty, which impeded the development of the mind, and to promote the education of the masses. "Intelligence, far more than necessity," Ward wrote, "is the mother of invention," and "the influence of knowledge as a social factor, like that of wealth, is proportional to the extent of its distribution." Intellect, rightly informed by science, could plan successfully. In the benevolent "sociocracy" of the future, legislatures would function mainly to sanction decisions worked out in the sociological laboratory.

REALISM IN FACT AND FICTION

PRAGMATISM   Around the turn of the century, the concept of evolutionary development found expression in a philosophical principle set forth in mature form by William James in his book *Pragmatism: A New*

Name for Some Old Ways of Think-ing. James, a professor of philosophy and psychology at Harvard, shared Lester Frank Ward's concern with the role of ideas in the process of evolution. Truth, to James, arose from the testing of new ideas, the value of which lay in their practical consequences. Thus, scientists could test the validity of their ideas in the laboratory and judge their import by their applications. Pragmatism re-flected a quality often looked upon as genuinely American: the inven-tive, experimental spirit.

William James.

John Dewey, who would become the chief philosopher of pragmatism after James, preferred the term "instrumentalism," by which he meant that ideas were instruments for action, especially for social reform. Dewey, unlike James, threw himself into movements for the rights of la-bor and women, the promotion of peace, and the reform of education. He believed that education was the process through which society would gradually progress toward the goal of economic democracy.

THE LOCAL COLORISTS   Writers of fiction in the post–Civil War decades responded in different ways to the changes in American life and thought. What came to be called the local color movement ex-pressed the nostalgia of people moving from a rural to an urban culture, and longing for those places where the old folkways survived. Sarah Orne Jewett depicted the down-easters of her native Maine most en-duringly in the stories and sketches collected in *The Country of the Pointed Firs* (1896). Jewett's creative vision was always backward-looking and affectionate. She looked upon her parents' "generation as the one to which I really belong—I who was brought up with grandfathers and granduncles and aunts for my best playmates."

Once the passions of war and Reconstruction were spent, the South became for many northern readers an inexhaustible gallery of quaint types. George Washington Cable exploited the local color of the Louisiana Creoles and Cajuns in *Old Creole Days* (1879), *The*

Grandissimes (1880), and other books. Joel Chandler Harris, a newsman and columnist, wove authentic African-American folk tales into the unforgettable stories of Uncle Remus, gathered first in *Uncle Remus: His Songs and His Sayings* (1880).

CLEMENS   The best of the local colorists could find universal truths in common life, and Samuel Langhorne Clemens (Mark Twain) transcended them all. A native of Missouri, he was forced to work at age twelve, becoming first a printer and then a Mississippi riverboat pilot. When the Civil War shut down the river traffic, he briefly joined a Confederate militia company, then left with his brother, Orion, for Nevada. He moved on to California in 1864 and first gained widespread notice with his tall tale of the gold country, "The Celebrated Jumping Frog of Calaveras County" (1865). In 1867 the San Francisco *Alta Californian* staked him to a tour of the Mediterranean, and his humorous reports on the trip, revised and collected into *Innocents Abroad* (1869), established him as a funny man much in demand on the lecture circuit. With the success of *Roughing It* (1871), an account of his western years, he moved to Hartford, Connecticut, and was able to establish himself as a full-time author and hilarious lecturer.

Mark Twain illustrated in the frontispiece to his novel Tramp Abroad, *1880.*

Clemens was the first great American writer born and raised west of the Appalachians. His early writings accentuated his western background, but for his greatest books he drew heavily upon his boyhood in a border slave state and the tall-tale tradition of southwestern humor. In *The Adventures of Tom Sawyer* (1876) he evoked in fiction the prewar Hannibal, Missouri, where his own boyhood was cut so short. Clemens's masterpiece, *The Adventures of Huckleberry Finn* (1884), created unforgettable characters in Huck Finn, his shiftless father, the slave Jim, the Widow

Douglas, the "King," and the "Duke." The product of an erratic upbringing, Huck Finn embodied the instinct of every red-blooded American boy to "light out for the territory" whenever polite society set out to civilize him. Huck's effort to help his friend Jim escape bondage expressed well the moral dilemmas imposed by slavery on everyone. Many years later another great American writer, Ernest Hemingway, would claim that "All modern American literature comes from one book by Mark Twain, called *Huckleberry Finn.*"

LITERARY NATURALISM   During the 1890s, a new literary school known as naturalism shocked genteel sensibilities. The naturalists were young literary rebels who imported scientific determinism into literature, viewing people as part of the animal world, prey to natural forces and internal drives without control or full knowledge of them.

Stephen Crane in *Maggie: A Girl of the Streets* (1893) and *The Red Badge of Courage* (1895) portrayed people caught up in environmental situations beyond their control. *Maggie* depicted a tenement girl driven to prostitution and death amid scenes so sordid that Crane had to finance publication himself. *The Red Badge of Courage,* his masterpiece, told the story of a young man going through his baptism of fire in the Civil War, and evoked nobility and courage amid the ungovernable carnage of war.

Two of the naturalists achieved a degree of popular success: Jack London and Theodore Dreiser. London was both a professed socialist and a believer in the German philosopher Friedrich Nietzsche's doctrine of the superman. In adventure stories such as *The Call of the Wild* (1903) and *The Sea Wolf* (1904), London celebrated the triumph of brute force and the will to survive. He reinforced his point about animal force in *The Call of the Wild.* The novel's protagonist is not a superman but a superdog that reverted to the wild in Alaska and ran with a wolf pack.

Theodore Dreiser shocked the genteel public probably more than the others, presenting protagonists who sinned without remorse and without punishment. *Sister Carrie* (1900), a counterpoint to Crane's *Maggie,* departed from it by having Carrie Meeber survive illicit loves and go on to success on the stage. In *The Financier* (1912) and *The Titan* (1914), Dreiser's main character was a sexual athlete and a man of elemental force who rose to a dominant position in business and society.

SOCIAL CRITICISM   Behind their dogma of determinism, the naturalists harbored intense outrage at human misery and social injustice. Other writers shared their indignation but addressed themselves more directly to protest and reform. One of the most influential of these activists was Henry George, a California printer and journalist. During a visit to New York he was shocked by the contrast the city offered between wealth and poverty. "Once, in daylight, and in a city street, there came to me a thought, a vision, a call. . . . And there and then I made a vow" to seek out the cause of poverty in the midst of progress. The basic social problem, he reasoned, was the "unearned increment" in wealth that came to those who owned land. The fruit of his thought, *Progress and Poverty* (1879), a thick and difficult book, sold slowly at first, but by 1905 had sold about 2 million copies in several languages.

George held that everyone had as much right to the use of the land as to the air they breathed. Nobody had a right to the value that accrued from the land, since that was created by the community, not by its owner. George proposed simply to tax the "unearned" increment in the value of the land, or the rent. George's idea was widely propagated and actually affected tax policy here and there, but his influence on the thinking of the day came less from his "single-tax" panacea than from the paradox he posed in his title, *Progress and Poverty.*

The journalist and freelance writer Henry Demarest Lloyd addressed himself to what many found a more vital issue than Henry George's, not the monopoly in land but industrial monopoly. His best-known book, *Wealth Against Commonwealth* (1894), drew on more than a decade of studying the Standard Oil Company. Lloyd, like Lester Frank Ward, saw the key to progress in cooperation rather than competition. Economic activities in their cooperative aspects demonstrated a civilizing process; Lloyd argued that "the spectacle of the million or more employees of the railroads . . . dispatching trains, maintaining tracks, collecting fares and freights . . . is possible only where civilization has reached a high average of morals and culture." But those in charge of huge corporations were concerned only with wealth, not with promoting civilization. To avoid destruction, civilization required changes. The cooperative principle should be applied "to all toils in which private sovereignty has become through monopoly a despotism over the public." Where monopoly had developed, it should be transferred to public operation in the public interest. In 1903, just before his death, Lloyd joined the Socialist party.

Thorstein Veblen brought to his social criticism a background of formal training in economics and a purpose of making economics more an evolutionary or historical science. By all accounts he taught miserably, even inaudibly, and seldom held a job for long, but he wrote brilliantly. In his best-known work, *The Theory of the Leisure Class* (1899), he examined the pecuniary values of the middle classes and introduced phrases that have since become almost clichés: "conspicuous consumption" and "conspicuous leisure." With the advent of industrial society, Veblen argued, property became the conventional basis of reputation. For the upper classes, moreover, it became necessary to consume time nonproductively as evidence of the ability to afford a life of leisure. In this and later works Veblen held that the division between industrial experts and business managers was widening to a dangerous point. The businessman's interest in profits combined with his ignorance of efficiency produced wasteful organization and a failure to realize the full potential of modern technology.

THE SOCIAL GOSPEL

While novelists, journalists, and commentators were writing about the rising social tensions and injustices of late-nineteenth-century America, more and more people were addressing these problems through direct social action. Some reformers focused on legislative solutions to social problems; others stressed philanthropy or organized charity. A few militants promoted socialism or anarchism. Whatever the method or approach, however, social reformers were on the march at the turn of the century, and their activities gave to American life a new urgency and energy.

RISE OF THE INSTITUTIONAL CHURCH   The churches responded slowly to the mounting social concerns, for American Protestantism had become one of the main props of the established order. The Reverend Henry Ward Beecher, pastor of the fashionable Plymouth Congregational Church in Brooklyn, preached success, Social Darwinism, and the unworthiness of the poor. As the middle classes moved out to

A Salvation Army group in Flint, Michigan, 1894.

the streetcar suburbs, their churches followed. In the years 1868–1888, for instance, seventeen Protestant churches abandoned the areas below Fourteenth Street in Manhattan. In the center of Chicago 60,000 residents had no church, Protestant or Catholic. Where churches became prosperous they fell easily under the spell of respectability and do-nothing Social Darwinism.

However, many churches responded to the human needs of the time by devoting their resources to community service and care for the unfortunate. The Young Men's Christian Association had entered the United States from England in the 1850s and grew rapidly after 1870; the Salvation Army, founded in London in 1876, came to the United States four years later. Churches in urban districts began to develop institutional features that were more social than strictly religious in function. After the Civil War, churches acquired gymnasiums, libraries, lecture rooms, and other facilities for social programs. Russell Conwell's Baptist Temple in Philadelphia included, among other features, a night school for working people that grew into Temple University.

RELIGIOUS REFORMERS   Other church leaders who feared that Christianity was losing influence in the cities preached what came to be called the social gospel. Washington Gladden of Columbus, Ohio, preached that true Christianity lies not in rituals, dogmas, or even in the mystical experience of God, but in the principle that "Thou shalt love thy neighbor as thyself." Christian law should govern the workplace, with worker and employer united in serving each other's interest. He argued for labor's right to organize and complained that class distinctions split congregations as well.

The acknowledged intellectual leader of the social gospel movement, however, was the Baptist Walter Rauschenbusch, professor at the Colgate–Rochester Theological Seminary. In *Christianity and the Social Crisis* (1907) and other works, he developed a theological basis for the movement in the Kingdom of God. This kingdom existed in the churches themselves, but it embraced far more than these: "It is the Christian transfiguration of the social order. The church is one social institution alongside of the family, the industrial organization of society, and the State. The Kingdom of God is in all these, and realizes itself through them all." The church was indispensable to religion, but "the greatest future awaits religion in the public life of humanity."

EARLY EFFORTS AT URBAN REFORM

THE SETTLEMENT HOUSE MOVEMENT   While preachers of the social gospel dispensed inspiration, other dedicated reformers attacked the problems of the slums from residential and community centers called settlement houses. By 1900 perhaps a hundred settlement houses existed in the United States, some of the best known being Jane Addams's and Ellen Starr's Hull House in Chicago (1889), Robert A. Woods's South End House in Boston (1891), and Lillian Wald's Henry Street Settlement (1895) in New York.

The settlement houses were staffed mainly by young middle-class idealists, a majority of them college-trained women who had few other outlets for meaningful work outside the home. Settlement workers sought to broaden the horizons and improve the lives of slum dwellers in diverse ways. At Hull House, for instance, workers enrolled the neighborhood children into clubs and kindergartens, and set up a nursery to care for the infant children of working mothers. The program gradually expanded as Hull House sponsored health clinics, lectures, music and art studios, an employment bureau, men's clubs, training in

Jane Addams.

skills such as bookbinding, a gymnasium, and a savings bank.

Settlement house leaders realized, however, that the spreading slums made their work as effective as bailing out the ocean with a teaspoon. They therefore organized political support for housing laws, public playgrounds, juvenile courts, mothers' pensions, workers' compensation laws, and legislation against child labor. Lillian Wald promoted the establishment of the federal Children's Bureau in 1912, and Jane Addams, for her work in the peace movement, received late in her life the Nobel Peace Prize for 1931.

The settlement house movement, however, was not immune to criticism. Critics accused them of subtle and not-so-subtle forms of social control and of attempts to assimilate the ethnic poor to white, middle-class Protestant standards. The cultural gap between middle-class social workers and slum dwellers could often lead to misunderstanding, and in the effort to "Americanize" immigrants, the settlement houses and agencies of education sometimes lacked sensitivity to the values of other cultures. But on balance their contributions were more positive than negative. By the end of the century both the Catholic church and Jewish agencies were taking up the settlement house movement.

WOMEN'S EMPLOYMENT AND SUFFRAGE   Settlement house workers, insofar as they were paid, made up but a fraction of all gainfully employed women. With the growth of population, the number of employed women steadily increased, as did their percentage of the labor force and of the total female population. The greatest leaps forward came in the decades of the 1880s and the 1900s, both of which were also peak decades of immigration, a correlation that can be explained by the immigrant's need for income. The number of employed women went from over 2.6 million in 1880 to 4 million in 1890, then from 5.1 million in 1900 to 7.8 million in 1910. "Between 1880 and 1900 the employment of women in most parts of the economy became an established fact," wrote one historian. "This was surely the most significant event in the modern history of women." Through all those years domestic work remained the largest category of employment for women; teaching and nursing also remained among the leading fields. The main change was that clerical work (bookkeeping, stenographic work, and the like) and sales jobs became increasingly available to women.

These changes in occupational status had little connection with the women's rights movement, which increasingly focused on the issue of suffrage. Immediately after the Civil War, Susan B. Anthony, a seasoned veteran of the movement, demanded that the Fourteenth Amendment guarantee the vote for women as well as black males. She made little impression on the defenders of masculine prerogative, however, who insisted that women belonged in the domestic sphere.

In 1869 the unity of the women's movement was broken in a manner reminiscent of the antislavery rift three decades before. The question once again was whether the movement should concentrate on one overriding issue. Anthony and Elizabeth Cady Stanton founded the National Woman Suffrage Association to promote a women's suffrage

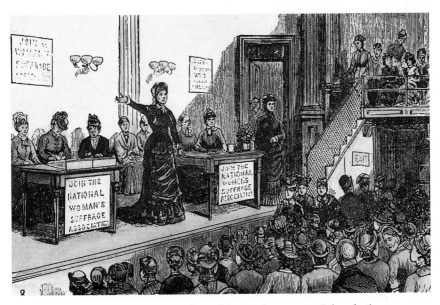

Elizabeth Cady Stanton is pictured speaking in the center of the platform at a meeting of the National Woman Suffrage Association in Chicago, 1880.

amendment to the Constitution, but they looked upon the vote as but one among many feminist causes to be promoted. Later that same year, Lucy Stone, Julia Ward Howe, and other leaders formed the American Woman Suffrage Association, which focused single-mindedly on the suffrage as the first and basic reform.

It would be another half century before the battle could be won, and the long struggle focused the women's cause ever more on the primary objective of the vote. In 1890, after three years of negotiation, the rival groups united as the National American Woman Suffrage Association, with Elizabeth Cady Stanton as president for two years, to be followed by Susan B. Anthony until 1900. The work thereafter was carried on by a new generation of activists, led by Anna Howard Shaw and Carrie Chapman Catt. Over the years the movement achieved some local and some partial victories, as a few states granted women suffrage in school board or municipal elections, or bond referenda. In 1869 the Territory of Wyoming granted full suffrage to women, and after 1890 it retained women's suffrage when it became a new state. Three other western states soon followed suit: Colorado in 1893, Utah and Idaho in 1896. But women's suffrage lost in a California referendum in 1896 by a dishearteningly narrow margin.

The movement remained in the doldrums thereafter until the cause easily won a Washington state referendum in 1910, and then carried California by a close majority in 1911. The following year three more western states—Arizona, Kansas, and Oregon—joined in to make a total of nine western states with full suffrage. In 1913 Illinois granted women presidential and municipal suffrage. Yet not until New York acted in 1917 did a state east of the Mississippi adopt universal suffrage. In 1878 California's Senator A. A. Sargent introduced the "Anthony Amendment," a women's suffrage provision that remained before Congress until 1896 and then vanished until 1913, when it was finally ratified (see Chapter 26).

Despite the focus on the vote, women did not confine their public work to that issue. In 1866 a Young Women's Christian Association, a parallel to the YMCA, appeared in Boston and spread elsewhere. The New England Women's Club, started in 1868 by Julia Ward Howe and others, was an early example of the women's clubs that then proliferated to the extent that a General Federation of Women's Clubs tied them together in 1890. Many women's clubs confined themselves to

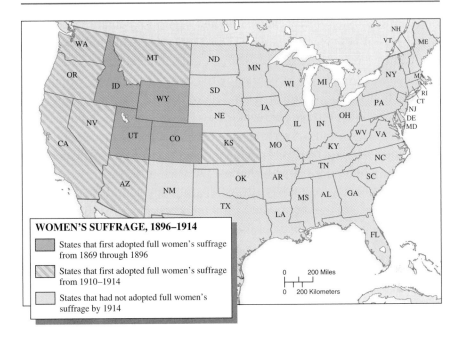

WOMEN'S SUFFRAGE, 1896–1914

States that first adopted full women's suffrage from 1869 through 1896

States that first adopted full women's suffrage from 1910–1914

States that had not adopted full women's suffrage by 1914

"literary" and social activities, but others became deeply involved in charities and reform. The New York Consumers League, formed in 1890, and the National Consumers League, formed nine years later, sought to make the buying public, chiefly women, aware of labor conditions. One of its devices was the "White List" of firms that met its minimum standards. The National Women's Trade Union League, founded in 1903, performed a similar function of bringing educated and middle-class women together with working women for the benefit of women unionists.

These and the many other women's groups of the time may have aroused the fear in opponents to women's suffrage that voting women would tilt toward reform. This was the fear of the brewing and liquor interests, large business interests generally, and political machine bosses. Others, mainly in the South, opposed women's suffrage on the ground that black women would be enfranchised, or because of states'-rights views.

TOWARD A WELFARE STATE   Even without the support of voting women in most places, the states adopted rudimentary measures to regulate big business and labor conditions in the public interest. By the end of the century, nearly every state had begun to regulate railroads, if not always effectively, and had moved to supervise banks and insurance companies. Between 1887 and 1897, by one count, the states and terri-tories passed over 1,600 laws relating to conditions of work, which lim-ited the hours of labor, provided special protection for women, limited or forbade child labor, required regular wage payments in cash, and called for factory inspections. Nearly all states had boards or commissioners of labor, and some had boards of conciliation and arbitration. Still, conserv-ative judges limited the practical impact of such new laws.

In thwarting new regulatory efforts, the Supreme Court used a revised interpretation of the Fourteenth Amendment clauses forbidding the states to "deprive any person of life, liberty or property without due pro-cess of law" or to deny any person "the equal protection of the laws." Two significant steps of legal reasoning turned the due-process clause into a bulwark of private property. First, the judges reasoned that the word "per-son" in the clause included corporations, which in other connections were legally artificial persons with the right to own property, buy and sell, sue and be sued like natural persons. Second, the courts moved away from the old view that "due process" referred only to correct procedures and toward a doctrine of "substantive due process," which allowed courts to review the substance of an action. The principle of substantive due process enabled judges to overturn laws that deprived persons of property to an unreasonable degree, and thereby violated due process.

From the due-process clause the Court also derived a new doctrine of "liberty of contract," defined as being within the liberties protected by the due-process clause. Liberty, the Court ruled in 1897, involved "not only the right of the citizen to be free from the mere physical re-straint of his person, . . . but the term is deemed to embrace the right of the citizen to be free in the enjoyment of all his faculties," and free "to enter into all contracts" proper to carrying out such purposes. When it came to labor laws, this translated into an employee's "liberty" to contract for work under the most oppressive conditions without interference from the state. The courts continued to apply such an interpretation well into the twentieth century.

At the end of the nineteenth century, opinion in the country stood poised between such conservative rigidities and a growing sense that new corporate structures and social problems required more progres-sive action. "By the last two decades of the century," wrote one observer, "many thoughtful men had begun to march under various banners declaring that somewhere and somehow the promise of the American dream had been lost—they often said 'betrayed'—and that drastic changes needed to be made to recapture it."

The last two decades of the nineteenth century had already seen a slow erosion of laissez-faire values, which had found their most secure home in the courts. From the social philosophy of the reformers, Social Gospelers, and Populists there emerged a concept of the general-welfare state, which, in the words of one historian, sought "to promote the general welfare not by rendering itself inconspicuous but by taking such positive action as is deemed necessary to improve the condition under which its citizens live and work." The reformers supplied no agreed-upon blueprint for a general-welfare utopia, but "simply assumed that government could promote the public interest by appropriate positive action . . . whenever the circumstances indicated that such action would further the common weal." The conflict between this notion and laissez-faire values went on into the new century, but by the mid–twentieth century, after the Progressive movement, the New Deal, and the Fair Deal, the conflict would be "resolved in theory, in practice, and in public esteem in favor of the general-welfare state."

MAKING CONNECTIONS

- As the next chapter shows, the presidential election of 1896 was in many ways a contest between the new urban values discussed in this chapter and those of a more traditional rural American society.

- The reform impulse you've read about in this chapter finds voice again in the discussion of the Progressive movement in Chapter 24.

- The nativist thinking discussed in this chapter fueled the immigration restriction laws enacted in the 1920s (Chapter 26).

FURTHER READING

For a survey of urbanization, see David Goldfield's *Urban America* (1990). Gunther P. Barth discusses the emergence of a new urban culture in *City People: The Rise of Modern City Culture in Nineteenth Century America* (1980). John Bodnar offers a synthesis of the urban immigrant experience in *The Transplanted: A History of Immigrants in Urban America* (1985). Walter Nugent's *Crossings: The Great Transatlantic Migrations, 1870– 1914* (1992) provides a wealth of demographic information and insight.

For the growth of urban leisure and sports, see Roy Rosenzweig's *Eight Hours for What We Will: Workers and Leisure in an Industrial City, 1870–1920* (1983) and Steven A. Riess's *City Games: The Evolution of American Urban Society and the Rise of Sports* (1989). Saloon culture is examined in Nathan Ward's *Faces Along the Bar: The Workingman's Saloon, 1870–1920* (1998).

Richard Hofstadter's *Social Darwinism in American Thought* (rev. ed., 1992) and Cynthia E. Russett's *Darwin in America* (1976) examine the impact of the theory of evolution. On the rise of realism in thought and the arts during the second half of the nineteenth century, see David Shi's *Facing Facts: Realism in American Thought and Culture, 1850– 1920* (1995).

Eleanor Flexner's *Century of Struggle: The Woman's Rights Movement in the United States* (rev. ed., 1975) surveys the condition of women in the late nineteenth century.

22 ⤔ GILDED-AGE POLITICS AND AGRARIAN REVOLT

*I*n 1873 writers Mark Twain and Charles Dudley Warner created an enduring label for the post–Civil War era when they collaborated on a novel entitled *The Gilded Age*. The book depicted an age of widespread political corruption, personal greed, and social excess. Perspectives on the times would eventually mellow, but generations of political scientists and historians have since reinforced the two novelists' judgment. As a young college graduate in 1879, Woodrow Wilson described the state of the American political system: "No leaders, no principles; no principles, no parties." Indeed, the real movers and shakers of the Gilded Age were not the men who sat in the White House or the Congress but the captains of industry who crisscrossed the continent with railroads and decorated its cities with plumed smokestacks and gaudy mansions.

PARADOXICAL POLITICS

Throughout the last third of the nineteenth century, political inertia reigned on the national level. A fairly even division between Republicans and Democrats in Congress created a sense of stalemate. Neither party was willing to embrace controversial issues or take bold initiatives because their relative strength was so precarious. Many observers then and since considered this a time of political mediocrity in which the parties refused to confront "real issues" such as the runaway growth of an unregulated economy and its attendant social injustices.

Voters of the time nonetheless thought politics was very important. Voter turnout during the Gilded Age was commonly about 70 to 80 percent, even in the South, where the disenfranchisement of blacks was not yet complete. (By contrast, the turnout for the 2000 presidential election was 51 percent.) The paradox of such high voter participation in the face of the inertia at the national political level raises an obvious question: How was it that leaders who failed to address the "real issues" of the day presided over the most highly organized and politically active electorate in American history?

The answer is partly that the politicians and the voters believed that they *were* dealing with crucial issues: the tariff, monopolies, the currency, civil service reform, and immigration. But the answer also reflects the extreme partisanship of the times and the essentially local nature of political culture during the Gilded Age. While people expected little from their national government, they demanded much from their local and state officials.

PARTISAN POLITICS   Most Americans after the Civil War were intensely loyal to one of the two major parties, Democratic or Republican. In the midst of the social and economic disruptions caused by the second industrial revolution, the political parties gave people an anchor of activity and loyalty in an unstable world. Local party officials took care of those who voted their way, and they distributed appointive public offices and other favors to party loyalists. These "city machines" used patronage and favoritism to get and keep the loyalty of business supporters, while providing jobs or food or fuel to working-class voters who had fallen on hard times.

The political parties were also a key source of entertainment for activist and ordinary voters. The party faithful eagerly took part in rallies and picnics, deriving a sense of camaraderie as well as recreation that offered a welcome relief from their usual workday routine.

Party loyalties and voter turnout in the late nineteenth century reflected religious and ethnic divisions as well as geographic differences. The Republican party attracted mainly Protestants of British descent. Their native seat was New England, and their other strongholds were New York and the upper Midwest, both of which were populated with Yankee stock. Legitimate heirs to the abolitionist tradition, Republicans drew to their ranks a host of reformers and moralists, spiritual descendants of the perfectionists who championed the revivals and the reform movements of the antebellum years. The party's heritage of anti-Catholic nativism would also make a comeback in the 1880s. And the Republicans, the party of Abraham Lincoln, could also rely on the votes of blacks and Union veterans of the Civil War.

The Democrats, by contrast, tended to be a heterogeneous, often unruly coalition embracing southern whites, immigrants and Catholics of any origin, Jews, freethinkers, skeptics, and all those repelled by the "party of morality." As one Chicago Democrat explained, "A Republican is a man who wants you t' go t' church every Sunday. A Democrat says if a man wants to have a glass of beer on Sunday he can have it."

In the Midwest, especially, tensions over religious and social issues, such as Sunday closing laws and liquor prohibition, created intense political allegiances. Republicans pressed nativist causes, calling for restrictions on immigration and on the employment of foreigners, and greater emphasis on the teaching of the "American" language in the schools. Prohibitionism revived along with nativism in the 1880s. Among the immigrants who crowded into the growing cities were many Irish, Germans, and Italians who enjoyed alcoholic beverages. Republicans increasingly saw saloons as the central social evil around which all others revolved, including vice, crime, political corruption, and neglect of families, and they associated these problems with the ethnic groups that frequented the saloons.

POLITICAL STALEMATE AT THE NATIONAL LEVEL Between 1869 and 1913, from the presidencies of Ulysses S. Grant to William Howard Taft, Republicans monopolized the White House except during the two nonconsecutive terms of Grover Cleveland, but Republican domination was more apparent than real. Between 1872 and 1896, no president won a majority of the popular vote. In each of those presidential elections, sixteen states invariably voted Republican and fourteen voted Democratic, leaving a pivotal six states whose results might change. The important swing-vote role that two of these states, New York and Ohio, played helps explain the election of seven presidents from these states from 1870 to 1912.

Deferential presidents also contributed to the political stalemate. No chief executive between Lincoln and Theodore Roosevelt could be described as a "strong" president. None seriously challenged the prevailing view that Congress, not the White House, should formulate policy. Senator John Sherman of Ohio expressed the widely held notion that the legislative branch should take initiative in a republic: "The President should merely obey and enforce the law."

Republicans controlled the Senate, and Democrats controlled the House during the Gilded Age. Only during 1881–1883 and 1889–1891 did a Republican president have a Republican Congress, and only between 1893 and 1895 did a Democratic president enjoy a Democratic Congress.

Political stasis thus led Congress to postpone making major decisions or launching new programs and to concentrate instead on partisan maneuvering over procedural issues. The almost equal strength of the parties in Congress and the fear in each party of alienating key factions worked against any vigorous new initiatives in Congress. Because most bills required bipartisan support to pass both houses, and legislators tended to vote along party lines, the Democrats and Republicans pursued a policy of evasion on the national issues of the day. Only the tariff provoked clear-cut divisions between protectionist Republicians and low-tariff Democrats, but there were individual exceptions even on that. On the important questions of the currency, regulation of big business, farm problems, civil service reform, and immigration, the parties differed very little. As a result, they primarily became vehicles for seeking office and dispensing patronage in the form of government jobs and contracts.

STATE AND LOCAL INITIATIVES   Unlike today, people during the Gilded Age expected little direct support from the federal government. Most of the significant political activity occurred at the state and local levels. In the western territories, prior to their receiving statehood, people were largely forced to fend for themselves rather than to rely on federal authorities. They formed towns, practiced vigilante justice, and made laws on their own. Once incorporated into the Union, these former territories retained much of their autonomy.

Much more than the national Congress, state governments after the Civil War were dynamic centers of political activity and innovation. Over 60 percent of the nation's spending and taxing were exercised by state and local authorities. Then, unlike today, the large cities spent far more on local services than did the federal government. And three-fourths of all public employees worked for state and local governments. Local issues such as prohibition, Sunday closing laws, and parochial school funding generated far more excitement than complex debates over tariffs and monetary policies. It was state and local governments rather than the national government that first sought to curb the power and restrain the abuses of corporate interests.

CORRUPTION AND REFORM

In this period states made rudimentary attempts to regulate big business; most of these regulations were overturned by the courts, however. A close alliance developed between business and political leaders. This was not necessarily perceived by the public as inappropriate, since many politicians favored business interests out of conviction. Nor were people as sensitive to conflicts of interest as they would later become. Congressman James G. Blaine of Maine, for example, and many of his supporters, saw nothing wrong in his accepting stock certificates from an Arkansas railroad after helping it win a land grant from Congress. Railroad passes, free entertainment, and a host of other favors were freely provided to politicians, editors, and other leaders in positions to influence public opinion or affect legislation.

The Bosses of the Senate. *This 1889 cartoon bitingly portrays the alliance between big business and politics in this period.*

On the local level, the exchange of favors for votes was not perceived as improper either. People voted for their party because of their intense partisan loyalty. Although they looked to their parties to supply them with favors, entertainment, and even jobs, they did not see themselves as "selling their votes." This was simply the practice of patronage democracy, in which local party officials awarded party loyalists with contracts and public jobs such as heads of the customs houses and post offices.

Both Republican and Democratic leaders squabbled over the "spoils" of office. These were the appointive offices that were available on both the local and the national levels. After each election, it was expected that the party that had won would throw out the appointees from the defeated party and appoint their own men to office in their stead. Each party had its share of corrupt officials willing to buy and sell government appointments or congressional votes, yet each also witnessed the emergence of factions promoting honesty in government. This struggle for clean government soon became one of the foremost issues of the day.

HAYES AND CIVIL SERVICE REFORM   In the aftermath of Reconstruction, Rutherford B. Hayes admirably embodied the "party of morality." Hayes brought to the White House in 1877 a new style of uprightness, a sharp contrast to the graft and corruption of the Grant administration. The son of an Ohio farmer, Hayes became one of the early Republicans, was wounded four times in the Civil War, and was promoted to major-general. Elected governor of Ohio in 1867, he served three terms. Honest and respectable, competent and dignified, he lived in a modest style with his wife, who was nicknamed "Lemonade Lucy" because of her refusal to serve alcohol at White House functions.

Yet Hayes's presidency suffered from the supposed secret deal that awarded him victory over Democrat Samuel Tilden in the 1876 election. Snide references to him as "His Fraudulence" dogged his steps and denied him any chance at a second term, which he renounced from the beginning. Hayes's own party was split between so-called Stalwarts and Half-Breeds, led respectively by Senators Roscoe Conkling of New York and James G. Blaine of Maine. The difference between these Republican factions was murkier than that between the parties. The Stalwarts generally supported Grant, a Radical southern policy, and the spoils system. The Half-Breeds took a contrary view on the first two and even vaguely supported civil service reform.

For the most part, the two Republican factions were loose alliances designed to advance the careers of Conkling and Blaine. The two men could not abide each other. Blaine once referred to Conkling as displaying a "majestic, supereminent, overpowering, turkey-gobbler strut." He was right. Tall and lordly, with a pointed beard, thick, auburn hair, and upturned jaw and nose, Conkling boasted good looks, fine clothes, and an arrogant manner. He dressed and lived flamboyantly, sporting pastel bow ties, silk scarves, moon-colored vests, and patent-leather shoes. Yet underneath his glamorous facade he was a ruthless power broker. Conkling viewed politics as a brute struggle for control. Politics "is a rotten business," he declared. "Nothing counts except to win."

Hayes thought otherwise, and he aligned himself with the growing public discontent over the corruption that characterized the era. American leaders were just learning about the merit system for public employees long established in the bureaucracies of France and Germany, and the new British practice in which civil service jobs were filled by competitive examination. Prominent leaders such as James A. Garfield in the House and Carl Schurz in the Senate embraced civil service reform, and Hayes raised the issue during the campaign of 1876.

Although Hayes failed to get civil service legislation, he did mandate his own rules for political appointments based on merit: those already in office would be dismissed only for the good of the government and not for political reasons; party members would have no more influence in appointments than other respectable citizens; no assessments of government employees for political contributions would be permitted; and no officeholder could manage election campaigns for political organizations, although all could vote and express opinions.

The issue of honest and effective government administration culminated in a dispute over the federal customs houses. They were notorious centers of corrupt politics, filled with political appointees with little or nothing to do but draw salaries and run political machines. Importers sometimes found that they might gain favor by cooperating with corrupt customs officials, and might be punished for making trouble. An inquiry into operations at the New York Customs House revealed that both collector Chester A. Arthur and naval officer Alonzo Cornell were guilty of "laxity" and of using the customs house for political management on behalf of Senator Roscoe Conkling's organization. When Hayes hinted that resignations would be welcomed, Conkling accused the president and other civil service reformers of being blinded by a "canting self-righteousness."

On October 15, 1877, after removing Arthur and Cornell, Hayes named replacements, only to have the nominees rejected when Conkling appealed to the "courtesy of the Senate," an old custom whereby senators might control appointments in their own states. During a recess in the summer of 1878, however, Hayes appointed new replacements. When Congress reassembled, the administration put pressure on senators and, with Democratic support, the nominations were approved. Even this, however, did not end the New York Customs House episode; it would flare up again under the next president.

For all Hayes's efforts to clean house, his vision of government's role remained limited. On the economic issues of the day he held to a conservative line that would guide his successors for the rest of the century. His solution to labor troubles, demonstrated in the Great Railroad Strike of 1877, was to send in federal troops and break the strike. His answer to demands for an expansion of the currency was to veto the Bland-Allison Act, which required only a limited expansion of silver currency through the government's purchase for coinage of $2 million to $4 million worth of silver per month. (The act passed anyway when Congress overrode Hayes's veto.)

GARFIELD AND ARTHUR   With Hayes unavailable for a second term, the Republicans were forced to look elsewhere in 1880. The Stalwarts, led by Conkling, brought Grant forward for a third time, still a strong contender despite the tarnish of his administration's scandals. For two days the Republican convention in Chicago was deadlocked, with Grant holding a slight lead over Blaine. When Wisconsin suddenly switched its votes to Senator-elect James A. Garfield, the convention stampeded to the dark-horse candidate, carrying him to the nomination. As a sop to the Stalwarts, the convention named Chester A. Arthur, the deposed collector of the New York Customs House for vice-president.

The Democrats selected Winfield Scott Hancock, a Union commander at Gettysburg, to counterbalance the Republicans' Major-General Garfield and thus ward off "bloody-shirt" attacks on their party as the vehicle of Rebellion. Former rebels, nevertheless, advised their constituents to "vote as you shot"—that is, against Republicans. In an election characterized by widespread bribery, Garfield eked out a plurality of only 39,000 votes with 48.5 percent of the vote, but with a comfortable margin of 214 to 155 in the electoral college.

A native of Ohio, Garfield distinguished himself during the Civil War and was mustered out as a major-general when he went to Congress in 1863. Noted for his oratory and parliamentary skills, he became one of the outstanding leaders in the House and eventually its Speaker.

On July 2, 1881, President Garfield was walking through the Washington, D.C., rail station when a deranged office seeker named Charles Guiteau shot him in the back. "I am a Stalwart," Guiteau explained to the arresting officers. "Arthur is now President of the United States," an announcement that would prove crippling to the Stalwarts. Garfield lingered near death for two months. On September 19, he died of complications resulting from the shooting, having been president for a little over six months.

One of the chief henchmen of Stalwart leader Roscoe Conkling was now president. "Chet Arthur, President of the United States?" one of his friends exclaimed, "Good God!" Little in Arthur's past, except for his record as an abolitionist lawyer who had helped secure the freedom of a fugitive slave, raised hopes that he would rise above customs-house politics.

But Arthur surprisingly proved to be a competent president. He distanced himself from Conkling and the Stalwarts and established a genuine independence. As president, Arthur vigorously prosecuted the Star Route Frauds, a kickback scheme on contracts for postal routes that involved his old political cronies. The president further surprised old-guard Republicans in 1882 with the veto of an $18 million river and harbors bill, a "pork-barrel" measure that included something for most congressional districts. He also vetoed the Chinese Exclusion Act (1882), which in his view violated the Burlingame Treaty of 1868. Congress proceeded to override both vetoes.

Most startling of all was Arthur's emergence as something of a civil service and tariff reformer. Stalwarts had every reason to expect him to oppose the merit system of government appointments, but instead he allied himself with the reformers. While the assassin Guiteau had unwittingly added a certain urgency to the public support of reform, the defeat of a reform bill in 1882 sponsored by "Gentleman George" Pendleton, Democratic senator from Ohio, aroused public opinion further.

The Pendleton Civil Service Act finally passed in 1883, setting up a three-member Civil Service Commission independent from the regular

Invitation to the Inaugural Reception for President James A. Garfield. Garfield, on the left, and Chester Arthur, on the right, flank a portrait of George Washington at the center.

cabinet departments, the first such federal agency established on a permanent basis. About 14 percent of all government jobs would now be filled on the basis of competitive examinations rather than political favoritism. What was more, the president could enlarge the class of affected jobs at his discretion. This had important consequences over the years, because after each of the next four presidential elections the "outs" emerged as victors. Each new president thus had a motive to enlarge this category of government jobs, because it would shield his own appointees from political removal.

The high protective tariff, a heritage of the Civil War, designed to deter foreign imports by taxing them, had by the early 1880s raised federal revenues to the point that the government actually enjoyed an embarrassment of riches, a surplus that drew money into the Treasury and out of circulation, thus constricting economic growth. Some argued that lower tariff rates would reduce prices and the cost of living, and at the same time leave more money in circulation to fuel economic growth. In 1882 Arthur named a special commission to study the problem. The Tariff Commission recommended a 20 to 25 percent rate reduction, which gained Arthur's support, but Congress's effort to enact the proposal was marred by logrolling (the trading of votes to benefit different legislators' local interests), resulting in the "Mongrel Tariff" of 1883, so called because of its diverse rates for different commodities. Overall, the tariff provided for a slight rate reduction, perhaps by 5 percent, but it actually raised the duty on some articles.

SCURRILOUS CAMPAIGN   When the 1884 presidential campaign began, Arthur's record might have commended him to the voters, but it did not please leaders of his party. So the Republicans dumped Arthur and turned to the glamorous Senator James G. Blaine of Maine, long-time leader of the Half-Breeds. Blaine was the consummate politician. He never forgot a name or a face, he inspired the party faithful with his oratory, and at the same time he knew how to wheel and deal in the back rooms. He managed eloquence even when spouting the platitudes of party loyalty, waving the bloody shirt by reminding voters that Democrats had led the South out of the Union and into the Confederacy, and criticizing British foreign policy—the last of which held special appeal for the Irish, a group not normally drawn to Republicans. Blaine did

Senator James G. Blaine of Maine.

have his enemies, however. Democratic newspapers, for example, turned up evidence of his corruption. Based on references in the "Mulligan letters," they claimed that Blaine was in the pocket of the railroad barons, and that he had sold his votes on measures favorable to their interests.

During the campaign, more letters surfaced with disclosures embarrassing to Blaine. For the reform element of the Republican party, this was too much, and prominent leaders and supporters of the party bolted the ticket. Party regulars scorned them as "goo-goos"—the "good-government" crowd who ignored partisan realities—and the editor of the *New York Sun* jokingly called them Mugwumps, after an Algonquian word meaning a great chieftain. To party regulars, in what soon became a stale joke, Mugwumps were unreliable Republicans who had their "mugs" on one side of the fence and their "wumps" on the other.

The rise of the Mugwumps, however, influenced the Democrats to nominate Stephen Grover Cleveland as a reform candidate. Cleveland rose rapidly from obscurity to the White House. One of many children in the family of a small-town Presbyterian minister, he had been forced by his father's death to go to work at an early age. He won a job as clerk in a law office, read law, passed the bar examination, and became an assistant state attorney-general in New York in 1863 and later sheriff of Erie County. He first attracted national attention as the anti-corruption mayor of Buffalo, where he was elected in 1881. In 1882 he was elected as governor, and he continued to build a reform record by fighting New York's corrupt Tammany Hall organization. As mayor and as governor, he repeatedly vetoed what he considered special-privilege bills serving selfish interests.

A stocky 250-pound man, Cleveland seemed the stolid opposite of Blaine. He possessed little charisma, but impressed the public with his stubborn integrity. Then a scandal erupted when the *Buffalo Evening Telegraph* revealed that as a bachelor Cleveland had had an affair with

Another Voice for Cleveland. *This 1884 cartoon attacks "Grover the Good" for fathering an illegitimate child.*

an attractive Buffalo widow, who had named him as the father of a child born to her in 1874. Cleveland took responsibility and provided for the child. When supporters asked Cleveland what to say, he answered "Tell the truth." The respective escapades of Blaine and Cleveland provided some of the most colorful battle cries in American political history. "Blaine, Blaine, James G. Blaine, the continental liar from the state of Maine," Democrats chanted. Republicans countered with "Ma, ma, where's my pa? Gone to the White House, ha, ha, ha!"

Near the end of the campaign, Blaine and his supporters committed two fateful blunders. The first occurred at New York's fashionable Delmonico's restaurant, where Blaine went to a private dinner with several millionaire bigwigs to discuss campaign finances. Cartoons and accounts of "Belshazzar's Feast" festooned the opposition press for days.

The second fiasco cost Blaine much of the Irish vote when a delegation of Protestant ministers visited Republican headquarters in New York, and one of them referred to the Democrats as the party of "rum, Romanism, and rebellion." The judgment had a certain validity, but the tone was insolent. Blaine, who was present, let pass the implied insult to Catholics—a fatal oversight, since he had always cultivated

Irish-American support with his anti-British talk and public reminders that his mother was Catholic. Democrats spread word that Blaine was at heart anti-Irish and anti-Catholic.

The incident may have tipped the election. The electoral vote in Cleveland's favor stood at 219 to 182, but the popular vote ran far closer: Cleveland's plurality was fewer than 30,000 votes.

CLEVELAND AND THE SPECIAL INTERESTS   For all of Cleveland's hostility to the spoils system and politics as usual, he represented no sharp break with the conservative policies of his predecessors, except in opposing governmental favors to business. "A public office is a public trust" was one of his favorite mottoes. He held to a strictly limited view of government's role in both economic and social matters, a rigid philosophy illustrated by his 1887 veto of the Texas Seed Bill, an effort to appropriate funds to meet the urgent need of drought victims for seed grain. Back to Congress it went with a lecture on the need to limit the powers and functions of government—"though the people support the government the government should not support the people," Cleveland asserted.

Despite his strong philosophical convictions, Cleveland had a mixed record on the civil service. He had good intentions, but he also led a party hungry for partisan appointments, with the first Democratic president since the election of James Buchanan in 1856. Before his inauguration Cleveland repeated his support for the Pendleton Act; he would not remove able government workers simply on partisan grounds. But he inserted one significant exception: those who had used federal jobs to forward the interests of the opposition party. In many cases, especially in the post offices, he thus had ample excuse to remove people who had practically made their offices into Republican headquarters.

Party pressures gradually forced Cleveland's hand. When he left office about two-thirds of the federal officeholders were Democrats, including all internal revenue collectors and nearly all the heads of customs houses. At the same time, however, Cleveland had extended the number of federal jobs subject to civil service regulation to about 27,000 employees, almost double the number that had been covered when he came in. Yet he satisfied neither Mugwumps nor spoilsmen; indeed, he managed to antagonize both.

On other matters Cleveland's stubborn courage and concern for protecting the public Treasury led him into conflicts with predatory interests, conflicts that eventually cost him the White House. One such dispute arose over misuse of government-owned land in the West. Cleveland's secretary of the interior and the commissioner of the General Land Office uncovered one case after another of fraud and mismanagement: bogus surveys by government surveyors; public lands used fraudulently by lumber companies, mine operators, and cattle ranchers with the collusion of government officials; and at least 30 million acres of land grants given to railroads that never built the required lines.

The administration sued railroads to recover such lands. It also nullified exploitive leases of Indian lands. Cattle barons were ordered to remove fences enclosing water holes and grasslands on the open range. In all, during Cleveland's first term about 81 million acres of public lands were restored to the federal government.

Cleveland incurred the wrath of Union military veterans by his firm stand against their pension raids on the Treasury. Congress had passed the first Civil War pension law in 1862 to provide for Union veterans disabled in service and for the widows, orphans, and dependents of veterans. By 1882 the Grand Army of the Republic, an organization of Union veterans and a powerful pressure group, was trying to get pensions paid for any disability, even if unrelated to military service. Meanwhile many veterans succeeded in pushing private pension bills through an obliging Congress. In Washington, lawyers built careers on filing claims and pressing for special laws to benefit veterans.

Insofar as time permitted, Cleveland examined such bills critically and vetoed the dubious ones. Although he signed more than any of his predecessors, running pension costs up from $56 million to $80 million, he also vetoed more. A climax came in 1887 when Congress passed the Dependent Pension Bill, which provided funds for veterans dependent upon manual labor and unable to work for any reason, whether or not the reason was connected to military service. Cleveland sent it back with a ringing veto, declaring that the pension list would become a refuge for frauds rather than a "roll of honor."

About the middle of his term Cleveland assaulted new special interests, leading to the adoption of an important new policy, railroad regulation. Since the late 1860s, states had adopted railroad regulatory laws, and from the early 1870s, Congress had debated federal legislation. In

1886 a Supreme Court decision finally spurred action. In the case of *Wabash Railroad* v. *Illinois*, the Court denied the state's power to regulate rates on interstate traffic. Cleveland thereupon urged that since this "important field of control and regulation [has] thus been left entirely unoccupied," Congress should act.

It did, and in 1887 Cleveland signed into law an act creating the Interstate Commerce Commission (ICC), the first such independent regulatory commission. The law empowered the five ICC members to investigate railroads and prosecute violators. All freight rates had to be "reasonable and just." Railroads were forbidden to grant secret rebates to preferred shippers, discriminate against persons, places, and commodities, or enter into pools (secret agreements among competing railroads to fix rates). The commission's actual powers, however, proved to be weak when first tested in the courts. Though creating the ICC seemed to conflict with Cleveland's fear of big government, it accorded with his fear of big business. The Interstate Commerce Act, to his mind, was a legitimate exercise of sovereign power.

THE TARIFF ISSUE   Cleveland's most dramatic challenge to special interests focused on tariff reform. Why was the tariff such an important and controversial issue? By the late nineteenth century, Republicans and business leaders had come to assume that American prosperity and high tariffs were tightly linked. Others disagreed. Many observers had concluded that the formation of huge corporate "trusts" was not a natural development of a maturing capitalist system. Instead, they charged that government policies had fostered big business at the expense of small producers and retailers. Among those policies favoring corporate interests was a tariff so high that it effectively shut out foreign imports, thereby enabling corporations to dominate their markets. "The mother of all trusts is the tariff bill," proclaimed one

Grover Cleveland made the issue of tariff reform central to the politics of the late 1880s.

leading business executive. By shielding American manufacturers from foreign competition, the tariff, critics argued, made it easier for them to combine into ever-larger entities. The high tariff also enabled large corporations to restrict production and fix prices. "The heart of the trust problem is in our tariff system of plunder," declared the head of the New England Free Trade League. "The quickest and most certain way of reaching the evils of trusts is not by direct legislation against them, or by constitutional amendment, but by the abolition of tariff duties."

Cleveland agreed. He concluded that the tariff rates were too high and included many inequities. Near the end of 1887 Cleveland devoted his entire annual message to the subject. He did so in the full knowledge that he was focusing attention on a political minefield on the eve of an election year, against the warnings of his advisers. "What is the use of being elected if you don't stand for something?" he asked.

Cleveland's message noted that tariff revenues had bolstered the surplus, making the Treasury "a hoarding place for money needlessly withdrawn from trade and the people's use." The tariff pushed up prices for everybody, and while it was supposed to protect American workers against the competition of cheap foreign labor, the most recent census showed that of 17.4 million Americans gainfully employed, only 2.6 million were in "such manufacturing industries as are claimed to be benefitted by a high tariff."

It was evident, moreover, that competition in every industry produced better prices for buyers. Business combinations could push prices up to the artificial level set by the prices of dutied foreign goods, but prices often fell below that level when domestic producers were in competition, "proof that someone is willing to accept lower prices for such commodity and that such prices are remunerative." Congress, Cleveland argued, should reduce the tariff rates. Blaine and other Republicans denounced Cleveland's message as pure "free trade," a doctrine all the more suspect because it was also British policy. If Cleveland's talk accomplished his purpose of drawing party lines more firmly, it also confirmed the fears of his advisers. The election of 1888 for the first time in years highlighted a difference between the major parties on an issue of substance.

Cleveland was the obvious nominee of his party. The Republicans turned to the obscure Benjamin Harrison, who had all the attributes of availability. The grandson of President William Henry Harrison, and a flourishing lawyer in Indiana, the diminutive Harrison resided in a pivotal state and also had a good war record. There was little in his political record to offend any voter. He had lost a race for governor and served one term in the Senate (1881–1887). The Republican platform accepted Cleveland's challenge to make the protective tariff the chief issue, and promised generous pensions to veterans.

As insurance against tariff reduction, manufacturers gave generously to the Republican campaign fund, which was used to denounce Cleveland's un-American "free trade" and his pension vetoes. Personal attacks too were leveled against Cleveland. On the eve of the election Cleveland suffered a more devastating blow from the phony "Murchison letter." A California Republican had written British minister Sir Lionel Sackville-West using the false name "Charles F. Murchison." Posing as an English immigrant, he asked advice on how to vote. Sackville-West, engaged at the time in sensitive negotiations over British and American access to Canadian fisheries, hinted that he should vote for Cleveland. The letter aroused a storm of protest against foreign intervention and further linked Cleveland to British free-traders. Democratic explanations never caught up with the public's original sense of outrage.

Still, the outcome was close. Cleveland won the popular vote by 5,538,000 to 5,447,000, but that was poor comfort. The distribution of votes was such that Harrison, with the key states of Indiana and New York on his side by virtue of the sordid, but common practice of paying voters, carried the electoral college by 233 to 168. When his campaign manager reported the election returns, Harrison exclaimed fervently: "Providence has given us the victory." The cynical adviser later remarked that Harrison "ought to know that Providence hadn't a damn thing to do with it" and opined that the president "would never know how close a number of men were compelled to approach a penitentiary to make him president."

REPUBLICAN REFORM UNDER HARRISON   As president, Benjamin Harrison became a competent and earnest figurehead, overshadowed by his secretary of state, James G. Blaine. Harrison had aroused the hopes of civil service reformers when he declared that "fitness and not party service should be the essential and discriminating test" for government employment. Nevertheless he appointed a wealthy Philadelphia merchant as his postmaster-general, allegedly as a reward for a

generous contribution. The first assistant postmaster-general announced
less than a year later: "I have changed
31,000 out of 55,000 fourth-class
postmasters and I expect to change
10,000 more before I finally quit."
Harrison made a few feckless efforts
to resist partisan pressures, but the
party leaders had their way. His most
significant gesture at reform was to
name young Theodore Roosevelt to
the Civil Service Commission.

BILLION- DOLLARISM) HOLE

In an attack on Benjamin Harrison's
spending policies, this cartoon shows
Harrison pouring Cleveland's huge
surplus down a hole.

Harrison owed a heavy debt to
Union Civil War veterans, which he
discharged by naming an officer of
the Grand Army of the Republic to
the position of pension commis-
sioner. "God help the surplus," the new commissioner reportedly exclaimed. He proceeded to approve pensions for veterans with such
abandon that the secretary of the interior removed him six months and
several million dollars later. In 1890 Congress passed, and Harrison
signed, the Dependent Pension Act, substantially the same measure
that Cleveland had vetoed. The pension rolls almost doubled between
1889 and 1893.

During the first two years of Harrison's term, the Republicans controlled the presidency and both houses for only the second time in the
twenty years between 1875 and 1895. They were positioned to have
pretty much their own way, and they made the year 1890 memorable for
some of the most significant legislation enacted in the entire period. In
addition to the Dependent Pension Act, Congress and the president approved the Sherman Anti-Trust Act, the Sherman Silver Purchase Act,
the McKinley Tariff, and the admission of Idaho and Wyoming as new
states, which followed the admission of the Dakotas, Montana, and
Washington in 1889.

Both parties had pledged themselves to do something about the
growing power of trusts and monopolies. The Sherman Anti-Trust Act,
named for Ohio senator John Sherman, chairman of the Senate Judiciary Committee that drafted it, sought to incorporate into federal law a

long-standing principle against activities in "restraint of trade." It forbade contracts, combinations, or conspiracies in restraint of trade or in the effort to establish monopolies in interstate or foreign commerce. A broad consensus put the vague law through, but its passage turned out to be largely symbolic. During the next decade successive administrations rarely enforced the new law in part because of the ambiguity about what exactly constituted "restraint of trade." From 1890 to 1901 only eighteen lawsuits were instituted, and four of those were against labor unions.

Congress meanwhile debated currency legislation against the backdrop of growing economic distress in the farm regions of the West and South. Hard-pressed farmers were agitating for an increased coinage of silver to inflate the currency, which would raise commodity prices, making it easier for farmers to earn the money with which to pay their debts.

The silverite forces were also strengthened, especially in the Senate, by members from the new western states that had silver-mining interests. Congress passed the new Sherman Silver Purchase Act in 1890, replacing the Bland-Allison Act of 1878. It required the Treasury to purchase 4.5 million ounces of silver each month and to issue in payment Treasury notes redeemable in either gold or silver. But the act failed to satisfy the demands of the silverites, in part because most people opted to redeem their silver certificates in gold. Although the amount of silver purchased doubled, it was still too little to have an inflationary impact on the economy. Eastern business and financial groups, on the other hand, saw a threat to the gold reserve in the growth of paper currency that holders could redeem in gold at the Treasury. The stage was set for the currency issue to eclipse all others in a panic that would sweep the country three years later.

Republicans viewed their victory over Cleveland as a mandate not just to maintain the protective tariff but to raise it. Piloted through by William McKinley, House Ways and Means chairman, and Senator Nelson W. Aldrich, the McKinley Tariff of 1890 raised duties on manufactured goods to an average of about 50 percent, the highest to that time. And it included three new departures. First, the protectionists reached out for farmers' votes with high duties on agricultural products. Second, they sought to lessen the tariff's impact on consumers by putting sugar, a universal necessity, on the duty-free list—thus reducing its cost—and then compensating Louisiana and Kansas sugar growers with a bounty of 2¢ a pound out of the federal Treasury. And third, they included a reciprocity section, which empowered the president to hike duties on sugar, molasses, tea, coffee, and hides to pressure countries exporting those items into reducing unreasonably high duties on American goods.

The absence of a public consensus for higher tariffs became clearly visible in the 1890 midterm elections. The voters repudiated the McKinley Tariff with a landslide of Democratic votes. In the new House, Democrats outnumbered Republicans by almost three to one; in the Senate, the Republican majority was reduced to eight.

One of the election casualties was McKinley himself, the victim of tricks the Democrats used to reinforce the widespread revulsion against the increased tariff duties. But there was more to the election than the tariff. Voters also reacted against the baldly partisan measures of the Harrison administration and its extravagant expenditures on military pensions and other programs. With expenditures rising and revenues dropping, largely because the McKinley tariff was so high as to discourage imports, the nation's Treasury surplus was rapidly shrinking.

The large Democratic vote in 1890 may have also been a reaction to Republican efforts to legislate against alcohol. Between 1880 and 1890, sixteen out of twenty-one states outside the South held referenda on constitutional prohibition of alcoholic beverages. Only six states voted for prohibition, however. Teetotaling Republicans were playing a losing game, arousing wets (anti-Prohibitionists) on the Democratic side. Another issue that served to mobilize Democratic resistance was the Republican attempt to eliminate funding for state-supported Catholic schools. In 1889 Wisconsin Republicans pushed through a law that held that a school could be accredited only if it taught the basic subjects in English. That was the last straw: it turned large numbers of outraged immigrants into Democratic activists. In 1889 and 1890 the Democrats swept state after state.

THE FARM PROBLEM AND AGRARIAN PROTEST MOVEMENTS

The 1890 election reflected more than a reaction against the Republican tariff, patronage politics, extravagant spending, and moralizing. The Democratic victory revealed a deep-seated unrest in the farming communities of the South and West. As the Democrats took power, the beginnings of an economic crisis appeared on the horizon. Farmers' debts mounted as crop prices plummeted.

Frustrated by the unwillingness of Congress to meet their demands and ease their plight, disgruntled farmers began to organize for political action. Like so many of their counterparts laboring in urban factories, they realized that social change required demonstrations of power, and power lay in numbers. But unlike labor unions, farm organizations faced a more complex array of economic variables affecting their livelihood. They had to deal with more than just management; bankers, processors, railroad and grain elevator operators, as well as the world commodities market, all affected the agricultural sector. So too did the unpredictable forces of nature: droughts, blizzards, insects, and erosion.

There were also many important obstacles to collective action by farmers. The farmers' rugged individualism and physical isolation made communication and organization especially difficult. American farmers had long prided themselves on their self-reliant hardihood, and many balked at sacrificing their independence. Another hurdle was the fact that after the Civil War agricultural interests had diverged and in some cases conflicted with one another. In the Great Plains, for example, the railroads were the largest landowners. In addition, there were large absentee landowners, some foreign, who leased out vast tracts of land. There were also huge "bonanza" farms that employed hundreds of seasonal workers. Yet the majority of farmers were simple rural folk in the South and West who were moderate-size landowners, small land speculators, small landowners, tenant farmers, and hourly wage workers. It was the middle-size landowners who experienced rapidly rising land values and rising indebtedness. Such farmers were concerned with land values and crop prices, while tenants, sharecroppers, and farm hands supported land distribution schemes that would give them access to their own land.

Given such a diversity of interests, farm activists discovered that it was often difficult to develop and maintain a cohesive organization. Yet, for all the difficulties, they persevered, and the results were dramatic, if not completely successful. Thus, for example, the deep-seated unrest in the farming communities of the South and West began to find voice in the Granger movement, the Alliance movement, and in the new

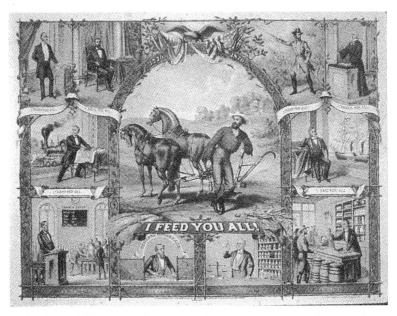

"I Feed You All," a poster showing the farmer at the center of society, first published in Prairie Farmer *in 1869.*

People's party, agrarian movements of considerable political and social significance.

ECONOMIC CONDITIONS   For some time, farmers in the South and Midwest had been subject to worsening economic and social conditions. The source of their problems was a long-term decline in commodity prices from 1870 to 1898, the product of domestic overproduction and growing international competition for world markets. The vast new lands brought under cultivation in the West poured an ever-increasing supply of farm products into the market, driving down prices. This effect was reinforced as innovations in transportation and communications brought American farmers ever more into international competition, further increasing the supply of farm commodities. Considerations of abstract economic forces, however, puzzled many farmers. How could one speak of overproduction when so many remained in need? Instead, they reasoned, there must be a screw loose somewhere in the system.

The railroads and the processors who handled the farmers' products were seen as the prime villains. Farmers resented the high railroad rates that prevailed in farm regions with no alternative forms of transportation.

Individual farmers could not get the rebates on freight charges that the big corporations could extract from railroads, and they could not exert the political influence wielded by the railroad lobbies. In other ways farmers found themselves with little bargaining power as either buyers or sellers. When they tried to sell wheat or cotton, the buyer set the price; when they went to buy a plow point, the seller set the price.

High tariffs operated to farmers' disadvantage because they protected manufacturers against foreign competition, allowing them to raise the prices of factory goods on which farmers depended. Farmers, however, had to sell their wheat, cotton, and other staples in foreign markets, where competition lowered prices. Tariffs inflicted a double blow on farmers because insofar as they hampered imports, they indirectly hampered exports by making it harder for foreign buyers to get the necessary American currency or exchange to purchase American crops.

Debt, too, had been a perennial problem of agriculture. After the Civil War, farmers became ever more enmeshed in debt—western farmers incurred mortgages to cover the costs of land and machinery, while southern farmers used crop liens. As commodity prices dropped, the burden of debt grew because farmers had to cultivate more wheat or cotton to raise the same amount of money; and by growing more they furthered the vicious cycle of surpluses and price declines.

THE GRANGER MOVEMENT   When the Department of Agriculture sent Oliver H. Kelley on a tour of the postbellum South in 1866, it was the isolation of farm folk that most impressed him. Resolving to do something about it, Kelley and some government clerks in 1867 founded the Patrons of Husbandry, better known as the Grange (an old word for granary), as each chapter was called. In the next few years the Grange mushroomed, reaching a membership as high as 1.5 million by 1874. The Grange started as a social and educational response to the farmers' isolation, but as it grew it began to promote farmer-owned cooperatives for the buying and selling of crops. Their ideal was to free themselves from the conventional marketplace.

The Grange soon became indirectly involved in politics through independent third parties, especially in the Midwest during the early 1870s. The Grangers' chief political goal was to regulate the rates charged by railroads and warehouses. In five states they brought about the passage of "Granger Laws," which at first proved relatively ineffective, but laid a foundation for stronger legislation to follow. Owners subject to their regulation challenged these laws in cases that soon advanced to the Supreme Court, where the plaintiffs in the "Granger Cases" claimed to have been deprived of property without due process of law. In a key case involving warehouse regulation, *Munn* v. *Illinois* (1877), the Supreme Court ruled that the state under its "police powers" had the right to regulate property in the interest of the public good where that property was clothed with a public interest. If regulatory power were abused, the ruling said, "the people must resort to the polls, not the courts." Later, however, the courts would severely restrict state regulatory powers.

The Granger movement gradually declined (but never vanished) as members' energies were drawn off into cooperatives, many of which failed, and into political action. Out of the independent political movements of the time there grew in 1875 a party calling itself the Independent National party, more commonly known as the Greenback party because of its emphasis on the virtues of paper money. In the 1878 midterm elections it polled over 1 million votes and elected fifteen congressmen. But in 1880 the party's fortunes declined, and it disintegrated after 1884.

FARMERS' ALLIANCES   As the Grange lost energy, other farm organizations known as the Farmers' Alliances grew in size and significance. Like the Grange, the Farmers' Alliances offered social and recreational opportunities, but they also emphasized political action. Farmers throughout the South and Midwest, where tenancy rates were highest, rushed to join the Alliance movement. They saw in collective action a way to seek relief from the hardships created by chronic indebtedness, declining prices, and devastating droughts. Unlike the Grange, which was a national organization that tended to attract larger and more prosperous farmers, the Alliance was a grassroots local organization representing marginal farmers.

The Alliance movement swept across the cotton belt and established strong positions in Kansas and the Dakotas. In 1886, a white minister in Texas, which had one of the largest and most influential Alliance movements, responded to the appeals of black farmers and organized the Colored Alliance. The white leadership of the Alliance movement in Texas endorsed this development because the Colored Alliance stressed

Members of the Texas Alliance, 1870s. Alliance groups united local farmers, fostered a sense of community, and influenced political policies.

that its objective was economic justice, not social equality. By 1890, the Alliance movement had members from New York to California numbering about 1.5 million, and the Colored Farmers' Alliance claimed over 1 million members.

A powerful attraction for many isolated, struggling farmers and their families was the sense of community provided by the Alliance. An Alliance gathering resembled what one observer described as "a religious revival . . . a pentecost . . . in which the tongue of flame sat upon every man, and each spake as the spirit gave him utterance." The Alliance movement welcomed rural women and men over sixteen years old who displayed a "good moral character," believed in God, and demonstrated "industrious habits." The slogan of the Southern Alliance was "Equal rights to all, special privileges to none." Women eagerly embraced such equal opportunities to engage economic and political issues. One North Carolina woman expressed her appreciation for the "grand opportunities" the Alliance provided women to emerge from traditional domesticity. "Drudgery, fashion, and gossip," she declared, "are no longer the bounds of woman's sphere." One of the Alliance publications made the point explicitly: "The Alliance has come to redeem woman from her enslaved condition, and place her in her proper sphere." The number of women in the Alliance movement grew rapidly, and many assumed key leadership roles in the "grand army of reform."

The Alliance movement sponsored an ambitious social and educational program, and about 1,000 affiliated newspapers. But unlike the Grange, the Alliance also proposed from the start an elaborate economic program. In 1890 Alliance agencies and exchanges in some eighteen states claimed a business of $10 million, but they soon went the way of the Granger cooperatives, victims of discrimination by wholesalers, manufacturers, railroads, and bankers, and also of their own inexperienced management and overextended credit.

The Alliance movement also was ready to enter the political fray to help farmers. In Texas, for example, in 1886 a devastating drought brought matters to a head. When President Grover Cleveland vetoed a bill to aid Texas farmers, Alliance leaders resolved to challenge the Democratic party at the polls. Although some members whose primary allegiance was to the Democratic party left the movement, most remained to carry out the fight both locally and nationally.

In 1887 Charles W. Macune, the new Alliance president, proposed that Texas farmers create their own Alliance Exchange in an effort to free themselves from their dependence on processors and banks. Members of the Exchange would sign joint notes, borrow money from banks, and purchase their goods and supplies from a new corporation created by the Alliance in Dallas. The Exchange would also build its own warehouses to store and market the crops of members. While their crops were being stored, member farmers could obtain credit from the warehouse cooperative so they could buy household goods and supplies.

This grand "cooperative" scheme collapsed when the Texas banks refused to accept the joint notes from Alliance members. Macune and others then focused their energies on what Macune called a "subtreasury plan." Under this plan, farmers would be able to store their crops in new government warehouses and obtain government loans for up to 80 percent of their crops' value at 1 percent interest. Besides providing immediate credit, the plan would allow the farmer the leeway to hold a crop for a better price later, since he would not have to sell it at harvest time to pay off debts. The plan would also promote inflation because these loans to farmers would be made in new legal-tender notes.

The subtreasury plan went before Congress in 1890 but was never adopted. Its defeat as well as setbacks to other proposals convinced many farm leaders that they needed more political power to secure railroad regulation, currency inflation, state departments of agriculture, antitrust laws, and farm credit.

FARM POLITICS   In the West, where hard times had descended after the blizzards of 1887, farmers were ready for third-party action. In the South, however, white Alliance members hesitated to bolt the Democratic party, seeking instead to influence or control it. Both approaches gained startling success. Independent parties under various names upset the political balance in western states, almost electing a governor under the banner of the People's party (also known as the Populist party) in Kansas (a Populist was elected governor in 1892) and taking control of one house of the legislature there and both houses in Nebraska. In South Dakota and Minnesota, Populists gained a balance of power in the legislatures, while Kansas sent a Populist to the Senate.

The farm protest movement produced colorful leaders, especially in Kansas, where Mary Elizabeth Lease advised farmers "to raise less corn and more hell." Born in Pennsylvania to parents who were political exiles from Ireland, she grew up within a family devastated by the Civil War. Her two brothers were killed in battle, and her father died in Georgia's notorious Andersonville Prison. Afterward Lease migrated to Kansas, taught school, raised a family, and finally failed at farming in the mid-1880s. She then studied law, "pinning sheets of notes above her wash tub," and through strenuous effort became one of the state's first female lawyers. At the same time, she took up public speaking on behalf of various causes ranging from Irish nationalism to temperance to women's suffrage. By the end of the 1880s, Lease had joined the Alliance as well as the Knights of Labor, and she soon applied her

Mary Elizabeth Lease, 1890.

gifts as a fiery speaker to the cause of free silver. A tall, proud, and imposing woman, Lease drew attentive audiences. "The people are at bay," she warned in 1894, "let the bloodhounds of money beware."

"Sockless Jerry" Simpson was an equally charismatic agrarian radical. Born in Canada, he had served as a seaman on Great Lakes steamships before buying a farm in northern Kansas. He, his wife, and young daughter made a go of the farm, but when he saw his child crushed to death in a sawmill accident, he and his wife relocated to the southern part of the state. There he raised cattle for several years before losing his herd in a blizzard.

Simpson embraced the Alliance movement, and in 1890 he campaigned for Congress. A shrewd man with huge, callused hands and pale blue eyes, he simplified the complex economic and political issues of the day. "Man must have access to the land," he maintained, "or he is a slave." He warned Republicans: "You can't put this movement down by sneers or by ridicule, for its foundation was laid as far back as the foundation of the world. It is a struggle between the robbers and the robbed." Simpson dismissed his Republican opponent, a wealthy railroad lawyer, as an indulgent pawn of the corporations whose "soft white hands" and "silk hosiery" betrayed his true priorities. His outraged opponent thereupon shouted that it was better to have silk socks than none at all, providing Simpson with his folksy nickname. "Sockless Jerry" won a seat in Congress, and so too did many other friends of "the people" in the Midwest.

In the South, the Alliance won equal if not greater success by forcing the Democrats to nominate candidates pledged to their program. The southern states elected four pro-Alliance governors, seven pro-Alliance legislatures, forty-four pro-Alliance congressmen, and several senators. Among the most respected of the southern Alliance leaders was Tom Watson of Georgia. The son of prosperous slaveholders who lost everything after the Civil War, he became a successful lawyer and orator on behalf of the Alliance cause. Watson took the lead in appealing to black tenant farmers and sharecroppers to join with their white counterparts in ousting the white political elite. "You are kept apart," he told black and white farmers, "that you may be separately fleeced of your earnings."

THE POPULIST PARTY AND THE ELECTION OF 1892 The success of the Alliances led many to consider the formation of a third political party on the national level. In 1891 a conference in Cincinnati brought together delegates from farm, labor, and reform organizations to discuss strategy. The meeting endorsed a national third party and formed a national executive committee of the People's party. Few southerners were at the Cincinnati conference, but many approved of the third-party idea after their failure to move the Democratic party toward the subtreasury plan. In 1892 a larger meeting in St. Louis called for a national convention of the People's party at Omaha to adopt a platform and choose candidates.

The platform focused on issues of finance, transportation, and land. Its financial program demanded implementation of the subtreasury plan, free and unlimited coinage of silver at the 16 to 1 ratio, an increase in the amount of money in circulation to $50 per capita, a graduated income tax, and postal savings banks to protect depositors who otherwise risked disastrous losses in small-town banks vulnerable to farm depression. As to transportation, the time had come "when the railroad corporations will either own the people or the people must own the railroads." Let government therefore nationalize the railroads, and the telephone and telegraph systems as well. The Populists called for the government to reclaim from railroads and other corporations lands "in excess of their actual needs," and to forbid land ownership by immigrants who had not yet gained citizenship. Finally, the platform endorsed the eight-hour workday and restriction of immigration. The party took these last positions to win

A Populist gathering in Callaway, Nebraska, 1892.

support from the urban workers, whom Populists looked upon as fellow "producers."

The party's platform turned out to be more exciting than its candidate. Iowa's James B. Weaver, an able, prudent man, carried the stigma of his defeat on the Greenback ticket twelve years before. To balance Weaver, who had been a Union general, the party named a former Confederate general for vice-president.

The Populist party was the startling new feature of the 1892 campaign. The major parties renominated the candidates of 1888, Democrat Grover Cleveland and Republican Benjamin Harrison. The tariff issue monopolized their attention. Both major candidates polled over 5 million votes, but Cleveland carried a plurality of the popular votes and a majority of the electoral college. Weaver polled over 1 million votes, and carried Colorado, Kansas, Nevada, and Idaho, for a total of twenty-two electoral votes. Alabama was the banner Populist state of the South, with 37 percent of its vote for Weaver.

THE ECONOMY AND THE SILVER SOLUTION

While the farmers were funneling their discontent into politics and businessmen were consolidating their holdings, a fundamental weakness in the economy would soon cause a major economic collapse.

AN INADEQUATE CURRENCY   The nation's money supply in the late nineteenth century lacked the flexibility to grow along with America's expanding economy. From 1865 to 1890, the amount of currency in circulation per capita decreased about 10 percent. Currency deflation then contributed to the cost of borrowing money, as a tight money supply caused bankers to hike interest rates on loans.

Metallic currency dated from the Mint Act of 1792, which authorized free and unlimited coinage of silver and gold at a ratio of 15 to 1. The ratio meant that the amount of precious metal in a silver dollar weighed fifteen times as much as that in a gold dollar. This reflected the relative values of gold and silver at the time. The phrase "free and unlimited coinage" simply meant that owners of precious metals could have any quantity of their gold or silver coined free, except for a nominal fee to cover costs.

A fixed ratio of values, however, could not reflect fluctuations in the market value of the metals. When gold rose to a market value higher than that reflected in the official ratio, owners ceased to present it for coinage. The country was actually on a silver standard until 1837, when Congress changed the ratio to 16 to 1, which soon reversed the situation. Silver became more valuable in the open market than in coinage, and the country drifted to a gold standard. This state of affairs prevailed until 1873, when Congress passed a general revision of the coinage laws and dropped the then-unused provision for the coinage of silver.

This occurred, however, just when silver production began to increase, reducing its market value through the growth in supply. Under the old laws, this would have induced owners of silver to present it at the mint for coinage. Soon advocates of currency inflation began to denounce the "crime of '73," which they had scarcely noticed at the time. Gradually suspicion grew that bankers and merchants had conspired in 1873 to ensure a scarcity of money. But the pro-silver forces had little more legislative success than the advocates of greenback inflation. The Bland-Allison Act of 1878 and the Sherman Silver Purchase Act of 1890 provided for some silver coinage, but too little in each case to offset the overall contraction of the currency.

THE DEPRESSION OF 1893   Just before Grover Cleveland started his second term, one of the most devastating business crises in history erupted when the Philadelphia and Reading Railroad declared bankruptcy and set off a panic on Wall Street. Not only business was affected, but also entire farm regions were devastated by the spreading depression. One-quarter of the cities' unskilled workers lost their jobs, and by the fall of 1893 over six hundred banks had closed. By 1894 the economy had reached bottom. That year some 750,000 workers went on strike; millions found themselves unemployed; and railroad construction workers, laid off in the West, began tramping east and talked of marching on Washington, D.C.

Few of them made it to the capital. One protest group that did reach Washington was "Coxey's Army," led by Jacob S. Coxey, a wealthy Ohio quarry owner turned Populist who demanded that the federal government provide unemployed people with meaningful work. Coxey, his wife, and their son, Legal Tender Coxey, rode in a carriage ahead of some 400 hardy protesters who finally straggled into Washington. There

Coxey was arrested for walking on the grass. Although his ragtag army dispersed without any violent incidents, its march on Washington as well as the growing political strength of populism struck fear into the hearts of many Americans. Critics portrayed Populists as "hayseed socialists" whose election would endanger property rights.

The 1894 congressional elections took place amid this climate of anxiety. The elections amounted to a severe setback for the Democrats, who paid politically for the economic downturn, and the Republicans were the chief beneficiaries. The Populists emerged with six senators and seven representatives. They had polled 1.5 million votes for their congressional candidates and still expected the festering discontent to carry them to national power in 1896.

SILVERITES VS. GOLDBUGS   The course of events, however, would dash that hope. In the mid-1890s events conspired to focus all concerns on the currency issue. One of the causes of the 1893 depression had been the failure of a major British bank, which led many British investors to unload their American holdings in return for gold. Soon after Grover Cleveland's inauguration, the gold reserve fell below $100 million. To plug this drain on the Treasury, the president sought repeal of the Sherman Silver Purchase Act to stop the issuance of silver notes redeemable in gold. Cleveland won the act's repeal in 1893, but at the cost of irreparable division in his own party. One embittered pro-silver Democrat labeled the president a "Benedict Arnold."

Western silver interests now escalated their demands for silver coinage, which presented a strategic dilemma for Populists: Should the party promote the long list of varied reforms it had originally advocated, or should it try to ride the silver issue into power? The latter seemed the practical choice. As a consequence, the Populist leaders decided, over the protest of more radical members, to hold their 1896 nominating convention last, confident that the two major parties would at best straddle the silver issue and that the Populists would then reap a harvest of bolting silverite Republicans and Democrats.

THE ELECTION OF 1896   Contrary to these expectations, the major parties took opposite positions on the currency issues. The Republicans, as expected, chose William McKinley on a gold-standard platform.

McKinley, a former congressman and governor of Ohio, symbolized the mainstream Republican values that had served the party well.

On the Democratic side, the pro-silver forces captured the convention for their platform. William Jennings Bryan arranged to give the closing speech for the silver plank. A fervent Baptist moralist, Bryan was a two-term congressman from Nebraska who had been swept out in the Democratic losses of 1894; he had distinguished himself mainly with an exhausting three-hour speech against repeal of the Sherman Silver Purchase Act. In the months

William Jennings Bryan, whose "Cross of Gold" speech at the 1896 Democratic convention roused the delegates and secured him the party's presidential nomination.

before the convention he had traveled throughout the South and West, speaking for free silver and against Cleveland's "do-nothing" response to the depression. Bryan's rehearsed phrases swept the convention into a frenzy:

> I come to speak to you in defense of a cause as holy as the cause of liberty—the cause of humanity. . . . We have petitioned, and our petitions have been scorned. We have entreated, and our entreaties have been disregarded. We have begged, and they have mocked when our calamity came. We beg no longer; we entreat no more; we petition no more. We defy them!

By the time Bryan reached his free-silver conclusion, there was little doubt that he would get the nomination: "You shall not press down upon the brow of labor this crown of thorns. You shall not crucify mankind upon a cross of gold!"

The next day Bryan won the nomination on the fifth ballot, and in the process the Democratic party was fractured beyond repair. Disappointed pro-gold, pro-Cleveland Democrats walked out of the convention and nominated their own candidate, Senator John M. Palmer of Illinois.

"Fellow Democrats," he announced, "I will not consider it any great fault if you decide to cast your vote for [Republican] William McKinley."

When the Populists met in St. Louis two weeks later, they faced an impossible choice. They could name their own candidate and divide the silver vote, or they could endorse Bryan and probably lose their identity. In the end they backed Bryan, but chose their own vice-presidential candidate, former representative Thomas E. Watson of Georgia, and invited the Democrats to drop their vice-presidential nominee—an action that Bryan refused to countenance.

The thirty-six-year-old Bryan launched a whirlwind campaign. He crisscrossed the country, exploiting his spellbinding eloquence on behalf of "the struggling masses" of workers, farmers, and small-business owners. McKinley, meanwhile, conducted a "front-porch campaign," receiving selected delegations of supporters at his home in Canton, Ohio, and giving only prepared responses. McKinley's campaign manager, Mark Hanna, shrewdly portrayed Bryan as a radical whose "communistic spirit" would ruin the capitalist system. Many observers agreed with the portrait. The *New York Tribune* denounced Bryan as a "wretched rattle-pated boy, posing in vapid vanity and mouthing resounding rottenness." Theodore Roosevelt had equally strong opinions. "The silver craze surpasses belief," he wrote a friend. "Bryan's election would be a great calamity."

By preying upon such fears, the McKinley campaign raised vast sums of money to finance an army of Republican speakers who traveled the country in support of McKinley. In the end the Democratic-Populist-Silverite candidates were overwhelmed by the well-organized and well-financed Republican campaign. McKinley won the popular vote by 7.1 million to 6.5 million and the electoral college vote by 271 to 176.

Bryan carried most of the West and the South, but found little support in the metropolitan centers east of the Mississippi and north of the Ohio and Potomac Rivers. In the critical midwestern battleground, from Minnesota and Iowa eastward to Ohio, Bryan carried not a single state. Many Catholic voters, normally drawn to the Democrats, were no doubt repelled by Bryan's Baptist evangelical style. Farmers in the Northeast, moreover, were less attracted to agrarian radicalism than were farmers in the wheat and cotton belts, where there were higher rates of tenancy and a narrower range of crops. Among factory workers in the cities, Bryan found even less support. They found it easier to

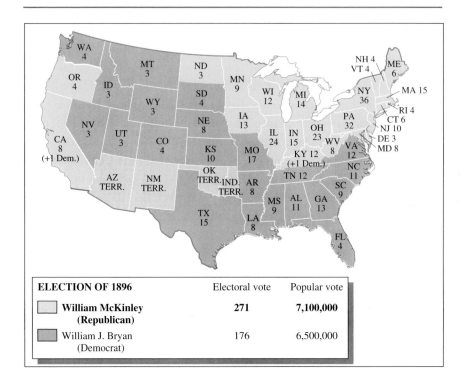

ELECTION OF 1896	Electoral vote	Popular vote
William McKinley (Republican)	271	7,100,000
William J. Bryan (Democrat)	176	6,500,000

identify with McKinley's "full dinner pail" than with Bryan's free silver panacea. Some workers may have been intimidated by business owners' threats to close shop if the "Demopop" heresies triumphed.

A NEW ERA The election of 1896 had been a climactic political struggle. Urban-industrial values had indeed taken firm hold of the political system. The first important act of the McKinley administration was to call a special session of Congress to raise the tariff again. The Dingley Tariff of 1897 became the highest to that time.

By 1897 economic prosperity was returning, helped along by inflation of the currency, which bore out the arguments of greenbackers and silverites. But the inflation came, in one of history's many ironies, from neither greenbacks nor silver, but from a new flood of gold into the market and into the mints. During the 1880s and 1890s, discoveries of gold in South Africa, in the Canadian Yukon, and in Alaska led to spectacular new gold rushes. In 1900, Congress passed a Gold Standard Act, which marked an end to the silver movement.

At the close of the nineteenth century, the old issues of tariff and currency policy that had dominated national politics since the Civil War gave way to global concerns: the outbreak of the Spanish-American War and the American acquisition of territories outside the Western Hemisphere. At the same time, the advent of a new century brought new social and political developments. Even though the Populist movement faded with William Jennings Bryan's defeat, most of the agenda promoted by Bryan Democrats and Populists, dismissed as too radical and controversial in 1896, was implemented over the next two decades. Bryan's impassioned candidacy had helped transform the Democratic party into a vigorous instrument of "progressive" reform during the early twentieth century. Democrats began to promote antitrust prosecutions, state laws to limit the working hours of women and children, the establishment of a minimum wage, and measures to support farmers and protect labor union organizers. As the United States looked ahead to a new century, it began to place more emphasis on the role of government in society and the economy.

MAKING CONNECTIONS

- The laissez-faire policies of the Gilded Age were challenged by Progressive reform activists, as discussed in Chapter 24.

- William Jennings Bryan was one of the most prominent figures in American politics and political culture for thirty years. He will again be discussed in Chapters 24 and 26.

FURTHER READING

A good overview of the Gilded Age is Vincent P. DeSantis's *The Shaping of Modern America, 1877–1920* (2000). Nell Painter's *Standing at Armageddon: The United States, 1877–1919* (1987) focuses on the experience of the working classes.

Scholars have also examined various Gilded-Age issues and interest groups. Gerald W. McFarland's *Mugwumps, Morals, and Politics,*

1884–1920 (1975) examines the issue of reforming government service. Tom E. Terrill's *The Tariff, Politics, and American Foreign Policy, 1874–1901* (1973) lends clarity to that complex issue. The finances of the Gilded Age are covered in Walter T. K. Nugent's *Money and American Society, 1865–1880* (1968).

One of the most controversial works on populism is Lawrence Goodwyn's *The Populist Movement: A Short History of the Agrarian Revolt in America* (1978). A more balanced account is Robert C. McMath, Jr.'s *American Populism: A Social History, 1877–1898* (1993).

PART SIX

MODERN AMERICA

The United States entered the twentieth century on a wave of unrelenting change. In 1800 the nation had been a rural, agrarian society largely detached from the concerns of international affairs. By 1900, the United States had become a highly industrialized, urban culture with a growing involvement in world politics and commerce. In other words, the nation was on the threshold of modernity.

The prospect of modernity both excited and scared Americans. Old truths and beliefs clashed with unsettling new scientific discoveries and social practices. People debated the legitimacy of Darwinism, the existence of God, the dangers of jazz, and the federal effort to prohibit alcoholic beverages. The automobile and airplane helped shrink distance, and communications innovations such as radio and film contributed to a national consciousness. In the process, the United States began to emerge from its isolationist shell. Throughout most of the nineteenth century, policy makers had sought to isolate America from the intrigues and conflicts of the great European powers. As early as 1780, John Adams had warned Congress against involving the United States in the affairs of Europe. "Our business with them, and theirs with us," he wrote, "is commerce, not politics, much less war." George Washington echoed this sentiment in his farewell address upon leaving the presidency, warning Americans to avoid "entangling alliances" with foreign governments.

With only a few exceptions, American statesmen during the nineteenth century followed such advice. Noninvolvement in foreign wars and nonintervention in the internal affairs of foreign governments formed the pillars of American foreign policy until the end of the century. During the 1890s, however, expanding commercial interests around the world led Americans to expand the horizons of their concerns. Imperialism was the order of the day among the great European powers, and a growing number of American expansionists demanded that the United States also adopt a global ambition and join in the hunt for new territories and markets. Such motives helped spark the Spanish-American War of 1898 and helped to justify the resulting acquisition of American colonies outside the continental United States. Entangling alliances with European powers soon followed.

The outbreak of the Great War in Europe in 1914 posed an even greater challenge to the American tradition of isolation and nonintervention. The prospect of a German victory over the French and British threatened the European balance of power, which had long ensured the security of the United States. By 1917 it appeared that Germany might emerge triumphant and begin to menace the Western Hemisphere. Woodrow Wilson's crusade to use American intervention in World War I to transform the world order in accordance with his idealistic principles dislodged American foreign policy from its isolationist moorings. It also spawned a prolonged debate about the role of the United States in world affairs, a debate that World War II would resolve for a time on the side of internationalism.

While the United States was entering the world stage as a great military power, it was also becoming a great industrial power. Cities and factories sprouted across the landscape. An abundance of new jobs served as a magnet attracting millions of immigrants from every corner of the globe. They were not always welcomed nor were they readily assimilated. Ethnic and racial strife, as well as labor agitation, increased at the turn of the century. In the midst of such social turmoil and unparalleled economic development, American reformers made their first sustained attempt to adapt their political and social institutions to the realities of the industrial age. The worst excesses and injustices of urban-industrial development—corporate monopolies, child labor, political corruption, hazardous working conditions, urban ghettos—were finally addressed in a comprehensive way. During the Progressive Era (1900–1917), local, state, and federal governments sought to rein in the excesses of industrial capitalism and develop a more rational and efficient public policy.

A conservative Republican resurgence challenged the notion of the new regulatory state during the 1920s. Free enterprise and corporate capitalism witnessed a dramatic revival. But the stock market crash of 1929 helped propel the United States and many other nations into the worst economic downturn in history. The unprecedented severity of the Great Depression renewed public demands for federal government programs to protect the general welfare. "This nation asks for action," declared President Franklin D. Roosevelt in his 1933 inaugural address. The many New Deal initiatives and agencies instituted by Roosevelt and his Democratic administration created the framework for a welfare state that has since served as the basis for American public policy.

The New Deal helped revive public confidence and put people back to work, but it did not end the Great Depression. It took a world war to restore full employment. The necessity of mobilizing the nation in support of the Second World War also served to accelerate the growth of the

federal government. And the unparalleled scope of the war helped cata-
pult the United States into a leadership role in world politics. The use of
atomic bombs ushered in a new era of nuclear diplomacy that held the
fate of the world in the balance. For all of the new creature comforts asso-
ciated with modern life, Americans in 1945 found themselves living amid
an array of new anxieties.

23 AN AMERICAN EMPIRE

CHAPTER ORGANIZER

This chapter focuses on:

• the circumstances that led to America's "new imperialism."

• the causes of the Spanish-American War.

• Theodore Roosevelt's foreign policy in Asia and Latin America.

hroughout the nineteenth century, most Americans displayed what one senator called "only a languid interest" in foreign affairs. Indeed, the overriding concerns of the time were industrial development, western settlement, and domestic politics. Compared to these concerns, foreign relations simply were not important to the vast majority of Americans. After the Civil War, an isolationist mood swept across the United States as the country basked in its geographic advantages: wide oceans as buffers on either side, the British navy situated between America and the powers of Europe, and militarily weak neighbors in the Western Hemisphere.

Yet the notion of America having a "Manifest Destiny" ordained by God to expand its territory and influence remained alive in the decades after the end of the Civil War. Several prominent political and business leaders argued that the rapid industrial development of the United States required the acquisition of foreign territories to gain easier access to vital raw materials. In addition, as their exports grew, American companies and farmers became increasingly intertwined in the world economy. This, in turn, required an expanded naval presence to protect the shipping lanes. And a modern steam-powered navy needed bases where its ships could replenish their coal and water. For these reasons and others, the United States during the last quarter of the nineteenth century began to expand its military presence beyond the Western Hemisphere.

TOWARD THE NEW IMPERIALISM

By the late nineteenth century, European powers had already unleashed a new surge of imperialism in Africa and Asia, where they had seized territory, established colonies and protectorates, and had begun a systematic program of economic exploitation and Christian evangelism. Writing in 1902, the British economist J. A. Hobson declared that imperialism was "the most powerful factor in the current politics of the Western world."

IMPERIALISM IN A GLOBAL CONTEXT Western imperialism had economic roots, and the new imperialism was above all a quest for markets and raw materials. The second industrial revolution generated such dramatic increases in production that business leaders felt compelled to find new markets for their burgeoning supply of goods and new sources of investment for their growing supply of capital. Manufacturers, on the other hand, were eager to find new sources of raw materials to supply their expanding needs. At the same time, the aggressive nationalism and bitter rivalries of the European powers made all of them compete with the others as they expanded their empires.

The result was a widespread process of imperial expansion into Africa and Asia, often with brutal consequences for the indigenous peoples. Beginning in the 1880s, the British, French, Belgians, Italians, Dutch, Spanish, and Germans used military force and political guile to conquer regions of Africa and Asia. Each of the imperial nations, including the United States, dispatched Christian missionaries to convert the native peoples. By 1900, some 18,000 Christian missionaries were scattered around the world. Often the conversion to Christianity was the first step in the loss of a culture's indigenous traditions. The Western religious efforts also influenced the colonial power structure. A British nationalist explained the global ambitions of the imperialist nations: "Today, power and domination rather than freedom and independence are the ideas that appeal to the imagination of the masses—and the national ideal has given way to the imperial." Unfortunately, this imperial outlook also set in motion clashes among the Western powers that would lead to unprecedented conflict in the twentieth century.

AMERICAN IMPERIALISM   As the European nations expanded their control over much of the rest of the world, Americans also began to acquire territories outside the continental United States. Most Americans became increasingly aware of world markets as developments in transportation and communication quickened the pace of commerce and diplomacy. From the first, agricultural exports had been the basis of economic growth. Now the conviction grew that American manufacturers had matured to the point that they could outsell foreign competitors in the world market. But should the expansion of markets lead to territorial expansion as well? Or to intervention in the internal affairs of other countries? On such points Americans disagreed, but a small yet vocal and influential group of public officials embraced the idea of overseas possessions, regardless of the implications. These expansionists included Senators Albert J. Beveridge of Indiana and Henry Cabot Lodge of Massachusetts, Theodore Roosevelt, and not least of all, naval Captain Alfred Thayer Mahan.

During the 1880s, Captain Mahan became a leading advocate of sea power and Western imperialism. In 1890 he published *The Influence of Sea Power upon History, 1660–1783*, in which he argued that national greatness and prosperity flowed from maritime power. To Mahan, modern economic development called for a powerful navy, a strong merchant marine, foreign commerce, colonies, and naval bases. Mahan, a self-described "imperialist," championed America's "destiny" to control the Caribbean, build an isthmian canal to connect the Pacific and Caribbean, and spread Western civilization in the Pacific. His ideas were widely circulated in popular journals and within the American government. Theodore Roosevelt ordered a copy for every American ship.

Even before Mahan's writings became influential, a gradual expansion of the American navy had begun. In 1880 the nation had fewer than a hundred seagoing vessels, many of them rusting or rotting at the docks. By 1896, eleven powerful new battleships had been built or authorized.

IMPERIALIST THEORY   Certain intellectual concepts bolstered the new imperialist spirit and buttressed claims of racial superiority. Spokesmen in each country, including the United States, used the arguments of Social Darwinism to justify economic exploitation. Among nations as among individuals, expansionists claimed, the fittest survive and prevail. John Fiske, the historian and popular lecturer on Darwinism, developed racial corollaries from Darwin's ideas. In *American Political Ideas* (1885), he stressed the superior character of "Anglo-Saxon" institutions and peoples. The English "race," he argued, was destined to dominate the globe in the institutions, traditions, language, even in the blood of the world's peoples. Josiah Strong, a Congregationalist minister, added the sanction of religion to theories of racial and national superiority. In his book *Our Country: Its Possible Future and Its Present Crisis* (1885), Strong asserted that "Anglo-Saxon" embodied two great ideas: civil liberty and "a pure spiritual Christianity." The Anglo-Saxon was "divinely commissioned to be, in a peculiar sense, his brother's keeper."

EXPANSION IN THE PACIFIC

For Josiah Strong and other expansionists, Asia offered an especially alluring temptation. President Andrew Johnson's secretary of state, William H. Seward, had predicted in 1866 that the United States must inevitably exercise commercial domination "on the Pacific Ocean, and its islands and continents." Eager for American manufacturers to exploit Asian markets, Seward believed the United States first had to remove all foreign interests from the northern Pacific coast and gain access to that region's valuable ports. To that end, he cast covetous eyes on the British crown colony of British Columbia, sandwiched between Russian America (Alaska) and Washington Territory.

Late in 1866, while encouraging annexation sentiment among the British Columbians, Seward learned of Russia's desire to sell Alaska. He leaped at the opportunity, and in 1867 the United States bought

In a critical comment on Seward's 1867 purchase, this cartoon represents Alaska as a big block of ice labeled "Russian America."

Alaska for $7.2 million, thus removing Russia, the most recent colonial power, from the New World. Critics scoffed at "Seward's folly" of buying the Alaskan "icebox," but it proved in time to be the biggest bargain for the United States since the Louisiana Purchase.

Seward's successors at the State Department sustained his expansionist vision, and acquiring key ports in the Pacific Ocean remained the major focus of overseas activity through the rest of the nineteenth century. Two island groups occupied especially strategic positions about twenty degrees from either side of the equator: Samoa on the south and Hawaii (the Sandwich Islands) on the north. Both had major harbors, Pago Pago and Pearl Harbor, respectively. In the years after the Civil War, American interest in these islands gradually deepened.

SAMOA   In 1878, the Samoans signed a treaty with the United States that granted a naval base at Pago Pago and extraterritoriality for Americans (meaning that in Samoa they remained subject only to American law), exchanged trade concessions, and called for the United States to extend its good offices in case of a dispute with another nation. The Senate ratified this accord, and in the following year the German and British governments worked out similar arrangements with other islands of the Samoan group. There matters rested until civil war broke out in 1887. The Germans backed a pretender against the native Samoan king and finally installed him under a German protectorate. The sequel to this incident was a conference in Berlin (1889) that established a tripartite protectorate over Samoa, with Germany, Great Britain, and the United States in an uneasy partnership.

HAWAII   In Hawaii, the Americans had a clearer field to exploit. The islands, a united kingdom since 1795, had a sizable settlement of American missionaries and planters and were strategically more important to the United States than Samoa. Occupation by another major power might have posed a threat to American commercial interests and even to American defense.

In 1875 the kingdom entered a reciprocal trade agreement under which Hawaiian sugar would enter the United States duty free and under which Hawaii promised that none of its territory would be leased or granted to a third power. This agreement resulted in a boom in sugar production, and American settlers in Hawaii soon formed an economic elite. White planters in Hawaii built their fortunes on cheap immigrant labor, mainly Chinese, Japanese, and Portuguese. By the 1890s, the native population had been reduced to a minority by smallpox and other foreign diseases, and Asians quickly became the most numerous group in Hawaii.

In 1887, the Americans on the islands forced the king to accept a new constitution that created a constitutional government, which they dominated. In 1890, however, the McKinley Tariff destroyed Hawaii's favored position in the sugar trade by putting the sugar of all countries on the free list and granting growers in the continental United States a 2¢ subsidy per pound of sugar. This led to an economic crisis in Hawaii and affected the political situation as well.

In 1891, when the king's sister, Liliuokalani, ascended the throne, she tried to reclaim a measure of power and to eliminate white control of the government. Hawaii's white population then revolted against Queen Liliuokalani early in 1893 and seized power. The American minister brought in marines to support the coup. As he cheerfully reported to Washington, "The Hawaiian pear is now fully ripe, and this is the golden hour for the United States to pluck it." Within a month, a committee of the new government turned up in Washington with a treaty of annexation.

The treaty, however, appeared just weeks before President Benjamin Harrison left office, and Democratic senators blocked ratification. President Cleveland withdrew the treaty and sent a special commissioner to investigate. He removed the American marines and reported that the Americans in Hawaii had acted improperly. Most Hawaiians opposed annexation to the United States, the commissioner found. He concluded that the revolution had been engineered mainly by the American sugar planters hoping to get the subsidy for sugar grown in

Queen Liliuokalani.

the United States. Cleveland proposed to restore the queen to power in return for amnesty to the revolutionists. The provisional government refused to give up power, however, and on July 4, 1894, it proclaimed the islands the Republic of Hawaii, which had in its constitution a standing provision for American annexation. When McKinley became president in 1897, he was looking for an excuse to annex the islands. "We need Hawaii," he claimed, "just as much and a good deal more than we did California. It is manifest destiny." This excuse was found when the Japanese, also hoping to take over the islands, sent warships to Hawaii. McKinley responded by sending American warships and asked the Senate to approve a treaty to annex Hawaii. When the Senate could not muster the two-thirds majority needed to approve the treaty, McKinley used a joint resolution of the House and Senate to achieve his aims. The resolution passed by simple majorities in both houses, and Hawaii was annexed in the summer of 1898.

THE SPANISH-AMERICAN WAR

Until the 1890s, a certain ambivalence about overseas possessions had checked America's drive to expand. Suddenly, in 1898 and 1899, the inhibitions collapsed, and American power thrust its way to the far reaches of the Pacific. The occasion for this explosion of

José Martí, leader of the Cuban revolt against Spanish rule.

imperialism lay neither in the Pacific nor in the quest for bases and trade, but to the south in Cuba. The chief motive was a sense of outrage at another country's imperialism.

"CUBA LIBRE" Throughout the second half of the nineteenth century, Cubans had repeatedly revolted against Spanish rule, only to be ruthlessly suppressed. One of Spain's oldest colonies, Cuba was a major export market for the mother country. American investments in Cuba, mainly in sugar and mining, were steadily rising. The United States in fact traded more with Cuba than Spain did.

On February 24, 1895, insurrection broke out again. Simmering discontent with Spanish rule had been aggravated by the Wilson-Gorman Tariff of 1894, which took sugar off the free list in the midst of a depression already damaging to the market for Cuban sugar. Raw sugar prices collapsed, putting Cubans out of work and thereby rekindling their desire for rebellion. Public feeling in the United States supported the Cuban rebels.

Cuban insurrectionists waged guerrilla warfare and sought to damage the economic life of the island, which in turn would excite the concern of American investors. The strategy dictated hit-and-run attacks on trains, railways, and plantations. Americans often compared the insurrection to their own War of Independence. In 1896 Spanish general Valeriano Weyler adopted a policy of gathering Cubans behind Spanish lines, often in detention (*reconcentrado*) centers so that no one could join the insurrections by night and appear peaceful by day. In some of the centers, a combination of tropical climate, poor food, and unsanitary conditions quickly brought a heavy toll of disease and death. The American press promptly christened the Spanish commander "Butcher" Weyler.

Events in Cuba supplied exciting copy for the popular press. William Randolph Hearst's *New York Journal* and Joseph Pulitzer's *New York World* were at the time locked in a monumental competition for readers. "It was a battle of gigantic proportions," one journalist later wrote, "in which the sufferings of Cuba merely chanced to furnish some of the most convenient ammunition." The newspaper sensationalism came to be called "yellow journalism."

At the outset, the Cleveland administration tried to protect American rights in Cuba but avoided involvement beyond an offer of mediation. Mounting public sympathy for the cause, however, prompted concern in Congress. By concurrent resolution on April 6, 1896, the two houses endorsed official recognition of the Cuban belligerents and urged the president to seek a peace on the basis of Cuban independence. Cleveland, however, denied any designs against Spanish rule and offered to cooperate with Spain in bringing peace on the basis of allowing Cubans a measure of self-governance. The Spanish politely refused.

PRESSURE FOR WAR   America's posture of neutrality changed sharply when William McKinley entered office. He had been elected on a platform that endorsed Cuban independence as well as American control of Hawaii and the construction of an isthmian canal. In 1897 Spain offered Cuba autonomy (self-government without formal independence) in return for peace. What the Cubans might once have welcomed, however, they now rejected, insurrectionists and Spanish loyalists alike. Spain was impaled on the horns of a dilemma, unable to end the rebellion and unready to give up Cuba.

Early in 1898 events moved rapidly to arouse opinion against Spain. On January 25, the American battleship *Maine* docked in Havana Harbor, ostensibly on a courtesy call. On February 9 Hearst's *New York Journal* released the text of a letter from Spanish minister Depuy de Lôme to a friend in Havana, stolen from the post office by a Cuban spy. In the letter de Lôme called President McKinley "weak and a bidder for the admiration of the crowd, besides being a would-be politician who tries to leave a door open behind himself while keeping on good terms with the jingoes of his party." This was hardly more extreme than what McKinley's outspoken assistant secretary of the navy, Theodore Roosevelt, had said about him: that the "white-livered" president had "no more backbone than a chocolate eclair." But that comment had remained private. De Lôme resigned to prevent further embarrassment to his government.

Six days later, during the night of February 15, 1898, the *Maine* exploded in tranquil Havana Harbor and sank with a loss of 266 men. The ship's captain, one of only 84 survivors, scribbled a telegram to Washington: "*Maine* blown up in Havana Harbor at nine forty tonight and destroyed. Many wounded and doubtless more killed or drowned. . . . Public opinion should be suspended until further report."

But those eager for a war with Spain saw no need to withhold judgment. Theodore Roosevelt called the sinking "an act of dirty treachery on the part of the Spaniards." A naval court of inquiry reported that an external mine had set off an explosion in the ship's magazine. Lacking hard evidence, the court made no effort to fix the blame, but the yellow press had no need of evidence. The outcry against Spain reached a crescendo in the words "Remember the *Maine!*" Never mind that Spain could have derived little benefit from such an act. A comprehensive study in 1976 concluded that the sinking of the *Maine* was an

An American cartoon depicts the sinking of the Maine *in Havana Harbor. The uproar created by the incident and its coverage in the "yellow press" edged McKinley toward war.*

accident, the result of an internal explosion triggered by a fire in its coal bunker.

Under the mounting pressure of public excitement, McKinley tried to maintain a steady course. But the weight of outraged public opinion and militants in his own party such as Theodore Roosevelt and Henry Cabot Lodge eroded his neutrality. On March 9, the president coaxed from Congress a $50 million appropriation for defense. Still, McKinley sought to avoid war, as did most business leaders. Such caution infuriated Roosevelt. "We will have this war for the freedom of Cuba," he fumed on March 26, "in spite of the timidity of the commercial interests."

The Spanish government, sensing the growing militancy in the United States, announced a unilateral cease-fire in early April 1898. On April 10 the Spanish minister gave the State Department a message that amounted to a surrender: the United States should indicate the nature and duration of the armistice; Cuba would have an autonomous government; and the two countries would submit the question of the sinking of the *Maine* to arbitration. The United States minister to Spain then cabled from Madrid: "I hope nothing will now be done to humiliate Spain, as I am satisfied that the present government is going, and is loyally ready to go, as fast and as far as it can." McKinley, he predicted, could win a settlement by August 1 on any terms: autonomy, independence, or cession of Cuba to the United States.

But the message came too late. The following day McKinley asked Congress for power to use armed forces in Cuba to protect American property and trade. On April 20 a joint resolution of Congress went beyond endorsing the use of the armed forces: it declared Cuba independent and demanded withdrawal of Spanish forces. The Teller Amendment, added on the Senate floor, disclaimed any American designs on Cuban territory. McKinley signed the war resolution, and a copy went off to the Spanish government, with notice that McKinley would execute it unless Spain gave a complete and satisfactory response by noon, April 23. Meanwhile, on April 22 the president announced a blockade of Cuba's northern coast and the port of Santiago. Under international law this was an act of war. Rather than give in to an ultimatum, the Spanish government declared war on April 24. Congress then, determined to be first, declared war on April 25, retroactive to April 21, 1898.

Why such a rush into war after the American minister had predicted that Spain would cave in before the summer was out? Chiefly because too much momentum and popular pressure had already built up for a confidential message to change the course of events. Also, leaders of the business community were now demanding a quick resolution of the problem. Many lacked faith in the willingness or ability of the Spanish government to carry out a moderate policy in the face of a hostile public opinion. Still, it is fair to ask why McKinley did not take a stand for peace. He might have defied Congress and public opinion, but in the end he decided that the political risk was too high. The ultimate blame for war, if blame must be levied, belongs to the American people for letting themselves be whipped up into such a hostile frenzy.

DEWEY TAKES MANILA   The war itself lasted only 114 days. John Hay, soon to be secretary of state, called it "a splendid little war." The war's end was also the end of Spain's once great New World empire. It marked as well the emergence of the United States as a world power. The United States liberated Spain's colonies, yet in some cases it would substitute Spanish oppression with its own. If war with Spain saved many lives by ending the insurrection in Cuba, it also led to American involvement in another insurrection, in the Philippines, and created a host of problems that persisted into the twentieth century.

The Spanish-American war was barely under way before the navy produced a spectacular victory in an unexpected quarter—Manila Bay. While public attention focused on Cuba, young Theodore Roosevelt was thinking of the Spanish-controlled Philippines. As assistant secretary of the navy, he had Commodore George Dewey appointed commander of the small American squadron in Asia, and had ordered it to engage Spain in the Philippines in case of war. President McKinley had approved those orders.

Arriving late on April 30 with four cruisers and two gunboats, Dewey destroyed or captured all the Spanish warships in Manila Bay. The Spanish force lost 381 men, while Dewey's squadron suffered only 8 wounded. Dewey, without an occupation force, was now in awkward possession of Manila Bay. Promised reinforcements, he stayed while German and British warships hung about the scene like watchful vultures, ready to take over the Philippines if the United States did not do so. Land reinforcements finally arrived, and with the help of Filipino insurrectionists under Emilio Aguinaldo, Dewey's forces entered Manila on August 13.

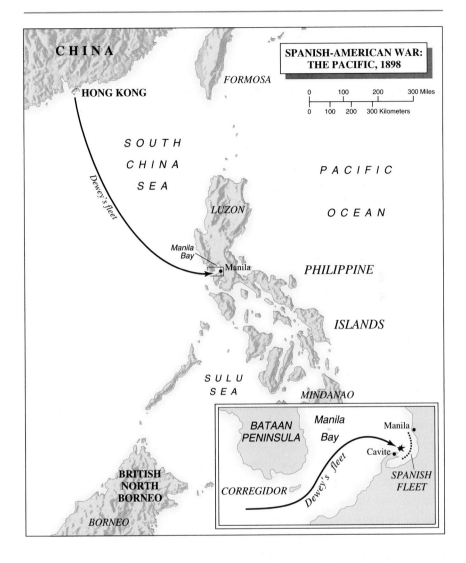

THE CUBAN CAMPAIGN While these events transpired halfway around the world, the fighting in Cuba reached a surprisingly quick climax. The U.S. navy blockaded the Spanish navy at Santiago. Although the navy was fit, the army could muster only an ill-assorted guard of 28,000 regulars and about 100,000 militiamen. Altogether during the war about 200,000 more militiamen were recruited, chiefly as state volunteers. The armed forces suffered badly from both inexperience and maladministration, with the result that more died from disease than from enemy action.

A force of some 17,000 American troops hastily assembled at Tampa, Florida. One significant unit was the First Volunteer Cavalry, better known as the "Rough Riders" and best remembered because Lieutenant-Colonel Theodore Roosevelt was second in command. Eager to get "in on the fun," and "to act up to my preachings," Roosevelt had quit the Navy Department soon after war was declared. He ordered a custom-fitted uniform from Brooks Brothers and rushed to help organize a volunteer regiment of Ivy League athletes, leathery ex-convicts, Indians, and southwestern sharpshooters. Their landing at the southeastern tip of Cuba was a mad scramble, as the horses were mistakenly sent elsewhere, leaving the "Rough Riders" to become the "Weary Walkers."

Land and sea battles around Santiago broke Spanish resistance. On July 1, about 7,000 American soldiers took the fortified village of El Caney from about 600 of the enemy garrison. While a much larger force attacked San Juan Hill, a smaller unit, including the dismounted Rough Riders, together with black soldiers from two cavalry units, seized the enemy position atop nearby Kettle Hill. Roosevelt later claimed that he "would rather have led that charge than served three terms in the U.S. Senate." A friend wrote to Roosevelt's wife that her husband was "revelling in victory and gore."

The two battles put American forces atop heights from which to the west and south they could bring Santiago and the Spanish fleet under siege. On July 3 the Spanish navy made a gallant run for it, but its decrepit ships were little more than sitting ducks for the newer American fleet, which included five battleships and two cruisers. The casualties were as one-sided as at Manila: 474 Spanish were killed and wounded and 1,750 were taken prisoner, while only one American was killed and one wounded. Santiago surrendered on July 17. On July 25 an American force moved into Spanish-held Puerto Rico against minor resistance.

The next day the Spanish government sued for peace. After discussions lasting two weeks, an armistice was signed on August 12, less than four months after the war's start and the day before Americans entered Manila. The peace protocol specified that Spain should give up Cuba, and that the United States should annex Puerto Rico and occupy Manila pending the transfer of power in the Philippines.

In all, over 60,000 Spanish soldiers died of disease or wounds in the four-month war. Among more than 274,000 Americans who served during the war and the ensuing demobilization, some 6,000 died, but only 379 in battle. Most succumbed to malaria, typhoid, dysentery, or yellow fever. At such a cost the United States was launched onto the world scene as a great power, with all the benefits—and burdens—of a new colonial power.

THE DEBATE OVER ANNEXATION   The United States and Spain signed the Treaty of Paris on December 10, 1898. But the fundamental question of the status of the Philippines remained unanswered. McKinley, who claimed that at first he himself could not locate the islands on a map, gave ambiguous signals to the peace commission. The commission itself was divided.

There had been no demand for annexation of the Philippines before the war, but Commodore Dewey's victory quickly kindled expansionist fever. Businessmen began thinking of the commercial possibilities in the nearby continent of Asia, such as oil for the lamps of China and textiles for its millions. Missionary societies saw the chance to bring Christianity to the "little brown brother." The Philippines promised to provide a useful base for all such activities. It was neither the first nor

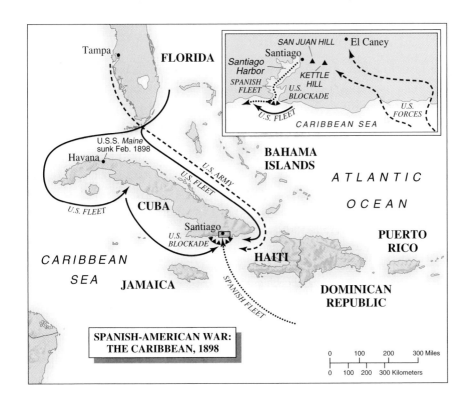

SPANISH-AMERICAN WAR:
THE CARIBBEAN, 1898

"Well, I Hardly Know Which to Take First." *At the end of the nineteenth century, it seemed that Uncle Sam had developed a considerable appetite for foreign territory.*

the last time that Americans would get caught up in fantasies of "saving" Asia or getting rich there. McKinley pondered the alternatives and later explained his reasoning to a group of Methodists:

> And one night late it came to me this way—I don't know how it was, but it came: (1) that we could not give them back to Spain—that would be cowardly and dishonorable; (2) that we could not turn them over to France or Germany—our commercial rivals in the Orient—that would be bad business and discreditable; (3) that we could not leave them to themselves—they were unfit for self-government—and they would soon have anarchy and misrule over there worse than Spain's was; and (4) that there was nothing left for us to do but to take them all, and to educate the Filipinos, and uplift and civilize and Christianize them, and by God's grace do the very best we could by them, as our fellowmen for whom Christ also died. And then I went to bed, and went to sleep and slept soundly.

In one brief statement he had summarized the motivating ideas of imperialism: (1) national honor, (2) commerce, (3) racial superiority, and

(4) altruism. Spanish negotiators raised the delicate point that American forces had no claim by right of conquest, and had even taken Manila after the armistice. American negotiators finally offered the Spanish compensation of $20 million. The treaty thus added to American territory Puerto Rico, Guam (a Spanish island in the Pacific), and the Philippines.

Meanwhile Americans had taken other giant steps in the Pacific. Hawaii had been annexed in the midst of the war. Within a year of the peace treaty, in 1899, after another outbreak of fighting over the royal succession in Samoa, Germany and the United States agreed to partition the Samoa Islands. The United States annexed the easternmost islands; Germany took the rest, including the largest island. Britain ceded its claims in Samoa in return for German concessions in the Pacific and in Africa. Meanwhile, in 1898 the United States had laid claim to Wake Island, located between Guam and the Hawaiian islands, which would become a vital link in a future trans-Pacific cable line.

The Treaty of Paris had yet to be ratified in the Senate, where most Democrats and Populists, and some Republicans, opposed it. Anti-imperialists argued that acquisition of the Philippines would undermine democracy. They stressed traditional isolationism, American principles of self-government, the inconsistency of liberating Cuba and annexing the Philippines, the involvement in foreign entanglements that would undermine the logic of the Monroe Doctrine, and the danger that the Philippines would become an Achilles heel, expensive if not impossible to defend. The prospect of incorporating so many alien peoples into American life was not the least of some people's worries. "Bananas and self-government cannot grow on the same piece of land," one senator claimed.

The opposition might have been strong enough to kill the treaty had not the populist Democrat William Jennings Bryan influenced the vote for approval. Ending the war, he argued, would open the way for the future independence of Cuba and the Philippines. Finally, ratification came on February 6, 1899, by a margin of more than two to one. A week later, the deciding vote of the vice-president defeated a resolution for Philippine independence. That same month in *McClure's* magazine the British poet Rudyard Kipling published "The White Man's Burden," in which he called the American people to a new duty:

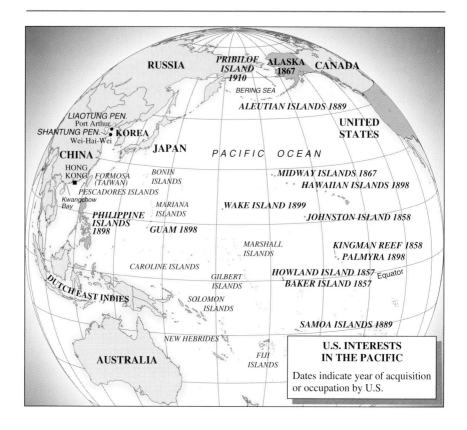

RUSSIA

PRIBILOF ISLAND 1910

ALASKA 1867

CANADA

BERING SEA

ALEUTIAN ISLANDS 1889

LIAOTUNG PEN.
Port Arthur
SHANTUNG PEN.
Wei-Hai-Wei

KOREA

UNITED STATES

CHINA

JAPAN

PACIFIC OCEAN

HONG KONG
FORMOSA (TAIWAN)
PESCADORES ISLANDS
Kwangchow Bay

BONIN ISLANDS

MIDWAY ISLANDS 1867

HAWAIIAN ISLANDS 1898

MARIANA ISLANDS

WAKE ISLAND 1899

JOHNSTON ISLAND 1858

PHILIPPINE ISLANDS 1898

GUAM 1898

KINGMAN REEF 1858

PALMYRA 1898

MARSHALL ISLANDS

CAROLINE ISLANDS

GILBERT ISLANDS

HOWLAND ISLAND 1857

BAKER ISLAND 1857

Equator

DUTCH EAST INDIES

SOLOMON ISLANDS

SAMOA ISLANDS 1889

NEW HEBRIDES

AUSTRALIA

FIJI ISLANDS

U.S. INTERESTS IN THE PACIFIC

Dates indicate year of acquisition or occupation by U.S.

> Take up the White Man's burden—
> Send forth the best ye breed—
> Go, bind your sons to exile
> To serve your captive's need;
> To wait in heavy harness
> On fluttered folk and wild—
> Your new-caught sullen peoples,
> Half devil and half child.

By this time Americans had already clashed with Filipino insurrectionists near Manila. The Filipino leader, Emilio Aguinaldo, had been in exile until Commodore Dewey brought him back to Luzon to make trouble for the Spanish. Since Aguinaldo's forces were more or less in control of the islands outside of Manila, what followed was largely an American war of conquest that lasted more than two years. Organized Filipino resistance collapsed by the end of 1899, but even after the

Emilio Aguinaldo (seated third from right) *and other leaders of the Filipino insurgents.*

capture of Aguinaldo in 1901, sporadic guerrilla action lasted until mid-1902. It was a sordid little war, with massacres and torture on both sides. In the end it took 63,000 American troops, 4,300 American deaths, and almost three years to crush the revolt.

Against the backdrop of this nasty guerrilla war the great debate over imperialism continued in the United States. The treaty debates inspired a number of anti-imperialist groups, which united in 1899 as the American Anti-Imperialist League. The league attracted members representing many shades of opinion; the main thing they had in common was that most belonged to an older generation. Andrew Carnegie footed the bills, but on imperialism at least union leader Samuel Gompers agreed with him. Presidents Charles Eliot of Harvard and David Starr Jordan of Stanford supported the group, along with social reformer Jane Addams. The drive for imperialism, said the philosopher William James, had caused the nation to "puke up its ancient soul."

ORGANIZING THE NEW ACQUISITIONS   Such criticism, however, did not faze the expansionists. Senator Beveridge boasted in 1900: "The Philippines are ours forever. And just beyond the Philippines are China's illimitable markets. We will not retreat from either. . . . The power that rules the Pacific is the power that rules the world. That power will forever be the American Republic."

In the Philippines McKinley had already moved toward setting up a civil government. In 1900 he dispatched a commission under Judge William Howard Taft with instructions to set up a system of government. Unlike some of the Americans on the scene, Taft seemed to like the Filipinos, encouraged them to participate, and eventually convinced Filipino representatives to sit on the commission itself.

On July 4, 1901, American military government in the Philippines ended. Under an act of Congress, Taft became the civil governor. The Philippine Government Act, passed by Congress in 1902, declared the Philippine Islands an "unorganized territory" and made the inhabitants citizens of the Philippines. In 1916 the Jones Act affirmed America's intention to grant the Philippines independence at an indefinite date. Finally, the Tydings-McDuffie Act of 1934 offered independence after a tutelary period of ten more years. A constitution was drafted and ratified, and in September 1934, Manuel Quezon was elected the first president of the Philippines. Independence finally took effect on July 4, 1946.

Puerto Rico had been acquired in part to serve as an American outpost on the approaches to the Caribbean and any future isthmian canal. On April 12, 1900, the Foraker Act established a civil government on the island. The president appointed a governor and eleven members of an executive council, and an elected House of Delegates made up the lower house of the legislature. Residents of the island were citizens of Puerto Rico but not of the United States until 1917, when the Jones Act granted United States citizenship and made both houses of the legislature elective. In 1947 the governor also became elective, and in 1952 Puerto Rico became a commonwealth with its own constitution and elected officials, a unique status. Like a state, Puerto Rico is free to change its constitution insofar as it does not conflict with the United States Constitution.

The Foraker Act of 1900 also levied a temporary duty on imports from Puerto Rico. The tariff was challenged in the federal courts on the grounds that the island had become part of the United States, but the Supreme Court upheld the tariff. In this and other "Insular Cases" federal judges faced a question that went to the fundamental nature of the American Union and to the civil and political rights of the people in

America's new possessions: Does the Constitution follow the flag? The Court ruled in effect that it did not unless Congress extended it.

Having liberated the Cubans from Spanish rule, the Americans found themselves propping up a shaky new Cuban government whose economy was in a state of collapse. Bad relations between American soldiers and Cubans erupted almost immediately. When McKinley set up a military government for the island late in 1898, it was at odds with rebel leaders from the start.

Many Europeans expected annexation, and General Leonard Wood, who became Cuba's military governor in 1899, thought this the best solution. But the United States finally did fulfill the promise of independence for Cuba after the military regime had restored order, gotten schools under way, and improved sanitary conditions. The problem of disease in Cuba provided a focus for the work of Dr. Walter Reed, who made an outstanding contribution to the health of people in tropical climates around the world. Named head of the Army Yellow Fever Commission in 1900, he directed experiments with volunteers that proved the theory of a Cuban physician that yellow fever was carried by stegomyia mosquitoes. These experiments led the way to effective control of the disease.

In 1900, at President McKinley's order, General Wood called an election for a Cuban constitutional convention, which drafted a basic law modeled on that of the United States. The Platt Amendment to the Army Appropriations Bill passed by Congress in 1901, however, sharply restricted the independence of the new government. The amendment required Cuba never to impair its independence by treaty with a third power, to maintain its debt within the government's power to repay out of ordinary revenues, and to acknowledge the right of the United States to intervene for the preservation of Cuban independence and the maintenance of "a government adequate for the protection of life, property, and individual liberty." Finally, Cuba was called upon to sell or lease to the United States lands to be used for coaling or naval stations—a proviso that led to an American naval base at Guantanamo Bay, a base still in operation.

Under pressure, the Cuban delegates added the Platt Amendment as an appendix to their own constitution. As early as 1906 an insurrection arose against the new government, and President Theodore Roosevelt responded by sending Secretary of War William Howard Taft to suppress the rebels. Backed up by American armed forces, Taft assumed full governmental authority, as he had in the Philippines, and the American army stayed until 1909, when a new Cuban president was peacefully elected. Further interventions would follow for more than two decades.

IMPERIAL RIVALRIES IN EAST ASIA

During the 1890s, not only the United States but also Japan emerged as a world power. Commodore Matthew Perry's voyage of 1853–1854 had opened Japan to Western ways, and the country began modernization in earnest after the 1860s. Flexing its new muscles, Japan defeated China's stagnant empire in the Sino-Japanese War (1894–1895) and as a result picked up the Pescadores Islands and the island of Taiwan (renamed Formosa). China's weakness, demonstrated in the war, brought the great powers into a scramble for "spheres of influence" on that remaining frontier of imperialist expansion. Russia secured the privilege of building a railroad across Manchuria and established itself in Port Arthur and the Liaotung Peninsula. The Germans moved into Shantung, the French into Kwangchow Bay, the British into Wei-Hai-Wei.

The bright prospect of American trade with China dimmed with the possibility that the great powers would throw up tariff barriers in their own spheres of influence. The British, ensconced at Hong Kong since 1840, had more to lose though, for they already had the largest foreign trade with China. Just before the Spanish-American War, in 1898, the British suggested joint action with the United States to preserve the integrity of China, and renewed the proposal early in 1899. Both times the Senate rejected the request because it risked an entangling alliance.

CHINA AND THE "OPEN DOOR"   In its origins and content, what soon came to be known as the Open Door Policy resembled the Monroe Doctrine. In both cases the United States proclaimed unilaterally a hands-off policy, which the British had earlier proposed as a joint statement. The policy outlined in Secretary of State John Hay's Open Door Note, dispatched in 1899 to London, Berlin, and St. Petersburg, and a little later to Tokyo, Rome, and Paris, proposed to keep China open to trade with all countries on an equal basis. More specifically it called upon foreign powers, within their spheres of influence: (1) not to interfere with any treaty port (a port open to all by treaty) or any vested interest, (2) to permit Chinese authorities to collect tariffs on an equal basis, and (3) to show no favors to their own nationals in the matter of harbor dues or railroad charges. Hay's request that each of the powers accept these principles was, one diplomat later wrote, like asking everyone who believes in truth to stand: the liars would be the first on their feet. As it turned out, none except Britain accepted Hay's principles, but none rejected them, either. So Hay simply announced that all powers had accepted the policy. None stood to deny it.

The Open Door Policy, if rooted in the self-interest of American businesses eager to exploit Chinese markets, also tapped the deep-seated sympathies of those who opposed imperialism, especially as it endorsed China's territorial integrity. But it had little more legal standing than a pious affirmation. When the Japanese, concerned about Russian pressure in Manchuria, asked how the United States intended to enforce the policy, Hay replied that America was "not prepared . . . to enforce these views on the east by any demonstration which could present a character of hostility to any other power." So it would remain for forty years, until continued Japanese expansion in China would bring America to war in 1941.

American troops marching in Beijing after putting down the Boxer Rebellion.

THE BOXER REBELLION   A new crisis arose in 1900, when a group of Chinese nationalists known to the Western world as Boxers ("Fists of Righteous Harmony") rebelled against foreign encroachments on China and laid siege to foreign embassies in Peking. An international expedition of British, German, Russian, Japanese, and American forces mobilized to relieve the embassy compound. Hay, fearful that the intervention might become an excuse to dismember China, took the opportunity to further refine the Open Door Policy. The United States, he said in a letter of July 3, 1900, sought a solution that would "preserve Chinese territorial and administrative integrity" as well as "equal and impartial trade with all parts of the Chinese Empire."

Six weeks later, the expedition reached Peking and quelled the Boxer Rebellion. The occupying powers then agreed to settle for an indemnity from China of approximately $333 million. Of this total the United States received $25 million, of which nearly $11 million was refunded to China once all claims were paid. Most of this the Chinese government put into a fund to support Chinese students in American colleges.

ROOSEVELT'S BIG STICK DIPLOMACY

More than any other American of his time, Theodore Roosevelt helped transform the role of the United States in world affairs. The country had emerged from the Spanish-American War a world power, and he insisted that this entailed major new responsibilities. To ensure that his country accepted such international obligations, Roosevelt stretched both the Constitution and executive power to the limit. In the process he pushed a reluctant nation onto the center stage of world affairs.

ROOSEVELT'S RISE   Born in 1858, the son of a wealthy New York merchant and a Georgia belle, Roosevelt grew up in Manhattan in cultured comfort, visited Europe as a child, spoke German fluently, and graduated Phi Beta Kappa from Harvard in 1880. A sickly, scrawny boy with poor eyesight, he built himself up into a physical and intellectual athlete who became a lifelong practitioner of the "strenuous life." Rigorous exercise and outdoor activities became an integral part of his life. A boxer, wrestler, mountain climber, hunter, and outdoorsman, he was also a dedicated bird watcher, renowned historian and essayist, and outspoken moralist. His energy and fierce competitive spirit were both inexhaustible and infectious, and he was ever willing to express opinions on any and all subjects.

Within two years of graduating from Harvard, Roosevelt won election to the New York legislature and published *The Naval War of 1812*, the first of a number of historical, biographical, and other writings to flow from his pen. But with the world seemingly at his feet, disaster struck. In 1884 his beloved mother, only forty-eight years old, died. Eleven hours later, in the same house, his twenty-two-year-old wife struggled with kidney failure and died in his arms, soon after giving birth to their first child. Roosevelt was distraught and bewildered. That night he drew a large cross over the entry in his diary: "The light has gone out of my life." The double funeral was so wrenching that the officiating minister wept throughout his prayer.

In an attempt to recover from this "strange and terrible fate," Roosevelt turned his baby daughter over to his sister, quit his political career, sold the family house, and moved west to take up cattle ranching on the Dakota frontier. The blue-blooded New Yorker relished hunting, leading roundups, capturing outlaws, fighting Indians—and reading novels by the campfire. When a drunken cowboy, a gun in each hand, tried to bully the tinhorn Roosevelt, teasing him about his glasses, the feisty Harvard dude laid him out with one punch. Although his western career lasted only two years, he never quite got over being a cowboy.

Back in New York City, Roosevelt ran for mayor in 1886 and lost, and later served six years as civil service commissioner and two years as New York City's police commissioner. In the latter capacity he loved to don a black cloak and broad-brimmed hat and patrol the streets at midnight. When he came upon a sleeping policeman, Roosevelt would rap the man with his nightstick. In 1897, McKinley appointed Roosevelt assistant secretary of the navy. After serving in Cuba and hastening into print his own account of the Rough Riders, Roosevelt easily won the governorship of New York, arousing audiences with his impassioned speeches and powerful personality.

In the 1900 presidential contest, the Democrats turned once again to William Jennings Bryan, who sought to make imperialism the "paramount issue" of the campaign. The Democratic platform condemned the Philippine conflict as "an unnecessary war" that had "placed the United States, previously known and applauded throughout the world as the champion of freedom, in the false and un-American position of crushing with military force the efforts of our former allies to achieve liberty and self-government."

The Republicans welcomed the issue. They renominated McKinley and named Roosevelt his running mate. After his role in the military action in the Philippines and Cuba, Roosevelt had virtually become "Mr. Imperialism." McKinley outpolled Bryan by 7.2 million to 6.4 million in the popular vote and by 292 to 155 in the electoral vote. But less than a year later, on September 6, 1901, while McKinley attended a reception at the Pan American Exposition in Buffalo, New York, a fanatical anarchist named Leon Czolgosz approached him with a gun concealed in a bandaged hand and fired at point-blank range. McKinley died eight days later, and Theodore Roosevelt was suddenly elevated to the White House. "Now look," Mark Hanna, the Ohio businessman and politico, erupted, "that damned cowboy is President of the United States!"

Six weeks short of his forty-third birthday, Roosevelt was the youngest man ever to reach the White House, but he brought to it more experience in public affairs than most and perhaps more vitality than any. One observer compared him to Niagara Falls, "both great wonders of nature." Roosevelt's glittering spectacles, glistening teeth, and overflowing gusto were a godsend to the cartoonists, who added another trademark when he pronounced the adage: "Speak softly, and carry a big stick."

This 1900 cartoon shows the Republican vice-presidential candidate, Theodore Roosevelt, overshadowing his running mate, President McKinley.

Along with Roosevelt's boundless energy went an unshakable right-eousness and a tendency to cast every issue in moral and patriotic terms. He considered the presidency his "bully pulpit," and he delivered fist-smacking speeches on the virtues of righteousness, honesty, civic duty, and strenuosity. Yet his boundless energy left a false impression of impulsiveness, and his moral earnestness cloaked a cautious pragmatism. Roosevelt could get carried away on occasion, but as he said of his foreign policy steps, this was likely to happen only when "I am assured that I shall be able eventually to carry out my will by force." Indeed, nowhere was President Roosevelt's forceful will more evident than in his conduct of foreign affairs.

BUILDING THE PANAMA CANAL   After the Spanish-American War, the United States became more deeply involved in the Caribbean area. One issue overshadowed every other in the region: the Panama Canal. The narrow isthmus of Panama had excited dreams of an interoceanic canal ever since Balboa's crossing in 1513. Admiral Mahan regarded a canal as important to American commerce and naval power, a point dramatized in 1898 by the long voyage of the battleship *Oregon* around South America's Cape Horn to join the American fleet off Cuba.

Transit across the isthmus had first become a strong concern of the United States in the 1840s, when it became an important route to the California gold fields. Two treaties dating from that period loomed years later as obstacles to construction of a canal. The Bidlack Treaty (1848) with Colombia (then New Granada) guaranteed both Colombia's sovereignty over Panama and the neutrality of the isthmus, so that "free transit . . . not be embarrassed in any future time." In the Clayton-Bulwer Treaty (1850) the British agreed to acquire no more Central American territory, and the United States joined them in agreeing to build or fortify a canal only by mutual consent.

After the Spanish-American War, Secretary of State Hay commenced talks with the British ambassador to establish such consent. The outcome was the Hay-Pauncefote Treaty of 1900, but the Senate rejected it on the grounds that it forbade fortification of the canal and required that the canal be neutral even in time of war. By then a bill was already pending in Congress for a Nicaraguan canal, and the British apparently decided to accept the inevitable. In 1901 the Senate

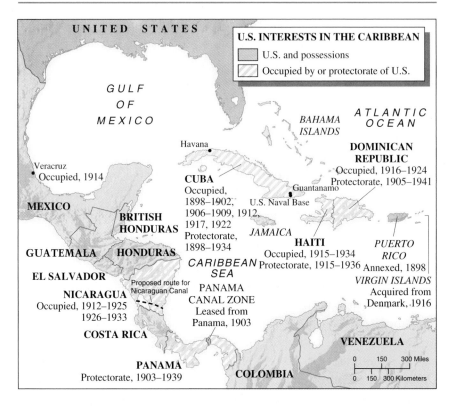

U.S. INTERESTS IN THE CARIBBEAN

☐ U.S. and possessions

▨ Occupied by or protectorate of U.S.

UNITED STATES

GULF
OF
MEXICO

ATLANTIC
OCEAN

BAHAMA
ISLANDS

Havana

DOMINICAN
REPUBLIC
Occupied, 1916–1924
Protectorate, 1905–1941

Veracruz
Occupied, 1914

CUBA
Occupied,
1898–1902,
1906–1909, 1912,
1917, 1922
Protectorate,
1898–1934

Guantanamo
U.S. Naval Base

MEXICO

BRITISH
HONDURAS

JAMAICA

HAITI
Occupied, 1915–1934
Protectorate, 1915–1936

PUERTO
RICO
Annexed, 1898

GUATEMALA   HONDURAS

CARIBBEAN
SEA

VIRGIN ISLANDS
Acquired from
Denmark, 1916

EL SALVADOR

Proposed route for
Nicaraguan Canal

PANAMA
CANAL ZONE
Leased from
Panama, 1903

NICARAGUA
Occupied, 1912–1925
1926–1933

COSTA RICA

VENEZUELA

PANAMA
Protectorate, 1903–1939

COLOMBIA

0   150   300 Miles
0 150 300 Kilometers

ratified a second Hay-Pauncefote Treaty, which simply omitted reference to the former limitations.

Other obstacles remained, however. From 1881 to 1887 a French company under Ferdinand de Lesseps, who had engineered the Suez Canal in 1877, had spent nearly $300 million and some 20,000 lives to dig less than a third of the canal through Panama, then under the control of Colombia. The company now wanted $109 million for its holdings. An Isthmian Canal Commission, appointed by President McKinley, reported in 1901 that a Nicaraguan route would be cheaper. When the House of Representatives quickly passed an act for construction there, the French company lowered its price to $40 million, and the Canal Commission switched to Panama.

Meanwhile Secretary Hay had opened negotiations with Ambassador Thomas Herrán of Colombia. In return for a Canal Zone six miles wide, the United States agreed to pay $10 million in cash and a rental fee of $250,000 a year. The United States Senate ratified the

Hay-Herrán Treaty in 1903, but the Colombian Senate held out for $25 million in cash. At this action of those "foolish and homicidal corruptionists in Bogotá," Theodore Roosevelt, by then president, flew into a rage punctuated by references to "dagoes" and "contemptible little creatures." Meanwhile in Panama, an isolated province long at odds with the remote Colombian authorities in Bogotá, feeling was heightened by Colombia's rejection of the treaty. One Manuel Amador, an employee of the French canal company, then hatched a plot in close collusion with the company's representative, Philippe Bunau-Varilla. He visited Roosevelt and Hay and, apparently with inside information, informed the conspirators that the U.S.S. *Nashville* would call at Colón in Panama on November 2.

With an army of some 500 Panamanians, Amador staged a revolt the next day. Colombian troops, who could not penetrate the overland jungle, found American ships blocking the sea lanes. On November 13 the Roosevelt administration received its first ambassador from Panama, whose name happened to be Philippe Bunau-Varilla, and he signed a treaty that extended the Canal Zone from six to ten miles in width. For $10 million down and $250,000 a year, the United States received "in perpetuity the use, occupation and control" of the zone. The U.S. attorney-general, asked to supply a legal opinion upholding Roosevelt's actions, responded wryly: "No, Mr. President, if I were you I would not have any taint of legality about it."

In 1904 Congress created a new Isthmian Canal Commission to direct construction. Despite sanitary problems, the biggest obstacle at first, Roosevelt instructed the commission to make the "dirt fly." He later explained: "I took the Canal Zone and let Congress debate; and while the debate goes on the Canal does also."

By needlessly offending Latin American sensibilities, Roosevelt had committed one of the greatest blunders in American foreign policy. Colombia eventually got its $25 million from the Harding administration in 1921, but only once America's interest in Colombian oil had lubricated the wheels of diplomacy. There was no apology, but the payment was made to remove "all misunderstandings growing out of the political events in Panama, November, 1903." The canal opened on August 15, 1914, less than two weeks after the outbreak of World War I in Europe.

President Theodore Roosevelt photographed operating a steam shovel during his 1906 visit to the Panama Canal.

THE ROOSEVELT COROLLARY   Even without the canal, the United States would have been concerned about the stability of the Caribbean area, and particularly with the activities of any hostile power there. A prime excuse for intervention in those days was to force the collection of debts owed to foreign nationals. In 1904 a crisis over the debts of the Dominican Republic gave Roosevelt an opportunity to formulate American policy in the Caribbean. In his annual address to Congress in 1904, he set forth what came to be known as the Roosevelt Corollary to the Monroe Doctrine: the principle, in short, was that since the Monroe Doctrine prohibited intervention in the region by Europeans, the United States was justified in intervening first to forestall the actions of outsiders.

In the president's words, the Roosevelt Corollary held that: "Chronic wrongdoing . . . may in America, as elsewhere, ultimately require intervention by some civilized nation, and in the Western Hemisphere the adherence of the United States to the Monroe Doctrine may force the United States, however reluctantly, in flagrant cases of such wrongdoing or impotence, to the exercise of an international police power." As put into practice by mutual agreement with the Dominican Republic in 1905, the Roosevelt Corollary called for the United States to install and protect a collector of customs who would apply 55 percent of the revenues to debt payments.

THE RUSSO-JAPANESE WAR In East Asia, meanwhile, the principle of equal trading rights embodied in the Open Door Policy received a serious challenge when rivalry between Russia and Japan flared into a fight. By 1904 the Japanese had grown convinced that the Russians threatened their own ambitions in China and Korea. On February 8, Japan launched a surprise attack that devastated the Russian fleet. The Japanese then occupied Korea and drove the Russians back into Manchuria. But neither side could score a knockout blow, and neither relished a prolonged war. Roosevelt sought to maintain a balance between the two powers and offered to mediate their conflict. When the Japanese signaled that they would welcome a negotiated settlement, Roosevelt agreed to sponsor a peace conference in Portsmouth, New Hampshire. In the Treaty of Portsmouth, signed on September 5, 1905, the concessions all went to the Japanese. Russia acknowledged Japan's "predominant political, military, and economic interests in Korea" (Japan would annex the kingdom in 1910), and both powers agreed to evacuate Manchuria.

AMERICA'S RELATIONS WITH JAPAN Japan's show of strength against Russia raised doubts among American leaders about the security of the Philippines. During the Portsmouth talks, Roosevelt sent William Howard Taft to meet with the Japanese foreign minister in Tokyo. The two men negotiated the Taft-Katsura Agreement of July 29, 1905, in which the United States accepted Japanese control of Korea and Japan disavowed any designs on the Philippines. Three years later, the Root-Takahira Agreement, negotiated by Secretary of State Elihu Root and the Japanese ambassador, endorsed the status quo and reinforced the Open Door Policy by supporting "the independence and integrity of China" and "the principle of equal opportunity for commerce and industry in China."

Behind the diplomatic facade of goodwill, however, lay mutual distrust. For many Americans the Russian threat in East Asia now gave way to the "yellow peril" of Japan.* Racial animosities on the West Coast helped sour relations with Japan. In 1906 the San Francisco school board ordered students of Chinese, Japanese, and Korean descent to attend a separate public school. The Japanese government sharply

---

*The term "yellow peril" was apparently coined by Kaiser Wilhelm II of Germany.

The World's Constable. *Theodore Roosevelt, shown here as the world's police-man, wields the "big stick" symbolizing his approach to diplomacy.*

protested such prejudice, and President Roosevelt managed to talk the school board into changing its mind after making sure that Japanese authorities would not issue passports to "laborers" except former residents of the United States, the parents, wives, or children of residents, or those who already possessed an interest in an American farming enterprise. This "Gentlemen's Agreement" of 1907, the precise terms of which have never been revealed, halted the influx of Japanese immigrants and brought some respite to racial agitations in California.

THE UNITED STATES AND EUROPE   During the years of expansionism, the United States cast its gaze westward and southward. But events in Europe also required attention. While Roosevelt was moving toward mediation of the Russo-Japanese War in 1905, another dangerous crisis began brewing in Morocco. There, on March 31, 1905, German kaiser Wilhelm II stepped ashore at Tangier and gave a saber-rattling speech criticizing French and British interests in North Africa. The kaiser's speech aroused a diplomatic storm of dangerous proportions. Roosevelt felt that the United States had something at stake in preventing the outbreak of a major war. At the kaiser's behest, he talked the French and British into attending an international conference at Algeciras, Spain, with American delegates present. Roosevelt then maneuvered the Germans into accepting his lead.

The Act of Algeciras, signed in 1906, affirmed the independence of Morocco and guaranteed an open door for trade there, but provided for the training and control of Moroccan police by France and Spain. The United States Senate ratified the agreement, but only with the proviso that it was not to be construed as a departure from America's traditional policy of noninvolvement in European affairs. It was a departure, of course, and one that may well have prevented a general war, or at least postponed it until 1914. Roosevelt received the Nobel Peace Prize in 1906 for his work at Portsmouth and Algeciras. Despite his bellicosity on other occasions, he had earned it.

Before Roosevelt left the White House, he celebrated America's rise to world power with one great flourish. In 1907 he sent the entire fleet of the United States navy, by then second in strength only to the British, on a grand tour around the world, their commander announcing he was ready for "a feast, a frolic, or a fight." He got mostly the first two, and none of the last. At every port of call the "Great White Fleet" set off rousing celebrations, down the Atlantic coast of South America, up the West Coast, out to Hawaii, and down to New Zealand and Australia. It was the first such show of American naval might in the Pacific, and many feared the reaction of the Japanese, for whose benefit Roosevelt had in fact staged the show. They need not have worried, for in Japan the flotilla got the greatest welcome of all. Thousands of schoolchildren turned out waving tiny American flags and singing "The Star-Spangled Banner" in English. The triumphal procession continued home by way of the Mediterranean and steamed back into American waters in 1909, just in time to close out Roosevelt's presidency on a note of success.

But it was a success that would have mixed consequences. As one insightful student of Roosevelt's role in America's rise to world power wrote: "One comes away from the study with admiration for Roosevelt's ability, his energy, and his devotion to his country's interests as he saw them but with a sense of tragedy that his abilities were turned toward imperialism and an urge for power, which were to have consequences so serious for the future." Roosevelt had influenced the United States "in a direction that . . . was to bring her face to face with grave dangers" before the mid–twentieth century.

MAKING CONNECTIONS

- The Spanish-American War marked a turning point in American foreign policy. America's emergence as a global power is a central theme in the twentieth century.

- Theodore Roosevelt's foreign policy displayed an activist approach to the presidency. In the next chapter, we see the connections between his foreign policies and his approach to domestic affairs.

FURTHER READING

An excellent survey of the diplomacy of the era is Charles Campbell's *The Transformation of American Foreign Relations, 1865–1900* (1976). For background to the events of the 1890s, see Walter LeFeber's *The American Search for Opportunity, 1865–1913* (1993) and David Healy's *U.S. Expansionism: The Imperialist Urge in the 1890s* (1970). The dispute over American policy concerning Hawaii is covered in Thomas J. Osborne's *"Empire Can Wait": American Opposition to Hawaiian Annexation, 1893–1898* (1981).

Ivan Musicant's *Empire by Default: The Spanish-American War and the Dawn of the American Century* (1998) is the most comprehensive volume on the conflict. For the war's aftermath in the Philippines, see Stuart C. Miller's *"Benevolent Assimilation": American Conquest of the Philippines, 1899–1903* (1982). Robert L. Beisner's *Twelve Against Empire: The Anti-Imperialists, 1898–1900* (1985) handles the debate over annexation.

A good introduction to American interest in China is Michael H. Hunt's *The Making of a Special Relationship: The United States and China to 1914* (1983). Kenton J. Clymer's *John Hay: The Gentleman as Diplomat* (1975) examines the role of this key secretary of state in forming policy.

For American policy in the Caribbean and Central America, see Walter LeFeber's *Inevitable Revolutions: The United States in Central America* (1993). David McCullough's *The Path between the Seas: The Creation of the Panama Canal, 1870–1914* (1977) presents the fullest account of how the United States secured the Panama Canal.

24 ∽ THE PROGRESSIVE ERA

CHAPTER ORGANIZER

This chapter focuses on:

- the social bases of progressivism.

- the basic elements of progressive reform.

- the presidencies of Theodore Roosevelt, William H. Taft, and Woodrow Wilson.

- the significance of the election of 1912.

*T*heodore Roosevelt's emergence as a national leader coincided with the onset of what historians have labeled the Progressive Era (1900–1917). The Progressive movement arose in response to many changes in society, the most powerful of which was the devastating depression of the 1890s and its attendant social unrest. The depression brought hard times to the cities and provoked both the fears and consciences of the rapidly growing middle and upper-middle classes. By the turn of the century, so many activists were at work seeking to improve social conditions that people began to speak of a "Progressive Era," a time of fermenting idealism and constructive social, economic, and political change.

ELEMENTS OF REFORM

Progressivism was a reform movement so varied and comprehensive it almost defies definition. Political progressives crusaded against the abuses of urban political bosses and corporate robber barons. Their goals were greater democracy, honest and efficient government, more effective regulation of business, and greater social justice for working people. They believed that the scope of local, state, and federal government authority should be expanded to accomplish these goals. Doing so, they hoped, would ensure the "progress" of American society. The "real heart of the movement," declared one self-described progressive reformer, was "to use the government as an agency of human welfare."

But the Kansas editor William Allen White hinted at a paradox in the movement when he said that progressivism was just populism that had "shaved its whiskers, washed its shirt, put on a derby [hat], and moved up into the middle class." As White suggested, urban business and professional leaders brought to progressivism a certain respectability and political savvy that the Populists had lacked. They also brought a more businesslike, efficient approach to reform. While one strand in the varied fabric of progressivism retained the resonant appeal of agrarian democracy and its antitrust traditions, a new emphasis on efficiency soon gained ascendancy.

Another paradox in the Progressive movement was that it contained an element of conservatism. In some cases, the regulation of business turned out actually to be regulation proposed *by* business leaders who preferred regulated stability to the chaos and uncertainty of unrestrained competition. In addition, many progressives were motivated by religious beliefs that led them to concentrate on "reforms" such as prohibition of alcoholic beverages and Sunday closing laws. In sum, progressivism was diverse in both origins and agendas. Few people adhered to all of the varied progressive causes. What reformers shared was a common assumption that the complex social ills and tensions generated by the urban-industrial revolution required new responses. Governments were now called upon to extend a broad range of direct services: schools, good roads (a movement propelled first by cyclists and then by automobilists), conservation, public health and welfare, care of the handicapped, farm loans and demonstration agents (county workers who visited farm families to demonstrate new technology), among other things. Such initiatives represented the first tentative steps toward what would become known during the 1930s and after as the welfare state.

ANTECEDENTS TO PROGRESSIVISM   Populism was indisputably one of the catalysts of progressivism. The Populist platform of 1892 outlined many reforms that would be accomplished in the Progressive Era. After the collapse of the farmers' movement and the revival of the agricultural sector at the turn of the century, the reform spirit shifted to cities, where middle-class activists had for years attacked the problems of political bossism and urban development. The Mugwumps, those gentlemen reformers who had fought the spoils system and promoted a civil service based on merit, supplied the Progressive movement with an important element of its thinking, the honest-government ideal. Over the years, their ranks had been supplemented and the honest-government outlook broadened by leaders who confronted such new urban problems as crime, vice, and the efficient provision of gas, electricity, water, sewers, mass transit, and garbage collection.

Finally, another significant force in fostering the spirit of progressivism was the growing familiarity with socialist doctrines and their critiques of living and working conditions. The Socialist party of the time served as the left wing of progressivism. Most progressives found socialist remedies unacceptable, and the progressive reform impulse grew in part from a desire to counter the growing influence of socialist doctrines. More important in spurring progressive reform were social critics who dramatized the need for reform.

THE MUCKRAKERS   Poverty, unsafe working conditions, and child labor in mills, mines, and factories were complex social issues; remedying them required raising public awareness that would in turn spur political action. The writers who thrived on exposing social ills got their name when Theodore Roosevelt compared them to a character in John Bunyan's *Pilgrim's Progress:* "A man that could look no way but downwards with a muckrake in his hands." The "muckrakers are often indispensable to . . . society," Roosevelt said, "but only if they know when to stop raking the muck."

Henry Demarest Lloyd is sometimes cited as the first of the muckrakers for his critical examination of the Standard Oil Company and other monopolies in his book, *Wealth against Commonwealth* (1894).

Another early muckraker was Jacob Riis, a Danish immigrant who, as an influential New York journalist, exposed slum conditions in *How the Other Half Lives* (1890). The chief outlets for these social critics were the inexpensive popular magazines that began to flourish in the 1890s, such as the *Arena* and *McClure's* magazine.

The golden age of muckraking is sometimes dated from 1902 when *McClure's* began to run articles by the reporter Lincoln Steffens on municipal corruption, later collected into a book: *The Shame of the Cities* (1904). *McClure's* also ran Ida M. Tarbell's *History of the Standard Oil Company* (1904). Tarbell provided a more detailed treatment than the earlier book by Lloyd, but it was all the more damaging in its detail. Other reform-minded books that began as magazine articles exposed corruption in the stock market, the meat industry, the life insurance business, and the political world.

Without the muckrakers, progressivism surely would never have achieved the popular support it had. In feeding the public's appetite for sordid facts about the new urban-industrial society, the muckrakers demonstrated one of the salient features of the Progressive movement, and one of its central failures: the progressives were stronger on diagnosis than on remedy. They professed a naive faith in the power of democracy. Let the people know, expose corruption, and bring government close to the people, reformers believed, and the correction of evils would follow automatically. The cure for the ills of democracy, it seemed, was a more informed and active democracy.

THE MAIN FEATURES OF PROGRESSIVISM

DEMOCRACY The most important reform with which the progressives tried to democratize government was the direct primary, or the nomination of candidates by the vote of party members. Under the existing convention system, only a small proportion of the voters attended the local caucuses or precinct meetings that sent delegates to county, and in turn to state and national, conventions. While this traditional method allowed seasoned leaders to sift the candidates, it also lent itself to domination by political professionals who were able to come early and stay late. Direct primaries at the local level had been held sporadically since the 1870s, but after South Carolina adopted the first statewide primary in 1896, the movement spread within two decades to nearly every state.

The party primary was but one expression of a broad movement for greater public participation in the political process. In 1898 South Dakota became the first state to adopt the *initiative* and *referendum,* procedures that allowed voters to enact laws directly. If a designated number of voters petitioned to have a measure put on the ballot (the initiative), the electorate could then vote it up or down (the referendum). Oregon adopted a whole spectrum of reform measures, including a voter registration law (1899); the initiative and referendum (1902); the direct primary (1904); a sweeping corrupt-practices act (1908); and the recall (1910), whereby public officials could be removed by petition and vote. Within a decade nearly twenty states had adopted the initiative and referendum and nearly a dozen the recall.

Most states adopted the party primary even in the choice of United States senators, heretofore selected by state legislatures. Nevada was first, in 1899, to let voters express a choice that state legislators of their party were expected to follow in choosing senators. The popular election of senators required a constitutional amendment, and the House of Representatives, beginning in 1894, four times adopted such an amendment, only to see it defeated in the Senate, which came under increasing attack as a "millionaire's club." By 1912 thirty states had provided party primary elections. The Senate in that year finally accepted the inevitable and agreed to the Seventeenth Amendment, authorizing popular election of senators. The amendment was ratified in 1913.

Poster to encourage on-the-job productivity, 1920s. With a series of posters, the Mather Poster Company aimed to keep workers focused, productive, and loyal.

EFFICIENCY A second major theme of progressivism was the "gospel of efficiency." In the business world during the early twentieth century, Frederick W. Taylor, the original "efficiency expert," was developing the techniques he summed up in his book *The Principles of Scientific Management* (1911): efficient management of production time and costs, the proper routing and scheduling of work, standardization of tools and equipment, and the like. "Taylorism," as scientific management came to be known, promised to reduce waste through the careful analysis of labor processes. By breaking down the production process into separate steps and by meticulously studying the time it took each worker to perform a task, Taylor sought to discover the optimum technique for the average worker and establish performance standards for each job classification. The promise of higher wages, he believed, would motivate workers to exceed the "average" expectations.

Instead, many workers resented Taylor's innovations. They saw in scientific management a tool for employers to make them work faster than was healthy or fair. Yet Taylor's system brought concrete improvements in productivity—especially among those industries whose production processes were highly standardized and where jobs were rigidly defined. "In the future," Taylor predicted in 1911, "the system [rather than the individual workers] will be first."

In government, the efficiency movement demanded the reorganization of agencies to eliminate redundancy, to establish clear lines of authority, and to assign responsibility and accountability to specific officials. Two new ideas for making municipal government more efficient gained headway in the first decade of the new century. The commission system, first adopted by Galveston, Texas, in 1901, when local government there collapsed in the aftermath of a devastating hurricane and tidal wave, placed ultimate authority in a board composed of elected administrative heads of city departments—commissioners of sanitation, police, utilities, and so on. The more durable idea, however, was the city-manager plan, under which a professional administrator ran the government in accordance with policies set by the elected council and mayor. Staunton, Virginia, first adopted the plan in 1908. By 1914 the National Association of City Managers heralded the arrival of a new profession.

When America was a pre-industrial society, Andrew Jackson's notion that any reasonably intelligent citizen could perform the duties of any public office may have been true. By the early twentieth century, many functions of government and business had come to require expert specialists.

Robert M. La Follette.

This principle of government by experts was promoted by Governor Robert M. La Follette of Wisconsin, who advocated progressivism and established a Legislative Reference Bureau to provide research, advice, and help in the drafting of legislation. The "Wisconsin Idea" of efficient government was widely publicized and copied. La Follette also pushed for such reforms as the primary, stronger railroad regulation, the conservation of natural resources, and workmen's compensation.

REGULATION   Of all the problems facing American society at the turn of the century, one engaged a greater diversity of reformers, and elicited more—and more controversial—solutions than any other: the regulation of giant corporations, which became a third major theme of progressivism. Bipartisan concern over the concentration of economic power had brought passage of the Sherman Anti-Trust Act in 1890, but the act had turned out to be more symbolic than effective.

The problem of economic power and its abuse offered a dilemma for progressives. Four broad solutions were available, but of these, two were extremes that had limited support: letting business work out its own destiny under a policy of laissez-faire, or adopting a socialist program of public ownership of big businesses. At the municipal level, however, the socialist alternative was rather widely adopted in public utilities and transportation—so-called gas and water socialism—but otherwise was not seriously considered as a general policy. The other choices were either to adopt a policy of trust-busting in the belief that restoring old-fashioned competition would best prevent economic abuses, or to accept big business in the belief that it brought economies of scale, but to regulate it to prevent abuses.

Efforts to restore the competition of small firms proved unworkable, partly because breaking up large corporations was complex and difficult. The trend over the years was toward regulation rather than dissolution of big business. To some extent regulation and "stabilization" won acceptance among business leaders who, whatever respect they paid to competition in the abstract, preferred not to face it in practice. As time passed, however, regulatory agencies often came under the influence or control of those they were supposed to regulate. Railroad executives, for instance, generally had more intimate knowledge of the intricate details involved in their business, giving them the advantage over the outsiders who might be appointed to the Interstate Commerce Commission.

SOCIAL JUSTICE   A fourth important feature of the progressive spirit was the impulse toward social justice, which motivated diverse actions—from promotion of private charities to campaigns against child labor and liquor. The settlement house movement of the late nineteenth century had spawned a corps of social workers and genteel reformers devoted to the uplift of slum dwellers. But with time it became apparent that social evils extended beyond the reach of private charities and demanded government intervention.

Labor legislation was perhaps the most significant reform to emerge from the drive for social justice. It emerged first at the state level. The National Child Labor Committee, organized in 1904, led a movement for laws banning the still widespread employment of young children. Through publicity, the organization of state and local committees, and a telling documentation of the evils of child labor by the photographer Lewis W. Hine, the committee within ten years brought about legislation in most states banning the labor of underage children (the minimum age varied from twelve to sixteen) and limiting the working hours of older children.

Closely linked with the child-labor reform movement was a concerted effort to regulate the hours of work for women. Spearheaded by Florence

Kelley, the head of the National Consumers League, this progressive crusade prompted the passage of state laws to ameliorate the distinctive hardships that long working hours imposed on women who were wives and mothers. Many states also outlawed night work and labor in dangerous occupations for both women and children. But numerous exemptions and inadequate enforcement often virtually nullified the laws.

The Supreme Court pursued a curiously erratic course in ruling on state labor laws. In *Lochner* v. *New York* (1905), the Court voided a ten-hour-

A young girl working as a spinner in a cotton mill in Vermont, 1910.

workday law because it violated workers' "liberty of contract" to accept any terms they chose. But in *Muller* v. *Oregon* (1908), the high court upheld a ten-hour law for women largely on the basis of sociological data regarding the effects of long hours on the health and morals of women. In *Bunting* v. *Oregon* (1917), the Court accepted a ten-hour day for both men and women, but held out for twenty more years against state minimum-wage laws.

Legislation to protect workers against avoidable accidents gained impetus from disasters such as the 1911 fire at the Triangle Shirtwaist Company in New York in which 146 people, mostly women, died for want of adequate exits. They either were trapped on the three upper floors of a ten-story building, or they plunged to the street below. Stricter building codes and factory inspection acts followed. One of the most important advances along these lines was the series of workers' compensation laws enacted after Maryland led the way in 1902. Accident insurance systems replaced the old common-law principle that an injured worker was entitled to compensation only if he could prove employer negligence, a costly and capricious procedure from which the worker was likely either to win nothing or to be granted excessive awards from overly sympathetic juries.

PROHIBITION   For many progressive activists the cause of liquor prohibition was a fifth area for action. Opposition to strong drink was an
ideal cause in which to merge the older religious-based ethics with the
new social ethics. Given the importance of saloons as arenas for local
politics, prohibitionists could equate the "liquor traffic" with progressive
suspicion of bossism and "special interests." When reform pressures
mounted, prohibition offered an easy outlet, bypassing the complexities
of corporate regulation.

The battle against booze dated far back into the nineteenth century.
The Women's Christian Temperance Union had promoted the cause
since 1874, and a Prohibition political party had entered the elections
in 1876. But the most successful political action followed the formation
in 1893 of the Anti-Saloon League, an organization that pioneered the
strategy of the single-issue pressure group. Through its singleness of
purpose, it forced the prohibition issue into the forefront of state and
local elections. At its "Jubilee Convention" in 1913 the Anti-Saloon
League endorsed a prohibition amendment to the Constitution, adopted
by Congress that year. By the time it was ratified six years later, state
and local action already had dried up areas occupied by nearly three-
fourths of the nation's population.

ROOSEVELT'S PROGRESSIVISM

While most progressive initiatives originated at the state and local
levels, calls for national progressive efforts began to appear around 1900.
Theodore Roosevelt brought to the White House in 1901 an expansive
vision of the presidency that was admirably suited to the cause of progressive reform. In one of his first addresses to Congress, he stressed the
need for a new political approach. When the Constitution was first
drafted, he explained, the nation's social and economic conditions were
quite unlike those at the dawn of the twentieth century. "The conditions
are now wholly different and wholly different action is called for."

More than any other president since Lincoln, Roosevelt possessed
an activist bent. Still, his initial approach to reform was cautious. He
sought to avoid the extremes of socialism on the one hand and laissez-
faire individualism on the other. A skilled political maneuverer, he cultivated party leaders in Congress and steered away from such divisive

Theodore Roosevelt as an apostle of prosperity (top) and as a Roman tyrant (bottom). Roosevelt's energy, spirit, righteousness, and impulsiveness led people to have distinct reactions to his personality.

issues as the tariff and regulation of the banks. And when he did approach the explosive issue of the trusts, he always took care to reassure the business community. For him, politics was the art of the possible. Unlike the more radical progressives and the doctrinaire "lunatic fringe," as he called them, he would take half a loaf rather than none at all.

EXECUTIVE ACTION   At the outset of his presidency in 1901, Roosevelt promised to sustain McKinley's policies. He worked with Republican leaders in Congress, against whom the minority of new progressives was as yet powerless. Yet Roosevelt would accomplish more by vigorous executive action than by passing legislation, and in the exercise of executive power he would not be inhibited by points of legal detail. He argued that, as president, he might do anything not expressly forbidden by the Constitution.

In 1902 Roosevelt carried the trust issue to the people on a tour of New England and the Midwest. He endorsed a "square deal" for all, calling for enforcement of existing antitrust laws and stricter controls on big business. From the outset, however, Roosevelt balked at wholesale trust-busting. Effective regulation of corporate giants was better than a futile effort to restore small business, which might be achieved only at a cost to the efficiencies of scale gained in larger operations.

Because Congress boggled at regulatory legislation, Roosevelt sought to force the issue by a more vigorous prosecution of the Sherman Anti-Trust Act. He chose his target carefully. In the case against the sugar trust (*United States* v. *E. C. Knight and Company,* 1895), the Supreme Court had declared manufacturing a strictly intrastate activity. Railroads, however, were beyond question engaged in interstate commerce and thus subject to federal authority.

In 1902 Roosevelt ordered his attorney-general to break up the Northern Securities Company, a giant conglomerate of railroads. The company, formed the previous year, had taken shape during a gigantic battle between E. H. Harriman of the Union Pacific and James J. Hill and J. P. Morgan of the Great Northern and Northern Pacific for the stock of the Northern Pacific, which was crucial to shipping in the Northwest. The stock battle raised the threat of a panic on the New York Stock Exchange and led to a settlement in which the chief contenders made peace. They formed Northern Securities as a holding company to control the Great Northern and Northern Pacific. The merger of such rival rail lines essentially ended competition by forging a monopoly. In 1904 the Supreme Court ordered the railroad combination dissolved.

THE 1902 COAL STRIKE   Support for Roosevelt's use of the "big stick" against corporations was strengthened by the stubbornness of mine owners in the anthracite coal strike of 1902. On May 12 the United Mine Workers (UMW) walked off the job in Pennsylvania and West Virginia, demanding a 20 percent wage increase, a reduction in daily hours from ten to nine, and official union recognition by the mine owners. The mine operators, having granted a 10 percent raise two years before, dug in their heels against further concessions, and shut down the mines in preparation for a long struggle to starve out the miners, many of whom were immigrants from eastern Europe. One of the mine owners expressed the attitude of many of them when he proclaimed: "The miners don't suffer—why, they can't even speak English."

Facing the prospect of a nationwide coal shortage, Roosevelt called both sides to a conference at the White House. The mine owners attended but refused even to speak to the UMW leaders. The "extraordinary stupidity and temper" of the "wooden-headed" owners infuriated Roosevelt. The president wanted to grab the spokesman for the mine owners "by the seat of his breeches" and "chuck him out" a White House window. After the conference ended in an impasse, Roosevelt threatened to take over the mines and run them with the army. When a congressman questioned the constitutionality of such a move, an exasperated Roosevelt roared: "To hell with the Constitution when the people want coal!" Militarizing the mines would have been an act of dubious legality, but the owners feared that Roosevelt might actually do it and that public opinion would support him.

The coal strike ended in October 1902 with an agreement to submit the issues to an arbitration commission named by the president. The agreement enhanced Roosevelt's prestige, although it produced only a partial victory for the miners. By the arbitrators' decision in 1903, the miners won a nine-hour day but only a 10 percent wage increase, and no union recognition.

EXPANDING FEDERAL POWER   Roosevelt continued to use his executive powers to enforce the Sherman Anti-Trust Act, but he drew back from further antitrust legislation. Altogether his administration initiated about twenty-five antitrust suits; the most notable victory came in *Swift and Company* v. *United States* (1905), a decision against the "beef trust" through which most of the meat packers had avoided competitive bidding in the purchase of livestock. In this decision, the Supreme Court put forth the "stream-of-commerce" doctrine, which overturned its previous holding that manufacturing was strictly intrastate. Since both livestock and the meat products of the packers moved in the stream of interstate commerce, the Court reasoned, they were subject to federal regulation. This interpretation of the interstate commerce power would be broadened in later years until few enterprises would remain beyond the reach of federal regulation.

In 1903 Congress passed the Elkins Act, which made it illegal for railroads to take as well as to give secret rebates to their favorite customers. All shippers would be charged the same price. In that same year, Congress created a new Bureau of Corporations to study and report on the activities of interstate corporations. Its findings could lead to antitrust suits, but its purpose was rather to help corporations correct malpractices and avoid the need for lawsuits. Many companies, among them United States Steel and International Harvester, worked closely with the bureau, but others held back. When Standard Oil refused to turn over its records, the government brought an antitrust suit that

A cartoon that depicts Theodore Roosevelt as a lion-tamer, confronting the business beasts of the steel trust, oil trust, beef trust, and others, in the arena of Wall Street.

resulted in its breakup in 1911. The Supreme Court broke up the American Tobacco Company at the same time. This approach fell short of the direct regulation that Roosevelt preferred, but without a congressional will to pass such laws, little more was possible. Trusts that cooperated were left alone; others had to run the gauntlet of antitrust suits.

ROOSEVELT'S SECOND TERM

Roosevelt's policies built a coalition of progressive- and conservative-minded voters that assured his election in his own right in 1904. The Republican convention chose him by acclamation. The Democrats, having lost with Bryan twice, turned to Alton B. Parker who, as chief justice of New York, had upheld labor's right to the closed shop (requiring that all employees be union members) and the state's right to limit hours of work. Despite his liberal record, party leaders presented him as a safe conservative, and his acceptance of the gold standard as "firmly and irrevocably established" bolstered such a view. The effort to present a candidate more conservative than Roosevelt proved a futile gesture for the party that had twice nominated William Jennings Bryan. Despite Roosevelt's trust-busting proclivities, most business executives, according to the *New York Sun,* preferred the "impulsive candidate of the party of conservatism to the conservative candidate of the party which the business interests regard as permanently and dangerously impulsive." Even business tycoons J. P. Morgan and E. H. Harriman contributed handsomely to Roosevelt's campaign chest.

An invincible popularity plus the sheer force of his personality swept Roosevelt to an impressive victory by a popular vote of 7.6 million to 5.1 million. Parker carried only the Solid South of the former Confederacy and two border states, Kentucky and Maryland (with an electoral vote of 336 for Roosevelt and 140 for Parker). On election night, Roosevelt announced that he would not run again, a statement he later would regret.

LEGISLATIVE LEADERSHIP   Elected in his own right, Roosevelt approached his second term with heightened confidence and a stronger commitment to progressive reform. In 1905 he devoted most of his annual message to the regulation and control of business. This understandably irked many of his corporate contributors. Said steel baron

Henry Frick, "We bought the son of a bitch and then he did not stay put." The independent-minded Roosevelt took aim at the railroads first. The Elkins Act of 1903, finally outlawing rebates, had been a minor step. Railroad executives themselves welcomed it as an escape from shippers clamoring for special favors. But a new proposal for railroad regulation endorsed by Roosevelt was something else again. It sought to extend the authority of the Interstate Commerce Commission (ICC) and give it effective control over freight rates.

Enacted in 1906, the Hepburn Act for the first time gave the ICC power to set maximum freight rates. The commission no longer had to go to court to enforce its decisions. While the carriers could challenge the rates in court, the burden of proof now rested on them rather than on the Interstate Commerce Commission. In other ways, too, the Hepburn Act enlarged the mandate of the ICC. Its reach now extended beyond railroads to pipelines, express companies, sleeping-car companies, bridges, and ferries, and it could prescribe a uniform system of bookkeeping to provide uniform statistics.

Railroads took priority, but a growing movement for the regulation of meat packers, food processors, and makers of drugs and patent medicines reached fruition, as it happened, on the very day after passage of the Hepburn Act. Discontent with abuses in these industries had grown rapidly as a result of the muckrakers' revelations. They supplied evidence of harmful preservatives and adulterants in the preparation of "embalmed meat" and other food products. The *Ladies' Home Journal* and *Collier's* published evidence of false claims and dangerous ingredients in patent medicines. One of the more notorious "medicines," Lydia Pinkham's Vegetable Compound, was advertised to work wonders in the relief of "female complaints"; it was no wonder, for the compound was 18 percent alcohol.

Perhaps the most telling blow against such abuses was struck by Upton Sinclair's novel *The Jungle* (1906). Sinclair meant the book to promote socialism, but its main impact came from its portrayal of filthy conditions in Chicago's meat-packing industry: "It was too dark in these storage places to see well, but a man could run his hand over these piles of meat and sweep off handfuls of the dried dung of rats. These rats were nuisances, and the packers would put poisoned bread out for them, they would die, and then rats, bread, and meat would go into the hoppers together." Roosevelt read *The Jungle*—and reacted

Pigs strung up along the hog scraping rail at the Armour's Packing Plant in Chicago, 1909.

quickly. He sent two agents to Chicago, and their report confirmed all that Sinclair had said: "We saw meat shovelled from filthy wooden floors, piled on tables rarely washed, pushed from room to room in rotten box carts, in all of which processes it was in the way of gathering dirt, splinters, floor filth, and the expectoration of tuberculous and other diseased workers."

Congress and Roosevelt acted quickly to address the problem. The Meat Inspection Act of 1906 required federal inspection of meats destined for interstate commerce and empowered officials in the Agriculture Department to impose sanitation standards. The Pure Food and Drug Act, enacted the same day, placed restrictions on the makers of prepared foods and patent medicines, and forbade the manufacture, sale, or transportation of adulterated, misbranded, or harmful foods, drugs, and liquors.

CONSERVATION   One of the most enduring legacies of the Roosevelt years was his energetic support for the conservation movement. Concern for protecting the environment grew with the rising awareness that exploitation of natural resources was despoiling the nation's natural wonders. As early as 1872, Yellowstone National Park had been set aside as a public reserve (the National Park Service would be created in 1916 after other parks had been added). In 1881 Congress had created

Yellowstone, Wyoming, photographed by William Henry Jackson during the 1870s.

a Division of Forestry in the Department of Agriculture, and Roosevelt's appointment of Gifford Pinchot, one of the country's first scientific foresters, as chief brought vigorous administration of forests on public lands. The president strove to halt the unchecked destruction of the environment by providing a barrier of federal regulation and protection. To do so, Roosevelt added fifty federal wildlife refuges, approved five new national parks, and initiated the system of designating national monuments such as the Grand Canyon. He also used the Forest Reserve Act (1891) to exclude from settlement or harvest some 172 million acres of timberland. Lumber barons were irate, but Roosevelt held firm. As he bristled, "I hate a man who would skin the land."

Forestry chief Gifford Pinchot worked vigorously, with the president's support, to develop programs and public interest in conservation. Congressional resistance to their proposals led Pinchot and Roosevelt to publicize the cause through a White House Conference on Conservation in 1908, and later that year by setting up a National Conservation Commission, which proposed a thorough survey of the nation's resources in minerals, water, forests, and soil. Within eighteen months, some forty-one state conservation commissions had sprung up, and a number of private groups took up the cause. The movement remained divided, however, between those who wanted to conserve resources for continuous human use and those who wanted to set aside areas as wilderness preserves. Pinchot, for instance, provoked the wrath of famous naturalist John Muir in 1906 when he endorsed a water reservoir in the wild Hetch Hetchy Valley of Yosemite National Park to supply the needs of San Francisco.

From Roosevelt to Taft

Toward the end of his second term, Roosevelt declared "I have had a great time as president." Although eligible to run again, he opted for retirement. Unlike most presidents, he was strong enough to handpick a successor to carry out "the policies." He decided that the heir to the White House should be Secretary of War William Howard Taft, and the Republican convention ratified the choice on its first ballot in 1908. The Democrats, whose conservative strategy had backfired in 1904, decided to give William Jennings Bryan one more chance at the highest office. Still vigorous at forty-eight, Bryan retained a faithful following, but struggled to attract a national following. Roosevelt advised Taft: "Do not answer Bryan; *attack* him. Don't let him make the issues." Taft followed Roosevelt's advice, declaring that Bryan's election would result in a "paralysis of business."

The Republican platform declared its support of Roosevelt's policies, including conservation and further strengthening of the Interstate Commerce Commission. On the tariff and the use of labor injunctions, the platform made vague references to revision but without any specifics. The Democratic platform hardly differed on regulation, but it endorsed a lower tariff and an AFL-supported plank opposing court injunctions against labor actions. In the end, the voters opted for Roosevelt's chosen successor: Taft swept the electoral college by 321 to 162. The real surprise of the election, however, was the strong showing of the Socialist party candidate, labor hero Eugene V. Debs. His 421,000 votes revealed the depth of working-class resentment in the United States.

Once out of office, still only fifty, Roosevelt went on a big-game hunt in Africa, prompting his old foe J. P. Morgan to mutter, "Let every lion do his duty." The new president he left behind was an entirely different kind of political animal, in fact hardly a political animal at all. Offspring of a prominent Cincinnati family—his father had been Grant's attorney-general—Taft had progressed through appointive offices, from judge in Ohio to solicitor in the Justice Department, federal judge, commissioner and governor-general in the Philippines, and secretary of war. The presidency was the only elective office he ever held. Later he would be chief justice of the Supreme Court (1921–1930), a job more suited to his temperament.

William Howard Taft.

Taft detested politics and never felt comfortable in the White House. He once observed that whenever someone said "Mr. President," he looked around for Roosevelt. The political dynamo in the family was his wife, Nellie, who had wanted the White House more than he. One of the major tragedies of Taft's presidency was that Helen "Nellie" Taft suffered a debilitating stroke soon after they entered the White House, and for most of his term she remained unable to serve as his political adviser.

TARIFF REFORM   Taft's domestic policies generated a storm of controversy within his own party. Contrary to Republican tradition, he preferred a lower tariff, and he made this the first important issue of his presidency. But if in pressing an issue that Roosevelt had skirted Taft seemed the bolder of the two, he proved less skillful in dealing with Congress.

A tariff bill passed the House with surprising ease. It lowered rates less than Taft would have preferred but made some important reductions and enlarged the number of items that were duty free. But the chairman of the Senate Finance Committee, Nelson W. Aldrich, guided through a drastically revised bill that included more than 800 changes. What came out of a conference committee was a measure close to the final Senate version, although Taft did get some tariff reductions on important items: hides, iron ore, coal, oil, cottons, boots, and shoes.

In response to the higher rates in Aldrich's bill, a group of midwestern Republicans took the Senate floor to fight what they considered a corrupt throwback to the days when the Republican party had done the bidding of big business. In all, ten progressive Republicans joined the Democrats in an unsuccessful effort to defeat the bill. Taft at first agreed with them; then, fearful of a party split, he backed the majority and agreed to an imperfect bill. He lacked Roosevelt's love of a grand battle as well as his gift for working both sides of the street. Temperamentally conservative, inhibited by scruples about interfering too much with the legislative process, he drifted into the orbit of the Republican Old Guard and quickly alienated the progressive wing of his party, whom he tagged "assistant Democrats." He made things worse by labeling the new bill the best tariff the Republican party had ever passed.

BALLINGER AND PINCHOT   In 1910 Taft's policies drove the wedge deeper between the conservative and progressive Republican factions. What came to be called the Ballinger-Pinchot controversy made Taft appear to be a less reliable custodian of Roosevelt's conservation policies than he actually was. Taft's secretary of the interior, Richard A. Ballinger of Seattle, was well aware that many westerners opposed conservation programs on the ground that they held back full development of the region. The strongest conservation leaders were often easterners such as Roosevelt and Gifford Pinchot of Pennsylvania. Ballinger threw open to commercial use more than a million acres of waterpower sites that Roosevelt had withdrawn in the guise of ranger stations. Ballinger's reasoning was that the withdrawal had "gone far beyond legal limitations," and Taft agreed. At about the same time, Ballinger turned over certain federal coal lands in Alaska to a group of Seattle tycoons, some of whom he had represented as a lawyer. Apparently without Ballinger's knowledge, this group had already agreed to sell part of the lands to a banking syndicate.

Chief of Forestry Pinchot reported the collusion to Taft, who refused to intervene. When Pinchot went public with the controversy, Taft fired him for insubordination early in 1910. A joint congressional investigation exonerated Ballinger from all charges of fraud or corruption, but progressive suspicions created such pressure that he resigned in 1911.

In firing Pinchot, Taft acted on the strictly legal view that his training had taught him to value, but circumstances tarnished his image in the public mind. "In the end," one historian has written, "the Ballinger-Pinchot affair had more impact on politics than it did on conservation." Taft had been elected to carry out the Roosevelt policies, his opponents said, and he was carrying them out—"on a stretcher."

Meanwhile, in the House of Representatives rebellion had broken out among the more progressive Republicans. When the regular session opened in 1910, the insurgents joined Democrats in voting to investigate Ballinger. Flushed with that victory, they resolved to clip the wings of Speaker Joseph G. Cannon (R-Ill.), a conservative who held almost a stranglehold on procedures by his power to appoint all committees and their chairmen, and especially by his control of the Rules Committee, of which he was a member. A coalition of Democrats and progressive Republicans overrode a ruling from the Speaker and proceeded to adopt new rules offered by George W. Norris (R-Neb.) that enlarged the Rules Committee from five to fifteen members, made them elective by the House, and excluded the Speaker as a member. About forty Republicans joined the Democratic minority in the move. In the next Congress the rules would be further changed to make all committees elective.

Events had conspired to cast Taft in a conservative role at a time when progressive sentiment was riding high in the country. The result was a severe rebuke to the president in the congressional elections of 1910, first by the widespread defeat of pro-Taft candidates in the Republican primaries, then by the election of a Democratic majority in the House and of enough Democrats in the Senate that progressive Republicans could wield the balance of power.

TAFT AND ROOSEVELT   In 1910 Theodore Roosevelt had returned from his extended travels abroad. He had been reading news accounts and letters about the Taft "betrayal," but unlike some of his supporters, he refused to break with his successor. With rather severe politeness, however, Roosevelt refused an invitation to visit the White House. But, he wrote Taft: "I shall keep my mind open as I keep my mouth shut." Neither was easy for Roosevelt, whose followers urged him to action. Soon he was rallying support for the Republican gubernatorial candidate in New York, and then he was off on a speaking tour of the

West in advance of the congressional elections. In Kansas, he gave a catchy name to his latest principles, the "New Nationalism." Roosevelt issued a stirring call for an array of new federal regulatory laws, a social-welfare program, and new measures of direct democracy, including the old Populist demands for the initiative, recall, and referendum. His purpose was not to revolutionize American life but to save it from the threat of revolution. "What I have advocated," he explained a few days later, "is not wild radicalism. It is the highest and wisest kind of conservatism."

Relations between Roosevelt and Taft remained tense, but it was another year before they came to an open break. The split happened in the fall of 1911, when the Taft administration announced an antitrust suit against United States Steel, citing specifically as cause the company's acquisition of the Tennessee Coal and Iron Company in 1907, a move to which Roosevelt had given tacit approval in the belief that it would avert a business panic. In mid-November Roosevelt published a sharp attack on Taft's "archaic" attempt to restore competition. The only sensible response to the problem, he argued, was to accept business combinations under modern circumstances but to enlarge the government's power to regulate them. Roosevelt's entry into the next presidential campaign was now only a matter of time.

Not all progressive Republicans wanted Roosevelt back in the White House. A sizable number proposed to back Senator Robert La Follette in 1912, but some of La Follette's supporters were ready to switch if Roosevelt entered the race. An opening came on February 2, 1912, when La Follette showed signs of nervous exhaustion in a rambling speech in Philadelphia. As his following began to drop away, a group of seven Republican governors met in Chicago and called on Roosevelt to become a candidate. On February 24 Roosevelt decided to enter the race. "I hope that so far as possible the people may be given the chance, through direct primaries," Roosevelt wrote the governors, "to express their preference." He had decided that Taft had "sold the Square Deal down the river," and he now dismissed Taft as a "hopeless fathead."

The rebuke implicit in Roosevelt's decision to run against Taft, his chosen successor, was in many ways undeserved. During Taft's first year in office one political tempest after another left his image irreparably damaged. The three years of solid achievement that followed came too late to restore its luster or to reunite his divided party. Taft had at least attempted tariff reform, which Roosevelt had never dared. He replaced Ballinger and Pinchot with men of impeccable credentials in conservation matters. He won from Congress the power to protect public lands for any reason, and was the first president to withdraw oil lands from use. Under the Appalachian Forest Reserve Act (1911), he enlarged the national forest by purchase of lands in the East. In the end his administration withdrew more public lands in four years than Roosevelt's had in nearly eight, and brought more antitrust suits, by a score of eighty to twenty-five.

In 1910, with Taft's support, Congress passed the Mann-Elkins Act, which empowered the Interstate Commerce Commission for the first time to initiate rate changes, extended regulation to telephone and telegraph companies, and set up a Commerce Court to expedite appeals from the ICC rulings. Taft also established the Bureau of Mines and the Federal Children's Bureau (1912), and he called for statehood for Arizona and New Mexico and territorial government for Alaska (1912). The Sixteenth Amendment (1913), authorizing a federal income tax, was ratified with Taft's support before he left office, and the Seventeenth Amendment (1913), providing for the popular election of senators, was ratified soon after he left office.

Despite this progressive record, Roosevelt now hastened Taft's demise. In all but two of the thirteen states that held presidential primaries, Roosevelt won, even in Taft's Ohio. But the groundswell of popular support was no match for Taft's decisive position as sitting president and party leader. In state conventions the party regulars held the line, so that Roosevelt entered the Republican national convention about 100 votes short of victory. The Taft forces proceeded

A skeptical view of Roosevelt, the Bull Moose candidate in 1912.

to nominate their man by the same "steamroller" tactics that had nominated Roosevelt in 1904.

Outraged at such "naked theft," the Roosevelt delegates assembled in a rump convention. "If you wish me to make the fight I will make it," Roosevelt told the delegates, who then issued a call for a Progressive party convention, which assembled in Chicago on August 5. Roosevelt appeared before the delegates, feeling "fit as a bull moose." He was "stripped to the buff and ready for the fight," he said. "We stand at Armageddon and we battle for the Lord." But few professional politicians turned up. Progressive Republicans decided to preserve their party credentials and fight another day. For the time being, with the disruption of the Republican party, the progressive torch was about to be passed on to the Democrats.

Wilson's Progressivism

WILSON'S RISE   The emergence of Thomas Woodrow Wilson as the Democratic nominee in 1912 climaxed a political rise even more rapid than that of Grover Cleveland. In 1910, before his nomination and election as governor of New Jersey, Wilson had been president of Princeton University, but he had never run for public office. Born in Staunton, Virginia, in 1856, the son of a "noble-saintly mother" and a stern Presbyterian minister, he had grown up in Georgia and the Carolinas during the Civil War and Reconstruction.

Young Wilson, tall and slender, with a lean, long, sharply chiseled face, inherited his father's unquestioning piety, once declaring that "so far as religion is concerned, argument is adjourned." Wilson also developed a consuming ambition to "serve" humankind. Driven by a sense of destiny and duty, as well as by a certain moral fastidiousness, he once confessed: "I am too intense." Wilson nurtured a righteous commitment to principle that would prove to be his Achilles' heel.

Wilson graduated from Princeton in 1879, and after law school at the University of Virginia he tried a brief, unfulfilling, and profitless legal practice in Atlanta. From there he went to the new Johns Hopkins University in Baltimore, where he found his calling in the study of history and political science.

Wilson's doctoral dissertation, *Congressional Government,* published in 1885, argued that the president, like the British prime minister, should be the leader of party government, as active in directing legislation as in the administration and enforcement of laws. In calling for a strong presidency he expressed views closer to those of Roosevelt than those of Taft. He also shared Roosevelt's concern that politicians should promote the general welfare rather than narrowly serve special interests. And, like Roosevelt, he was critical of big business, organized labor, socialists, and agrarian radicalism.

After Johns Hopkins, Wilson taught at Bryn Mawr and then Wesleyan College before moving to Princeton in 1890. There he quickly earned renown for his scintillating lectures, vigorous mind, and sharp debating skills. In 1902 he was unanimously elected president of the university. In that position he showed the first evidence of reform views. "We are not put into this world to sit still and know," he stressed in his inaugural address. "We are put into it to act." And act he did. At Princeton Wilson modernized the curriculum, expanded and improved the faculty, introduced the tutorial system, and raised admissions standards. But he failed in his attempt to restructure the elitist social clubs of Princeton undergraduates.

Wilson's urge for reform increasingly brought him head to head with university administration and alumni, however, and when, the Democratic boss of New Jersey offered Wilson his support for the 1910 gubernatorial nomination, Wilson accepted. The party leaders sought a respectable candidate to help them ward off progressive challengers, but they discovered too late that the schoolmaster actually had an iron will of his own. Like Roosevelt, Wilson had come to shed some of his original conservatism and to view progressive reform as a necessary expedient in order to stave off more radical social change. Elected as a reform candidate, Governor Wilson promoted progressive measures and pushed them

Wilson campaigning from a train platform.

through the legislature. He pressured lawmakers to enact a workers' compensation law, a corrupt-practices law, measures to regulate public utilities, and ballot reforms. Such strong leadership in a state known as the "home of the trusts" for its lenient corporation laws brought Wilson to national attention.

In the spring of 1911 a group of southern Democrats in New York opened a Wilson presidential campaign headquarters, and Wilson set forth on strenuous tours into all regions of the country, denouncing special privilege and political bossism. But by convention time, despite a fast start, the Wilson campaign seemed headed for defeat by Speaker of the House Bennett Champ Clark of Missouri. Clark had enough for a majority in the early ballots, but the Wilson forces combined with supporters of Oscar Underwood of Alabama to prevent a two-thirds majority. On the fourteenth ballot, William Jennings Bryan came over to Wilson. When the Democratic boss of Illinois deserted Clark on the forty-second ballot and the Underwood delegates went over to Wilson on the forty-sixth, he clinched the nomination.

THE ELECTION OF 1912 The 1912 presidential campaign involved four candidates: Wilson and Taft represented the two major parties while Eugene Debs ran as a Socialist and Roosevelt headed the Progressive party ticket. No sooner did the formal campaign open than Roosevelt's candidacy almost ended. While entering a car on his way to deliver a speech in Milwaukee, he was shot by a fanatic. The bullet went through Roosevelt's overcoat, spectacles case, and folded speech, then fractured a rib before lodging just below his right lung. "Stand back, don't hurt the man," he yelled at the crowd as they mobbed the attacker. Roosevelt then demanded that he be driven to the auditorium to deliver his speech. In a dramatic gesture, he showed the audience his bloodstained shirt and punctured text and vowed: "It takes more than this to kill a bull moose."

As the campaign developed, Taft quickly lost ground. "There are so many people in the country who don't like me," he lamented. The campaign settled down to a running debate over the competing ideologies of the two front-runners: Roosevelt's "New Nationalism" and Wilson's "New Freedom." The inchoate ideas that Roosevelt fashioned into his New Nationalism had first been presented systematically in *The Promise of American Life* (1909) by Herbert Croly, a then-obscure New York journalist. Its central point was often summarized in a useful catchphrase: "Hamiltonian means to achieve Jeffersonian ends," meaning that Alexander Hamilton's program of governmental activism on behalf of business interests should be used to achieve democratic and egalitarian Jeffersonian goals. The times required people to give up Jeffersonian prejudices against big government and use a strong central government to achieve democratic ends in the interest of the people.

The old nationalism had been used "by the sinister . . . special interests," Roosevelt said. His New Nationalism would enable government to promote social justice and to effect such reforms as graduated income and inheritance taxes, workers' compensation, regulation of the labor of women and children, and a stronger Bureau of Corporations. These ideas and more went into the platform of the Progressive party, which called for a federal trade commission with sweeping authority over business and a tariff commission to set rates on a "scientific basis."

Before the end of his administration, Wilson would be swept into the current of New Nationalism too. But initially he adhered to the decentralizing antitrust traditions of his party. Before the start of the campaign, Wilson conferred with Louis D. Brandeis, a progressive lawyer from Boston who focused Wilson's thought much as Croly had focused Roosevelt's. Brandeis's design for the New Freedom differed from Roosevelt's New Nationalism in its belief that the federal government should restore the competition among small economic units rather than regulate huge monopolies. This required a vigorous antitrust policy, lowering tariffs to allow competition with foreign goods, and breaking up the concentration of financial power in Wall Street. But Brandeis and Wilson saw the vigorous expansion of federal power as only a temporary necessity, not a permanent condition. Roosevelt, who was convinced that both corporate concentration and an expanding federal government were permanent developments, dismissed the New Freedom as mere fantasy.

The Republican schism between Taft and Roosevelt opened the way for Woodrow Wilson to win by 435 electoral votes to 88 for Roosevelt and 8 for Taft. But in popular votes, Wilson had only 42 percent of the total. Roosevelt received 27 percent, Taft 23 percent, and Debs 6 percent. It was the victory of a minority over a divided opposition.

The 1912 election was significant in several ways. First, it was a high-water mark for progressivism. The election was the first to feature presidential primaries. The two leading candidates debated the basic issues of progressivism in a campaign unique for its focus on vital alter-

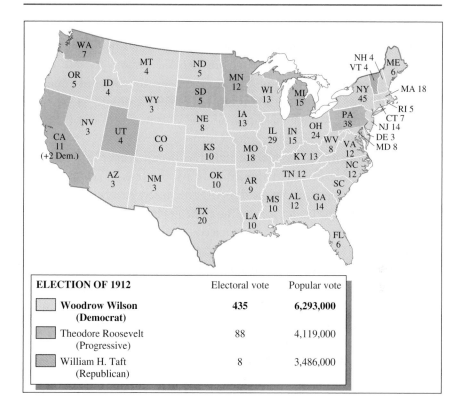

ELECTION OF 1912	Electoral vote	Popular vote
Woodrow Wilson (Democrat)	**435**	**6,293,000**
Theodore Roosevelt (Progressive)	88	4,119,000
William H. Taft (Republican)	8	3,486,000

natives and for its high philosophical tone. Taft, too, despite his temperament and associations, showed his own progressive instincts. And the Socialist party, the left wing of progressivism, polled over 900,000 votes for Eugene V. Debs, its highest proportion ever.

Second, the election gave Democrats effective national power for the first time since the Civil War. For two years during the second Grover Cleveland administration, 1893–1895, they had held the White House and majorities in both houses of Congress, but they had fallen quickly out of power during the severe depression of the 1890s. Now, under Wilson, they again held the presidency and were the majority in both the House of Representatives and the Senate.

Third, the election of Wilson brought southerners back into the orbit of national and international affairs in a significant way for the first time since the Civil War. Five of Wilson's ten cabinet members were born in the South, three still resided there, and William Jennings Bryan, the secretary of state, was an idol of the southern masses. At the president's right hand, and one of the most influential members of the Wilson circle, at least until 1919, was Colonel Edward M. House of Texas. Wilson described House as "my second personality. He is my independent self." On Capitol Hill southerners, by virtue of their seniority, held the lion's share of committee chairmanships. As a result, much of the progressive legislation of the Wilson era would bear the names of the southerners who guided it through Congress.

Fourth and finally, the election of 1912 had begun to alter the character of the Republican party. Even though most party professionals remained, the defection of the Bull Moose Progressives had weakened the party's progressive wing. The leaders of the Republican party that would return to power in the 1920s would be more conservative in tone and temperament.

WILSONIAN REFORM   Wilson's inaugural address voiced in eloquent tones the ideals of social justice that animated many progressives. "We have been proud of our industrial achievements," he said, "but we have not hitherto stopped thoughtfully enough to count the human cost . . . the fearful physical and spiritual cost to the men and women and children upon whom the dead weight and burden of it all has fallen pitilessly the years through." He promised specifically a lower tariff and a new banking system. "This is not a day of triumph; it is a day of dedication. Here muster, not the forces of party, but the forces of humanity."

If Roosevelt had been a strong president by force of personality, Wilson became a strong president by force of conviction. The president, he wrote in *Congressional Government*, "is . . . the political leader of the nation, or has it in his choice to be. The nation as a whole has chosen him, and is conscious that it has no other political spokesman. His is the only national voice in affairs."

Wilson courted popular support, but he also courted members of Congress through personal contacts, invitations to the White House, and visits to the Capitol. He used patronage power to reward friends and punish enemies. He might have acted through a progressive coalition, but chose instead to rely on party loyalty. "I'd rather trust a machine Senator when he is committed to your program," he told his navy secretary, "than a talking Liberal who can never quite go along with others because of his admiration of his own patented plan of reform." Wilson therefore made use of the party caucus, in which disagreements among Democrats were settled.

THE TARIFF   Wilson's leadership faced its first big test on the issue of tariff reform. He summoned Congress into special session and addressed it in person—the first president to do so since John Adams. (Roosevelt was said to have asked, "Why didn't I think of that?") Congress acted vigorously on tariff reductions. Only four Democrats bolted the party line as the new bill passed the House easily.

The crunch came in the Senate, the traditional graveyard of tariff reform. Swarms of lobbyists got so thick in Washington, Wilson said, that "a brick couldn't be thrown without hitting one of them." The president turned the tables with a public statement that focused the spotlight on the "industrious and insidious" tariff lobby.

The Underwood-Simmons Tariff became law in 1913. It reduced import duties on most goods and lowered the overall average duty from about 37 percent to about 29 percent. A list of some 300 items exempted from tariff duties included important consumer goods and raw materials: sugar, wool, iron ore, steel rails, agricultural implements, cement, coal, wood and wood pulp, and many farm products. The act lowered tariff rates but raised federal revenues with the first income tax levied under the newly ratified Sixteenth Amendment: 1 percent on incomes over $3,000 ($4,000 for married couples) and a surtax graduated from 1 percent on incomes of about $20,000 to 6 percent on incomes above $500,000. The highest total tax rate thus would be 7 percent.

THE FEDERAL RESERVE ACT   Before the new tariff had cleared the Senate, the administration proposed the first major banking and currency reform since the Civil War. The Glass-Owen Federal Reserve Act of 1913 created a new national banking system, with regional reserve banks supervised by a central board of directors. There would be twelve Federal Reserve Banks, each owned by member banks in its district. All national banks became members; state banks and trust companies could join if they wished. Each member bank had to subscribe 6 percent of its capital to the Federal Reserve Bank and deposit a portion of its reserves there, the amount depending on the size of the community.

These "bankers' banks" dealt with their members and not at all with individuals. Along with other banking functions, the chief service to member banks was to rediscount their loans, that is, to take them over in exchange for Federal Reserve Notes, which member banks might then

Reading the Death Warrant. *Wilson's plan for banking and currency reform spells the death of the "Money Trust," according to this cartoon.*

use to make further loans. The Federal Reserve Notes in turn were based 40 percent on government gold and 60 percent on commercial and agricultural paper (the promissory notes signed by borrowers). This arrangement made it possible to expand both the money supply and bank credit in times of high business activity, or as the level of borrowing increased. A Federal Reserve Board named three of the nine members on each Reserve Bank's board (member banks chose the remaining six) and carried out general supervision, including review of the rediscount rates. These rates might be raised to fight inflation by tightening credit, or lowered to stimulate business by making credit more easily available.

This new system corrected three great defects in the previous arrangement. Now bank reserves could be pooled, affording greater security; both the currency and bank credit became more elastic; and the concentration of reserves in New York was lessened. The system represented a new step in active governmental intervention and control in one of the most sensitive segments of the economy.

ANTITRUST LAWS Wilson made trust-busting the central focus of the New Freedom. The concentration of economic power had continued to grow despite the Sherman Anti-Trust Act and the federal watchdog agency, the Bureau of Corporations. Wilson's solution to the problem was revision of the Sherman Act to define more explicitly what counted as "restraint of trade." He decided to make a strong Federal Trade Commission (FTC) the cornerstone of his antitrust program. Created in 1914, the five-member commission replaced Roosevelt's

Bureau of Corporations and assumed new powers to define "unfair trade practices" and to issue "cease-and-desist" orders when it found evidence of unfair competition.

Having now embraced the principle of "controlled competition," Wilson seemed to lose interest in the antitrust bill drafted by Henry D. Clayton (D-Ala.) of the House Judiciary Committee, which followed the president's original idea of defining specific acts in restraint of trade. The Clayton Antitrust Act, passed in 1914, outlawed such practices as price discrimination (charging different customers different prices for the same goods), "tying" agreements that limited the right of dealers to handle the products of competing manufacturers, interlocking directorates connecting corporations with a capital of more than $1 million (or banks with more than $5 million), and corporations' acquisition of stock in competing corporations. In every case, however, conservative forces in the Senate qualified these provisions by tacking on the weakening phrase "where the effect may be to substantially lessen competition" or words of similar effect. And conservative southern Democrats and northern Republicans amended the act to allow for broad judicial review of the Federal Trade Commission's decisions, thus further weakening its freedom of action. In accordance with the president's recommendation, however, corporate officials were made individually responsible for any violations. Victims of price discrimination and tying agreements could sue for compensation equaling three times the amount of damages suffered.

Agrarian activists, in alliance with organized labor, won a stipulation that supposedly exempted farm labor organizations from the antitrust laws, but actually only declared them not to be, per se, unlawful combinations in restraint of trade. Injunctions in labor disputes, moreover, were not to be handed down by federal courts unless "necessary to prevent irreparable injury to property." Though hailed by Samuel Gompers as labor's "Magna Carta," these provisions were actually little more than pious affirmations, as later court decisions would demonstrate. Wilson himself remarked that the act did little more than affirm the right of unions to exist by forbidding their dissolution for being in restraint of trade.

Administration of the antitrust laws generally proved disappointing to the more vehement progressives under Wilson. The president reassured business that his purposes were friendly. As his secretary of commerce put it later, Wilson hoped to "create in the Federal Trade Commission a counsellor and friend to the business world." But its first chairman lacked forcefulness, and under its next head, a Chicago industrialist, the FTC practically abandoned its function of watchdog. The Justice Department meanwhile offered help and advice to businessmen interested in arranging matters so as to avoid antitrust prosecutions. The appointment of conservative men to the Interstate Commerce Commission and the Federal Reserve won plaudits from the business world and profoundly disappointed progressives.

SOCIAL JUSTICE   Wilson had never been a strong progressive of the social-justice persuasion. He had carried out promises to lower the tariff, reorganize the banking system, and strengthen the antitrust laws. Swept along by the course of events and the pressures of more far-reaching progressives, he was pushed further than he intended to go on some points. The New Freedom was now complete, he wrote late in 1914; the future would be "a time of healing because a time of just dealing." Although Wilson endorsed state action for women's suffrage, he declined to support a suffrage amendment because his party platform had not. He withheld support from federal child-labor legislation because he regarded it as a state matter. He opposed a bill for federal support of rural credits (low-interest loans to farmers) on the ground that it was "unwise and unjustifiable to extend the credit of the government to a single class of the community."

Not until the second anniversary of his inauguration (March 4, 1915) did Wilson sign an important piece of social-justice legislation, the La Follette Seamen's Act. The product of stubborn agitation by the eloquent president of the Seamen's Union, the act strengthened shipboard safety requirements, reduced the power of captains, set minimum food standards, and required regular wage payments. Seamen who jumped ship before their contracts expired, moreover, were relieved of the charge of desertion.

PROGRESSIVISM FOR WHITES ONLY   Like many other progressives, Woodrow Wilson showed little interest in the plight of African Americans. In fact, he shared many of the racist attitudes prevalent at the time. Although Wilson denounced the Ku Klux Klan's "reign of terror," he sympathized with its motives to restore white rule in the postwar South and to relieve whites of the "ignorant and hostile" power of the black vote. As a student at Princeton, Wilson detested the enfranchisement of blacks, arguing that Americans of Anglo-Saxon origin would always resist domination by "an ignorant and inferior race."

Later, as a politician, Wilson courted black voters, but he rarely consulted African-American leaders and repeatedly avoided opportunities to associate with them in public. Many of the southerners he appointed to his cabinet were uncompromising racists who systematically began segregating the employees in their agencies, even though the agencies had been integrated for over fifty years. Workplaces were segregated by race, as were toilets, drinking fountains, and areas for work breaks. When black leaders protested these actions, Wilson replied that such racial segregation was intended to eliminate "the possibility of friction" in the federal workplace.

PROGRESSIVE RESURGENCE   The need to weld a winning coalition in 1916 pushed Wilson back onto the road of reform. Progressive Democrats were restless, and after war broke out in Europe in August 1914, further divisions arose over defense and foreign policy. At the same time, the Republicans were repairing their own rift, as the Progressive party showed little staying power in the midterm elections and Roosevelt showed little will to preserve it. It was plain to most observers that Wilson could gain reelection only by courting progressives of all parties. In 1916 Wilson scored points with them when he nominated Louis D. Brandeis to the Supreme Court. Conservatives waged a vigorous battle against Brandeis, but Senate progressives rallied to win confirmation of the social-justice champion, the first Jewish member of the Supreme Court.

Meanwhile Wilson began to embrace a broad program of farm and labor reforms. The agricultural sector continued to suffer from a shortage of capital. To address the problem, Wilson supported a proposal to set up land banks to sponsor long-term farm loans. The Federal Farm Loan Act became law in 1916. Under the control of a Federal Farm Loan Board, twelve Federal Land Banks paralleled the Federal Reserve Banks and offered farmers loans of five to forty years' duration at low interest rates.

Thus the dream of cheap rural credits, sponsored by a generation of Alliance members and Populists, finally came to fruition. Democrats never embraced the Populist subtreasury plan, but made a small step in that direction with the Warehouse Act of 1916. This measure authorized federal licensing of private warehouses, and federal backing made their receipts for stored produce more acceptable as collateral for short-term bank loans to farmers. Other concessions to farm demands came in the Smith-Lever Act of 1914 and the Smith-Hughes Act of 1917, both of which passed with little controversy. The first provided federal grants-in-aid for farm demonstration agents under the supervision of land-grant colleges. The measure made permanent a program that had started a decade before in Texas and that had already spread to many localities. The second measure extended agricultural and mechanical education to high schools through grants-in-aid.

Farmers with automobiles had more than a passing interest as well in the Federal Highways Act of 1916, which provided dollar-matching contributions to states with highway departments that met certain federal standards. The measure authorized distribution of $75 million over five years, and marked a sharp departure from Jacksonian opposition to internal improvements at federal expense, just as the Federal Reserve System departed from Jacksonian banking principles. Although the argument that highways were one of the nation's defense needs weakened constitutional scruples against the act, it still restricted support to "post roads" used for the delivery of mail. A renewal act in 1921 would mark the beginning of a systematic network of numbered U.S. highways.

The progressive resurgence of 1916 broke the logjam on labor reforms as well. Advocates of child-labor legislation persuaded Wilson that social-justice progressives would regard his stand on the issue as an important test of his humanitarian concerns, and Wilson overcame doubts of its constitutionality to support and sign the Keating-Owen Child Labor Act, which excluded from interstate commerce goods manufactured by children under fourteen. Both the Keating-Owen Act and a later act of 1919 to achieve the same purpose with a prohibitory tax were ruled unconstitutional by the Supreme Court on the ground that regulation of interstate commerce could not extend to the conditions of labor. Effective action against the social evil of child labor had to await the New Deal of the 1930s, although it seems likely that discussion of the issue contributed to the sharp reduction in the number of underage workers during the next few years.

Another important accomplishment was the eight-hour workday for railroad workers, a measure that the Supreme Court upheld. The Adamson Act of 1916 was brought about by a threatened strike of railroad unions demanding the eight-hour workday and other concessions.

Wilson, who objected to some of the union demands, nevertheless went before Congress to request action on the hours limitation. The resulting Adamson Act required an eight-hour workday, with time and a half for overtime, and appointed a commission to study the problem of working conditions in the railroad industry.

In Wilson's first term progressivism reached its zenith. Progressivism had conquered the old dictum that the government is best which governs least. From two decades of ferment (three, if the Populist years are counted) the great contribution of progressive politics was the firm establishment and general acceptance of the public-service concept of government.

THE LIMITS OF PROGRESSIVISM

The Progressive Era was an optimistic age in which reformers of various hues assumed that no problem lay beyond solution. But like all great historic movements, progressivism displayed elements of paradox and irony. Despite its talk of greater democracy, it was the age of disenfranchisement for southern blacks—an action seen by many whites as "progressive." The first two decades of the twentieth century also witnessed a new round of anti-immigrant prejudice. The initiative and referendum, supposedly democratic reforms, proved subject to manipulation by well-financed publicity campaigns. And much of the public policy of the time came to be formulated by experts and members of appointed boards, not by broad segments of the population. There is a fine irony in the fact that the drive to increase the political role of ordinary people moved parallel with efforts to strengthen executive leadership and exalt government expertise. This age of efficiency and bureaucracy, in business as well as government, brought into being a society in which more and more of the decisions affecting people's lives were made by unelected policy makers.

Progressivism was largely a middle-class movement in which the poor and unorganized had little influence. The supreme irony was that a movement so dedicated to the rhetoric of democracy should experience so steady a decline in voter participation. In 1912, the year of the Bull Moose campaign, voting dropped off by between 6 and 7 percent. The new politics of issues and charismatic leaders proved to be less effective in turning out voters than party organizations and bosses had been. And by 1916 the optimism of an age that looked to infinite progress was already confronted by a vast slaughter. Europe had already stumbled into war, and America would soon be drawn in. The twentieth century, which dawned with such bright hopes, held in store episodes of unparalleled horror.

MAKING CONNECTIONS

- Many of the progressive reforms described in this chapter—particularly business regulation and the growth of the welfare state—provided the seeds for the New Deal reforms of the 1930s (Chapter 28).

- After World War I the progressive impulse manifested itself in reforms such as Prohibition and women's suffrage, but the moralistic strain in progressivism took an ugly turn in the Red Scare and immigration restriction.

- The next chapter shows how Wilson's foreign policy in Latin America and Europe reflected the same moralism that guided his domestic policy.

FURTHER READING

A splendid analysis of progressivism is John Chambers's *The Tyranny of Change: America in the Progressive Era, 1890–1920* (2000). The evolution of government policy toward business is examined in Martin J. Sklar's *The Corporate Reconstruction of American Capitalism, 1890–1916: The Market, the Law, and Politics* (1988). Mina Carson's *Settlement Folk: Social Thought and the American Settlement Movement, 1885–1930* (1990) and Jack M. Holl's *Juvenile Reform in the Progressive Era* (1971) examine the problem of social problems in the cities. An excellent study of the role of women in progressivism's emphasis on social justice is Kathryn Kish Sklar's *Florence Kelley and the Nation's Work: The Rise of Women's Political Culture, 1830–1900* (1995). Robert Kanigel's *The One Best Way: Frederick Winslow Taylor and the Enigma of Efficiency* (1997) highlights the role of efficiency in the Progressive Era.

25 ✎ AMERICA AND THE GREAT WAR

Throughout the nineteenth century, the United States reaped the benefits of its geographic distance from the wars that plagued Britain and Europe. The Atlantic Ocean provided a welcome buffer. During the early twentieth century, however, events combined to end the nation's comfortable isolation. Spectacular industrial development and ever-expanding world trade entwined American national interests with the fate of Europe. In addition, the development of steam-powered ships and submarines meant that foreign navies could threaten American security. At the same time, the election of Woodrow Wilson in 1912 brought to the White House a stern moralist determined to impose his standards for right conduct on renegade nations. This combination of circumstances led the outbreak of war in Europe in 1914 to become a profound crisis for the United States, a crisis that in the end would transform the nation's role in international affairs.

WILSON AND FOREIGN AFFAIRS

Woodrow Wilson brought to the presidency little background in international relations. The former college professor admitted as much when he remarked just before taking office, "It would be an irony of fate if my administration had to deal chiefly with foreign affairs." But events in Latin America and Europe were to make the irony all too real. From the summer of 1914, when a catastrophic world war erupted, foreign relations increasingly overshadowed all else, including Wilson's domestic program.

AN IDEALIST'S DIPLOMACY   Although lacking in international experience, Wilson did not lack ideas or convictions about global issues. He saw himself as a man of destiny who would help create a new world order governed by morality and idealism rather than by crass national interests. The product of a Calvinist past, he brought to diplomacy a version of progressivism animated by righteousness. His election had put him on a course charted "by no plan of our conceiving, but by the hand of God who led us into this way." Both Wilson and his secretary of state, William Jennings Bryan, believed that America had a religious duty to advance democracy and moral progress in the world. If they did not always follow principle at the expense of national self-interest, they did in many respects try to develop a diplomatic policy based on pious idealism.

During 1913–1914, Bryan negotiated some thirty "cooling-off" treaties under which participating nations pledged not to go to war over any disagreement for a period of twelve months pending discussion by an international arbitration panel. The treaties, however, were of little consequence, soon forgotten in the revolutionary sweep of world events that would make the twentieth century the bloodiest in recorded history.

INTERVENTION IN MEXICO   Mexico, which had been in the throes of rival revolutions for nearly three years, presented a thorny problem for Wilson soon after he took office. For most of the thirty-five years from 1876 to 1911, President Porfirio Díaz had dominated Mexico. As military dictator he had suppressed opposition and showered favors on his wealthy allies and on foreign investors, who piled up holdings in Mexican mines, petroleum, railroads, and agriculture. But eventually the dictator's hold slipped, and in 1910 popular resentment boiled over into revolt. A year later, revolutionary armies occupied Mexico City, and Díaz fled.

The leader of the rebellion, Francisco I. Madero, proved unable to manage the tough adversaries attracted by the scramble for power. In 1913 General Victoriano Huerta assumed power, and Madero was murdered soon afterward. Confronted with a military dictator ruling Mexico, Wilson enunciated a new doctrine of nonrecognition: "We hold . . . that just government rests upon the consent of the governed." Official recognition by the United States government, formerly extended routinely to governments that exercised *de facto* power, now might depend on judgments of their legality; an immoral government presumably would not pass muster.

Wilson expressed sympathy with the revolutionary movement and began to put diplomatic pressure on Huerta. Early in 1914 he removed an embargo on arms to Mexico in order to help an insurgent faction under Venustiano Carranza of the Constitutionalist party and stationed American warships off Veracruz to halt arms shipments to Huerta. "I am going to teach the South American republics to elect good men," Wilson vowed to a British diplomat. On April 9, 1914, several American sailors gathering supplies in Tampico strayed into a restricted area and were arrested. Mexican officials quickly released them and sent an apology to the American naval commander. There the incident might have ended, but the naval officer demanded that the Mexicans salute the American flag. Wilson backed him up and won from Congress authority to use force to bring Huerta to terms. Before the Tampico incident could be resolved, Wilson sent a naval force to Veracruz. American marines and sailors went ashore on April 21, 1914, and occupied the town at a cost of nineteen killed. The Mexicans lost at least two hundred killed.

In Mexico the American occupation aroused the opposition of all factions, and Huerta tried to rally support against foreign invasion. At this juncture, Wilson accepted an offer of mediation by the ABC powers (Argentina, Brazil, and Chile), which proposed withdrawal of United States forces, the removal of Huerta, and installation of a provisional government sympathetic to reform. Huerta refused, but the moral effect of the proposal and the growing strength of his foes forced him to leave office. The Carranzistas entered Mexico City, and the Americans left Veracruz in late 1914. A year later, the United States and several Latin American governments recognized Carranza as president of Mexico.

Still, the troubles south of the border continued. The prolonged upheaval had spawned independent gangs of bandits, Pancho Villa's among the wildest. All through 1915, fighting between the forces of Villa and Carranza continued sporadically. In 1916 Villa seized a train and murdered sixteen American mining engineers in a deliberate attempt to provoke American intervention, discredit Carranza, and build himself up as an opponent of the "gringos." That failing, he crossed the border on raids into Texas and New Mexico. On March 9 he entered Columbus, New Mexico, burned the town, and killed seventeen Americans.

Pancho Villa (center) and his followers rebelled against the president of Mexico and antagonized the United States with violent attacks against "gringos."

Wilson then had to abandon his policy of "watchful waiting." With the reluctant consent of Carranza, he sent General John J. Pershing across the border with a force of 11,000 men and mobilized 150,000 National Guardsmen along the frontier. For nearly a year Pershing's troops went on a fruitless chase after Villa through northern Mexico. They had no luck and were ordered home in 1917. Carranza then pressed his own war against the bandits and put through a new liberal constitution in 1917. Mexico was by then well on the way to a more orderly government, almost in spite of Wilson's actions rather than because of them.

PROBLEMS IN THE CARIBBEAN   In the Caribbean, Wilson found it as hard to act on his ideals as in Mexico. The "dollar diplomacy" practiced by the Taft administration encouraged bankers in the United States to aid debt-plagued governments in Haiti, Guatemala, Honduras, and Nicaragua. Despite Wilson's public stand against using military force to back up American investments, he kept the marines in Nicaragua, where they had been sent by President Taft in 1912, to prevent renewed civil war. Then in 1915 he dispatched more marines to Haiti after two successive revolutions and subsequent governmental disarray. "I suppose," Wilson told Secretary of State Bryan, "there is nothing to do but to take the bull by the horns and restore order." The American forces stayed in Haiti until 1934. Disorders in the Dominican Republic brought American marines to that country in 1916; they remained until 1924. The presence of these additional U.S. military forces in the region only exacerbated the Yankee phobia among many Latin Americans. And as the *New York Times* charged, Wilson's frequent interventions made Taft's dollar diplomacy look like "ten cent diplomacy."

AN UNEASY NEUTRALITY

Problems in Latin America and the Caribbean loomed larger in Wilson's thinking than the gathering storm in Europe. When the thunderbolt of war struck Europe in the summer of 1914, most Americans, one North Carolinian wrote, saw it "as lightning out of a clear sky." Whatever the troubles in Mexico, whatever disorders and interventions agitated other countries, it seemed unreal that civilized Europe could descend into such an orgy of destruction. Since the fall of Napoleon in

1815, Europe had known local wars but only as interruptions of a general peace that contributed to a century of unprecedented material progress.

But peace ended with the assassination of Austrian archduke Franz Ferdinand. He was shot by an Austrian citizen of Serbian descent who wanted an independent Serbia. Austria-Hungary's determination to punish Serbia for the murder provoked Russia to mobilize its army in sympathy with its Slavic friends in Serbia. This in turn triggered a European system of alliances: the Triple Alliance or Central Powers (Germany, Austria-Hungary, and Italy) and the Triple Entente or Allied Powers (France, Great Britain, and Russia). When Russia refused to stop its army's mobilization, Germany, which backed Austria-Hungary, declared war on Russia on August 1, 1914, and on Russia's ally France two days later. Germany then invaded Belgium to get at France, which brought Great Britain into the war on August 4. Japan, eager to seize German holdings in the Pacific, declared war on August 23, and Turkey entered on the side of the Central Powers in October. Although allied with the Central Powers, Italy initially stayed out of the war, and then struck a bargain under which it joined the Allied Powers in 1915.

As the fighting unfolded, it quickly became apparent that the First World War was unlike any previous conflict in its scope and carnage because military tactics had not kept up with military technology. Machine guns, high-velocity rifles, aerial bombing, poison gas, flame throwers, land mines, long-range artillery, and armored tanks changed the nature of warfare and produced massive casualties and widespread destruction. Over 61 million men served in the armed forces on both sides, and over 9 million combatants were killed in action. Another 19 million were wounded.

The battlefields of World War I were surrealistic in their horrors. During the Battle of Verdun in France, lasting from February to December 1916, some 32 million artillery shells were fired—1,500 shells for every square meter of the battlefield. Such devastating firepower turned farm land and forests into wasteland.

Trench warfare gave the First World War its lasting character. Most of the great battles of the war involved hundreds of thousands of men crawling out of their muddy, rat-infested trenches and then crossing "no-man's-land" to attack enemy positions, only to be pushed back a day or a week later. The 475 miles of trenches provided protection and

EUROPE AT WAR, 1914
- Central Powers (Triple Alliance)
- Allied Powers (Triple Entente)
- Neutral countries

living space as well as a jumping-off point for large- and small-scale attacks by day or night.

Life in the trenches was miserable. In addition to the dangers of enemy fire, soldiers on both sides were forced to deal with flooding and diseases such as trench fever and trench foot, which could lead to amputation. Lice and rats were constant companions. The stench was unbearable. Soldiers on both sides ate, slept, and fought among the dead, and amid the reek of death.

AMERICA'S INITIAL REACTIONS As the trench war along the Western Front in Belgium and in France stalemated, the casualties mounted and pressure for American intervention increased. On the first day of the Battle of the Somme, on July 1, 1916, 20,000 British soldiers were killed and 40,000 others were wounded—all in less than twenty-four hours. Shock in the United States over the sudden outbreak of war in Europe gave way to gratitude that an ocean stood between America and the killing fields. "Our isolated position and freedom from entangling alliances," said the *Literary Digest,* "inspire our press with cheering assurance that we are in no peril of being drawn into the European quarrel." President Wilson repeatedly urged the American people to be "neutral in thought as well as in action."

That was more easily said than done. In the 1910 population of 92 million, more than 32 million were "hyphenated Americans," first- or second-generation immigrants who retained ties to their old countries. Among the more than 13 million immigrants from the countries at war, by far the largest group was German American, numbering 8 million. And 4 million Irish Americans harbored a deep-rooted enmity to England. These groups instinctively leaned toward the Central Powers.

But old-line Americans, largely of British origin, supported the Allied Powers. If, as has been said, Britain and the United States were divided by a common language, they were united by ties of culture and tradition. Americans identified also with France, which had contributed to American culture and ideas, and to independence itself. Britain and France, if not their ally Russia, seemed the custodians of democracy, while Germany more and more seemed the embodiment of autocracy and militarism. If not a direct threat to the United States, Germany would pose at least a potential threat if it destroyed the balance of power in Europe. High officers of the United States government were pro-British in thought from the outset of the war. Robert Lansing, first counselor of the State Department, Walter Hines Page, ambassador to London, and Colonel Edward

Most Americans leaned toward the Allied Powers, but all were shocked at the outbreak of the Great War. In this cartoon, the Samson-like War pulls down the temple of Civilization.

House, Wilson's close adviser, saw in German militarism a potential danger to America.

The Germans and the British launched intensive propaganda campaigns to influence American opinion. The British gained a supreme advantage when they cut the undersea cable that ran from Germany to the United States. Nearly all news from the battlefronts, therefore, had to clear through London. Highly exaggerated reports of German atrocities were convincing to Americans, and there were real atrocities enough in the German occupation of Belgium to excite American outrage.

A STRAINED NEUTRALITY   At first the war in Europe brought a slump in American exports and the threat of a depression, but by the spring of 1915 the Allies' demand for supplies generated a wartime boom. The Allies at first financed their purchases by disposing of American securities, but ultimately they needed loans. Early in the war, Secretary of State William Jennings Bryan informed banker J. P. Morgan that loans to any warring nation were "inconsistent with the true spirit of neutrality." Yet Wilson quietly began approving short-term credits to sustain trade with the Allies. When in the fall of 1915 it became apparent that the Allies could no longer carry on without long-term credit, the administration removed all restrictions, and J. P. Morgan soon extended a loan of $500 million to England and France. American investors would advance over $2 billion to the Allies before the United States entered the war, and only $27 million to Germany.

The administration nevertheless clung to the fond hope of neutrality through two and a half years of warfare in Europe and tried to uphold the traditions of "freedom of the seas," which had guided American policy since the Napoleonic Wars. As the German drive through Belgium and toward Paris finally ground down into the stalemate of trench warfare, trade on the high seas assumed a new importance. In a war of attrition, survival depended on access to supplies, and in such a war British naval power counted for a great deal. With the German fleet outnumbered and bottled up almost from the outset, the war in many ways assumed the pattern that had once led America into war with Britain in 1812.

On August 6, 1914, Secretary of State Bryan called upon the belligerents to accept the Declaration of London, drafted and signed in 1909 by leading powers but never ratified by the British. That document, reduced the list of contraband (war-related) items and specified that a blockade was legal only when effective just outside enemy ports. The Central Powers promptly accepted the Declaration of London. The British almost as promptly refused, lest they lose some of their advantage in sea power. Beginning with an Order in Council of August 20, 1914, Britain gradually extended the list of contraband goods to include all sorts of things formerly excluded, such as food, cotton, wood, and certain ores. President Wilson protested, but U.S. ambassador Page, personally pro-British, assured British foreign secretary Sir Edward Grey that the two could find ways of getting around the problem. The British consequently gave little serious heed to further protests.

In November 1914 the British declared the whole North Sea a war zone, sowed it with mines, and ordered neutral ships to enter only by the Strait of Dover, where they could be easily searched. In March 1915 they further announced that they would seize ships carrying goods with a presumed enemy destination, ownership, or origin. Previous policies had required search on the high seas and this, combined with Britain's new policy, caused extended delays, sometimes running into months. The same Order in Council also directed British ships to stop vessels carrying German goods via neutral ports. When the State Department protested, Grey reminded the Americans that this was the same doctrine of "continuous voyage" on which the United States had acted in the 1860s to keep British goods out of the Confederacy.

NEUTRAL RIGHTS AND SUBMARINES British actions, including blacklisting of American companies that traded with the enemy and censorship of the mails, raised some old issues of neutral rights, but the German reaction introduced an entirely new question. With the German fleet bottled up by the British blockade, few surface vessels could venture out to harass the enemy. On February 4, 1915, in response to the "illegal" British blockade, the German government proclaimed a war zone around the British Isles. Enemy merchant ships in those waters were liable to sinking by submarines, the Germans declared, "although it may not always be possible to save crews and passengers." As the chief advantage of U-boat (*Unterseeboot*) warfare was in surprise, it violated the established procedure of stopping enemy vessels on the high seas and providing for the safety of passengers and crews

Americans were outraged when a German torpedo sank the Lusitania *on May 7, 1915.*

before sinking the vessel. Since the British sometimes flew neutral flags as a ruse, neutral ships in the zone would also be in danger.

The United States pronounced the German policy "an indefensible violation of neutral rights" and warned that Germany would be held to "strict accountability" for any destruction of American lives and property. Then on May 7, 1915, the captain of the German submarine U-20 sighted a four-stack liner moving slowly through the Irish Sea and fired a torpedo. It hit the mark, and the ship exploded and sank within a few minutes. Only as it tipped into the waves was the German commander able to make out the name *Lusitania* on the stern. Before the British Cunard liner left New York bound for Liverpool, the German embassy had published warnings in the American press against travel to the war zone, but among the 1,198 persons lost were 128 Americans.

Americans were outraged. The sinking was an act of piracy, Theodore Roosevelt declared. To quiet the uproar, Wilson urged patience: "There is such a thing as a man being too proud to fight. There is such a thing as a nation being so right that it does not need to convince others by force that it is right." But his previous demand for "strict accountability" forced him to make a strong response. On May 13 Secretary of State

Bryan reluctantly signed a note demanding that the Germans abandon unrestricted submarine warfare, disavow the sinking, and pay reparations. The Germans responded that the ship had been armed (which it was not) and secretly carried a cargo of small arms and ammunition (which it did). A second note on June 9 repeated American demands in stronger terms. The United States, Wilson asserted, was "contending for nothing less high and sacred than the rights of humanity." Bryan, unwilling to risk war over the issue, resigned in protest and joined the peace movement as a private citizen. His successor, Robert Lansing, signed the note.

In response to the uproar over the *Lusitania,* the German government had secretly ordered U-boat captains to avoid sinking large passenger vessels. When, despite the order, two American lives were lost in the sinking of the British liner *Arabic,* bound for New York, the Germans paid an indemnity and offered a public assurance on September 1, 1915: "Liners will not be sunk by our submarines without warning and without safety of the lives of non-combatants, provided that the liners do not try to escape or offer resistance." With this *Arabic* pledge, Wilson's resolute stand seemed to have resulted in a victory for his policy.

During the fall of 1915, Wilson's trusted adviser Edward M. House proposed to renew a mediation effort he had explored on a visit to London, Paris, and Berlin the previous spring—before the *Lusitania* sinking. In early 1916 House visited those capitals again but found neither side ready to begin serious negotiations. The French and British would soon be engaged in massive battles at Verdun and the Somme, and both were determined to fight until they could bargain from strength.

Peace advocates in Congress now challenged the administration's policy on neutral rights. In 1916 resolutions were introduced in the House and Senate warning Americans against traveling on armed belligerent vessels. Such surrender to the German threat, Wilson asserted, would be a "deliberate abdication of our hitherto proud position as spokesmen, even amidst the turmoil of war, for the law and the right." He warned that if the United States accepted a single abatement of neutral rights, then "the whole fine fabric of international law might crumble under our hands piece by piece." The administration managed to defeat both resolutions by a solid margin. On March 24, 1916, a U-boat torpedoed the French steamer *Sussex,* injuring two

Helping the President. *In this 1915 cartoon, Wilson holds to the middle course between the pacifism of Bryan (shown on left with a sign "Let us avoid unnecessary risks") and the belligerence of Roosevelt (shown on right with a sign "Let us act without unnecessary delay").*

Americans. When Wilson threatened to break off relations, Germany renewed its pledge that U-boats would not torpedo merchant and passenger ships. This *Sussex* pledge implied the virtual abandonment of submarine warfare.

THE DEBATE OVER PREPAREDNESS   The *Lusitania* incident, and more generally the quarrels over neutral commerce, contributed to a growing demand for a stronger American army and navy. On December 1, 1914, the champions of preparedness had organized the National Security League to promote their cause. After the *Lusitania* sinking, Wilson asked the War and Navy Departments to draft proposals for expansion.

Progressives and pacifists, as well as many residents in the rural South and West, were opposed to military expansion. Their antiwar sentiments tapped into the traditional American suspicion of military establishments, especially of standing armies, which dated back to the colonial period. The new Democratic leader in the House opposed "the big Navy and big Army program of the jingoes and war traffickers." In the East, leaders of the peace movement organized a League to Limit Armament. Jane Addams and suffragist Carrie Chapman Catt organized a Women's Peace party.

The administration's plan to enlarge the regular army and create a national reserve force of 400,000 ran into stubborn opposition in the

House Military Affairs Committee. Wilson was forced to accept a compromise between advocates of an expanded force under federal control and advocates of a traditional citizen army. The National Defense Act of 1916 expanded the regular federal army from 90,000 to 175,000 and permitted gradual enlargement to 223,000. It also expanded the National Guard to 440,000, made provision for their training, and gave federal funds for summer training camps for civilians.

The bill for an increased navy aroused less opposition because of the general feeling expressed by the navy secretary that there was "no danger of militarism from a relatively strong navy such as would come from a big standing army." The Naval Construction Act of 1916 authorized between $500 million and $600 million for a three-year expansion program.

Forced to relent on military preparedness, progressive opponents of a buildup determined that the financial burden should rest on the wealthy people they held responsible for promoting the military expansion. The income tax became their weapon. Supported by a groundswell of popular support, they wrote into the Revenue Act of 1916 changes that doubled the basic income tax rate from 1 to 2 percent, lifted the surtax to a maximum of 13 percent (for a total of 15 percent) on incomes over $2 million, added an estate tax, levied a 12.5 percent tax on gross receipts of munitions makers, and added a new tax on corporation capital, surplus, and excess profits. The new taxes on wealth amounted to the most clear-cut victory of radical progressives in the entire Wilson period, a victory further consolidated and advanced after America entered the war. It was the capstone to the progressive legislation that Wilson supported in preparation for the election of 1916.

THE ELECTION OF 1916 As the 1916 election approached, Republicans hoped to regain their normal electoral majority, and Theodore Roosevelt hoped to be their leader again. But he had committed the deadly sin of bolting his party in 1912 and, what was more, he expressed a bellicosity on war issues that would scare off voters. Needing somebody who would draw Bull Moose Progressives back into the fold, the Republican regulars turned to Justice Charles Evans Hughes, who had a progressive record as governor of New York from 1907 to 1910. On the Supreme Court since then, he had neither taken a stand in 1912 nor spoken out on foreign policy. The remnants of the Progressive party gathered in Chicago at the same time as the Republicans. Roosevelt had held out the vain hope of getting both nominations, but he now declined to lead a third party. Two weeks later the Progressive National Committee disbanded the party and endorsed Hughes; a minority, including their vice-presidential nominee, came out for Wilson.

The Democrats, as expected, chose Wilson again, and in their platform endorsed a program of social legislation, neutrality, and reasonable preparedness. The party further commended women's suffrage to the states, denounced groups that placed the interests of other countries above those of the United States, and pledged support for a postwar League of Nations to enforce peace with collective security measures against aggressors. The Democrats found their most popular issue, however, when the keynote speaker, a former New York governor, got an unexpected response to his recital of historic cases in which the United States had refused under provocation to go to war. As he mentioned successive examples, the crowd chanted "What did we do? What did we do?" and the speaker responded: "We didn't go to war! We didn't go to war!" The peace theme, refined into the slogan "He kept us out of war," became the rallying cry of the Wilson campaign, one that had the merit of taking credit without making any promises for the future.

Republican progressives found themselves drawn in large numbers to Wilson. The impression of Democratic purpose and effectiveness was heightened by Republican feuding and ineptitude. On foreign policy, Hughes worked both sides of the street. While trying to keep the votes of German Americans and other "hyphenates," Hughes refused to disavow Theodore Roosevelt, who was traveling the country denouncing the kaiser. On social-reform issues Wilson was far ahead of Hughes, and Hughes found himself often the captive of old-line Republican bosses more eager to punish Bull Moose Progressives than to win the election for Hughes.

In the end, Wilson's twin pledges of peace and progressivism, a unique combination of issues forged in the legislative and diplomatic crucibles of 1916, brought a narrow victory. Early returns showed a Republican sweep in the East and Midwest, signaling a victory for Hughes, but the outcome remained in doubt until word came that Wilson had carried California by 3,772 votes. The final vote showed a Democratic sweep of the Far West and South, enough for victory in the electoral college by 277 to 254, and in the popular vote by 9 million to 8.5 million.

Peace with Honor. *Wilson's neutral policies proved popular in the 1916 campaign.*

LAST EFFORTS FOR PEACE   Immediately after the election, Wilson again offered to mediate an end to the war in Europe, whereupon the German government announced on December 12 its readiness to begin discussion of peace terms. Six days later Wilson sent identical notes to the belligerent powers, asking each to state its war aims. The Germans responded promptly that they would state their war demands only to a conference of the warring states at a neutral site (although it soon became clear that they intended to seize new territory along the Baltic Sea, in the Congo of Africa, and in France, Belgium, and Luxembourg). In January 1917 the Allies made it plain that they intended to require reparations (payments to the victors), break up the Austro-Hungarian and Ottoman Empires, and destroy German power.

Wilson then decided to make one more appeal, in the hope that public opinion would force the hands of the warring governments. Speaking before the Senate on January 22, 1917, he asserted the right of the United States to a share in laying the foundations for a lasting peace, which would have to be a "peace without victory," for only a "peace among equals" could endure. The peace must be based on the principles of government by the consent of the governed, freedom of the seas, and disarmament, and must be enforced by an international league for peace established to make another such catastrophe impossible.

Although Wilson did not know it, he was already too late. Exactly two weeks before he spoke, impatient German military leaders had decided to wage unrestricted submarine warfare. They took the calculated risk of provoking American anger in the hope of scoring a quick knockout. On January 31 the new policy was announced, effective the next day. All vessels in the war zone, belligerent or neutral, would be sunk without warning. "Freedom of the seas," said the *Brooklyn Eagle,* "will now be enjoyed [only] by icebergs and fish."

On February 3, 1917, Wilson told a joint session of Congress that the United States had broken diplomatic relations with the German government. Three weeks later he asked for authority to arm American merchant ships and "to employ any other instrumentalities or methods" necessary and "to protect our ships and our people." There was little quarrel with arming merchant ships, but bitter opposition to Wilson's vague reference to "any other instrumentalities or methods." A group of eleven or twelve die-hard noninterventionists filibustered the measure until the legislative session expired on March 4. A furious Wilson decided to outflank Congress. On March 12 the State Department announced that a forgotten law of 1792 allowed the arming of merchant ships regardless of congressional inaction.

On February 25 Wilson had learned that the British had intercepted and decoded an important message from German foreign secretary Arthur Zimmermann to his minister in Mexico. The note instructed the envoy to offer an alliance and financial aid to Mexico in case of war between the United States and Germany. In return for diversionary action against the United States, Mexico would recover "the lost territory in Texas, New Mexico, and Arizona."

On March 1, news of the Zimmermann Telegram broke in the American press and infuriated the public. Then, later in March, a revolution overthrew Russia's czarist government and established the provisional government of a Russian Republic. The fall of the czarist autocracy allowed Americans the illusion that all the major Allied Powers were now fighting for constitutional democracy. Not until November 1917 was this illusion shattered, when the Bolsheviks, led by Vladimir Lenin, seized power in Russia.

AMERICA'S ENTRY INTO THE WAR

In March 1917, German submarines sank five American merchant vessels in the North Atlantic. On March 20 Wilson's cabinet unanimously endorsed a declaration of war, and the following day the president called a special session of Congress. When it met on April 2, Wilson asked Congress to recognize the war that Imperial Germany was already waging against the United States. The German government had revealed itself as a natural foe of liberty, and therefore "The world must be made safe for democracy." The war resolution passed the Senate by a vote of 82 to 6 on April 4. The House concurred, 373 to 50, and Wilson signed the measure on April 6, 1917.

How had it come to this less than three years after Wilson's proclamation of neutrality? Prominent among the various explanations of America's entrance into the war were the effects of British propaganda and America's deep involvement in trade with the Allies, which some observers then and later credited to the intrigues of war profiteers and munitions makers. Some Americans thought German domination of Europe would be a threat to American security, especially if it meant the destruction or capture of the British navy. But whatever the influence of such factors, they likely would not have been decisive without the issue of submarine warfare. Once Wilson had taken a stand for the traditional rights of neutrals and noncombatants, he was to some extent at the mercy of decisions by the German high command.

AMERICA'S EARLY ROLE   The scope of America's role in the European war remained unclear. Few on either side of the Atlantic expected more from the United States than a token military effort. Despite Congress's preparedness measures, the army remained small and untested. The navy also was largely undeveloped. This began to change, however, when Rear Admiral William S. Sims assumed command of American ships in European waters. He then systematically built up the United States Navy, bringing the first contingent of six American destroyers to Queenstown, Ireland, in May 1917, and more later. The Americans, in addition, made two important contributions to Allied naval strategy. Previously, merchant ships had survived submarine attack through speed and evasive action. Sims persuaded the Allies to adopt a convoy system of escorting merchant ships in groups. The result was a sharp

Remember Your First Thrill of
AMERICAN LIBERTY

YOUR DUTY-*Buy*
United States Government *Bonds*
2nd Liberty Loan of 1917

This Liberty Loan poster urges immigrants to do their duty to their new country by buying government bonds.

decrease in Allied shipping losses. Later the United States Navy laid a gigantic minefield across the North Sea that limited the U-boats' access to the North Atlantic.

Within a month of the declaration of war, British and French officials arrived in the United States. They first requested money with which to buy supplies, a request Congress had already anticipated in the Liberty Loan Act, which added $5 billion to the national debt in "Liberty Bonds." Of this amount, $3 billion could be loaned to the Allied Powers. The United States was also willing to furnish naval support, credits, supplies, and munitions. But to raise and train a large army, equip it, and send it across a submarine-infested ocean seemed out of the question. The French nevertheless insisted that the United States send a token force to bolster morale, and on June 26, 1917, the first contingent of Americans, about 14,500 men commanded by General John J. Pershing, began to disembark on the French coast. Pershing and his troops reached Paris by July 4. Pershing soon advised the War Department to send a million American troops by the following spring. It was done—through strenuous efforts.

When the United States entered the war, the combined strength of the regular army and National Guard was only 379,000; at the end it would be 3.7 million. The need for such large numbers of troops converted Wilson to the idea of conscription. Under the Selective Service Act of 1917, all men aged twenty-one to thirty (later, from eighteen to forty-five) had to register for military service. All told, about 2 million American troops crossed the Atlantic and about 1.4 million saw some combat.

Wilson and his secretary of war, Newton D. Baker, as well as many others, saw the mobilization of hundreds of thousands of young men as an opportunity for social engineering. To improve the recruits' character while preparing them for war, Wilson and Baker created the Commission on Training Camp Activities (CTCA). The idea was to inculcate middle-class "progressive" virtues and values into recruits while they were undergoing their military training. The CTCA produced sex education programs to prevent the spread of venereal diseases, worked with local authorities to police "red-light" districts near the military bases and to arrest prostitutes, and sponsored sporting events and entertainment programs, dances and religious services, all designed to minister to the physical and moral well-being of the trainees.

MOBILIZING A NATION   Complete economic mobilization on the home front was also necessary to conduct the war efficiently. The Army Appropriation Act of 1916 had created a Council of National Defense, which in turn led to the creation of other wartime agencies. The Lever Food and Fuel Control Act of 1917 created a Food Administration, headed by Herbert Hoover, a future president. Hoover, a mining engineer and former head of the Commission for Relief in Belgium, sought to raise agricultural production while reducing civilian use of foodstuffs. "Food will win the war" was the slogan. Hoover directed a propaganda campaign promoting "Meatless Tuesdays," "Wheatless Wednesdays," "Porkless Saturdays," the planting of victory gardens, and the creative use of leftovers.

The War Industries Board (WIB), established in 1917, soon became the most important of all the mobilization agencies. It was headed by Bernard Baruch, a brilliant Wall Street speculator, who exercised a virtual dictatorship over the economy. Under Baruch the purchasing bureaus of the United States and Allied governments submitted their needs to the board, which set priorities and planned production. The board could allocate raw materials, tell manufacturers what to produce, order construction of new plants, and, with the approval of the president, fix prices.

A NEW LABOR FORCE   The closing off of foreign immigration, and the movement of 4 million men from the workforce into the armed services created a labor shortage during World War I. To meet it, women, blacks, and other ethnic minorities were encouraged to enter industries and agricultural activities heretofore dominated by white males. Northern businesses sent recruiting agents into the Deep South to find workers for their factories and mills, and over 400,000 southern blacks began the "Great Migration" northward during the war years, a mass movement that continued unabated through the 1920s. Mexican Americans followed the same migratory pattern. Recruiting agents and newspaper editors portrayed the North as the "land of promise" for southern blacks suffering from their region's depressed agricultural economy and rising racial intimidation and violence. The African-American newspaper *Chicago Defender* exclaimed: "To die from the bite of frost is far more glorious than at the hands of a mob." By 1930 the number of African Americans living in the North had tripled from 1910 levels.

But the newcomers were not always welcomed above the Mason-Dixon line. Many native white workers resented the new arrivals, and racial tensions sparked riots in cities across the country. In 1917 over forty African Americans and nine whites were killed during a riot over employment in a defense plant in East St. Louis. Two years later the toll of a Chicago race riot was nearly as high, with twenty-three black and fifteen white deaths. In these and other incidents of racial violence the pattern was the same. Whites angered by the influx of blacks into their communities would seize upon an incident to rampage through black neighborhoods, killing, burning, and looting, while white policemen looked the other way or encouraged the hooliganism.

American intervention in World War I also had a significant impact on women. Initially, women supported the war effort in traditional ways. They helped organize war-bond and war-relief drives, conserved foodstuffs and war-related materials, supported the Red Cross, and joined the Army nurse corps. But as the scope of the war widened, both government and industry sought to mobilize women workers for service on farms, loading docks, and railway crews, as well as in armaments industries, machine shops, steel and lumber mills, and chemical plants. Many women leaders saw such opportunities as a real breakthrough. "At last, after centuries of disabilities and discrimination," said a speaker at a Women's Trade Union League meeting in 1917, "women are coming into the labor and festival of life on equal terms with men." A black woman who exchanged her job as a live-in servant for work in a factory declared: "I'll never work in nobody's kitchen but my own any more. No indeed, that's the one thing that makes me stick to this job."

Women working at the Bloomfield International Fuse Company, New Jersey, 1918.

In fact, however, war-generated changes in female employment were limited and brief. About a million women participated in "war work," but most of them were young and single and already working outside the home. Most returned to their previous jobs once the war ended. In fact, male-dominated unions encouraged women to revert to their stereotypical domestic roles after the war ended. The Central Federated Union of New York insisted that "the same patriotism which induced women to enter industry during the war should induce them to vacate their positions after the war." The anticipated gains of women in the workforce failed to materialize. In fact, by 1920 the 8.5 million working women made up a smaller percentage of the labor force than they had in 1910. Still, one lasting result of women's contributions to the war effort was Woodrow Wilson's decision to endorse female suffrage. In the fall of 1918 he told the Senate that giving women the vote was "vital to the winning of the war."

WAR PROPAGANDA The exigencies of winning the war led the government to mobilize more than economic life: the progressive gospel of efficiency suggested mobilizing public opinion as well. On April 14,

1917, eight days after the declaration of war, an executive order established the Committee on Public Information, composed of the secretaries of state, war, and the navy. Its executive head, George Creel, a Denver newsman, sold Wilson on the idea that the best approach to influencing public opinion was "expression, not repression"—propaganda instead of censorship. Creel organized a propaganda machine to convey the Allies' war aims to the people, and above all to the enemy, where it might encourage the forces of moderation. To sell the war, Creel gathered a remarkable group of journalists, photographers, artists, entertainers, and others useful to his purpose. A film division produced such pictures as *The Beast of Berlin*. Hardly any public group escaped a harangue by one of the 75,000 Four-Minute Men, organized to give short speeches on Liberty Bonds, the need to conserve food and fuel, and other timely topics.

CIVIL LIBERTIES   By arousing public opinion to such a frenzy, however, the war effort channeled the zeal of progressivism into grotesque campaigns of "Americanism" and witch-hunting. Wilson had foreseen such consequences. "Once lead this people into war," he said, "and they'll forget there even was such a thing as tolerance." Popular prejudice equated anything German with disloyalty. Symphonies refused to perform Bach and Beethoven, schools dropped courses in the German language, and patriots translated "sauerkraut" into "liberty cabbage," "German measles" into "liberty measles," and "dachshunds" into "liberty pups."

While mobs hunted spies and chased rumors, the federal government stalked bigger game, with results often as absurd. Under the Espionage and Sedition Acts, Congress in effect outlawed criticism of government leaders and war policies. The Espionage Act of 1917 set penalties of up to $10,000 and twenty years in prison for those who gave aid to the enemy, who tried to incite insubordination, disloyalty, or refusal of duty in the armed services, or who circulated false reports and statements with intent to interfere with the war effort. The postmaster-general could bar from the mails anything that violated the act or advocated treason, insurrection, or forcible resistance to any United States law. The Sedition Act of 1918 extended the penalties to those who did or said anything to obstruct the sale of Liberty Bonds or to advocate cutbacks in production, and—just in case something had been overlooked—for saying, writing, or printing anything "disloyal, profane, scurrilous, or abusive" about the American form of government, the Constitution, or the army and navy.

The Espionage and Sedition Acts generated more than 1,000 convictions. Socialists and other radicals were the primary targets. In Chicago over 100 members of the Industrial Workers of the World went on trial for opposing the war effort. All were found guilty, and the IWW never fully recovered from the blow. Victor Berger, Socialist congressman from Milwaukee, received a twenty-year sentence for editorials in the *Milwaukee Leader* that called the war a capitalist conspiracy. Eugene V. Debs, who had polled over 900,000 votes for president in 1912, ardently opposed American intervention. He repeatedly urged American men to refuse to serve in the military, even though he knew he could be prosecuted for such remarks under the Espionage Act. "I would a thousand times rather be a free soul in jail than a sycophant and a coward in the streets," he told a Socialist gathering in 1918. He received his wish. Two weeks later Debs was arrested and eventually given a twenty-year prison sentence for encouraging draft resistance. In 1920, still in jail, he polled nearly 1 million votes for president.

In two important decisions just after the war, the Supreme Court upheld the Espionage and Sedition Acts. *Schenck v. United States* (1919) reaffirmed the conviction of a man for circulating antidraft leaflets among members of the armed forces. In this case Justice Oliver Wendell Holmes said: "Free speech would not protect a man in falsely shouting fire in a theater, and causing a panic." The act applied where there was "a clear and present danger" that speech in wartime might create evils Congress had a right to prevent. In *Abrams v. United States* (1919) the Court upheld the conviction of a man who circulated pamphlets opposing American intervention in Russia to oust the Bolsheviks. Here Holmes and Louis Brandeis dissented from the majority view. The "surreptitious publishing of a silly leaflet by an unknown man," they argued, posed no danger to government policy.

"THE DECISIVE POWER"

American troops played little more than a token role in the European fighting until early 1918. Before that they were parceled out in quiet sectors mainly for training purposes. All through 1917 the Allies remained on the defensive, and late in the year their situation turned desperate. In October the Italian lines collapsed and were overrun by Austrian forces. With the help of Allied troops from France, the Italians finally held their ground. In November the Bolshevik Revolution overthrew the infant Russian Republic, and the new Soviet government dropped out of the war. With the Central Powers now free to concentrate their forces on the Western Front, the American war effort became a "race for France" to restore the balance of strength. French premier Georges Clemenceau appealed to the Americans to accelerate their mobilization: "A terrible blow is imminent," he predicted to an American journalist. "Tell your Americans to come quickly."

THE WESTERN FRONT On March 21, 1918, Clemenceau's prediction came true when the Germans began the first of several offensives to try to end the war before the Americans arrived in force. On the Somme River they broke through the British and French sectors and penetrated thirty-five miles, nearly to Amiens. Farther north, the Germans struck in Flanders, where the Allies still held a corner of Belgium. At this critical point, on April 14 the Allies made French general Ferdinand Foch the supreme commander of all Allied forces.

American soldiers in Argonne, France.

THE WESTERN FRONT, 1918
- - - The Western Front, March 1918
······· German offensive, spring 1918
→ Allied counteroffensive
—— The Western Front, November 1918

On May 27 the Germans began their next drive along the Aisne River, took Soissons, and pushed on to the Marne River along a forty-mile front. By May 1918 there were 1 million fresh American troops in Europe, and for the first time they made a difference. In a counterattack American forces retook Cantigny on May 28 and held it. A week later, on June 2–3, a marine brigade blocked the Germans at Belleau Wood. American army troops took Vaux and opposed the Germans at Château-Thierry. Though these actions had limited military significance, their effect on Allied morale was immense. Each was a solid American success, and together they reinforced General Pershing's demand for a separate American army.

Before that could come to pass, the turning point in the western campaign came on July 15, 1918, in the Second Battle of the Marne. On both sides of Reims, the eastern end of a great bulge toward Paris, the Germans commenced their push against the French lines. Within three days, however, they had stalled, and the Allies, mainly with American troops, went on the offensive.

Soon the British, French, and Americans began to roll the German front back into Belgium. Then on August 10 the first U.S. Army was organized and assigned the task of liquidating the Germans at St. Mihiel, southeast of Verdun. There, on September 12, an army of more than 500,000 staged the first strictly American offensive of the war. Within three days the Germans had pulled back. The great Meuse-Argonne offensive, begun on September 26, then employed American divisions in a drive toward Sédan and its railroad, which supplied the entire German front. The largest American action of the war, it involved 1.2 million American troops and cost 117,000 American casualties, including 26,000 dead. But along the front from Sédan to Flanders the Germans were in retreat. "America," wrote German general Erich Ludendorff, "thus became the decisive power in the war."

THE BOLSHEVIKS AND THE WAR   When the war broke out in 1914, Russia was one of the Allied Powers. Over the next three years, the Russians suffered some 5.5 million casualties. By 1917, there were shortages of ammunition for Russian troops and food for the Russian people. The czarist government was in disarray, and after the czar's abdication, it first gave way to a provisional republican government, which in turn succumbed in November 1917 to a revolution led by Vladimir Lenin and his Bolshevik party, who promised war-weary Russians "Peace, Land, and Bread."

Once in control of the government, the Bolsheviks unilaterally stopped fighting. With German troops deep in Russian territory, and with armies of "White" Russians (anti-Bolsheviks) organizing resistance to their power, on March 3, 1918, the Bolsheviks concluded a separate peace with Germany in the Treaty of Brest-Litovsk. In an effort to protect Allied supplies and to encourage anti-Bolshevik forces in the developing Russian civil war, Wilson sent American forces into Russia's Arctic ports to prevent military supplies from falling into German hands. Troops were also sent to eastern Siberia, where they remained until April 1920 in an effort to curb the growing Japanese ambitions there.

A gun crew firing on entrenched German positions, 1918.

The Allied intervention in Russia failed because the Bolsheviks were able to consolidate their power. Russia took no further part in World War I and did not participate in the peace settlement. The intervention also generated among Soviets a long-lasting suspicion of the West.

THE FOURTEEN POINTS   As the conflict in Europe was ending, the question of war aims arose again. Neither the Allies nor the Central Powers, despite Wilson's prodding, had stated openly what they hoped to gain through the fighting. Wilson repeated that the Americans had no selfish ends. "We desire no conquest, no dominion," he stressed in his war message of 1917. "We seek no indemnities for ourselves, no material compensation for the sacrifices we shall freely make. We are but one of the champions of the rights of mankind." Unfortunately for his purpose, after the Bolsheviks seized power in November 1917, they published copies of secret treaties in which the Allies had promised territorial gains in order to win Italy, Romania, and Greece to their side. When an Interallied Conference in Paris late in 1917 failed to agree on a statement of war aims, Colonel House advised Wilson to formulate his own.

Salvation Army worker writing a letter home for a wounded soldier.

During 1917 House had been drawing together an informal panel of American experts called "the Inquiry" to formulate plans for peace. With advice from these experts, Wilson himself drew up a statement that would become the famous Fourteen Points. These he delivered to a joint session of Congress on January 8, 1918, "as the only possible program" for peace. The first five points in general terms called for open diplomacy, freedom of the seas, removal of trade barriers, reduction of armaments, and an impartial adjustment of the victor's colonial claims based on the interests of the populations involved. Most of the remaining points dealt with territorial claims: they called on the Central Powers to evacuate occupied lands and to allow self-determination for various nationalities, a crucial principle for Wilson. Point 13 proposed an independent Poland with access to the sea. Point 14, the capstone in Wilson's thinking, called for the creation of a "league" of nations to secure guarantees of independence and territorial integrity to all countries, great and small.

The Fourteen Points embodied Wilson's sincere commitments, but they also served the purposes of psychological warfare. One of their aims was to keep Russia in the war by a more liberal statement of purposes—a vain hope, as it turned out. Another was to reassure the Allied peoples that they were involved in a noble cause. A third was to drive a wedge between the governments of the Central Powers and their peoples by the offer of a reasonable peace. Wilson's promise of "autonomous development" for the subject nationalities of Austria-Hungary (Point 10) might have weakened the polyglot Hapsburg Empire, though he did not intend to break up the empire. But the chaos into which central Europe descended in 1918, and the national aspirations of the Hapsburg Empire's peoples, took matters out of his hands.

On September 29, 1918, German general Ludendorff advised his government to seek the best peace terms possible. On October 3, a new chancellor made the first German overtures for peace on the basis of the Fourteen Points. A month of diplomatic fencing followed between Colonel House and Allied representatives. Finally, when he threatened to pursue separate negotiations with Germany, the Allies accepted the Fourteen Points as a basis of peace, but with two significant reservations: they reserved the right to discuss limiting freedom of the seas, and they demanded reparations for war damages.

Meanwhile the German home front was being torn apart by a loss

Celebration of the Armistice ending World War I, New York City, November 1918.

of morale, culminating in a naval mutiny at Kiel. Germany's allies dropped out of the war: Bulgaria on September 29, 1918, Turkey on October 30, and Austria-Hungary on November 3. On November 9, 1918, the kaiser abdicated, and a German Republic was proclaimed. On November 11, at 5 A.M., an armistice was signed. Six hours later, at the eleventh hour of the eleventh day of the eleventh month, the guns fell silent. Under the Armistice the Germans had to evacuate occupied territories, pull back behind the Rhine River, and surrender their naval fleet, railroad equipment, and other materials. The Germans were assured that the Fourteen Points would be the basis for the peace conference.

THE FIGHT FOR THE PEACE AT HOME AND ABROAD

DOMESTIC UNREST   Woodrow Wilson made a fateful decision to attend in person the peace conference that convened in Paris on January 18, 1919. It shattered precedent for a president to leave the country for so long, but it dramatized all the more Wilson's messianic vision and his desire to ensure his goal of a lasting peace. From one viewpoint it was a shrewd move, for his prestige and determination made a difference in Paris. But he lost touch with political developments at home. His progressive coalition was already unraveling under the pressures of wartime discontent (a state of war officially existed until 1921). Western farmers complained about the government's control of wheat prices while southern cotton producers rode the wartime inflation. Eastern businessmen chafed at revenue policies designed, according to the *New York Sun,* "to pay for the war out of taxes raised north of the Mason and Dixon Line." Organized labor, despite manifest gains, was unhappy with inflation and the problems of reconversion to a peacetime economy.

In the midterm elections of 1918, Wilson made matters worse by urging voters to elect a Democratic Congress on the grounds that Democrats would loyally support his foreign policies. Republicans, who for the most part had supported war measures, took affront. In elections held on November 5, a week before the Armistice, the Democrats lost control of both houses of Congress. With an opposition majority in the new Congress, Wilson further weakened his standing by failing to involve a single prominent Republican in the peace negotiations. Former president Taft groused that Wilson's real intention in going to Paris was "to hog the whole show."

When Wilson reached Europe in December 1918, enthusiastic demonstrations greeted him in Paris. The cheering millions saw in the American idealist a prophet of peace and a spokesman for humanity. Their heartfelt support no doubt strengthened his hand at the conference, but Wilson had to deal with some tough-minded statesmen.

The Paris peace conference included delegates from all countries that had declared war or broken diplomatic relations with Germany. It was controlled by the Big Four: the prime ministers of Britain, France, and Italy, and the president of the United States. Japan restricted its interests to Asia and the Pacific. French premier Georges Clemenceau was a stern realist who had little patience with Wilson's utopianism. "God gave us the Ten Commandments and we broke them," Clemenceau sneered. "Wilson gave us the Fourteen Points—we shall see." Clemenceau insisted on harsh measures to weaken Germany and ensure French security. British prime minister David Lloyd George was a gifted politician fresh from electoral victory on the slogan "Hang the

Woodrow Wilson (second from left) *with Georges Clemenceau of France and Arthur Balfour of Great Britain at the Paris Peace Conference.*

Kaiser." Vittorio Orlando, prime minister of Italy, was there to pick up the spoils promised in the secret Treaty of London (1915).

THE LEAGUE OF NATIONS   Wilson insisted that his cherished League of Nations must come first, in the conference and in the treaty. Whatever compromises he might have to make regarding territorial boundaries and financial claims, whatever mistakes might result, Wilson believed that a permanent agency of collective security would ensure international stability. Wilson presided over the commission set up to work out a charter for the League.

Article X of the covenant, which Wilson called "the heart of the League," pledged members to consult on military and economic sanctions against aggressors. The use of arms would be a last (and an improbable) resort. The League, it was assumed, would exercise enormous moral influence that would make military action unnecessary. The League structure allowed each member an equal voice in the Assembly; the Big Five (Britain, France, Italy, Japan, and the United States) and four other nations would make up the Council; the administrative staff in Geneva would make up the Secretariat; and finally, a Permanent Court of International Justice (set up in 1921 and usually called the World Court) could "hear and determine any dispute of an international character."

On February 14, 1919, Wilson presented the finished draft of the League covenant to the plenary session of the conference and departed the next day for a month-long visit home. Already he faced rumblings of opposition, and shortly before his return to Paris, Henry Cabot Lodge, the chairman of the Senate Foreign Relations Committee, announced that the League covenant was unacceptable. His statement bore the signatures of thirty-nine Republican senators or senators-elect, more than enough to block ratification.

TERRITORY AND REPARATIONS   Back in Paris, Wilson grudgingly acceded to French demands for territorial concessions and reparations from Germany that would keep it weak for years to come. Wilson clashed sharply with Clemenceau, and after the president threatened to leave the conference, they settled on a demilitarized Rhineland (up to fifty kilometers [thirty-one miles] beyond the Rhine River), Allied occupation of this zone for fifteen years, and League administration of the Saar Basin. France could use Saar coal mines for fifteen years, after which a plebiscite would determine the region's status.

In other territorial matters Wilson had to compromise his principle of national self-determination. There was in fact no way to make Europe's boundaries correspond to ethnic divisions. The folk wanderings of centuries had left mixed populations scattered throughout central Europe. In some areas, moreover, national self-determination yielded to other interests: the Polish Corridor, for instance, gave Poland its much-needed outlet to the sea through German territory, and the South Tyrol, home for some 200,000 German-speaking Austrians, gave Italy a more defensible frontier at the Brenner Pass. One part of the Austro-Hungarian Empire became Czechoslovakia, which included the German-speaking Sudetenland, an area favored with good defenses. Another part of the empire united with Serbia to create the kingdom of Yugoslavia. Still other substantial parts passed to Poland (Galicia), Romania (Transylvania), and Italy (Trentino and Trieste). All in all, despite aberrations, the new boundaries more nearly followed the ethnic divisions of Europe than the prewar lines.

EUROPE AFTER VERSAILLES
- ········ 1914 boundaries
- New nations
- Plebiscite areas
- Occupied area

The discussion of reparations (payments by the vanquished to the victors) was among the longest and most bitter at the conference. Despite a pre-Armistice agreement that Germany would be liable only for civilian damages, Clemenceau and Lloyd George proposed reparations for the entire cost of the war, including veterans' pensions. On this point Wilson made perhaps his most fateful concessions. He accepted in the treaty a clause by which Germany confessed responsibility for the war and thus for its entire costs. The "war guilt" clause offended Germans and caused persistent bitterness.

On May 7, 1919, the victorious powers presented the treaty to the German delegates, who returned three weeks later with 443 pages of criticism protesting that the terms violated the Fourteen Points. A few changes were made, but when the Germans still refused to sign, the French prepared to move their army across the Rhine. Finally, on

June 28, 1919, the Germans gave up and signed the treaty in the Hall of Mirrors at Versailles.

WILSON'S LOSS AT HOME   Wilson returned home with the Versailles Treaty on July 8, 1919. Two days later he called on the Senate to accept "this great duty." The force of Wilson's idealism struck deep, and he returned amid a great clamor of popular support. A third of the state legislatures had endorsed the League, as had thirty-three of forty-eight governors.

Yet, Senator Henry Cabot Lodge, powerful chairman of the Senate Foreign Relations Committee, harbored doubts. He did not want the United States to withdraw from world affairs, but he felt that the outcome at Versailles exhibited the weakness in "the beautiful scheme of making mankind virtuous by a statute or a written constitution." Americans, thought Lodge, were too prone to promise more than they could deliver when great principles entailed great sacrifices. Foreign policy would have to be built up from what the public would sustain rather than be imposed from above. A staunch Republican with an intense dislike for Wilson, Lodge sharpened his partisan knives. He knew the undercurrents already stirring up opposition to the treaty: the resentment of German, Italian, and Irish groups in the United States, the disappointment of liberals at Wilson's compromises on reparations and territories, the distractions of demobilization and the resulting domestic problems, and the revival of isolationism. Lodge's close friend, Theodore Roosevelt, still a popular figure, lambasted the League, noting

The League of Nations Argument in a Nutshell. *J. N. "Ding" Darling's summation of the League controversy.*

that he keenly distrusted a "man who cares for other nations as much as his own."

Others agreed. In the Senate a group of "irreconcilables," fourteen Republicans and two Democrats, were unwilling to allow America to enter the League on any terms. They were mainly western or midwestern progressives who feared that foreign commitments threatened domestic reforms. The irreconcilables would be useful to Lodge's purpose, but he belonged to a larger group of "reservationists" who insisted on limiting American participation in the League and its actions. Wilson pointed out to them that the agreement already stipulated that with a veto in the League Council the United States could not be obligated to do anything against its will.

Lodge, who set more store by the old balance of power than by the new idea of collective security, brought forward a set of amendments or reservations. Wilson responded by agreeing to interpretive reservations, but to nothing that would reopen the negotiations. He especially opposed weakening Article X of the League covenant, which provided for collective action against aggression.

By September, with momentum for the treaty slackening, Wilson decided to go to the people and, as he put it, "purify the wells of public opinion." Against the advice of doctors and friends he set forth on a tour through the Midwest to the West Coast. In all he traveled 8,000 miles in twenty-two days, gave thirty-two major addresses and eight informal ones.

For a while Wilson seemed to be regaining the initiative, but then, on October 2, 1919, Wilson suffered a severe stroke and paralysis on his left side, leaving him an invalid for the rest of his life. For more than seven months he did not meet the cabinet. His protective wife kept him isolated from all but the most essential business. Wilson's disability intensified his stubbornness. He might have done better to stay in the White House and secure the best compromise possible, but now he refused to yield anything. As he scoffed to an aide, "Let Lodge compromise."

Lodge was determined to amend the treaty before it was ratified. The Senate adopted fourteen of his reservations, most having to do with the League. Wilson especially opposed the revision of Article X, which he said, "does not provide for ratification but, rather, for the nullification of the treaty." As a result, the Wilsonians found themselves thrown into an unlikely combination with irreconcilables, who opposed the treaty under any circumstances. The Senate vote was 39 for and 55 against. On the question of taking the treaty without reservations, irreconcilables and reservationists combined to defeat ratification again, with 38 for and 53 against.

In the face of public reaction, however, the Senate voted to reconsider. But the stricken Wilson remained adamant: "Either we should enter the League fearlessly, accepting with responsibility and not fearing the role of leadership which we now enjoy, contributing our efforts toward establishing a just and permanent peace, or we should retire as gracefully as possible from the great concert of powers by which the world was saved." On March 19, 1920, twenty-one Democrats deserted the intransigent Wilson and joined the reservationists, but the treaty once again fell short of a two-thirds majority by a vote of 49 yeas and 35 nays. The real winner was the smallest of the three groups in the Senate, neither the Wilsonians nor the reservationists but the irreconcilables.

When Congress declared the war at an end by joint resolution on May 20, 1920, Wilson vetoed the action; it was not until July 2, 1921, after he left office, that a joint resolution ended the state of war with Germany and Austria-Hungary. Peace treaties with Germany, Austria, and Hungary were ratified on October 18, 1921, but by then Warren Gamaliel Harding was president of the United States.

LURCHING FROM WAR TO PEACE

The Versailles Treaty, for all the time it took in the Senate, was but one issue clamoring for public attention in the turbulent period after the war. Demobilization of the armed forces and war industries proceeded in haphazard fashion. The sudden cancellation of war contracts left workers and business leaders to cope with reconversion on their own. Wilson's leadership was missing. He had been preoccupied by the war and the League, and once bedridden by his illness, he became strangely grim and peevish. His administration floundered through its last two years.

THE SPANISH FLU   Amid the confusion of postwar life many Americans confronted a virulent menace that produced far more casualties than the war itself. It became known as the Spanish flu, and its contagion spread around the globe. Erupting in the spring of 1918 and lasting a year, the pandemic killed more than 22 million people throughout the world, twice as many as the number who died in World War I. In the United States alone the flu accounted for more than 500,000 deaths, five times the number of combat deaths in France.

American servicemen returning from France brought the flu with them, and it raced through the congested army camps and naval bases. Still, no one seemed alarmed, for the flu remained a common if severe ailment. But then the hospitalized men started dying by the dozens, and it became obvious that this was no ordinary flu virus. In addition to the usual symptoms—coughing, chills, fever, body aches—the afflicted suffered from vomiting, dizziness, labored breathing, nosebleeds, and profuse sweating. Many contracted pneumonia as well, and a startling number of patients died. Some 43,000 American servicemen died of influenza in 1918.

By September 1918 the epidemic had spread to the civilian population. In that month alone 10,000 Americans died from the disease. "Nobody seemed to know what the disease was, where it came from or how to stop it," observed the editors of *Science* magazine in 1919. Millions of people began wearing surgical masks to work. Phone booths were locked up, as were other public facilities such as dance halls, poolrooms, and theaters. Even churches and saloons in many communities were declared off limits. Still the death toll rose. In Philadelphia 528 people were buried in a single day. From September 1918 to June 1919 some 675,000 Americans died of flu and pneumonia, and fully one-quarter of the population had contracted the illness. Life insurance companies nearly went bankrupt, hospitals were besieged, and cemeteries ran out of burial space.

Yet by the spring of 1919 the pandemic had run its course. It ended as suddenly—and as inexplicably—as it had begun. Although another outbreak occurred in the winter of 1920, the population had grown more resistant to its assaults. No disease, plague, war, famine, or natural catastrophe in world history killed so many people in such a short time. The most remarkable aspect of the flu pandemic was that people for the most part took it in stride. People seemed resigned to biological forces beyond their control while issues of war and peace in Europe and the home-front economy continued to dominate the headlines.

Office workers with gauze masks during the Spanish flu epidemic, 1918.

THE ECONOMIC TRANSITION   The problems of postwar readjustment were worsened by general labor unrest. Prices continued to
rise after the war, and discontented workers, released from wartime
constraints, were more willing to strike for their demands. In 1919,
more than 4 million workers went on strike in thousands of disputes.
Some workers in the East won their demands early in the year, but
after a general strike in Seattle, public opinion began to turn against
labor's demands. The Seattle mayor denounced the walkout of
60,000 workers as evidence of Bolshevik influence. The strike lasted
only five days, but public alarm over the affair damaged the cause of
unions across the country.

An AFL campaign to organize steelworkers suffered from charges
of radicalism against its leader, William Z. Foster, who had joined
the Socialists in 1900 and later emerged as a Communist. Attention
to Foster's radicalism obscured the squalid conditions that had
marked the steel industry since the Homestead Strike of 1892. The
twelve-hour day, often combined with a seven-day week, was common for steelworkers. On September 22, 1919, after U.S. Steel refused to talk, about 340,000 workers walked out. But the union gave

up the strike four months later. When information about working conditions became widely known, public opinion turned in favor of the steelworkers, but too late: the strike was over. Steelworkers remained unorganized until the 1930s.

The most celebrated postwar labor dispute was the Boston Police Strike. Though less significant than the steel strike in the numbers involved, it inadvertently launched a presidential career. On September 9, 1919, most of Boston's police force went out on strike. Governor Calvin Coolidge mobilized the National Guard to keep order, and after four days the strikers were ready to return, but the police commissioner refused to take them back. When labor leader Samuel Gompers appealed for their reinstatement, Coolidge responded in words that suddenly turned him into a national figure: "There is no right to strike against the public safety by anybody, anywhere, any time."

RACIAL FRICTION   The summer of 1919 also brought a season of race riots, both in the North and South. What black leader James Weldon Johnson called "the Red Summer" ("Red" here signified blood.) began in July, when whites invaded the black section of Longview, Texas, in search of a teacher who had allegedly accused a white woman of a liaison with a black man. They burned shops and houses and ran several African Americans out of town. A week later in Washington, D.C., reports of black assaults on white women aroused white mobs, and for four days gangs of white and black rioters waged race war in the streets until soldiers and driving rains ended the fighting. These were but preliminaries to the Chicago riot of late July in which 38 people were killed and 537 injured. The climactic disorders of the summer occurred

A victim of racial rioting in Chicago, July 1919.

in the rural area around Elaine, Arkansas, where black tenant farmers tried to organize a union. According to official reports, 5 whites and 25 blacks died, but whites told one reporter in the area that in reality more than 100 blacks died. Altogether twenty-five race riots erupted in 1919.

THE RED SCARE   Public reaction to the wave of labor strikes and race riots reflected the impact of the Bolshevik Revolution. A minority of radicals thought America's domestic turbulence, like that in Russia, was the first scene in a drama of world revolution. A much larger public was persuaded that they might be right. After all, a tiny faction in Russia had exploited confusion to impose its will. In 1919 the Socialist party, already depleted by wartime persecution, suffered the further defection of radicals inspired by the Russian example. Left-wing members formed the Communist and the short-lived Communist Labor parties. Wartime hysteria against all things German was readily transformed into a postwar Red Scare.

Fears of revolution in America might have remained latent except for the actions of a lunatic fringe. In April 1919 the post office intercepted nearly forty bombs addressed to prominent citizens. One slipped through and blew off the hands of a Georgia senator's maid. In June another destroyed the front of Attorney-General A. Mitchell Palmer's house in Washington. The random violence of these criminals formed no part of Bolshevik tactics, but many Americans saw Red on all sides and condoned attacks on all kinds of minorities in retaliation.

Soon the government itself was promoting witch-hunts. Attorney-General Palmer harbored an entrenched distrust of aliens and a strong desire for the presidency. In 1919 the Justice Department decided to deport radical aliens, and Palmer set up as the head of the new General Intelligence Division the young J. Edgar Hoover, who began to collect an index file on radicals. Raids began on November 7, 1919, when agents swooped down on the Union of Russian Workers in twelve cities. On December 22 the transport ship *Buford*, dubbed the "Soviet Ark," left New York for Finland with 249 people, including assorted anarchists, criminals, and public charges. All were deported to Russia without benefit of a court hearing. On January 2, 1920, a series of police raids in dozens of cities swept up some 5,000 suspects, many taken from their houses without arrest warrants, of whom more than half were kept in custody. That same month the New York legislature expelled five duly elected Socialist members.

Basking in popular approval, Palmer continued to warn of the Red menace, but like other fads and alarms, the mood passed. By the summer of 1920 the Red Scare had begun to evaporate. Communist revolutions in Europe died out, leaving Bolshevism isolated in Russia; bombings tapered off; the wave of strikes and race riots receded. The attorney-general began to seem more threatening to civil liberties than a handful of radicals. By September 1920, when a bomb explosion at the corner of Broad and Wall Streets in New York killed thirty-eight people, Americans were ready to take it for what it was, the work of a crazed mind and not the start of a revolution. The Red Scare nevertheless left a lasting mark on American life. Part of its legacy was the continuing crusade for "100 percent Americanism" and restrictions on immigration. It left a stigma on labor unions and contributed to the anti-union open-shop campaign—the "American Plan," its sponsors called it. But for many Americans the chief residue of the Great War and its disordered aftermath was a profound disillusionment that pervaded American thought in the postwar decades.

MAKING CONNECTIONS

- The Red Scare at the end of World War I led to a wave of nativism and immigration restriction, outlined in the next chapter.

- This chapter ends by noting the "profound disillusionment" Americans felt with efforts to reform the world. The political aspect of that disillusionment—the turn to "normalcy" of the 1920s—is discussed in Chapter 27.

- The treaty ending World War I was designed to cripple Germany's military strength. But as Chapter 29 shows, within two decades Adolf Hitler was leading a rebuilt German military force into World War II.

FURTHER READING

A lucid and thoughtful overview of international events covered in this chapter is Daniel M. Smith's *The Great Departure: The United States and World War I, 1914–1920* (1965).

On Wilson's stance toward war, see Ross Gregory's *The Origins of American Intervention in the First World War* (1971). A notable recent biography is August Heckscher's *Woodrow Wilson: A Biography* (1991).

Edward M. Coffman's *The War to End All Wars: The American Military Experience in World War I* (1968) is a detailed presentation of America's military involvement. David M. Kennedy's *Over Here: The First World War and American Society* (1980) surveys the impact of the war on the home front. Maurine Weiner Greenwald's *Women, War, and Work: The Impact of World War I on Women Workers in the United States* (1980) discusses the role of women. Ronald Schaffer's *America in the Great War: The Rise of the War Welfare State* (1991) shows the effect of war mobilization on business organization. Richard Polenberg's *Fighting Faiths: The Abrams Case, the Supreme Court, and Free Speech* (1987) examines the prosecution of a case under the 1918 Sedition Act.

How American diplomacy fared in the making of peace has received considerable attention. The role of the president is treated in Robert H. Ferrell's *Woodrow Wilson and World War I, 1917–1921* (1985). Thomas J. Knock interrelates domestic affairs and foreign relations in his explanation of Wilson's peacemaking in *To End All Wars: Woodrow Wilson and the Quest for a New World Order* (1992).

The problems of the immediate postwar years are chronicled by a number of historians. On the Spanish flu, see Alfred W. Crosby's *America's Forgotten Pandemic: The Influenza of 1918* (1990). Labor tensions are examined in David E. Brody's *Labor in Crisis: The Steel Strike of 1919* (1965) and Francis Russell's *A City in Terror: 1919, the Boston Police Strike* (1975). On racial strife, see William Tuttle, Jr.'s *Race Riot: Chicago in the Red Summer of 1919* (1970). The fear of Communists is analyzed in Robert K. Murray's *Red Scare: A Study in National Hysteria, 1919–1920* (rev. ed., 1980).

26 THE MODERN TEMPER

CHAPTER ORGANIZER

This chapter focuses on:

- the reactionary strains of the 1920s.

- the social ferment of the 1920s.

- the influence of modernism in American culture.

The horrors of World War I dealt a shattering blow to the widespread belief that Western civilization was progressing, a myth that had dominated the public consciousness for a century and that had been so powerful a stimulant to progressivism. The editors of *Presbyterian Magazine* announced in 1919 that the "world has been convulsed . . . and every field of thought and action has been disturbed. . . . The most settled principles and laws of society have been attacked."

The war's unimaginable carnage produced a postwar disillusionment among young intellectuals that challenged old values. A new "modernist" sensibility emerged among artists, writers, and intellectuals. At once a mood and a movement, modernism emerged first in Europe at the end of the nineteenth century and became a pervasive international force by 1920. It arose out of a widespread recognition that Western civilization had entered an era of bewildering change. New technologies, new modes of transportation and communication, and new scientific discoveries such as quantum mechanics and relativity theory combined to rupture perceptions of reality and generate new forms of artistic expression. "One must never forget," declared Gertrude Stein, the experimentalist poet, "that the reality of the twentieth century is not the reality of the nineteenth century, not at all." Modernism introduced a whole series of intellectual and artistic movements: impressionism, futurism, dadaism, surrealism, Freudianism. As the French painter Paul Gauguin acknowledged, the upheavals of modernism produced "an epoch of confusion."

At the same time that the war and its turbulent aftermath provided an accelerant for modernism, it also stimulated political and social radicalism. The postwar wave of strikes, bombings, anti-Communist hysteria, and race riots convinced many that America had entered a frightening new era of diversity and change. Defenders of tradition located the germs of radicalism in the polyglot cities teeming with immigrants and foreign ideas. The defensive mood of the 1920s fed on a growing tendency to connect American nationalism with nativism, Anglo-Saxon racism, and militant Protestantism.

REACTION IN THE TWENTIES

NATIVISM   The foreign connections of so many political radicals strengthened the sense that the seeds of sedition were foreign born. In the early 1920s, over half the white men and a third of the white women working in manufacturing industries were foreign born, most of them from central or eastern Europe. That socialism and anarchism were popular in these regions made such immigrant workers especially suspicious in the eyes of "old stock" Americans.

The most celebrated criminal case of the times seemed to prove the connection. It involved two Italian-born anarchists, Nicola Sacco and Bartolomeo Vanzetti. Arrested on May 5, 1920, for a robbery and murder in South Braintree, Massachusetts, they were brought for trial before a judge who privately referred to the defendants as "those anarchist bastards." A belief persists in some quarters that they were sentenced

Sacco and Vanzetti. *From a series of paintings by Ben Shahn, 1931–1932.*

for their political ideas and their ethnic origins rather than for any crime they had committed. The case became a great radical and liberal cause célèbre of the 1920s, but despite public demonstrations around the world on behalf of the two men, Sacco and Vanzetti went to the electric chair on August 23, 1927. More recent investigations have pointed to their guilt.

The surging postwar nativism generated new efforts to restrict immigration. A pseudo-scientific racism bolstered anti-immigration groups. It found expression in a widely read book, Madison Grant's *The Passing of the Great Race* (1916)—the great race being the Nordics of northern Europe, threatened by the Slavic and Latin people of eastern and southern Europe. The flow of immigrants, slowed by the war, rose again at its end. From June 1920 to June 1921, more than 800,000 persons entered the country, 65 percent of them from southern and eastern Europe; and more were on the way.

An alarmed Congress passed the Emergency Immigration Act of 1921, which restricted new arrivals each year to 3 percent of the foreign-born of any nationality as shown in the 1910 census. A new quota law in 1924 reduced the number to 2 percent based on the 1890 census, which included fewer of the "new" immigrants. This law set a permanent limitation, which became effective in 1929, of slightly over 150,000 new arrivals per year based on the "national origins" of the American people as of 1920. Since national origins could not be determined with precision, officials were called upon to use available statistics on migration, natural increase, and "such other data as may be found reliable." However inexact the quotas, their purpose was clear: to tilt the balance in favor of immigrants from northern and western Europe, who were assigned about 85 percent of the total. The law completely excluded people from East Asia—a gratuitous insult to the Japanese, who were already kept out of the United States by their "Gentlemen's Agreement" with Theodore Roosevelt.

On the other hand, the law left the gate open to new arrivals from Western Hemisphere countries, so that an ironic consequence was a great increase in the Hispanic Catholic population of the United States. The legal arrivals from Mexico peaked at 89,000 in 1924. Lower figures after that date merely reflect policies of the Mexican government to clamp down on the outflow of labor and stronger American enforcement of old regulations such as the 1882 exclusion of those immigrants likely to become public charges. Waves of illegal immigrants continued to come, however, in response to southwestern agriculture's demand for "stoop" labor. People of Latin American descent (chiefly Mexicans, Puerto Ricans, and Cubans) became the fastest-growing ethnic minority in the country.

THE KLAN   During the postwar years, the nativist tradition took on a new form, a revived Ku Klux Klan modeled on the group founded during Reconstruction. The new Klan was devoted to "100 percent Americanism" and restricted its membership to native-born white Protestants. It was determined to protect its warped notion of the American way of life not only from African Americans, but also from Roman Catholics, Jews, and immigrants. America was no melting pot, the Klan's founder William J. Simmons warned: "It is a garbage can! . . . When the hordes of aliens walk to the ballot box and their votes outnumber yours, then that alien horde has got you by the throat." A habitual joiner and promoter of fraternal orders, Simmons had gathered a hooded group near Atlanta on Thanksgiving night, 1915. There, "bathed in the sacred glow of the fiery cross, the invisible empire was called from its slumber of half a century to take up a new task."

In going nativist, the Klan had gone national and was no longer restricted to the South. Its appeal reached areas as widely scattered as Oregon and Maine. It thrived in small towns and cities in the North, and especially in the Midwest. It flourished outside the South among the urban social mainstream, attracting clergymen, engineers, accountants, managers and superintendents, small businessmen, and store owners. And it was preoccupied with the defense of white ("native") women and Christian morals. The robes, the flaming crosses, the eerie processionals, the kneeling recruits, the occult liturgies—all tapped a deep urge toward mystery and brought drama into the dreary routine of a thousand communities.

The Klan was a vicious reaction to shifting moral standards, the declining influence of churches, and the broadmindedness of city dwellers and college students. In the Southwest, it became more than anything else a moral crusade. "It is going to drive the bootleggers forever out of this land," declared a Texan. "It is going to bring clean

In 1925 the Ku Klux Klan staged a 40,000-man parade down Pennsylvania Avenue in Washington, D.C.

moving pictures . . . clean literature . . . break up roadside parking . . . enforce the laws . . . protect homes." To achieve such moral goals, the Klan terrorized and assaulted blacks.

Estimates of its peak membership, probably inflated, range from 3 million to 8 million, but the Klan's influence evaporated as quickly as its numbers grew. For one thing, the Klan suffered from a decline in nativist excitement after passage of the 1924 immigration law. For another, it suffered recurrent factional quarrels and schisms, and its willing use of violence tarnished its moral pretensions.

FUNDAMENTALISM   While the Klan saw a threat mainly in the "alien menace," many adherents of the old-time religion saw threats from modernism in the churches: new ideas that the Bible should be studied in the light of modern scholarship (the "higher criticism") or that it could be reconciled with biological theories of evolution. Fearing that such notions had infected schools and even pulpits, orthodox Christians took on a militant new fundamentalism. The fundamentalists were distinguished less by their belief in a faith that many others shared than by their posture of hostility toward any other belief.

Among rural fundamentalist leaders only former secretary of state William Jennings Bryan had the following, prestige, and eloquence to make the movement a popular crusade. Although advancing age had cost Bryan his commanding physical presence, he remained as optimistic, pious, and silver-tongued as ever. In 1921 Bryan sparked a drive for laws to prohibit the teaching of evolution in the public schools. He denounced Darwin with the same zeal he had once directed against William McKinley. "Evolution," he said, "by denying the need or possibility of spiritual regeneration, discourages all reforms, for reform is always based upon the regeneration of the individual." Anti-evolution bills began to turn up in legislatures, but the only victories came in the South—and there were few of those. Some officials took direct action without legislation. Governor Miriam "Ma" Ferguson of Texas outlawed textbooks upholding Darwinism. "I am a Christian mother," she declared, "and I am not going to let that kind of rot go into Texas schoolbooks."

The climax came in Tennessee, where in 1925 the legislature passed a bill outlawing the teaching of evolution in public schools and colleges. The governor, unwilling to endanger a pending school program, signed

Courtroom Scene during the Scopes Trial. *The media, food vendors, and other assorted characters flocked to Dayton, Tennessee, to hear the case against John Scopes, the teacher who taught evolution.*

the bill with the hope that it would probably never be applied. He was wrong. In Dayton, Tennessee, citizens convinced a young high school teacher, John T. Scopes, to accept an offer from the American Civil Liberties Union to defend a test case—chiefly to put their town on the map. They succeeded beyond their wildest hopes: the publicity was worldwide, and enduring. Before the opening day of the "monkey trial" on July 13, 1925, the streets of Dayton swarmed with publicity hounds, curiosity seekers, evangelists, atheists, a blind mountaineer who proclaimed himself the world's greatest authority on the Bible, hot-dog and soda-pop hucksters, and a miscellany of reporters.

The two stars of the show—Bryan, who had offered his services to the prosecution, and Clarence Darrow, renowned trial lawyer of Chicago and confessed agnostic—united at least in their determination to make the trial an exercise in public education. When the judge ruled out scientific testimony, however, the defense called Bryan as an expert witness on biblical interpretation. In his dialogue with Darrow, he repeatedly entrapped himself in literal-minded interpretations and indeed his ignorance of biblical history and scholarship. He insisted that a "great fish" actually swallowed Jonah, that Joshua literally made the sun stand still, that the world was created in 4004 B.C.—all, according to Darrow, "fool ideas that no intelligent Christian on earth believes." It was a bitter scene. At one point the two men, their patience exhausted in the broiling summer heat, lunged at each other, shaking their fists, prompting the judge to adjourn court.

The next day testimony ended. The only issue before the court, the judge ruled, was whether Scopes had taught evolution, and no one denied that he had. He was found guilty, but the Tennessee supreme court, while upholding the state's anti-evolution statute, overruled the $100 fine on a legal technicality. The chief prosecutor accepted the higher court's advice against "prolonging the life of this bizarre case" and dropped the issue. With more prescience than he knew, Bryan had described the trial as a "duel to the death." A few days after it closed, he died suddenly of a heart condition aggravated by heat and fatigue.

After the Dayton trial, the fundamentalists had spent their fury. Their very victories were self-defeating, for they served to publicize evolution, the doctrine they opposed as heresy. The states that went through the fiercest controversies became prime markets for books on evolution, and the movement roused a liberal defense of academic freedom.

PROHIBITION Prohibition of alcoholic beverages offered another example of reforming zeal channeled into a drive for moral righteousness and social conformity. Around 1900, however, the leading temperance organizations, the Women's Christian Temperance Union and the Anti-Saloon League, had converted from efforts to change individuals to a campaign for a national Prohibition law. Building upon the general moral disrepute of saloons, they were able to equate the "liquor traffic" with the trusts and "special interests." At the same time, contrary to certain old-time folk beliefs that alcohol was beneficial, medical and scientific opinion now showed that it did more harm than good. By the 1910s, the Anti-Saloon League had become one of the most effective pressure groups in American history, mobilizing Protestant churches behind its single-minded battle to elect "dry" candidates.

At its "Jubilee Convention" in 1913, the league endorsed a national Prohibition Amendment to the Constitution. The 1916 elections finally produced two-thirds majorities for Prohibition in both houses of Congress. Soon the wartime spirit of sacrifice, the need to use grain for food, and wartime hostility to German-American brewers transformed the cause virtually into a test of patriotism. On December 18, 1917, Congress sent to the states the Eighteenth Amendment which, one year after ratification on January 16, 1919, banned the manufacture, sale, or transport of intoxicating liquors.

By then, however, about three-fourths of the American people already lived in states and counties that were legally dry. In 1919 the Volstead Act defined as "intoxicating" all beverages containing more than 0.5 percent alcohol, which became illegal once the Eighteenth Amendment went into effect in 1920.

But the new amendment did not convince people to stop drinking. Instead it provoked them to use ingenious—and illegal—ways to satisfy their thirst for alcohol. The Eighteenth Amendment had been in effect fewer than eight months when authorities found a still with a daily capacity of 130 gallons near Austin, Texas, on a farm belonging to Morris Shepard, the "Father of National Prohibition." Congress never supplied adequate enforcement, if such was indeed possible given the public thirst, the spotty support of local officials, and the

A police raid on a speakeasy in 1926.

profits to be made in bootlegging. In Detroit, across the river from Ontario, where liquor was still legal, the liquor industry during the Prohibition Era was second in size only to the auto industry. Speakeasies, hip flasks, and cocktail parties were among the social innovations of the Prohibition Era, along with increased drinking by women.

It would be too much to say that Prohibition gave rise to organized crime, for systematic vice, gambling, and extortion had long been practiced, and often tied in with the saloons. But Prohibition supplied criminals with a new source of enormous income, while the automobile and the submachine gun provided greater mobility and firepower. Gangland leaders showed remarkable gifts for exploiting loopholes in the law, when they did not simply bribe policemen and politicians.

The most celebrated gangster and racketeer (a word coined in the 1920s) was "Scarface" Al Capone, who moved from New York to Chicago in 1920 and within a few years became the city's leading bootlegger and gambling and vice lord. In 1927 his bootlegging, prostitution, and gambling empire brought him an income of $60 million, which he flaunted in expensive suits and silk pajamas, a custom-upholstered and bulletproof Cadillac, an entourage of bodyguards, and lavish support for city charities. Capone always insisted that he was merely providing the public with goods and services it demanded: "They say I violate the prohibition law. Who doesn't?" He neglected to say that he himself had also bludgeoned to death several conspiring police lieutenants and ordered the execution of dozens of his rival criminals. Law-enforcement officials led by FBI agent Eliot Ness began to smash his bootlegging operations in 1929, but they were unable to pin anything on Capone until a Treasury agent infiltrated his gang and uncovered evidence that nailed him for tax evasion. Tried in 1931, Capone was sentenced to eleven years in prison.

In light of the illegal activities of Capone and other organized-crime members, it came as no great surprise in 1931 when a commission under former attorney-general George W. Wickersham reported evidence that enforcement of Prohibition had broken down. Of the commission's eleven members, only five approved continued efforts to enforce Prohibition without change, four favored modifications, and two personally favored repeal. Still, the commission as a whole voted for further efforts to make Prohibition work, and President Hoover chose to stand by what he called the "experiment, noble in motive and far-reaching in purpose."

THE ROARING TWENTIES

In many ways the defensive temper of the 1920s and the repressive movements it spawned seemed the dominant trends of the times, but they arose in part as reactions to a social and intellectual revolution that threatened to rip America away from its old moorings. In various labels given to the times, it was an era of excess, the Jazz Age, the Roaring Twenties, the ballyhoo years, the aspirin age. During those years, a new cosmopolitan, urban America confronted an old insular, rural America, and cultural conflict reached new levels of tension.

Leading young urban intellectuals developed an active disdain for the old-fashioned rural/small-town values of the hinterlands. Sinclair Lewis's novel *Main Street* (1920) portrayed the stifling, mean, cramped life of the prairie town, depicting a "savorless people, gulping tasteless food, and sitting afterward, coatless and thoughtless, in rocking chairs prickly with inane decorations, listening to mechanical music, saying mechanical things about the excellence of Ford automobiles, and viewing themselves as the greatest race in the world."

The banality of small-town life became a pervasive theme in much of the literature of the time. In *Look Homeward, Angel* (1929), Thomas Wolfe scandalized his native Asheville, North Carolina, with his unrelenting drive to escape the encircling hills and flee to the "billion-footed city." Writing for the *Smart Set* and *American Mercury*, the Baltimore journalist H. L. Mencken was the most merciless in his attacks on the American "booboisie." The daily panorama of America, he wrote, had become "so inordinately gross and preposterous . . . that only a man who was born with a petrified diaphragm can fail to laugh himself to sleep every night, and to awake every morning with all the eager, unflagging expectation of a Sunday-school superintendent touring the Paris peep-shows." The hinterlands responded with counterimages of cities infested with vice, crime, corruption, and foreigners.

THE JAZZ AGE   Writer F. Scott Fitzgerald dubbed the postwar era the "Jazz Age" because young people were willing to experiment with

Frankie "Half Pint" Jackson and His Band at the Sunset Cafe, Chicago, 1920s. *Jazz emerged during this period as an especially American expression of the modernist spirit. Black artists bent musical conventions to give fuller rein to improvisation.*

new forms of recreation and sexuality. The new jazz music bubbling up in New Orleans, Kansas City, Memphis, New York City, and Chicago blended African and European musical traditions into a distinctive sound characterized by improvisation, "blue notes," and polyrhythms. The syncopated rhythms of jazz were immensely popular among rebellious young adults and helped spawn carefree new dance steps such as the Charleston and Black Bottom, gyrations that shocked guardians of morality.

If people were not listening to "ragtime" or "jazz" music or to the family radio shows that became the rage in the 1920s, they were frequenting movie theaters. By 1930 there were more than 23,000 of them around the country, and they drew more than 95 million customers each week. In Muncie, Indiana, a small city of 35,000 people, there were nine movie theaters operating seven days a week. Movies were by far the most popular form of mass culture in the twenties, and films became even more favored after the introduction of sound in 1927.

THE NEW MORALITY   Much of the shock to old-timers during the Jazz Age came from the revolution in manners and morals, evidenced first among young people, and especially on the college campuses. In *This Side of Paradise* (1920), a novel of student life at Princeton, F. Scott Fitzgerald wrote of "the great current American phenomenon, the 'petting party.'" None of the Victorian mothers, he said, "had any idea how casually their daughters were accustomed to be kissed." From such novels and from magazine pieces, the heartland learned about the wild parties, bathtub gin, promiscuity, speakeasies, "shimmy dancers," and the new uses to which automobiles were put on secluded lovers' lanes.

Writers also informed the nation about the "new woman" eager to exercise new freedoms. These independent females discarded corsets, sported bobbed hair, heavy makeup, and skirts above the ankles; they smoked cigarettes and drank beer, drove automobiles, and in general, defied old Victorian expectations for womanly behavior.

Sex came to be discussed with a new frankness during the 1920s. Much of the talk derived from a spreading awareness of Dr. Sigmund Freud, the Viennese father of psychoanalysis. When in 1909 Freud visited Clark University in Massachusetts, he was surprised to find himself so well known "even in prudish America." By the 1920s, his ideas had begun to percolate into the popular awareness, and the talk spread in society and literature about libido, inhibitions, Oedipus complexes, and repression.

Fashion also reflected the rebellion against prudishness and a loosening of inhibitions. In 1919 women's skirts were typically six inches above the ground; by 1927 they were at the knees, and the "flapper" was providing a shocking model of the new feminism. The name derived from the way fashionable women allowed their galoshes to "flap" about their ankles. Conservative moralists saw the flappers as just another sign of a degenerating society. Others saw in the "new women" an expression of American individualism. "By sheer force of violence," explained the *New York Times* in 1929, the flapper has "established the feminine right to equal representation in such hitherto masculine fields of endeavor as smoking and drinking, swearing, petting, and upsetting the community peace."

By 1930, however, the thrill of rebellion was waning; the revolution against Victorian codes had run its course. Its extreme expressions aroused doubts that the indulgence of lust equaled liberation. Still, some new folkways had come to stay. In *Middletown* (Muncie, Indiana),

Teaching Old Dogs New Tricks. *A Life magazine cover by John Held, Jr. A young flapper is shown attempting to teach an elderly gentleman how to dance the Charleston.*

the subject of Robert and Helen Lynd's classic community study in the mid-1920s, a young man told them on their return in 1935 that young people had "been getting more and more knowing and bold. The fellows regard necking as a taken-for-granted part of a date." In the late 1930s, a survey disclosed that among college women almost half (47 percent) had yielded their virginity before marriage, but of these, three-quarters had had sexual relations only with their future spouses.

The most pervasive change brought by the new moral code was in its views of marriage. The old code had made the husband head and master of the family, responsible for its support, while limiting the wife's "sphere" to the care of the home and children and the nurturing of the husband. By the 1930s, a code exalting romantic love and companionship as the basis for marriage had gained ascendancy. One sociologist announced that the "breaking of the former taboo on sex has made possible for younger men and women a healthier attitude toward marital relationship" and a greater chance for mutual happiness. More important than breaking taboos may have been the social and economic evolution of a century that had taken away functions the family once had and delivered them to the factory, the school, and other institutions. People expressed alarm in the 1920s at the rising divorce rate. The rate declined briefly with the onset of the Great Depression in 1929, but picked up again during the later 1930s and 1940s. The divorce rate reflected perhaps less an increase in unsatisfactory marriages than a greater willingness and ability to abandon an intolerable situation.

MARGARET SANGER AND BIRTH CONTROL Perhaps the most controversial women's issue of the Jazz Age was birth control. Margaret Sanger, a New York nurse concerned about the adverse effects of frequent childbirths, miscarriages, and abortions, began to distribute birth-control information to working-class women in 1912. Through her steadfast efforts, women for the first time began to gain easy access to contraception.

Sanger embraced reproductive freedom in part because of her personal experiences. Born Margaret Higgins in upstate New York in 1879, the child of Irish immigrants, she blamed her mother's premature death from tuberculosis on her frequent pregnancies and the demands of caring for a large family. Margaret entered the nursing program at White Plains Hospital in 1900. Two years later she married architect William Sanger, and in 1910 the Sangers moved to New York City. There they immersed themselves in the bohemian culture and radical idealism of Greenwich Village. Margaret Sanger soon became a militant Socialist and cultural radical. She joined the Socialist party and participated in labor protests organized by the Industrial Workers of the World.

When not protesting and politicking, Sanger worked as a nurse and midwife in the working-class tenements on the Lower East Side of Manhattan. She saw many struggling young mothers who often did not have enough money to provide basic support for their growing families. She also witnessed firsthand the consequences of unwanted pregnancies, tragic miscarriages, and amateur abortions. Sanger resolved to spend the rest of her life helping women gain control of their own bodies. "No woman can call herself free until she can choose consciously whether she will or will not be a mother," she asserted.

Yet basic information about contraception was not readily available, especially to working-class women. Mailing such material was a criminal offense under the Comstock Law, named after Anthony Comstock, a self-appointed anti-vice crusader. In 1873 he had convinced Congress that contraceptive information was as "obscene" as pornography and should be banned from the postal system.

In 1914 Sanger defied the Comstock Law by publishing *The Woman Rebel,* a monthly journal that advocated militant feminism, including the right to practice "birth control," a term she coined. Each

Birth-control activist Margaret Sanger.

issue of the new journal proclaimed it a woman's duty to "look the whole world in the face with a go-to-hell look in the eyes; to have an ideal; to speak and act in defiance of convention." Six months after the journal appeared, the police arrested Sanger for violating postal obscenity laws. Unwilling to risk a lengthy imprisonment, she jumped bail and escaped to England. The flamboyant crusader returned to New York a year later, eager to garner media attention through a sensational trial. The case, however, never made it to court.

When Sanger's only daughter died suddenly of pneumonia, sympathetic publicity convinced the attorney-general to drop the prosecution. He did not want to make the grieving Sanger a "martyr." Denied the forum of a public trial, Sanger launched a nationwide tour to promote birth control. Arrested in several cities, the single-minded reformer with a genius for self-promotion attracted widespred publicity for the cause of birth control.

Back in New York, Sanger opened the nation's first family-planning clinic in Brooklyn in 1916. To promote its opening, she distributed fliers in English, Yiddish, and Italian, asking, "Mothers! Can you afford to have a large family? Do you want any more children? If not, why do you have them? Do not kill, do not take life, but prevent!" Hundreds of women flocked to the new clinic, arousing intense opposition from the Catholic church. On its tenth day of operation, police raided the clinic and arrested Sanger and her staff. The judge offered her clemency if she would promise to stop circulating information about contraception. She refused and spent thirty days in jail.

Sanger attracted growing public support. In 1921 Sanger organized the American Birth Control League, which in 1942 changed its name to Planned Parenthood. The League distributed birth-control information to doctors, social workers, women's clubs, and the scientific community, as well as to thousands of individual women.

During World War I, birth control had been a radical notion promoted by cultural liberals. In the 1920s contraception became a conservative instrument of social control. Advocates of eugenics, the popular "science" of improving hereditary qualities by socially controlling human reproduction, promoted birth control as a means of regulating the "promiscuous" lower classes whose birth rates were soaring. Twenty states passed forced sterilization laws, eugenics was taught in universities, and many leading reformers and thinkers endorsed the idea. In 1927, the Supreme Court ruled in *Buck* v. *Bell* that states could sterilize the disabled, insane, or epileptic.

During the 1920s Margaret Sanger alienated supporters, then and since, by endorsing sterilization for the mentally incompetent and those with hereditary deficiencies. Birth control, she stressed, was "the most constructive and necessary of the means to racial health." In 1928 Sanger angrily resigned as president of the American Birth Control League over issues related to the eugenics movement and her own autocratic style of leadership. For all of her faults, Sanger never lost her focus on women's freedom and its wider implications for social justice. She insisted that women should direct their own lives. Although Sanger did not succeed by 1929 in legalizing the distribution of contraceptives and contraceptive information through the mails, she had laid the foundation for such efforts in the future. In 1936 a federal court ruled that physicians could prescribe contraceptives—a vital step in Sanger's efforts to realize her slogan, "Every child a wanted child."

THE WOMEN'S MOVEMENT Voting rights for women arrived in 1920. The suffrage movement, which had been in the doldrums since 1896, sprang back to life in the second decade of the new century. In 1912 Alice Paul, a Quaker social worker, returned from an apprenticeship with the militant suffragists of England, and became head of the National American Woman Suffrage Association's Congressional Committee. Paul told female activists to picket state legislatures, target and "punish" politicians who failed to endorse suffrage, chain themselves to public buildings, provoke police into arresting them, and undertake hunger strikes.

Paul's militant tactics and single-minded focus on the federal amendment increasingly drove a wedge between her and the larger national group. The Congressional Union, formed by her committee in 1913, became a separate organization in 1915 and changed its name to the Woman's Party in 1916. This group copied the British suffragists in holding the party in power responsible for failure to act, a reasonable stance under a parliamentary system but one that led them to oppose every Democrat, which the mainline suffragists found self-defeating in America. Alice Paul nevertheless knew how to get publicity for the cause. By 1917 she and her followers were picketing the White House and deliberately provoking arrests, after which they went on hunger strikes in prison. The authorities obligingly cooperated in making martyrs. They arrested them by the hundreds.

In 1915 Carrie Chapman Catt had once again become head of the National Woman Suffrage Association (NWSA). For several years, President Woodrow Wilson had evaded the issue of an amendment, but he voted for suffrage in a New Jersey referendum and supported a plank

A parade in New York, 1916, in which suffragettes carry a banner that declares "Women have full suffrage in Wyoming, Colorado, Utah & Idaho."

in the 1916 Democratic platform endorsing state action for women's suffrage. He also addressed the NWSA that year, and thereafter worked closely with its leaders.

Finally, in 1918, after the House had passed the "Susan B. Anthony Amendment," Wilson went before the Senate to plead for its passage there. The Senate fell short of the needed two-thirds majority by two votes, but the attention centered on the issue helped defeat two anti-suffrage senators. On June 4, 1919, the Senate finally adopted the amendment by a bare two-thirds majority. Ratification of the Nineteenth Amendment took another fourteen months. The Tennessee legislature had the distinction of completing the ratification, on August 21, 1920. It was one of the climactic achievements of the Progressive Era.

Meanwhile, the NWSA began transforming itself into the League of Women Voters, founded in 1920, and women thereafter entered politics in growing numbers. But, it was often noted, this did not usher in a sudden release of women from all the trammels of custom and law. What was more, the lack of further advancements for women after the suffrage victory left the broader feminist movement disillusioned. Carrie Chapman Catt, former head of the NWSA, wrote that suffragists were disappointed "because they miss the exaltation, the thrill of expectancy, the vision which stimulated them in the suffrage campaign. They find none of these appeals to their aspiration in the party of their choice."

One group, however, wanted to take matters further. Alice Paul and the Woman's Party set a new feminist goal, first introduced in Congress in 1923: an Equal Rights Amendment that would eliminate any remaining legal distinctions between the sexes—including the special legislation for the protection of working women put on the books in the previous fifty or so years. It would be another fifty years before Alice Paul would see Congress adopt her amendment in 1972; she did not live, however, to see it fall short of ratification.

The sharp increase in the number of women in the workforce during World War I proved short-lived, but in the longer view a steady increase in the numbers of employed women occurred in the 1920s and, surprisingly, continued through the depression decade of the 1930s. By 1910 they made up almost a quarter of all nonagricultural workers, and in 1920 they were found in all but 35 of the 572 job categories listed by the census. The continued entry of women into the workforce brought their numbers up from 8 million in the 1920 census to 10 million in 1930, and 13 million in 1940. Still, these women remained concentrated in traditional occupations: domestics, office workers, teachers, clerks, salespeople, dressmakers, milliners, and seamstresses. On the eve of World War II, women's work was little more diversified than it had been at the turn of the century, but by 1940 it was on the verge of a great transformation.

THE "NEW NEGRO" The discriminations experienced by African Americans and women have many parallels, and the loosening of restraints for both have often coincided. The most significant development in black life during the early twentieth century was the Great Migration northward. The movement of blacks to the North began in 1915–1916, when rapidly expanding war industries were experiencing a labor shortage at a time when the war prevented replacement by foreign immigrants; legal restrictions on immigration continued the movement in the 1920s. Altogether, between 1910 and 1920, the Southeast lost some 323,000 blacks, or 5 percent of the native black population, and by 1930 it had lost another 615,000, or 8 percent of the native black population in 1920. With the migration, a slow but steady growth in black political influence set in. Blacks were freer to speak and act in a northern setting; they also gained political leverage by concentrating in large cities located in states with many electoral votes.

Along with political activity came a bristling spirit of protest among blacks, a spirit that received cultural expression in a literary and artistic movement known as the "Harlem Renaissance." Claude McKay, a Jamaican immigrant, was the first significant writer of the movement, which featured a rediscovery of black folk culture and an emancipation from the genteel tradition. Poems collected in McKay's *Harlem Shadows* (1922) expressed defiance in such titles as "If We Must Die" and "To the White Fiends." Other emergent writers included Langston Hughes, Zora Neale Hurston, Countée Cullen, and James Weldon Johnson. Perhaps the greatest single creation of the time was Jean Toomer's novel *Cane,* which pictured the lives of simple folk in Georgia's black belt and the sophisticated African-American middle class in Washington, D.C.

A Negro Family Just Arrived in Chicago from the Rural South, 1922. *Between 1910 and 1930 almost 1 million blacks left the South.*

The spirit of the "New Negro" also found expression in what came to be called "Negro nationalism," which exalted blackness, black cultural expression, and black exclusiveness. The leading spokesman for such views was the flamboyant Marcus Garvey. In 1916 he brought to New York the Universal Negro Improvement Association (UNIA), which he had started in his native Jamaica two years before. His organization grew rapidly amid the racial tensions of the postwar years. Racial bias, Garvey said, was so ingrained in whites that it was futile to appeal to their sense of justice. He told American blacks to liberate themselves from the surrounding white culture. "We have outgrown slavery," he declared, "but our minds are still enslaved to the thinking of the Master Race." He saw every white person as a "potential Klansman" and therefore endorsed the "social and political separation of all peoples to the extent that they promote their own ideals and civilization."

Such a separatist message appalled other black leaders. W. E. B. Du Bois, for example, labeled Garvey "the most dangerous enemy of the

Marcus Garvey, founder of the Universal Negro Improvement Association and a leading spokesman for "Negro nationalism" in the 1920s.

Negro race." Garvey and his aides created their own black version of Christianity, organized their own fraternal lodges and community cultural centers, started their own businesses, and published their own newspaper. Garvey's message of racial pride and self-reliance appealed to many blacks who had arrived in the northern cities during the Great Migration and had grown frustrated and embittered with the hypocrisy of American democracy during the postwar economic slump.

Delivering the keynote address at the first convention of the UNIA in 1920, Garvey declared that the only lasting hope for blacks was to flee America and build their own republic in Africa. Garvey quickly enlisted half a million members and claimed as many as 6 million by 1923. At that point he was charged with fraudulent use of the mails in fund-raising. Found guilty, he was sent to prison in 1925, where he remained until President Calvin Coolidge pardoned and deported him to Jamaica in 1927. Garvey died in obscurity in London in 1940, but the memory of his movement kept alive an undercurrent of racial nationalism that would reemerge later under the slogan of "black power."

A more lasting and influential force for racial equality was the National Association for the Advancement of Colored People (NAACP), founded in 1910 by white liberals and black activists. Black participants came mainly from a group associated with W. E. B. Du Bois and called the Niagara Movement, which had met each year since 1905 at a place associated with antislavery (Niagara Falls, Oberlin, Boston, Harper's Ferry) and issued a defiant statement against discrimination.

Although most white progressives did not embrace the NAACP, the new group took seriously the progressive idea that the solution to social problems began with informing the people, and it planned an active press bureau to accomplish this. Du Bois became its director of publicity and research, and editor of its journal, *The Crisis*. The NAACP's main strategy was to focus on legal action designed to bring the Fourteenth and Fifteenth Amendments back to life. One early victory came with *Guinn* v. *United States* (1915). The Supreme Court struck down Oklahoma's grandfather clause, used in the state to deprive blacks of the vote. In *Buchanan* v. *Worley* (1917) the Court invalidated a residential segregation ordinance in Louisville, Kentucky.

In 1919 the NAACP launched a campaign against lynching, a still-common form of vigilante racism. An anti-lynching bill to make mob murder a federal offense passed the House in 1922, but it lost to a filibuster by southern senators. The bill stayed before the House until 1925, and NAACP field secretary James Weldon Johnson believed the continued agitation of the issue did more than the bill's passage would have to reduce lynchings, which decreased to a third of what they had been in the previous decade.

The emergent black political renaissance found its most important expression in two events: Oscar DePriest's election from a Chicago district in 1928 as the first black congressman since 1901, the first ever from the North; and the fight against the confirmation of Judge John J. Parker for the Supreme Court in 1930. When President Herbert Hoover submitted Parker's name, the NAACP found that, as the 1920 Republican candidate for governor of North Carolina, Parker had pronounced Negro suffrage "a source of evil and danger." The NAACP conducted its campaign, Du Bois said, "with a snap, determination, and intelligence never surpassed in colored America." Parker lost by the close vote of 41 to 39; his defeat represented the first instance of a significant black impact on Congress since Reconstruction.

THE CULTURE OF MODERNISM

After 1920, changes in the realms of science and social thought were perhaps even more dramatic than those affecting women and blacks. As the twentieth century advanced, the easy faith in progress and reform expressed by progressives fell victim to a series of frustrations and disasters, including the Great War, the failure of the League of Nations, Woodrow Wilson's physical and political collapse, and the failure of prohibition. Startling new findings in physics further shook prevailing assumptions of order and certainty.

SCIENCE AND SOCIAL THOUGHT   Physicists of the early twentieth century altered the image of the cosmos in ways that seemed almost a conspiracy against common sense. Since Isaac Newton, conventional wisdom had held the universe to be governed by laws that the scientific method could ultimately uncover. A world of such certain order had bolstered hopes of infinite progress in human knowledge.

This rational world of order and certainty disintegrated at the turn of the century when Albert Einstein, a young German physicist, announced his theory of relativity, which maintained that space, time, and mass were not absolutes but relative to the location and motion of the observer. Isaac Newton's eighteenth-century mechanics, according to Einstein's relativity theories, worked well enough at relatively slow speeds, but the more nearly one approached the velocity of light (about 186,000 miles per second) the more all measuring devices would change accordingly, so that yardsticks would become shorter, clocks and heartbeats would slow down, even the aging process would ebb.

Certainty dissolved the farther one reached out into the universe and the farther one reached down into the minute world of the atom. The discovery of radioactivity in the 1890s showed that atoms were not irreducible units of matter but that some of them emitted particles of energy. This meant, Einstein noted, that mass and energy were not separate phenomena but interchangeable.

Meanwhile, the German physicist Max Planck had discovered that electromagnetic emissions of energy, whether as electricity or light, came in little bundles that he called quanta. The developed of quantum theory suggested that atoms were far more complex than once believed and, as another pioneering German physicist, Werner Heisenberg, stated in his uncertainty principle in 1927, ultimately indescribable. One could never know both the position and the velocity of an electron, Heisenberg concluded, because the very process of observation would inevitably affect the behavior of the particle, altering its position or velocity.

Heisenberg's thesis meant that human knowledge had limits. "The physicist thus finds himself in a world from which the bottom has dropped clean out," a Harvard mathematician wrote in 1929. The

Albert Einstein.

scientist had to "give up his most cherished convictions and faith. The world is not a world of reason, understandable by the intellect of man, but as we penetrate ever deeper, the very law of cause and effect, which we had thought to be a formula to which we could force God Himself to subscribe, ceases to have any meaning." Hard for the public to grasp, such findings proved too troubling even for Einstein, who spent much of the rest of his life in search of an explanation that would unify the relativity and quantum theories. "I shall never believe that God plays dice with the world," Einstein asserted.

Just as Enlightenment thinkers drew on Isaac Newton's laws of gravitation two centuries before to formulate their views on the laws governing society, the ideas of relativity and uncertainty in the twentieth century provoked people to deny the relevance of absolute values in any sphere of society, which undermined the concepts of personal responsibility and absolute standards. Anthropologists aided the process by transforming the world *culture,* which had before meant refinement, into a term for the whole system of ideas, folkways, and institutions within which any group lived. Even the most primitive groups had cultures and, all things being relative, one culture should not impose its value judgments on another. Two anthropologists, Ruth Benedict and Margaret Mead, were especially effective in spreading this viewpoint.

MODERNIST ART AND LITERATURE   The cluster of scientific ideas associated with Charles Darwin, Sigmund Freud, and Albert Einstein inspired a revolution in the minds of intellectuals and creative artists, which they expressed in a new "modernism." The modernist world was one in which, as Karl Marx said, "All that is solid melts into air." Whereas nineteenth-century writers and artists took for granted an accessible world that could be readily observed and accurately represented, self-willed modernists viewed the "real" as something to be created rather than copied, expressed rather than reproduced. They thus concluded that the subconscious regions of the psyche were more interesting and potent than reason, common sense, and logic.

In the various arts, related technical features appeared: abstract painting that represented an inner mood rather than a recognizable image of an object, atonal music, free verse in poetry, stream-of-consciousness narrative, and interior monologues in stories and novels. Writers showed an intense concern with new forms in language in an effort to avoid outmoded forms and structures and to violate expectations and shock their audiences.

The search for the new centered in America's first major artistic bohemias in Chicago and New York, especially the area in lower Manhattan known as Greenwich Village. In 1913 the Armory Show in New York, which went then to Chicago, Philadelphia, and Boston, shocked traditionalists with its display of the latest works by experimental and non-representational artists: post-impressionists, expressionists, primitives, and cubists. Pablo Picasso's work made its American debut there. The show aroused shock, indignation, and not a little good-natured ridicule, but it was a huge success.

The chief American prophets of modernism were in neither Chicago nor New York, but were American expatriates in Europe: Ezra Pound and T. S. Eliot in London and Gertrude Stein in Paris, all deeply concerned with creating new and often difficult styles of modernist expression. Pound, as foreign editor for *Poetry*, became the conduit through which many American poets achieved publication in America and Britain. At the same time, he became the leader of the imagist movement, a revolt against the ornamental verbosity of Victorian poetry in favor of the concrete image.

Pound's most important protégé was T. S. Eliot, who in 1915 contributed to *Poetry* his first major poem, "The Love Song of J. Alfred Prufrock," the musings of an ineffectual man who "after tea and cakes and ices" could never find "the strength to force the moment to its crisis." Eliot's *The Waste Land* (1922) made few concessions to readers in its arcane allusions, its juxtaposi-

Pablo Picasso's portrait of Gertrude Stein, 1906.

tion of unexpected metaphors, its deep sense of postwar disillusionment and melancholy, and its suggestion of a burned-out civilization; but it became for a generation almost the touchstone of the modern temper, along with the Irishman James Joyce's stream-of-consciousness novel *Ulysses,* published the same year. As poet and critic in the *Criterion,* which he founded in 1922, Eliot became the arbiter of modernist taste in Anglo-American literature.

Gertrude Stein, in voluntary exile since 1903, was with her brother, Leo, an early champion of modern art and a collector of early Cézannes, Matisses, and Picassos. Long regarded as no more than the literary eccentric who wrote "A rose is a rose is a rose is a rose," she came later to be recognized as one of the chief promoters of modernist prose style, beginning with *Three Lives* (1906). Stein sought to capture interior moods in her writing, developing in words the equivalent of nonrepresentational painting.

But Stein was long known chiefly through her influence on such other expatriates as Ernest Hemingway, whom she told: "All of you young people who served in the war, you are the lost generation." The earliest chronicler of that generation, F. Scott Fitzgerald, blazed up

The Fitzgeralds Celebrate Christmas. *F. Scott Fitzgerald and his wife, Zelda, lived in and wrote about the "greatest, gaudiest spree in history."*

brilliantly and then quickly flickered out, like all the tinseled, sad young people of his novels. Successful and famous at age twenty-four with *This Side of Paradise* (1920), along with his wife, Zelda, he lived in and wrote about the "greatest, gaudiest spree in history," and then both had their crack-up in the Great Depression. What gave depth to the best of his work was what a character in *The Great Gatsby* (1925), his finest novel, called "a sense of the fundamental decencies" amid all the surface gaiety—and almost always a sense of impending doom.

Ernest Hemingway's novels *The Sun Also Rises* (1926) and *A Farewell to Arms* (1929), depict a desperate search for "real" life and the doomed, war-tainted love affairs of young Americans of the "lost generation." These novels contain the frenetic, hard-drinking lifestyle and the cult of athletic masculinity (epitomized by the bullfighter), which became the stuff of the public image Hemingway cultivated for himself and the hallmark of such novels as *Death in the Afternoon* (1932), *To Have and Have Not* (1937), *For Whom the Bell Tolls* (1940), and *The Old Man and the Sea* (1952). Hundreds of writers tried to imitate Hemingway's terse style, but few had his gift, which lay less in what he had to say than in the way he said it.

THE SOUTHERN RENAISSANCE As modernist literature arose in response to the changes taking place in the United States and Europe, so did southern literature of the twenties reflect a mythic world in the midst of rebirth. A southern renaissance in writing emerged from the conflict between the dying world of tradition and the modern, commercial world struggling to be born in the aftermath of the Great War. While in the South the conflict of values aroused the Ku Klux Klan and fundamentalist furies that tried desperately to bring back the world of tradition, it also inspired the vitality and creativity of the South's young writers.

In Nashville, *The Fugitive: A Journal of Poetry* (1922–1925) announced the arrival of the most influential group of American writers since the New England transcendentalists. The Fugitive poets began as a group of student intellectuals at Vanderbilt University who first gathered for discussions in 1915, then regrouped after the war with young Professor John Crowe Ransom as their dean and mentor. Four of the group eventually stood out in their commitment to literature as a profession: Ransom, Donald Davidson, Allen Tate, and Robert Penn Warren. The Fugitives admired T. S. Eliot and were committed to the new doctrines of modernism in literature.

"One may reasonably argue," wrote a critic in 1930, "that the South is the literary land of promise today." Just the previous year two vital figures had emerged: Thomas Wolfe, with *Look Homeward, Angel,* and William Faulkner, with *Sartoris* and *The Sound and the Fury.* Fame rushed in first on Wolfe and his native Asheville, North Carolina, which became in the 1920s a classic example of the scandalized community. "Against the Victorian morality and the Bourbon aristocracy of the South," Wolfe had "turned in all his fury," newspaper editor Jonathan Daniels, a former classmate, wrote. The reaction was not an uncommon response to the works of the southern renaissance, created by authors who had outgrown their "provincial" hometowns and looked back from new perspectives acquired through travel and education.

Despite his gargantuan lust for experience and knowledge, his demonic drive to escape the encircling hills for the "fabled" world outside, Wolfe never completely severed his roots in the South. *Look Homeward, Angel,* his first novel, remained his most successful; it was the lyrical

William Faulkner.

and searching biography of Eugene Gant's (actually Wolfe's) youth in Altamont (Asheville) and his college days in Pulpit Hill (Chapel Hill). It established him as "the giant among American writers of sensitive youth fiction."

William Faulkner's achievement, more than Wolfe's, was rooted in the coarsely textured social world that produced him. Born near Oxford, Mississippi, he grew up there and transmuted his hometown into the fictional Jefferson, Yoknapatawpha County. After a brief stint with the Royal Canadian Air Force he passed the postwar decade in what seemed to fellow townspeople an aimless drifting. He briefly attended classes at the University of Mississippi, worked at odd jobs, and went to New Orleans where he wrote *Soldiers' Pay* (1926), a novel of postwar disillusionment, and *Mosquitoes* (1927), a caricature of the New Orleans bohemians yachting on Lake Pontchartrain. Between books he shipped out briefly for Europe, and after knocking around the Gulf coast, returned to Oxford.

There, in writing *Sartoris* (1929), he began to discover that his "own little postage stamp of native soil was worth writing about" and that he "would never live long enough to exhaust it." With *Sartoris* and the creation of his mythical land of Yoknapatawpha, Faulkner kindled a blaze of creative energy. Next, as he put it, he wrote his gut into *The Sound and the Fury* (1929). It was one of the triumphs of the modernist style, but most early readers, taking their cue from the title instead of the critics, found it signified nothing.

Modernism and the southern literary renaissance, both of which emerged from the crucible of the Great War and its aftermath, were products of the 1920s. But the widespread alienation felt by the artists of the 1920s did not survive the decade. The onset of the Great Depression in 1929 sparked a renewed sense of commitment and affirmation in the arts, as if people could no longer afford the art-for-art's-sake affectations of the 1920s. Alienation would give way to social purpose in the decade to come.

MAKING CONNECTIONS

- The next chapter discusses the growing consumer culture of the 1920s, an economic offshoot of the "Roaring Twenties" described in this chapter.

- Chapter 28 describes the changes in American literary culture wrought by the Great Depression—from the modernism discussed in this chapter to a recognition of the social role of literature and the cultural "rediscovery of America" in the 1930s.

- The status of women in the workforce did not improve in the 1920s, despite the successes of the women's movement. That status changed, at least temporarily, during World War II. Chapter 30 traces the increase in women in the workforce.

FURTHER READING

For a lively survey of the interwar period, start with William E. Leuchtenburg's *The Perils of Prosperity, 1914–1932* (rev. ed., 1993). The best introduction to the culture of the 1920s remains Loren Baritz's *The Culture of the Twenties* (1970). See also Lynn Dumenil's *The Modern Temper: American Culture and Society in the 1920s* (1995).

John Higham's *Strangers in the Land: Patterns of American Nativism, 1860–1925* (rev. ed., 1988) details the story of immigration restriction. The controversial Sacco and Vanzetti case is thoroughly explored in Richard Newby's *Kill Now, Talk Forever: Debating Sacco and Vanzetti* (2002). For analysis of the revival of Klan activity, see Nancy MacLean's *Behind the Mask of Chivalry: The Making of the Second Ku Klux Klan* (1994).

Women's suffrage is treated extensively in Eleanor Flexner's *Century of Struggle: The Women's Rights Movement in the United States* (rev. ed., 1975). See Charles F. Kellogg's *NAACP: A History of the National*

Association for the Advancement of Colored People (1967) for his analysis of the pioneering court cases against racial discrimination. Nathan I. Huggins's *Harlem Renaissance* (1971) assesses the cultural impact of the Great Migration in New York. On the migration to Chicago, see James R. Grossman's *Land of Hope: Chicago, Black Southerners, and the Great Migration* (1989). Nicholas Lemann's *The Promised Land* (1991) is a fine exposition of the changes brought about by the Great Migration in both the South and North.

On "modernism," see Daniel J. Singal's *The War Within: From Victorian to Modernist Thought in the South, 1919–1945* (1982). Stanley Coben's *Rebellion against Victorianism: The Impetus for Cultural Change in 1920s America* (1991) surveys the appeal of "modernism" among writers, artists, and intellectuals.

27 ⟶ REPUBLICAN RESURGENCE AND DECLINE

CHAPTER ORGANIZER

This chapter focuses on:

- the conservatism in the presidencies of Harding, Coolidge, and Hoover.

- growth in the American economy in the 1920s.

- the causes of the Great Depression.

*T*he progressive political coalition that reelected Woodrow Wilson in 1916 proved to be quite fragile, and by 1920 it had fragmented. It unraveled for several reasons. Radicals and other opponents of the war grew disaffected with America's entrance into the conflict and the war's aftermath. Organized labor resented the administration's unsympathetic attitude toward the strikes of 1919–1920. Farmers of the Great Plains and the West thought that wartime price controls had discriminated against them. Intellectuals also drifted away from their former support of progressivism. They became disillusioned with the emphases on grassroots democracy because of popular support for Prohibition and the anti-evolution movements. The larger middle class became preoccupied with building a new business civilization "based not upon monopoly and restriction," in the words of one historian, "but upon a whole new set of business values— mass production and consumption, short hours and high wages, full employment, welfare capitalism." Progressivism's final triumphs at the national level were already pretty much foregone conclusions before the war's end: the Eighteenth Amendment, ratified in 1919, which imposed national Prohibition, and the Nineteenth Amendment, ratified in 1920, which extended women's suffrage to the entire country.

Progressivism, however, did not disappear in the 1920s. Progressives dominated Congress during much of the decade even while the White House was in conservative Republican hands. The progressive impulse for "good government" and broader public services remained strong, especially at the state and local levels, where movements for good roads, education, public health, and social welfare all gained momentum during the decade. Much of the progressive impulse for reform, however, was transformed into the drive for moral righteousness and conformity animating the Ku Klux Klan as well as the fundamentalist and prohibitionist movements.

"NORMALCY"

HARDING'S ELECTION   After World War I, most Americans had grown weary of idealistic crusades and were suspicious of leaders promoting widespread reforms. Woodrow Wilson himself recognized this fact. "It is only once in a generation," he remarked, "that a people can be lifted above material things. That is why conservative government is in the saddle two-thirds of the time."

When the Republicans met in Chicago in 1920, the Old Guard party regulars found their man in the affable Ohio senator Warren Gamaliel Harding, who had set the tone of his campaign when he told a Boston audience: "America's present need is not heroics, but healing; not nostrums, but normalcy; not revolution, but restoration; not agitation, but adjustment; not surgery, but serenity; not the dramatic, but the dispassionate; not experiment, but equipoise; not submergence in internationality, but sustainment in triumphant nationality."

Harding's promise of a "return to normalcy" reflected his own conservative values and folksy personality. The son of an Ohio farmer, he described himself not as an intellectual or a crusader but "just a plain fellow" who was "old-fashioned and even reactionary in matters of faith and morals." But such a description suggests a certain puritan regimen that Harding never practiced. Far from being an old-fashioned moralist in his personal life, he drank bootleg liquor in the midst of Prohibition, smoked and chewed tobacco, relished weekly poker games, and had numerous liaisons with women other than his austere wife, whom he called "Duchess." The general public, however, remained unaware of Harding's escapades. Instead the voters saw him as a handsome, charming, gregarious, and lovable politician. A man of self-confessed limitations in vision, leadership, and intellectual power, he once admitted that "I cannot hope to be one of the great presidents, but perhaps I may be remembered as one of the best loved." He got his wish.

The Democrats in 1920 hoped that Harding would not be president at all. James Cox, former newsman and former governor of Ohio, won the presidential nomination of an increasingly fragmented Democratic party on the forty-fourth ballot. For vice-president the convention named Franklin D. Roosevelt, who as assistant secretary of the navy occupied the same position his Republican cousin Theodore Roosevelt had held before him.

The Democrats suffered from the breakup of the Wilsonian coalition and the conservative postwar mood. In the words of progressive journalist William Allen White, Americans in 1920 were "tired of issues, sick at heart of ideals, and weary of being noble." The country voted overwhelmingly for Harding's promised "return to normalcy." Harding got 16 million votes to 9 million for Cox, who carried no state outside the Solid Democratic South.

EARLY APPOINTMENTS AND POLICY   Harding in office had much in common with Ulysses Grant. His cabinet, like Grant's, mixed some of the "best minds" in the party, whom he had promised to seek out, with some of the worst, cronies who sought him out. Charles Evans Hughes, like Grant's Hamilton Fish, became a distinguished secretary of state. Herbert Hoover in the Commerce Department, Andrew W. Mellon in the Treasury Department, and Henry C. Wallace in the Agriculture Department functioned efficiently and made policy on their own. Other cabinet members and administrative appointees, however, were not so conscientious. The secretary of the interior landed in prison and the attorney-general narrowly escaped serving time. Many lesser offices went to members of the "Ohio Gang," a group with which Harding met in a "Little House on K Street" to get away from the pressures of the White House.

Until he became president, Harding had loved politics. He was the party hack par excellence, "bloviating" (a verb of his own making, which meant speaking with gaseous eloquence) on the stump, jollying it up in the clubhouse and cloakroom, hobnobbing with the great and near-great in Washington. As president, however, Harding was simply in over his head, and self-doubt overwhelmed him. "I don't think I'm big enough for the Presidency," he confided to a friend. Harding much preferred to get away with the "Ohio Gang," who shared his taste for whiskey, poker, and women.

Harding and his friends set about dismantling or neutralizing as many of the social and economic components of progressivism as they could. To that end, Harding took advantage of four Supreme Court vacancies by appointing conservatives, including Chief Justice William Howard Taft, who announced that he had been "appointed to reverse a few decisions." During the 1920s, the Taft Court struck down a federal child-labor law and a minimum-wage law for women, issued numerous injunctions against striking unions, and passed rulings limiting the powers of federal regulatory agencies.

The Harding administration established a pro-business tone reminiscent of the McKinley White House. To sustain economic growth, Secretary of the Treasury Mellon instituted a Republican policy of reduced government spending and lower taxes. To get a better handle on expenditures, he persuaded a lukewarm Congress to pass the Budget and Accounting Act of 1921, which created a new Bureau of the Budget, headed by a Chicago banker, to prepare a unified federal budget, and a General Accounting Office to audit the accounts. This act realized a long-held progressive desire to bring greater efficiency and nonpartisanship to the budget preparation process. General tax reductions from the wartime level were warranted, but Mellon insisted that they should go mainly to the rich, on the principle that wealth in the hands of the few would augment the general welfare through increased capital investment. Mellon's admirers tagged him "the greatest Secretary of the Treasury since Alexander Hamilton."

In Congress a group of western Republicans and southern Democrats fought a dogged battle to preserve the graduated scale built into wartime taxes, but Mellon, in office through the 1920s, eventually won out. At his behest, Congress in 1921 repealed the wartime excess-profits tax and lowered the maximum rate on personal income from 65 to 50 percent. Subsequent revenue acts lowered the maximum rate to 40 percent in 1924 and 20 percent in 1926. The Revenue Act of 1926 extended further benefits to high-income groups by lowering estate taxes and repealing the gift tax. Unfortunately, much of the tax money released to wealthy people seems to have fueled the speculative excess of the late 1920s as much as it fostered gainful enterprise. Mellon, however, did balance the federal budget for a time. Governmental expenditures fell, as did the national debt.

In addition to tax cuts, Mellon favored the time-honored Republican policy of high tariffs, and innovations in the chemical and metal industries revived the argument for protection of infant American industries from foreign competition. The Fordney-McCumber Tariff of 1922 increased rates on chemical and metal products as a safeguard against the revival of German industries that had previously commanded the field. To please the farmers, who historically benefited little from tariffs, the new act further extended the duties on farm products.

Higher tariffs, however, had unexpected consequences. During the war, the United States had been transformed from a debtor to a creditor nation. In former years foreign capital had flowed into the United States, playing an important role in the economic expansion of the nineteenth century. But the private and public credits given the Allies to purchase American supplies during the war had reversed the pattern. Mellon insisted that the European powers must repay all that they had borrowed. But the tariff walls erected around the country made it all the harder for other nations to sell in the United States and thus acquire the dollars or credits with which to repay their war debts. For nearly a decade, further extensions of American loans and investments sent more dollars abroad, postponing the reckoning.

Rounding out the Republican economic program during the 1920s was a more lenient attitude toward government regulation of corporations. Neither Harding nor his successor, Calvin Coolidge, could dissolve the regulatory agencies, but they named commissioners who promoted "friendly" regulation. Harding named conservative advocates of big business to the Interstate Commerce Commission, the Federal Reserve Board, and the Federal Trade Commission. Senator George Norris characterized the new appointments as "the nullification of federal law by a process of boring from within." Senator Henry Cabot Lodge agreed, boasting that "we have torn up Wilsonism by the roots."

A CORRUPT ADMINISTRATION   Republican conservatives such as Lodge and Mellon were at least operating out of a philosophical conviction intended to benefit the nation. Members of the "Ohio Gang," however, used White House connections to line their own pockets. In 1923 Harding learned that an official of the Veterans Bureau was systematically looting medical and hospital supplies. The official fled to Europe and resigned. Harding's general counsel then committed suicide.

Not long afterward, a close buddy of the attorney-general also shot himself. The corrupt crony held no government appointment, but had set up an office in the Justice Department from which he peddled influence for a fee. The attorney-general himself was implicated in the fraudulent handling of German assets seized after the war. When discovered, he refused to testify on the ground that he might incriminate himself. Twice brought to court, he was never indicted, for want of evidence, possibly because he had destroyed pertinent records. These were but the most visible among many scandals that touched the Justice Department, the Prohibition Bureau, and other agencies under Harding.

But one major scandal rose above all others. Teapot Dome, like the Watergate break-in fifty years later, became the catchword for a climate of corruption. An oil deposit under the sandstone Teapot Rock in Wyoming, Teapot Dome had been set aside as a naval oil reserve administered by the Interior Department under Albert B. Fall. At the time the move seemed a sensible attempt to unify control over public reserves. But once Fall had control, he signed contracts letting private interests exploit the oil deposits: Harry Sinclair's Mammoth Oil Company at Teapot Dome, Wyoming, and Edward L. Doheny's Pan-American Petroleum and Transport Company at Elk Hills, California. Fall argued that these contracts were in the government's interest. Yet why did Fall act in secret, without allowing competitive bids?

Suspicion grew when Fall's personal standard of living suddenly rose. It turned out that he had taken loans of about $400,000 (which came in "a little black bag") from Sinclair and Doheny. For the rest of his life, Fall insisted that the loans were unrelated to the oil leases, and that he had contrived a good deal for the government, but at best the circumstances revealed a fatal blindness to his impropriety.

Juggernaut. *This 1924 cartoon shows the dimensions of the Teapot Dome scandal.*

Harding himself avoided the humiliation of public disgrace. How much he knew of the scandals swirling about him is unclear, but he knew enough to become visibly troubled. "My God, this is a hell of a job!" he confided to a friend. "I have no trouble with my enemies, I can take care of my enemies all right. But my damn friends, my God-damn friends.... they're the ones that keep me walking the floor nights!" In 1923 Harding left on what would be his last journey, a western speaking tour and a trip to the Alaska Territory. Back in Seattle, he suffered an attack of food poisoning, recovered briefly, and then died in a San Francisco hotel.

Not since the death of Abraham Lincoln had there been such an outpouring of grief for a "beloved President," for the kindly, ordinary man who found it in his heart (as Wilson had not) to pardon Eugene Debs, the Socialist who had been jailed for opposing U.S. entry into World War I. As the black-streamered funeral train moved toward Washington, D.C., then back to Ohio, millions stood by the tracks to honor their lost leader. Eventually, however, grief yielded to scorn and contempt. For nearly a decade, the revelations of scandal within the Harding administration were paraded before investigating committees and then courts.

Harding's long extramarital affair with Nan Britton came to light, first the birth of their illegitimate child, and later their couplings in a White House closet. Harding's love letters to another man's wife also surfaced. As a result of his amorous detours and corrupt associates, Harding's foreshortened administration came to be widely viewed as one of the worst in American history.

More recent assessments of Harding's presidency, however, suggest that the scandals obscured some real accomplishments. Some historians credit Harding for leading the nation out of the turmoil of the postwar years and creating the foundation for the decade's remarkable economic boom. These revisionists also stress that he was a hardworking president who played a far more forceful role than previously assumed in shaping his administration's economic and foreign policies and in shepherding legislation through Congress. Harding also promoted diversity and civil rights. He appointed Jews to key federal positions and spoke out forcefully against the Ku Klux Klan as well as other "factions of hatred and prejudice and violence." No president promoted women's rights as forcefully as did Harding. But even Harding's foremost scholarly defender admits that he lacked good judgment and "probably should never have been president."

"SILENT CAL" The news of Harding's death came when Calvin Coolidge was visiting his father in the isolated mountain village of Plymouth, Vermont, his birthplace. There at 2:47 on the morning of August 3, 1923, by the light of a kerosene lamp, Colonel John Coolidge administered the oath of office to his son. The rustic simplicity of Plymouth, the very name itself, evoked just the image of traditional roots and solid integrity that the country would long for amid the coming disclosures of corruption in the Harding administration.

Coolidge brought to the White House a clear conviction that the presidency should revert to its Gilded-Age stance of passive deference to Congress. "Four-fifths of our troubles," Coolidge predicted, "would disappear if we would sit down and keep still." He abided by this rule, insisting on twelve hours of sleep and an afternoon nap. H. L. Mencken asserted that Coolidge "slept more than any other president, whether by day or by night. Nero fiddled, but Coolidge only snored."

Americans embraced the unflappability of "Silent Cal." Although a man of few words, he was not as bland or as dry as critics claimed. Yet

Warren Harding (left) *and Calvin Coolidge* (right).

he was conservative. Even more than Harding, Coolidge identified the nation's welfare with the success of big business. "The chief business of the American people is business," he intoned. "The man who builds a factory builds a temple. The man who works there worships there." Where Harding had sought to balance the interests of labor, agriculture, and industry, Coolidge focused on industrial development at the expense of the other two areas. He sought to unleash the free-enterprise system and, even more than Harding, he strove to end government regulation of business and industry and reduce taxes as well as the national debt. His pro-business stance led the *Wall Street Journal* to exult: "Never before, here or anywhere else, has a government been so completely fused with business."

THE 1924 ELECTION   In filling out Harding's unexpired term, Calvin Coolidge successfully distanced himself from the scandals of the administration, and put in charge of the prosecutions two lawyers of undoubted integrity. A man of honesty and ability, a good administrator who delegated well and managed Republican factions adroitly, he quietly took control of the party machinery and seized the initiative in the campaign for nomination, which he won with only token opposition.

The Coolidge luck held as the Democrats fell victim to continuing internal dissensions, which prompted humorist Will Rogers's classic statement: "I am a member of no organized political party. I am a Democrat." The party's fractiousness illustrated the deep divisions between the new urban culture of the 1920s and the more traditional hinterland, a gap that the Democrats could not bridge. After much factional fighting, it took the Democrats 103 ballots to bestow the tarnished nomination on John W. Davis, a Wall Street lawyer from West Virginia who could nearly outdo Coolidge in conservatism.

While the Democrats bickered, a new farmer-labor coalition was mobilizing a third-party effort. Meeting in Cleveland on July 4, 1924, activists organized the Progressive party and nominated Robert M. La Follette for president. The Wisconsin reformer also won the support of the Socialist party and the American Federation of Labor.

In the campaign Coolidge focused on La Follette, whom he called a dangerous radical who would turn America into a "communistic and socialistic state." The country preferred to "keep cool with Coolidge," who swept both the popular and electoral votes by decisive majorities. Davis took only the Solid South, and La Follette carried only his native Wisconsin. The popular vote went 15.7 million for Coolidge, 8.4 million for Davis, and 4.8 million for La Follette—the largest popular vote ever polled by a third-party candidate. The electoral college result was 382 to 136 to 13, respectively.

THE NEW ERA

Business executives interpreted the Republican victory in 1924 as a vindication of their leadership, and Coolidge saw the economy's surging prosperity as a confirmation of his philosophy. In fact, the prosperity and technological achievements of the time known as the New Era had much to do with Coolidge's victory over the Democrats and Progressives. Those in the large middle class who before had formed an important part of the Progressive party coalition were now absorbed instead in the new world created by advances in communications, transportation, and business organization.

A GROWING CONSUMER CULTURE   American economic and social life was changing markedly during the 1920s. More people than ever before had the money and leisure to indulge their consumer fancies, and a growing advertising industry fueled the appetites of this new moneyed class. By the mid-1920s advertising had become both a huge enterprise and a major institution of social power. Old-time values of thrift and saving gave way to a new economic ethic that made spending a virtue. The innovation of installment buying made increased consumption feasible for many. A newspaper editorial insisted that the American's "first importance to his country is no longer that of citizen but that of consumer. Consumption is a new necessity."

A dispirited Charlie Chaplin in a still image from his classic 1921 film, The Kid.

Consumer-goods industries fueled much of the boom from 1922 to 1929. Moderately priced creature comforts, including items such as hand cameras, wristwatches, cigarette lighters, vacuum cleaners, washing machines, and linoleum, became increasingly available. Inventions in communications and transportation, such as motion pictures, radio, telephones, and automobiles, not only fueled the boom but also brought transformations in society.

In the 1890s a quick sequence of inventions had made it possible for a New York audience to see the first moving picture show in 1896. By 1905 the first movie house opened in Philadelphia, and within three years there were nearly 10,000 scattered across the nation. By 1915 Hollywood had become the center of movie production, grinding out Westerns and the timeless comedies of Mack Sennett's Keystone Studios, where a raft of slapstick comedians, most notably Charlie Chaplin, perfected their art into a form of social criticism.

Birth of a Nation, directed in 1915 by D. W. Griffith, became a triumph of cinematic art that marked the arrival of the modern motion picture and at the same time perpetuated a grossly distorted image of Reconstruction. Based on Thomas Dixon's novel *The Clansman*, the movie featured

The radio brings this family together and connects them to the outside world. By the end of the 1930s, millions would tune in to newscasts, soap operas, sporting events, and church services.

stereotypes of villainous carpetbaggers, sinister mulattoes, blameless white southerners, and faithful "darkies." The blatantly racist film grossed $18 million and revealed the movie industry's enormous potential as a social force. By the mid-1930s, every American city and most small towns had theaters, and movies replaced oratory as the chief mass entertainment of Americans. A further advancement in technology came with the "talkies." The first movie with sound accompaniment appeared in 1926, but the success of talking pictures was established by *The Jazz Singer* (1927), starring Al Jolson.

Radio broadcasting had an even more spectacular growth. Except for experimental broadcasts, radio served only for basic communication until 1920. In that year station WWJ in Detroit began transmitting news bulletins from the *Detroit Daily News,* and KDKA in Pittsburgh, owned by the Westinghouse Company, began regular programs. The first radio commercial aired in New York in 1922. By the end of that year, there were 508 stations and some 3 million receivers in use. In 1926 the National Broadcasting Company (NBC) a subsidiary of RCA, began linking stations into a network; the Columbia Broadcasting System (CBS) entered the field the next year. In 1927 a Federal Radio Commission was established to regulate the industry; in 1934 it became the Federal Communications Commission, with authority over other forms of communication as well. Calvin Coolidge was the first president to address the nation by radio, and he did so monthly, paving the way for Franklin Roosevelt's "fireside chats."

AIRPLANES, AUTOMOBILES, AND THE ECONOMY Advances in transportation were equally significant. Wilbur and Orville Wright of Dayton, Ohio, owners of a bicycle shop, built and flew the first airplane at Kitty Hawk, North Carolina, in 1903. But the use of planes advanced slowly until the outbreak of war in 1914, after which the Europeans rapidly developed the plane as a military weapon. When the United States entered the war, it still had no combat planes—American pilots did battle in British or French planes. An American aircraft industry developed during the war but foundered in the postwar demobilization. Under the Kelly Act of 1925, however, the government began to subsidize the industry through airmail contracts. The Air Commerce

Orville Wright pilots the first flight of a power-driven airplane, while his brother, Wilbur, runs alongside.

Act of 1926 started a program of federal aid to air transport and navigation, including aid in establishing airports.

The infant aviation industry received a psychological boost in 1927 when Charles A. Lindbergh, Jr., made the first transatlantic solo flight from New York to Paris in thirty-three hours and thirty minutes. The heroic deed, which won him a prize of $25,000, was dramatic. He flew through a dense fog for part of the way and at times dropped to within ten feet of the water before sighting the Irish coast and regaining his bearings. The parade down Broadway in Lindbergh's honor surpassed even the celebration of the Armistice.

Four years later New York City honored another pioneering American aviator—Amelia Earhart. In 1931 she became the first woman to fly solo across the Atlantic Ocean. Born in Kansas in 1897, she made her first solo flight in 1921 and began working as a barnstorming stunt pilot at air shows across the country. A tall, thin, gray-eyed young woman with short, tousled blond hair and a "boyish" smile, she looked remarkably like Lindbergh. Earhart's popularity soared after her own transatlantic solo flight from Newfoundland to Northern Ireland. The fifteen-hour feat led Congress to award her the Distinguished Flying Cross, and she was named Outstanding American Woman of the Year.

Caught up in the fervor of the time for such dramatic exploits, Earhart began preparing in 1935 for "just one more long flight." Two years later she and a male navigator left Miami, Florida, and headed east on a round-the-world flight. The trip went smoothly until July 2, 1937, when they attempted the most difficult leg: from New Guinea to a tiny atoll in the Pacific 2,556 miles away. A Coast Guard vessel anchored near the island picked up weakening signals indicating that Earhart's plane was losing fuel. The plane disappeared, and despite extensive searches, no trace of it or the aviators was ever found. It remains the most intriguing mystery in aviation history. The accomplishments of Earhart and Lindbergh helped catapult the aviation industry into prominence. By 1930 there were forty-three American airline companies in operation.

By far the most significant economic and social development of the early twentieth century was the automobile. The first motor car had been manufactured for sale in 1895, but the founding of the Ford Motor Company in 1903 revolutionized the industry. Ford's reliable Model T

Ford Motor Company's Highland Park Plant, 1913. *Gravity slides and chain conveyors aided the mass production of automobiles.*

(the celebrated "tin lizzie") came out in 1908 at a price of $850 (in 1924 it would sell for $290). Ford vowed "to democratize the automobile. When I'm through everybody will be able to afford one, and about everyone will have one."

He was right. In 1916 the total number of cars manufactured passed 1 million; by 1920 more than 8 million were registered, and in 1929 more than 23 million. The production of automobiles consumed large amounts of the nation's steel, rubber, glass, and textile output, among other materials. It gave rise to a gigantic market for oil products just as the Spindletop gusher (1901) in Texas heralded the opening of vast southwestern oil fields. It quickened the movement for good roads, financed in large part from a gasoline tax, speeded transportation, encouraged the sprawl of suburbs, and sparked real-estate booms in California and Florida.

By virtue of its size and importance, the automobile industry became the leading example of mass production. When Ford brought out the Model T in 1908, demand ran far ahead of production. Ford then hired a factory expert who, by rearranging the plant and installing new equipment, met his production goal of 10,000 cars in twelve months. The next year Ford's new Highland Park plant was planned with job analysis in mind. In 1910 gravity slides were installed to move parts from one workbench to the next, and by the end of 1913 the system was complete, with endless chain conveyors pulling the parts along feeder lines and the chassis down the final assembly line.

STABILIZING THE ECONOMY   During the 1920s, the drive for efficiency, which had been a prominent feature of the progressive impulse, powered the wheels of mass production and consumption, and became a cardinal belief of Republican leaders. Herbert Hoover, who served as secretary of commerce through the Harding-Coolidge years, was himself an engineer who had made a fortune in far-flung mining operations in Australia, China, Russia, and elsewhere. Out of his experiences in business and his management of Belgian relief, the Food Administration, and other wartime activities, Hoover had developed a philosophy that he set forth in his book *American Individualism* (1922). The idea might best be called "cooperative individualism," or in one of his favorite terms, "associationalism." The principle also owed something to his Quaker upbringing, which taught him the virtue of the work ethic and mutual help. When he applied it to the relations of government and business, Hoover prescribed a kind of middle way between the regulatory and trust-busting traditions, a way of voluntary cooperation.

As secretary of commerce under Harding and Coolidge, Hoover transformed the trifling Commerce Department into the government's most dynamic agency. During a period of governmental retrenchment, he was engaged in expansion. Through an enlarged Bureau of Foreign and Domestic Commerce he sought out new markets for business. A Division of Simplified Practice in the Bureau of Standards sponsored more than a thousand conferences on design, production, and distribution, carried forward the wartime move toward standardization of everything from automobile tires and paving bricks to bedsprings and toilet paper. In 1926 Hoover created a Bureau of Aviation and the next year set out to bring order into the new field of radio with the Federal Radio Commission.

Hoover's priority was the burgeoning trade-association movement. Through trade associations, business leaders competing in a given field would gather and disseminate information on everything: sales, purchases, shipments, productions, and prices. This information allowed them to make plans with more confidence, the advantages of which included predictable costs, prices, and markets, as well as more stable employment and wages. Sometimes abuses crept in as trade associations engaged in price-fixing and other monopolistic practices, but the

Supreme Court in 1925 held the practice of sharing information as such to be within the law.

THE BUSINESS OF FARMING   During the 1920s, agriculture remained a weak sector in the economy, in many ways as weak as its position in the 1890s, when cities flourished and agriculture languished. Briefly after the war, the farmers' hopes soared on wings of prosperity. The wartime boom lasted into 1920, and then prices collapsed as world agricultural production returned to prewar levels. Wheat went in eighteen months from $2.50 a bushel to less than $1; cotton from 35¢ per pound to 13¢. Low commodity prices persisted into 1923, especially in the wheat and corn belts, and after that improvement was spotty. A bumper cotton crop in 1926 resulted only in a price collapse and an early taste of depression in much of the South, where foreclosures and bankruptcies spread.

Yet in many ways farmers shared the entrepreneurial outlook of the New Era. The most successful farms, like corporations, were getting larger, more efficient, and more mechanized. By 1930 about 13 percent of all farmers had tractors, and the proportion was even higher on the

Farm mechanization played an increasing role in early-twentieth-century agriculture. Here, a silo leader stands at the center of this Wisconsin farm scene.

western plains. Better plows, harvesters, and other machines were part of the mechanization process that accompanied improved crop yields, fertilizers, and animal breeding.

Farm organizations of the mid- to late 1920s moved away from the alliance with urban labor that marked the Populist Era and toward a new view of farmers as businessmen. During the postwar farm depression, the idea of marketing cooperatives became the farmer's equivalent of the corporate trade-association movement. Farm groups formed regional commodity-marketing associations that pushed for ironclad contracts with producers to deliver their crops over a period of years. They also promoted "orderly marketing," which required standards and grades, efficient handling of commodities and advertising, and a businesslike setup with professional technicians and executives.

But if concern with marketing co-ops and other businesslike approaches drew farmers farther away from populism, it was still inevitable that farm problems should invite political solutions. The most effective political response to the falling crop prices of the early 1920s was the formation of the farm bloc, a coalition of western Republicans and southern Democrats that put through a program of legislation from 1921 to 1923. The farm bloc pushed legislation to prevent collusion designed to keep farm prices down. It won an act to exempt farm cooperatives from antitrust laws, and another that set up twelve intermediate credit banks on the model of the Federal Land Banks. The new banks filled the gap of six months to three years between the provisions of short-term loans under the Federal Reserve System and long-term loans by the Federal Land Banks, and could lend to cooperative producing and marketing associations.

Meanwhile a new panacea appeared on the horizon. In 1924 Senator Charles L. McNary of Oregon and Representative Gilbert N. Haugen of Iowa introduced the first McNary-Haugen Bill. It sought to secure "equality for agriculture in the benefits of the protective tariff." Complex as it would have been in operation, it was simple in conception: in short, a plan to dump American farm surpluses on the world market in order to raise prices in the home market. The goal was to achieve "parity"—that is, to raise domestic farm prices to a point where they would have the same purchasing power relative to other prices they had had between 1909 and 1914, a time viewed in retrospect as a golden age of American agriculture.

A McNary-Haugen Bill passed both houses of Congress in 1927, only to be vetoed by President Coolidge. The process was repeated in 1928. Coolidge pronounced the measure an unsound effort at price-fixing, and un-American and unconstitutional to boot. In a broader sense, however, McNary-Haugenism did not fail. The debates made the farm problem into an issue of national policy and defined it as a problem of surpluses. The evolution of the McNary-Haugen plan, moreover, revived the idea of an alliance between the South and West, a coalition that in the next decade became a dominant influence on national farm policy.

SETBACKS FOR UNIONS   Urban workers shared more than farmers in the affluence of the 1920s. "A workman is far better paid in America than anywhere else in the world," a French visitor wrote in 1927, "and his standard of living is enormously higher." Non-farm workers gained about 20 percent in real wages between 1921 and 1928, while farm income rose only 10 percent. The benefits of this rise, however, were distributed unevenly. Miners and textile workers suffered a decline in real wages. In these and other trades, technological unemployment followed the introduction of new methods and machines, because technology destroyed as well as created jobs.

Organized labor, however, did no better than organized agriculture in the 1920s. Even though President Harding supported the practice of collective bargaining and tried to reduce the twelve-hour workday and the six-day workweek so that the working class "may have time for leisure and family life," he ran into stiff opposition in Congress. Overall, unions suffered a setback after the growth years of the war. The Red Scare and strikes of 1919 left the uneasy impression that unions practiced subversion, an idea that the enemies of unions promoted. The brief postwar depression of 1921 further weakened the unions, and they felt the severe impact of open-shop associations that proliferated across the country after the war, led by chambers of commerce and other business groups. In 1921 business groups in Chicago designated the open shop the "American Plan" of employment. While the open shop in theory implied only the employer's right to hire anyone, in practice it meant discrimination against unionists and refusal to recognize unions even in shops where most of the workers belonged to one.

To suppress unions, employers used intimidation. They often required "yellow-dog" contracts that forced workers to agree to stay out of unions. Owners also used labor spies, blacklists, intimidation, and coercion. Some employers tried to kill the unions with kindness. They introduced programs of "industrial democracy" guided by company unions or various schemes of "welfare capitalism" such as profit-sharing, bonuses, pensions, health programs, recreational activities, and the like. The benefits of such programs were often considerable.

Prosperity, propaganda, welfare capitalism, and active hostility combined to cause union membership to drop from about 5 million in 1920 to 3.5 million in 1929. In 1924 Samuel Gompers, founder and longtime president of the AFL, died; William Green of the mine workers, who took his place, embodied the conservative, even timid, attitude of unions during the period. The outstanding exception to the anti-union policies of the decade was passage of the Railway Labor Act in 1926, which abolished the Railway Labor Board and substituted a new Board of Mediation. The act also provided for the formation of railway unions "without interference, influence, or coercion," a statement of policy not extended to other workers until the 1930s.

THE GASTONIA STRIKE OF 1929 Anti-union sentiment was fiercest in the South during the 1920s. In 1929 a wave of violent strikes swept across the region. Most of the unrest centered in the large textile mills that had come to dominate the southern economy since the 1880s. During World War I, the desperate need for military clothing brought rapid expansion and high profits to the textile industry. After the war, however, demand for cotton cloth sagged and prices plummeted. Military demobilization, changing women's fashions—rising hemlines—and foreign competition combined to erode the profit margins of the textile companies. In response, owners closed mills, slashed wages, and raised production quotas. They installed new machinery and adopted new production techniques to improve efficiency and reduce the workforce. They operated the mills around the clock and established rigid production quotas (piecework) for each worker.

This onerous "stretch-out" system finally provoked workers to rebel. Many of them joined the AFL's United Textile Workers (UTW) union. Strikes and work stoppages followed, and the powerful mill owners, supported by security guards, local police, and state militia, forcefully suppressed union efforts. Few of the strikes lasted more

These female textile workers pit their strength against that of a National Guardsman during the strike of the Loray mill in Gastonia, North Carolina, 1929.

than a week at most, but the 1929 walkout at the huge Loray mill in Gastonia, North Carolina, escalated into a prolonged conflict that involved two deaths.

Gaston County then had more textile plants than any other county in the nation. The red brick Loray mill was the largest in the South. At its peak, it employed 3,500 workers, almost half of them women. During 1927 and 1928, however, the workforce was slashed. Those who kept their jobs were required to work longer (eleven hours a day, six days a week) and tend more machines for lower wages (averaging about $15 a week for men; $6 for women). A night shift was also added. On April 1, 1929, over 1,000 exhausted Loray workers walked off the job. They were encouraged to do so by the National Textile Workers Union (NTWU), a Communist party–led rival to the UTW. Local officials were outraged that mill workers were collaborating with Communists. Equally shocking was the large number of young women among the strikers. Gastonia, a Charlotte newspaper reported, had discovered that "militant women were within its bounds."

But perhaps most upsetting to local prejudices was the NTWU's commitment to racial equality. Only 1 percent of the Loray employees were black, but the Communist party organizers who traveled to Gastonia insisted that racial justice be included among the strike's demands. A northern union spokesman told strikers: "Our union has no color line, although the bosses wish you did." In fact, however, few of the white strikers embraced racial equality. Some of them abandoned the union and the strike because of racial prejudices. While willing to allow blacks to join the union, the local leaders required them to meet in a separate room. Leaders in the black community, especially the clergy, feared a racial backlash and discouraged African Americans from joining the strike or the union. Race remained a more divisive issue than class in the twentieth-century South.

The Loray mill's managers refused to negotiate or even meet with the strikers. Community sentiment endorsed the anti-union stance. The editor of the *Gastonia Daily Gazette* could not believe what was happening: "How our good mill people can be led by these people [northern Communist agitators] who are not our kind, who defy God, flout religion, denounce our government and who are working for social equality among white and black is a mystery." The southern people, he accurately predicted, "will never for one instance tolerate such a thing."

As tensions in Gastonia rose, the North Carolina governor, himself a textile-mill owner, dispatched National Guard units to protect the plant and break the strike. Vigilante groups took matters into their own hands. A gang of masked men destroyed the union's strike headquarters and assaulted workers. When police entered the strikers' tent city to search for weapons, a skirmish erupted and someone shot and killed Gastonia's police chief. Police then arrested seventy-five of the strike leaders, thirteen of whom were eventually charged with murder. The Communist party turned the ensuing trial into a national crusade. Reporters from across the nation and the world descended on Gastonia. After the first court action ended in a mistrial, vigilantes again attacked the union headquarters and later assaulted a convoy of strikers headed to a rally. Shots were fired, and twenty-nine-year-old Ella May Wiggins, a folk-singing labor organizer and mother of nine, was killed.

Despite a lack of concrete evidence, seven strikers were eventually convicted of conspiracy to commit murder in the death of the police chief and sentenced to long prison terms. By contrast, those accused of shooting

Ella May Wiggins were found not guilty. The release of the accused killers provoked a firestorm of criticism in the northern press, but to no avail.

The Loray strike had collapsed by the end of May 1929. The infant NTWU did not have enough funds to feed the strikers. After missing their first paycheck, most laborers had no choice but to drift sullenly back to work. Within a few months, the mill's owners were sponsoring an essay contest, inviting workers to compete for prizes by describing "Why I Enjoy Working at the Loray."

PRESIDENT HOOVER, THE ENGINEER

HOOVER VS. SMITH   On August 2, 1927, while on vacation in the Black Hills of South Dakota, President Coolidge passed out slips of paper to reporters with the curious statement: "I do not choose to run for President in 1928." Exactly what he meant puzzled observers then and since. Apparently he at least half hoped for a convention draft, but his statement cleared the way for Herbert Hoover to mount an active campaign for the nomination. Well before the 1928 Republican convention in Kansas City, Hoover was too far in the lead to be stopped. The platform took credit for prosperity, cost-cutting ("raised to a principle of government"), debt and tax reduction, and the protective tariff ("as vital to American agriculture as it is to manufacturing"). It rejected the McNary-Haugen program, but promised a farm board to manage surpluses more efficiently.

The Democratic nomination went to Governor Alfred E. Smith of New York. The party's farm plank, while not endorsing McNary-Haugen, did pledge "economic equality of agriculture with other industries." Like the Republicans, the Democrats promised to enforce the Volstead Prohibition Act and, aside from calling for stricter regulation of water-power resources, promised nothing that departed from the conservative position of the Republicans.

The two candidates projected sharply different images that obscured the essential likeness of their programs. Hoover was the Quaker son of middle America, the successful engineer and businessman, the architect of Republican prosperity, while Smith was the prototype of those things rural/small-town America distrusted: the son of Irish immigrants, Catholic, and anti-Prohibition. Outside the large cities all those attributes were handicaps he could scarcely surmount, for all his affability and wit. The religious right launched a furious assault on Smith. The Klan, for example, mailed thousands of postcards proclaiming that the Catholic New Yorker was the "Antichrist."

In the election Hoover won in the third consecutive Republican landslide, with 21 million popular votes to Smith's 15 million, and an even more top-heavy electoral vote majority of 444 to 87. Hoover even cracked the Solid South, leaving Smith only six Deep South states plus Massachusetts and Rhode Island. The election was above all a vindication of Republican prosperity. But the shattering defeat of the Democrats concealed a portentous realignment in the making. Smith had nearly doubled the vote for John W. Davis, the Democratic candidate of four years before. Smith's image, though a handicap in the hinterlands, swung big cities back into the Democratic column. In the farm states of the West there were signs that some disgruntled farmers had switched over to the Democrats. A coalition of urban workers and unhappy farmers was in the making.

HOOVER IN CONTROL   The milestone year 1929 dawned with high hopes. Business seemed good, incomes were rising, and the chief architect of Republican prosperity was about to enter the White House.

"I have no fears for the future of our country," Herbert Hoover told his audience at his inauguration in 1929.

"I have no fears for the future of our country," Hoover told the audience at his inauguration. "It is bright with hope." For Hoover the presidency crowned a career of steady ascent, first in mining, then in public service. Hoover's image combined the benevolence fitting a director of wartime relief and the efficiency of a businessman and administrator.

Hoover's program to stabilize business carried over into his program for agriculture, the most visibly weak sector of the economy. To treat the malady of glutted markets he offered two main remedies: federal help for cooperative marketing and higher tariffs on imported farm products. In 1929 he pushed through a special session of Congress the Agricultural Marketing Act, which set up a Federal Farm Board with a revolving loan fund of $500 million to help farm cooperatives market the major commodities. The act also provided a program in which the Farm Board could set up "stabilization corporations" empowered to buy surpluses off the market. Unluckily for any chance of success the plan might have had, it got under way almost simultaneously with the onset of the depression that fall.

Farmers gained even less from tariff revision. What Hoover won after fourteen months of struggle with competing local interests was in fact a general upward revision of duties on manufactures as well as farm goods. The Hawley-Smoot Tariff of 1930 carried duties to an all-time high. Rates went up on some 70 farm products and more than 900 manufactured items. More than 1,000 economists petitioned Hoover to veto the bill because, they said, it would raise prices to consumers, damage the export trade and thus hurt farmers, promote inefficiency, and provoke foreign reprisals. Events proved them right, but Hoover felt that he had to go along with his party in an election year.

THE ECONOMY OUT OF CONTROL   The tariff did nothing to check a deepening crisis of confidence in the economy. After the slump of 1921, the idea grew that the American economy had entered a New Era of *permanent* growth. But greed propelled a growing contagion of get-rich-quick schemes. Speculative mania fueled the Florida real-estate boom that began when the combination of Coolidge prosperity and Ford's "tin lizzies" gave people extra money and made Florida an accessible playground. Thousands of people invested in Florida real estate, eager for quick profits in the nation's fastest growing state. In the fanfair of fast turnover the reckless speculator was, if anything, more likely to gain than the prudent investor. In mid-1926, however, the Florida bubble burst.

For the losers it was a sobering lesson, but it proved to be but an audition for the Great Bull Market in stocks. Until 1927 stock values had gone up with profits, but then they began to soar on wings of pure speculation. Treasury Secretary Mellon's tax reductions had released money that, with the help of aggressive brokerage houses, found its way to Wall Street. Instead of speculating in real estate, one could buy stock on margin—that is, make a small down payment (the "margin") and borrow the rest from a broker who held the stock as security against a down market. If the stock declined and the buyer failed to meet a margin call for more money, the broker could sell the stock to cover his loan. Brokers' loans more than doubled from 1927 to 1929.

Gamblers in the market ignored warning signs. By 1927 residential construction and automobile sales were catching up to demand, business inventories rose, and the rate of consumer spending slowed. By mid-1929 production, employment, and other measures of economic activity were declining. Still the stock market rose.

By 1929 the market had entered a fantasy world. Conservative financiers and brokers who counseled caution were ignored. President Hoover was worried about the "orgy of mad speculation," and he urged stock exchange and Federal Reserve officers to discourage speculation. In August the Federal Reserve Board raised the rate on loans to member banks (the rediscount rate) to 6 percent, but with no effect. On September 4 stock prices wavered, and the day after that they dropped, opening a season of fluctuations. The Great Bull Market staggered on into October, trending downward but with enough good days to keep hope alive. On October 22 a leading bank president told reporters: "I know of nothing fundamentally wrong with the stock market or with the underlying business and credit structure."

THE CRASH AND ITS CAUSES   The next day stock values crumbled, and the day after that a wild scramble to unload stocks lasted until word arrived that leading bankers had formed a pool to buy stocks and halt the slide. Prices steadied for the rest of the week, but after a weekend to think the situation over, stockholders began to unload on Monday. On Tuesday, October 29, the most devastating single day in the market's history, brokers reported sales of 16.4 million shares (at the time 3 million shares traded was a busy day). The plunge in prices fed on itself as brokers sold the shares they held for buyers who failed

Apprehensive crowds gathered on the steps of the Subtreasury Building, across from the New York Stock Exchange, as news of a stock collapse spread, October 29, 1929.

to meet their margin calls. During October, stocks on the New York Exchange fell in value by 37 percent.

Business and government leaders initially expressed hope. According to President Hoover, "the fundamental business of the country" was sound. Some speculators who got out of the market went back in for bargains but found themselves caught in a slow, tedious erosion of values. By March 1933, the value of stocks on the New York Exchange was less than a fifth of the value at the market's peak. The *New York Times* stock average, which stood at 452 in September 1929, bottomed at 52 in July 1932.

Caution became the watchword for consumers and business executives. Buyers held out for lower prices, orders fell off, wages fell or ceased altogether, and the decline in purchasing power brought further cutbacks in business activity. From 1929 to 1932 Americans' personal incomes declined by more than half. Unemployment continued to rise. Farmers, already in trouble, faced catastrophe. More than 9,000 banks closed during the period, hundreds of factories and mines shut down, and thousands of farms were foreclosed for debt and sold at auction. A cloak of gloom fell over the nation.

The stock market crash did not cause the Great Depression, but it did reveal major structural flaws in the economy and government policies. Too many businesses had maintained prices and taken profits while holding down wages. As a result, about one-third of the personal income went to only 5 percent of the population. By plowing most profits back into expansion rather than wage increases, business brought on a growing imbalance between rising productivity and declining purchasing power. As the demand for goods declined, the rate of investment in the new plants began to decline. For a time the softness of purchasing power was concealed by greater use of installment buying, and the deflationary effects of high tariffs were concealed by the volume of loans and investments abroad that supported foreign demand for American goods. But the flow of American capital abroad began to dry up when the stock market began to look more attractive. Swollen profits and dividends, together with the Treasury Secretary Mellon's tax policies, enticed the rich into market speculation. When trouble came, the bloated corporate structure collapsed.

Governmental policies also contributed to the debacle. Mellon's tax reductions brought oversaving among the general public, which helped diminish demand for consumer goods. The growing money supply fed the fever of speculation. Hostility toward labor unions discouraged collective bargaining and may have worsened the prevalent imbalances in income. High tariffs discouraged foreign trade. Lax enforcement of antitrust laws encouraged concentration, monopoly, and high prices.

Another culprit was the gold standard. The world monetary system remained fragile throughout the 1920s. When economic output, prices, and savings began dropping in 1929, policy makers—certain that they had to keep their currencies tied to gold at all costs—either did nothing or tightened money supplies, thus exacerbating the downward spiral. The only way to restore economic stability within the constraints of the gold standard was to let prices and wages continue to fall, allowing the downturn, in Andrew Mellon's words, to "purge the rottenness out of the system." What happened instead was that such passivity turned a recession into the world's worst depression.

THE HUMAN TOLL OF DEPRESSION   The devastating collapse of the economy caused immense social hardships throughout the nation. By 1933 there were over 13 million people out of work. Millions more who kept their jobs saw their hours and wages reduced. Factories shut down, banks closed, farms went bankrupt, and millions of people found themselves not only jobless, but also homeless and penniless. Hungry people lined up at churches and soup kitchens; others rummaged through trash cans behind restaurants. Many slept on park benches or in back alleys. Others congregated in makeshift shelters in vacant lots. Thousands of desperate men in search of jobs "rode the rails." These "hobos" or "tramps," as they were derisively called, sneaked onto empty railway cars and rode from town to town looking for work. During the winter, homeless people wrapped themselves in newspapers to keep warm, referring to them sarcastically as "Hoover blankets." Some grew weary of their grim fate and ended their lives. Suicide rates soared during the 1930s. America had never before experienced social distress on such a scale.

HOOVER'S EFFORTS AT RECOVERY   Although the policies of public officials helped to bring on economic collapse, few public leaders even acknowledged that there was an unprecedented crisis: all that was needed, they thought, was a slight correction of the market. Those who held to the dogma of limited government thought the economy would cure itself. The best policy, Treasury Secretary Mellon advised, would be to "liquidate labor, liquidate stocks, liquidate the farmers, liquidate real estate." Hoover himself had little patience with speculators, but he was unwilling now to sit by and let events take their course. Hoover in fact did more than any president had ever done before in such dire economic circumstances. Still, his own philosophy, now hardened into dogma, set limits to governmental action, and he was unready to set it aside even to meet an emergency.

Hoover believed that the nation's fundamental business structure was sound and that the country's main need was confidence. In speech after speech, he exhorted the public to keep up hope, and he asked business owners to keep the mills and shops open, maintain wage rates, and spread the work to avoid layoffs—in short to let the first shock fall on corporate profits rather than on purchasing power. In return, union leaders, who had little choice, agreed to refrain from wage demands and strikes. As it happened, however, words were not enough, and the prediction that good times were just around the corner (actually made by the vice-president, though attributed to Hoover) eventually became a sardonic joke.

Hoover did more than try to reassure the American public. He hurried the building of government construction projects in order to provide jobs, but state and local cutbacks more than offset new federal

spending. At Hoover's demand the Federal Reserve returned to an easier credit policy, and Congress passed a modest tax reduction to put
more purchasing power in people's pockets. The Federal Farm Board
stepped up its loans and its purchases of farm surpluses, only to face
bumper crops in 1930 despite droughts in the Midwest and Southwest.
The high Hawley-Smoot Tariff, proposed at first to help farmers,
brought reprisals abroad, devastating foreign trade.

As always, a depressed economy hurt the party in power. Democrats
exploited Hoover's predicament for all it was worth, and more. In 1930
the floundering president was easy game. During the war, "to Hoover-
ize" had signified patriotic sacrifice; now the president's name signified
distress. Near the city dumps, along the railroad tracks, the dispos-
sessed huddled in shacks of tarpaper and galvanized iron, old packing
boxes, and abandoned cars. These squalid settlements became known
as "Hoovervilles"; a "Hoover flag," was an empty pocket turned inside
out. In November 1930 the Democrats gained their first national vic-

These two children set up shop in a Hooverville in Washington, D.C.

tory since 1916, winning a majority in the House and enough gains in the Senate to control it in coalition with western agrarians.

One irony of the time was that the great humanitarian of wartime relief was recast as the stubborn opponent of depression relief. But Hoover was still doing business at the same old stand: his answer to the economic crisis remained voluntarism. When the head of the Emergency Committee for Employment strongly recommended a governmental spending program for road building and other public works, the president turned it down. His annual message to Congress in December 1930 demanded that each community and state undertake the relief of distress "with that sturdiness and independence which built a great Nation."

In the first half of 1931 economic indicators rose, renewing hope for an upswing. Then, as recovery beckoned, another shock occurred. In May 1931 the failure of Austria's largest bank triggered panic in central Europe. To ease concerns, President Hoover proposed a one-year moratorium on both reparations and war-debt payments by the European nations. The major European nations accepted the moratorium and later also a temporary "standstill" on settlement of private obligations between banks. The general shortage of monetary exchange drove Europeans to withdraw their gold from American banks and dump their American securities. One European country after another abandoned the gold standard and devalued its currency. Even the Bank of England went off the gold standard. The United States meanwhile slid into the third bitter winter of depression.

CONGRESSIONAL INITIATIVES   With a new Congress in session, demands for federal action impelled Hoover to stretch his individualistic philosophy to its limits. He was ready now to use governmental resources at least to shore up the financial institutions of the country. In 1932 the new Congress set up the Reconstruction Finance Corporation (RFC) with $500 million (and authority to borrow $2 billion more) for emergency loans to banks, life insurance companies, building and loan societies, farm mortgage associations, and railroads. Under former vice-president Charles G. Dawes, it authorized $1.2 billion in loans within six months. The RFC staved off bankruptcies, but Hoover's critics found in it favoritism to business, the most damaging instance of which was a $90 million loan to Dawes's own Chicago bank, made soon after he left the RFC in 1932. The RFC nevertheless remained a key agency through the New Deal and World War II.

Further help to the financial structure came with the Glass-Steagall Act of 1932, which broadened the definition of commercial loans that the Federal Reserve would support. The new arrangement also released about $750 million in gold formerly used to back Federal Reserve Notes, countering the effect of foreign withdrawals and domestic hoarding of gold at the same time that it enlarged the supply of credit. For home-owners the Federal Home Loan Bank Act of 1932 created with Hoover's blessing a series of discount banks for home mortgages. They provided for savings and loan and other mortgage agencies a service much like that the Federal Reserve System provided to commercial banks.

Hoover's critics said all these measures reflected a dubious "trickle-down" theory. If government could help banks and railroads, asked New York senator Robert G. Wagner, "is there any reason why we should not likewise extend a helping hand to that forlorn American, in every village and every city of the United States, who has been without wages since 1929?" The contraction of credit devastated debtors such as farmers and those who made purchases on the "installment plan" or who held "balloon-style" mortgages whose monthly payments increased over time. By 1932 members of Congress were filling the hoppers with bills for federal measures to provide relief to individuals. At that point Hoover might have pleaded "dire necessity" and taken the leadership of the relief movement and salvaged his political fortunes.

Instead he held back and only grudgingly edged toward federal relief. On July 21, 1932, Hoover signed the Emergency Relief and Construction Act, which avoided a direct federal dole to individuals but gave the RFC $300 million for relief loans to the states, authorized loans of up to $1.5 billion for state and local public works, and appropriated $322 million for federal public works.

FARMERS AND VETERANS IN PROTEST   Government relief for farmers had long since been abandoned. In mid-1931 the government quit buying crop surpluses and helplessly watched prices slide. Faced with the loss of everything, desperate farmers began to defy the law. Angry mobs stopped foreclosures and threatened to lynch the judges sanctioning them. In Nebraska farmers burned corn to keep warm. Iowans formed the militant Farmers' Holiday Association, which called a farmers' strike and forcibly blocked deliveries of produce.

In the midst of the crisis, there was desperate talk of revolution. "Folks are restless," Mississippi governor Theodore Bilbo told reporters in 1931. "Communism is gaining a foothold. . . . In fact, I'm getting a little pink myself." Across the country the once-obscure Communist party began to draw crowds to its rallies and willing collaborators into its "hunger marches." Yet, for all the sound and fury, few Americans were converted to communism during the 1930s. Party membership in America never rose much above 100,000.

Fears of organized revolt arose when unemployed veterans converged on Washington in the spring of 1932. The "Bonus Expeditionary Force" grew quickly to more than 15,000. Their purpose was to get immediate payment of the bonus to world-war veterans that Congress had voted in 1924. The House approved a bonus bill, but when the Senate voted it down, most of the veterans went home. The rest, having no place to go, camped in vacant government buildings and in a shantytown at Anacostia Flats, within sight of the Capitol.

Eager to disperse the squatters, Hoover convinced Congress to pay for their tickets home. More left, but others stayed even after Congress adjourned, hoping at least to meet with the president. Late in July the administration ordered the government buildings cleared. In the ensuing melee, one policeman panicked, fired into the crowd, and killed two veterans. The president then ordered in about 700 soldiers under General Douglas MacArthur, aided by junior officers Dwight D. Eisenhower and

Unemployed veterans, members of the "Bonus Expeditionary Force," clash with Washington, D.C., police at Anacostia Flats, July 1932.

George S. Patton, Jr. The soldiers drove out the unarmed veterans and their families, injuring dozens and killing one, an eleven-week-old boy born at Anacostia, who died from exposure to tear gas.

General MacArthur claimed that the "mob," animated by "the essence of revolution," was about to seize control of the government. The administration insisted that the Bonus Army consisted mainly of Communists and criminals, but neither a grand jury nor the Veterans Administration could find evidence to support the charge. One observer wrote before the incident: "There is about the lot of them an atmosphere of hopelessness, of utter despair, though not of desperation. . . . They have no enthusiasm whatever and no stomach for fighting."

Their mood, and the mood of the country, echoed that of Hoover himself. He worked hard, but took no joy from his labors. The stress took its toll on his health and morals. "I am so tired," he sometimes said, "that every bone in my body aches." News conferences became more strained and less frequent. When friends urged him to seize the reins of leadership, he said, "I can't be a Theodore Roosevelt," or "I have no Wilsonian qualities." The gloom, the sense of futility, communicated itself to the country. In a mood more despairing than rebellious, people waited to see what another presidential campaign would produce.

MAKING CONNECTIONS

- This chapter discussed setbacks for labor unions during the Republican administrations of the 1920s. In the next chapter, unions win new protections under Franklin Roosevelt's New Deal.

- An element of the "normalcy" discussed in this chapter was American isolationism from global affairs. Chapter 29 discusses that isolationism in the context of the coming of World War II.

- Compare the characteristics of 1920s American society with the postwar society and culture of the 1950s, discussed in Chapter 32.

FURTHER READING

A fine synthesis of events immediately following the First World War is Ellis W. Hawley's *The Great War and the Search for a Modern Order: A History of the American People and Their Institutions, 1917–1933* (1979).

For an introduction to Harding, see Robert K. Murray's *The Harding Era: Warren G. Harding and His Administration* (2000). On Coolidge, see Donald R. McCoy's *Calvin Coolidge: The Silent President* (1967). Studies on Hoover include Joan Hoff Wilson's *Herbert Hoover: Forgotten Progressive* (1975) and George Nash's multivolume work, *The Life of Herbert Hoover* (1983–1987).

Overviews of the depressed economy are found in Charles P. Kindleberger's *The World in Depression, 1929–1939* (rev. ed., 1986) and Peter Fearon's *War, Prosperity and Depression: The U.S. Economy, 1917–1945* (1987). John A. Garraty's *The Great Depression: An Inquiry into the Causes, Course, and Consequences of the Worldwide Depression of the Nineteen-Thirties* (1986) describes how people survived the depression.

28 ∞ NEW DEAL AMERICA

CHAPTER ORGANIZER

This chapter focuses on:

- the social effects of the Great Depression and Roosevelt's efforts at relief, recovery, and reform.

- criticism of the New Deal, from both the right and the left.

- how the New Deal greatly expanded the federal government's authority and responsibilities.

- the change in cultural direction in the 1930s.

Upon arriving in the White House in 1933, Franklin Roosevelt inherited a nation mired in the third year of an unprecedented economic depression. No other economic slump had been so deep, so long, or so painful. One out of every four Americans in 1932 was unemployed, and in many large cities nearly half of the adults were out of work. Some 500,000 Americans had lost their homes or farms because they could not pay their mortgages. Thousands of banks had failed; millions of depositors lost their life savings. The worldwide depression helped accelerate the rise of fascism and communism. Totalitarianism was on the march—and democratic capitalism was on the defensive. "The situation is critical," political analyst Walter Lippmann warned President-elect Roosevelt. "You may have to assume dictatorial powers."

Roosevelt did not become a dictator, but he did take decisive action. He and a supportive Congress immediately adopted bold measures to relieve the human suffering and promote economic recovery. Such initiatives provided the foundation for what came to be called welfare capitalism.

FROM HOOVERISM TO THE NEW DEAL

FDR'S ELECTION   On June 14, 1932, while the ragtag Bonus Army was still encamped in Washington, D.C., Republicans gathered in Chicago to renominate Hoover. The delegates went through the motions in a mood of defeat. By contrast, the Democrats converged on Chicago confident that they would nominate the next president. New York governor Franklin D. Roosevelt was already the front-runner with most of the delegates lined up, and he went over the top on the fourth ballot.

In a bold gesture, Roosevelt appeared before the convention in person to accept the nomination instead of awaiting formal notification. "Let it . . . be symbolic that . . . I broke traditions," he told the delegates. "Republican leaders not only have failed in material things, they have failed in national vision, because in disaster they have held out no hope. . . . I pledge you, I pledge myself to a new deal for the American people." What the New Deal would be in practice Roosevelt had little idea as yet, but he was much more flexible and willing to experiment than Hoover. What was more, his upbeat personality communicated joy and hope. His campaign song was "Happy Days Are Here Again."

Born in 1882 into a wealthy family, educated by governesses and tutors at Springwood, his father's rambling estate along the Hudson River in New York, young Franklin led the cosmopolitan life of a young patrician. After attending Groton, an elite Connecticut boarding school, he earned degrees from Harvard and Columbia University Law School. While a law student, he married his distant cousin, Anna Eleanor Roosevelt, the niece of his fifth cousin, Theodore Roosevelt, then president of the United States.

Franklin Roosevelt began work with a prominent Wall Street law firm, but soon lost interest in legal affairs and decided to enter politics. In 1910 he won a Democratic seat in the New York State Senate. As a freshman legislator he displayed the contradictory qualities that would always characterize his political career: an aristocrat with a sincere affinity for common folk; a traditionalist with a penchant for experiment; an affable charmer with a luminous smile and upturned chin who also harbored profound convictions; and a skilled political tactician with a shrewd sense of timing and a distinctive willingness to listen to and learn from others.

Tall, handsome, and athletic, Roosevelt seemed destined for greatness. In 1912 he had backed Wilson, and for both of Wilson's terms he served as assistant secretary of the navy. Then, in 1920, largely on the strength of his name, he became Democrat James Cox's running mate. The following year, at age thirty-nine, his career seemed cut short by an attack of polio that left him permanently crippled, unable to stand or walk without braces. But the struggle for recovery transformed the young aristocrat. He became less arrogant, less superficial, more focused, and more interesting. A friend recalled that he emerged from his struggle with polio "completely warm-hearted, with a new humility of spirit" that led him to identify with the poor and suffering. Justice Oliver Wendell Holmes, Jr., later summed up his qualities this way: "A second-class intellect—but a first-class temperament."

For seven years, aided by his talented wife Eleanor, Roosevelt strengthened his body to compensate for his disability, and in 1928 he won the governorship of New York. Reelected by a whopping majority of 700,000 in 1930, Roosevelt became the favorite for president in 1932.

Partly to dispel doubts about his health, Roosevelt set forth on a grueling campaign tour. He blamed the depression on Hoover and the Republicans, and he began to define what he meant by the "New Deal." Like Hoover, Roosevelt promised to balance the budget, but he was willing to incur short-term deficits to prevent starvation and restore the economy. On the tariff, he was evasive. On farm policy, he offered several options pleasing to farmers and ambiguous enough not to alarm city dwellers. He called for strict regulation of utilities and for at least some government development of electricity, and he consistently stood by his party's pledge to repeal the Prohibition Amendment. Perhaps most important, he recognized that a mature economy would require national planning.

Governor Franklin D. Roosevelt, the Democratic nominee for president, campaigning in Topeka, Kansas. Roosevelt's confidence inspired voters.

"The country needs, and, unless I mistake its temper, the country demands bold, persistent experimentation. . . . Above all, try something."

What came across to voters, however, was less the content of Roosevelt's speeches than the confidence of the man. By contrast, Hoover lacked vitality and assurance. He could turn a neat phrase, but many elegant passages suffered from his pedestrian delivery. Democrats, Hoover argued, ignored the international causes of the depression. They were taking a reckless course. Roosevelt's policies, he warned, "would destroy the very foundations of our American system." Pursue them, and "grass will grow in the streets of a hundred cities, a thousand towns." But few were listening. Amid the persistent depression, the country wanted a new course, a new leadership, a new deal.

Some people took a dim view of both major candidates. Those who believed that only a radical departure would suffice went over to Socialist Norman Thomas, who polled 882,000 votes, and a few preferred the Communist party candidate, who got 103,000. The wonder is that a desperate people did not turn in greater numbers to radical candidates.

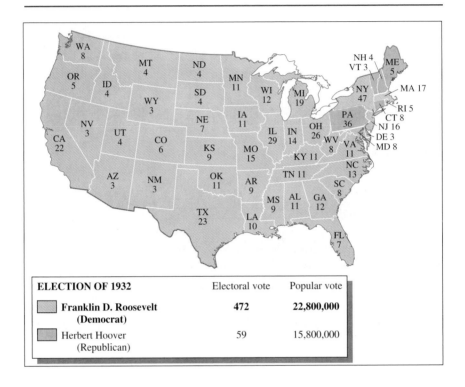

ELECTION OF 1932	Electoral vote	Popular vote
Franklin D. Roosevelt (Democrat)	472	22,800,000
Herbert Hoover (Republican)	59	15,800,000

Instead they swept Roosevelt into office with 22.8 million votes to Hoover's 15.8 million. Hoover carried only four states in New England plus Pennsylvania and Delaware, and lost in the electoral college by 472 to 59.

THE INAUGURATION   For the last time, the country waited four months, until March 4, for a new president and Congress to take office. The Twentieth Amendment, ratified on February 6, 1933, provided that presidents would thereafter take office on January 20 and the newly elected Congress on January 3.

The bleak winter of 1932–1933 witnessed spreading destitution and misery. Unemployment continued to rise, and panic struck the banking system. As bank after bank announced closure and did not have adequate cash to repay depositors, people rushed to their own bank to remove their deposits. Many discovered that they, too, were caught short. When the Hoover administration ended, four-fifths of the nation's banks were closed, and the country teetered on the brink of economic paralysis.

The profound crisis of confidence that greeted Roosevelt when he took the oath of office on March 4, 1933, gave way to a mood of expectancy.

The new president asserted "that the only thing we have to fear is fear itself—nameless, unreasoning, unjustified terror which paralyzes needed efforts to convert retreat into advance." If need be, he said, "I shall ask the Congress for . . . broad executive power to wage a war against the emergency as great as the power that would be given me if we were in fact invaded by a foreign foe." It was a measure of the country's mood that this call received the loudest applause.

COMPETING SOLUTIONS   When Roosevelt and his corps of "New Dealers" arrived in Washington, they confronted three major challenges: reviving the economy, relieving the human misery, and rescuing the farm sector and its families. His "brain trust" of advisers developed conflicting opinions about how best to rescue the economy from depression. Some promoted vigorous enforcement of the antitrust laws as a means of restoring competition; others argued just the opposite, saying that antitrust laws should be suspended so as to enable large corporations to collaborate with the federal government and thereby better manage the overall economy. Still others called for a massive expansion of welfare programs and a prolonged infusion of increased government spending to address the profound human crisis and revive the economy.

Roosevelt was willing to try some elements of each of these approaches without ever embracing one completely. In part, this reflected the political reality that conservative southern Democrats controlled the Congress, and Roosevelt could not risk alienating these powerful figures who were committed to balanced budgets and suspicious of federal programs. Roosevelt's inconsistencies also reflected his own outlook. He was a pragmatist rather than an ideologue. As he once explained, "Take a method and try it. If it fails admit it frankly and try another." Roosevelt's "New Deal," therefore, would take the form of a series of trial-and-error actions.

Roosevelt and his advisers initially settled on a three-pronged strategy as their first attempt at addressing the problems facing the nation. First, they sought to remedy the financial crisis and to provide short-term emergency relief for the jobless. Second, they tried to promote industrial recovery through increased federal spending and cooperative agreements between management and organized labor. Third, they attempted to raise commodity prices (and thereby farm income) by paying farmers to reduce crops and herds. By reducing the overall supply of farm products, prices would rise. None of these initiatives worked perfectly, but their combined effect was to restore hope and energy to a nation paralyzed by fear and uncertainty.

STRENGTHENING THE MONETARY SYSTEM   The first order of business for the new administration was to free up the channels of finance. On his second day in office, Roosevelt displayed his penchant for action when he called Congress to meet in special session on March 9, and then declared a four-day banking holiday. It took Congress only seven hours to pass the Emergency Banking Relief Act, which permitted sound banks to reopen and provided managers for those that remained in trouble. On March 12, in the first of his radio "fireside chats," the president insisted that it was safer to "keep your money in a reopened bank than under the mattress." His reassurances soothed a nervous nation. The following day, deposits in reopened banks exceeded withdrawals, and by March 15 banks controlling nine-tenths of the nation's banking resources were once again open. The crisis had ended, and the new administration was ready to get on with its broader program.

In rapid order Roosevelt undertook to meet two specific pledges in the Democratic platform. At his behest, Congress passed an Economy Act granting the executive branch the power to cut government salaries, reduce payments to military veterans for non-service-connected

The Galloping Snail. *A vigorous Roosevelt drives the Congress to action in this* Detroit News *cartoon, March 1933.*

disabilities, and reorganize federal agencies in the interest of reducing federal expenses. The Beer-Wine Revenue Act amended the Volstead Act to permit sale of beverages with an alcoholic content of 3.2 percent. The Twenty-first Amendment, already submitted by Congress to the states, would be declared ratified on December 5, thus ending the "noble experiment" of Prohibition.

The measures of March were but the beginning. During the session from March 9 to June 16, the so-called Hundred Days, Congress received and enacted fifteen major proposals from the president with a dizzying speed unlike anything seen before in American history:

March 9	The Emergency Banking Relief Act
March 20	The Economy Act
March 31	Establishment of the Civilian Conservation Corps
April 19	Abandonment of the gold standard
May 12	The Federal Emergency Relief Act
May 12	The Agricultural Adjustment Act, including the Thomas Amendment, which gave the president powers to expand the money supply
May 12	The Emergency Farm Mortgage Act, providing for the refinancing of farm mortgages
May 18	The Tennessee Valley Authority Act, providing for the unified hydroelectric development of the Tennessee Valley
May 27	The Federal Securities Act, requiring full disclosure in the issue of new securities
June 5	The Gold Repeal Joint Resolution, which abrogated the gold clause in public and private contracts
June 13	The Home Owners' Loan Act, setting up the Home Owners' Loan Corporation to refinance home mortgages
June 16	The National Industrial Recovery Act, providing for a system of industrial self-regulation under federal supervision and for a $3.3 billion public-works program
June 16	The Glass-Steagall Banking Act, separating commercial and investment banking and establishing the Federal Deposit Insurance Corporation
June 16	The Farm Credit Act, which reorganized the agricultural credit system

With the banking crisis over, there remained an acute debt problem for farmers and homeowners, and a lingering distrust of the banks, which might yet be aroused again. By executive decree, Roosevelt reorganized all farm credit agencies into the Farm Credit Administration (FCA). By the Emergency Farm Mortgage Act and the Farm Credit Act, Congress authorized extensive refinancing of farm mortgages at lower interest rates.

The Home Owners' Loan Act provided a similar service to city dwellers through the new Home Owners' Loan Corporation (HOLC). The HOLC refinanced mortgage loans at lower monthly payments for strapped homeowners. This helped slow the rate of foreclosures. The Glass-Steagall Banking Act further shored up confidence in the banking system. It created the Federal Deposit Insurance Corporation (FDIC) to guarantee bank deposits up to $5,000. To prevent speculative abuses, it separated investment and commercial banking corporations and extended the Federal Reserve's regulatory power over credit. The Federal Securities Act required the full disclosure of information about new stock and bond issues, at first by registration with the Federal Trade Commission, and later with the Securities and Exchange Commission (SEC), which was created to regulate the stock and bond markets.

Throughout 1933 Roosevelt tinkered with devaluation of the currency as a way to raise prices and thus ease the debt burden on strapped investors and farmers. On April 19 the government officially abandoned the gold standard: the consequent decline in the value of the dollar increased the prices of commodities and stocks at home.

RELIEF MEASURES   Another urgent priority in 1933 was relieving the widespread personal distress caused by the Great Depression. Hoover had stubbornly resisted using the federal government to provide direct relief for the unemployed. Roosevelt was more flexible. As he once remarked, the "test of our progress is not whether we add to the abundance of those who have much. It is whether we provide enough for those who have too little." As a first step toward such relief Congress created the Civilian Conservation Corps (CCC), which was designed to give work to unemployed and unmarried young men aged eighteen to twenty-five.

Nearly 3 million young men took to the woods to work at a variety of CCC jobs in forests, parks, recreational areas, and soil conservation

A group of jocular CCC enrollees, on a break from work at Saint Joseph National Forest, 1933.

projects. As part of the CCC, they built roads, bridges, campgrounds and fish hatcheries, planted trees, taught farmers how to control soil erosion, and fought fires. They were paid a nominal sum of $30 a month, of which $25 went home to their families. The enrollees could also take education courses and earn high school diplomas. Directed by army officers and foresters, they worked under a semi-military discipline. Like the military at the time, the CCC camps were racially segregated. In Texas, African Americans were initially told that the camps were for whites only, and this falsehood helps explain the low number of blacks enrolled. Only 400 black Texans, less than 5 percent of the total number of men enrolled, participated in the CCC.

The Federal Emergency Relief Administration (FERA), created with an authorization of $500 million, addressed the broader problems of human distress. Harry L. Hopkins, a tough-talking, big-hearted social worker who had directed Roosevelt's state relief efforts in New York, pushed the program with a boundless energy. The FERA expanded the assistance to the unemployed that had begun under

Hoover's RFC, but with a difference. Federal monies flowed to the states in grants rather than "loans." While FERA continued to channel aid through state agencies to relief clients mainly in the form of direct cash payments, Hopkins enlarged its scope by gradually developing work programs for education, student aid, rural rehabilitation, and for the many jobless wanderers across the country. He pushed an "immediate work instead of dole" approach on local officials, but they preferred the dole (direct cash payments to individuals) as an easier and quicker way to reach the needy.

The first large-scale experiment with *federal* work relief, which put people directly on the government payroll at competitive wages, came with the formation of the Civil Works Administration (CWA). Created in November 1933, when it had become apparent that the state-sponsored programs under the FERA would not prevent widespread privation, the CWA provided federal jobs and wages to those unable to find work that winter. It was hastily conceived and implemented, but during its four-month existence, it put to work over 4 million people. In Chicago alone, some 70,000 people gathered before sunrise to register for the CWA on its opening day. The agency spent over $900 million (mostly in wages) for a variety of useful projects, from making highway repairs and laying sewer lines to constructing or improving more than 1,000 airports and 40,000 schools, to providing 50,000 teaching jobs that helped keep rural schools open. As the number of people employed by the CWA soared, the program's costs skyrocketed to over a billion dollars. Roosevelt balked at such high expenditures, and he worried that people would become dependent on federal jobs. He ordered the CWA dissolved in the spring of 1934. By April some 4 million workers were again unemployed.

Roosevelt, however, continued to favor work relief over the dole. He thought the dole was an addictive "narcotic, a subtle destroyer of the human spirit." Real jobs, on the other hand, nurtured "self-respect and self-reliance." In 1935 he asked Congress for an array of new federal job programs, and it responded by passing a $4.8 billion Emergency Relief Appropriation Act providing work relief for the jobless. To manage these programs, Roosevelt created the Works Progress Administration (WPA) headed by Harry L. Hopkins, to replace the FERA. Hopkins was told to provide millions of jobs quickly, and as a result some of the new jobs appeared to be make-work or mere "leaning on shovels." But before the

This mural painted by a WPA artist depicts a bustling New Deal–era street scene.

WPA died during World War II, it left permanent monuments on the landscape in the form of buildings, bridges, hard-surfaced roads, airports, and schools.

The WPA also employed a wide range of talents in the Federal Theatre Project, the Federal Art Project, Federal Music Project, and the Federal Writers' Project. Talented writers such as Ralph Ellison, John Cheever, and Saul Bellow found work writing travel guides to the United States, and Orson Welles directed Federal Theatre productions. Critics charged that these programs were frivolous, but Hopkins replied that writers and artists needed "to eat just like other people." The National Youth Administration (NYA), under the WPA, provided part-time employment to students, set up technical training programs, and aided jobless youth. Twenty-seven-year-old Lyndon Johnson was director of an NYA program in Texas, and Richard Nixon, a penniless Duke University law student, found work through the local NYA at thirty-five cents an hour. Although the WPA took care of only about 3 million out of some 10 million jobless at any one time, in all it helped some 9 million clients weather desperate times before it expired in 1943.

RECOVERY THROUGH REGULATION

In addition to rescuing the banks and providing relief to the unemployed, Roosevelt and his advisers promoted the long-term recovery of agriculture and business. The languishing economy needed a boost—a big one. There were 13 million people without jobs. Members of Franklin Roosevelt's "brain trust" were largely heirs to Theodore Roosevelt's New Nationalism. Like the earlier progressives, they insisted that the trend toward economic concentration was inevitable. Big businesses were not going to go away. They also believed that the mistakes of the 1920s showed that the only way to operate an integrated economy at capacity and in the public interest was through efficient regulation and organized central planning, not through trust-busting. The success of centralized planning during World War I reinforced such ideas, and new recovery programs sprang from these beliefs.

AGRICULTURAL RECOVERY: THE AAA   The sharp decline in commodity prices after 1929 meant that many farmers could not afford to plant or harvest their crops. Farm income had plummeted from $6 billion in 1929 to $2 billion in 1932. The Agricultural Adjustment Act of 1933 contained nearly every major plan applicable to farm relief, but only some of its provisions were implemented by the new federal agency, the Agricultural Adjustment Administration (AAA). The act sought to control farm production by compensating farmers for voluntary cutbacks in production in an effort to restore farm prices. The act covered seven "basic commodities," a number later enlarged, and the money for benefit payments came from a processing tax levied on each—at the cotton gin, for example, or the flour mill.

By the time Congress acted, however, the growing season was already advanced. The prospect of another bumper cotton crop forced the AAA to sponsor a plow-under program. To destroy a growing crop was a "shocking commentary on our civilization," Agriculture Secretary Henry A. Wallace lamented. "I could tolerate it only as a cleaning up of the wreckage from the old days of unbalanced production." Moreover, given the oversupply of hogs, some 6 million pigs were slaughtered "before they could reach the full hogness of their hogdom." It could be justified, Wallace said, only as a means of helping farmers to do with pigs what steelmakers did with pig iron—cut production to fit the market and therefore raise prices.

For a while these farm measures worked. By the end of 1934, Secretary of Agriculture Wallace could report significant declines in wheat, cotton, and corn production and a simultaneous increase in commodity prices. Farm income increased by 58 percent between 1932 and 1935. The AAA, however, was only partially responsible for such gains. The devastating drought that settled over the Plains states between 1932 and 1935 played a major role in reducing production and creating the epic "dust bowl" migrations so poignantly evoked in John Steinbeck's *Grapes of Wrath*. Many of these migrant families had actually been driven off the land by AAA benefit programs that encouraged large farmers to take the lands worked by tenants and sharecroppers out of cultivation first.

Although it created unexpected problems, the AAA achieved real successes in boosting the overall farm economy. But conservatives opposed its sweeping powers. On January 6, 1936, in *United States v. Butler,* the Supreme Court, by a vote of six to three, declared the AAA's tax on food processors unconstitutional. The administration hastily devised a new plan in the Soil Conservation and Domestic Allotment Act, which it pushed through Congress in six weeks. The new act omitted processing taxes and acreage quotas, but provided benefit payments for soil conservation practices that took land out of soil-depleting staple crops, thus indirectly achieving crop reduction. The act boosted a eveloping conservation movement directed by the Soil Conservation Service, which had been created in 1935.

The act was an almost unqualified success as an engineering and educational project because it helped heal the scars of erosion and the plague of dust storms. But soil conservation nevertheless failed as a device for limiting production. With their worst lands taken out of production, farmers cultivated their fertile acres more intensively. In response, Congress passed the Second Agricultural Adjustment Act in 1938, which reestablished the earlier programs but left out the processing taxes. Benefit payments would come from general funds. By the time the second AAA reached a test in the Supreme Court, changes in the Court's personnel had altered its outlook. This time the law was upheld as a legitimate exercise of the interstate commerce power. Agriculture, like manufacturing, was now held to be in the stream of commerce.

INDUSTRIAL RECOVERY: THE NRA   The industrial counterpart to the AAA was the National Industrial Recovery Act (NIRA), passed on June 16, 1933, the two major parts of which dealt with economic recovery and public-works projects designed to put people to work. The latter part, Title II, created the Public Works Administration (PWA) with $3.3 billion for public buildings, highway programs, flood control, and other improvements. Under the direction of Interior Secretary Harold L. Ickes, the PWA indirectly served the purpose of work relief. Ickes directed it toward well-planned permanent improvements, and he used private contractors rather than placing workers directly on the government payroll. PWA workers built Virginia's Skyline Drive, New York's Triborough Bridge, the Overseas Highway from Miami to Key West, and Chicago's subway system.

The more controversial and ambitious part of the NIRA created the National Recovery Administration (NRA), headed by Hugh S. Johnson, a colorful retired army general. Its purposes were twofold: first, to stabilize business by reducing chaotic competition through the implementation

In this cartoon employer and employee agree to cooperate in the spirit of unity that inspired the National Recovery Administration.

of codes that set wages and prices, and second, to generate more purchasing power for consumers by providing jobs, defining labor standards,
and raising wages. In each major industry, committees representing management, labor, and government drew up the codes of fair practice.
Code Number 1, which dealt with the textile industry, imposed restraints on plant expansion, limited operations to eighty hours a week,
and required reports on operations every four weeks. The labor standards featured in every code set a forty-hour workweek and minimum
weekly wages of $13 ($12 in the South, where living costs were lower),
which more than doubled earnings in some cases. Announcement of a
proviso against child labor under the age of sixteen did "in a few minutes
what neither law nor constitutional amendment had been able to do in
forty years," Johnson said.

As the drafting of other industry codes began to drag, Johnson proposed a "blanket code" pledging employers generally to observe the
same labor standards as applied to cotton textiles. He launched a crusade to whip up popular support for the NRA and its symbol of compliance, the "Blue Eagle," which had been modeled on an Indian
thunderbird and embellished with the motto "We do our part." The
eagle decal was displayed in shop windows and stamped on products.
It was a gamble, but the public responded. Some 2 million employers
signed the pledge, and the impact of the campaign broke the logjam in
code making.

Labor unions, already hard pressed by the economic downturn and
the loss of members were understandably concerned about the NRA's
efforts to reduce competition by allowing businesses to cooperate in fixing wages and prices. To gain their support, the NRA included a provision that guaranteed the right of workers to organize unions. But while
prohibiting employers from interfering with labor organizing efforts, the
NRA did not create adequate enforcement measures, nor did it require
employers to bargain in good faith with labor representatives.

For a time the NRA worked, perhaps because a new air of confidence had overcome the depression blues and the downward spiral of
wages and prices had subsided. But as soon as economic recovery began, the honeymoon ended. The daily annoyances of code enforcement inspired growing hostility among business owners. Charges
mounted that the larger companies dominated the code authorities
and that price-fixing robbed small producers of the chance to compete.

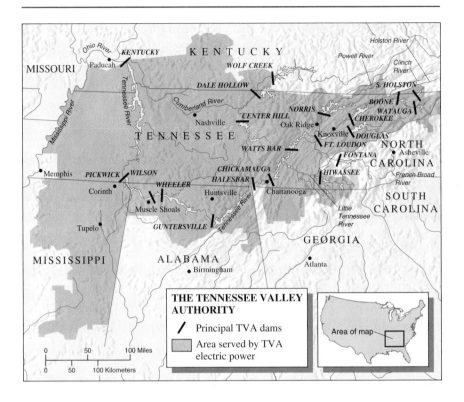

THE TENNESSEE VALLEY
AUTHORITY

/ Principal TVA dams

■ Area served by TVA
electric power

Area of map

In 1934 an investigating committee substantiated at least some of the charges. Limiting industrial production, moreover, had discouraged investment. And because the NRA wage codes excluded agricultural workers and domestic workers, three out of every four employed blacks derived no direct benefit from the program. By 1935 the NRA had developed more critics than friends. When it died in May 1935, struck down by the Supreme Court as unconstitutional, few paused to mourn.

The NRA experiment was generally a failure, but it left an enduring mark. With dramatic suddenness the codes had set new workplace standards, such as the forty-hour workweek and the end of child labor, from which it was hard to retreat. The NRA's endorsement of collective bargaining spurred the growth of unions. The codes, moreover, advanced trends toward stabilization and rationalization that were becoming the standard practice of business at large and that, despite misgivings about the concentration of power, would be further promoted by trade associations. Yet as 1934 ended, economic recovery was nowhere in sight.

The massive Norris Dam in Tennessee connected many TVA projects in an effort to expand power production, 1936.

REGIONAL PLANNING: THE TVA   The wide-ranging scope of the New Deal embraced several pathbreaking ideas. The creation of the Tennessee Valley Authority (TVA) was a truly bold and original venture. The TVA differed from most of the measures of Roosevelt's first Hundred Days, which were efforts to redress the ills of depression, in that it refuted the idea that the economy had reached its full measure of mature development. The Tennessee River Valley was one of the most underdeveloped and poverty-stricken regions of the country, and illiteracy and disease were rampant. On May 18, 1933, Congress created the TVA as a multipurpose public corporation. Mobilizing local support under Director David E. Lilienthal's slogan of "grassroots democracy," the TVA won almost universal loyalty among the people of the poverty-stricken region. By 1936 it had six dams completed or underway, and a master plan to build nine high dams on the Tennessee River, which would create the "Great Lakes of the South," and other dams on the tributaries. The agency, moreover, opened the rivers for navigation, fostered soil conservation and forestry, experimented with fertilizers, drew new industry to the region, encouraged the formation of labor unions, improved schools and libraries, and sent cheap electric power pulsating through the valley for the first time.

Cheap public power, Lilienthal's main passion, became more and more the TVA's reason for being—a purpose that would become all the more important during World War II. The TVA's success at generating greater power consumption and lower rates awakened private utilities to the mass consumer markets. Cheap power transported farmers of the valley from the age of kerosene to the age of electricity. The TVA's first rural cooperative, set up at Corinth, Mississippi, in 1934, pointed the way to the electrification of the nation's farms in the decade that followed. The Rural Electrification Administration (REA), formed as a relief agency by presidential order in 1935, achieved a permanent statutory basis in 1936. By 1940 it had extended loans of more than $321 million to rural electrical cooperatives.

THE HUMAN COST OF THE DEPRESSION

Although New Deal programs helped ease the devastation wrought by the depression, they did not restore prosperity or end the widespread human suffering. The depression continued to take a toll on ordinary Americans—factory workers, farmers, bankers, and professionals remained in the throes of a shattered economy that only slowly was working its way back to health.

CONTINUING HARDSHIPS As late as 1939, some 9.5 million workers (17 percent of the labor force) remained unemployed. Prolonged economic hardship continued to create personal tragedies and tremendous social strains. Poverty led desperate people to do desperate things. Petty theft soared during the 1930s, as did street-corner begging and prostitution. Although the divorce rate dropped during the decade, in part because couples could not afford to live separately or pay the legal fees to obtain divorces, all too often husbands down on their luck simply deserted their wives. In 1940 a survey revealed that 1.5 million husbands had left home. With their future uncertain, married couples often decided not to have children; the birthrate plummeted during the depression. Those parents with children sometimes could not support them. In 1933 the Children's Bureau reported that one out of every five children was not getting enough to eat. Often, struggling parents sent their children to live with relatives or friends.

Some 900,000 other children simply left home and joined the army of homeless "tramps."

DUST BOWL MIGRANTS   Uprooted farmers and their families formed a migratory stream rushing from the South and Midwest toward California, buoyed by currents of hope and desperation. The West Coast was rumored to have plenty of jobs. So off they went on a cross-country trek. One couple claimed they had heard "how much money a man could make out there and we wanted to go."

Although frequently lumped together as "Okies," most of the dust bowl refugees were actually from cotton-belt communities in Arkansas, Texas, and Missouri, as well as Oklahoma. During the 1930s and 1940s, some 800,000 people left those four states and headed to the Far West. Not all were farmers; many were white-collar workers and re-tailers whose jobs had been tied to the health of the agricultural sector. Most of the dust bowl migrants were white, and most were young adults in their twenties and thirties who relocated with spouses and children. Some traveled on trains or buses, others hopped a freight train

Dust Storm Approaching, *1930s. When a dust storm blew in, it would bring complete darkness as well as sand and grit that would soon cover every surface, both inside and out.*

or hitched a ride; most rode in their own cars, the trip taking four to five days on average.

Most of the dust bowl migrants who had come from cities gravitated to California's urban areas—Los Angeles, San Diego, or San Francisco. Half of the newcomers, however, moved into the San Joaquin Valley, the agricultural heartland of the state. There they discovered that California was no paradise. Only a few of the migrants could afford to buy land. Most (men and women) found themselves competing with local Hispanics and Asians for seasonal work as pickers in the cotton fields or orchards of large corporate farms. Living in tents or crude cabins and frequently on the move, they suffered from exposure and from poor sanitation.

They also felt the sting of social prejudice. John Steinbeck explained that "Okie us'ta mean you was from Oklahoma. Now it means you're a dirty son-of-a-bitch. Okie means you're scum. Don't mean nothing in itself, it's the way they say it." Such hostility drove a third of the "Okies" to return to their home states. Most of the farm workers who stayed tended to fall back upon their old folkways rather than assimilate themselves into their new surroundings. These gritty "plain folk" brought with them their own prejudices against blacks and ethnic minorities as well as a potent tradition of evangelical Protestantism and a distinctive style of music variously labeled "country," "hillbilly," or "cowboy." This "Okie" subculture remains a vivid part of California society today.

MINORITIES AND THE NEW DEAL   The depression was especially traumatic for the most disadvantaged groups in American society. However progressive Roosevelt was on social issues, he failed to assault long-standing patterns of racism and segregation for fear of alienating southern Democrats in Congress. As a result, many of the New Deal programs were for whites only. The Federal Housing Administration (FHA), for example, refused to guarantee mortgages on houses purchased by blacks in white neighborhoods. The Civilian Conservation Corps and the Tennessee Valley Authority both practiced racial segregation.

The efforts of the Roosevelt administration to raise crop prices by reducing production proved especially devastating for blacks and Mexican Americans. To earn the federal payments for reducing crops as provided by the AAA and other New Deal agricultural programs, many farm owners would first take out of cultivation the marginal lands worked by tenants and sharecroppers. This would drive the landless off farms and cost the jobs of many migrant workers. Over 200,000 black tenant farmers nationwide were displaced by the AAA.

Mexican Americans suffered even more. Thousands of Mexicans had migrated to the United States during the 1920s, most of them settling in California, New Mexico, Arizona, Colorado, Texas, and the midwestern states. But because many Mexican Americans were unable to prove their citizenship, either out of ignorance of the regulations or because their migratory work hampered their ability to meet residency requirements, they were denied access to the new federal relief programs under the New Deal. As economic conditions worsened, government officials called for the deportation of Mexican-born Americans to avoid the costs of providing them with public services and relief. By 1935, over 500,000 Mexican Americans and their American-born children had returned to Mexico. The state of Texas alone returned over 250,000 people.

Deportation became such a popular solution in part because of the rising level of involvement of Mexican-American workers in union activities. In 1933 Mexican-American women in El Paso, Texas, formed the Society of Female Manufacturing Workers to protest wages as low as 75¢ a day. In the same year, some 18,000 Mexican cotton pickers went on strike in California's San Joaquin Valley. Police crushed the strike by burning the workers' camps.

Native Americans were especially devastated by the Great Depression. They initially were encouraged by Roosevelt's appointment of John Collier as the commissioner of the Bureau of Indian Affairs (BIA). Collier steadily increased the number of Native Americans employed by the BIA and lobbied strenuously with the heads of New Deal agencies to ensure that Indians gained access to the various relief programs. Collier's primary objective, however, was passage of the Indian Reorganization Act. He wanted the new legislation to replace the provisions of the Dawes General Allotment Act (1887), which had sought to "Americanize" the Indians by breaking up their tribal lands and allocating them to individuals. Collier insisted that the Dawes Act had produced only widespread poverty and demoralization among the Indians. Collier hoped to reinvigorate traditional Indian cultural traditions by restoring land to tribes, granting Indians the right to charter business enterprises and establish self-governing constitutions, and providing federal funds for vocational training and economic development. The act that Congress finally passed, however, was a much diluted

Heywood Patterson (center), *one of the defendants in the Scottsboro case, is seen here with his attorney, Samuel Liebowitz* (left) *in Decatur, Alabama, 1933.*

version of Collier's original proposal, and the "Indian New Deal" brought only a partial improvement in the lives of Native Americans.

COURT DECISIONS AND BLACK VOTERS   During the 1930s, the NAACP's legal campaign against racial prejudice gathered momentum. A major setback occurred in *Grovey v. Townsend* (1935), which upheld the Texas Democrats' white primary as the practice of a voluntary association and thus not subject to state action. But the *Grovey* decision held up for only nine years and marked the end of major decisions that for half a century had narrowed application of the Reconstruction amendments. A trend in the other direction had already set in. Two important precedents rose from the celebrated Scottsboro case in 1931, in which nine black youths were convicted of raping two white women while riding a freight train in Alabama. The first verdict failed, the high court ruled in *Powell v. Alabama* (1932), because the judge had not ensured that the accused were provided adequate defense attorneys." Another verdict fell to a judgment in *Norris v. Alabama* (1935) that the systematic exclusion of blacks from Alabama juries had denied the defendants equal protection of the law—a principle that had significant and widespread impact on state courts.

Like Woodrow Wilson, Franklin Roosevelt did not give a high priority to racial issues. As a consequence, many of his New Deal programs failed to help minorities, and in a few instances the new initiatives discriminated against those least able to help themselves. Nevertheless, Roosevelt included people in his administration who did care deeply about racial issues. As his first term drew to a close in 1936, Roosevelt found that there was a de facto "Black Cabinet" of some thirty to forty advisers in government departments and agencies, people who were wrestling with racial issues and the plight of African Americans. Moreover, by 1936, many black voters were fast transferring their political loyalty from Republicans to Democrats and would vote accordingly in the coming presidential election.

CULTURE IN THE THIRTIES

In view of the celebrated—if exaggerated—alienation of writers, artists, and intellectuals rebelling against the materialistic world of the 1920s, one might have expected the onset of the Great Depression to deepen the despair of such cultural leaders. Instead it brought a renewed sense of militancy and affirmation, as if people could no longer afford the art-for-art's sake outlook of the 1920s. Said one writer early in 1932: "I enjoy the period thoroughly. The breakdown of our cult of business success and optimism, the miraculous disappearance of our famous American complacency, all this is having a tonic effect."

In the early 1930s the "tonic effect" of commitment sometimes took the form of allegiance to revolution. By the summer of 1932, even the "golden boy" of the lost generation, writer F. Scott Fitzgerald, declared that "to bring on the revolution, it may be necessary to work within the Communist party." But few remained Communists for long. Being a notoriously independent lot, most writers rebelled at demands to hew to a shifting party line. And many abandoned communism upon learning that Soviet leader Joseph Stalin practiced a tyranny more horrible than anything under the czars.

LITERATURE AND THE DEPRESSION Among the writers who addressed themes of immediate social significance two novelists deserve special notice: John Steinbeck and Richard Wright. The single piece of fiction that best captured the ordeal of the depression, Steinbeck's *The Grapes of Wrath* (1939), treated workers as people rather than just a variable in a political formula. Steinbeck had traveled with displaced "Okies" driven from the Oklahoma dust bowl by bankers and farm machines to pursue the illusion of good jobs in the fields of California's Central Valley. This first-hand experience allowed him to create a vivid tale of the Joad family's painful journey west from Oklahoma.

Among the most talented new young novelists emerging in the 1930s was Richard Wright, a black writer born near Natchez, Mississippi. The grandson of four former slaves and the son of a Mississippi sharecropper who deserted the family, Wright ended his formal schooling with the ninth grade (as valedictorian of his class). He then worked in Memphis and greedily devoured books he borrowed on a white friend's library card, all the while saving up to go North to escape the racism of the segregated South. In Chicago, where he arrived on the eve of the depression, the Federal Writers' Project gave him a chance to develop his talent. His period as a Communist from 1934 to 1944 gave him an intellectual framework that did not, however, overpower his fierce independence.

Native Son (1940), Wright's masterpiece, was set in the Chicago he had come to know before moving to New York. It was the story of Bigger Thomas, a product of the black ghetto, a man hemmed in and finally impelled to murder by forces beyond his control. Somehow Wright managed to sublimate into literary power his bitterness and rage at what he called "The Ethics of Living Jim Crow."

POPULAR CULTURE DURING THE DEPRESSION   While many of America's most talented writers and artists dealt directly with the human suffering and social tensions provoked by the Great Depression, the more popular cultural outlets such as radio programs and movies provided patrons with a welcome "escape" from the decade's grim realities.

By the 1930s, radio had become a major source of family entertainment. More than 10 million families owned a radio, and by the end of the decade the number had tripled. "There is radio music in the air, every night, everywhere," reported a San Francisco newspaper. "Anybody can hear it at home on a receiving set which any boy can put up in an hour." Franklin Roosevelt was the first president to take full advantage of the popularity of radio broadcasting. He hosted sixteen "fireside chats" to generate public support for his New Deal initiatives.

In the late 1920s, what had been "silent" films were transformed by the introduction of sound. The "talkies" made the movie industry by far the most popular form of entertainment during the 1930s—much more popular than today. The introduction of double features in 1931 and the construction of outdoor drive-in theaters in 1933 also boosted interest and attendance. More than 60 percent of the population—70 million people—saw at least one movie each week. Adults paid a quarter and children a dime for their tickets.

Films of the 1930s rarely dealt directly with hard times. Exceptions were the film version of *The Grapes of Wrath* (1940) and the classic documentaries by Pare Lorenz entitled *The River* (1937) and *The Plow That Broke the Plains* (1936). Much more common were movies intended for pure entertainment; they transported viewers into the realm of adventure, spectacle, and fantasy. People relished "shoot 'em up" gangster films, Walt Disney's animated cartoons, spectacular musicals, "screwball" comedies, and classic horror films such as *Dracula* (1931), *Frankenstein* (1931), *The Werewolf* (1932), and *The Mummy* (1932).

But the best way to escape the daily troubles of the depression was to watch one of the zany comedies of the Marx Brothers, former vaudeville performers. As one Hollywood official explained, the movies during the

The Marx Brothers performing one of their many madcap routines.

1930s were intended to "laugh the big bad wolf of the depression out of the public mind." *The Cocoanuts* (1929), *Animal Crackers* (1930), and *Monkey Business* (1931) introduced Americans to the anarchic antics of Chico, Groucho, Harpo, and Zeppo Marx. These madcap comedians combined slapstick humor with verbal wit to create plotless master-pieces filled with irreverent satire.

THE SECOND NEW DEAL

During Roosevelt's first year in office his programs and his personal charms aroused massive support. The president's travels and speeches, his twice-weekly press conferences, and his "fireside chats" over the ra-dio generated vitality and warmth from a once-remote White House. In the congressional elections of 1934, the Democrats actually increased their strength in both the House and the Senate, an almost unprece-dented midterm victory for the party in power. When it was over, only seven Republican governors remained in office throughout the country.

ELEANOR ROOSEVELT   One of the reasons for Roosevelt's unprece-dented popularity was his wife, Eleanor, who had increasingly become an enormous political asset and would prove to be one of the most influen-tial and revered leaders of her time. From an early age, Eleanor had chan-neled her energies into social service. As a teen, she had volunteered in a New York settlement house, doing what she could to help the poor and suffering. As an adult, she remained ardently concerned about issues of human welfare and rights for women and blacks. Her compassion resulted in part from the loneliness she had experienced as she was growing up and in part from the sense of betrayal she had felt when she discovered in 1918 that her husband was engaged in an extramari-tal affair with Lucy Mercer, her personal secretary. "The bottom dropped out of my own particular world," she recalled. Upon learning of the affair, she had asked Franklin if he wanted a divorce. Absolutely not, he replied, in part because his mother threatened to disown him, and he promised Eleanor that he would end his relationship with Mercer (he did not).

In the face of personal setbacks, Eleanor Roosevelt "lived to be kind." Compassionate without being maudlin, more stoic than sentimental,

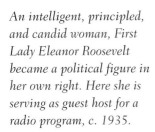

An intelligent, principled, and candid woman, First Lady Eleanor Roosevelt became a political figure in her own right. Here she is serving as guest host for a radio program, c. 1935.

she exuded warmth and sincerity, and she challenged the complacency of the comfortable and the affluent. "No woman," observed a friend, "has ever so comforted the distressed or so distressed the comfortable."

After FDR's election, Eleanor could not be satisfied with the traditionally passive role of First Lady. She was an activist who redefined the role of presidential spouse. She was the first woman to address a national political convention, to write a nationally syndicated column, and to hold regular press conferences. A tireless advocate and agitator, Eleanor crisscrossed the nation, representing the president and the New Deal, defying local segregation ordinances to meet with black leaders, supporting women's causes and organized labor, highlighting the plight of unemployed youth, and imploring Americans to live up to their egalitarian and humanitarian ideals. An opinionated and outspoken woman who occasionally used her syndicated column to criticize Franklin's policy decisions, she was especially forceful in prodding officials to ease racial discrimination in federal programs and housing.

Eleanor Roosevelt also became her husband's most visible and effective liaison with many liberal groups, bringing labor leaders, women activists, and black spokesmen into the White House after hours, and serving to deflect criticism of the president by taking progressive stands and running political risks he himself dared not. He was the politician, she once remarked, she was the agitator.

CRITICISM OF THE NEW DEAL   Public criticism of the New Deal during Roosevelt's first year in office was muted, but not for long. The depression's downward slide had been halted, but unemployment remained high (10 million in 1935, more than 20 percent of the workforce) and prosperity remained elusive. "We have been patient and long suffering," said a farm leader in October 1933. "We were promised a New Deal. . . . Instead we have the same old stacked deck." Even more unsettling to some was the dramatic growth of executive power and the emergence of welfare capitalism, whereby workers developed a sense of entitlement to federal support programs. In 1934 a group of conservative businessmen and politicians, including Al Smith and John W. Davis, two previous Democratic presidential candidates, formed the American Liberty League to oppose New Deal measures as violations of personal and property rights.

More potent threats to Roosevelt came from the hucksters of social panaceas, old and new. The most flamboyant of the group was Louisiana's "Kingfish," Senator Huey P. Long, Jr. A short, strutting man, Long sported pink suits and pastel shirts, red ties, and two-toned shoes. He seemed like a clown to some observers, and he loved to make people think he was a country bumpkin. But underneath all the carefully designed hoopla was a shrewd lawyer and consummate politician. First as Louisiana governor, then as political boss of the state, Long had delivered to its citizens tax favors, roads, schools, free textbooks, charity hospitals, and better public services. That he had become a sort of state dictator in the process, using bribery, physical intimidation, and blackmail to achieve his ends seemed irrelevant to many of his ardent supporters.

In 1933 Long joined Roosevelt in Washington as a Democratic senator. He initially supported the New

The "Kingfish," Huey Long, governor of Louisiana.

Deal but quickly grew suspicious of the NRA's collusion with big business. He also had grown jealous of Roosevelt's mushrooming popularity, having himself developed aspirations for the Oval Office. Promoting himself as a radical egalitarian, a true, if self-indulgent, friend of the people, Long had his own plan for dealing with the Great Depression.

Long's Share Our Wealth program was tantalizingly generous and simple. In one version he proposed to confiscate large personal fortunes, guarantee every family a cash grant of $5,000 and every worker an annual income of $2,500, provide pensions to the aged, reduce working hours, pay veterans' bonuses, and ensure a college education for every qualified student. It did not matter to him that his figures failed to add up or that his program offered little to promote an economic recovery. As he told a group of distressed Iowa farmers, "Maybe somebody says I don't understand it. Well, you don't have to. Just shut your damn eyes and believe it. That's all." Whether he had a workable plan or not, by early 1935 the charismatic Long was claiming 7.5 million supporters.

Another popular social scheme was hatched by a gray-haired California doctor, Francis E. Townsend. Outraged by the sight of three haggard old women raking through garbage cans in Long Beach, Townsend proposed government pensions for the aged. In 1934 he began promoting the Townsend Plan of paying $200 a month to every citizen over sixty who retired from employment and who promised to spend the money within the month. The plan had the lure of providing both financial security for the aged and job openings for the young. Critics noted that the cost of his program for 9 percent of the population would be more than half the national income. Yet Townsend was indifferent to such factors. "I'm not in the least interested in the cost of the plan," he blandly told a House committee.

A third huckster of panaceas, Father Charles E. Coughlin, the Roman Catholic "radio priest," founded the National Union for Social Justice in 1934. In broadcasts over the CBS network, he promoted schemes for the coinage of silver and made attacks on bankers that carried growing overtones of anti-Semitism.

Coughlin, Townsend, and Long drew support largely from desperate lower-middle-class Americans. Of the three, Long had the widest following. A 1935 survey showed that he could draw 5 to 6 million votes as a third-party candidate for president in 1936, perhaps enough to under-mine Roosevelt's chances of reelection. Beset by pressures from both ends of the political spectrum, Roosevelt hesitated for months before deciding to "steal the thunder" from the left by instituting new programs of reform and social security. "I'm fighting Communism, Huey Longism, Coughlinism, Townsendism," Roosevelt told a reporter in early 1935. He needed "to save our system, the capitalist system," from such "crackpot ideas." Political pressures impelled Roosevelt to move left, but so did the growing influence within the administration of Supreme Court Justices Louis Brandeis and Felix Frankfurter. These powerful advisers urged Roosevelt to be less cozy with big business and to push for restored competition and heavy taxes on large corporations.

OPPOSITION FROM THE COURT   A series of Supreme Court decisions finally galvanized the president into action. On May 27, 1935, the Court killed the National Industrial Recovery Act by unanimous vote. In *Schechter Poultry Corporation* v. *United States,* quickly tagged the "sick chicken" case, the defendants had been convicted of selling an "unfit chicken" and violating other NRA code provisions. The high court ruled that Congress had delegated too much power to the executive branch when it granted the code-making authority to the NRA, and Congress had exceeded its power under the commerce clause by regulating *intrastate* commerce. The poultry in question, the Court decided, had "come to permanent rest within the state," although it earlier had been moved across state lines. In a press conference soon afterward, Roosevelt fumed: "We have been relegated to the horse-and-buggy definition of interstate commerce." The same line of reasoning, he warned, might endanger other New Deal programs.

LEGISLATIVE ACHIEVEMENTS OF THE SECOND NEW DEAL   To rescue his legislative program from such judicial and political challenges, Roosevelt in 1935 ended the stalemate in Congress and launched the so-called Second New Deal. He demanded several pieces of "must" legislation, most of which were already pending. During the next two months, Congress passed another cluster of significant—and quite controversial—legislation.

The National Labor Relations Act, often called the Wagner Act for its sponsor, New York senator Robert Wagner, gave workers the right to bargain through unions of their own choice and prohibited employers from interfering with union activities. A National Labor Relations Board of five members could supervise plant elections and certify unions as bargaining agents where a majority of the workers approved. The board could also investigate the actions of employers and issue "cease and desist" orders against specified unfair practices.

The Social Security Act of 1935, Roosevelt announced, was the New Deal's "cornerstone" and "supreme achievement." Indeed, it has proven to be the most significant and far-reaching of all the New Deal initiatives. The concept was by no means new. Progressives during the early 1900s had proposed a federal system of social security for the aged, indigent, disabled, and unemployed. Other nations had already enacted such programs, but the United States remained steadfast to its tradition of individual self-reliance. The Great Depression, however, revived the idea, and Roosevelt masterfully guided the legislation through Congress.

A poster distributed by the government to educate the public about the new Social Security Act.

The Social Security Act included three major provisions. Its centerpiece was a pension fund for retired people over the age of sixty-five and their survivors. Beginning in 1937, workers and employers contributed payroll taxes to establish the fund. Benefit payments started in 1940 and averaged $22 per month, a quite modest sum even for those depressed times. Roosevelt knew this, and he stressed that the pension program was not intended to guarantee a comfortable retirement; it was designed to supplement other sources of income and protect the elderly from some of the "hazards and vicissitudes of life." Only later did American voters and politicians come to perceive Social Security as the *primary* source of retirement income for most of the aged. By 2002, the average monthly payment was about $875.

The Social Security Act also set up a shared federal-state unemployment insurance program, financed by a payroll tax on employers.

In addition, the new legislation committed the national government to a broad range of social welfare activities based on the assumption that "unemployables"—people who were unable to work—would remain a state responsibility, while the national government would provide work relief for the able-bodied. To that end, the law inaugurated federal grants-in-aid for three state-administered public assistance programs— old age assistance, aid for dependent children, aid for the blind—and further aid for maternal, child welfare, and public health services.

Relatively speaking, the new federal program was quite conservative. It was the only government pension program in the world financed by taxes on the earnings of current workers. Most other countries funded such programs out of general revenues. The Social Security payroll tax was also a regressive tax in that it entailed a single fixed rate for all, regardless of income level. It thus hurt the poor more than the rich, and it also hurt Roosevelt's efforts to revive the economy because it removed from circulation a significant amount of money. The new Social Security tax took money out of workers' pockets and placed it into a trust fund, thus exacerbating the shrinking money supply that was one of the main causes of the depression. By taking discretionary income away from workers, the government blunted the sharp increase in public consumption needed to restore the health of the economy. In addition, the Social Security system initially excluded 9.5 million workers who needed it the most: farm laborers, domestic servants, and the self-employed, a disproportionate percentage of whom were black.

Roosevelt recognized and regretted such limitations, but he knew that they were necessary compromises in order to see the Social Security Act through Congress and to enable it to withstand court challenges. As he replied to an aide who criticized funding the pension program through employee contributions, "I guess you're right on the economics, but those taxes were never a problem of economics. They are politics all the way through. We put those payroll contributions there so as to give the contributors a moral, legal, and political right to collect their pensions and their unemployment benefits. With those taxes in there, no damn politician can ever scrap my Social Security program."

The last of the major bills making up the "Second New Deal" was the Revenue Act of 1935, sometimes called the Wealth Tax Act, but popularly known as the "Soak the Rich" tax. The Revenue Act raised tax rates on incomes above $50,000. Estate and gift taxes also rose, as did the corporate tax on all but small corporations (those with less than $50,000 annual income).

Business leaders fumed over Roosevelt's tax and spending policies. The wealthy resented their loss of status and the growing power of government and labor. They railed against the New Deal and Roosevelt, whom they called "a traitor to his own class." By "soaking" the rich, Roosevelt stole much of the thunder from the political left, although the results of his tax policy fell short of the promise. The new "soak the rich" tax failed to increase federal revenue significantly, nor did it result in a significant redistribution of income. Still, the prevailing view was that Roosevelt had moved in a radical direction. Newspaper editor William Randolph Hearst growled that the Wealth Tax was "essentially communism. This bastard proposal should be ascribed to a composite personality which might be labeled Stalin Delano Roosevelt."

The extent of the new departure taken by the Second New Deal is easy to exaggerate. Such measures as Social Security, utility regulation, and higher taxes on the wealthy had long been in the works in Congress and had already been adopted by most other industrial nations. Roosevelt himself stressed his own basic conservatism and asserted that he had no love for socialism. "I am fighting communism. . . . I want to save our system, the capitalistic system." Yet he added that to save it from revolutionary turmoil required a more equal "distribution of wealth."

ROOSEVELT'S SECOND TERM

On June 27, 1936, Roosevelt accepted the Democratic party's presidential nomination for a second term. He promised to continue to promote a government motivated by "a spirit of charity" rather than a government "frozen in the ice of its own indifference."

THE 1936 ELECTION The popularity of Roosevelt and the New Deal impelled the Republican convention in 1936 to avoid candidates too closely identified with the "hate-Roosevelt" contingent. The party chose Governor Alfred M. Landon of Kansas, a bland and genial former Bull Moose Progressive. A fiscal conservative, Landon had nevertheless endorsed many New Deal programs. He was probably more liberal than most of his backers, and clearly more so than the party's platform, which accused the New Deal of usurping power.

The Republicans hoped that the followers of Long, Coughlin, Townsend, and other dissidents would combine to draw enough votes away from Roosevelt to throw the election to them. But that possibility faded when an assassin, the son-in-law of a Louisiana judge whom Long had sought to remove, gunned down the "Kingfish" in 1935. Coughlin, Townsend, and a remnant of the Long movement supported Representative William Lemke of North Dakota on a Union party ticket, but it was a forlorn effort that polled only 882,000 votes.

In 1936 Roosevelt forged a new electoral coalition that would affect national politics for years to come. While holding the support of most traditional Democrats North and South, FDR made strong gains among beneficiaries of the AAA farm program in the West. In the northern cities, he held on to the ethnic groups helped by New Deal welfare measures. Middle-class voters, whose property had been saved by New Deal measures, flocked to Roosevelt's support, along with in-tellectuals stirred by the ferment of new governmental ideas. The re-vived labor movement threw its support to Roosevelt, and in the most profound new departure of all, black voters for the first time cast the majority of their ballots for a Democratic president. "My friends, go home and turn Lincoln's picture to the wall," a black Pittsburgh jour-nalist told black Republicans. "That debt has been paid in full." The fi-nal vote tally revealed that 81 percent of those with incomes under $1,000 a year opted for Roosevelt, as did 79 percent of those earning between $1,000 and $2,000. By contrast, only 46 percent of those earning $5,000 voted for FDR.

In his acceptance speech to the Democratic convention, Roosevelt had dropped efforts to reassure corporate leaders. As the Americans of 1776 had sought freedom from political autocracy, he noted, the Americans of 1936 sought freedom from the "economic royalists." He later claimed that never before had the business leaders been "so united against one candidate." They were "unanimous in their hate for me—and I welcome their hatred." Roosevelt wound up carrying every state except Maine and Vermont, with a popular vote of 27.7 million to Landon's 16.7 million. Democrats would also dominate Republicans in the new Con-gress, by 77 to 19 in the Senate and 328 to 107 in the House. After the lopsided victory, Roosevelt rode a wave of popularity into a second term.

THE COURT-PACKING PLAN   Soon after his landslide reelection, however, Roosevelt found himself deluged in a sea of troubles. His second inaugural address, delivered on January 20, 1937, suggested that he was ready to enact even greater reforms. The challenge to American democracy, he maintained, was that millions of citizens "at this very moment are denied the greater part of what the very lowest standards of today call the necessities of life. . . . I see one-third of a nation ill-housed, ill-clad, ill-nourished." The election of 1936 had been a mandate for even more extensive governmental action, he argued, and the overwhelming Democratic majorities in Congress ensured their passage. But one major roadblock stood in the way: the Supreme Court.

By the end of the 1936 term, the Court had ruled against New Deal laws in seven of the nine major cases it reviewed. Suits against the Social Security and Wagner Labor Relations acts were also pending. Given the established trend of rulings, the Second New Deal seemed in danger of being nullified like the first.

For that reason, Roosevelt resolved to change the Court's philosophy by enlarging it, a move for which there was ample precedent and power. Congress, not the Constitution, determines the size of the Court,

An editorial cartoon commenting on Roosevelt's grandiose plan to enlarge the Supreme Court.

which at different times had numbered six, seven, nine, and ten jus- tices, and in 1937 numbered nine. On February 5 Roosevelt sent his plan to Congress, without having consulted congressional leaders. He wanted to create up to fifty new federal judges, including six new Supreme Court justices, and to diminish the power of the judges who had served ten or more years or reached the age of seventy.

But the "court-packing" maneuver, as opponents quickly tagged it, backfired on Roosevelt. It was a shade too contrived, much too brazen, and far too political. The normally pro-New Deal *New York World-Telegram* dismissed Roosevelt's court-packing scheme as "too clever, too damned clever." By implying that some judges were impaired by senility, Roosevelt affronted the elder statesmen of Congress and the Court, especially Justice Louis D. Brandeis, who was both the oldest and the most liberal of the Supreme Court judges. It also ran headlong into a deep-rooted public veneration of the courts and aroused fears that an- other president might use the precedent for quite different purposes.

As it turned out, unforeseen events blunted Roosevelt's drive to change the Court. A sequence of Court decisions during the spring of 1937 reversed previous judgments in order to uphold the Wagner Act and the Social Security Act. In addition, a conservative justice resigned, and Roosevelt named to the vacancy one of the most consistent New Dealers, Senator Hugo Black of Alabama.

Roosevelt later claimed he had lost the battle but won the war. The Court had reversed itself on important New Deal legislation, and Roosevelt was able to appoint justices in harmony with the New Deal. But the episode created dissension in his party and blighted Roosevelt's prestige. For the first time, Democrats in large numbers deserted the "champ," and the Republican opposition found a powerful issue. During the first eight months of 1937, the momentum of Roosevelt's great 1936 victory was lost. As Henry Wallace later remarked, "The whole New Deal really went up in smoke as a result of the Supreme Court fight."

A NEW DIRECTION FOR LABOR   Rebellions erupted on other fronts even while the court-packing bill pended. Under the impetus of the New Deal, the dormant labor movement stirred anew. When Section 7a of the National Industrial Recovery Act demanded in every industry code a statement of the workers' right to organize, alert unionists quickly translated it to mean "The President wants you to join the union."

John L. Lewis of the United Mine Workers was among the first to exploit the spirit of the NIRA. Leading a union decimated by depression, he rebuilt it from 150,000 members to 500,000 within a year. Spurred by the mine workers' example, Sidney Hillman of the Amalgamated Clothing Workers and David Dubinsky of the International Ladies' Garment Workers joined Lewis in promoting a campaign to organize workers in the mass-production industries. As leaders of some of the few industrial unions (made up of all workers) in the AFL, they found the more restrictive craft unions (made up of skilled male workers) to be obstacles to organizing the basic industries.

In 1935, with passage of the Wagner Act, the industrial unionists formed a Committee for Industrial Organization (CIO), and craft unionists began to fear submergence by the mass unions. Jurisdictional disputes divided them, and in 1936 the AFL expelled the CIO unions, which then formed a permanent structure called after 1938 the Congress of Industrial Organizations. The rivalry spurred both groups to greater efforts.

The CIO's major organizing drives in the automobile and steel industries began in 1936, but until the Supreme Court upheld the Wagner Act in 1937 there was little compliance with unions on the part of industry. Companies used blacklisting, private detectives, labor spies, vigilante groups, and intimidation to fight the unions. Early in 1937 automobile workers spontaneously adopted a new technique, the "sit-down strike," in which workers refused to leave the workplace until the employers granted collective-bargaining rights.

Led by the fiery young autoworker and union organizer Walter Reuther, thousands of employees at General Motors' assembly plants in Flint, Michigan, occupied the factories and stopped all production. Women workers supported their male counterparts by picketing at the plant entrances. The wives, daughters, and mothers of the strikers formed a Women's Auxiliary to feed the workers who slept at the plants. Management refused to recognize the union efforts. Company officials called in police to harass the strikers, sent spies to union meetings, and threatened to fire the workers. They also pleaded with Roosevelt to dispatch federal troops. He refused, while at the same time expressing his displeasure with the sit-down strike. The standoff lasted over a month. Then, on February 11, the company relented and signed a contract recognizing the United Auto Workers (UAW). Other automotive companies

CIO pickets jeering at nonstriking workers entering a mill, 1941.

soon followed suit. And the following month, United States Steel capitulated to the Steel Workers Organizing Committee (later the United Steelworkers of America), granting it recognition, a 10 percent wage hike, and a forty-hour workweek.

The Wagner Act put the power of the federal government behind the principle of unionization. In Congress, a Senate subcommittee under Robert M. La Follette, Jr., exposed violent practices against unions. President Roosevelt refused to use force against sit-down strikers, though he was opposed to the tactic. The unions, he said, would soon learn that they could not continue to use a "damned unpopular" tactic. Roosevelt himself had come late to the support of unions and sometimes took exception to their behavior. In the fall of 1937 he became so irritated with the warfare between the mercurial John L. Lewis and Republic Steel that he pronounced "a plague on both your houses." The grandiloquent Lewis, who for a year had been trying to organize a union for steelworkers, responded: "It ill behooves one who has supped at labor's table and who has been sheltered in labor's house to curse with equal fervor and fine impartiality both labor and its adversaries when they become locked in a deadly embrace." In 1940 an angry Lewis would back the Republican presidential candidate, but he would be unable to carry the labor vote with him. As workers became more organized, they more closely identified with the Democratic party. By August 1937 the CIO claimed over 3.4 million members, more than the AFL. The unions made a difference. Through their efforts, wages rose, and working conditions improved. Whether by design or accident, Roosevelt and the Democratic party were the beneficiaries of the labor movement. Workers became active voters and reliable Democrats.

A SLUMPING ECONOMY The years 1935 and 1936 had seen steady economic improvement. By the spring of 1937 output had moved above the 1929 level. The prosperity of early 1937 was achieved largely through governmental spending. On top of relief and public-works outlays, Congress in 1936 provided for cash payments of veterans' bonuses upon demand. But in 1937 Roosevelt, worried about deficits and inflation, ordered sharp cuts in spending. At the same time the Treasury began to diminish disposable income by collecting $2 billion in Social Security taxes. Private spending could not fill the gap left by reductions in government spending, and business still lacked the faith to risk large investments. The result was that the economy suddenly stalled, and then slid into a business slump deeper than that in 1929. The Dow Jones stock average fell some 40 percent between August and October. By the end of the year 2 million people had been thrown out of work; scenes of the earlier depression reappeared.

The recession provoked a fierce debate within the administration. One group, led by Treasury Secretary Henry Morgenthau, Jr., favored less spending and a balanced budget. The slow pace of recovery, Morgenthau thought, resulted from the reluctance of business to invest, and that resulted in turn from fear that federal spending would bring inflation and heavy taxes. The other group, which included Harry Hopkins and Harold Ickes, argued for renewed government spending. The recession, they noted, had come just when the budget was brought into balance. This view echoed that of the English economist John Maynard Keynes, who had given extended development to the idea in his book *The General Theory of Employment, Interest and Money* (1936). Keynesian economics offered a convenient theoretical justification for what New Dealers had already done in pragmatic response to existing conditions.

ECONOMIC POLICY AND LATE REFORMS   Roosevelt waited as the rival theorists sought his approval. When the spring of 1938 failed to bring recovery, he endorsed the ideas of the spenders. On April 14, 1938, he asked Congress to adopt a large-scale spending program, and Congress voted $33 billion, mainly for public works by the PWA and the WPA, with lesser amounts for other programs. In a short time the increase in spending reversed the economy's decline, but the recession and Roosevelt's reluctance to adopt the truly massive, sustained government spending called for in Keynesian theory forestalled the achievement of full recovery. Only during World War II would employment reach pre-1929 levels.

The court-packing fight, the sit-down strikes, and the recession in 1937 all undercut Roosevelt's prestige and dissipated the mandate of the 1936 elections. When the 1937 congressional session ended, the only major new reforms enacted for the benefit of the "ill-housed, ill-clad, [and] ill-nourished" were the Wagner-Steagall National Housing Act and the Bankhead-Jones Farm Tenant Act. In 1938 the Democratic Congress enacted three more major reforms, the last of the New Deal era: the Second Agricultural Adjustment Act; the Food, Drug and Cosmetic Act; and the Fair Labor Standards Act.

The Housing Act set up the United States Housing Authority (USHA) in the Department of the Interior, which extended long-term loans to local agencies willing to assume part of the cost for slum clearance and public housing. The agency also subsidized low rents. Later, during World War II, it financed housing in connection with defense projects.

The Farm Tenant Act addressed the problem of rural poverty. In some ways the New Deal's larger farm program, the AAA, had aggravated the problem; although tenants were supposed to be kept on in spite of government-sponsored cutbacks in production, landlords often simply evicted workers and pocketed their shares of benefit payments. The Tenant Act was administered by a new agency, the Farm Security Administration (FSA). The program made available rehabilitation loans to shore up marginal farmers and prevent their sinking into tenancy. It also made loans to tenants for purchase of their own farms. In the end, however, the FSA proved to be little more than another relief operation that tided a few farmers over difficult times. A more effective answer to the problem, sadly, awaited mobilization for war, which took many tenants off into the military services or defense industries, broadened their horizons, and taught them new skills.

The Agricultural Adjustment Act of 1938 was a response to renewed crop surpluses and price declines during the recession. It reenacted the basic devices of the earlier AAA with some new twists. Before the government could apply marketing quotas to a given crop, for instance, the growers had to approve in a vote. The new Food, Drug and Cosmetic Act broadened the coverage of the 1906 Pure Food and Drug Act and forbade the use of false or misleading advertising. Enforcement of the advertising provision became the responsibility of the Federal Trade Commission. The Fair Labor Standards Act applied to enterprises that operated in or affected interstate commerce. It set a minimum wage of 40¢ an hour and a maximum workweek of forty hours, to be put into effect over several years. The act also prohibited child labor under the age of sixteen, and prohibited it under eighteen in hazardous occupations.

THE LEGACY OF THE NEW DEAL

SETBACKS FOR THE PRESIDENT   As the New Deal turned its focus from recovery to reform, an effective opposition to Roosevelt emerged within the president's party, especially in the conservative southern wing. Local power elites in the South felt that the New Deal jeopardized their position. They felt threatened, too, when in 1936 the Democratic convention eliminated the two-thirds rule for nominations, thereby removing the South's veto power, and seated African-American delegates. Southern Democrats were at best uneasy bedfellows with organized labor and northern blacks. Senator "Cotton" Ed Smith of South Carolina and several other southern delegates walked out of the convention, with Smith declaring that he would not support any party that views "the Negro as a political and social equal." Some disgruntled southern Democrats drifted toward coalition with conservative Republicans. By the end of 1937, a bipartisan conservative bloc had coalesced against the New Deal.

In 1938 the conservative opposition stymied an executive reorganization bill amid cries that it would lead to dictatorship. They also secured drastic cuts in the undistributed-profits and capital gains taxes to help restore business "confidence." The House also set up a Committee on Un-American Activities chaired by Martin Dies of Texas, who took to the warpath against Communists. Soon he began to brand New Dealers as Red dupes. "Stalin baited his hook with a 'progressive' worm," Dies wrote in 1940, "and New Deal suckers swallowed bait, hook, line, and sinker."

As the political season of 1938 advanced, Roosevelt unfolded a new idea as momentous as the court-packing plan—a proposal to reshape the Democratic party in the image of the New Deal. He announced his purpose to intervene in Democratic primaries as the party leader, "charged with the responsibility of carrying out the definitely liberal declaration of principles set forth in the 1936 Democratic platform." He wanted his own supporters nominated. Instead of succeeding, however, the effort backfired and broke the spell of presidential invincibility, or what was left of it. As in the court-packing fight, Roosevelt had risked his prestige while handing his adversaries a persuasive issue. His opponents tagged his intervention in the primaries as an attempt to "purge" the Democratic party of its southern conservatives; the word evoked visions of Adolf Hitler and Joseph Stalin, tyrants who had purged their Nazi and Communist parties in blood.

The elections of November 1938 handed the administration another setback, a result partly of the friction among Democrats. Roosevelt had failed utterly in his efforts to liberalize the Democratic party by ousting southern conservatives. The Democratic majority in the House fell from 229 to 93, in the Senate from 56 to 42. The margins remained large, but the president headed a restive and divided party. In his State of the Union message in 1939, Roosevelt for the first time proposed no new reforms, but spoke of the need "to invigorate the process of recovery, in order to *preserve* our reforms." In the same year, the administration won an extension of Social Security and finally put through a diluted version of its reorganization plan. Under the Administrative Reorganization Act, the president could "reduce, coordinate, consolidate, and reorganize" the agencies of government. Thereafter, however, Roosevelt lost widespread congressional and popular support. The conservative coalition and the administration had reached a standoff. As one observer noted, the New Deal "has been reduced to a movement with no program, with no effective political organization, with no vast popular party strength behind it."

A HALFWAY REVOLUTION   The New Deal had lost momentum, but it had wrought several enduring changes. By the end of the 1930s, the power of the national government was vastly enlarged over what it had been in 1932, and hope had been restored to people who had grown fatalistic. But the New Deal entailed more than just bigger government and revived public confidence. It also constituted a significant change from the older liberalism embodied in the progressivism of Theodore Roosevelt and Woodrow Wilson. Those earlier reformers, despite their sharp differences, had assumed that the function of progressive government in the American republic was to ensure through aggressive regulation that the people had equal opportunity to pursue their notions of happiness.

Franklin Roosevelt and the New Dealers went beyond this regulatory-state concept by insisting that the government should not simply *respond* to social crises but take positive steps to *avoid* them. To this end, the New Deal's various welfare and benefit programs conferred on government the responsibility to ensure a minimum level of well-being for all Americans. The New Deal had established minimum qualitative standards for labor conditions and public welfare and helped middle-class Americans hold on to their savings, their homes, and their farms. The protection afforded by bank deposit insurance, unemployment pay, and Social Security pensions would come to be universally accepted as a safeguard against future depressions.

The old progressive formulation of regulation versus trust-busting was now superseded by the rise of the "broker state," a powerful federal government that mediated among major interest groups. Government's role was to act as an honest broker protecting a variety of interests, not just business but workers, farmers, consumers, small business, and the unemployed.

In implementing his domestic program, Roosevelt steered a zigzag course between the extremes of laissez-faire capitalism and socialism. The first New Deal had experimented for a time with a managed economy under the NRA, but had abandoned that experiment for a turn toward enforcing competition and priming the economy with increased government spending. This finally produced full employment during World War II.

Roosevelt himself, impatient with political theory, was flexible in developing policy: he kept what worked and discarded what did not. The result was, paradoxically, both profoundly revolutionary and profoundly conservative. Roosevelt sharply increased the regulatory functions of the federal government and laid the foundation for what would become an expanding welfare state. But despite what his critics charged, his initiatives fell far short of socialism; they left the basic capitalistic structure in place. In the process of such bold experimentation and dynamic preservation, the New Deal represented a "halfway revolution" that permanently altered the social and political agenda.

MAKING CONNECTIONS

- In the mid-1930s, just as Roosevelt was getting the New Deal into place, the growing conflict in Europe began to consume more and more of his (and America's) attention: Chapter 29 shows how Roosevelt went from combating the depression to leading the United States into World War II.

- Harry Truman, Roosevelt's successor in the White House, tried unsuccessfully to expand the idea of the New Deal into new areas (national health insurance and federal aid to education, for example), a topic covered in Chapter 31.

FURTHER READING

An engaging introduction to the decade of the New Deal is Anthony J. Badger's *The New Deal: The Depression Years, 1933–1940* (1989). A comprehensive overview is David M. Kennedy's *Freedom from Fear: The American People in Depression and War* (1999). Alan Brinkley's *The End of Reform: New Deal Liberalism in Recession and War* (1995) suggests that the New Deal reformers did not go far enough in their efforts to curb big business. On the critics of the New Deal, see Alan Brinkley's *Voices of Protest: Huey Long, Father Coughlin, and the Great Depression* (1982).

James M. Gregory's *American Exodus: The Dust Bowl Migration and Okie Culture in California* (1989) describes the migratory movement's effect on American culture.

29 $\mathcal{L}$ FROM ISOLATION
TO GLOBAL WAR

CHAPTER ORGANIZER

This chapter focuses on:

• isolationism and peace movements between the two world wars.

• America's response to German aggression in Europe.

• how events in Asia led to Japan's attack on Pearl Harbor and America's entry into the global war.

*I*n the late 1930s, as the winds of war swept across Asia and Europe, the focus of American politics moved abruptly from domestic to foreign affairs. Another Democratic president had to shift attention from social reform to military preparedness and war. And the public again had to wrestle with the painful choice: involve the country in volatile world affairs or remain aloof and officially neutral.

POSTWAR ISOLATIONISM

THE LEAGUE AND THE UNITED STATES   Between Woodrow Wilson and Franklin Roosevelt lay two decades of relative isolation from foreign entanglements. The postwar mood of detached indifference to global affairs expressed in the election of 1920 set the pattern. The voters yearned for a restored isolationism, and President-elect Harding lost little time in disposing of the League of Nations. "You just didn't want a surrender of the United States," he told the people in his victory speech. "That's why you didn't care for the League, which is now deceased." The spirit of isolation found other expressions as well: the higher tariff walls, the Red Scare, the rage for "100 percent Americanism," and restrictive immigration laws by which a nation of immigrants all but shut the door to any more newcomers.

The United States may have felt the urge to insulate itself from a wicked world, but it could hardly ignore its global interests. American business, despite the tariff walls, now had worldwide connections. American investments and loans abroad put in circulation the dollars that purchased American exports. Overseas possessions, moreover, directly involved the country in world affairs, especially in the Pacific. Even the League of Nations was too great a fact to ignore, although messages from the League at first went unanswered by American diplomats. By the end of 1922, however, the United States had "unofficial observers" at the League's headquarters in Geneva, and after 1924 American diplomats gradually entered into joint efforts on such matters as the international trade in drugs and arms, the criminal traffic in women and children, and a variety of economic, cultural, and technical conferences.

WAR DEBTS AND REPARATIONS Probably nothing did more to heighten American isolationism—or anti-American feeling in Europe—than the war-debt tangle. When in 1917 the Allies had begun to exhaust their ability to pay for American military supplies, the United States government had advanced them funds first for the war effort and then for postwar reconstruction. A World War Foreign Debt Commission, created by Congress in 1922, renegotiated the Allied debt to America to a total of about $11.5 billion. Adding the interest payable over sixty-two years to this principal, the Allied debt totaled over $22 billion.

To most Americans it all seemed a simple matter of obligation, but Europeans commonly had a different perception. In the first place, Americans who thought their loan money had flowed to Europe were wrong: most of it went toward purchases of military supplies in the United

States, which fueled American prosperity. Then, too, the Allies held off the enemy at great cost while the United States was raising an army. American states, the British noted, had repudiated debts to British investors after the American Revolution; the French pointed out that they had never been repaid for helping the American side in the Revolution. But most difficult were the practical problems of repayment. To get dollar exchange, European debtor nations had to sell their goods to the United States, but American tariff walls went higher in 1921 and 1922, and again in 1930, making European goods more expensive and debt payment harder.

The French and British insisted that they could pay America only as they collected reparations from defeated Germany. Twice during the 1920s the resulting strain on Germany brought the structure of international payments to the verge of collapse, and both times the Reparations Commission called in private American bankers to work out rescue plans.

The whole structure finally did collapse during the Great Depression. In 1931 President Hoover negotiated a moratorium on both German reparations and Allied payment of war debts, thereby indirectly accepting the connection between the two. The purpose, among other things, was to shore up American private loans of several billion dollars in Germany, which for the time had kept the international credit structure intact. Once the United States had accepted the connection between reparations and war debt, the Allies virtually canceled German reparations. At the end of 1932, after Hoover's debt moratorium ended, most of the European countries defaulted on their war debts to the United States. In retaliation, Congress passed the Johnson Debt Default Act of 1934, which prohibited even private loans to any government that had defaulted on its debts to the United States.

ATTEMPTS AT DISARMAMENT   Yet, for all the isolationist sentiment of the time, Wilsonian internationalism had struck a responsive chord in many Americans. A lingering doubt, tinged with guilt, haunted many Americans about their rejection of membership in the League. Before long, Harding's advisers hit upon a happy substitute—disarmament. The conviction had grown after World War I that excessive armaments had been the war's cause, and that arms limitation would bring lasting peace. The United States had no intention of maintaining a large army, but under the building program begun in 1916, it constructed a navy second only to that of Britain. Neither the British nor the Americans had much stomach for the cost of a naval armaments race with each other, but both shared a common concern with the alarming growth of Japanese power.

During and after the war, Japanese-American relations grew increasingly strained. The United States objected to continued Japanese encroachments in Asia. During the war Japan had tried to expand its presence in China. In 1915 the cabinet in Tokyo issued what came to be known as the Twenty-one Demands, which would have brought China virtually under Japanese control. The United States protested, and fortunately the Japanese decided not to force their most rigorous demands. In 1917, after the United States entered the war, Viscount Kikujiro Ishii visited Washington to secure American recognition of Japan's expanding claims in Asia. Secretary of State Robert Lansing entered an ambiguous agreement that recognized Japan's "special interests [translated by the Japanese as 'paramount interests'] in China." Americans were unhappy with the Lansing-Ishii Agreement, but it seemed the only way to preserve the appearance of friendship.

After the war ended, Japanese-American relations grew more strained. To address the problem, President Warren Harding invited

The Washington Armaments Conference, 1921. *The Big Five at the conference were* (from left): *Prince Tekugawa (Japan), Arthur Balfour (Great Britain), Charles Evans Hughes (United States), M. Briand (France), and H. E. Carlo Sanchez (Italy).*

eight principal foreign powers to the Washington Armaments Conference in 1921. The American secretary of state Charles Evans Hughes,
in what was expected to be a perfunctory greeting, announced that "the
way to disarm is to disarm." The only way out of an armaments race, he
said, "is to end it now." It was one of the most dramatic moments in
American diplomatic history. In less than fifteen minutes, one electrified reporter said, Hughes had destroyed more tonnage "than all the admirals of the world have sunk in a cycle of centuries."

Delegates from the United States, Britain, Japan, France, and Italy
signed a Five-Power Naval Treaty (1922) incorporating Hughes's plan
for tonnage limits and a moratorium of ten years during which no battleships would be built. These powers also agreed to refrain from further fortification of their Pacific possessions. The agreement in effect
partitioned the world: U.S. naval power became supreme in the Western Hemisphere, Japanese power in the western Pacific, and British
power from the North Sea to Singapore.

Two other major agreements emerged from the Washington Conference. With the Four-Power Treaty, the United States, Britain, Japan,
and France agreed to respect each other's possessions in the Pacific,
and to refer any disputes or any outside threat to consultation. The
Nine-Power Treaty for the first time formally pledged the signers to
support the principle of the Open Door enunciated by Secretary of
State John Hay at the turn of the century. The Open Door enabled all
nations to compete for trade and investment opportunities in China
on an equal footing rather than allow individual nations to create economic monopolies in particular regions of the country. The signers of
the Nine-Power Treaty also promised to respect the territorial
integrity of China. The nations involved, in addition to those signing
the Five-Power Treaty, were China, Belgium, Portugal, and the
Netherlands.

With these agreements in hand, Harding could boast of a brilliant
diplomatic stroke that relieved taxpayers of the need to pay for an enlarged navy, and warded off potential conflicts in the Pacific. Yet the
agreements were uniformly without obligation and without teeth. The
signers of the Four-Power Treaty agreed only to consult, not to help
each other militarily. The formal endorsement of the Open Door in the
Nine-Power Treaty was just as ineffective, and the American people
remained unwilling to uphold the principle with anything but pious

affirmation. The naval disarmament treaty set limits only on capital ships (battleships and aircraft carriers); the race to build cruisers, destroyers, submarines, and other smaller craft continued. Expansionist Japan withdrew from the agreement in 1934. Thus, twelve years after the Washington Conference, the dream of naval disarmament died.

THE KELLOGG-BRIAND PACT   During and after World War I, the fanciful ideal of abolishing war caught the American imagination. In 1921 a wealthy Chicagoan founded the American Committee for the Outlawry of War. "We can outlaw this war system just as we outlawed slavery and the saloon," said one of the more enthusiastic converts.

The glorious vision of abolishing war at the stroke of a pen culminated in the signing of the Kellogg-Briand Pact in 1928. This unique treaty started with an initiative from French foreign minister Aristide Briand, who in 1927 proposed to Secretary of State Frank B. Kellogg an agreement that the two countries would never go to war against each other. This innocent-seeming proposal was actually a clever ploy to draw the United States into the French security system by the back door. In any future war, for instance, such a pact would inhibit the United States from reprisals against any French intrusions on neutral rights. Kellogg gave the idea a cool reception, and was outraged to discover that Briand had urged leaders of the American peace movements to put pressure on the government to sign.

Finally Kellogg turned the tables on Briand. He countered with a scheme to have all nations sign the pact, an idea all the more acceptable to the peace organizations. Caught in a trap of his own making, the French foreign minister finally relented. The Pact of Paris (its official name), signed on August 27, 1928, solemnly declared that the signatories "condemn recourse to war . . . and renounce it as an instrument of national policy." Eventually sixty-two nations adhered to the pact, but all explicitly or tacitly reserved "self-defense" as an escape hatch. The United States Senate included a reservation declaring the preserving of the Monroe Doctrine necessary to self-defense, and then ratified the agreement by a vote of 85 to 1. One senator who voted for "this worthless, but perfectly harmless peace treaty" wrote a friend later that he feared it would "confuse the minds of many good people who think that peace may be secured by polite professions of neighborly and brotherly love."

THE "GOOD NEIGHBOR" POLICY In
Latin America the spirit of peace and
noninvolvement helped allay resentments against "Yankee imperialism,"
which had been freely practiced in the
Caribbean during the first two decades
of the century. The Harding administration agreed in 1921 to pay the republic
of Colombia the $25 million it had once
demanded for America's use of Panama
Canal rights. In 1924 American troops
left the Dominican Republic, occupied
since 1916, although United States officials continued to collect customs duties there for another twenty-five years.

*Nicaraguan rebel leader César
Augusto Sandino.*

The marines left Nicaragua in 1925,
but returned a year later at the outbreak
of disorders and civil war. There in 1927,
the Coolidge administration brought
both parties into an agreement for American-supervised elections, but
one rebel leader, César Augusto Sandino, held out, and the marines
stayed until 1933. The unhappy legacies of this intervention were enmity toward the United States and a ruthless, corrupt Nicaraguan National Guard, created to keep order after the marines left, but used in
1936 to set up the dictatorship of Anastasio Somoza.

The troubles in Nicaragua increased strains between the United
States and Mexico. Relations were already soured by repeated Mexican
threats to expropriate American oil properties in Mexico. In 1928, however, the American ambassador was able to get an agreement protecting
American rights acquired before 1917. Expropriation did in fact occur
in 1938, but the Mexican government then agreed to reimburse American
owners.

In 1928, with problems apparently clearing in Mexico and Nicaragua,
President Coolidge traveled to Havana to open the Pan-American Conference. It was an unusual gesture of friendship, and so was the choice
of Charles Evans Hughes, the former secretary of state, to head the
American delegation. Hughes announced the United States' intention
to withdraw its marines from Nicaragua and Haiti as soon as possible,

although he did block a resolution declaring that "no state has the right to intervene in the affairs of another."

At the end of 1928 President-elect Hoover began a tour of ten Latin American nations. Once in office he reversed Wilson's policy of refusing to recognize "bad" regimes and reverted to the older policy of recognizing governments in power, regardless of their behavior. In 1930 he generated more goodwill by permitting publication of a memorandum drawn up in 1928 by Undersecretary of State J. Ruben Clark. The Clark Memorandum denied that the Monroe Doctrine justified American intervention in Latin America. Although Hoover never endorsed the Clark Memorandum, he never intervened in the region. Before he left office, steps had already been taken to withdraw American forces from Nicaragua and Haiti.

Franklin D. Roosevelt likewise embraced "the policy of the good neighbor" and soon advanced it in practice. In 1933, at the Seventh Pan-American Conference, the United States supported a resolution saying "No state has the right to intervene in the internal or external affairs of another." Under President Roosevelt the marines completed their withdrawals from Nicaragua and Haiti, and in 1934 the president negotiated with Cuba a treaty that abrogated the Platt Amendment and thus ended the last formal claim to a right of intervention in Latin America. Roosevelt reinforced hemispheric goodwill in 1936, when he opened the Eighth Pan-American Conference with a speech declaring that outside aggressors "will find a Hemisphere wholly prepared to consult together for our mutual safety and our mutual good."

WAR CLOUDS

JAPANESE INCURSIONS IN CHINA   The lessening of irritants in the Western Hemisphere during the 1930s proved an exception in an otherwise dismal world scene, as war clouds thickened over Europe and Asia. Actual conflict erupted first in Asia, where unsettled conditions in China had invited foreign encroachments since before the turn of the century. In 1929 Chinese nationalist aspirations and China's subsequent clashes with Russia convinced the Japanese that their own extensive investments in Manchuria, including the South Manchurian Railway, were in danger.

Japanese occupation of Manchuria began with the Mukden Incident of 1931, when an explosion destroyed a section of railway track near that city. The Japanese "Kwantung Army," based in Manchuria to guard the railway, blamed the incident on the Chinese and used it as a pretext to begin its occupation, which it extended during the winter of 1931–1932 to all of Manchuria. In 1932 the Japanese converted Manchuria into the puppet empire of "Manchukuo."

The Manchuria Incident, as the Japanese called their undeclared war, flagrantly violated the Nine-Power Treaty, the Kellogg-Briand Pact, and Japan's pledges as a member of the League of Nations. But when China asked the League and the United States for help, neither responded. President Hoover was unwilling to invoke either military or economic sanctions. Secretary of State Henry Stimson, who would have preferred to do more, warned in 1932 that the United States refused to recognize any treaty, agreement, or situation that violated American treaty rights, the Open Door, the territorial integrity of China, or any situation brought about by violation of the Kellogg-Briand Pact. This statement, later known as the Stimson Doctrine, had no effect on

Japan's seizure of Manchuria in 1931 prompted this American condemnation.

Japanese action, for soon the Japanese navy attacked and briefly occupied Shanghai, China's great port city.

Indiscriminate bombing of Shanghai's civilian population aroused indignation but no further Western action. When the League of Nations condemned Japanese aggression in 1933, Japan withdrew from the League. During the spring of 1933, hostilities in Manchuria gradually subsided and ended with a truce. Then an uneasy peace settled upon East Asia for four years, during which time the leaders of Japan's military further extended their political sway in Tokyo.

ITALY AND GERMANY The rise of the Japanese militarists paralleled the rise of fascist dictators in Italy and Germany. In 1922 Benito Mussolini had seized power in Italy. After returning from World War I as a wounded veteran, he had organized the fascist movement, a hybrid of nationalism and socialism. The fascist program, and above all Mussolini's promise to restore order and pride in a country fragmented by dissension, enjoyed a wide appeal. Once in power, Mussolini largely abandoned the socialist part of his platform and gradually suppressed all political opposition. By 1925 he wielded dictatorial power as Il Duce (the leader).

There was always something ludicrous about the strutting Mussolini. Italy, after all, was a minor power. But Germany was another matter, and Americans were not amused, even at the beginning, by Il Duce's counterpart, Adolf Hitler. Hitler's National Socialist (Nazi) party duplicated the major features of Italian fascism, including the ancient Roman salute. The impotence of Germany's democratic Weimar Republic in the face of world depression offered Hitler his opening. Made chancellor on January 30, 1933, he swiftly intimidated the opposition, won dictatorial powers from a subservient Reichstag (parliament), and in 1934 assumed the title of Reichsführer (national leader) with absolute powers. The Nazi police state cranked up the engines of tyranny, persecuting socialists and Jews, whom Hitler blamed for all Germany's troubles, and rearming in defiance of the Versailles Treaty. Hitler flouted international agreements, pulled Germany out of the League of Nations in 1933, and proclaimed his intention to extend control over all German-speaking peoples. Despite one provocation after another, the European democracies lacked the will to resist his bold grab for power.

Mussolini and Hitler in Munich, Germany, June 1940.

THE MOOD IN AMERICA   Most Americans, absorbed by the problems of the depression, chose to retreat all the more into isolationism
during the early 1930s. In the 1932 presidential campaign, Roosevelt
renounced his support for the United States joining the League of
Nations.

The chief exception to the administration's isolationism was Secretary of State Cordell Hull's grand scheme of reciprocal trade agreements. Hull, a former Tennessee judge and congressman, believed that
free trade among all nations would advance understanding and peace.
In 1934 the administration threw its support behind Hull's pet project,
and over the objections of business interests and Republicans, Congress adopted the Trade Agreements Act, which authorized the president to lower tariff rates as much as 50 percent for countries that made
similar concessions on American products. Agreements were made with
fourteen countries by the end of 1935, reaching a total of twenty-nine
by 1945. The economic results are hard to measure, since the intervening years were so troubled.

Another scheme for building foreign markets, diplomatic recognition
of Soviet Russia, won more support in business quarters than had the
reciprocity plan. By 1933 the reasons for American refusal to recognize
the Bolshevik regime had grown stale. Japanese expansionism in Asia,
moreover, gave Russia and the United States a common concern. Given

an opening by the shift of opinion, Roosevelt invited Maxim Litvinov, Soviet commissar for foreign affairs, to visit Washington. After nine days of talks, a formal exchange of notes on November 16, 1933, signaled the renewal of diplomatic relations. Litvinov promised that his country would abstain from propaganda in the United States, extend religious freedom to Americans in the U.S.S.R., and reopen the question of czarist debts to America.

THE EXPANDING AXIS   But a catastrophic chain of events in Asia and Europe sent the world hurtling toward disaster. In 1934 Japan renounced the Five-Power Naval Treaty. The next year, Mussolini commenced an Italian conquest of Ethiopia. The same year a referendum in the Saar Basin, held in accordance with the Versailles Treaty, delivered that coal-rich region into the hands of Hitler. In 1936 Hitler reoccupied the Rhineland with armed forces, in violation of the Versailles Treaty but without any forceful response from the French. The year 1936 also brought the Spanish Civil War, which began with an uprising of the Spanish armed forces in Morocco, led by General Francisco Franco. In three years Franco had established a fascist dictatorship with help from Hitler and Mussolini while the democracies stood by and left the Spanish Republic to its fate. On July 7, 1937, Japanese and Chinese troops clashed at the Marco Polo Bridge near Beijing. The incident quickly developed into a full-scale war that the Japanese persisted in calling the "China Incident." It was the beginning of World War II in Asia, two years before war erupted in Europe. That same year Japan joined Germany and Italy in the "Anti-Comintern Pact," allegedly directed at the Communist threat, thus establishing the Rome-Berlin-Tokyo "Axis."

By 1938 the peace of Europe trembled in the balance. Having rebuilt German military force, Hitler forced the *Anschluss* (union) of Austria with Germany in March 1938, and six months later took the Sudeten territory from Czechoslovakia after signing an agreement at Munich under which Britain and France abandoned a country that had probably the second-best army in central Europe. The mountainous Sudetenland, largely German in population, was vital to the defense of Czechoslovakia. Having promised that this was his last territorial demand, Hitler in March 1939 brazenly violated his pledge and occupied the remainder of Czechoslovakia and seized formerly German territory from Lithuania. In quick succession the Spanish Republic finally collapsed, and

Mussolini seized the kingdom of Albania. Finally, during the summer, Hitler heated up a "war of nerves" over control of the free city of Danzig and the Polish Corridor, and on September 1 launched his conquest of Poland. A few days before, he had signed a nonaggression pact with Soviet Russia. Having deserted Czechoslovakia, Britain and France now honored their commitment to go to war if Poland were invaded.

DEGREES OF NEUTRALITY During these years of deepening crisis, the Western democracies seemed paralyzed, hoping in vain that each concession would appease the appetites of fascist dictators. The Americans retreated more deeply into isolation. The prevailing mood was reinforced by a Senate inquiry into the role of bankers and munitions makers in World War I. Under Senator Gerald P. Nye of North Dakota, a progressive Republican, the committee sat from 1934 to 1937, and concluded that bankers and munitions makers had made scandalous profits from the war. Although Nye never showed that greed for profit had actually impelled Woodrow Wilson into war, millions of Americans became convinced that Uncle Sam had been duped by the "merchants of death."

Like generals who are said to be always preparing for the last war, Congress occupied itself with keeping out of the last war. Neutrality laws of the 1930s moved the United States toward complete isolation from the quarrels of Europe. Americans wanted to keep out of war, but their sympathies were more strongly than ever with the Western democracies, and the triumph of fascist aggression aroused growing fears for national security.

In 1935 President Roosevelt signed the first of five formal neutrality laws intended to keep the United States out of war. The Neutrality Act of 1935 forbade the sale of arms and munitions to all warring nations whenever the president proclaimed that a state of war existed. Americans who traveled on belligerent ships did so at their own risk. Roosevelt would have preferred discretionary authority to levy an embargo only against aggressors, but reluctantly accepted the act because it would be effective only for six months.

A 1938 cartoon showing U.S. foreign policy entangled by the serpent of isolationism.

On October 3, 1935, just weeks after Roosevelt signed the Neutrality Act, Italy invaded Ethiopia and the president invoked the Neutrality Act. One shortcoming in its provisions became apparent right away: the key problem was neither weapons traffic nor passenger travel, but trade in war materials not covered by the Neutrality Act. While Italy did not need to buy arms, it did need to buy raw materials, such as oil, which were not covered by the Neutrality Act. So the sanctions imposed under the Neutrality Act had no deterrent effect on Mussolini or his suppliers. In the summer of 1936, Il Duce completed his conquest of Ethiopia.

When Congress reconvened in 1936, it extended the arms embargo and added a provision forbidding loans to nations at war. Then in July 1936, while Italian troops mopped up the last resistance in Ethiopia, the Spanish army led by Francisco Franco revolted against the republican government in Madrid. Ironically, Roosevelt now became more isolationist than some of the isolationists. Although the Spanish Civil War involved a fascist uprising against a recognized, democratic government, Roosevelt accepted the French and British position that only nonintervention would localize the fight. There existed, moreover, a strong bloc of pro-Franco Catholics in America who worried that the Spanish Republic was a threat to the church. They feared an atheistic Communist influence in the Spanish government; intrigues by Spanish Communists did prove divisive and the Soviet Union in fact did supply aid to the Republic, but nothing like the quantity of German and Italian assistance to Franco.

Roosevelt sought another "moral embargo" on the arms trade, and asked Congress to extend the neutrality laws to cover civil wars. Congress did so in 1937 with only one dissenting vote. The Western democracies then stood witness while German and Italian soldiers, planes, and armaments supported Franco's overthrow of Spanish democracy, which was completed in 1939.

In the spring of 1937 isolationist sentiment peaked in the United States. A Gallup poll found that 94 percent of its respondents preferred efforts to keep out of war over efforts to prevent war. That same spring Congress passed the fourth neutrality law. It continued restraints on arms sales and loans, forbade Americans to travel on the ships of nations at war, and prohibited the arming of American merchant ships trading with those nations. The president also won discretionary authority to require that goods other than arms or munitions exported to

Japanese troops enter Beijing after the clash at the Marco Polo Bridge, July 1937.

warring nations be sold on a cash-and-carry basis (that is, the purchaser of the goods would have to pay in cash and then carry them away in its own ships). This was an ingenious scheme to preserve a profitable trade without running the risk of war.

The new law faced its first test in July 1937, when Japanese and Chinese forces clashed at the Marco Polo Bridge west of Peking (Beijing). Since neither side declared war, Roosevelt was able to use his discretion about invoking the neutrality law. He decided to wait, and in fact never invoked it because its net effect would have favored the Japanese. Trade in munitions to China flourished as ships carried arms across the Atlantic to England, where they were reloaded onto British ships bound for Hong Kong. Roosevelt, by inaction, had challenged strict isolationism.

Then, on December 12, 1937, Japanese planes bombed and sank the American gunboat *Panay,* which had been lying at anchor in China on the Yangtze River and prominently flying the American flag; Japan also attacked three Standard Oil tankers. Two members of the *Panay* crew and an Italian journalist died; thirty more were injured. Though the Japanese government apologized and paid reparations, the incident reinforced American animosity toward Japan. The private boycott of

Japanese goods spread, but isolationist sentiment continued strong, as was vividly demonstrated by support for the Ludlow Amendment in Congress. The proposed constitutional amendment would have required a public referendum for a declaration of war except in case of attack on American territory. Only by the most severe pressure from the White House, and a vote of 209 to 188, was consideration of the measure tabled in 1938.

After the German occupation of Czechoslovakia in 1939, Roosevelt no longer pretended impartiality in the impending European struggle. He began trying to educate the American public about the menace of fascism. He urged Congress to repeal the embargo and permit the United States to sell arms on a cash-and-carry basis to Britain and France, but to no avail. When the Germans attacked Poland on September 1, 1939, Roosevelt proclaimed neutrality, but in a radio talk said that he did not, like Woodrow Wilson in 1914, ask Americans to remain neutral in thought because "even a neutral has a right to take account of the facts."

Roosevelt summoned Congress into special session and asked it once again to amend the Neutrality Act. "I regret the Congress passed the Act," the president said. "I regret equally that I signed the Act." This time he got what he wanted, however. Under the Neutrality Act of 1939, Britain and France could send their own freighters to the United States, buy supplies with cash, and take away arms or anything else they wanted. American ships, on the other hand, were excluded from the ports of warring nations and from specified war zones. Roosevelt then designated as a war zone the Baltic Sea and the waters around Great Britain and Ireland from Norway south to the coast of Spain. One effect of this move was to relieve Hitler of any inhibitions against using unrestricted submarine warfare to blockade Britain.

Once the great democracies of western Europe faced war, American public opinion, appalled at Hitler's tyranny, supported measures short of war to help their cause. "What the majority of the American people want," an editor wrote in the *Nation*, "is to be as un-neutral as possible without getting into war." After Hitler overran Poland in less than a month, the war in Europe settled into a stalemate that began to be called the "phony war." What lay ahead, it seemed, was a long war of attrition in which Britain and France would have the resources to outlast Hitler. The illusion lasted through the winter.

The Storm in Europe

BLITZKRIEG   In the spring of 1940 the winter's long *Sitzkrieg* suddenly erupted into *Blitzkrieg*—lightning war. At dawn on April 9, without warning, Nazi troops occupied Denmark and disembarked along the Norwegian coast. Denmark fell in a day, Norway within a few weeks. On May 10 Hitler unleashed his dive bombers and panzer tank divisions on neutral Belgium and the Netherlands. On May 21 German troops reached the English Channel, cutting off a British force sent to help the Belgians and French. A desperate evacuation from the French beaches at Dunkirk enlisted every available British boat from warship to tug. Amid the chaos, some 338,000 men, about a third of them French, escaped to England.

Having outflanked the forts on France's eastern defense perimeter, the Maginot Line, the German forces rushed ahead, cutting the French armies to pieces and spreading panic. On June 14 the swastika flew over Paris. Eight days later, French delegates, in the presence of Hitler, submitted to his terms in the same railroad car in which German delegates had been forced to sign the Armistice of 1918. "The Battle of France is over," Winston Churchill told a somber House of Commons. "I expect that the Battle of Britain is about to begin."

AMERICA'S GROWING INVOLVEMENT   Britain now stood alone, but in Parliament the new prime minister, Winston Churchill, breathed defiance. "We shall go on to the end," he said; "we shall never surrender." Despite the grim resolution of the British, America seemed suddenly vulnerable as Hitler turned his air force against Britain. President Roosevelt called for a military buildup and the production of 50,000 combat planes a year. By October 1940, Congress had voted more than $17 billion for defense. In response to Churchill's appeal for military supplies, the War and Navy Departments reluctantly followed Roosevelt's orders and began releasing stocks of arms, planes, and munitions to the British.

The world crisis transformed Roosevelt. Having been stalemated for much of his second term by congressional opposition, he was revitalized by the war in Europe. Nervous cabinet officers, military leaders, and diplomats now encountered a decisive and forceful president willing to exert executive authority on behalf of Britain. Roosevelt acted with remarkable boldness in the face of an American public that still held staunchly to the doctrine of isolationism. In June 1940 the president set up the National Defense Research Committee to coordinate military research, including a top-secret look into the possibility of developing an atomic bomb, suggested the previous fall by Albert Einstein and other scientists. To bolster national unity, Roosevelt named two Republicans to the defense posts in his cabinet: Henry L. Stimson as secretary of war and Frank Knox as secretary of the navy.

St. Paul's Cathedral looms above the destruction wrought by German bombs during the Blitz. Churchill's response: "We shall never surrender."

The summer of 1940 brought the desperate Battle of Britain, in which the Royal Air Force, with the benefit of the new technology of radar, outfought the numerically superior German Luftwaffe and finally forced the Germans to postpone plans to invade England. Submarine warfare meanwhile strained the resources of the battered Royal Navy. To relieve the pressure, Churchill urgently requested the transfer of American destroyers. Secret negotiations led to an executive agreement under which fifty "overaged" American destroyers went to the British in return for ninety-nine-year American leases on naval and air bases in Newfoundland, Bermuda, the Bahamas, Jamaica, St. Lucia, Trinidad, Antigua, and British Guiana. Roosevelt disguised the action as being necessary for hemisphere defense. On September 16 Congress adopted the first peacetime conscription in American history, requiring the registration of all 16 million men aged twenty-one to thirty-five for a year's military service within the United States.

The new state of affairs prompted vigorous debate between "internationalists," who believed national security demanded aid to Britain, and isolationists, who charged that Roosevelt was drawing the United

States into a needless war. In 1940 the nonpartisan Committee to Defend America by Aiding the Allies was organized. It drew its strongest support from the East and West Coasts and the South. On the other hand, isolationists formed the America First Committee, which included among its members Herbert Hoover and Charles A. Lindbergh, Jr. The isolationists argued that the war involved, in Senator William E. Borah's words, "nothing more than another chapter in the bloody volume of European power politics," and that a Nazi victory, while distasteful, would pose no threat to national security.

A THIRD TERM FOR FDR   In the midst of these terrible global crises, the quadrennial presidential campaign came due. Isolationist sentiment was strongest in the Republican party and both the leading Republican candidates were noninterventionists, but neither loomed as a man of sufficient stature to challenge the "champ," assuming Roosevelt made the unprecedented decision to run for a third term. Senator Robert A. Taft of Ohio, son of the former president, lacked popular appeal, and New York district attorney Thomas E. Dewey, who had won fame as a "racket buster," at thirty-eight seemed young and unseasoned. This left an opening for an inspired group of political amateurs to promote the dark-horse candidacy of Wendell L. Willkie of Indiana.

Willkie seemed at first an unlikely choice: a former Democrat who had voted for Roosevelt in 1932, a utilities president who had fought the TVA, but in origins a Hoosier farm boy whose disheveled charm inspired strong loyalty. Unlike the Republican front-runners, he openly supported aid to the Allies, and the Nazi *Blitzkrieg* had brought many other Republicans to the same viewpoint. When the Republicans met at Philadelphia on June 28, six days after the French surrender, the convention was stampeded by the cry of "We Want Willkie" from the galleries.

The Nazi victory in France also ensured another nomination for Roosevelt. Had war not erupted in Europe, Roosevelt would have probably followed custom and retired after his second term. But the crisis led him to run again. The president cultivated party unity behind his foreign policy and kept a sphinx-like silence about his intentions regarding the war. The world crisis reconciled southern conservatives to the man whose foreign policy, at least, they supported. At the July convention in Chicago Roosevelt won nomination for a third term with only token opposition.

Through the summer Roosevelt assumed the role of a man above the political fray, busy rather with urgent matters of defense and diplomacy: Pan-American agreements for mutual defense, the destroyer-bases deal, and visits to defense facilities that took the place of campaign trips. Willkie was reduced to attacks on New Deal red tape and promises to run the new federal programs better. In the end, however, he switched to an attack on Roosevelt's conduct of foreign policy. In October he warned: "If you re-elect him you may expect war in April, 1941." To this Roosevelt responded, "I have said this before, but I shall say it again and again and again: Your boys are not going to be sent into any foreign wars." Neither man distinguished himself with such hollow statements, since both knew the risks of all-out aid to Britain, which both supported.

Roosevelt won the election by a comfortable margin of 27 million votes to Willkie's 22 million, and a wider margin of 449 to 82 in the electoral college. Even so, it was Roosevelt's narrowest victory. Willkie polled five million more votes than Landon had four years before, a telling indicator of Roosevelt's declining stature. But given the dangerous world situation, a majority of the voters still agreed with the Democrats' slogan: "Don't switch horses in the middle of the stream."

THE "ARSENAL OF DEMOCRACY" Bolstered by the mandate for an unprecedented third term, Roosevelt moved quickly for greater measures to aid Britain. Since the outbreak of war Roosevelt had corresponded with Winston Churchill, the feisty British leader, who soon after the election informed Roosevelt that British cash was fast running out. Since direct American loans would arouse memories of earlier war-debt defaults—the Johnson Act of 1934 forbade such loans anyway—the president created an ingenious device to bypass that issue and yet supply British needs, the "lend-lease" program.

In a fireside radio chat, Roosevelt told the nation that it must become "the great arsenal of democracy" because of the threat of Britain's fall. And this required new efforts to help the British purchase American supplies. The Lend-Lease Bill, introduced in Congress on January 10, 1941, authorized the president to sell, transfer, exchange, lend, lease, or otherwise dispose of arms and other equipment and supplies to "any country whose defense the President deems vital to the defense of the United States."

For two months a bitter debate over the Lend-Lease Bill raged in Congress and the country. Isolationists saw it as the point of no return. "The lend-lease-give program," said Senator Burton K. Wheeler, "is the New Deal's triple A foreign policy; it will plow under every fourth American boy." Roosevelt pronounced this "the rottenest thing that has been said in public life in my generation." Administration supporters denied that lend-lease would lead to war, but it did manifestly increase the risk. Lend-lease became law in March. Almost all of the dissenting votes were Republican senators and congressmen from the staunchly isolationist Midwest.

While the nation debated, the war expanded. Italy had officially entered the war in June 1940 as Germany's ally. In October 1940, when the presidential campaign approached its climax, Mussolini launched attacks on Greece and, from Italian Libya, on the British in Egypt. But he miscalculated, and his forces had to fall back in both cases. In the spring of 1941, German forces under General Erwin Rommel joined the Italians in Libya, forcing the British, whose resources had been drained to help Greece, to withdraw into Egypt. In April 1941 Nazi

Women picketing the White House to urge defeat of the lend-lease program. Like Senator Burton Wheeler they feared that lend-lease would "plow under every fourth American boy."

armored divisions overwhelmed Yugoslavia and Greece, and by the end of May airborne forces subdued the Greek island of Crete, putting Hitler in a position to menace the entire Middle East. With Hungary, Romania, and Bulgaria forced into the Axis fold, Hitler controlled nearly all of Europe.

On June 22, 1941, German armies suddenly fell upon Soviet Russia, their ally. Frustrated in the purpose of subduing Britain, Hitler sought to eliminate the potential threat on his rear with another lightning stroke. The Russian plains offered an ideal theater for *Blitzkrieg,* or so it seemed. With Romanian and Finnish allies, the Nazis massed 3.6 million troops and thousands of tanks and planes along a 2,000-mile front from the Arctic to the Black Sea. Then, after four months, the Russian soldiers rallied in front of Leningrad, Moscow, and Sevastopol. During the winter of 1941–1942, Hitler's legions began to learn the bitter lesson the Russians had taught Napoleon and the French in 1812. Still, in the summer of 1941 the Nazi juggernaut appeared unstoppable.

Winston Churchill had already decided to offer British support to the Soviet Union in case of such an attack. "If Hitler invaded Hell," he said, "I would make at least a favorable reference to the Devil in the House of Commons." Roosevelt adopted the same policy, offering American aid two days after the German attack. Stalinist Russia, so long as it held out, ensured the survival of Britain. American aid was now indispensable to Europe's defense, and the logic of lend-lease led on to deeper American involvement. To deliver aid to Britain, goods had to be maneuvered through the German U-boat "wolf packs" in the North Atlantic. So in April 1941, Roosevelt informed Churchill that the United States Navy would extend its patrol areas in the North Atlantic nearly all the way to Iceland.

In August 1941 Roosevelt and Churchill held a secret naval meeting off Newfoundland, where they drew up a statement of principles known as the Atlantic Charter. It called for the self-determination of all peoples, equal access to raw materials, economic cooperation, freedom of the seas, and a new system of general security. In September it was announced that fifteen anti-Axis nations, including the Soviet Union, had endorsed the statement.

Thus Roosevelt had led the United States into a joint statement of war aims with the anti-Axis powers. It was not long before shooting incidents involved Americans in the North Atlantic. The first attack on an American warship occurred on September 4 when a German submarine fired two torpedoes at the destroyer *Greer*. The president announced a week later orders to "shoot on sight" any German or Italian raiders ("rattlesnakes of the Atlantic") that ventured into American defensive waters. Five days later, the United States Navy began convoying merchant vessels all the way to Iceland.

Then on October 17, while the destroyer *Kearny* was attacking German submarines, it sustained severe damage and loss of eleven lives from a German torpedo. Two weeks later, a submarine torpedoed and sank the destroyer *Reuben James*, with a loss of 115 seamen, while it was on convoy duty west of Iceland. This action hastened Congress into making the changes in the Neutrality Act already requested by the president. On November 17 the legislation was in effect repealed when the bans on arming merchant vessels and allowing them to enter combat zones and the ports of nations at war were removed. Step by step the United States had given up neutrality and embarked on naval warfare against Germany. Still, the American people hoped to avoid taking the final step into all-out war. The decision for war came in an unexpected quarter—the Pacific.

THE STORM IN THE PACIFIC

JAPANESE AGGRESSION   After the Nazi victories in the spring of 1940, America's relations with Japan also took a turn for the worse. Japanese militarists, bogged down in the vastness of China, now eyed new temptations in South Asia: French Indochina (Vietnam, Laos, Cambodia), the Dutch East Indies (Indonesia), British Malaya (Malaysia), and Burma (Myanmar), where they could cut off one of China's last links to the West, the Burma Road. What was more, they could incorporate into their "Greater East Asia Co-Prosperity Sphere" the oil, rubber, and other strategic materials that the crowded Japanese homeland lacked. As it was, Japan depended on the United States for important supplies, including 80 percent of its fuel.

In 1940 Japan and the United States began a series of escalating moves that provoked but failed to restrain the other, all the while pushing each side toward war. During the summer of 1940, Japan forced the helpless French government at Vichy to permit the construction of Japanese airfields in French-controlled northern Indochina and to cut off the railroad into South China. The United States responded with a loan to China and the Export Control Act of July 2, 1940, which authorized the president to restrict the export of arms and other strategic materials to Japan. Gradually Roosevelt extended embargoes on aviation gas, scrap iron, and other supplies.

On September 27, 1940, the Tokyo government signed a Tripartite Pact with Germany and Italy, by which each pledged to declare war on any nation that attacked any of them. The pact could have been directed against either the United States or the Soviet Union. The Germans hoped to persuade Japan to enter Siberia when Nazi forces entered the Soviet Union from the west. The Soviet presence in Siberia did inhibit the Japanese impulse to move southward, but on April 13, 1941, while the Nazis were sweeping through the Balkans, Japan signed a nonaggression pact with the Soviet Union and, once the Nazis invaded Russia in June, the Japanese were freed of any threat from the north.

In July 1941 Japan announced that it was assuming a protectorate over all of French Indochina. Roosevelt took three steps in response: he froze all Japanese assets in the United States; he restricted oil exports to Japan; and he merged the armed forces of the Philippines with the Army of the United States and put their commander, General Douglas MacArthur, in charge of all United States forces in East Asia. By September the oil restrictions had tightened into an embargo. The Japanese estimated that their oil reserves would last two years at most, eighteen months in case of an expanded war. Forced by the embargo to secure other oil supplies, the Japanese army and navy began to perfect plans for attacks on the Dutch and British colonies to the south.

Actions by both sides put the United States and Japan on the way to a war that neither wanted. In his regular talks with the Japanese ambassador, Secretary of State Cordell Hull demanded that Japan withdraw from Indochina and China as the price of renewed trade. A more flexible position might have strengthened the moderates in Japan. The Japanese were not then pursuing a concerted plan of aggression comparable to Hitler's. The Japanese military had stumbled crazily from one act of aggression to another without approval from the government in Tokyo. Premier Fumimaro Konoye, however, while known as a man of

liberal principles who preferred peace, caved in to pressures from the militants. Perhaps he had no choice.

The Japanese warlords, for their part, seriously misjudged the United States. The desperate wish of Americans to stay out of war might still have enabled the Japanese to conquer the British and Dutch colonies before an American decision to act. But the warlords decided that they dared not leave the American navy intact and the Philippines untouched on the flank of their new lifeline to the south.

TRAGEDY AT PEARL HARBOR   Thus a tragedy began to unfold with a fatal certainty—mostly out of sight of the American people, whose attention was focused on the war in the Atlantic. Late in August 1941 Premier Konoye proposed a personal meeting with President Roosevelt. Secretary of State Hull advised Roosevelt not to meet unless agreement on fundamentals could be reached in advance. Soon afterward, on September 6, a Japanese imperial conference approved preparations for a surprise attack on Hawaii and gave Premier Konoye six more weeks to reach a settlement.

The Japanese emperor's clear displeasure with the risks of an attack afforded the premier one last chance to pursue a compromise, but the stumbling block was still the presence of Japanese troops in China. In October Konoye urged War Minister Hideki Tojo to consider withdrawal while saving face by keeping some troops in North China. Tojo countered with his "maximum concession" that Japanese troops would stay no longer than twenty-five years if the United States stopped aiding China. Faced with this rebuff and with Tojo's threat to resign and bring down the cabinet, Konoye himself resigned on October 15; Tojo became premier the next day. The war party now assumed complete control of the government.

On the very day that Tojo became premier, a special Japanese envoy conferred with Hull and Roosevelt in Washington. The envoy's arrival was largely a cover for Japan's war plans, although neither he nor the Japanese ambassador knew that. On November 20 they presented Tojo's final proposal. Japan would occupy no more territory if the United States would cut off aid to China, restore trade, and help Japan get supplies from the Dutch Indies. In that case Japan would pull out of southern Indochina immediately and abandon the remainder once peace had been established with China—presumably on Japanese terms. Tojo expected the United States to refuse such demands. On November 26 Hull repeated the demand that Japan withdraw altogether from China. War now seemed inevitable. "The question," Secretary of War Stimson thought, "was how we should maneuver them into the position of firing the first shot without allowing too much danger to ourselves." That same day a Japanese naval force began heading secretly across the North Pacific toward Pearl Harbor, the key American military base in the Pacific.

Officials in Washington already knew that war was imminent. Reports of Japanese troop transports moving south from Formosa prompted Washington to send warnings to American commanders in the Pacific, and to the British government. The massive movements southward clearly signaled attacks on the British and the Dutch possessions. American leaders had every reason to expect war in the southwest Pacific, but none expected that Japan would commit most of its aircraft carriers to another attack 5,000 miles away at Pearl Harbor.

The Attack on Pearl Harbor. *The view from an American airfield shows the destruction and confusion brought on by the surprise attack.*

In the early morning of December 7, 1941, Americans decoded the last part of a fourteen-part Japanese message breaking off the negotiations. Japan's ambassador was instructed to deliver the message at 1 P.M. (7:30 A.M. in Honolulu), about a half hour before the Japanese attack, but delays held up delivery until more than an hour later than scheduled. The War Department sent out an alert at noon that something was about to happen, but the message, which went by commercial telegraph because radio contacts were broken, arrived in Hawaii eight and a half hours later. Even so, the decoded Japanese message had not mentioned Pearl Harbor, and everyone still assumed that any Japanese move would be in Southeast Asia.

It was still a sleepy Sunday morning when the first Japanese planes roared down the west coast and the central valley of Oahu to begin their assault. For nearly two hours the Japanese planes pummeled an unsuspecting Pacific Fleet. Of the eight battleships in

Pearl Harbor, three were sunk, one grounded, one capsized, and the others badly battered. Altogether nineteen ships were sunk or disabled. At the adjoining Hickam Field and other airfields on the island the Japanese found planes parked wing to wing, and destroyed in all about 180 of them. Few were able to get airborne, and Japanese losses numbered fewer than thirty planes. Before it was over the raid had killed more than 2,400 American servicemen and civilians, and wounded 1,178 more.

The surprise attack fulfilled the dreams of its planners, but it fell short of total success in two ways. The Japanese ignored the onshore facilities and oil tanks in Hawaii that supported the U.S. fleet, without which the surviving ships might have been forced back to the West Coast, and they missed the American aircraft carriers that had fortuitously left a few days earlier. In the naval war to come, these carriers would prove decisive.

Later the same day (December 8 in the western Pacific) Japanese forces invaded the Philippines, Guam, Midway, Hong Kong, and the Malay Peninsula. With one stroke the Japanese had silenced America's debate on neutrality, and a suddenly unified and vengeful nation prepared for the struggle. The next day President Roosevelt delivered his war message to Congress in a speech long remembered by most Americans:

> Yesterday, December 7, 1941—a date which will live in infamy—the United States of America was suddenly and deliberately attacked by naval and air forces of the Empire of Japan. . . .

Congress voted for the war resolution unanimously, with the sole exception of Representative Jeanette Rankin, a pacifist who was unable in good conscience to vote for war in 1917 or 1941. For several days it was uncertain whether war with the other Axis Powers would follow. The Tripartite Pact was ostensibly for defense only, and it carried no obligation for them to enter, but Hitler, impatient with continuing American aid to Britain, willingly joined his Asian allies. On December 11, Germany and Italy impetuously declared war on the United States. The separate wars that were being waged by armies in Asia and Europe had become one global conflict—and American isolationism was cast aside.

MAKING CONNECTIONS

- The United States tried to stake out a neutral position in the growing world conflict. Compare this to earlier American attempts at neutrality, from the Napoleonic Wars era of Jefferson's administration onward.

- The American alliance with the Soviet Union described in this chapter proved to be temporary: after the war, the Americans and the Soviets would be adversaries in a great cold war, the beginnings of which are outlined in Chapter 31.

- The Japanese conquest of French Indochina (Vietnam) would play an important role in the events leading to American involvement in the region, a topic discussed in Chapter 33.

FURTHER READING

The best overview of interwar diplomacy remains Selig Adler's *The Uncertain Giant: American Foreign Policy between the Wars* (1965). Joan Hoff Wilson's *American Business and Foreign Policy, 1920–1933* (1971) highlights the efforts of Republican administrations during the 1920s to promote international commerce. Robert Dallek's *Franklin D. Roosevelt and American Foreign Policy, 1932–1945* (1995) provides a judicious assessment of Roosevelt's foreign policies during the 1930s.

A noteworthy study of America's entry into World War II is Waldo Heinrichs's *Threshold of War: Franklin D. Roosevelt and American Entry into World War II* (1988). Bruce M. Russett's *No Clear and Present Danger* (1972) provides a critical account of American actions.

On Pearl Harbor, see Gordon W. Prange's *Pearl Harbor: The Verdict of History* (1986). Japan's perspective is described in Akira Iriye's *The Origins of World War II in Asia and the Pacific* (1987).

30 ∽ THE SECOND WORLD WAR

CHAPTER ORGANIZER

This chapter focuses on:

- the social and economic effects of World War II, especially in the West.

- how the Allied forces won the war.

- the efforts of the Allies to shape the postwar world.

*T*he Japanese attack on Pearl Harbor ended a period of tense neutrality for the United States, and it launched America into an epochal event that would cost the lives of over 400,000 Americans and transform the nation's social and economic life as well as its position in international affairs. The Second World War would become the most destructive and far-reaching conflict in history. It was so terrible and capricious, so surreal in its intensity and obscene in its cruelties, that it altered the image of war itself. Devilish new instruments of destruction were invented—plastic explosives, flame throwers, proximity fuses, rockets, jet airplanes, and atomic weapons—and systematic genocide emerged as an explicit war aim of the Nazis. Racist propaganda flourished on both sides, and excited hatred of the enemy caused many military and civilian prisoners to be executed. The scorching passions of such an all-out war blanched many moral niceties from the conduct of war. Over 50 million deaths were attributed to the war worldwide, and the physical destruction was incalculable. Whole cities were leveled, nations dismembered, and societies transformed. Latin America was the only region to escape the war's fury. The world is still coping with the consequences of the war.

AMERICA'S EARLY BATTLES

SETBACKS IN THE PACIFIC   For months after the attack on Pearl Harbor, the news from the Pacific was "all bad," as President Roosevelt frankly confessed. In quick sequence the Japanese captured numerous Allied outposts before the end of December 1941: Guam, Wake Island, the Gilbert Islands, and Hong Kong. The fall of Rangoon in Burma (present-day Myanmar) cut off the Burma Road, the main supply route to China. In the Philippines, where General Douglas MacArthur abandoned Manila on December 27, the main American forces, outmanned and outgunned, held out on Bataan Peninsula until April 9, and then on "The Rock," the fortified island of Corregidor. MacArthur slipped away in March, when he was ordered to Australia to take command of Allied forces in the southwest Pacific. By May 6, 1942, when American forces surrendered Corregidor, Japan controlled a new empire that stretched from Burma eastward through the Dutch East Indies (present-day Indonesia) and extending to Wake Island and the Gilberts.

American prisoners of war, captured by the Japanese in the Philippines, 1942.

The Japanese might have consolidated an almost impregnable empire with the resources they had seized. But the Japanese navy succumbed to what one of its admirals later called "victory disease." Its leaders resolved to push on into the South Pacific, isolate Australia, and strike again at Hawaii. Japanese planners hoped to draw out and destroy the American navy before the productive power of the United States could be brought to bear on the war effort.

A Japanese mistake and a stroke of American luck, however, enabled the United States Navy to frustrate the plan. Japan's failure to destroy the shore facilities at Pearl Harbor left the base relatively intact, and most of the ships damaged on December 7 lived to fight another day. The aircraft carriers at sea during the attack spent several months harassing Japanese outposts. Their most spectacular exploit, an air raid on Tokyo itself, was launched on April 18, 1942. B-25 bombers took off from the carrier *Hornet* and, unable to land on its deck, proceeded to China. The raid caused only token damage but did much to lift American morale amid a series of defeats elsewhere.

CORAL SEA AND MIDWAY   American forces finally halted the Japanese advance toward Australia in two decisive naval battles. The Battle of the Coral Sea (May 7–8, 1942) stopped a fleet convoying Japanese troop transports toward New Guinea. The Japanese sought to gain control of the Coral Sea and thereby isolate Australia. Planes from the *Lexington* and *Yorktown* sank one Japanese carrier, damaged another, and destroyed smaller ships. American losses were greater, but the Japanese threat against Australia was repulsed.

Less than a month after the Coral Sea engagement, Admiral Isoruku Yamamoto, the Japanese naval commander, decided to force a showdown in the central Pacific. He wanted to inflict a major defeat on the American navy that might force the United States to seek a negotiated peace. With nearly every ship under his command, he headed for Midway Island, from which he hoped to render Pearl Harbor helpless. This time it was the Japanese who were the victims of surprise. American cryptanalysts had by then broken the Japanese naval code, and Admiral Chester Nimitz, commander of the central Pacific, knew what was up. He reinforced Midway with planes and carriers.

The first Japanese foray against Midway, on June 4, 1942, severely damaged the island's defenses, but at the cost of about a third of the Japanese planes. American torpedo planes and dive bombers struck back before another Japanese attack could be mounted. The Japanese lost their four best aircraft carriers; the Americans, a carrier and a destroyer. The Japanese navy was forced into retreat less than six months after the attack on Hawaii. Midway was the turning point of the Pacific war. It demonstrated that aircraft carriers, not battleships, were the decisive elements of modern naval warfare.

SETBACKS IN THE ATLANTIC   Early American setbacks in the Pacific were matched by setbacks in the Atlantic. Since the *Blitzkrieg* of 1940, German submarine "wolf packs" had wreaked havoc in the North Atlantic. In 1942, after an ominous lull, German submarines suddenly appeared off American shores and began to sink coastal shipping. Nearly 400 ships were lost in American waters before effective countermeasures brought the problem under control. The naval command accelerated the building of small escort vessels, meanwhile pressing into patrol service all kinds of surface craft and planes, some of them civilian. During the second half of 1942, the losses diminished to a negligible number.

MOBILIZATION AT HOME

The Pearl Harbor attack ended not only the long debate between isolation and intervention but also the long depression that had ravaged the economy in the 1930s. The war effort would require all of America's immense productive capacity and full employment of the workforce.

Mobilization was in fact already further along than preparedness had been in 1916–1917. The Selective Service had been in effect for more than a year, and the army had grown to more than 1.4 million men by July 1941. With America's entry into the war, men between eighteen and forty-five now became subject to the draft. The average soldier or sailor was twenty-six years old, stood five feet eight inches, and weighed 144 pounds, an inch taller and eight pounds heavier than the typical recruit in World War I. Less than half of the GIs had finished high school. Altogether more than 15 million men and women would serve in the armed forces over the course of the conflict.

ECONOMIC CONVERSION   The economy, too, was already partially mobilized by lend-lease and defense efforts. The War Powers Act of 1941 had given the president the authority to reshuffle government

Mobilization for war deflected many New Deal programs.

agencies, and a Second War Powers Act empowered the government to allot materials and facilities as needed for defense, with penalties for those who failed to comply.

The War Production Board (WPB), created in 1942 on the model of its counterpart during the First World War, directed the conversion of industrial manufacturing to war production. Auto makers switched to producing tanks, shirt factories began to make mosquito netting, and the manufacturers of refrigerators, stoves, and cash registers began to produce munitions. The Reconstruction Finance Corporation, a New Deal agency, financed the construction of war plants. Roosevelt established staggering production goals: 60,000 warplanes in 1942 and twice as many the following year; 55,000 anti-aircraft guns; and tens of thousands of tanks. His purpose was to confront the enemy with a "crushing superiority of equipment."

The war effort required conservation as well as production. "Use it up, wear it out, make do or do without," became the prevailing slogan encouraging the public to sacrifice on behalf of the war effort. People collected scrap metal and grew their own food in backyard "victory gardens." Tire and gasoline rationing began in earnest. Through the Office of Scientific

Research and Development, Dr. Vannevar Bush mobilized thousands of scientists to create and modify radar, sonar, the proximity fuse, the bazooka, means to isolate blood plasma, and numerous other innovations.

The pressure of wartime needs and the stimulus of government spending sent the gross national product soaring from $100 billion in 1940 to $214 billion in 1945, a rise of 114 percent. The figure for total government expenditures was twice as great as the total of all previous federal spending in the history of the republic, about 10 times what America spent in World War I, and 100 times the expenditures during the Civil War.

FINANCING THE WAR   To cover the war's huge cost the president preferred raising taxes to borrowing. The wartime Congress, however, dominated by conservatives, feared taxes more than deficits and refused to go more than halfway with Roosevelt's fiscal prudence. The Revenue Act of 1942 provided for only about $7 billion in increased revenue, less than half that recommended by the Treasury. It also greatly broadened the tax structure. Whereas in 1939 only about 4 million people filed returns, the new act made everyone a taxpayer.

The federal government paid for about 45 percent of its 1939–1946 costs with tax revenues. Roosevelt would have preferred to cover more, but the figure compared favorably with 30 percent for World War I and 23 percent for the Civil War. To cover the rest of its costs, the government borrowed from the public. War-bond drives, including a Victory Drive in 1945, induced citizens to invest more than $150 billion in bonds. Financial institutions picked up most of the rest of the government's debt. In all, by the end of the war the national debt had grown to about $260 billion, about six times its size at the time of Pearl Harbor.

The basic economic problem was no longer finding jobs but finding workers for the booming shipyards, aircraft factories, and gunpowder mills. Millions of people, especially women, who had lived on the margin of the economic system were now brought fully into the economy. Stubborn pockets of poverty did not disappear, but for most of those who stayed home the war spelled neither hardship nor suffering but a better life than ever before, despite shortages and rationing.

ECONOMIC CONTROLS   Increased family incomes and government spending during the war raised the specter of inflation. Some of the available money went into taxes and war bonds, but even so, more was sent chasing after consumer goods just as production was converting to war needs. Consumer durables such as cars, washing machines, and nondefense housing in fact ceased to be made at all. It was apparent that only strict restraints would keep prices of scarce commodities from soaring out of sight. In 1942, Congress authorized the Office of Price Administration (OPA) to set price ceilings. With prices frozen, goods had to be allocated through rationing, with coupons doled out for sugar, coffee, gasoline, automobile tires, and meats.

Wages and farm prices, however, were not controlled, and this complicated things. War prosperity offered farmers a chance to recover from two decades of distress, and farm-state congressmen fought successfully to raise both floors and ceilings on farm prices. Higher food prices reinforced worker demands for higher wages, but the War Labor Board tried to hold the line. Finally, under the Stabilization Act of 1942, the president won new authority to control wages and farm prices. At the same time, he set up the Office of Economic Stabilization under James F. Byrnes, who left his seat on the Supreme Court to coordinate the effort. Stabilization proved to be one of the most complex jobs of the war effort, subject to constant sniping by special interests.

Both businesses and workers chafed at the wage and price controls. On occasion the government seized industries threatened by strike. The coal mines and railroads both came under government operation for a short time in 1943, and in 1944 the government briefly took over the Montgomery-Ward Company. Soldiers had to carry its chairman bodily out of his office when he stubbornly defied orders of the War Labor Board. Despite these problems, the government effort to stabilize wages and prices succeeded. By the end of the war, consumer prices had risen about 31 percent, a record far better than the World War I rise of 62 percent.

DOMESTIC CONSERVATISM Despite government efforts to promote patriotic sacrifice among the public, discontent with price controls, labor shortages, rationing, and a hundred other petty vexations spread. In 1942 the congressional elections registered a national swing against the New Deal. Republicans gained forty-six seats in the House and nine in the Senate, chiefly in the farm areas of the midwestern states. Democratic losses outside the South strengthened the southern delegation's position within the party, and the delegation itself reflected conservative victories in southern primaries. A coalition of conservatives proceeded to dismantle "nonessential" New Deal agencies. In 1943 Congress abolished the Works Progress Administration, the National Youth Administration, the Civilian Conservation Corps, and the National Resources Planning Board.

Organized labor, despite substantial gains during the war, felt the impact of the conservative trend. In the spring of 1943, when John L. Lewis led the coal miners out on strike, Congress passed the Smith-Connally War Labor Disputes Act, which authorized the government to seize plants useful to the war. In 1943 a dozen states adopted laws variously restricting picketing and other union activities, and in 1944 Arkansas and Florida set in motion a wave of "right-to-work" legislation that outlawed the closed shop (requiring that all employees be union members).

SOCIAL EFFECTS OF THE WAR

MOBILIZATION AND THE DEVELOPMENT OF THE WEST The dramatic expansion of defense production after 1940 and the mobilization of millions of men into the armed forces accelerated economic development and the population boom in the western states. Nearly 8 million people moved into the states west of the Mississippi River between 1940 and 1950. The Far West experienced the fastest rate of urban growth in the country. Small cities such as Phoenix and Albuquerque mushroomed, while Seattle, San Francisco, Los Angeles, and San Diego witnessed dizzying growth. San Diego's population, for example, increased by 147 percent between 1941 and 1945.

Abundant jobs at high wages enticed people to the western states. California alone garnered 10 percent of all the defense contracts during the war years. In Texas, manufacturing employment almost doubled between 1940 and 1945. Los Angeles, which in 1939 was the seventh largest manufacturing center in the nation, had by 1943 become second only to Detroit in industrial activity. City services could not keep up with the influx of workers and military personnel. Employees at Seattle's shipyards and the Boeing airplane plant lived in tents because of a housing shortage. To address the problem, Congress authorized financing for over a million new temporary housing units across the country. Yet this federal housing program did not meet the demand. Some women workers at a San Diego defense plant lived eight to a room in a company dormitory.

The migration of workers to new defense jobs in the West had significant demographic effects. Communities that earlier had few African Americans witnessed an influx of blacks. Lured by news of job openings and higher wages, African Americans from Texas, Oklahoma, Arkansas, and Louisiana headed west. During the war years Seattle's black population jumped from 4,000 to 40,000, Portland's from 2,000 to 15,000.

CHANGING ROLES FOR WOMEN   The war marked an important watershed in the changing status of women. The proportion of women working had barely altered from 1910 to 1940, but with millions of men going into military service, the demand for labor shook up old prejudices about sex roles in the workplace—and in the military.

Nearly 200,000 women served in the Women's Army Corps (WAC) and the navy's equivalent, Women Accepted for Volunteer Emergency Service (WAVES). Lesser numbers joined the Marine Corps, the Coast Guard, and the Army Air Force. Over 6 million women entered the workforce during the war, an increase of over 50 percent and in manufacturing alone of some 110 percent. Old barriers fell overnight as women became toolmakers, machinists, crane operators, lumberjacks, stevedores, blacksmiths, and railroad track workers.

By 1944 women made up 14 percent of all workers in shipbuilding and 40 percent in aircraft plants. The government launched an intense publicity campaign to draw

Women in the Military. *This navy recruiting poster urged women to join the WAVES (Women Accepted for Volunteer Emergency Service).*

women into traditional male jobs. "Do your part, free a man for service," one ad pleaded. "Rosie the Riveter," a beautiful model dressed in overalls, became the cover girl for the recruiting campaign.

One striking feature of the new labor scene was the larger proportion of older, married women in the workforce. In 1940 about 15 percent of married women went into gainful employment; by 1945 it was 24 percent. In the workforce as a whole, married women for the first time outnumbered single women.

Many men opposed this new trend. One disgruntled male legislator asked what would happen to traditional domestic tasks if women flocked to factories: "Who will do the cooking, the washing, the mending, the humble homey tasks to which every woman has devoted herself; who will rear and nurture the children?" Many women, however, were eager to get away from the grinding routine of domestic life. One female welder remembered that her wartime job "was the first time I had a chance to get out of the kitchen and work in industry and make a few bucks. This was something I had never dreamed would happen." And it was something that many women did not want to relinquish after the war.

EXPANDED PARTICIPATION OF BLACKS   The most volatile issue ignited by the war was African-American participation in the defense effort. From the start, black leaders demanded full recognition in the armed forces and defense industries. Eventually about a million African Americans served in the armed forces, but usually in segregated units. Every army camp had separate facilities and periodic racial "incidents." The most important departure was a 1940 decision to integrate officer candidate schools, except those for air force cadets. A separate flight school at Tuskegee, Alabama, trained about 600 black pilots, many of whom distinguished themselves in combat.

War industries were even less hospitable to black influence and participation. "We will not employ Negroes," said the president of North American Aviation. In 1941 A. Philip Randolph, the tall, gentlemanly head of the Brotherhood of Sleeping Car Porters, organized a March on Washington Movement to demand an end to racial discrimination in defense industries. The administration then struck a bargain. The Randolph group called off its march in return for an executive order that forbade discrimination in defense work and training

Tuskegee Airmen, 1942. *One of the last segregated military training schools, the flight school at Tuskegee trained African-American men for combat during World War II.*

programs by requiring a nondiscrimination clause in defense contracts, and set up the Fair Employment Practices Commission (FEPC). The FEPC's authority was chiefly moral, since it had no power to enforce directives. It nevertheless offered willing employers the chance to say they were following government policy in giving jobs to black citizens.

Blacks quickly broadened their drive for wartime participation into a more inclusive social and political front. Early in 1942 the *Pittsburgh Courier* endorsed the "Double V," which stood for victory at home and abroad. The slogan became immensely popular in black communities, and blacks began to challenge more openly all kinds of discrimination, including racial segregation itself. Membership in the NAACP grew during the war from 50,000 to 450,000. Blacks could look forward to greater political participation after the Supreme Court, in *Smith* v. *Allwright* (1944), struck down Texas's white primary on the ground that Democratic primaries were part of the election process and thus subject to the Fifteenth Amendment.

The growing militancy of blacks promoting civil rights aroused antagonism from some whites. Racial violence during this period did not approach the level of that in World War I, but growing tensions on a hot summer afternoon in Detroit sparked incidents at a park. Fighting raged through June 20–21, 1943, until federal troops arrived on the second evening. Twenty-five blacks and nine whites had been killed.

HISPANICS IN THE LABOR FORCE   As rural folk moved to the western cities, the farm counties experienced a labor shortage. In an ironic about-face, local and federal government authorities who before the war strove to force Mexican alien laborers back across the border now recruited them to harvest crops. The Mexican government, however, first insisted that the United States ensure minimum work and living conditions before it would assist in providing the needed workers. The result was the creation of the *bracero* program in 1942. Mexico agreed to provide seasonal farm workers in exchange for a promise by the American government not to draft them into military service. The workers were hired on year-long contracts that offered wages at the prevailing rate, and American officials provided transportation from the border to their job sites. Under this *bracero* program, some 200,000 Mexican farm workers entered the western United States. At least that many more crossed the border as illegal aliens.

This population influx created new tensions. The rising tide of Mexican Americans in Los Angeles provoked a growing stream of anti-Hispanic editorials and incidents. Even though Mexican Americans fought in the war with great valor, earning seventeen Congressional Medals of Honor, there was constant conflict between servicemen and Mexican-American gang members and teenage "zoot-suiters" in southern California. "Zoot suits" were the flamboyant clothes worn by some young Mexican-American men. In 1943, several thousand off-duty sailors and soldiers, joined by hundreds of local white civilians, rampaged through downtown Los Angeles streets, assaulting Hispanics, blacks, and Filipinos. The violence lasted a week and came to be labeled the "zoot suit" riots.

NATIVE AMERICANS AND THE WAR EFFORT   Indians may have supported the war effort more fully than any other group in American society. Almost a third of eligible Native American men, over 25,000 people, served in the armed forces. Another one-fourth worked in defense-related industries. Thousands of Indian women volunteered as nurses or joined the WAVES (Women Accepted for Volunteer Emergency Service). As was the case with African Americans, Indians benefited from the broadening experiences afforded by the war. Those who left reservations to work in defense plants or to join the military gained new vocational skills as well as a greater awareness of American society and how to succeed within it.

Why did Native Americans fight for a nation that had stripped them of their lands and decimated their heritage? Some felt that they had no choice. Mobilization for the war effort ended many New Deal programs that had provided Indians with jobs. Reservation Indians thus faced the necessity of finding new jobs elsewhere. Many viewed the Nazis and Japanese warlords as threats to their own homeland. The most common sentiment, however, seems to have been a genuine sense of patriotism.

Whatever the reasons, Indians distinguished themselves in the military during the war. Unlike their African-American counterparts, Indian servicemen were integrated within the regular units. Perhaps the most distinctive activity performed by Indians was their service as "code talkers." Every military branch used Indians—Oneidas, Chippewas, Sauks, Foxes, Comanches, and Navajos—to encode and decipher messages.

INTERNMENT OF JAPANESE AMERICANS   The record on civil liberties during World War II was on the whole better than that during World War I, if only because there was virtually no domestic opposition to the war effort after the attack on Pearl Harbor. Neither German Americans nor Italian Americans faced the harassments meted out to their counterparts in the previous war; few had much sympathy for Hitler or Mussolini. The shameful exception to an otherwise improved record was the treatment given to more than 100,000 Americans of Japanese descent (Nisei), who were forcibly removed from homes and businesses on the West Coast and transported to "War Relocation Camps" in the interior. Caught up in the war hysteria and racial prejudice provoked by the attack on Pearl Harbor, President Roosevelt initiated the removal of Japanese Americans when he issued Executive Order 9066 on February 19, 1942. More than 60 percent of the internees were U.S. citizens; a third were under the age of nineteen. Forced to sell their farms and businesses at great losses, the internees lost not

This young Japanese American and her parents are being forced to relocate from Los Angeles to Owens Valley, 1942.

only their liberty but also their property. Few, if any, were disloyal, but all were victims of fear and racial prejudice.

This was especially the case in the months following the attack on Pearl Harbor. Idaho's governor declared: "A good solution to the Jap problem would be to send them all back to Japan, then sink the island." As one Japanese American poignantly complained, "What really hurts most is the constant reference to us evacuees as 'Japs.' 'Japs' are the guys we are fighting. We're on this side and we want to help. Why won't America let us?" Many did support the effort. Japanese-American Hawaiians and mainlanders made up two of the most celebrated infantry units in the war, fighting with distinction on the Italian front. Other thousands of Nisei served as interpreters and translators, the "eyes and ears" of the American armed forces in the Pacific. Not until 1983 did the government finally recognize the injustice of the internment policy. That year it authorized granting those Nisei still living $20,000 each in compensation.

THE ALLIED DRIVE TOWARD BERLIN

By mid-1942, the "home front" began to get news from the war fronts that some of the lines were holding at last. Japanese naval losses at the Coral Sea and Midway had secured Australia and Hawaii. By mid-year a motley fleet of American air and sea sub-chasers was ending six months of happy hunting for German U-boats off the Atlantic coast. This was all the more important because war plans called for the defeat of Germany first.

WAR AIMS AND STRATEGY   There were many reasons for giving top priority to defeating Hitler. Nazi forces in western Europe and the Atlantic posed a more direct threat to the Western Hemisphere; German war potential was greater than Japan's, and German science was more likely to come up with some devastating new weapon. Lose in the Atlantic, General George Marshall grimly predicted, and you lose everywhere. Despite such assumptions, Japanese attacks involved Americans directly in the Pacific war from the start, and as a consequence, during the first year of fighting more Americans went to the Pacific than across the Atlantic.

The Pearl Harbor attack brought British prime minister Winston Churchill to Washington for lengthy talks about a common war plan. Thus began a wartime alliance between the United States and Great Britain, a partnership marked almost as much by disagreement and suspicion as it was by common purposes. As Churchill later remarked, "There is only one thing worse than fighting with allies, and that is fighting without them." Although he and Roosevelt admired each other, they disagreed about military strategy and the likely makeup of the postwar world.

Initially, at least, such differences of opinion were masked by the need to make basic decisions related to the conduct of the war. In Washington on January 1, 1942, representatives of twenty-six governments then at war with the Axis signed the Declaration of the United Nations, affirming the principles of the Atlantic Charter, pledging their full resources to the war, and promising not to make separate peace with the common enemies. The meetings between Churchill and Roosevelt in Washington in 1942 produced several major decisions, including the one to name a supreme commander in each major theater of war. Each commander would be subject to orders from the British-American Combined Chiefs of Staff. Other joint boards allotted munitions, raw materials, and shipping. Finally, in the course of their talks, the British and American leaders reaffirmed the priority of war against Germany.

Agreement on war aims, however, did not bring agreement on strategy. Roosevelt and Churchill, meeting at the White House again in June 1942, could not agree on where to hit first. American military planners wanted to strike directly across the English Channel before the end of 1942, secure a beachhead in France, and move against

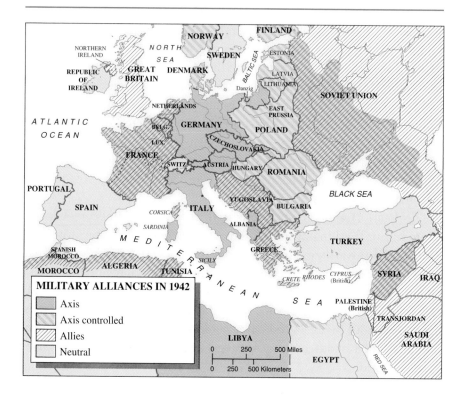

NORWAY · FINLAND
NORTHERN IRELAND · NORTH SEA · SWEDEN · ESTONIA
REPUBLIC OF IRELAND · GREAT BRITAIN · DENMARK · LATVIA · LITHUANIA
Danzig
BALTIC SEA
SOVIET UNION
ATLANTIC OCEAN · NETHERLANDS · EAST PRUSSIA
BELG. · GERMANY · POLAND
LUX.
FRANCE · CZECHOSLOVAKIA
SWITZ · AUSTRIA · HUNGARY · ROMANIA
PORTUGAL · YUGOSLAVIA · BLACK SEA
SPAIN · CORSICA · ITALY · BULGARIA
SARDINIA · ALBANIA
MEDITERRANEAN · TURKEY
SPANISH MOROCCO · SICILY · GREECE
MOROCCO · ALGERIA · TUNISIA · CRETE · RHODES · CYPRUS (British) · SYRIA · IRAQ

MILITARY ALLIANCES IN 1942
- Axis
- Axis controlled
- Allies
- Neutral

SEA · PALESTINE (British)
TRANSJORDAN
LIBYA · SAUDI ARABIA
0 250 500 Miles
0 250 500 Kilometers
EGYPT
RED SEA

Germany in 1943. The British preferred to keep the Germans off balance with hit-and-run raids and air attacks while continuing to build up their forces. With vivid memories of the last war, the British feared a mass bloodletting in trench warfare if they struck prematurely. The Russians, bearing the brunt of the German attack in the east, insisted that the Western Allies must do something to relieve the pressure. Finally, the Americans accepted Churchill's proposal to invade French North Africa.

THE NORTH AFRICA CAMPAIGN   On November 8, 1942, British and American forces under the command of American general Dwight D. Eisenhower landed at Casablanca in Morocco and at Oran and Algiers in Algeria. Completely surprised, French forces under the Vichy government (which collaborated with the Germans) had little will to resist. Hitler therefore occupied the whole of France and sent German forces into French Tunisia. By chance Admiral Jean-François Darlan, second to Marshal Pétain in the collaborationist Vichy government, was visiting in Algiers and was persuaded by the Allies to order a cease-fire.

Farther east, General Bernard Montgomery's British forces were pushing the brilliant German tank commander General Erwin Rommel back across Libya, and green American forces confronted seasoned Nazis pouring into Tunisia. Before spring, however, Montgomery had taken Libya, and the Germans were caught in a gigantic pincers. Hammered from all sides, unable to retreat across the Mediterranean, an army of 275,000 surrendered on May 13, 1943, leaving all of North Africa in Allied hands.

While the battle of Tunisia unfolded, in January 1943 Roosevelt and Churchill and the Combined Chiefs of Staff met at Casablanca. Stalin declined to leave Russia for the meeting but continued to press for a second front in western Europe. For the time, however, they decided to postpone the cross-Channel invasion and invade Sicily. Meanwhile, Admiral Chester Nimitz and General Douglas MacArthur were authorized to start an offensive to dislodge the Japanese from the Pacific islands. Top priority, however, went to an antisubmarine campaign in the Atlantic.

Before leaving Casablanca, Roosevelt announced, with Churchill's endorsement, that the war would end only with the "unconditional surrender" of all enemies. This decision was designed to quiet Soviet suspicions that the Western Allies might negotiate separately with the enemy. The announcement owed a good bit also to the determination that, as Roosevelt put it, "every person in Germany should realize that this time Germany is a defeated nation." This dictum was later criticized for having stiffened enemy resistance, but it probably had little effect; in fact neither the Italian nor the Japanese surrender would be totally unconditional. But the decision did have one unexpected result: it opened an avenue for eventual Soviet control of eastern Europe because it required Russian armies to pursue Hitler's forces all the way to Germany. And as they liberated the countries of eastern Europe, the Soviets created new governments in their own image.

THE BATTLE OF THE ATLANTIC While fighting raged in North Africa, the more crucial Battle of the Atlantic reached its climax on the high seas. By early 1943 there were in the western half of the North

Major-General George S. Patton, commander of American invasion forces on Sicily.

Atlantic at any one time an average of 31 convoys with 145 escorts and 673 merchant ships, and a number of heavily escorted troopships. None of the troopships going to Britain or the Mediterranean was lost. Patrols by land-based planes covered much of the Atlantic from airfields in Britain, the Azores, and elsewhere. The U-boats kept up the Battle of the Atlantic until the war's end; when Germany finally collapsed, at least forty-nine were still at sea. But their commander later admitted that the Battle of the Atlantic was lost by the end of May 1943. He credited the difference largely to radar. What he did not know then was that the Allies had a secret weapon. By early 1943 their cryptanalysts were routinely decoding secret messages and telling their sub-hunters where to look for German U-boats.

SICILY AND ITALY On July 10, 1943, after the Allied victory in North Africa, about 250,000 British and American troops landed on Sicily. It was the largest single amphibious action in the war to that time. The entire island was in Allied hands by August 17, although some 40,000 Germans escaped to the mainland. Allied success in Sicily ended Mussolini's twenty years of fascist rule. Italians had never had much heart for the war into which he had dragged them. On July 25, 1943, Italy's King Victor Emmanuel III dismissed Mussolini as premier. A new regime startled the Allies when it offered not only to surrender but to switch sides in the war. Unfortunately, mutual suspicions prolonged talks until September 3, while the Germans poured reinforcements into Italy and seized key points. In the confusion the Italian army disintegrated, although most of the navy escaped to Allied ports. A few army units later joined the Allied effort. Mussolini, plucked from imprisonment by a daring German airborne raid, became head of a shadowy puppet government in northern Italy.

Allied landings on the Italian mainland therefore did not turn into a walkover. Although American and British troops secured beachheads within a week and soon captured Naples, fighting stalled in the Apennine Mountains. Finally, on June 4, 1944, the U.S. Fifth Army entered Rome. The capture of Rome provided only a brief moment of glory, however, for the long-awaited cross-Channel landing in France came two days later. Italy, always a secondary front, faded from the limelight of world attention.

"Joe, yestiddy ya saved my life an' I swore I'd pay ya back. Here's my last pair of dry socks." *From Bill Mauldin's "Willie and Joe," a cartoon strip that appeared in the GI newspaper* Yank, *about two infantrymen slogging their way through the Italian campaign.*

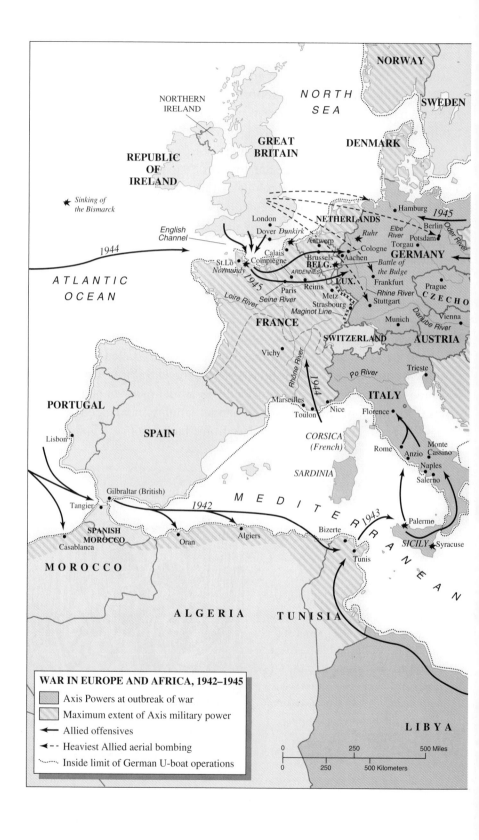

NORTHERN
IRELAND

NORTH
SEA

NORWAY

SWEDEN

GREAT
BRITAIN

DENMARK

REPUBLIC
OF
IRELAND

★ *Sinking of
the Bismarck*

*English
Channel*

London
Dover *Dunkirk*

NETHERLANDS

Hamburg *1945*

Berlin

Elbe
River

Potsdam

Ruhr

Antwerp

Cologne

Torgau

GERMANY

ATLANTIC

OCEAN

1944

Calais
St.Lô Compiègne
Normandy

Brussels
BELG.
ARDENNES

Aachen

*Battle of
the Bulge*

Frankfurt

Prague

CZECHO

1945

Paris

Reims

LUX.

Metz

Rhine River

Loire River

Seine River

Strasbourg

Stuttgart

Maginot Line

Munich

Danube River

Vienna

FRANCE

Vichy

SWITZERLAND

AUSTRIA

Rhône River

Po River

Trieste

1944

ITALY

PORTUGAL

Marseilles

Toulon

Nice

Florence

SPAIN

CORSICA
(French)

Rome

Monte
Cassino

Anzio

Lisbon

Naples

SARDINIA

Salerno

Gibraltar (British)

M E D I T E R R

1942

Tangier

SPANISH
MOROCCO

Casablanca

Oran

Algiers

Bizerte

1943

Palermo

SICILY ★ Syracuse

Tunis

MOROCCO

A N E A N

ALGERIA

TUNISIA

LIBYA

WAR IN EUROPE AND AFRICA, 1942–1945

Axis Powers at outbreak of war

Maximum extent of Axis military power

← Allied offensives

◄--- Heaviest Allied aerial bombing

········· Inside limit of German U-boat operations

0   250   500 Miles

0   250   500 Kilometers

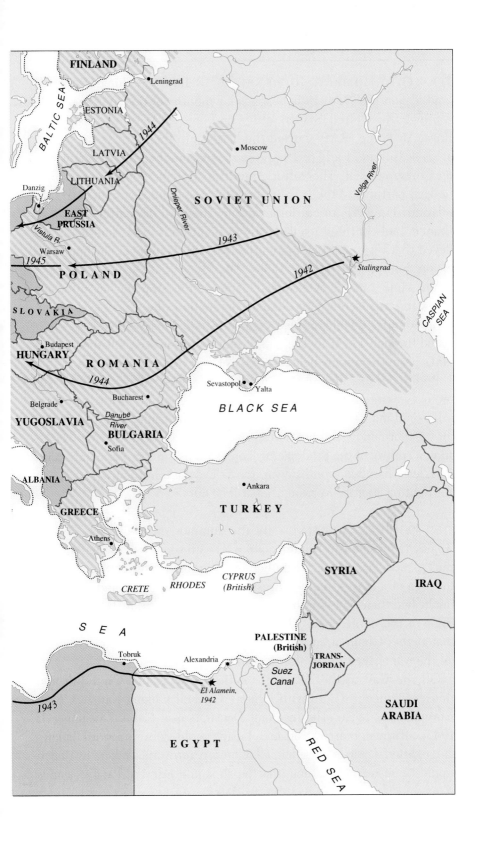

FINLAND

BALTIC SEA

•Leningrad

ESTONIA

LATVIA

1944

LITHUANIA

Danzig

•Moscow

SOVIET UNION

Dnieper River

Volga River

EAST
PRUSSIA

Vistula R.

Warsaw •

1945

1943

★ Stalingrad

POLAND

1942

CASPIAN
SEA

SLOVAKIA

Budapest •

HUNGARY

ROMANIA

1944

Sevastopol •
• Yalta

Belgrade •

Bucharest •

BLACK SEA

YUGOSLAVIA

Danube
River

BULGARIA

Sofia •

ALBANIA

GREECE

• Ankara

TURKEY

Athens •

CYPRUS
(British)

CRETE   RHODES

SYRIA

IRAQ

S E A

Tobruk •

Alexandria •

PALESTINE
(British)

TRANS-
JORDAN

★
El Alamein,
1942

Suez
Canal

SAUDI
ARABIA

1943

EGYPT

RED SEA

STRATEGIC BOMBING OF EUROPE   Behind the long-postponed landings on the Normandy beaches lay months of preparation. While waiting, the United States Army Air Force (AAF) and the British Royal Air Force (RAF) carried the battle into the German-controlled areas of Europe. Early in 1943 Americans launched their first air raid on Germany itself. Thereafter, American strategic bombers were full-fledged partners of the RAF in the effort to pound Germany into sub-mission. The RAF, to cut losses during the hard days after the fall of France, had confined itself mostly to night raids. The Americans believed that they could be more effective with high-level daylight "precision" bombing.

Yet while causing widespread damage, the strategic air offensive failed to cut severely into German production; the strikes also, some contend, were unable to break civilian morale. Heavy Allied losses persisted through 1943. By the end of that year, however, jettisonable gas tanks permitted escort fighters to go as far as Berlin and back.

Berlin became the object of repeated Allied raids. With air supremacy assured, the Allies were free to concentrate on their primary urban and industrial targets, and when the time came, to provide cover for the Normandy landings. On April 14, 1944, General Eisenhower assumed control of the Strategic Air Forces for use in the Normandy landings, less than two months away. On D-Day he told the troops: "If you see fighting aircraft over you, they will be ours."

THE TEHERAN MEETING   By the summer of 1943, the growing American presence in Britain, combined with successes in the Battle of the Atlantic and the strategic bombing, brought Churchill around on the idea of a cross-Channel invasion. Late in the fall he and Roosevelt finally had their first joint meeting with Joseph Stalin, in Teheran, Iran. Prior to the conference, when England and America gave assurance that a cross-Channel invasion was coming, the Soviets promised to enter the war against Japan after Germany's defeat.

On the way to the Teheran meeting with Stalin, Churchill and Roosevelt met in Cairo with China's General Chiang Kai-shek from November 22 to 26. The resultant Declaration of Cairo (December 1, 1943) affirmed that war against Japan would continue until Japan's unconditional surrender, that all Chinese territories taken by Japan would be restored to China, that Japan would lose the Pacific islands acquired after 1941, and that "in due course Korea shall become free and independent."

From November 28 to December 1, the Big Three leaders conferred in Teheran. Their chief subject was the planned invasion of France and a Russian offensive timed to coincide with it. Stalin repeated his promise to enter the war against Japan, and the three leaders agreed to create an international organization to maintain peace after the war.

D-DAY AND AFTER   In early 1944 General Dwight D. Eisenhower arrived in London to take command at Supreme Headquarters, Allied Expeditionary Forces (SHAEF). Already battle-tested in North Africa and the Mediterranean, he now faced the supreme task of planning and conducting Operation "Overlord," the cross-Channel assault on Hitler's "Atlantic Wall." German forces using captive Europeans for laborers had created what seemed to be an impregnable series of fortifications along the French coastline.

The prospect of an amphibious assault against such defenses in a single huge battle unnerved some of the Allied planners. As D-Day approached, Eisenhower's chief of staff predicted only a 50-50 chance of success. Operation Overlord prevailed largely because Eisenhower and the Allies surprised the Germans. They fooled Hitler's generals into believing that the invasion would come at Pas de Calais, on the French-Belgian border, where the English Channel was narrowest. Instead, the landings occurred in Normandy, almost 200 miles south. In April and May 1944, while the vast invasion forces made final preparations, the Allied air forces disrupted the transportation network of northern France, smashing railroads and bridges. By early June all was ready, and D-Day fell on June 6, 1944.

On the evening of June 5, Eisenhower visited some of the 16,000 American paratroopers preparing to land behind the German lines to create chaos and disrupt communications. The men noticed his look of grave concern and tried to lift his spirits. "Now quit worrying, General," one of them said, "we'll take care of this thing for you." After the planes took off, Eisenhower returned to his car with tears in his eyes. "Well," he said quietly to his driver, "it's on." He knew that many of his troops would die within a few hours.

Airborne forces dropped behind the beaches while planes and battleships pounded the coastal defenses. At dawn the invasion fleet of some

General Dwight D. Eisenhower instructing paratroopers just before they board their airplanes to launch the D-Day assault.

4,000 ships and 150,000 men (57,000 Americans) filled the horizon off the Normandy coast. Overhead, thousands of Allied planes supported the invasion force. Sleepy German soldiers awoke to see the vast armada arrayed before them. For several hours, the local German commanders interpreted the Normandy landings as merely a diversion for the "real" attack at Pas de Calais. When Hitler learned of the Allied landings, he boasted that "the news couldn't be better. As long as they were in Britain, we couldn't get at them. Now we have them where we can destroy them."

Despite Eisenhower's meticulous planning and the imposing array of Allied troops and firepower, the D-Day invasion almost failed. Cloud cover and German antiaircraft fire caused many of the paratroopers and glider pilots to miss their landing zones. Oceangoing landing craft delivered their troops to the wrong locations. Low clouds also led the Allied planes assigned to soften up the seaside defenses to drop their bombs too far inland. The naval bombardment was equally ineffective. Rough seas caused many of the soldiers to become seasick and capsized dozens of landing craft. Over a thousand men drowned. On Utah Beach the American invaders made it in against relatively light opposition, but farther east, on a four-mile segment designated Omaha Beach, bombardment had failed to take out German defenders, and the Americans were caught in heavily mined water. The first units ashore lost over 90 percent of their troops. In many cases, no one even made it off the landing ships. Once ashore, they then had to cross a fifty-yard beach exposed to machine guns in concrete pillboxes before they could huddle under a seawall and begin to root out the defenders. In one rifle company 197 out of 205 men were killed or wounded within ten minutes. By nightfall there were some 5,000 killed or wounded Allied soldiers strewn across the sand and surf of Normandy.

German losses were even more incredible. Entire units were decimated or captured. Operation Overlord was the greatest military invasion in the annals of warfare, and the climactic battle of World War II. With the beachhead secured, the Allied leaders knew that victory was now in their grasp. "What a plan!" Churchill exclaimed to the British parliament. Stalin, who had been clamoring for the cross-Channel invasion for years, applauded the Normandy operation and heaped praise on the Allies. He declared that the "history of warfare knows no other like undertaking from the point of view of its scale, its vast conception and its orderly execution."

The landing at Normandy, D-Day, June 6, 1944.

Within two weeks the Allies had landed a million troops, 556,000 tons of supplies, and 170,000 vehicles. They had seized a beachhead sixty miles wide and five to fifteen miles deep. They continued to pour men and supplies onto the beaches and to edge inland through the marshes and hedgerows. The German commanders advised withdrawal to defenses behind the Seine River, but a stubborn Hitler issued disastrous orders to contest every inch of land. General Erwin Rommel, convinced that all was lost, began to intrigue for a separate peace. Other like-minded German officers, convinced that the war was hopeless, tried to kill Hitler at his headquarters on July 20, 1944, but the Führer survived the bomb blast, and hundreds of conspirators and suspects were tortured to death. Rommel was granted the option of suicide, which he took.

Meanwhile, the Führer's tactics brought calamity to the German forces in western France. On July 25 American units broke out westward into Brittany and eastward toward Paris. On August 15 a joint American-French invasion force landed on the French Mediterranean coast and raced up the Rhône Valley. German resistance in France collapsed. A Free French division, aided by American forces, had the honor of liberating Paris on August 25. Nazi forces retired pell-mell toward the German border, and by mid-September most of France and Belgium were cleared of enemy troops.

SLOWING MOMENTUM   Events had moved so much faster than expected, in fact, that the Allies were running out of gas. Neither their plans nor their supply system could keep up with the rapid movement of tanks and men. British and Canadian forces under General Bernard Montgomery had moved forward into Belgium, where they took Antwerp on September 4. From there, Montgomery argued, a quick fatal thrust toward Berlin could end things. On the right flank, General George Patton was just as sure he could take the American Third Army all the way to Berlin. Eisenhower reasoned, however, that a swift, narrow thrust into Germany would be cut off, counterattacked, and defeated. Instead he advocated advancing along a broad front. Prudence demanded getting his supply lines in order first, which required clearing out stubborn German forces and opening a supply channel to Antwerp—a long, hard battle that lasted until the end of November.

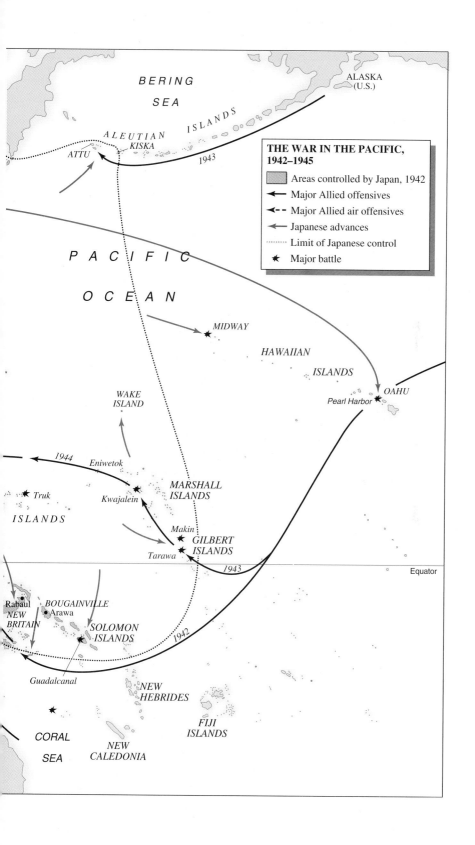

BERING SEA

ALASKA (U.S.)

ALEUTIAN ISLANDS

ATTU   KISKA   1943

PACIFIC

OCEAN

THE WAR IN THE PACIFIC, 1942–1945

Areas controlled by Japan, 1942
Major Allied offensives
Major Allied air offensives
Japanese advances
Limit of Japanese control
★ Major battle

MIDWAY

HAWAIIAN ISLANDS

WAKE ISLAND

OAHU
Pearl Harbor

1944   Eniwetok

Truk

Kwajalein

MARSHALL ISLANDS

ISLANDS

Makin

GILBERT ISLANDS

Tarawa

1943   Equator

Rabaul   BOUGAINVILLE
NEW   Arawa
BRITAIN

SOLOMON ISLANDS

1942

Guadalcanal

NEW HEBRIDES

FIJI ISLANDS

CORAL

SEA

NEW CALEDONIA

troopships and ten warships bringing reinforcements. Thereafter the Japanese dared not risk sending transports to points under siege, making it possible to use the tactic of neutralizing Japanese strongholds with air and sea power, and moving on, leaving them to die on the vine. Some called it "leapfrogging," and Japanese leaders later acknowledged the strategy as a major cause of Allied victory. Meanwhile, in mid-April, before the offensive got under way, American fighter planes shot down a plane that code-breakers knew was carrying Admiral Yamamoto, Japan's naval commander and the planner of the Pearl Harbor attack. His death shattered Japanese morale.

NIMITZ IN THE CENTRAL PACIFIC   Admiral Nimitz's advance through the central Pacific had as its first target two tiny islands, Makin and Tarawa. After advance bombing raids, a fleet of 200 ships delivered infantry and marines ashore at dawn on November 20, 1943. Makin, where the Japanese had only a small force, was soon cleared. Tarawa, however, was one of the most heavily protected islands in the Pacific. There nearly 1,000 American soldiers, sailors, and marines lost their lives rooting out a determined resistance by 4,000 Japanese who refused to surrender. Invasion of the Marshall Islands, the next step "up the ladder" to Tokyo, began on January 31, 1944. American forces took Saipan in the Marianas on June 15, which brought the new American B-29 bombers within striking distance of Japan itself. The Japanese navy therefore had to resist with all it had, which was not enough, despite its crash program to build new aircraft carriers.

In the Battle of the Philippine Sea, fought mostly in the air on June 19 and 20, 1944, the Japanese lost three more aircraft carriers, two submarines, and over 300 planes. The battle secured the Marianas, and soon B-29s were winging their way to the first systematic bombings of the Japanese homeland. Defeat in the Marianas finally brought home to General Tojo the realization that the war was lost. On July 18, 1944, he and his entire cabinet resigned.

THE BATTLE OF LEYTE GULF   With New Guinea and the Marianas islands all but conquered, President Roosevelt met with General MacArthur and Admiral Nimitz in Honolulu on July 27–28, 1944, to decide the next major step. Previous plans had marked China as the essential springboard for invading Japan, but a Japanese offensive in April

General Douglas MacArthur (center) *staging his triumphant return to the Philippines, October 1944.*

1944 had taken most of the south China airfields from which American air power had operated. This strengthened MacArthur's belief that the Philippines would provide a safer staging area than Formosa (Taiwan). Sentimental and political considerations, as well as military, tipped the decision his way. MacArthur made his move into the Philippines on October 20, landing first on the island of Leyte. Wading ashore behind the first landings, he issued an announcement: "People of the Philippines: I have returned. . . . Rally to me. . . . Let no heart be faint."

The Japanese, knowing that loss of the Philippines would cut them off from the oil and other essential resources of the East Indies, brought in fleets from three directions. The three encounters that resulted on October 25, 1944, came to be known collectively as the Battle of Leyte Gulf. It proved to be the largest naval engagement in history. The Japanese lost most of their remaining sea power and the ability to defend the Philippines. The battle also brought the first of the suicide attacks by Japanese pilots who crash-dived into American carriers, sinking one and seriously damaging others. The "Kamikaze" units, named for the "Divine Wind" that centuries ago had saved Japan from Mongol invasion, inflicted severe damage on the American navy.

A New Age Is Born

ROOSEVELT'S FOURTH TERM   In 1944, war or no war, the calendar dictated another presidential election. This time the Republicans turned to the former crime-fighter and New York governor, Thomas E. Dewey, as their candidate. Once again no Democratic challenger rose high enough to contest Roosevelt, but a fight did develop over the second spot on the ticket. Vice-President Henry Wallace had earned the enmity of both southern conservative and northern city bosses who feared his ties with labor. Roosevelt finally fastened on the compromise choice of Missouri senator Harry S. Truman.

Dewey ran under the same handicap as Landon and Willkie before him. He did not propose to dismantle Roosevelt's programs, but argued that it was time for younger men to replace the tired old leaders of the New Deal. Roosevelt betrayed decided signs of illness and exhaustion, but nevertheless, on November 7, 1944, he was once again elected, this time by a popular vote margin of 25.6 million to 22 million and an electoral vote of 432 to 99.

CONVERGING MILITARY FRONTS   After their quick sweep across France, the Allies lost momentum in the fall of 1944 and settled down to slugging at the frontiers of Germany. Along this line the armies fought it out all winter. The Germans sprang a surprise in the rugged Ardennes Forest, where the Allied line was thinnest. Hitting on December 16, 1944, under clouds that prevented air reconnaissance, the Germans advanced along a fifty-mile bulge in Belgium and Luxembourg—hence the Battle of the Bulge. In ten days they penetrated nearly to the Meuse River on their way to Antwerp, but they stalled at Bastogne. Reinforced by the Allies just before it was surrounded, Bastogne held for six days against all the Germans could bring against it. On December 22 American general "Tony" McAuliffe gave his memorable answer to the demand for surrender: "Nuts." When a German major asked what the term meant, an American officer said, "It's the same as 'Go to Hell.' And I will tell you something else—if you continue to attack, we will kill every goddamn German that tries to break into this city." The American situation remained desperate until the next day when the clouds lifted, allowing Allied airpower to hit the Germans and drop in supplies. On December 26, American forces broke through to the relief of Bastogne, but it would be mid-January 1945 before the previous lines were restored.

Germany's sudden thrust upset Eisenhower's timetable, but the outcome shook Nazi power and morale. Their effort had weakened the eastern front, and in January 1945 the Russians began their final offensive. The destruction of Hitler's last reserve units at the Battle of the Bulge had also left open the door to Germany's heartland from the west. By early March, the Allies had reached the banks of the Rhine River, which runs nearly all the way from Holland to Switzerland. On March 6 they took Cologne, and the next day, by remarkable luck, the Allies seized the bridge at Remagen before the Germans could blow it up. Troops poured across the Rhine River.

The Allies then encircled the Ruhr Valley, center of Germany's heavy industry. By mid-April resistance there was over. Meanwhile the Soviet offensive had also reached Germany itself, after taking Warsaw on January 17 and Vienna on April 13.

With the British and American armies racing across western Germany and the Soviets moving in from the east, the attention of

German prisoners of war being corralled by American soldiers at the war's end.

the war planners turned to Berlin. Churchill had grown suspicious of the Soviets and worried that if they arrived in Berlin first, they would gain dangerous leverage in deciding the postwar map of Europe. He told Eisenhower of his concerns and urged him to get to Berlin first. Eisenhower, however, refused to mix politics with military strategy. He was convinced the Soviets would get to Berlin first. He also knew that the Allied leaders were envisioning separate occupation zones for Germany, and Berlin was in the Soviet zone. Why rush to liberate the German capital only to turn it over to the Soviets? Berlin, he decided, no longer was of military significance. His purpose remained the destruction of the enemy's ground forces. Churchill disagreed and appealed to Roosevelt, but the American leader, now seriously ill, left the decision to the supreme commander. Eisenhower then asked his trusted lieutenant, General Omar Bradley, to estimate what it would take to liberate Berlin before the Soviets. Bradley predicted that it would cost 100,000 Allied casualties, which he described as a "pretty stiff price to pay for a prestige objective." Eisenhower agreed, and they left Berlin for the Soviets to conquer.

YALTA AND THE POSTWAR WORLD   As the final offensives got under way, the Yalta Conference (February 4–11, 1945) brought the Big Three leaders together again in a czar's palace at a Crimean resort (it was the only place in Russia both warm enough in February and undamaged enough to be hospitable). While the focus at Teheran in 1943 had been on wartime strategy, it was now on the shape of the postwar world. Stalin was self-confident, assertive, demanding, and sarcastic. He knew that Soviet forces controlled key areas that would ensure his demands were met. Two aims loomed large in Roosevelt's thinking. One was the need to ensure that the Soviet Union join the war against Japan. The other was based on the lessons he drew from the previous world war. Chief among the mistakes to be remedied this time were the failure of the United States to join the League of Nations and the failure of the Allies to maintain a united front against the German aggressors.

The Yalta meeting began by calling for a conference to create a new world organization, to be held in the United States, beginning on April 25, 1945. With Hitler's "Thousand-Year Reich" stumbling to its doom, arrangements for the postwar governance of Germany also had to be made at Yalta. The war map dictated the basic pattern of occupation

The Yalta Conference, *February 1945. Churchill, Roosevelt, and Stalin confer on the shape of the postwar world.*

zones: the Soviets would control the east and the Western Allies would control the rich industrial areas of the west. Berlin, isolated within the Soviet zone, would be subject to joint occupation. Similar arrangements were made for Austria, with Vienna like Berlin under joint occupation within the Soviet zone. At the behest of Churchill and Roosevelt, liberated France received an occupation zone along its border with Germany and also in Berlin. Soviet demands for reparations of $20 billion, half of which would go to the Soviet Union, were referred to a Reparations Commission in Moscow. The commission never reached agreement, although the Soviets appropriated untold amounts of German machinery and equipment from their occupation zone.

With respect to eastern Europe, where Soviet forces were advancing on a broad front, there was little the Western Allies could do to influence events. Roosevelt was inhibited by his wish to win Soviet cooperation in the fight against Japan and in the effort to build the proposed United Nations organization. Poland became the main focus of Western concern. Britain and France had gone to war in 1939 to defend Poland, and now, six years later, the course of the war had left Poland's fate in the hands of the Soviets.

When Soviet forces reentered Poland in 1944, they placed civil administration under a Committee of National Liberation in Lublin, a puppet regime representing few Poles. As Soviet troops reached the gates of Warsaw, the underground resistance in the city rose against the Nazi occupiers. The Polish underground, however, supported the Polish government-in-exile in London. The Soviets then stopped their offensive for two months while the Nazis wiped out thousands of Poles, potential rivals to the Soviets' Lublin puppet government.

The belief that postwar cooperation could survive such events was a triumph of hope over experience. The Western Allies meeting at Yalta could do no more than acquiesce or stall. On the Soviet proposal to expand the Lublin Committee into a provisional government together with representatives of the London Poles, they acquiesced. On the issue of Poland's boundaries, they stalled. The Soviets proposed to keep eastern Poland for themselves, offering land taken from Germany as compensation. Roosevelt and Churchill accepted the proposal, but considered the western boundary at the Oder–Western Neisse Rivers only provisional. But the peace conference at which the western boundary of Poland was to be settled never took place because of later disagreements. The presence of the London Poles in the provisional government only lent a tone of legitimacy to a regime dominated by the Communists, who soon ousted their rivals.

At Yalta the Big Three promised to sponsor free elections, democratic governments, and constitutional safeguards of freedom throughout the rest of Europe. The Yalta Declaration of Liberated Europe reaffirmed faith in the principles of the Atlantic Charter, but in the end it made little difference. It may have postponed takeovers in eastern Europe for a few years, but before long Communist members of coalition governments had their hands on the levers of power and ousted the opposition. Aside from Czechoslovakia, though, the countries of eastern Europe lacked strong democratic traditions in any case. And Russia, twice invaded by Germany in the twentieth century, had reason for wanting buffer states between it and the Germans.

YALTA'S LEGACY   Critics later attacked the Yalta agreements for "giving" eastern Europe over to Soviet domination. But the course of the war shaped the actions at Yalta. The Soviet army controlled the region.

By suppressing opposition in the occupied territories, moreover, the Soviets were not acting under the Yalta accords, but in violation of them.

Perhaps the most bitterly criticized of the Yalta understandings was a secret agreement on the Far East, not made public until after the war. As the Big Three met, fighting still raged against the Japanese in the Philippines and Burma. The Combined Chiefs of Staff still estimated that Japan could hold out for eighteen months after the defeat of Germany. Costly campaigns lay ahead, and the atomic bomb was still an expensive and untested gamble. Roosevelt therefore accepted Stalin's demands on postwar arrangements in the Far East, subject technically to later agreement by Chiang Kai-shek. Stalin wanted continued Soviet control of Outer Mongolia through its puppet People's Republic there, acquisition of the Kurile Islands from Japan, and recovery of rights and territory lost after the Russo-Japanese War of 1905. Stalin in return promised to enter the war against Japan two or three months after the German defeat, to recognize Chinese sovereignty over Manchuria, and to conclude a treaty of friendship and alliance with the Chinese Nationalists. Roosevelt's concessions would later appear in a different light, but given their geographical advantages in Asia as in eastern Europe, the Soviets were in a position to get what they wanted in any case.

THE THIRD REICH COLLAPSES   By 1945 the collapse of Nazi resistance was imminent, but President Roosevelt did not live to join the celebrations. All through 1944 his health had been declining, and photographs from early 1945 reveal a very sick man. In the spring of 1945 he went to his second home in Warm Springs, Georgia, to rest up for the Charter Conference of the United Nations at San Francisco. On April 12, 1945, he died from a cerebral hemorrhage.

The end of Hitler's Germany came less than a month later. The Allied armies rolled up almost unopposed to the Elbe River, where they met advance detachments of Soviets on April 25. Three days later Italian partisans caught and killed Mussolini as he tried to flee. In Berlin, which was under siege by the Soviets, Hitler married his mistress, Eva Braun, in an underground bunker on the last day of April. He then killed her and himself. On May 2 Berlin fell to the Soviets. That same day German forces in Italy surrendered. Finally, on May 7, General Alfred Jodl, Chief of Staff of the German armed forces, signed an unconditional surrender in Allied headquarters at Reims, France. So ended

The celebration in New York's Times Square on V-E Day.

the Thousand-Year Reich, little more than twelve years after its Führer came to power.

Massive victory celebrations in Europe on V-E Day, May 8, 1945, were tempered by the tragedies that had engulfed the world: mourning for the lost American president and the death and mutilation of untold millions. Most shocking was the discovery of the Holocaust, scarcely believable until the Allied armies came upon the death camps in which the Nazis had sought to apply their "final solution" to the Jewish "problem": the wholesale extermination of some 6 million Jews along with more than 1 million others.

During the war, testimony from underground and neutral relief agencies had piled up growing evidence of the Nazis' systematic genocide against the Jews of Europe. Reports appeared in major American newspapers as early as 1942, but were nearly always buried on inside pages. The falsehoods of World War I propaganda had conditioned too many people to doubt all atrocity stories, and rumors of such horror seemed beyond belief.

American government officials, even some Jewish leaders, dragged their feet for fear that relief for Jewish refugees might stir up latent anti-Semitism at home. Under pressure, Roosevelt set up a War Refugee Board early in 1944, but with few resources at its disposal. It nevertheless

U.S. troops encounter surviving inmates at the Nazi concentration camp at Wobbelin, May 1945.

managed to rescue about 200,000 European Jews and some 20,000 others. More might have been done by broadcasts warning people in Europe that Nazi "labor camps" were really death traps. The Allies rejected bombing the rail lines into the largest camp, Auschwitz in Poland, although American planes hit industries five miles away. And few refugees were accepted into the United States. The Allied handling of the Holocaust was inept at best and disgraceful at worst.

A GRINDING WAR AGAINST JAPAN   The sobering thought that the defeat of Japan remained to be accomplished cast a further pall over the victory celebrations in Europe in the spring of 1945. American forces continued to penetrate and disrupt the Japanese Empire in the early months of 1945, but at heavy cost. While fighting went on in the Philippines, on February 19, 1945, marine assault forces invaded Iwo Jima, a speck of volcanic rock 750 miles from Tokyo. It was needed to provide fighter escort for bombers over Japan and a landing strip for disabled B-29 bombers. Nearly six weeks were required to secure an island five miles square from defenders hiding in underground caves. The cost was more than 20,000 American casualties, including nearly 7,000 dead.

The fight for Okinawa, beginning on Easter Sunday, April 1, was even bloodier. The largest island in the Ryukyu chain, Okinawa was large enough to afford a staging area for an invasion of Japan. It was the largest amphibious operation of the Pacific war, involving some 300,000 troops. The fight for Okinawa raged until late June, when the bloody attrition destroyed any further Japanese ability to resist. The Japanese lost an estimated 140,000 dead. Casualties also included about 42,000 Okinawans.

When resistance on Okinawa collapsed, the Japanese emperor instructed his new premier to seek peace terms. Washington had picked this up by decoding Japanese messages, which suggested either an effort to avoid unconditional surrender or perhaps just a stall.

THE ATOMIC BOMB   By this time, however, a new force had changed all strategic calculations: during the summer of 1945 President Truman learned of the first successful test explosion of an American atomic bomb, the result of several years of intensive work. The strands of scientific development that led to the bomb ironically ran back to Germany. Had the Nazi bigotry not driven scientists into exile, Germany might well have developed the atomic bomb first. Early in 1939 a scientific journal revealed that the uranium atom had been split in Berlin; experiments in Denmark and the United States soon confirmed the finding. On October 11, 1939, President Roosevelt learned of the matter when an emissary delivered a letter from physicist Albert Einstein and a memorandum explaining the potential of nuclear fission and warning that the Germans might develop a bomb first. Roosevelt quickly set up a committee to coordinate information in the field, and in 1940 some army and navy funds were diverted into research that grew ultimately into the $2 billion top-secret Manhattan Project.

On December 2, 1942, Dr. Enrico Fermi and other scientists achieved the first atomic chain reaction at the University of Chicago, removing any remaining doubts about the bomb's feasibility. Gigantic plants sprang up at Oak Ridge, Tennessee, and Hanford, Washington, to provide materials for atomic bombs, while a group of physicists under Dr. J. Robert Oppenheimer worked out the scientific and technical problems of bomb construction in a laboratory at Los Alamos, New Mexico. On July 16, 1945, the first atomic fireball rose from the desert. Oppenheimer said later that in the observation bunker "A few people laughed, a few people cried, most people were silent."

How to use this awful new weapon posed a profound dilemma. Some scientists, awed at the ghastly prospect, favored a demonstration in a remote area, but the decision went for military use because only two bombs were available, and even those might misfire. More consideration was given to the choice of targets. Four Japanese cities had been reserved from conventional bombing as potential targets. After Secretary of War Henry Stimson eliminated Kyoto, Japan's ancient capital and center of many national and religious treasures, and Kokura, priority went to Hiroshima, a port city of 400,000 people in southern Japan, which was a major assembly point for Japanese naval convoys and a center of war industries, headquarters of the Second General Army, and command center for the homeland's defenses. This met Truman's guidelines. He had written that only military personnel and installations rather than "women and children" should be targeted. Of course, he had no idea that the bomb would destroy virtually an entire city.

On July 25, 1945, President Harry S. Truman, who had been thrust into the presidency after Roosevelt's death in April, ordered the atomic bomb dropped if Japan did not surrender before August 3. Although an intense scholarly debate has emerged over the decision to drop the atomic bomb, Truman never considered not using it at the earliest opportunity. He "regarded the bomb as a military weapon and never had any doubt that it should be used." He was convinced that using the atomic bomb would in the end save lives by avoiding a costly American invasion against defenders who would fight like "savages, ruthless, merciless, and fanatic."

The ferocious Japanese defense of Okinawa had convinced American military planners that an amphibious invasion of Japan itself, scheduled to begin on November 1, 1945, could cost as many as 250,000 Allied casualties and even more Japanese losses. Moreover, some 100,000 Allied prisoners of war being held in Japan would be executed whenever an invasion began. It is important to remember as well that the bombing of cities and the consequent killing of civilians had become accepted military practice during 1945. Once the Japanese navy was destroyed, American ships were able to roam the Japanese coastline, shelling targets on shore. American planes bombed at will and mined the waters of the Inland Sea. Tokyo, Nagoya, and other major cities were devastated by firestorms created by incendiary bombs. The firebomb raids on Tokyo on a single night in March

1945 killed over 100,000 civilians and left over a million people homeless. By July more than sixty of Japan's largest cities had been firebombed, resulting in 500,000 deaths and 13 million civilians left homeless. The use of atomic bombs on Japanese cities was thus seen as a logical next step in an effort to end the war without an invasion of Japan. As it turned out, American scientists greatly underestimated the physical effects of the atomic bomb. They predicted that 20,000 people would be killed.

On July 26 the heads of the American, British, and Russian governments issued the Potsdam Declaration demanding that Japan surrender or face "prompt and utter destruction." The deadline passed, and on August 6, 1945, a B-29 bomber named the *Enola Gay*, with a crew commanded by Colonel Paul W. Tibbetts, took off at 2 A.M. from the island of Tinian and headed for Hiroshima. At 8:15 in the morning, flying at 31,600 feet, the *Enola Gay* released the five-ton uranium bomb nicknamed "Little Boy." Forty-three seconds later, as the *Enola Gay* turned sharply to avoid the blast, the bomb tumbled to an altitude of 1,900 feet, where it exploded as planned with the force of 15,000 tons of TNT. A blinding flash of light was followed by a fireball towering to 40,000 feet. The tail gunner on the *Enola Gay* described the scene: "It's like bubbling molasses down there . . . the mushroom is spreading out . . . fires are springing up everywhere . . . it's like a peep into hell."

The shock wave, firestorm, cyclonic winds, and radioactive rain killed some 80,000 people, including thousands of Japanese soldiers assigned to the Second General Army headquarters and 23 American prisoners of war housed in the city. Dazed survivors wandered the streets, so painfully burned that their skin began to peel in large strips. By the end of the year, the death toll had reached 140,000 as the effects of radiation burns and infection took their toll. In addition, 70,000 buildings were destroyed, and four square miles of the city turned to rubble.

In the United States, Americans greeted the first news with elation: the bombing promised a quick end to the long nightmare of war. "No tears of sympathy will be shed in America for the Japanese people," the *Omaha World Herald* predicted. "Had they possessed a comparable weapon at Pearl Harbor, would they have hesitated to use it?" Others were more circumspect. "Yesterday," journalist Hanson Baldwin wrote in the *New York Times*, "we clinched victory in the Pacific, but we sowed

This image shows the wasteland that remained after the atomic bomb "Little Boy" decimated Hiroshima, 1945.

the whirlwind." Only later would people realize that it marked the start of a more enduring nightmare, the atomic age.

Two days after the Hiroshima bombing, an opportunistic Russia, eager to share in the spoils of victory, hastened to enter the war. On August 9, the second atomic bomb exploded over the port city of Nagasaki, a ship-building and torpedo-factory center, killing 36,000 people. That night the emperor urged his cabinet to surrender on the sole condition that he remain as sovereign. The next day the United States government announced its willingness to let the emperor keep the throne, but under the authority of an Allied supreme commander. Frantic exchanges ended with Japanese acceptance on August 14, 1945, when the emperor himself broke precedent to record a radio message announcing the surrender to his people.

On September 2, 1945, General Douglas MacArthur and other Allied representatives accepted Japan's formal surrender on board the battle-ship *Missouri*. MacArthur then settled in at his occupation headquarters across from the Imperial Palace.

THE FINAL LEDGER

Thus ended the most deadly conflict in human history. One estimate has it that 70 million in all fought in the war, at a cost in human lives of 25 million military dead and more than 24 million civilian dead. The Soviet Union suffered the greatest losses of all, over 13 million military deaths, over 7 million civilians dead, and at least 25 million left homeless. World War II was more costly for the United States than any other of the country's foreign wars: 292,000 battle deaths and 114,000 other deaths. But in proportion to population, the United States suffered a far smaller loss than any of the major Allies or enemies, and American territory escaped the devastation visited on so many other parts of the world.

World War II had profound effects on American life and society. Mobilization for war stimulated a phenomenal increase in American productivity and brought full employment, thus ending the Great Depression and laying the foundation for a new era of unprecedented prosperity. New technologies and products developed for military purposes—radar, computers, electronics, plastics and synthetics, jet engines, rockets, atomic energy—soon began to transform the private sector as well. And new opportunities for women as well as for blacks and other minorities set in motion changes that would culminate in the civil rights movement of the 1960s and the feminist movement of the 1970s.

The Democratic party benefited from the war effort by solidifying its control of both the White House and Congress. The dramatic expansion of the federal government occasioned by the war continued after 1945. Presidential authority and prestige increased enormously at the expense of congressional and state power. The isolationist sentiment in foreign relations that had been so powerful in the 1920s and 1930s disintegrated as the United States emerged from the war with global responsibilities and interests.

The war's end opened a new era for the United States in the world arena. It accelerated the growth of American power while devastating all other world powers, leaving the United States economically and militarily the strongest nation on earth. But the Soviet Union, despite its human and material losses, emerged from the war with much new territory and enhanced influence, making it the greatest power on the whole Eurasian landmass. Just a little over a century after Frenchman Alexis de Tocqueville had predicted that western Europe would come to be overshadowed by the power of the United States and Russia, his prophecy had come to pass.

MAKING CONNECTIONS

- Compare the impact of World War II on the home front to that of World War I, especially the effects of war on race and gender relations.

- The growing domestic conservatism of the war years continued into the 1950s, a topic discussed in the next chapter.

- Dwight D. Eisenhower's success as American general and Allied leader led to his nomination and election as president in 1952. Compare Eisenhower's experience to that of General Grant in and after the Civil War, and to the political experiences of other American military leaders.

FURTHER READING

John Keegan's *The Second World War* (1990) surveys the European conflict, while Charles B. MacDonald's *The Mighty Endeavor: The American War in Europe* (rev. ed., 1992) concentrates on American involvement. Roosevelt's wartime leadership is analyzed in Eric Larrabee's *Commander in Chief: Franklin Delano Roosevelt, His Lieutenants and Their War* (1987).

Books on specific European campaigns include Stephen E. Ambrose's *D-Day, June 6, 1944: The Climactic Battle of World War II* (1994) and Charles B. MacDonald's *A Time for Trumpets: The Untold Story of the Battle of the Bulge* (rev. ed., 1997).

For the war in the Far East, see John Costello's *The Pacific War, 1941–1945* (1983), Ronald H. Spector's *Eagle against the Sun: The American War with Japan* (1984), John Dower's award-winning *War Without Mercy: Race and Power in the Pacific War* (1986), and Dan van der Vat's *The Pacific Campaign: The U.S.–Japanese Naval War, 1941–1945* (1992).

An excellent overview of the war's effects on the home front is Michael C. Adams's *The Best War Ever: America and World War II* (1993). On economic effects, see Harold Vatter's *The U.S. Economy in World War II* (1995).

Susan M. Hartmann's *The Home Front and Beyond: American Women in the 1940s* (1982) treats the new working environment for women. Neil Wynn looks at the participation of blacks in *The Afro-American and the Second World War* (rev. ed., 1993). The story of the oppression of Japanese Americans is told in Peter Irons's *Justice at War* (1983).

A sound introduction to American diplomacy during the conflict can be found in Gaddis Smith's *American Diplomacy during the Second World War, 1941–1945* (2nd ed., 1985). To understand the role that Roosevelt played in policy-making, consult Warren F. Kimball's *The Juggler: Franklin Roosevelt as Wartime Statesman* (1991).

The issues and events that led to the deployment of atomic weapons are addressed in Martin J. Sherwin's *A World Destroyed: The Atomic Bomb and the Grand Alliance* (1975).

PART SEVEN

THE AMERICAN AGE

The United States emerged from World War II the preeminent military and economic power in the world. At the end of the war, America enjoyed a commanding position in international trade and was the only nation in possession of the atomic bomb. While much of Europe and Asia struggled to recover from the horrific physical devastation of the war, the United States emerged virtually unscathed, its economic infrastructure intact and operating at peak efficiency. Jobs that were scarce in the 1930s were now available for the taking. By 1955 the United States, with only 6 percent of the world's population, was producing half of the world's goods. American capitalism not only demonstrated its economic strength, it became a dominant cultural force as well. In Europe, Japan, and elsewhere, American products, forms of entertainment, and fashion attracted excited attention.

Yet the specter of the "cold war" cast a pall over the buoyant revival of the American economy after World War II. The ideological contest with the Soviet Union and Communist China produced numerous foreign crises and sparked a domestic witch-hunt for Communists that far surpassed earlier episodes of political and social repression in the nation's history.

There was widespread acceptance in both major political parties of the geopolitical assumptions embedded in the ideological cold war with international communism. Both Republican and Democratic presidents affirmed the need to "contain" the spread of Communist influence around the world. This bedrock assumption eventually embroiled the United States in a tragic war in Southeast Asia that destroyed Lyndon Johnson's presidency and revived neo-isolationist sentiments. The Vietnam War also was the catalyst for a countercultural movement in which young idealists of the "baby-boom" generation sought alternatives to a government and a society that in their eyes had become oppressive and corrupt. The youth revolt provided energy for many overdue social reforms, including the civil rights and environmental movements, but it also contributed to an array of social ills, from street riots to drug abuse to sexual license. The social upheavals of the 1960s and early 1970s provoked a conservative backlash that overreached itself as well. In their efforts to restore "law and order," mayors failed to protect civil liberties in their cities. Richard Nixon's paranoid reaction to his critics led to the destruction of his presidency as a result of the Watergate investigations.

Through all of this turmoil, however, the basic premises of welfare state capitalism that Franklin Roosevelt had instituted with his New Deal programs remained essentially intact. With only a few exceptions, both Republicans and Democrats after 1945 came to accept the notion that the federal government must assume greater responsibility for the welfare of individuals than had heretofore been the case. Even Ronald Reagan, a sharp critic of liberal social-welfare programs, recognized the need for the federal government to provide a "safety net" for those who could not help themselves.

Yet this fragile consensus about public policy began to disintegrate in the late 1980s amid stunning international developments and less visible domestic events. The internal collapse of the Soviet Union and the disintegration of European communism surprised observers and sent policy makers scurrying to respond to a post–cold war world in which the United States remained the only legitimate superpower. After forty-five years, American foreign policy was no longer keyed to a single adversary, and world politics lost its bipolar quality. During the early 1990s, the two Germanies reunited, apartheid in South Africa finally ended, and Israel and the Palestinians signed a heretofore unimaginable peace treaty.

At the same time, American foreign policy began to focus less on military power and more on economic competition and technological development. In those arenas, Japan and a reunited Germany challenged the United States for preeminence. By reducing the public's fear of nuclear annihilation, the ending of the cold war also reduced public interest in foreign affairs. The presidential election of 1992 was the first since 1936 in which foreign policy issues played virtually no role. This was an unfortunate development, for post–cold war world affairs remained volatile and dangerous. The implosion of Soviet communism unleashed a series of ethnic, nationalist, and separatist conflicts. In the face of inertia among other governments and pleas for assistance, the United States found itself being drawn into crises in faraway lands such as Bosnia, Rwanda, Somalia, Chechnya, Afghanistan, and Iraq.

As the new multipolar world careened toward the end of a century and the start of a new millennium, fault lines began to appear in the American social and economic landscape. A gargantuan federal debt and rising annual deficits threatened to bankrupt a nation that was becoming top-heavy with retirees. Without fully realizing it, much less appreciating its cascading consequences, the American population was becoming disproportionately old. Those aged ninety-five to ninety-nine doubled between 1980 and 1990, and the number of centenarians increased 77 percent.

The proportion of the population aged sixty-five and older rose steadily during the 1990s. By the year 2000, half of the elderly population would be over the age of seventy-five. This demographic fact harbored profound social and political implications. It exerted increasing stress on health care costs, nursing home facilities, and the very survival of the Social Security system.

At the same time that the gap between young and old was increasing, so, too, was the disparity between rich and poor. This trend threatened to stratify a society already experiencing rising levels of racial and ethnic tension. Between 1960 and 1990, the gap between the richest 20 percent of the population and the poorest 20 percent doubled. Over 20 percent of all American children in 1990 lived in poverty, and the infant mortality rate rose. The infant death rate in Japan was less than half that in the United States. Despite the much-ballyhooed "war on poverty" programs initiated by Lyndon Johnson and continued in one form or another by all of his successors, the chronically poor in 1996 were more numerous and more bereft of hope than in 1964. Yet by the end of the century, a prolonged period of economic growth and a runaway stock market revived the myth of perennial prosperity.

31 & THE FAIR DEAL
AND CONTAINMENT

CHAPTER ORGANIZER

This chapter focuses on:

- the economic, social, and political aftermath of World War II and the origins and early development of the cold war.

- Truman's Fair Deal program.

- U.S. involvement in the Korean War.

- the roots of McCarthyism.

o sooner did the Second World War end than a "cold war" began. The uneasy wartime alliance between the United States and the Soviet Union collapsed completely by the fall of 1945. The two strongest nations to emerge from the carnage of World War II could not bridge their ideological differences over such basic issues as human rights, individual liberties, and religious beliefs. Mutual suspicion and a race to gain influence and control over the so-called Third World countries further polarized the two nations. The defeat of Japan and Germany created power vacuums that sucked the Soviet Union and America into an unrelenting war of words fed by clashing strategic interests. At the same time, the destruction of western Europe and the exhaustion of its peoples led to anticolonial uprisings in Asia and Africa that threatened to strip Britain and France of their once-great empires. The postwar world was thus an unstable one in which international tensions shaped the contours of domestic politics and culture as well as foreign relations.

DEMOBILIZATION UNDER TRUMAN

TRUMAN'S UNEASY START   "Who the hell is Harry Truman?" Roosevelt's chief of staff asked the president in the summer of 1944. The question was on more lips when, after less than twelve weeks as vice-president, Harry Truman took the presidential oath on April 12, 1945. Clearly he was not Franklin Roosevelt, and that was one of the burdens he would bear.

Roosevelt and Truman came from quite different backgrounds. For Truman there had been no inherited wealth, no early contact with the great and near-great, no European travel, no Harvard—indeed, no college at all. Born in 1884 in western Missouri, Truman grew up in Independence, an unglamorous town near Kansas City. Bookish and withdrawn, Truman after high school moved to his grandmother's farm, spent a few years working in Kansas City banks, and grew into an outgoing young man.

During World War I, Truman served in France as captain of an artillery battery. Afterward he and a partner went into the clothing business, but it failed in the recession of 1922, and Truman then became a professional politician under the tutelage of Kansas City's Democratic machine. In 1934 Missouri sent him to the United States Senate, where he remained fairly obscure until he became chairman of the committee to investigate war mobilization.

Something about Harry Truman evoked the spirit of Andrew Jackson: his decisiveness, his feisty character, his family loyalty. But that was a side of the man that the public came to know only as he settled into the presidency. On his first full day as president, he remained awestruck. "Boys, if you ever pray, pray for me now," he told a group of reporters. "I don't know whether you fellows ever had a load of hay fall on you, but when they told me yesterday what had happened, I felt like the moon, the stars and all the planets had fallen on me."

Truman favored much of the New Deal and was even prepared to extend its scope, but at the same time was uneasy with many New Dealers. Within ninety days he had replaced much of the Roosevelt cabinet with his own choices. On the whole they were more conservative in outlook and included several mediocrities. Truman suffered the further handicap of seeming to be a caretaker for the remainder of Roosevelt's term. Few, including Truman himself at first, expected him to run in 1948.

Truman gave one significant clue to his domestic policies on September 6, 1945, when he sent Congress a comprehensive peacetime program that in effect proposed to continue and enlarge the New Deal. Its twenty-one points included expansion of unemployment insurance, a higher minimum wage, a permanent Fair Employment Practices Commission, slum clearance and low-rent housing programs, regional development of the nation's river valleys, and a public-works program. "Not even President Roosevelt asked for so much at one sitting," said the House Republican leader. "It's just a plain case of out-dealing the New Deal." Beset by other problems, Truman soon saw his new domestic proposals mired in disputes over the transition to a peacetime economy.

CONVERTING TO PEACE   The raucous celebrations that greeted Japan's surrender signaled the habitual American response to victory: a rapid demobilization and a return to more congenial pursuits. The public demanded that the president and Congress bring the troops home. By 1947 the total armed forces were down from 12 million to 1.5 million. In his memoirs Truman termed this "the most remarkable demobilization in the history of the world, or 'disintegration' if you want to call it that." By early 1950 the army had fallen to 600,000 men.

The military veterans eagerly returned to schools, new jobs, wives, and babies. Population growth, which had dropped off sharply in the depression decade, now soared: the population increase of 9 million during the 1930s exploded to a growth of 19 million in the 1940s. Americans born during this postwar period composed what came to be known as the "baby-boom" generation, and that generation became a dominant force in the nation's social and cultural life.

The end of the war, with its sudden demobilization and reconversion to a peacetime economy, brought sharp dislocations but not the postwar depression that many feared. Several shock absorbers cushioned the

The Eldridge General Store, Fayette County, Illinois. *Postwar America quickly demobilized, turning its attention to the pursuit of abundance.*

economic impact of demobilization: unemployment pay and other Social Security benefits; the Servicemen's Readjustment Act of 1944, known as the "GI Bill of Rights," under which $13 billion was spent for veterans on education, vocational training, medical treatment, unemployment insurance, and loans for building houses or going into business; and, most important, the pent-up demand for consumer goods that was fueled by wartime deprivation. The gross national product first exceeded the 1929 level in 1940, when it reached $101 billion, but by annual increases (except in 1946) it had grown to $347 billion by 1952, Truman's last full year in office.

CONTROLLING INFLATION The most acute economic problem Truman faced was not depression but inflation. Released from wartime restraints, the demands of business owners and workers alike combined to frustrate efforts at controlling rising prices. Truman endorsed wage increases to sustain purchasing power. He felt that there was "room in the existing price structure" for business to grant such pay increases, a point management refused to concede. Within six weeks of war's end, corporations confronted a wave of union demands.

A series of strikes followed. The United Automobile Workers walked out on General Motors, with union chief Walter Reuther arguing that the company could afford a 30 percent pay hike without raising car prices. (The company denied this claim.) A strike in the steel industry finally gave rise to a formula for settling most of the disputes. President Truman suggested a pay raise of 18.5¢ per hour, which the Steel Workers accepted but management refused. To break the logjam, the administration in 1946 agreed to let the company increase its prices. That pattern then became the basis for settlements in other industries, and also set a dangerous precedent of price-wage spirals that would plague consumers in the postwar world.

Major disputes soon developed in the coal and railroad industries. John L. Lewis of the United Mine Workers wanted more than the 18.5¢-per-hour wage increase. He also demanded improved safety regulations and a union health and welfare fund. Mine owners refused the demands, and a strike followed. The government used its wartime powers to seize the mines; Truman's interior secretary then accepted nearly all the union's demands.

In the rail dispute, the unions and management reached an agreement, but two brotherhoods, the trainmen and locomotive engineers, held out for rule changes as well as higher wages. Truman seized the railroads and won a five-day postponement of a strike. But when the union leaders refused to budge further, the president lashed out against their "obstinate arrogance" and demanded authority from Congress to draft strikers into the armed forces. In the midst of this speech, he learned that the strike had been settled, but after telling a jubilant Congress, he went on with his message. The House passed a bill including the president's demands, but with the strike settled, it died in the Senate.

Into 1946 the wartime Office of Price Administration (OPA) maintained some restraint on price increases while gradually ending the rationing of most goods, and Truman asked for a one-year renewal of its powers. During the late winter and spring of 1946, however, business leaders mounted a massive campaign against price controls and other restraints. Just a week before controls were to expire at the end of June, Congress passed a bill to continue the OPA, but with such cumbersome new procedures as to cripple the agency. Truman vetoed the bill, allowing price controls to end. Congress finally extended controls in late July, but by then the cost of living had already gone up by 6 percent. When the OPA restored controls on meat prices, farmers responded by withholding beef from the market until they succeeded in forcing a reversal in October. After the congressional elections of 1946, Truman gave up the battle, ending all price controls except on rents, sugar, and rice.

PARTISAN COOPERATION AND CONFLICT The legislative history of 1946 was not all deadlock and frustration. Amid the turmoil Congress and the administration worked out two new departures, the Employment Act of 1946 and the Atomic Energy Commission. A program of "full employment" had been a Democratic promise in the campaign of 1944, a pledge reaffirmed by Truman in 1945. The administration backed an employment bill proposing that the government make an annual estimate of the investment and production necessary to ensure full employment, and key its spending to that estimate in order to raise production to full-employment levels. Conservatives objected to what they denounced as carte blanche for deficit spending, and proposed a nonpartisan commission to advise the president on the economy. Compromise resulted in the Employment Act of 1946, which dropped the commitment to full employment and set up a three-member Council of Economic Advisers to make appraisals of the economy and advise the president in an annual economic report. A new congressional Joint Committee on the Economic Report would propose legislation.

With regard to the new force that atomic scientists had released upon the world, there was little question that the public welfare required the control of atomic energy through a governmental monopoly. Disagreements over military versus civilian control were resolved when Congress, in 1946, created the civilian Atomic Energy Commission. The president alone was given power to order the use of atomic weapons in warfare. Technical problems and high costs, however, would delay for two decades the construction of nuclear power plants.

As congressional elections approached in the fall of 1946, public discontent ran high, most of it against the administration. Truman caught the blame for labor problems from both sides. A speaker at the CIO national convention tagged Truman "the No. 1 strikebreaker," while much of the public, angry at striking unions, also blamed the strikes on the White House. In 1946 Truman fired Henry A. Wallace as secretary of commerce in a disagreement over foreign policy, thus offending the Democratic left. At the same time, Republicans charged that Communists had infiltrated the government. Republicans had a field day coining slogans. "To err is Truman" was credited to Martha Taft, wife of Senator Robert Taft. In the elections Republicans won majorities in both houses of Congress for the first time since 1928.

Given the head of steam built up against organized labor, the new Republican Congress sought to curb the power of unions. The result was the Taft-Hartley Act of 1947, which banned the closed shop (in which nonunion workers could not be hired) but permitted a union shop (in which workers newly hired were required to join the union), unless banned by state law. It included provisions against "unfair" union practices such as secondary boycotts, jurisdictional strikes (by one union to exclude another from a given company or field), "featherbedding" (pay for work not done), refusal to bargain in good faith, and contributing to political campaigns. Unions' political action committees were allowed to function, but on a voluntary basis only, and union leaders had to take oaths that they were not members of the Communist party. Employers were permitted to sue unions for breaking contracts, to petition the National Labor Relations Board (NLRB) for votes for or against the use of specific unions as collective-bargaining agents, and to speak freely during union campaigns. The act forbade strikes by federal employees, and imposed a "cooling-off" period of eighty days on any strike that the president found to be dangerous to the national health or safety.

Truman's veto of the Taft-Hartley Bill, which unions called the "slave-labor act," restored his credit with labor, and many unionists who had gone over to the Republicans in 1946 returned to the Democrats. The bill, however, passed over Truman's veto.

"To the Rescue!" *Organized labor is being pulled under by the Taft-Hartley Act as Congress, which passed the bill over Truman's veto, makes sure there is no rescue.*

Its most severe impact probably was on the CIO's "Operation Dixie," a drive to win for unions a more secure foothold in the South. By 1954 fifteen states, mainly in the South, had used the Taft-Hartley Act's authority to enact "right-to-work" laws forbidding the union shop and other union security devices.

Truman clashed with the Republicans on other domestic issues, including tax reduction. Congress passed a tax cut, but Truman vetoed it on the principle that in times of high production and employment the federal debt should be reduced. In 1948, however, Congress finally managed to override his veto of a $5 billion tax cut at a time when government debt still ran high.

The conflicts between Truman and Congress obscured the high degree of bipartisan cooperation marking matters of governmental reorganization and foreign policy. In 1947 Congress passed the National Security Act. It created a National Military Establishment, headed by a secretary of defense with subcabinet departments of army, navy, and air force, and a new National Security Council (NSC), which included the president, heads of the defense departments, and the secretary of state, among others. The act made permanent the Joint Chiefs of Staff, which had been a wartime innovation, and established the Central Intelligence Agency (CIA), descended from the wartime Office of Strategic Service (OSS), to coordinate intelligence-gathering activities.

THE COLD WAR

BUILDING THE U.N.   The hope that the wartime military alliance would carry over into the postwar world proved but another great illusion. The pragmatic Roosevelt shared no such hope. To the contrary, he expected that the Great Powers in the postwar world would have separate spheres of influence, but felt he had to support an organization "which would satisfy widespread demand in the United States for new idealistic or universalist arrangements for assuring the peace."

On April 25, 1945, two weeks after Roosevelt's death and two weeks before the German surrender, delegates from fifty nations at war with the Axis met in San Francisco's Opera House to draw up the Charter of the United Nations (U.N.). Additional members could be admitted by a two-thirds vote of the General Assembly. This body, one of the two major agencies set up by the charter, included delegates from all member nations and was to meet annually in regular session to approve the budget, receive annual reports from U.N. agencies, and choose members of the Security Council and other bodies. The Security Council, the other major charter agency, would remain in permanent session and would have "primary responsibility for the maintenance of international peace and security." Its eleven (after 1965, fifteen) members included six (later ten) members elected for two-year terms and five permanent members: the United States, the Soviet Union, Britain, France, and China. Each permanent member had a veto on any question of substance. The Security Council might investigate any dispute, recommend settlement or reference to an International Court at The Hague, in the Netherlands, and take measures, including a resort to military force.

The Senate ratified the U.N. charter by a vote of 89 to 2 after only six days of discussion. The organization held its first meeting in London in 1946, and the next year moved to temporary quarters at Lake Success, New York, pending completion of its permanent home in New York City.

TRYING WAR CRIMINALS   There was also a consensus that those responsible for the atrocities of World War II should face trial and punishment. Both German and Japanese officials were tried for crimes against peace, against humanity, and against the established rules of war. At Nuremberg, site of the annual Nazi party rallies, twenty-one major German offenders faced an international military tribunal. After a ten-month trial filled with massive documentation of Nazi atrocities, the court acquitted three and sentenced eleven to death, three to life imprisonment, and four to shorter terms. In Tokyo, a similar tribunal put twenty-five Japanese leaders on trial in 1946, and pronounced death sentences on seven, life imprisonment on sixteen, and committed two for lesser prison terms. Other international tribunals tried thousands of others.

DIFFERENCES WITH THE SOVIETS   Since the end of World War II, historians have debated which side was more responsible for the onset of the cold war. The conventional or "orthodox" view declares that the Soviets, led by a paranoid dictator, tried to dominate the globe, and the United States had no choice but to stand firm in defense of democratic

Nazi leaders Hermann Goering (standing) *and Rudolf Hess* (seated, arms folded) *at Nuremberg, where they are on trial for war crimes.*

capitalist values. By contrast, those scholars known as "revisionists" argue that Truman and American economic imperialists were the culprits. Instead of maintaining Roosevelt's efforts to collaborate with Stalin and the Soviets, these scholars assert, Truman adopted an unnecessarily belligerent stance and activist foreign policy that sought to create American spheres of influence around the world. He and his military advisers exaggerated the Soviet threat, in part to justify an American military buildup. Their provocative policies thus crystallized the tensions between the two countries. Yet such an interpretation fails to recognize that Truman inherited a deteriorating relationship with the Soviets. Events of 1945 made compromise and conciliation more and more difficult, whether for Roosevelt or Truman.

There were signs of trouble in the Grand Alliance as early as the spring of 1945, as the Soviet Union moved to set up compliant governments in eastern Europe, violating the Yalta promises of democratic elections. On February 1 the Polish Committee of National Liberation, a puppet group already claiming the status of provisional government, moved from Lublin to Warsaw. In March the Soviets installed a puppet premier in Romania. Protests against such actions led to Soviet counterprotests that the British and Americans were negotiating German surrender in Italy "behind the back of the Soviet Union" and that German forces were being concentrated against the Soviet Union.

Such was the atmosphere when Truman entered the White House. A few days before the San Francisco conference to organize the United Nations, Truman gave Soviet foreign minister Vyacheslav Molotov a dressing-down in Washington on the Polish situation. "I have never been talked to like that in my life," Molotov said. "Carry out your agreements," Truman snapped, "and you won't get talked to like that."

On May 12, 1945, four days after victory in Europe, Winston Churchill sent a telegram to Truman: "What is to happen about Europe? An iron curtain is drawn down upon [the Russian] front. We do not know what is going on behind [it]. . . . Surely it is vital now to come to an understanding with Russia, or see where we are with her, before we weaken our armies mortally. . . ." Nevertheless, as a gesture of goodwill, and over Churchill's protest, the American forces withdrew from the German occupation zone assigned to the Soviet Union at Yalta. Americans still hoped that the Yalta agreements would be carried out, at least after a fashion, and that the Soviet Union would help defeat Japan.

Although the Soviets admitted British and American observers to their sectors of eastern Europe, there was little the Western powers could do to prevent Soviet control of the region, even if they had not let their military forces dwindle. The presence of Soviet armed forces frustrated the efforts of non-Communists to gain political influence in eastern European countries. The leaders of those opposed to Soviet influence were either exiled, silenced, executed, or imprisoned.

Secretary of State James F. Byrnes struggled on through 1946 with the problems of postwar settlements. In early 1947, the Council of Foreign Ministers finally produced treaties for Italy, Hungary, Romania, Bulgaria, and Finland. The treaties in effect confirmed Soviet control over eastern Europe, which in Russian eyes seemed but a parallel to American control in Japan and Western control over most of Germany and all of Italy. The Yalta guarantees of democracy in eastern Europe had turned out much like the Open Door Policy in China, little more than pious rhetoric sugar-coating the realities of raw power and national interest.

Byrnes's impulse to pressure Soviet diplomats by brandishing the atomic bomb only added to the irritations, intimidating no one. As early as April 1945, he had suggested to Truman that possession of the new weapon "might well put us in position to dictate our own terms at the end of the war." After becoming secretary of state he had threatened Soviet diplomats with America's growing arsenal of nuclear weapons. But they paid little notice.

CONTAINMENT   By the beginning of 1947, relations with the Soviet Union had become even more troubled. A year before, Stalin had already pronounced international peace impossible "under the present capitalist development of the world economy." His statement impelled George F. Kennan, counselor of the American embassy in Moscow, to send the secretary of state an 8,000-word dispatch in which he sketched the roots of Soviet policy and warned that the Soviet Union was "committed fanatically to the belief that . . . it is desirable and necessary that the internal harmony of our society be disrupted, our traditional way of life be destroyed, the international authority of our state be broken, if Soviet power is to be secure."

More than a year later, Kennan, now back at the State Department in Washington, spelled out his ideas for a proper response to the Soviets in a 1947 article published anonymously in *Foreign Affairs*. Kennan did not offer a cohesive strategy or an operational plan for combating communism but instead provided a psychological analysis of Soviet insecurity and intentions. He predicted that the Soviets would try to fill "every nook and cranny available . . . in the basin of world power." Yet their insecurity also meant that, in general, they would act cautiously and seek to reduce their risks. Therefore, he insisted, "the main element of any United States policy toward the Soviet Union must be that of a long-term, patient but firm and vigilant *containment* of Russian expansive tendencies. . . . Such a policy has nothing to do with

George F. Kennan, whose 1947 Foreign Affairs *article spelled out the doctrine of containment.*

outward histrionics: with threats or blustering or superfluous gestures of outward 'toughness.'" Americans, he argued, could hope for a long-term moderation of expansionist Soviet ideology and policy, so that in time tensions with the West would lessen. There was a strong possibility "that Soviet power, like the capitalist world of its conception, bears within it the seeds of its own decay, and that the sprouting of those seeds is well advanced."

Kennan's containment concept explained the new departure in foreign policy that America's political leaders had already decided to take. Behind this shift lay a growing fear that Soviet aims reached beyond eastern Europe, posing dangers in the eastern Mediterranean, the Middle East, and western Europe itself.

Indeed the Soviet Union was formulating a plan to gain access to the Mediterranean, long important to Russia for purposes of trade and defense. After the war the Soviet Union began to press Turkey for territorial concessions and the right to build naval bases on the Bosporus, an important gateway between the Black Sea and the Mediterranean. In 1946 civil war broke out in Greece between a government backed by the British and a Communist-led faction that held the northern part of Greece and drew supplies from Yugoslavia, Bulgaria, and Albania. In 1947 the British ambassador informed the American government that the British could no longer bear the economic and military burden of aiding Greece. When Truman conferred with congressional leaders on the situation, the chairman of the Senate Foreign Relations Committee recommended a strong appeal to the American people.

THE TRUMAN DOCTRINE AND THE MARSHALL PLAN   On March 12, 1947, President Truman appeared before Congress to request $400 million for economic aid to both Greece and Turkey and for the authority to send American personnel to train their soldiers. In his speech Truman enunciated what quickly came to be known as the Truman Doctrine. It justified aid to Greece and Turkey in terms more provocative than Kennan's idea of containment and more general than this specific case warranted. "I believe," Truman declared, "that it must be the policy of the United States to support free peoples who are resisting attempted subjugation by armed minorities or by outside pressures."

In 1947 Congress passed the Greek-Turkish aid bill, and by 1950 had spent $659 million on the program. Turkey achieved economic stability, and Greece defeated the Communist insurrection in 1949, partly because President Tito of Yugoslavia had broken with the Soviets in the summer of 1948 and ceased to aid the Greek Communists. But the principles embedded in the Truman Doctrine committed the United States to intervene throughout the world in order to "contain" the spread of communism, and this global commitment would produce tragic consequences as well as successes in the years to come.

The Truman Doctrine marked the beginning, or at least the open acknowledgment, of a contest that Bernard Baruch named in a 1947 speech to the legislature of his native South Carolina: "Let us not be deceived—today we are in the midst of a cold war." Greece and Turkey were but the front lines of an ideological struggle that would involve western Europe as well. There wartime damage and dislocation had devastated factory production, and severe drought in 1947, followed by a harsh winter, had destroyed crops. Coal shortages in London left only enough fuel to heat and light homes for a few hours each day. In Berlin, people were freezing or starving to death. The transportation system in Europe was in shambles. Bridges were out, canals clogged, and rail networks destroyed. Amid the chaos the Communist parties of France and Italy were flourishing. Aid from the United Nations had staved off starvation, but had provided little basis for economic recovery.

In the spring of 1947, George C. Marshall, who had replaced James Byrnes as secretary of state, called for a program of massive aid to rescue western Europe from disaster. The retired chairman of the Joint Chiefs of Staff who orchestrated the Allied victories over Germany and Japan, Marshall had been the highest-ranking army general during World War II. "He is the great one of the age," said Truman. Marshall used the occasion of the Harvard graduation ceremonies in 1947 to outline his plan for the reconstruction of Europe. "Our policy," he said, "is directed not against country or doctrine, but against hunger, poverty, desperation, and chaos." Marshall offered aid to all European countries, including the Soviet Union, and called upon them to take the lead in judging their own needs. On June 27 the foreign ministers of France, Britain, and the Soviet Union met in London to discuss Marshall's overture. Soviet foreign minister Molotov arrived with eighty advisers, but during the talks he got word from Moscow to withdraw from this "imperialist" scheme.

In December Truman submitted his proposal for the European Recovery Program to Congress. Two months later, a Communist insurgency in Czechoslovakia ended the last remaining coalition government in eastern Europe. Coming less than ten years after Munich, the Communist seizure of power in Prague assured congressional passage of the Marshall Plan. From 1948 until 1951 the Economic Cooperation Administration (ECA), which managed the Marshall Plan, poured $13 billion into European economic recovery.

DIVIDING GERMANY The Marshall Plan drew the nations of western Europe closer together, but the breakdown of the wartime alliance between the United States and the Soviet Union left the problem of postwar Germany unsettled. The German economy had stagnated, requiring the American army to support a staggering burden of relief. Slowly, zones of occupation evolved into functioning governments. In 1948 the British, French, and Americans united their zones. The West Germans then organized state governments and elected delegates to a federal constitutional convention.

Soviet leaders resented the Marshall Plan and the unification of West Germany. In April 1948 the Soviets began to restrict the flow of road and rail traffic into West Berlin; on June 23 they stopped all traffic. The next day Stalin cut electricity to the western sector. The Soviets hoped the blockade would force the Allies to give up either Berlin or the plan to unify West Germany. It

The Marshall Plan, which distributed aid throughout Europe, is represented in the background of this 1949 cartoon as a modern tractor. In contrast, a discouraged man is yoked to an old-fashioned "Soviet" plow in the foreground, forced to go over the ground of the "Marshal Stalin Plan" while Stalin tries to convince others that "it's the same thing without mechanical problems."

OCCUPATION OF GERMANY AND AUSTRIA

was war by starvation. But the American commander in Germany proposed to stand firm. "When Berlin falls, Western Germany will be next," he told the Pentagon. "If we mean . . . to hold Europe against communism, we must not budge."

Truman agreed, saying "We are going to stay—period." After considering the use of armed convoys to supply West Berlin, he opted for a massive airlift. At the time this seemed an enormous and perhaps impossible task. But the Allied air forces quickly brought in planes from around the world, and by October 1948 they were flying in up to 13,000 tons of food, medicine, coal, and equipment a day.

Finally, on May 12, 1949, after extended talks, the Soviets lifted the ten-month blockade. Before the end of the year the German Federal Republic had a government functioning under Chancellor Konrad Adenauer of the Christian Democratic party. At the end of May 1949, an independent German "Democratic" Republic arose in the eastern zone, formalizing the division of Germany. West Germany gradually acquired more authority, until the Western powers recognized its full sovereignty in 1955.

BUILDING NATO   As relations between the Soviets and western Europe chilled, transatlantic unity ripened into an outright military alliance. On April 4, 1949, the North Atlantic Treaty was signed at Washington by representatives of twelve nations: the United States, Britain, France, Belgium, the Netherlands, Luxembourg, Canada, Denmark, Iceland, Italy, Norway, and Portugal. Greece and Turkey joined the alliance in 1952, Germany in 1955, Spain in 1982. Senate ratification of the North Atlantic Treaty by a vote of 82 to 13 suggested that the isolationism of the prewar period no longer exerted a hold on the American people. The treaty pledged that an attack against any one of the signers would be considered an attack against all, and provided for a council of the North Atlantic Treaty Organization (NATO), which could establish other necessary agencies.

The eventful year 1948 produced one other foreign policy decision with long-term consequences. Palestine, as the biblical Holy Land had come to be known, was under Turkish rule until the League of Nations made it a British mandate after World War I. Over the early years of the twentieth century, many Zionists, who advocated a Jewish state in the region, had migrated there. More came after the British entered, and a greatly increased number arrived during the Nazi persecution in 1933 and after. Offered a promise by the British of a national homeland, the Jewish inhabitants demanded their own state.

Late in 1947, the U.N. General Assembly voted to partition Palestine into Jewish and Arab states, but this met fierce Arab opposition. Finally, the British mandate expired on May 14, 1948, and Jewish leaders proclaimed

NATO, a symbol of renewed strength for a battered Europe.

the independence of the state of Israel. President Truman, who had been in close touch with Jewish leaders, ordered recognition of the new state within minutes—the United States became the first nation to act. The neighboring Arab states thereupon went to war against Israel, which, however, held its own. U.N. mediators gradually worked out truce agreements with Israel's Arab neighbors, and an uneasy peace was restored by May 11, 1949, when Israel was admitted as a member of the United Nations. But the hard feelings and intermittent warfare between Israel and the Arab states have festered ever since, complicating American foreign policy, which has tried to maintain friendship with both sides, but has tilted toward Israel.

CIVIL RIGHTS DURING THE 1940S

The social tremors triggered by World War II and the onset of the cold war transformed America's racial landscape. The vicious racism of the German Nazis, Italian fascists, and Japanese imperialists focused attention on the need for the United States to improve its own race relations and to provide for equal rights under the law. As a *New York Times* editorial explained in early 1946, "This is a particularly good time to campaign against the evils of bigotry, prejudice, and race hatred because we have witnessed the defeat of enemies who tried to found a mastery of the world upon such cruel and fallacious policy." The postwar confrontation with the Soviet Union also gave Americans an added incentive to improve race relations in the United States. In the ideological contest for influence in Africa, American diplomats were at a disadvantage as long as racial segregation continued in the United States. The Soviets often compared segregation in the American South to the Nazis' treatment of Jews.

For most of his political career, Harry Truman had shown little concern about the plight of African Americans. He had grown up in western Missouri assuming that both blacks and whites preferred to be segregated from one another. As president, however, he began to reassess his convictions. In the fall of 1946 Truman hosted a delegation of civil rights activists from the National Emergency Committee Against Mob Violence. They urged the president to issue a public statement condemning the resurgence of the Ku Klux Klan and the lynching of blacks.

The delegation graphically described incidents of torture and intimidation against blacks in the South. Truman was aghast. He soon appointed a Committee on Civil Rights to investigate violence against African Americans and to recommend preventive measures.

The committee recommended the renewal of the Fair Employment Practices Committee (FEPC) and the creation of a permanent civil rights commission to investigate abuses. It also argued that federal aid be denied to any state that mandated segregated schools and public facilities.

On July 26, 1948, Truman banned racial discrimination in the hiring of federal employees. Four days later, he issued an executive order ending racial segregation in the armed forces. The air force and navy quickly complied, but the army dragged its feet until the early 1950s. By 1960 the armed forces were the most racially integrated of all American organizations. Desegregating the military was, Truman claimed, "the greatest thing that ever happened to America."

JACKIE ROBINSON Meanwhile, racial segregation was being confronted in a much more public field of endeavor—professional baseball. In April 1947, as the baseball season opened, the National

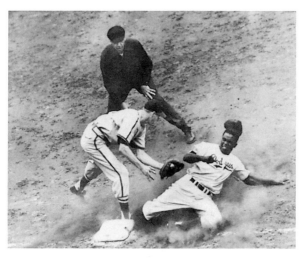

Jackie Robinson, 1949. *Racial discrimination remained widespread through the postwar period. In 1947 Jackie Robinson of the Brooklyn Dodgers became the first black to play major league baseball.*

League's Brooklyn Dodgers included on their roster the first black player to cross the color line in major league baseball: Jackie Robinson. Born in Georgia and raised in California, Robinson was an army veteran and baseball player in the Negro leagues. Branch Rickey, the courageous president of the Dodgers, selected Robinson to integrate professional baseball, not only for his athletic potential but because of his willingness to control his temper in the face of virulent racism. Rickey knew that the first black player in the major leagues would face a storm of abuse. Teammates and opposing players viciously baited Robinson, pitchers threw at him, base runners spiked him, and spectators booed and taunted him in every city. Hotels refused him rooms, and restaurants denied him service. Hate mail arrived by the bucket load. On the other hand, black spectators were electrified by Robinson's courageous example; they turned out in droves to see him play.

As time passed, Robinson won over many fans and opposing players through his quiet courage, self-deprecating wit, and determined performance. Soon, other teams began to sign black players. Baseball's pathbreaking efforts stimulated other professional sports such as football and basketball to integrate their rosters. Jackie Robinson vividly demonstrated that racism, not inferiority, impeded African-American advancement in the postwar era and that segregation need not be a permanent condition of American life.

SHAPING THE FAIR DEAL   The determination Truman projected in foreign affairs did not alter his weak image on the domestic front. By early 1948, after three years in the White House, Truman had yet to shake the impression that he was not up to the job. The Democratic party seemed about to fragment: southern conservatives resented Truman's outspoken support of civil rights, while the left had flared up in 1946 over his firing of Secretary of Commerce Henry Wallace after a speech critical of the administration's policy. "Getting tough [with the Soviet Union]," Wallace had argued, "never brought anything real and lasting—whether for schoolyard bullies or world powers. The tougher we get, the tougher the Russians will get." The left itself was splitting between the Progressive Citizens of America (PCA), formed in 1946, which supported Wallace, and the Americans for Democratic Action (ADA), formed in 1947, which also criticized Truman but took a firm anti-Communist stance.

Truman's support of civil rights for African Americans had its political costs, as this 1948 cartoon suggests.

Truman made an aggressive effort to shore up the New Deal coalition. He needed the midwestern and western farm belts, and had fairly strong support among farmers. In metropolitan areas, he needed to carry the labor and black vote, which he wooed by working closely with unions and liberals, and pressing the cause of civil rights.

Like other presidents, Truman used his State of the Union message in 1948 to set the agenda for an election year. The speech offered something to nearly every group the Democrats hoped to attract. The first goal, Truman said, was "to secure fully the essential human rights of our citizens," and he promised a special message later on civil rights. "To protect human resources," he proposed federal aid to education, increased and extended unemployment and retirement benefits, a comprehensive system of health insurance, more federal support for housing, and extension of rent controls. He continued to pile on the demands: for reclamation projects, more rural electrification, a higher minimum wage, laws to admit thousands of displaced persons to the United States, money for the Marshall Plan, and a "cost-of-living" tax credit.

THE 1948 ELECTION   The Republican-controlled Congress for the most part spurned the Truman program, an action it would later regret.

The opening of the 1948 Democratic National Convention is marked by demonstrations against racial segregation, led by A. Philip Randolph (left).

At the Republican party convention, New York governor Thomas E. Dewey won the nomination on the third ballot. The platform endorsed most of the New Deal reforms as accomplished fact and approved the administration's bipartisan foreign policy, but Dewey promised to run things more efficiently.

In July a glum Democratic convention gathered in Philadelphia, expecting to do little more than go through the motions, only to find itself doubly surprised: first by the battle over the civil rights plank, and then by Truman's acceptance speech. To keep from stirring southern hostility, the administration sought a platform plank that opposed racial discrimination only in general terms. Liberal Democrats, however, sponsored a plank that called on Congress for specific action and commended Truman "for his courageous stand on the issue of civil rights." Minneapolis mayor Hubert H. Humphrey electrified the delegates and set off a ten-minute demonstration when he declared: "The time has arrived for the Democratic party to get out of the shadow of states' rights and walk forthrightly into the bright sunshine of human rights." Segregationist delegates from Alabama and Mississippi walked, instead, out of the convention.

After the convention had nominated Truman, the president showed a new fighting style in his speeches. He pledged to "win this election and make the Republicans like it," and added "don't you forget it!" He also vowed to call Congress back into session "to get the laws the people need," many of which the Republican platform had endorsed.

On July 17 a group of rebellious southern Democrats met in Birmingham and nominated South Carolina governor Strom Thurmond on a States' Rights Democratic ticket, quickly dubbed the "Dixiecrat" ticket. The Dixiecrats hoped to draw enough electoral votes to preclude a majority for either major party, throwing the election into the House, where they might strike a sectional bargain. A few days later, on July 23, the left wing of the Democratic party gathered in Philadelphia to name Henry A. Wallace on a Progressive party ticket. These splits in the Democratic ranks seemed to spell the final blow to Truman. The special session of Congress petered out in futility.

But Truman, undaunted, set out on a 31,000-mile "whistle-stop" train tour during which he castigated the "do-nothing" Eightieth Congress.

The "Dixiecrats" nominate South Carolina governor Strom Thurmond (center) to lead their ticket in the 1948 election.

Friendly audiences shouted "Pour it on, Harry!" and "Give 'em hell, Harry." Truman responded: "I don't give 'em hell. I just tell the truth and they think it's hell." Dewey, in contrast, ran a restrained campaign, designed to avoid rocking the boat. By so doing he may have snatched defeat from the jaws of victory.

The polls and the pundits predicted a sure win for Dewey, but on election day Truman chalked up the biggest upset in American history, taking 24.2 million votes (49.5 percent) to Dewey's 22 million (45.1 percent) and winning a thumping margin of 303 to 189 in the electoral college. Thurmond and Wallace each got more than a million votes, but the revolt of right and left worked to Truman's advantage. The Dixiecrat rebellion reassured black voters who had questioned the Democrats' commitment to civil rights, while the Progressive movement made it hard to tag Truman as "soft on communism." Thurmond carried four Deep South states (South Carolina, Mississippi, Alabama, and Louisiana) with 39 electoral votes, including one electoral vote from a Tennessee elector who repudiated his state's decision for Truman. Thurmond's success started a momentous disruption of the Democratic

Truman's victory in 1948 was a huge upset, so much so that even the early edition of the Chicago Daily Tribune *was caught off guard, running the presumptuous headline "Dewey Defeats Truman."*

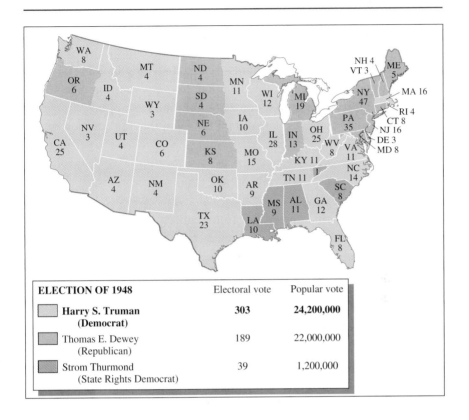

ELECTION OF 1948	Electoral vote	Popular vote
Harry S. Truman (Democrat)	303	24,200,000
Thomas E. Dewey (Republican)	189	22,000,000
Strom Thurmond (State Rights Democrat)	39	1,200,000

Solid South. But Truman's victory also carried Democratic majorities into Congress, where the new group of senators included Hubert Humphrey and, by eighty-seven disputed votes, "Landslide Lyndon" B. Johnson of Texas.

Truman viewed his victory as a vindication for the New Deal and a mandate for liberalism. "We have rejected the discredited theory that the fortunes of the nation should be in the hands of a privileged few," he said. His State of the Union message repeated the agenda he had set forth a year previously. "Every segment of our population and every individual," he declared, "has a right to expect from his government a fair deal." Whether deliberately or not he had invented a tag, the "Fair Deal," to set off his program from the New Deal.

Congress passed some of Truman's Fair Deal proposals, but they were mainly extensions or enlargements of New Deal programs already in place: a higher minimum wage, expansion of Social Security, coverage, extension of rent controls, increased farm price supports, and a sizable slum-clearance and public housing program. Despite Democratic majorities, however, the conservative coalition thwarted any drastic new departures in domestic policy. Congress rejected civil rights bills, national health insurance, federal aid to education, and a plan to provide subsidies that would hold up farm incomes rather than farm prices. Congress also turned down Truman's demand for repeal of the Taft-Hartley Act.

THE COLD WAR HEATS UP

Global concerns, never far from center stage in the postwar world, plagued Truman's second term, as they had his first. People began to live in real fear that the Communists were infiltrating American society and were intent upon world domination. In his inaugural address Truman called for a vigilant anti-Communist foreign policy to rest on four pillars: the United Nations, the Marshall Plan, NATO, and a "bold new plan" for technical assistance to underdeveloped parts of the world, a sort of global Marshall Plan that came to be known simply as "Point Four." This program to aid the postwar world never accomplished its goals, in part because other international problems soon diverted Truman's attention.

"LOSING" CHINA AND THE BOMB   One of the most intractable problems, the China tangle, was fast coming unraveled in 1949. The Chinese Nationalists led by Chiang Kai-shek had been fighting, Mao Tse-tung[*] and the Communists since the 1920s. The outbreak of war with Japan in 1937 halted the Chinese Civil War, and both, Roosevelt and Stalin believed that the Nationalists would organize China after the war.

But the commanders of American forces in China during World War II concluded that Chiang's government was hopelessly corrupt, tyrannical, and inefficient. After the war, American forces nevertheless ferried Nationalist Chinese armies back into the eastern and northern provinces

---

[*]*The traditional (Wade-Giles) spelling is used here. In 1958 the Chinese government adopted the "pinyin" transliterations that became more widely used after Mao's death in 1976, so that, for example, Mao Tse-tung became Mao Zedong, and Peking became Beijing.*

as the Japanese withdrew. U.S. policy during and immediately after the war promoted peace between the factions in China, but sporadic civil war broke out late in 1945.

It soon became a losing fight for the Nationalists, as the Communists won over the land-hungry peasantry. By the end of 1949, the Nationalist government had fled to the island of Formosa, which it renamed Taiwan. Administration critics now asked bitterly: "Who lost China?" A State Department study blamed Chiang for his failure to hold the support of the Chinese people. In fact it is hard to imagine how the United States government could have prevented a Communist victory short of massive military intervention, which would have been very risky and unpopular. The United States continued to recognize the Nationalist government on Taiwan as the rightful government of China, delaying formal relations with Communist China for thirty years. Seeking to shore up friendly regimes in Asia, in 1950 the United States recognized the French-supported regime of Emperor Bao Dai in Vietnam and shortly afterward extended aid to the French in their battle against Ho Chi Minh's guerrillas there.

As Mao and the Communists gained control of China, American intelligence in 1949 found an unusual level of radioactivity in the air, evidence that the Soviets had set off an atomic device. The American nuclear monopoly had lasted just four years. The discovery of the Soviet bomb provoked an intense reappraisal of the strategic balance in the world, causing Truman in 1950 to order the construction of a hydrogen bomb, a weapon far more frightful than the atomic bombs dropped on Japan, lest the Soviets make one first.

The discovery also led the National Security Council to produce a top-secret document, known as NSC-68, that called for rebuilding conventional military forces to provide options other than nuclear war. This represented a major departure from America's time-honored aversion to keeping large standing armies in peacetime, and was an expensive proposition. But the American public was growing more receptive to the nation's new role as world leader, and an invasion of South Korea by Communist forces from the north clinched the issue for most.

WAR IN KOREA   The Japanese had occupied Korea since 1910, and after their defeat and withdrawal in 1945, the victorious Allies faced the difficult task of creating a new nation. Complicating that task was the fact that Soviet troops had advanced into northern Korea and had accepted the surrender of Japanese forces above the 38th parallel, while American forces did the same south of the line. The Soviets quickly organized a Korean government along Stalinist lines, while the Americans set up a Western-style regime in the South.

The division of Korea at the end of World War II, like the division of Germany, began as a temporary expedient and ended as a permanent fact. In the hectic days of August 1945, the Soviets accepted an American proposal to divide Korea at the 38th parallel until steps could be taken to unify the war-torn country. With the onset of the cold war, however, it became clear that agreement on unification was no more likely in Korea than in Germany, and by the end of 1948 separate regimes had appeared in the two sectors and occupation forces had withdrawn. The weakened state of the American military contributed to the impression that South Korea was vulnerable. A growing body of evidence later gleaned from Soviet archives reveals that Stalin encouraged the North Koreans to use force to unify their country and oust the Americans from the peninsula. The Soviets helped design a war plan that called for North Korean forces to seize South Korea within a week. Stalin apparently assumed that the United States would not intervene.

Over 80,000 North Korean soldiers crossed the boundary on June 25, 1950, and swept down the peninsula. President Truman responded decisively. He and his advisers assumed that the North Korean attack was directed by Moscow and was a brazen indication of the aggressive designs of Soviet communism. "The attack upon Korea makes it plain beyond all doubt," Truman told Congress, "that communism has passed beyond the use of subversion to conquer independent nations and will now use armed invasion and war." Truman then made two critical decisions. First, he decided to wage war under the auspices of the United Nations rather than unilaterally. Second, he decided to wage war without asking Congress for a formal declaration of war.

An emergency meeting of the U.N. Security Council quickly censured the North Korean "breach of peace." The Soviet delegate, who held a veto power, was at the time boycotting the council because it would not seat Communist China in place of Nationalist China. On June 27, its first resolution having been ignored, the Security Council called on U.N. members to "furnish such assistance to the Republic of Korea as may be necessary to repel the armed attack and to restore international peace and security in the area." Truman ordered American air, naval, and ground forces into action. In all, some fourteen other U.N. members sent military units. General Douglas MacArthur was designated to take charge. The American defense of South Korea set a precedent of profound consequence: war by order of the president rather than by vote of Congress. Yet, it had the sanction of the U.N. Security Council, and could technically be considered a "police action," not a war. To be sure, other presidents had ordered American troops into action without a declaration of war, but never on such a scale.

Truman's conviction that the invasion of South Korea was orchestrated by Stalin led to two other decisions that had far-reaching consequences. Believing that the Korean conflict was actually a diversion for a Soviet invasion of western Europe, Truman began a major expansion of American forces in Europe. He also increased his assistance to the French in Indochina, creating the Military Assistance Advisory Group for Indochina. This was the start of America's deepening involvement in Vietnam.

Soldiers engaged in the recapture of Seoul from the North Koreans, September 1950.

For three months the fighting in Korea went badly for the Republic of Korea (ROK) and U.N. forces. By September the ROK and U.N. forces were barely hanging on to the Pusan perimeter in the southeast corner of Korea. Then, in a brilliant ploy, on September 15, 1950, MacArthur landed a new force to the North Korean rear at Inchon, the port city for Seoul. Synchronized with a breakout from Pusan, the sudden blow stampeded the enemy back across the border. At this point, MacArthur convinced Truman to allow him to push on and seek to reunify Korea. By now, the Soviet delegate was back in the Security Council, wielding his veto. So on October 7 the United States won approval for this course from the U.N. General Assembly, where the veto did not apply. United States forces had already crossed the boundary by October 1, and now continued northward against minimal resistance. President Truman, concerned about intervention by Communist China, flew 7,000 miles to Wake Island for a conference with General MacArthur on October 15. There the general discounted chances that the Red Chinese Army would act, but if it did, he predicted "there would be the greatest slaughter."

That same day Peking announced that China "cannot stand idly by." On October 20 U.N. forces had entered Pyongyang, the North Korean capital, and on October 26 advance units had reached Chosan on the Yalu River border with China. MacArthur predicted total victory by Christmas. On the night of November 25, however, some 260,000 Chinese "volunteers" counterattacked, and massive "human wave" attacks, with the support of tanks and planes, turned the tables on the U.N. forces, sending them into a desperate retreat just at the onset of winter. It had become "an entirely new war," MacArthur said. He criticized the administration for requiring that he conduct a limited war. He asked for thirty-four atomic bombs and proposed air raids on China's "privileged sanctuary" in Manchuria, a naval blockade of China, and an invasion of the Chinese mainland by the Taiwan Nationalists. MacArthur seemed to have forgotten altogether his onetime reluctance to bog down the country in a major war on the Asian mainland. Opposition to the war in Korea increased with each passing month. In December 1950, the editors of *Life* magazine warned that the news from Korea "is of disaster. World War III moves ever closer."

Truman opposed leading the United States into the "gigantic booby trap" of war with China, and the U.N. forces soon rallied. By January 1951 over 900,000 U.N. troops under General Matthew B. Ridgway

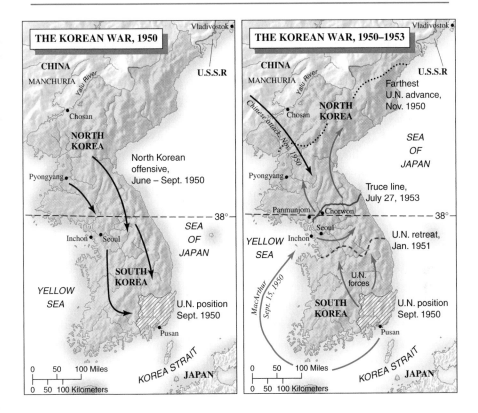

finally secured their lines below Seoul, and then launched a counterattack that in some places carried them back across the 38th parallel in
March. When Truman seized the chance and offered negotiations to restore the prewar boundary, MacArthur undermined the move by issuing
an ultimatum for China to make peace or be attacked. Truman then decided that MacArthur, whom he called "Mr. Prima Donna," would have
to go. On April 5, on the floor of the House, the Republican minority
leader read a letter in which MacArthur criticized the president and
said that "there is no substitute for victory." Such an act of open insubordination left the commander-in-chief no choice but to accept
MacArthur's policy or fire him. Civilian control of the military was at
stake, Truman later said, and he did not let it remain at stake very long.
On April 11, 1951, the president removed the popular MacArthur from
all his commands and replaced him with Ridgway.

Truman's action ignited an immediate uproar in the country, and a tumultuous reception greeted MacArthur upon his return home for the

first time since 1937. MacArthur's speech to a joint session of Congress provided the climactic event. He recalled a barracks ballad of his youth "which proclaimed most proudly that old soldiers never die, they just fade away." And like the old soldiers of that ballad, he said, "I now close my military career and just fade away, an old soldier who tried to do his duty as God gave him the light to see that duty." A Senate investigation brought out the administration's arguments, best summarized by General Omar Bradley, chairman of the Joint Chiefs of Staff. "Taking on Red China," he explained, would lead only "to a larger deadlock at greater expense." The MacArthur strategy "would involve us in the wrong war at the wrong place at the wrong time and with the wrong enemy." Most Americans found General Bradley's logic persuasive.

On June 24, 1951, the Soviet representative at the United Nations proposed a cease-fire and armistice along the 38th parallel; Secretary of State Dean Acheson accepted a few days later with the consent of the United Nations. China and North Korea responded favorably—at the time General Ridgway's "meat-grinder" offensive was inflicting severe losses—and truce talks started on July 10, 1951, at Panmunjom, only to drag on for another two years while the fighting continued. The chief snags were prisoner exchanges and the insistence of the South Korean president on unification. By the time a truce was finally reached on July 27, 1953, Truman had relinquished the White House to Dwight D. Eisenhower. The truce line followed the war front at that time, mostly a little north of the 38th parallel, with a demilitarized zone of two and a half miles separating the forces; repatriation of prisoners would be voluntary, supervised by a neutral commission. No final peace conference ever took place, and Korea, like Germany, remained divided. The war had cost the United States more than 33,000 battle deaths and 103,000 wounded and missing. South Korean casualties, all told, were about 1 million, and North Korean and Chinese casualties an estimated 1.5 million.

ANOTHER RED SCARE   In calculating the costs of the Korean War one must add in the far-reaching consequences of the Second Red Scare, which had grown since 1945 as the domestic counterpart to the cold war abroad and reached a crescendo during the Korean conflict. Since 1938, the House Un-American Activities Committee (HUAC) had kept up a drumbeat of accusations about subversives in government. On March 21, 1947, just nine days after he announced the Truman Doctrine, Truman signed an executive order setting up procedures for an employee loyalty program in the federal government. Every person entering civil employ would be subject to a background investigation. By early 1951 the Civil Service Commission had cleared over 3 million people, while over 2,000 had resigned and 212 had been dismissed for doubtful loyalty.

Perhaps the case most damaging to the administration involved Alger Hiss, president of the Carnegie Endowment for International Peace, who had served in several government departments. Whittaker Cham-

Alger Hiss, accused of leading a Soviet spy ring, testifying before the House Un-American Activities Committee in 1948.

bers, a former Soviet agent and later an editor of *Time* magazine, told the House Un-American Activities Committee in 1948 that Hiss had given him secret documents ten years earlier, when Chambers worked for the Soviets and Hiss worked in the State Department. Hiss sued for libel, and Chambers produced microfilms of the State Department documents he said Hiss had passed on to him. Hiss denied the accusation, whereupon he was indicted for perjury and, after one mistrial, convicted in 1950. The charge was perjury, but he was convicted of lying about espionage—for which he could not be tried because the statute of limitations on the crime had expired.

Most damaging to the administration was that President Truman, taking at face value the many testimonials to Hiss's integrity, called the charges against him a "red herring." The Hiss affair had another political consequence: it raised to national prominence a young California congressman, Richard M. Nixon, who doggedly insisted on pursuing the case and then exploited an anti-Communist stance to win election to the Senate in 1950.

More cases of Communist infiltration surfaced. In 1949 eleven top U.S. Communist party leaders were convicted under the Smith Act of 1940, which outlawed any conspiracy to advocate the overthrow of the government. The Supreme Court upheld the law under the doctrine of a "clear and present danger," which overrode the right to free speech. What was more, in 1950 the government unearthed the existence of a

British-American spy network that had fed information about the development of the atomic bomb to the Soviet Union. These disclosures led to the arrest of, among others, Klaus Fuchs in Britain and Julius and Ethel Rosenberg in the United States. The Rosenbergs, convicted of espionage, were executed in 1953.

MCCARTHY'S ANTI-COMMUNIST WITCH-HUNT   Such revelations of Soviet spying encouraged politicians to exploit public fears. If a man of such respectability as Hiss was guilty, many wondered, whom then could be trusted? The United States, which bestrode the world like a colossus in 1945, had since "lost" eastern Europe and Asia, and "lost" its atomic secrets to Russia. Early in 1950 a little-known Republican senator, Joseph R. McCarthy of Wisconsin, suddenly surfaced as the shrewdest and most ruthless exploiter of such anxieties. He took up the cause of anti-communism with a speech at Wheeling, West Virginia, on February 9, 1950, in which he said that the State Department was infested with Communists and that he held in his hand a list of their names. Later there was confusion as to whether he had said 205, 81, 57, or "a lot" of names, and even whether the sheet of paper carried a list. But such confusion always pursued McCarthy's charges.

Senator Joseph McCarthy (left) and his aide Roy Cohn (right) exchange comments during testimony.

Despite his outlandish claims, McCarthy never uncovered a single Communist agent in government. But with the United States at war with Korean Communists in mid-1950, it was easy for him to mobilize true believers. By 1951 he was riding so high as to list General George Marshall among the disloyal. His smear campaign went unchallenged until the end of the Korean War.

Fears of Communist espionage led the Congress in 1950 to pass the McCarran Internal Security Act over President Truman's veto. The act made it unlawful "to combine, conspire, or agree with any other person to perform any act which would substantially contribute to . . . the establishment of a totalitarian dictatorship." Communist and Communist-front organizations had to register with the attorney-general. Aliens who had belonged to totalitarian parties were barred from admission to the United States, a provision that discouraged any temptation for Communists to defect to the United States. The McCarran Act, Truman said in his veto message, would "put the Government into the business of thought control." He might in fact have said as much about the Smith Act of 1940, or even his own program of loyalty investigations. Yet documents recently uncovered in Russian archives and American security agencies reveal that the Soviets did indeed operate an extensive espionage ring in the United States. Russian agents recruited several hundred American spies to ferret out secrets regarding atomic weapons, defense systems, and military intelligence.

ASSESSING THE COLD WAR In retrospect, the onset of the cold war takes on an appearance of terrible inevitability. American and Soviet misunderstanding of each other's motives was virtually unavoidable. America's preference for international principles, such as self-determination and democracy, conflicted with the Soviet Union's preference for international spheres of influence. Russia, after all, had been invaded by Germany twice in the first half of the twentieth century, and Soviet leaders wanted tame buffer states on their borders for protection. The people of eastern Europe, as usual, were caught in the middle. But the Communists themselves held to a universal principle: world revolution.

If international conditions set the stage for the cold war, the actions of political leaders and thinkers set events in motion. President Truman may have erred in seeming to include all the world in his 1947 doctrine of Communist containment. The loyalty program, following on the heels of the Truman Doctrine, may have spurred on the anti-Communist hysteria of the times. Containment itself proved hard to contain, its author (George Kennan) later confessed, in part because he failed at the outset to spell out its limits.

The years after World War II were unlike any other postwar period in American history. Having taken on global burdens, the nation had become, if not a "garrison state," at least a country committed to a major and permanent national military establishment, along with the attendant National Security Council, Central Intelligence Agency, and by presidential directive in 1952, the enormous National Security Agency, entrusted with monitoring media and communications for foreign intelligence.

The policy initiatives of the Truman years had led the country to abandon its long-standing aversion to peacetime alliances. It was a far cry from the world of 1796, when George Washington in his farewell address warned his countrymen against "those overgrown military establishments which . . . are inauspicious to liberty" and advised his country "to steer clear of permanent alliances with any portion of the foreign world." But, then, Washington had warned only against participation in the "ordinary" combinations and collusions of Europe, and surely the postwar years had seen extraordinary events and unprecedented new alliances.

MAKING CONNECTIONS

- The cold war had a major impact on American society: among other things, it helped create the "conforming culture" described in the next chapter.

- The New Frontier and Great Society programs of Presidents Kennedy and Johnson accomplished much of what Truman tried to do through his Fair Deal policies. See Chapter 34.

- The world seemed a dangerous place at the height of the cold war, but when seen from the perspective of the post–cold war world of the 1990s (see Chapters 36 and 37), it had a certain stability that discouraged political violence.

FURTHER READING

The cold war remains a hotly debated topic. The traditional interpretation is best reflected in John L. Gaddis's *The United States and the Origins of the Cold War, 1941–1947* (1972) and *We Now Know: Rethinking Cold War History* (2001). Both superpowers, Gaddis argues, were responsible for causing the cold war, but the Soviet Union was more culpable. The revisionist perspective is represented by Gar Alperovitz's *Atomic Diplomacy* (rev. ed., 1994). He places primary responsibility for the conflict on the United States. Also see H. W. Brands's *The Devil We Knew: Americans and the Cold War* (1993) and Melvyn P. Leffler's *A Preponderance of Power: National Security, the Truman Administration, and the Cold War* (1992).

Arnold Offner indicts Truman for clumsy statesmanship in *Another Such Victory: President Truman and the Cold War* (2001). For a positive assessment of Truman's leadership, see Alonzo Hamby's *Beyond the New Deal: Harry S. Truman and American Liberalism* (1973). The domestic policies of the Fair Deal are treated in William C. Berman's *The Politics of Civil Rights in the Truman Administration* (1970), Richard M. Dalfiume's *Desegregation of the United States Armed Forces* (1969), and Maeva Marcus's *Truman and the Steel Seizure Case: The Limits of Presidential Power* (rev. ed., 1994). The most comprehensive biography of Truman is David McCullough's *Truman* (1992).

For an introduction to the tensions in Asia, see Akira Iriye's *The Cold War in Asia* (1974). For the Korean conflict, see Callum A. MacDonald's *Korea: The War before Vietnam* (1986) and Max Hasting's *The Korean War* (rev. ed., 1993).

The anti-Communist syndrome is surveyed in David Caute's *The Great Fear: The Anti-Communist Purge under Truman and Eisenhower* (1978). Arthur Herman's *Joseph McCarthy* (2000) covers McCarthy himself. For a well-documented account of how the cold war was sustained by superpatriotism, intolerance, and suspicion, see Stephen J. Whitfield's *The Culture of the Cold War* (1990).

32 ↷ THROUGH THE PICTURE WINDOW: SOCIETY AND CULTURE, 1945–1960

CHAPTER ORGANIZER

This chapter focuses on:

• the economic prosperity of America in the postwar period.

• the culture of the 1950s, with its strains of conformity and innovation.

• America's burgeoning consumer culture.

mericans emerged from World War II elated, proud of their military strength and industrial might. As the editors of *Fortune* magazine proclaimed in 1946, "This is a dream era, this is what everyone was waiting through the blackouts for. The Great American Boom is on." So it was, from babies to Buicks to Admiral television sets. An American public that had known mostly deprivation and sacrifice for the last decade and a half began to enjoy unprecedented prosperity. The postwar era witnessed tremendous economic growth and rising social contentment. Divorce and homicide rates fell, the birthrate soared, and the prevailing mood seemed aggressively upbeat—at least on the surface.

Amid such rising affluence and comfortable domesticity, however, many social critics, writers, and artists expressed a growing sense of unease. Was postwar American society becoming too complacent, too conformist, too materialistic? Such questions reflected the perennial tension in American life between idealism and materialism, a tension that arrived with the first settlers and remains with us today. Americans have always struggled to accumulate goods and cultivate goodness. During the postwar era, the nation again tried to do both. For a while, at least, it appeared to succeed.

PEOPLE OF PLENTY

The dominant feature of post–World War II American society was its remarkable prosperity. After a surprisingly brief postwar recession, the economy soared to record heights. The gross national product (GNP) nearly doubled between 1945 and 1960, and the 1960s witnessed an even more spectacular expansion of the economy. By 1970 the gap between living standards in the United States and the rest of the world had become a chasm: with 6 percent of the world's population, America produced and consumed two-thirds of the world's goods.

During the 1950s, government officials assured the citizenry that they should not fear another economic collapse. "Never again shall we allow a depression in the United States," President Eisenhower promised. The leading economists of the postwar era agreed that perpetual economic growth was possible, desirable, and, in fact, essential. The expectation of unending plenty became the reigning assumption of social thought in the postwar era.

Several factors contributed to this prolonged economic surge. The massive federal expenditures for military needs during World War II had catapulted the economy out of the Great Depression. High government spending continued in the postwar era, thanks to the tensions generated by the cold war and, in the early 1950s, the increase in defense spending provoked by the Korean conflict. The military budget after 1945 represented the single most important stimulant to the postwar economic boom. Defense research also helped spawn the new glamour industries of the postwar era: chemicals, electronics, and aviation.

Most of the other major industrial nations of the world—England, France, Germany, Japan, the Soviet Union—had been physically devastated during the war, which meant that American manufacturers enjoyed a virtual monopoly over international trade. In addition, technological innovations contributed to the "automation" of the workplace and thereby created spectacular increases in productivity. The wide-spread use of new and more efficient machinery and computers led to a 35 percent jump in worker productivity between 1945 and 1955. In 1945 it took 310 hours to make a car; in 1960, only 150.

The major catalyst in promoting economic expansion after 1945 was the unleashing of pent-up consumer demand. During the war, Americans had postponed purchases of such major items as cars and houses and in the process had saved over $150 billion. Now they were eager to buy. The United States after World War II experienced a purchasing frenzy.

THE GI BILL OF RIGHTS   Part of the purchasing frenzy was financed by the federal government. Fears that a sharp drop in military spending and the sudden influx of veterans as new workers would send the economy into a downward spiral and produce widespread unemployment led Congress to pass the Servicemen's Readjustment Act of 1944. Popularly known as the GI Bill of Rights (GI stood for the phrase "government issue" stamped on military uniforms and was slang for a serviceman), it led to the creation of a new government agency, the Veterans Administration, and it included provisions for mustering out pay, unemployment pay for veterans for one year, preference for civil service jobs, loans for home construction, access to government hospitals, and generous subsidies for college or professional training.

Between 1944 and 1956, almost 8 million veterans took advantage of $14.5 billion in GI Bill subsidies to attend college or job training programs. Some 5 million used GI Bill mortgage loans to buy new homes. The home loans required no down payment and provided up to twenty years for repayment. The infusion of funds into the economy provided by the GI Bill helped fuel the postwar prosperity. And the educational benefits encouraged people to consider pursuing higher education. Before World War II, approximately 160,000 Americans graduated from college each year. By 1950 the figure had risen to 500,000. In 1949 veterans accounted for 40 percent of all college enrollments, and the United States could boast the world's best-educated workforce.

The GI Bill democratized higher education. It provided a generation of working-class Americans with an opportunity to earn a college degree for the first time. In turn, a college education served as a lever into the middle class and economic security. But while the GI Bill helped erode class barriers, it was less successful in dismantling racial barriers. Many black veterans could not take equal advantage of the education benefits. Most colleges and universities after the war remained racially segregated, either by regulation or by practice. Of the 9,000 students enrolled at the University of Pennsylvania in 1946, for example, only 46 were African Americans. Those blacks who did manage to gain admission to white colleges or universities were barred from playing on athletic teams, attending dances and other social events, and joining fraternities or sororities.

The historically black colleges, most of which were in the South, could not expand quickly enough to meet the demand. In 1940 black colleges enrolled 43,000 students; in 1950 the number had soared to 77,000. Yet over 20,000 were denied admission because of overcrowded facilities. As a result, most black veterans did not get into a college. In

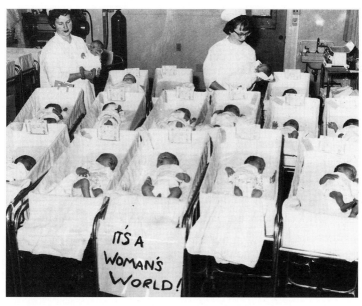

The Baby Boom. *Much of America's social history since the 1940s has been the story of the "baby-boom" generation.*

1946 only one-fifth of the 100,000 who had applied for educational benefits had enrolled. In other cases, black veterans were inadequately prepared for college-level work. As late as 1950, some 70 percent of black adults in the southern states had only a seventh-grade education or below.

The return of some 12 million veterans to private life also helped generate a postwar "baby boom," which peaked in 1957. Many young married couples who had delayed having children were intent on making up for lost time. Between 1945 and 1960, total population grew by some 40 million, an increase of almost 30 percent. Much of America's social history since the 1940s has been the story of the unusually large baby-boom generation and its progress through the stages of life. Initially, the postwar baby boom created a massive demand for diapers, baby food, toys, medicines, schools, books, teachers, furniture, and housing.

AN EXPANDING CONSUMER CULTURE   Postwar America soon became a hive of construction activity. The proportion of homeowners in the population increased by 50 percent between 1945 and 1960. And those new homes filled up with the latest appliances—refrigerators, washing machines, sewing machines, vacuum cleaners, freezers, electric mixers, carving knives, shoe polishers.

By far the most popular new household product was the television set. In 1946 there were only 7,000 primitive black-and-white TV sets in the country; by 1960 there were 50 million high-quality sets. Nine out of ten homes had one, and by 1970, 38 percent owned one of the new color sets. *TV Guide* was the fastest-growing new periodical of the 1950s. Watching television became an essential daily activity for millions of people.

What differentiated the affluence of the post–World War II era from earlier periods of prosperity was its ever-widening dispersion. Although rural and urban poverty persisted in every state, and were destined to explode in the 1960s, few commentators noticed such exceptions to the prevailing affluence during the 1950s. When George Meany was sworn in as head of the AFL-CIO in 1955, he proclaimed that "American labor never had it so good."

On the surface many blacks were also beneficiaries of the wave of prosperity that swept over postwar American society. By 1950, African Americans were earning on average more than four times their 1940 wages. One black journalist declared in 1951 that "the progressive

Mink Coat for Father. *An advertisement for a Ford Thunderbird claims that "What a mink coat does to perk up a lady, a Thunderbird does for a male."*

improvement of race relations and the economic rise of the Negro in the United States is a flattering example of democracy in action." But while gains had been made, blacks and other minority groups lagged behind whites in their rate of improvement. The gap between the average yearly income of whites and blacks widened during the decade of the 1950s. Yet such trends were rarely noticed amid the boosterism of the day. The need to present a united front against communism led commentators to ignore or gloss over issues of racial and economic injustice. Such corrosive neglect would fester and explode during the 1960s, but for now the emphasis was on consensus, conformity, and economic growth.

To perpetuate the postwar prosperity, marketing specialists accelerated their efforts to promote rising expectations and self-gratification. During the postwar era advertisers proved adept at exciting consumer desires and social envy. An advertisement for Ford automobiles assured customers, "You'll bask in the envious glances which Ford's Thunderbird styling draws." It then added, "Why not own two?" TV advertising expenditures increased 1,000 percent during the 1950s. Such startling results led the president of the National Broadcasting Company (NBC) to claim in 1956 that the primary reason for the postwar prosperity was that "advertising has created an American frame of mind that makes people want more things, better things, and newer things."

Paying for such "things" was no problem; the age of the credit card had arrived. Between 1945 and 1957, consumer credit soared 800 percent. Where families in other industrialized nations were typically saving 10 to 20 percent of their income, American families by the 1960s were saving only 5 percent. "Never before have so many owed so much to so many," *Newsweek* announced in 1953. "Time has swept away the Puritan conception of immorality in debt and godliness in thrift."

This consumer revolution had far-reaching cultural effects. Shopping became a major recreational activity. In 1945 there were only 8 shopping centers in the entire country; by 1960 there were 3,840. Much as life in a medieval town revolved around the cathedral, life in postwar America seemed to center on the new giant shopping centers and indoor malls.

THE SUBURBAN FRONTIER   The postwar era witnessed a mass migration to a new frontier—the suburbs. The burgeoning population created new communities and required an array of new services. Almost the entire population increase of the 1950s and 1960s (97 percent) was an urban or suburban phenomenon. Dramatic new technological advances in agricultural production reduced the need for manual laborers and thereby led 20 million Americans to leave the land for the city between 1940 and 1970.

Much of the urban population growth occurred in the South, the Southwest, and the West, in an arc that stretched from the Carolinas down through Texas and into California, diverse states that by the 1970s were being lumped together into the "Sunbelt." Air conditioning, developed by Willis Haviland Carrier in the first decade of the century, became a common household fixture in the 1950s and enhanced the appeal of warm climates. But the Northeast remained the most densely populated area; by the early 1960s, 20 percent of the national population lived in the corridor that stretched from Boston to Norfolk, Virginia.

While more concentrated in cities, post–World War II Americans were simultaneously spreading out within metropolitan areas. In 1950 the Census Bureau redefined the term "urban" to include suburbs as well as central cities. During the 1950s, suburbs grew six times faster than cities. By 1970, more Americans lived in suburbs (76 million) than in central cities (64 million). "Suburbia," proclaimed the *Christian Century* in 1955, "is now a dominant social group in American life." Suburban development required cars, highways, and government-guaranteed mortgages. It also required visionary entrepreneurs.

William Levitt, a brassy New York developer, led the suburban revolution. Levitt and his brother made a fortune during the depression by building houses. But the Levitts really struck it rich after the war, when the demand for new housing skyrocketed, and they developed an efficient system of mass production. In 1947, on 1,200 acres of Long Island farmland, they built 10,600 houses that were immediately sold and inhabited by more than 40,000 people—mostly adults under thirty-five and their children. Levitt's houses were affordable to the lower middle class. Bus drivers, schoolteachers, and steelworkers could purchase one with generous federal assistance.

Within a few years there were similar Levittowns in Pennsylvania and New Jersey, and other developers soon followed suit across the country.

Levittown. *Identical and affordable housing was built in Levittown, Long Island, to provide homes for veterans and families in the suburbs.*

This suburban revolution benefited greatly from federal government assistance. By insuring loans for up to 95 percent of the value of a house, the Federal Housing Administration made it easy for a builder to construct low-cost homes. Veterans got added benefits. A veteran could buy a Levitt house with no down payment and monthly mortgage installments of $56.

Expanded automobile production and highway construction also facilitated the rush to the suburbs, as more and more people were able to commute longer distances to work. Car production soared from 2 million in 1946 to 8 million in 1955, and a "car culture" soon transformed social behavior. As one commentator observed, the proliferation of automobiles "changed our dress, manners, social customs, vacation habits, the shape of our cities, consumer purchasing patterns, [and] common tastes." Widespread car ownership also necessitated an improved road network. Local and state governments built many new roads, but the guiding force was the federal government. In 1947 Congress authorized the construction of 37,000 miles of highways, and nine years later it funded over 42,000 additional miles in a new national system of interstate expressways.

Cars and roads provided access to the suburbs, and Americans—mostly middle-class white Americans—rushed to take advantage of the new living spaces. The motives for moving to the suburbs were numerous. The availability of more spacious homes as well as greater security and better educational opportunities for children all played a role. Racial considerations were also a factor. After World War II, African Americans migrated to the cities of the North and Midwest. As they moved in, many white residents moved out. Those engaged in "white flight" were usually eager to maintain residential segregation in their new suburban communities. As William Levitt explained, "We can solve a housing problem or we can try to solve a racial problem. But we can't combine the two." Contracts for houses in Levittown, Long Island, specifically excluded "members of other than the Caucasian race." Such discrimination, whether explicit or implicit, was widespread; the nation's suburban population in 1970 was 95 percent white.

THE GREAT BLACK MIGRATION   World War II, like World War I, helped spur a mass migration of rural southern blacks to the urban North and Midwest. This second migratory stream was much larger in scope than the first, and its social consequences were much more dramatic.

After 1945 more than 5 million southern blacks, mostly farm folk, left their native region in search of better jobs, higher wages, decent housing, and greater social equality. During the 1950s, for example, the black population of Chicago more than doubled. The South Side of Chicago soon became known as the capital of black America. It remains the largest concentration of African Americans in the country.

Most of these southern black migrants were sharecroppers and farm laborers from the Mississippi Delta, the richest cotton-producing land in the world. For over a century the Delta cotton culture had been dependent on black workers, first as slaves and then as sharecroppers and wage laborers. But a mechanical cotton picker invented in 1944 changed all that. The new machine could do the work of fifty people, thus making many farm workers superfluous. Displaced southern blacks, many of them illiterate and provincial, streamed northward in search of a new promised land, only to see many of their dreams dashed. The great writer Richard Wright, himself a migrant from the Delta to Chicago, observed that "never in history has a more utterly unprepared folk wanted to go to the city." In northern cities such as Chicago, Philadelphia, Newark, Detroit, New York, Boston, and Washington, D.C., rural blacks from the South confronted harsh new realities. Slumlords often gouged them for rent, many employers refused to hire them, and union bosses denied them membership. Soon the promised land had become for many an ugly nightmare of slum housing, joblessness, illiteracy, dysfunctional families, welfare dependency, street gangs, pervasive crime, and racism.

The unexpected tidal wave of black migrants severely taxed the resources of urban governments and the patience of white racists. For several nights during 1951, a white mob in a Chicago suburb assaulted a building into which a black family had moved. The National Guard had to quell the disturbance and disperse the crowd. Like other northern cities, Chicago sought to deal with the migrants and alleviate racial stress by constructing massive, all-black public housing projects to accommodate the newcomers. But these overcrowded racial enclaves were essentially segregated prisons. To be sure, many black migrants and their children did manage through extraordinary determination and ingenuity to "clear," that is, to climb out of the teeming ghettos and into the middle class. But most did not. As a consequence, the great black migration produced a web of complex social problems that in the 1960s would erupt into a crisis.

A CONFORMING CULTURE

In the 1950s, American social commentators mostly ignored people and cultures outside the middle-class mainstream. As evidenced in many of the new look-alike suburbs sprouting up across the land, much of middle-class social life during the two decades after the end of World War II exhibited an increasingly homogenized character. Fears generated by the cold war initially played a key role in encouraging orthodoxy. But McCarthyism was simply the most visible symbol of the many political and social forces promoting common standards of behavior. Suburban life itself encouraged uniformity. In new communities of strangers, people felt a need for companionship and a sense of belonging. Changes in corporate life as well as the influence of the consumer culture also played an important socializing role. "Conformity," predicted an editor in 1954, "may very well become the central social problem of this age."

CORPORATE LIFE   The composition of the American workforce and the very nature of work itself were dramatically changing during the postwar era. More time became available for leisure, as the standard workweek shrank from five and a half days to five days. Fewer people were self-employed, and manual labor was rapidly giving way to mental labor. By the mid-1950s, white-collar (salaried) workers outnumbered blue-collar (hourly-wage) workers for the first time in American history. Some 60 percent of the population enjoyed a "middle-class" standard of living (defined as annual family incomes of $3,000 to $10,000 in constant dollars). In 1929, before the stock market crash, only 31 percent were so designated. Managers, teachers, professors, researchers, salespeople, government employees, and office workers now constituted the bulk of the workforce, and they tended to work in larger and larger organizations.

This change happened because during World War II big business grew bigger. The government relaxed antitrust activity, and huge defense contracts tended to promote corporate concentration and consolidation. In 1940, for example, 100 companies were responsible for 30 percent of all manufacturing output; three years later, they were providing 70 percent. After the war, a wave of mergers occurred, and dominant corporate giants appeared in every major industry, providing the primary source of new jobs. By 1960, 38 percent of the workforce was employed

Office in a Small City. *Edward Hopper's 1953 painting suggests the alienation associated with white-collar work and a new corporate atmosphere in the 1950s.*

by organizations with more than 500 employees. In such huge companies, as well as similarly large government agencies and universities, the working atmosphere began to take on a distinctive new cast. The traditional notion of the hardworking, strong-minded individual advancing by dint of competitive ability and creative initiative gave way to the concept of a new managerial personality and an ethic of corporate cooperation and achievement.

WOMEN'S "PLACE" Increasing conformity in the middle-class workplace was mirrored in the middle-class home. A special issue of *Life* magazine in 1956 featured the "ideal" middle-class woman, a thirty-two-year-old "pretty and popular" suburban housewife, mother of four, who had married at age sixteen. She was described as an excellent wife, mother, volunteer, and "home manager" who made her own clothes, hosted dozens of dinner parties each year, sang in the church choir, worked with the school PTA and Campfire Girls, and was devoted to her husband. "In her daily round," *Life* reported, "she attends club or charity meetings, drives the children to school, does the weekly grocery shopping, makes ceramics, and is planning to study French."

A *Tupperware party in a middle-class suburban home.*

Life's description of the middle-class woman was symptomatic of a cult of feminine domesticity that witnessed a dramatic revival in the postwar era. The soaring birthrate reinforced the deeply embedded notion that a woman's place was in the home as tender of the hearth and guardian of the children. "Of all the accomplishments of the American woman," the *Life* cover story proclaimed, "the one she brings off with the most spectacular success is having babies."

Even though millions of women had responded to wartime appeals and joined the traditionally male workforce, afterward they were encouraged—and even forced—to turn their jobs over to the returning male veterans and resume their full-time commitment to home and family. A 1945 article in *House Beautiful* lectured women on their postwar responsibilities. The returning veteran, it said, was "head man again. . . . Your part in the remaking of this man is to fit his home to him, understanding why he wants it this way, forgetting your own preferences." Women were also to forget wartime-generated thoughts of their own career in the workplace. "Women must boldly announce," a Barnard College trustee asserted in 1950, "that no job is more exacting, more necessary, or more rewarding than that of housewife and mother."

SEARCH FOR COMMUNITY   Another illustration of the conformist tendencies of middle-class life during the Eisenhower years was the growth of membership in social organizations. Americans were on the move after World War II. Not only were they moving from the central cities to the suburbs, they were moving from suburb to suburb, farm to city, state to state. Some 20 percent of the population changed their place of residence each year. In Levittown an average of 3,000 homes per year turned over. A major cause of such mobility was the standard policy of the largest corporations to relocate their sales and managerial employees. IBM executives told friends that the company initials actually stood for "I've Been Moved." Such flux led people to search for a sense of community and rootedness. Hence middle-class Americans, even more than usual, tended to be joiners; they joined civic clubs, garden clubs, bridge clubs, carpools, and babysitting groups.

They also joined churches and synagogues in record numbers. The postwar era witnessed a massive renewal of religious participation. In 1940 less than half the adult population belonged to churches; by 1960 over 65 percent were official communicants. Sales of Bibles soared during the postwar era, and books, movies, and songs with religious themes were pervasive.

President Eisenhower repeatedly promoted a patriotic crusade to bring Americans back to God. "Recognition of the Supreme Being," he declared, "is the first, the most basic, expression of Americanism. Without God, there could be no American form of government, nor an American way of life." The president had himself first joined a church only in 1953, but he characterized himself as the "most intensely religious man I know." Not to be outdone, Congress in 1954 added the phrase "one nation under God" to the Pledge of Allegiance, and the following year made the statement "In God We Trust" mandatory on all American currency.

The prevailing tone of the popular religious revival during the 1950s was upbeat and soothing. Many ministers assumed that people were not interested in "fire-and-brimstone" harangues from the pulpit; they did not want their consciences overly burdened with a sense of personal sin or social guilt over such issues as racial segregation or inner-city poverty. Instead they wanted to be reassured that their own comfortable way of life was indeed God's will. As the Protestant Council of New York City explained to its corps of radio and television speakers, their

Billy Graham Preaches to Thousands, 1955. *Baptist evangelist Graham used both radio and television to promote his huge crusades, as droves of Americans, encouraged by the president, Congress, and even billboard advertising, joined churches and synagogues and attended revival meetings.*

addresses "should project love, joy, courage, hope, faith, trust in God, goodwill. Generally avoid condemnation, criticism, controversy. In a very real sense we are 'selling' religion, the good news of the Gospel."

The best salesman of this gospel of reassuring "good news" was the Reverend Norman Vincent Peale. Drawing on a long tradition of "positive thinking" in American social and religious thought, Peale perfected feel-good theology. No speaker was more in demand during the 1950s, and no writer was more widely read. Peale's book *The Power of Positive Thinking* (1952) was a phenomenal best-seller throughout the decade—and for good reason. It offered a simple "how-to" course in personal happiness. "Flush out all depressing, negative, and tired thoughts," Peale advised. "Start thinking faith, enthusiasm, and joy." By following this simple formula for success, he pledged, the reader could become "a more popular, esteemed, and well-liked individual."

NEO-ORTHODOXY   "Stop worrying and start living" was Peale's simple credo. But was it too simplistic? The "peace of mind" and "positive thinking" psychology promoted by Peale and other feel-good ministers struck some members of the religious community as shallow and misleading. They argued that the gospel of "good news" was just a way of sociability or "belonging," rather than a way of reorienting life toward God. These advocates of "neo-orthodoxy" criticized those who identified the United States as the only truly providential society and who used faith as a sanction for the social status quo.

The most significant spokesman for such "neo-orthodoxy" was Reinhold Niebuhr. A brilliant preacher-professor at New York's Union Theological Seminary, Niebuhr lambasted the "undue complacency and conformity" that had settled over American life in the postwar era. He found the popular religion of self-assurance and psychology of material success a woefully inadequate prescription for the ills of modern society. Spiritual peace, Niebuhr insisted, involves not the cheap comfort and sedating reassurance offered by Peale and other popular evangelists but the reality of pain, a pain "caused by love and responsibility" for the well-being of the entire human race.

CRACKS IN THE PICTURE WINDOW

Niebuhr was one of many who challenged the moral complacency and social conformity of American life during the 1950s and early 1960s. The widely publicized evidence of middle-class prosperity masked festering poverty in rural areas and urban ghettos. Moreover, one of the most striking aspects of postwar American life was the sharp contrast between the buoyant public mood and the increasingly bitter criticism of American life coming from intellectuals, theologians, novelists, playwrights, poets, and artists. As the philosopher and editor Joseph Wood Krutch recognized in 1960, "the gap between those who find the spirit of the age congenial and those who do not seems to have grown wider and wider."

THE LONELY CROWD   The criticism of postwar American life and values began in the early 1950s and quickly gathered momentum. Scores of books and articles swollen with mournful righteousness and unsettling truths decried virtually every area of the nation's social life. They shared a common fear: America in the age of Eisenhower was becalmed in a sea

Commuters on the 5:57, Park Forest, Illinois. *Postwar social critics commented on the overwhelming conformity of middle-class corporate and suburban life.*

of conformity, content to succumb to the soul-denying demands of the corporate "rat race," and eager to wallow in the consumer culture. In *The Affluent Society* (1958), for example, economist John Kenneth Galbraith attacked the prevailing notion that sustained economic growth would solve America's chronic social problems. The public sector was starved for funds, Galbraith argued, and public enterprises were everywhere deteriorating. He reminded readers that for all of America's vaunted postwar prosperity, the nation had yet to eradicate poverty.

Postwar cultural critics also questioned the supposed bliss of middle-class corporate and suburban life. John Keats, in *The Crack in the Picture Window* (1956), launched the most savage assault on life in the huge new suburban developments. He ridiculed Levittown and other such mass-produced communities as having been "conceived in error, nurtured in greed, corroding everything they touch." Locked into a monotonous routine, hounded by financial insecurity, and engulfed by mass mediocrity, suburbanites, he concluded, were living in a "homogeneous, postwar Hell."

Mass-produced suburban developments did exhibit a startling sameness. Levittown, for example, encouraged and even enforced uniformity.

The houses all sold for the same price—$7,990—and featured the same floor plan and accessories. Each had a picture window, a living room, bath, kitchen, and two bedrooms. A tree was planted every twenty-eight feet. Homeowners were required to cut their grass once a week, fences were prohibited, and laundry could not be hung out on weekends. However, Levittown was in many ways distinctive rather than representative. There were thousands of suburbs by the mid-1950s, and few were as regimented or as unvarying as Keats and other critics implied. Keats also failed to recognize the benefits that the suburbs offered those who would have otherwise remained in crowded urban apartments.

Still, there was more than a grain of truth to the charge that postwar American life was becoming oppressively regimented, and the huge modern corporation was repeatedly cited by social critics as the primary villain. The most comprehensive and provocative analysis of the docile new corporate character was David Riesman's *The Lonely Crowd* (1950). Riesman and his research associates detected a fundamental shift in the dominant American personality from what they called the "inner-directed" to the "other-directed" type. Inner-directed people possessed a deeply internalized set of basic values implanted by strong-minded parents or other elders. These values acted as a built-in stabilizer that kept inner-directed people on course.

Such an assured, self-reliant personality, Riesman argued, had been dominant in American life throughout the nineteenth century. But during the mid–twentieth century, an other-directed personality had displaced it. The new corporate culture demanded employees who could win friends and influence people rather than rugged individualists indifferent to personal popularity. Other-directed people were more concerned with being well liked than being independent. In the workplace they were always smiling, always glad-handing, always trying to please the boss.

Riesman amassed considerable evidence to show that the other-directed personality was not just an aspect of the business world; its premises were widely dispersed throughout middle-class life. Dr. Benjamin Spock's advice on raising children, Riesman pointed out, had become immensely influential. Spock's popular manual, *The Common Sense Book of Baby and Child Care,* sold a million copies a year between its first appearance in 1946 and 1960. Spock said that parents should foster in their children qualities and skills that would enhance their chances in what Riesman called the "popularity market."

By the mid-1950s, social commentators were growing increasingly concerned that such a managerial personality had come to dominate American life. In his influential study, *White Collar Society* (1956), the sociologist C. Wright Mills attacked the attributes and influence of modern corporate life. "When white-collar people get jobs," Mills explained, "they sell not only their time and energy, but their personalities as well. They sell by the week or month their smiles and their kindly gestures, and they must practice the prompt repression of resentment and aggression."

ALIENATION AND LIBERATION

THE STAGE   Many of the best dramatic plays of the postwar period reinforced David Riesman's image of modern American society as a "lonely crowd" of individuals without internal values, hollow at the core, groping for a sense of belonging and affection. Arthur Miller's play *Death of a Salesman* (1949), for example, was a powerful exploration of the theme. The play's protagonist, Willy Loman, an aging, confused salesman in decline, has centered his life and that of his family on the notion that material success is secured through personal popularity, only to be abruptly told by his boss that he is in fact a failure. Loman insists that it is "not what you say, it's how you say it—because personality always wins the day." He had tried to raise his sons, Biff and Happy, in his own image, encouraging them to be athletic, outgoing, popular, and ambitious. As he instructs them: "Be liked and you will never want." Yet Willy, for all his puffery about being well liked, admits in a fit of candor that he is "terribly lonely." He has no real friends; even his relations with his family are neither

In Arthur Miller's Death of a Salesman, *Willy Loman* (center, played by Lee J. Cobb) *destroys his life and family with the credo "Be liked and you will never want."*

honest nor intimate. When Willy finally realizes that he has been leading a counterfeit existence, he is so dumbfounded that he decides he can endow his life with meaning only by ending it.

THE NOVEL   The most enduring novels of the postwar period display a preoccupation with the individual's struggle for survival amid the smothering and disorienting forces of mass society. While millions were reading heartwarming religious epics such as *The Cardinal* (1950), *The Robe* (1953), and *Exodus* (1959), critics were praising the more disturbing writings of James Baldwin, Saul Bellow, John Cheever, Ralph Ellison, Joseph Heller, James Jones, Norman Mailer, Joyce Carol Oates, J. D. Salinger, William Styron, John Updike, and Eudora Welty. Their works had few happy endings—and even fewer celebrations of contemporary American life. The characters in novels such as Jones's *From Here to Eternity,* Bellow's *Dangling Man* and *Seize the Day,* Styron's *Lie Down in Darkness,* and Updike's *Rabbit, Run,* among many others, tended to be like Willy Loman—restless, tormented, and often socially impotent individuals who can find neither contentment nor respect in an overpowering or uninterested world.

African-American writer Ralph Ellison explored the theme of the lonely individual imprisoned in privacy in his kaleidoscopic novel *Invisible Man* (1952). By using a black narrator struggling to find and liberate himself in the midst of an oppressive white society, Ellison forcefully accentuated the problem of alienation. The narrator opens by confessing: "All my life I had been looking for something, and everywhere I turned someone tried to tell me what it was. I accepted their answers too, though they were often in contradiction and even self-contradictory. I was naive. I was looking for myself and asking everyone except myself questions which I, and only I, could answer."

Ralph Ellison, author of Invisible Man.

PAINTING   The artist Edward Hopper also explored the theme of desolate loneliness in postwar urban-industrial American life. Virtually all of his paintings of the period depict isolated individuals, melancholy, anonymous, motionless. A woman undressing for bed, a diner seated at a table in an all-night restaurant, a housewife in a doorway, a businessman at his desk, a lone passerby in the street—these are the characters of Hopper's world. The silence of his scenes is deafening, the monotony striking, the alienation absorbing.

A younger group of painters in New York City decided that postwar society was so chaotic that it precluded any attempt at literal representation. As Jackson Pollock maintained, "the modern painter cannot express this age—the airplane, the atomic bomb, the radio—in the old form of the Renaissance or of any past culture. Each age finds its own technique." The anarchic technique Pollock adopted came to be called abstract expressionism, and during the late 1940s and 1950s it dominated not only the American art scene but the international field as well. In addition to Pollock, its adherents included Robert Motherwell, Willem de Kooning, Arshile Gorky, Franz Kline, Clyfford Still, and Mark Rothko. "Abstract art," Motherwell explained, "is an effort to close the void that modern men feel." In practice this meant that the *act* of painting was as important as the final result.

THE BEATS   In Saul Bellow's novel *Dangling Man* (1946), a character concludes that the essence of life is the "desire for pure freedom." The desire to liberate self-expression, to surmount organizational constraints and discard traditional conventions, was an abiding goal of the abstract expressionists. It was also the central concern of a small but highly visible and controversial group of young writers, poets, painters, and musicians known as the Beats. These angry young men—Jack Kerouac, Allen Ginsberg, Gary Snyder, William Burroughs, and Gregory Corso, among others—rebelled against the regimented horrors of war and the mundane horrors of middle-class life. *Time* magazine called the Beats "a pack of oddballs who celebrate booze, dope, sex, and despair." The Beats, however, were not lost in despair; they strenuously embraced life. But it was life on their own terms, and those terms were shocking to most observers.

The self-described "Beats" grew out of the bohemian underground in New York's Greenwich Village. There they began their quest for a visionary

Allen Ginsberg, considered the poet laureate of the Beat generation, reading his uncensored poetry to a crowd in Washington Square Park in New York City.

sensibility and spontaneous way of life. Essentially apolitical throughout the 1950s, they were more interested in transforming themselves than in reforming the world. They sought personal rather than social solutions to their anxieties. Jack Kerouac defined the Beat generation as "basically a religious generation. Beat means beatitude, not beat up. You *feel* this. You feel it in a beat, in jazz—real cool jazz or a good gutty rock number." As Kerouac insisted, his friends were not beat in the sense of beaten; they were "mad to live, mad to talk, mad to be saved." Their road to salvation lay in hallucinogenic drugs and alcohol, sex, a penchant for jazz and the street life of urban ghettos, an affinity for Buddhism, and a restless, vagabond spirit that took them speeding back and forth across the country between San Francisco and New York during the 1950s.

This existential mania for intense experience and frantic motion provided the subject matter for the Beats' writings. Ginsberg's long prose-poem *Howl*, published in 1956, featured an explicit sensuality as well as an impressionistic attempt to catch the color, movement, and dynamism of modern life. Ginsberg howled at the "Robot apartments! invincible suburbs! skeleton treasuries! blind capitals! demonic industries!" Kerouac issued his autobiographical novel *On the Road* a year later. In frenzied prose and plotless ramblings, it portrayed the Beats' life of "bursting ecstasies" and maniacal traveling. At one point Dean Moriarty (Neal Cassady) has the following exchange with Sal Paradise (Kerouac): "We gotta go and never stop going till we get there." "Where we going, man?" "I don't know, but we gotta go."

Howl and *On the Road* provoked sarcasm and anger from many reviewers, but the books enjoyed brisk sales, especially among young people. *On the Road* made the best-seller list, and soon the term "Beat Generation" or "beatnik" referred to almost any young rebel who openly dissented from the comfortable ethos of middle-class life. Defiant, unruly actors such as James Dean and Marlon Brando were added to the pantheon of Beat "anti-heroes." The anarchic gaiety of the Beats played an important role in preparing the way for the more widespread youth revolt of the 1960s.

YOUTH CULTURE AND DELINQUENCY   Young people occupied a distinctive place in postwar American life. The children of the postwar baby boom were becoming adolescents during the 1950s, and in the process, a distinctive "teen" subculture began to emerge. Living amid such a prosperous era, teenagers had more money and free time than any previous generation.

A vast new teen market arose for goods ranging from transistor radios, Hula-Hoops, and "rock 'n' roll" records to cameras, surfboards, *Seventeen* magazine, and Pat Boone movies. Teenagers in the postwar era knew nothing of economic depressions or wartime rationing; immersed in abundance from an early age, the children of prospering parents took the notion of carefree consumption for granted.

To be sure, most young people during the 1950s embraced the values of their parents and the capitalist system. It was "the reassuring truth," reported *Collier's* magazine in 1951, "that the average young American is probably more conservative than you or your neighbor." One critic labeled the college students of the postwar era "the silent generation," content to cavort at fraternity parties and "sock hops" before landing a job with a large corporation, marrying, and settling down into the routine of middle-class suburban life.

Yet such general descriptions masked a great deal of turbulence. During the 1950s, a wave of juvenile delinquency swept across middle-class society. By 1956, over a million teens a year were being arrested.

A soda fountain in a drugstore from the 1950s, a popular outlet for teenage consumerism.

Car theft was the leading offense, but larceny, rape, beatings, and even murder, were not uncommon.

What was causing such delinquency? J. Edgar Hoover, the head of the FBI, insisted that the root of the problem was a lack of religious training. Others pointed to the growing number of urban slums. Such "bad" and "brutish" environments almost ensured that children would become criminals. The problem with such explanations was they failed to explain why so many middle-class kids from God-fearing families were becoming delinquents. One contributing factor may have been the unprecedented mobility of young people. Access to automobiles enabled teens to escape parental control, and in the words of a journalist, cars provided "a private lounge for drinking and for petting or sex episodes."

ROCK 'N' ROLL   Many concerned observers blamed the teen delinquency problem on a new form of music that emerged during the postwar era—rock 'n' roll. Rock music combined a strong beat with off-beat accents and repeated harmonic patterns to produce its distinctive sound, and the electric guitar provided the basic instrument. By the mid-1950s it had captured the imagination of young Americans. In 1955 *Life* magazine published a long article about a mysterious new "frenzied teenage music craze" that was creating "a big fuss."

Alan Freed, a Cleveland disc jockey, had coined the term "rock 'n' roll" in 1951. While visiting a record store, he had noticed an interesting new musical trend: white teenagers were buying rhythm and blues (R&B) records that had heretofore been purchased only by African Americans and Hispanic Americans. Freed wanted to take advantage of the new trend, but he realized that few white households would listen to a radio program featuring what was then called "race music." So he began playing R&B records but labeled the music rock 'n' roll (a phrase used in black communities to refer to dancing and sex) to surmount the racial barrier.

Freed's radio program was an immediate success, and its popularity helped bridge the gap between "white" and "black" music. African-American singers such as Chuck Berry, Little Richard, and Ray Charles, and Hispanic-American performers such as Ritchie Valens (Richard Valenzuela) suddenly were the rage among young, white middle-class audiences eager to claim their own cultural style and message.

At the same time, Elvis Presley, a young white truck driver and aspiring singer born in Tupelo, Mississippi, and raised in Memphis, Tennessee, began experimenting with "rockabilly" music, his own unique blend of gospel, country-and-western, and R&B rhythms and lyrics. In 1956 the twenty-one-year-old Presley released his smash hit "Heartbreak Hotel," and over the next two years the sensual baritone garnered fourteen gold records and emerged as the most popular musical entertainer in American history. Presley appeared on numerous television variety shows, starred in movies, and by the end of the decade had captured the attention of the world. His long hair and sideburns, his knowing grins and disobedient sneers, his leather jacket and tight blue jeans—all shouted defiance against adult conventions. His sexually suggestive stage performances featuring twisting hips and a gyrating pelvis drove teenagers wild.

Such hysterics prompted cultural conservatives to urge parents to destroy Presley's records because they promoted "a pagan concept of life." A Catholic cardinal denounced Presley as a vile symptom of a teenage "creed of dishonesty, violence, lust and degeneration." Patriotic groups

Elvis Presley, 1956. *The teenage children of middle-class America made rock 'n' roll a thriving industry in the 1950s and Elvis its first star.*

claimed that rock music was a tool of Communist insurgents designed to corrupt American youth. Yet rock 'n' roll survived such assaults, and it gave adolescents a self-conscious sense of being a unique social group with distinctive characteristics. It also represented an unprecedented intermingling of racial, ethnic, and class identities.

A PARADOXICAL ERA

Rock music would become one of the major vehicles of the youth revolt of the 1960s. In the 1950s, however, rock 'n' roll had little impact on the prevailing patterns of social and cultural life. The same held for most of the other critics who attacked the smug conformity and excessive materialism they saw pervading their society. The public had become weary of larger social or political concerns in the aftermath of the depression and the war. Instead Americans eagerly focused their efforts on personal and family goals and material achievements.

Yet those achievements, considerable as they were, eventually created a new set of problems. The benefits of abundance were by no means equally distributed, and millions of Americans still lived in poverty. For those more fortunate, unprecedented affluence and security fostered greater leisure and independence, which in turn provided opportunities for pursuing more diverse notions of what the good life entailed. Yet the conformist mentality of the cold war era discouraged experimentation. By the mid-1960s, tensions between innovation and convention would erupt into open conflict. Many members of the baby-boom generation would become the leaders of the 1960s rebellion against the corporate and consumer cultures. Ironically, the person who would warn Americans of the 1960s about the mounting dangers of the burgeoning "military-industrial complex" was the president who had long symbolized its growth—Dwight D. Eisenhower.

MAKING CONNECTIONS

- The culture of the 1950s laid the groundwork for the counterculture of the 1960s. See Chapters 34 and 35.

- There are fruitful comparisons between American culture in the 1950s and the earlier postwar period, the 1920s. See Chapter 26.

- The women's movement of the 1970s, discussed in Chapter 35, was led by women who rejected the cult of domesticity described in this chapter.

- The baby boom of the postwar period would have continuing economic, social, political, and cultural significance as this generation moved through the life cycle. Follow along in coming chapters.

FURTHER READING

Two excellent overviews of social and cultural trends in the postwar era are William H. Chafe's *The Unfinished Journey: America Since World War II* (rev. ed., 1995) and William E. Leuchtenburg's *A Troubled Feast: America Since 1945* (rev. ed., 1983). For insights into the cultural life of the 1950s, see Jeffrey Hart's *When the Going Was Good: American Life in the Fifties* (1982) and David Halberstam's *The Fifties* (1993).

The baby-boom generation and its impact are vividly described in Paul C. Light's *Baby Boomers* (1988). The emergence of the television industry is discussed in Erik Barnouw's *Tube of Plenty: The Evolution of American Television* (1982) and Ella Taylor's *Prime-Time Families: Television Culture in Postwar America* (1989).

A comprehensive account of the process of suburban development is Kenneth Jackson's *Crabgrass Frontier: The Suburbanization of the United States* (1985). Equally good is Tom Martinson's *American Dreamscape: The Pursuit of Happiness in Postwar America* (2000).

The middle-class ideal of family life in the 1950s is examined in Elaine Tyler May's *Homeward Bound: American Families in the Cold War Era* (1988). Thorough accounts of women's issues are found in Wini Breines Young's *Young, White and Miserable: Growing Up Female in the 1950s* (1992). For an overview of the resurgence of religion in the 1950s, see George Marsden's *Religion and American Culture* (1990).

A lively discussion of movies of the 1950s can be found in Peter Biskind's *Seeing Is Believing: How Hollywood Taught Us to Stop Worrying and Love the Fifties* (1983). The origins and growth of rock 'n' roll music are surveyed in Carl Belz's *The Story of Rock* (1972). Thoughtful interpretive surveys of postwar American literature include Josephine Hendin's *Vulnerable People: A View of American Fiction Since 1945* (1978) and Malcolm Bradbury's *The Modern American Novel* (1984). The colorful Beats are brought to life in Steven Watson's *The Birth of the Beat Generation: Visionaries, Rebels, and Hipsters, 1944–1960* (rev. ed., 1998).

33 CONFLICT AND DEADLOCK: THE EISENHOWER YEARS

CHAPTER ORGANIZER

This chapter focuses on:

- Eisenhower's "dynamic conservatism."

- American foreign policy in the 1950s.

- the civil rights movement in the 1950s.

- the background to the Vietnam War.

*T*he New Deal coalition established by Franklin Roosevelt and sustained by Harry Truman posed a formidable challenge to Republicans after World War II. To counter the unlikely but potent combination of "Solid South" white Democrats, blacks and ethnics, and organized labor, the Grand Old Party turned to General Dwight David Eisenhower, a military hero capable of attracting independent voters as well as tenuous Democrats. His commitment to a "moderate Republicanism" promised to slow the rate of federal government expansion while at the same time retaining many of the coveted social programs established by Roosevelt and Truman. His two terms as president are often characterized as representing a lull between two eras of Democratic activism. Eisenhower wanted to restore the authority of state and local governments and restrain the executive branch from political and social "engineering." In the process, he sought to renew traditional virtues and inspire people with a vision of a brighter future.

"TIME FOR A CHANGE"

By 1952 the Truman administration had piled up a heavy burden of political liabilities. Its bold stand in Korea had brought a bloody stalemate abroad, renewed wage and price controls at home, reckless charges of Communist subversion and disloyalty, and the exposure of corrupt lobbyists and influence peddlers who rigged favors in Washington. The disclosure of corruption led Truman to fire nearly 250 employees of the Bureau of Internal Revenue and, among others, an assistant attorney-general in charge of the Justice Department's Tax Division. But doubts lingered that Truman would ever finish the housecleaning.

EISENHOWER'S POLITICAL RISE   It was, Republicans claimed, "time for a change," and they saw public sentiment turning their way as the 1952 election approached. The Republican field quickly narrowed to two men, Ohio senator Robert A. Taft and General Dwight D. Eisenhower. Taft had become the foremost spokesman for domestic conservatism and for a foreign policy that his enemies branded as isolationist. His conservatism left room for federal aid to education and public housing, and his foreign policy, a "unilateralist" one, favored an active American role in opposing communism but opposed "entangling alliances" such as NATO.

Taft, however, inspired little enthusiasm beyond the party regulars. He projected a lackluster image, and as a leader used to taking controversial stands, he had made enemies. The eastern, internationalist wing of the party turned instinctively to Eisenhower, then the NATO commander. As a war hero he had the celebrity status that Taft lacked, and his captivating, unpretentious manner inspired confidence. His leadership had been tested in the fires of war, but as a professional soldier he had escaped the scars of political combat. He stood, therefore, outside and above the crass arena of public life, although his political instincts and skills were sharpened during his successful army career.

In 1952 Eisenhower affirmed that he was a Republican and permitted his name to be entered in party primaries. He then left his NATO post and joined the battle in person. An outpouring of public enthusiasm began to overwhelm Republican party regulars. Bumper stickers announced simply, "I like Ike." Eisenhower won the presidential nomination on the first ballot. He balanced the ticket with a youthful Californian, the thirty-nine-year-old Senator Richard M. Nixon, who had built a career on opposition to left-wing "subversives" and gained his greatest notoriety as the member of the House Un-American Activities Committee most eager in the pursuit of Alger Hiss.

THE 1952 ELECTION   The Twenty-second Amendment, ratified in 1951, forbade any president to seek a third term. The amendment exempted the current incumbent, Harry Truman, but weary of the war in Korea, harassed by charges of subversion and corruption in government, his popularity declining, Truman chose to withdraw and threw his support to Governor Adlai E. Stevenson of Illinois, who roused the Democratic delegates with an eloquent speech welcoming them to Chicago.

Good First Impression. *In the 1952 election the Republican party won significant support in the South for the first time.*

The campaign matched two of the most magnetic personalities ever pitted against each other in a presidential contest. Both Eisenhower and Stevenson attracted new followings among people previously apathetic about politics, but the race was uneven from the start. Eisenhower, though a political novice, was a world hero who had been in the public eye for a decade. Stevenson was hardly known outside of Illinois and was never able to escape the burden of Truman's liabilities. The genial general, who had led the crusade against

Hitler, now opened a domestic crusade to clean up "the mess in Washington." To this he added a promise, late in the campaign, that as president-elect he would go to Korea to secure "an early and honorable" peace. Stevenson possessed a lofty eloquence spiced with a quick wit, but he came across as just a bit too aloof, a shade too intellectual. The Republicans labeled him an "egghead" in contrast to Eisenhower, the man of the people, the general of decisive action.

In the end, Stevenson's humor and intellect were no match for Eisenhower's popularity. The war hero triumphed in a landslide of 34 million votes to Stevenson's 27 million, and 442 electoral votes to Stevenson's 89. The election marked a turning point in Republican fortunes in the South: for the first time since the 1850s the South was moving toward a two-party system. Stevenson carried only eight southern states plus West Virginia. Eisenhower picked up five states on the periphery of the Deep South: Florida, Oklahoma, Tennessee, Texas, and Virginia. In the former Confederacy the Republican ticket garnered 49 percent of the votes. The "nonpolitical" Eisenhower had made it respectable, even fashionable, to vote Republican in the South. Elsewhere, too, the former general made inroads in the New Deal coalition, attracting supporters among the ethnic and religious minorities in the major cities.

The voters, it turned out, liked Ike better than they liked his party. Democrats retained most of the governorships, lost control of the House by only eight votes, and broke even in the Senate, where only the vote of the vice-president ensured Republican control. The congressional elections two years later would weaken the Republican grip on Congress, and Eisenhower would have to work with a Democratic Congress until he left office.

EISENHOWER'S HIDDEN-HAND PRESIDENCY

IKE   Born in Denison, Texas, on October 14, 1890, Dwight David Eisenhower grew up in Abilene, Kansas. After finishing West Point, he spent nearly his entire adult life in the military service. During World War II, Eisenhower took command of American forces in the European theater and directed the invasion of North Africa in 1942. Two years later he assumed the post of supreme commander of Allied forces in

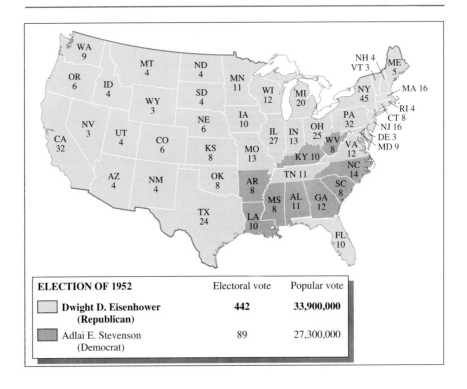

ELECTION OF 1952	Electoral vote	Popular vote
☐ **Dwight D. Eisenhower (Republican)**	**442**	**33,900,000**
☐ Adlai E. Stevenson (Democrat)	89	27,300,000

preparation for the invasion of the continent. After the war, by then a five-star general of the army, he became chief-of-staff and supreme commander of NATO forces, with a brief interlude as president of Columbia University.

Far from being a "do-nothing" president, as some have charged, Eisenhower was in fact an effective leader. The art of leadership, he once explained, did not require "hitting people over the head. Any damn fool can do that. . . . It's persuasion—and conciliation—and education—and patience. That's the only kind of leadership I know—or believe in—or will practice."

The public image of Ike was that of a man who rose above partisan politics. He was unpretentious, an ardent golfer, a common man with a winning smile who read little but Western novels, was uninformed about trends in intellectual and artistic life, and was prone to giving folksy advice. A diplomat labeled him "the nation's number one Boy Scout." But those who were closer to Ike have presented another side to the man. When provoked, he could release a fiery temper and scalding profanity. While Ike talked with genuine feeling about such traditional virtues as duty, honesty, and thrift, he was not above a calculated dis-simulation. One student of Eisenhower's techniques has spoken of a "hidden-hand presidency" in which Ike deliberately cultivated a public image of passivity to hide his active involvement in policy decisions.

"DYNAMIC CONSERVATISM" AT HOME   Like Ulysses Grant, Eisen-hower betrayed a weakness for hobnobbing with rich men. The presi-dent of General Motors became secretary of defense, and two auto distributors became secretary of the interior and postmaster-general, respectively. The New Dealers, Adlai Stevenson wryly remarked, "have all left Washington to make way for the car dealers."

Eisenhower called his domestic program "dynamic conservatism," which meant being "conservative when it comes to money and liberal when it comes to human beings." Budget cutting was a high priority for the new administration, which set out to slash both domestic programs and national defense spending. Eisenhower warned repeatedly against the dangers of "creeping socialism," "huge bureaucracies," and budget deficits. Eisenhower abolished the Reconstruction Finance Corpora-tion, ended wage and price controls, and reduced farm price subsidies. He also moved the government away from the Roosevelt-Truman com-mitment to public electric power. In fact, had Ike had his way the gov-ernment would have sold the Tennessee Valley Authority.

In 1954 the administration formulated tax reductions that resembled Republican programs of the 1920s in providing benefits mainly to cor-porations and individuals in the upper brackets. The new budget slashed expenditures by $6.5 billion, nearly 10 percent, and the Federal Reserve Board reinforced administration policy by tightening credit and raising interest rates to avert inflation. But a business slump followed, which reduced government revenues, making it harder to balance the budget. After that experience, Eisenhower's fiscal and monetary poli-cies became more flexible. The government accepted easier credit and deficits as necessary "countercyclical" methods.

Although Eisenhower chipped away at several New Deal programs, his presidency in the end served rather to sustain the New Deal by keeping its basic structure and premises intact during an era of prosperity. In a let-ter to his brother in 1954, Eisenhower observed: "Should any political party attempt to abolish Social Security and eliminate labor laws and farm programs, you would not hear of that party again in our political history."

In some ways, the administration not only maintained the New Deal but extended its reach, especially after 1954 when it had the help of Democratic Congresses. Amendments to the Social Security Act in 1954 and 1956 brought coverage to millions formerly excluded: professional people, domestic and clerical workers, farm workers, and members of the armed forces. In 1959 the program's benefits went up 7 percent. The federal minimum wage rose in 1955 from 75¢ to $1 an hour. Federal expenditures for public health rose steadily in the Eisenhower years, and the president went so far as to endorse federal participation in health insurance, but Congress twice refused to act. Low-income housing continued to be built with federal funds, although on a much reduced scale.

Some farm-related aid programs were expanded during the Eisenhower years. The president also continued to support federal construction projects for which he saw a legitimate need. Indeed, two such programs left major monuments to his presidency: the St. Lawrence Seaway and the interstate highways. The St. Lawrence Seaway opened the Great Lakes to oceangoing ships by means of locks and dredging. In 1956 a new federal highway construction act authorized the federal government to put up 90 percent of the cost of building 42,500 miles of limited-access interstate highways to serve the needs of commerce and defense, as well as private convenience. The states put up the remaining 10 percent. It was only afterward that people realized that the huge national commitment to the automobile might have come at the expense of America's railroad system, already in a state of advanced decay.

CONCLUDING AN ARMISTICE   America's new global responsibilities in the postwar world absorbed much of Eisenhower's attention. The most pressing problem when he entered office was the painful deadlock in the Korean peace talks. Many prisoners from North Korea wished to remain in South Korea. United Nations negotiators refused to agree to return prisoners of war who did not want to go back to the North. North Korean and Chinese negotiators insisted that all prisoners be returned regardless of their wishes. To break the deadlock, Eisenhower resolved upon a bold stand. In mid-May 1953 he stepped up aerial bombardment of North Korea, then had Secretary of State John Foster Dulles make a secret threat to Peking to remove all limits on weapons and targets. It was a thinly veiled warning of atomic warfare. Whether for that reason or others, negotiations then moved quickly toward an armistice along the established border just above the 38th parallel, and toward a complicated arrangement for prisoner exchange that allowed captives to accept or refuse repatriation.

On July 26, 1953, President Eisenhower announced the end of fighting in Korea. Whether Eisenhower had pulled a masterful bluff in getting the armistice has never become clear; no one knows if he would have used atomic weapons. Perhaps the more decisive factors in bringing about a settlement were rising Chinese Communist losses, which they increasingly found unacceptable, and the new spirit of uncertainty and caution felt by Russian Communists after the death of Joseph Stalin on March 5, 1953—six weeks after Ike's inauguration.

CONCLUDING A WITCH-HUNT   The Korean armistice helped to end another dismal episode: the meteoric career of Senator Joseph R. McCarthy, which had flourished amid the anxieties of wartime. Convinced that the government was infested with Communists and spies, the Wisconsin senator launched a one-man crusade to root them out. Eventually McCarthy's unscrupulous tactics led to his self-destruction, but not before he had left still more careers and reputations in ruins. The Republicans thought their victory in 1952 would curb his recklessness, but McCarthy actually grew more outlandish in his charges and his investigative methods. And many Americans caught up in the anti-Communist hysteria viewed him as a heroic knight doing battle against the forces of darkness.

McCarthy finally overreached himself when he made the absurd charge that the United States Army itself was "soft" on communism. From April 22 to June 17, 1954, the Army-McCarthy hearings displayed McCarthy to a large television audience at his capricious worst, bullying witnesses, dragging out lengthy irrelevancies, repeatedly calling "point of order." He became the perfect foil for the army's gentle but unflappable counsel, Joseph Welch of Boston, whose rapier wit repeatedly drew blood. When McCarthy tried to smear one of Welch's young associates, the counsel went into a cold rage: "Until this moment, Senator, I think I never really gauged your cruelty or your recklessness. . . . Have you no sense of decency, sir, at long last?" When the audience burst into applause, the confused, skulking senator was reduced to whispering, "What did I do?"

The Army-McCarthy Hearings, June 1954. *Joseph Welch* (hand on head) *listens incredulously after McCarthy's attempt to smear one of Welch's associates.*

On December 2, 1954, the Senate voted 67 to 22 to "condemn" McCarthy for contempt of the Senate. McCarthy was finished, and increasingly took to alcohol. Three years later, at the age of forty-eight, he was dead. McCarthyism, Ike joked, had become McCarthywasm, though not for those whose reputations and careers had been wrecked. To the end, Eisenhower kept his resolve not to "get down in the gutter with that guy" and sully the dignity of the presidency, but he did work resolutely against McCarthy behind the scenes. Eisenhower shared, nevertheless, the deeply held conviction of many citizens that espionage posed a real danger to national security. He denied clemency to Julius and Ethel Rosenberg, convicted of transmitting atomic secrets to the Russians, on the grounds that they "may have condemned to death tens of millions of innocent people." The Rosenbergs went to the electric chair on June 19, 1953.

INTERNAL SECURITY The anti-Communist crusade survived the downfall of McCarthy. Eisenhower stiffened the government security program that Truman had set up six years before. In 1953 an executive order broadened the basis for firing government workers by replacing Truman's criterion of "disloyalty" with the new category of "security risk." Under the new edict, federal workers could lose their jobs because of dubious associations or personal habits that might make them careless or vulnerable to blackmail.

The Supreme Court, however, modified some of the more extreme expressions of the Red Scare. In 1953 Eisenhower appointed former governor Earl Warren of California as chief justice, a decision the president later pronounced the "biggest damnfool mistake I ever made." Warren, who had seemed safely conservative while active in politics, proved to have a social conscience and a streak of libertarianism that another Eisenhower appointee, William J. Brennan, Jr., shared. The Warren Court (1953–1969), under the chief justice's influence, became an important agency of social and political change on through the 1960s.

In connection with security programs and loyalty requirements, the Court veered back in the direction of traditional individual rights. A 1957 opinion narrowly construed the Smith Act of 1940, aimed at conspirators against the government, to apply only to those advocating "revolutionary" action. Merely teaching revolutionary doctrine in the abstract could not be construed as a crime under the act. This, plus other decisions setting rigid standards for evidence, rendered the Smith Act a dead letter.

FOREIGN INTERVENTION

DULLES AND FOREIGN POLICY   The Eisenhower administration promised new departures in foreign policy under the direction of Secretary of State John Foster Dulles. Grandson of one former secretary of state and nephew of another, Dulles had pursued a lifetime career as an international lawyer and sometime diplomat. As counselor to the Truman State Department he had, among other things, negotiated the Japanese peace treaty. Son of a minister and himself an active Presbyterian layman, Dulles, in the words of the British ambassador, resembled those old zealots of the wars of religion who "saw the world as an arena in which the forces of good and evil were continuously at war." He gave the appearance of dour sternness and Calvinist righteousness, but he was also a man of immense energy, intelligence, and experience.

The foreign policy planks of the 1952 Republican platform, which Dulles wrote, showed both the moralist and the tactician at work. The Democratic policy of containment was needlessly defensive, Dulles thought. Containment implied contentment with the status quo. He saw no need for the United States to accept the Soviet presence in eastern Europe. Americans should instead work toward the "liberation" of eastern Europe from Soviet domination.

For all his bold talk of liberating eastern Europe from Soviet domination, Dulles made no significant departure from the strategy of containment created under Truman. Instead he institutionalized containment in the rigid mold of his cold war rhetoric and extended it to the military strategy of deterrence. His endorsement of "massive retaliation" was an effort to get, in the slogan soon current, "more bang for the buck." Budgetary considerations lay at the root of military plans, for Eisenhower and his cabinet feared that in the effort to build a superior war power the country could spend itself into bankruptcy. During 1953 members of the Joint Chiefs of Staff began planning a new military posture. The heart of their so-called New Look was the assumption that nuclear weapons could be used in limited-war situations, allowing reductions in conventional forces and thus budgetary savings. Dulles, who announced the policy in early 1954, explained that savings would come "by placing more reliance on deterrent power, and less dependence on local defensive power."

By this time both the United States and the Soviet Union had exploded hydrogen bombs. With the new policy of deterrence, what Winston Churchill called a "balance of terror" had replaced the old "balance of power." The threat of nuclear holocaust was terrifying, but the notion that the United States would actually risk such a disaster in response to local wars had little credibility.

"Don't Be Afraid—I Can Always Pull You Back." *Secretary of State Dulles pushes a reluctant America to the brink of war.*

Dulles's policy of "brinkmanship" depended for its strategic effect on those very fears of nuclear disaster. Dulles argued in 1956 that in following a tough policy of confrontation with communism, a nation sometimes had to "go to the brink" of war. Such a firm stand had halted further aggression in Korea in 1953 when America threatened to break the stalemate by removing restraints from the armed forces. Dulles had also employed brinkmanship in 1954 in Indochina when the United States sent aircraft carriers into the South China Sea "both to deter any Red Chinese attack against Indochina and to provide weapons for instant retaliation."

INDOCHINA: THE BACKGROUND TO WAR Dulles's use of brinkmanship in Indochina neglected the complexity of the situation there, which presented a special if not unique case of the nationalism that swept the old colonial world of Asia and Africa after World War II, damaging both the power and prestige of the colonial powers. By the early 1950s, most of British Asia was independent or on the way: India, Pakistan, Ceylon (later Sri Lanka), Burma (later Myanmar), and the Malay States (later the Federation of Malaysia). The Dutch and French, however, were less ready than the British to give up their colonies, which created a dilemma for American policy makers. Americans sympathized with colonial nationalists who sometimes invoked the example of 1776, but Americans also wanted Dutch and French help against communism. In order for the Dutch and French to maintain control of their colonial possessions, they had to reconquer areas that had passed from Japanese occupation into the hands of local patriots. The Truman administration felt obliged to answer their pleas for aid.

In the Dutch East Indies the Japanese had created a puppet Indonesian Republic, which emerged from World War II virtually independent. The Dutch effort to regain control met with resistance that exploded into open warfare. Eventually, American pressure persuaded the Dutch to accept Indonesian self-government under a Dutch-Indonesian Union in 1949, but that lasted only until 1954, when the Republic of Indonesia became independent. In 1955 the Bandung Conference in Indonesia, attended by delegates from twenty-nine independent countries of Asia and Africa, signaled the emergence of a "Third World" of underdeveloped countries, unaligned with either the United States or the Soviet bloc. Among other actions, the conference denounced

Ho Chi Minh.

"colonialism in all its manifestations," a statement that implicitly condemned both the Soviet Union and the West.

French Indochina, created in the nineteenth century out of the old kingdoms of Cambodia, Laos, and Vietnam, offered a variation on Third World nationalism. During World War II, when the Japanese controlled the area, they had supported French civil servants and had opposed the local nationalists. Chief among the latter were members of the Viet Minh (Vietnamese League for Independence), which fell under the influence of Communists led by Ho Chi Minh, a seasoned revolutionary and passionate Vietnamese nationalist obsessed by a single goal: independence for his country. At the end of the war, Ho's followers controlled part of northern Vietnam, and on September 2, 1945, Ho Chi Minh proclaimed a Democratic Republic of Vietnam, with its capital in Hanoi.

Ho's declaration of Vietnamese independence borrowed from Thomas Jefferson, opening with the words "We hold these truths to be self-evident. That all men are created equal." Ho had received secret American help against the Japanese during the war, but bids for further aid after the war went unanswered. Vietnam took low priority in American diplomatic concerns at the time, and Truman could not stomach aiding a professed Communist.

In 1946 the French government, preoccupied with domestic politics, recognized Ho's new government as a "free state" within the French union. Before the year was out, however, Ho's forces challenged French efforts to establish another colonial regime in the southern provinces, and this clash soon expanded into the First Indochina War. In 1949, having set up puppet rulers in Laos and Cambodia, the French reinstated former emperor Bao Dai as head of state in Vietnam. The victory of the Chinese Communists later in 1949 was followed by China's diplomatic recognition of the Viet Minh government in Hanoi, and then the recognition of Bao Dai by the United States and Britain.

The Viet Minh movement thereafter became more completely dominated by Ho Chi Minh and his Communist associates, and more dependent on the Soviet Union and China for help. In 1950, with the outbreak of fighting in Korea, the struggle in Vietnam became a major battleground in the cold war. When the Korean War ended, American aid to the French in Vietnam, begun by the Truman administration, continued. By the end of 1953, the Eisenhower administration was paying about two-thirds of the cost of the French effort in Indochina. By 1954 the United States found itself at the edge of the "brink" to which Dulles later referred. A major French force had been sent to Dien Bien Phu, near the Laos border, in the hope of luring Viet Minh guerrillas into the open and grinding them up with superior firepower. The French instead found themselves trapped by a Viet Minh force that threatened to overrun their stronghold.

In March 1954 the French government requested an American air strike to relieve the pressure on Dien Bien Phu. Eisenhower seemed to endorse forceful action, but when congressional leaders expressed reservations, he opposed American intervention unless the British lent support. When they refused, he backed away from unilateral action in Vietnam.

On May 7, 1954, the massive attacks loosed by Viet Minh general Vo Nguyen Giap finally overwhelmed the last French resistance at Dien Bien Phu. It was the very eve of the day that an international conference at Geneva took up the question of Indochina. Six weeks later, as French forces continued to suffer defeats in Vietnam, a new French government promised to get an early settlement. On July 20 representatives of France, Britain, the Soviet Union, the People's Republic of China, and the Viet Minh reached agreement on the Geneva Accords. The agreement proposed to neutralize Laos and Cambodia and to divide Vietnam at the 17th parallel. The Viet Minh would take power in the north, and the French would remain south of the line until elections in 1956 would reunify Vietnam. American and South Vietnamese representatives refused to join in the accord. This led the Soviet Union and China to back away from their earlier hints that they would guarantee the settlement.

Dulles responded to the growing Communist influence in Vietnam by organizing mutual defense arrangements for Southeast Asia. On September 8, 1954, at a meeting in Manila, the United States joined seven other countries in the Southeast Asia Treaty Organization (SEATO). The impression that it paralleled NATO was false, for SEATO was neither a common defense organization like NATO nor was it primarily Asian. The signers agreed that in case of attack on one, the others would act according to their "constitutional practices," and in case of threats or subversion they would "consult immediately." The members included only three Asian countries—the Philippines, Thailand, and Pakistan—together with Britain, France, Australia, New Zealand, and the United States. India and Indonesia, the two most populous countries in the region, refused to join. A special protocol added to the treaty extended coverage to Indochina. The treaty reflected what Dulles's critics called "pactomania," which by the end of the Eisenhower administration contracted the United States to defend forty-three other countries.

Eisenhower announced that though the United States "had not itself been party to or bound by the decision taken at the [Geneva] Conference," any renewal of Communist aggression "would be viewed by us as a matter of grave concern." (He failed to note that the United States had agreed at Geneva to "refrain from the threat or use of force to disturb" the agreements.) In Vietnam, when Ho Chi Minh took over the north, those who wished to leave for South Vietnam, mostly Catholics, did so with American aid. Power in the south gravitated to a new premier imposed on Emperor Bao Dai by the French at American urging: Ngo Dinh Diem, who had opposed both the French and the Viet Minh. In 1954 Eisenhower offered to assist Diem "in developing and maintaining a strong, viable state, capable of resisting attempted subversion or aggression through military means." In return, the United States expected Diem to enact democratic reforms and distribute land to the peasants. American aid took the form of CIA and military cadres charged with training Diem's armed forces and police.

Instead of instituting political and economic reforms, however, Diem suppressed opposition on both right and left, offering little or no land distribution, and permitting widespread corruption. In 1956 he refused to join in the elections to reunify Vietnam. After French withdrawal from the country, he ousted Bao Dai and installed himself as president. His efforts to eliminate all opposition played into the hands of the Communists, who found recruits among the discontented. By 1957 guerrilla forces known as the Viet Cong had begun attacks on the Diem

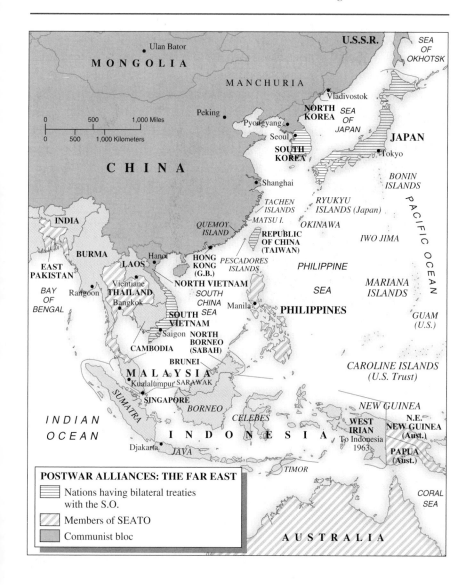

Ulan Bator
MONGOLIA
MANCHURIA
U.S.S.R.
SEA OF OKHOTSK
Vladivostok
Peking
NORTH KOREA
Pyongyang
Seoul
SOUTH KOREA
SEA OF JAPAN
JAPAN
Tokyo
CHINA
Shanghai
BONIN ISLANDS
TACHEN ISLANDS
RYUKYU ISLANDS (Japan)
MATSU I.
OKINAWA
IWO JIMA
QUEMOY ISLAND
REPUBLIC OF CHINA (TAIWAN)
PACIFIC OCEAN
INDIA
BURMA
Hanoi
HONG KONG (G.B.)
PESCADORES ISLANDS
PHILIPPINE SEA
EAST PAKISTAN
LAOS
NORTH VIETNAM
MARIANA ISLANDS
BAY OF BENGAL
Rangoon
Vientiane
THAILAND
Bangkok
SOUTH CHINA SEA
Manila
PHILIPPINES
GUAM (U.S.)
SOUTH VIETNAM
Saigon
NORTH BORNEO (SABAH)
CAMBODIA
BRUNEI
MALAYSIA
Kualalumpur
SARAWAK
SINGAPORE
BORNEO
CELEBES
CAROLINE ISLANDS (U.S. Trust)
INDIAN OCEAN
NEW GUINEA
WEST IRIAN
To Indonesia 1963
N.E. NEW GUINEA (Aust.)
Djakarta
JAVA
INDONESIA
PAPUA (Aust.)
TIMOR
CORAL SEA

POSTWAR ALLIANCES: THE FAR EAST
Nations having bilateral treaties with the S.O.
Members of SEATO
Communist bloc

AUSTRALIA

government, and in 1960 the resistance groups coalesced as the National Liberation Front. As guerrilla warfare gradually disrupted South Vietnam, the Eisenhower administration was helpless to do anything but "sink or swim with Ngo Dinh Diem."

PROTECTING TAIWAN   Just before the Manila Conference in 1954, Chinese artillery began shelling the South China Sea islands of Quemoy and Matsu, held by Chiang Kai-shek's Nationalists. On his way back from Manila, Secretary of State Dulles stopped in Taipei and worked out a mutual defense treaty that bound the United States to defend Taiwan and the nearby Pescadores Islands. In 1955 the president secured in Congress a resolution giving him full power to go to the defense of Taiwan and the Pescadores, and also authorizing him to secure and protect "related positions of that area now in friendly hands" in order to defend Taiwan. Congress's endorsement was overwhelming—the resolution drew only three negative votes in each house—for so sweeping a grant of power.

The Communist Chinese kept up their provocative activity nonetheless, and the islands of Quemoy and Matsu became symbols of the American will to protect Taiwan. The American chief of naval operations "leaked" word to journalists that the administration was considering a plan "to destroy Red China's military potential and thus end its expansionist tendencies." Soon afterward the Chinese backed away from the brink. At the Bandung Conference in April, with diplomatic encouragement from other Asian nations, Premier Chou En-lai said the People's Republic of China was ready to discuss the Formosa Strait issue directly with the United States. In 1955 representatives of the two governments began meetings in Geneva, and the guns fell silent.

REELECTION AND FOREIGN CRISES

As the United States continued to forge postwar alliances and to bring pressure to bear on foreign governments by practicing brinkmanship, a new presidential campaign unfolded. Despite having suffered a coronary seizure in the fall of 1955 and an operation for ileitis (an intestinal inflammation) in early 1956, Eisenhower decided to run for reelection. He retained public support and confidence, although the Democrats controlled Congress. Meanwhile, new crises in foreign and domestic affairs required him to take decisive action.

A LANDSLIDE FOR IKE   In 1956 the Republican convention renominated Eisenhower by acclamation and again named Richard Nixon as the vice-presidential candidate. The party platform endorsed Eisenhower's "modern Republicanism." The Democrats turned again to Adlai Stevenson. The platform revived old Democratic issues: less "favoritism" to big business, repeal of the Taft-Hartley Act, and tax relief for those in low-income brackets.

Neither candidate generated much excitement during the 1956 campaign. The Democrats centered their fire on the heir apparent, Richard Nixon, a "man of many masks." Stevenson roused little enthusiasm for two controversial proposals: to drop military conscription and rely on an all-volunteer army, and to ban H-bomb tests by international agreement. Both involved military questions that put Stevenson at a disadvantage by pitting his judgment against that of Eisenhower, a successful general.

During the last week of the campaign, fighting erupted along the Suez Canal in Egypt and in the streets of Budapest, Hungary. These twin crises were unrelated, but they occurred almost as if placed in malicious juxtaposition by some evil force. The attack on Egypt by Britain, France, and Israel disrupted the Western alliance and damaged any claim to moral outrage at Soviet actions in Hungary. For the Soviets, the Suez War afforded both a smokescreen for the subjugation of Hungary and a chance to enlarge their influence in the Middle East, an increasingly important source of oil.

The two crises led Stevenson to declare the administration's foreign policy "bankrupt." Most voters, however, reasoned that the crises spelled a poor time to switch horses, and they handed Eisenhower a landslide victory. He lost one border state, Missouri, but in carrying Louisiana became the first Republican to win a Deep South state since Reconstruction; nationally, he carried all but seven states. The decision was unmistakably clear: Eisenhower won more than 35 million popular votes to a little over 26 million for Stevenson, 457 electoral votes to the Democrat's 73.

In the euphoria of his landslide victory, Eisenhower declared on election night "that modern Republicanism has now proved itself. And America has approved of modern Republicanism." Eisenhower Republicans, it seemed clear, had assimilated the New Deal as an accomplished fact. But Eisenhower's decisive win failed to swing a congressional majority for his own party in either house, the first time this had happened since the election of Zachary Taylor in 1848.

CRISIS IN THE MIDDLE EAST   To forestall Soviet penetration into the Middle East, Dulles in 1955 had completed his line of alliances across the "northern tier" of the region. Under American sponsorship,

Britain had joined the Muslim states of Turkey, Iraq, Iran, and Pakistan in the Middle East Treaty Organization (METO), or Baghdad Pact, as the treaty was commonly called. By linking the easternmost NATO state (Turkey) to the westernmost SEATO state (Pakistan), METO had a certain superficial logic, but after Iraq, the only Arab member, withdrew in 1959, it became clear that the alliance had been bound to fail from the start. Below the northern tier, moreover, the Arab states remained aloof from the organization. These were the states of the Arab League (Egypt, Jordan, Syria, Lebanon, and Saudi Arabia), which had warred on Israel in 1948–1949 and remained committed to its destruction.

The most fateful developments in the region turned on the rise of Egyptian general Gamal Abdel Nasser after the overthrow of King Farouk in 1952. The bone of contention was the Suez Canal, which had opened in 1869 as a joint French-Egyptian venture. But in 1875 the British government had acquired the largest block of stock, and from 1882 on British forces were posted there to protect the British Empire's "lifeline" to India and other colonies. When Nasser's new nationalist

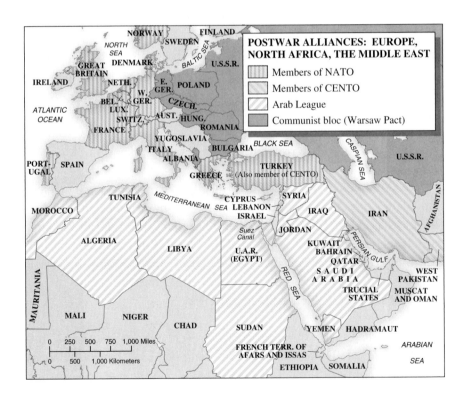

regime pressed for the withdrawal of British forces from the canal zone, Eisenhower and Dulles supported its demand, and in 1954 an Anglo-Egyptian treaty provided for British withdrawal within twenty months. Nasser, like other leaders of the Third World, remained unaligned in the cold war and sought to play both sides off against each other. The United States, meanwhile, courted Egyptian support by offering a loan to build a great hydroelectric plant at Aswan on the Nile River.

From the outset, the administration's proposal was opposed by Jewish constituencies concerned with Egyptian threats to Israel, and by southern congressmen who feared the competition from Egyptian cotton. When Nasser then increased trade with the Soviet bloc and recognized the People's Republic of China, Dulles abruptly canceled the loan offer in 1956. The outcome was far from a triumph of American diplomacy. The chief victims, it turned out, were Anglo-French interests in the Suez. Unable to retaliate against the United States, Nasser nationalized the Suez Canal Company. The British and French, faced with loss of control of the crucial Suez Canal, reacted strongly. Fruitless negotiations dragged out through the summer, and finally, on October 29, 1956, Israeli forces invaded the Gaza Strip and the Sinai peninsula. The Israelis invaded ostensibly to root out Arab guerrillas, but actually to synchronize with the British and French, who began bombing Egyptian air bases and occupied Port Said. Their actions, the British and French claimed, were meant to protect the canal against the opposing belligerents.

The Suez War put the United States in a quandary. Either the administration could support its Western allies and see the troublesome Nasser crushed, or it could stand on the United Nations charter and champion Arab nationalism against imperialistic aggression. Eisenhower opted for the latter course, with the unusual result that the Soviet Union sided with the United States. Once the threat of American embargoes had forced Anglo-French-Israeli capitulation, the Soviets capitalized on the situation by threatening to use missiles against the Western aggressors. This belated bravado won for the Soviet Union some of the credit in the Arab world for what the United States had actually accomplished.

REPRESSION IN HUNGARY   In the Soviet Union, Nikita Khrushchev had come out on top in the post-Stalinist power struggles. Khrushchev had delivered a "secret speech" on the crimes of the Stalin era in 1956

General Moshe Dayan (center), *commander of Israeli forces during the Sinai campaign, 1956.*

before the Communist Party Congress and hinted at relaxed policies and suggestions that different countries might take "different roads to socialism." This new policy of "de-Stalinization" put Stalinist leaders in the satellite countries of eastern Europe on the defensive and emboldened the more independent leaders to take action. Riots in the Polish city of Poznan led to the rise of Wladyslaw Gomulka, a Polish nationalist, to leadership of the Polish Communist party. Gomulka managed to win a greater degree of independence by avoiding an open break with the Soviets.

In Hungary, however, a similar movement got out of hand. On October 23, 1956, fighting broke out in Budapest, followed by the installation of Imre Nagy, a moderate Communist, as head of the government. Again the Soviets seemed content to let "de-Stalinization" follow its course, and on October 28 they withdrew their forces from Budapest. But Nagy's announcement three days later that Hungary would withdraw from the Warsaw Pact military alliance brought Soviet tanks back into Budapest. Although Khrushchev was willing to relax relations with the eastern European satellites, he refused to allow them to break with the Soviet Union or abandon their mutual defense obligations. In Hungary the Soviets installed a more compliant leader, Janos Kadar, and hauled Nagy off to Moscow, where a firing squad executed him in 1958. It was a tragic ending to a movement that, at the outset, promised the sort of moderation that might have vindicated George Kennan's policy of "containment," if not Dulles's notion of "liberation."

U.S. REACTIONS TO *SPUTNIK* On October 4, 1957, the Soviets launched the first satellite, called *Sputnik*. Less than a month later the Soviets launched *Sputnik II*, and it carried a dog wired up for monitoring. Americans, until then complacent about their technical primacy, suddenly discovered an apparent "missile gap." If the Soviets were so advanced in rocketry, then perhaps they could hit American cities. A Democratic senator demanded that Eisenhower call a special session of Congress to address the *Sputnik* crisis. The president refused, not wanting to heighten American anxiety.

All along Eisenhower knew that the "missile gap" was more illusory than real, but he could not reveal that high-altitude American spy planes were gathering this information. Even so, American missile development was in a state of disarray, with a tangle of agencies and committees engaged in waste and duplication.

The Soviet Union's success with *Sputnik* led to efforts in America to increase defense spending, to offer NATO allies intermediate-range ballistic missiles (IRBMs) pending development of long-range intercontinental ballistic missiles (ICBMs), to set up a new agency to coordinate space efforts, and to establish a crash program in science education. The "*Sputnik* syndrome," compounded by a sharp recession through the winter of 1957–1958, loosened the purse strings of frugal legislators, who added to the new budget more than Eisenhower wanted for both defense and domestic programs. During 1958, Britain, Italy, and Turkey accepted American missiles on their territory. In 1958 Congress created the

By the Rocket's Red Glare. *The Soviet success in space shocked Americans.*

National Aeronautics and Space Administration (NASA) to coordinate research and development in the field. Before the end of the year, NASA had a program to put a manned craft in orbit, but the first manned flight, by Commander Alan B. Shepard, Jr., did not take place until May 5, 1961. Finally, in 1958 Congress enacted the National Defense Education Act, which authorized federal grants for training in mathematics, science, and modern languages, as well as for student loans and fellowships.

FESTERING PROBLEMS ABROAD

Once the Suez and Hungary crises faded from the front pages, Eisenhower enjoyed eighteen months of smooth sailing in foreign affairs. Nonetheless, a brief flurry occurred in 1958 over hostile demonstrations in Peru and Venezuela against Vice-President Richard Nixon, who was on a goodwill tour of eight Latin American countries. Meanwhile, tensions in the Middle East and Europe continued to simmer, only to boil over in 1958.

CRISIS IN THE MIDDLE EAST In 1958 the president had secured from Congress authority for what came to be called the Eisenhower Doctrine, which promised to extend economic and military aid to Middle East nations, and to use armed forces if necessary to assist any such nation against armed aggression from any Communist country.

President Gamal Abdel Nasser of Egypt meanwhile had emerged from the Suez crisis with heightened prestige, and in 1958 he created the United Arab Republic (UAR) by merger (a short-lived one) with Syria. Then on July 14 a leftist coup in Iraq, supposedly inspired by Nasser and the Soviets, threw out the pro-Western government and killed the king, the crown prince, and the premier. In Lebanon, already unsettled by internal conflict, the government appealed to the United States for support against a similar fate. Eisenhower immediately ordered 5,000 marines into Lebanon. British forces meanwhile went into Jordan at the request of King Hussein. Once the situation stabilized, and the Lebanese factions reached a compromise, American forces (up to 15,000 at one point) withdrew in October.

CRISIS IN EAST ASIA   East Asia heated up again when, on August 23, 1958, the People's Republic of China renewed its shelling of the Chinese Nationalists on Quemoy and Matsu. In September the American Seventh Fleet began to escort Nationalist convoys, but stopped short of entering Chinese territorial waters. To abandon the islands, President Eisenhower said, would amount to a "Western Pacific 'Munich.'" But on October 1 he suggested that a cease-fire would provide "an opportunity to negotiate in good faith." China ordered such a cease-fire on October 6, and on October 25, which happened to be the day the last American forces left Lebanon, said that it would reserve the right to bombard the islands on alternate days. With that strange stipulation the worst of the crisis passed, but the tensions between Communist China and Taiwan continued to fester.

CRISIS IN BERLIN   The problem of Berlin festered too: Soviet premier Nikita Khrushchev called it a "bone in his throat." West Berlin provided a "showplace" of Western democracy and prosperity, a listening post for Western intelligence, and a funnel through which news and propaganda from the West penetrated what British leader Winston Churchill had called "the iron curtain." Although East Germany had sealed its western frontiers, refugees could still pass from East to West Berlin. On November 10, 1958, at a Soviet-Polish friendship rally in Moscow, Khrushchev threatened to give East Germany control of East Berlin and the air lanes into West Berlin. After the deadline he set, May 27, 1959, Western occupation authorities would have to deal with the East German government, in effect recognizing it, or face the possibility of another blockade.

Eisenhower refused to budge from his position on Berlin but sought a settlement. Khrushchev, it turned out, was no more eager for confrontation than Eisenhower. In talks with British prime minister Harold Macmillan, he

Soviet premier Nikita Khrushchev speaking on the problem of Berlin, 1959.

suggested that the main thing was to begin discussions of the Berlin issue, and not the May 27 deadline. Macmillan in turn won Eisenhower's consent to a meeting of the Big Four foreign ministers.

There was little hope of resolving different views on Berlin and German reunification, but the talks distracted attention from Khrushchev's deadline of May 27: it passed almost unnoticed. In September, after the Big Four talks had adjourned, Premier Khrushchev visited the United States, going to New York, Washington, Los Angeles, San Francisco, and Iowa, and dropping in on Eisenhower at Camp David. In talks there Khrushchev endorsed "peaceful coexistence," and Eisenhower admitted that the Berlin situation was "abnormal." They agreed that the time was ripe for a summit meeting in the spring.

THE U-2 SUMMIT   The summit meeting blew up in Eisenhower's face. On May 1, 1960, a Soviet rocket brought down an American spy plane. Such planes had been flying missions over the Soviet Union for three and a half years. Khrushchev set out to entrap Eisenhower and succeeded, by announcing first only that the plane had been shot down. When the State Department insisted that there had been no attempt to violate Soviet airspace, Khrushchev disclosed that the Soviets had American pilot Francis Gary Powers, "alive and kicking," and had his pictures of Soviet military installations. On May 11 Eisenhower abandoned his efforts to cover up the incident and finally took personal responsibility—an unprecedented action for a head of state—and justified the action on grounds of national security. In Paris, five days later, Khrushchev withdrew an invitation for Eisenhower to visit the Soviet Union and called on the president to repudiate the spy flights and "pass severe judgment on those responsible." When Eisenhower refused, Khrushchev left the meeting. (Later, in 1962, Powers was exchanged for a Soviet spy.)

CASTRO'S CUBA   The greatest thorn in Eisenhower's side was the Cuban regime of Fidel Castro, which came to power on January 1, 1959, after three years of guerrilla warfare against the dictator Fulgencio Batista. In their struggle against Batista, Castro's forces had the support of many Americans who hoped for a democratic government in Cuba. When American television covered trials and executions conducted by the victorious Castro, however, such hopes were dashed.

Fidel Castro (center) *became Cuba's first Communist premier in 1959 after three years of guerrilla warfare against the Batista regime.*

Staged before crowds of howling spectators, the trials vented anger against Batista's corrupt officials and police, but offered little in the way of legal procedure or proof. Castro, moreover, planned a social and agrarian revolution and opposed the widespread foreign control of the Cuban economy. When he began programs of land redistribution and nationalization of foreign-owned property, relations with the United States worsened. Some observers believed, however, that by rejecting Castro's requests for loans and other help, the American government lost a chance to influence the direction of the revolution, and by acting on the assumption that Communists already had the upper hand in his movement, the administration may have ensured that fact.

Castro, on the other hand, showed little reluctance to accept the Communist embrace. In 1960 he entered a trade agreement to swap Cuban sugar for Soviet oil and machinery. Then, after Cuba had seized three British-American oil refineries that refused to process Soviet oil, Eisenhower cut sharply the quota for Cuban sugar imports. Premier Khrushchev in response warned that any military intervention in Cuba would encounter Soviet rockets. The United States next suspended imports of Cuban sugar and embargoed most shipments to Cuba. One of Eisenhower's last acts as president was to suspend diplomatic relations with Cuba on January 3, 1961. The president also authorized the CIA to begin training a force of Cuban refugees (some of them former Castro stalwarts) for a new revolution. But the final decision on its use would rest with the next president, John F. Kennedy.

THE EARLY CIVIL RIGHTS MOVEMENT

While the cold war produced an uneasy stalemate by the mid-1950s, race relations in the United States threatened to explode the domestic tranquility masking years of injustice. Eisenhower entered office committed to civil rights in principle, and he pushed the issue in areas of federal authority. During his first three years, public services in Washington, D.C., were desegregated, as were navy yards and veterans' hospitals. Beyond that, however, two aspects of the president's philosophy limited progress with civil rights: his preference for state or local action over federal involvement, and his doubt that laws could change racial attitudes. "I don't believe you can change the hearts of men with laws or decisions," he said. For the time, then, leadership in the civil rights field came from the judiciary more than from the executive or legislative branch of the government.

In the 1930s, the National Association for the Advancement of Colored People (NAACP) had resolved to test the "separate but equal" doctrine that had upheld racial segregation since the *Plessy* decision in 1896. Charles H. Houston, dean of the Howard University Law School, laid the plans, and his former student, Thurgood Marshall, served as chief NAACP lawyer. They decided to begin their efforts to integrate American society with the expensive field of postgraduate study. In *Sweatt* v. *Painter* (1950) the Supreme Court ruled that a separate black law school in Texas failed to measure up because of intangible factors, such as its isolation from most of the future lawyers with whom its graduates would interact.

THE *BROWN* DECISION   By the early 1950s, challenges to state laws mandating segregation in the public schools were rising through the appellate courts. Five such cases, from Kansas, Delaware, South

Racial segregation began to be tested in the courts by the NAACP in the late 1930s.

Carolina, Virginia, and the District of Columbia—usually cited by reference to the first, *Brown* v. *Board of Education of Topeka, Kansas*—came to the Supreme Court for joint argument by NAACP attorneys in 1952. Chief Justice Earl Warren wrote the opinion, handed down on May 17, 1954, in which a unanimous Court declared that "in the field of public education the doctrine of 'separate but equal' has no place." In support of its opinion, the Court cited sociological and psychological findings—demonstrating that even if separate facilities were equal in quality, the mere fact of separating people by race engendered feelings of inferiority. A year later, after further argument, the Court directed "a prompt and reasonable start toward full compliance," ordering that the process of racial integration should move "with all deliberate speed."

Eisenhower refused to take any part in leading white southerners toward compliance with the Court's decisions. Privately he maintained "that the Supreme Court decision *set back* progress in the South *at least fifteen years.* The fellow who tries to tell me you can do these things by *force* is just plain *nuts.*" While token integration began as early as 1954 in the border states, hostility mounted in the Deep South and Virginia, led by the newly formed Citizens' Councils. The Citizens' Councils were middle- and upper-class versions of the Ku Klux Klan that spread quickly across the region and eventually enrolled 250,000 members. Instead of physical violence and intimidation, the Councils used economic coercion to discipline blacks who crossed racial boundaries. African Americans who defied white supremacy would lose their jobs, have their insurance policies canceled, or be denied personal loans or home mortgages. The Citizens' Councils grew so powerful that membership in them became almost a prerequisite for an aspiring white politician.

Before the end of 1955, moderate sentiment in the South gave way to surly reaction against desegregation of the schools. Virginia senator Harry F. Byrd supplied a rallying cry: "Massive Resistance." In 1956, 101 southern members of Congress signed a "Southern Manifesto," which denounced the Court's decision in the *Brown* case as "a clear abuse of judicial power." At the end of 1956, in six southern states, not a single black child attended school with whites.

THE MONTGOMERY BUS BOYCOTT   The essential role played by the NAACP and the courts in providing a legal lever for the civil rights movement often overshadows the courageous contributions of individual African Americans who took great personal risks to challenge segregation. For example, in Montgomery, Alabama, on December 1, 1955, Mrs. Rosa Parks, a black seamstress tired after a day's work, was arrested for refusing to give up her seat on a city bus to a white man. (As was the case in many southern communities, Montgomery had a local ordinance that required blacks to give up their bus or train seat to a white when asked.) The next night black community leaders met in the Dexter Avenue Baptist Church to organize a massive bus boycott under the aegis of the the the Montgomery Improvement Association.

In Dexter Avenue's twenty-six-year-old pastor, Martin Luther King, Jr., the movement found a charismatic leader. Born in Atlanta, the grandson of a slave and the son of a minister, King was endowed with intelligence, courage, and eloquence. After attending Morehouse College in Atlanta and then receiving a seminary degree, he earned a Ph.D. in philosophy from Boston University before accepting a call to preach in Montgomery. He brought the movement a message of nonviolent disobedience based on the Gospels, the writings of Henry David Thoreau, and the example of Mahatma Gandhi in India. "We must use the weapon of love," King told his supporters. "We must realize so many people are taught to hate us that they are not totally responsible for their hate." To his antagonists he said: "We will soon wear you down by our capacity to suffer, and in winning our freedom we will so appeal to your heart and conscience that we will win you in the process."

The bus boycott achieved a remarkable solidarity. For months blacks in Montgomery formed carpools, hitchhiked, or simply walked. But the white town fathers held out against the boycott and against the pleas of a bus company tired of losing money. The boycotters finally won a federal case they had initiated against bus segregation, and in 1956 the Supreme Court let stand without review an opinion of a lower court that "the separate but equal doctrine can no longer be safely followed as a correct statement of the law." The next day King and other blacks boarded the buses, but they still had a long way to travel before segregation ended.

To keep alive the spirit of the bus boycott, King and a group of associates in 1957 organized the Southern Christian Leadership Conference

Martin Luther King, Jr., here facing arrest for leading a civil rights march, advocated nonviolent resistance to racial segregation.

(SCLC). Several days later, King found an unexploded dynamite bomb on his front porch. Two hours later, he addressed his congregation: "I'm not afraid of anybody this morning. Tell Montgomery they can keep shooting and I'm going to stand up to them; tell Montgomery they can keep bombing and I'm going to stand up to them. If I had to die tomorrow morning I would die happy because I've been to the mountain top and I've seen the promised land and it's going to be here in Montgomery."

THE CIVIL RIGHTS ACT   Despite President Eisenhower's reluctance to take the lead in desegregating schools, he supported the right of blacks to vote. In 1956, hoping to exploit divisions between northern and southern Democrats and to reclaim some of the black vote for Republicans, Eisenhower proposed legislation that became the Civil Rights Act of 1957. The first civil rights law passed since Reconstruction, it finally got through the Senate, after a year's delay, with the help of Majority Leader Lyndon B. Johnson, a Texas Democrat who won southern acceptance by watering down the act. The act established for a period of two years the Civil Rights Commission, which was later extended indefinitely, and a new Civil Rights Division in the Justice Department, which could seek injunctions to prevent interference with the right to vote. Yet by 1959 the Civil Rights Act had not added a single southern black to the voting rolls. Neither did the Civil Rights Act of 1960, which provided for federal court referees to register blacks to vote where a court found a "pattern and practice" of discrimination, and also made it a federal crime to interfere with any court order. This bill, too, lacked teeth and depended upon vigorous presidential enforcement to achieve any tangible results.

DESEGREGATION IN LITTLE ROCK   A few weeks after the Civil Rights Act of 1957 passed, Arkansas governor Orval Faubus called out the National Guard to prevent nine black students from entering Little Rock's Central High School under federal court order. A conference between the president and the governor proved fruitless, but on court order Governor Faubus withdrew the National Guard. When the black students tried to enter the school, a hysterical white mob forced local authorities to remove the students. At that point Eisenhower, who had said two months before that he could not "imagine any set of circumstances that would ever induce me to send federal troops," ordered a thousand paratroopers to Little Rock to protect the black students, and placed the National Guard on federal service. The soldiers stayed through the school year.

The following year Faubus closed the high schools of Little Rock rather than allow integration, and court proceedings dragged on into 1959 before the schools could be reopened. In that year, massive resistance to integration in Virginia collapsed when both state and federal courts struck down state laws that had cut off funds from integrated schools. Thereafter, "massive resistance" for the most part was confined to the Deep South where five states, from South Carolina west through Louisiana, still opposed even token integration.

ASSESSING THE EISENHOWER YEARS

During Eisenhower's second term, the country experienced an economic slump, a drop in tax revenues, and a large federal deficit. The country also suffered the embarrassment of the spy plane incident and of Cuba falling into the Communist orbit. Emotional issues such as civil rights and defense policy and corrupt aides also compounded Eisenhower's troubles. As a result of domestic and foreign problems during his presidency, the Eisenhower administration did not draw much acclaim. One observer called the Eisenhower years "the time of the great postponement," during which the president left domestic and foreign policies "about where he found them in 1953."

Yet opinion about Eisenhower's presidency has improved with time. Even critics now grant that Eisenhower succeeded in ending the war in Korea and settling the dust raised by Joseph McCarthy. If Eisenhower failed to end the cold war and in fact institutionalized global confrontation, he did sense the limits of American power and kept its application to low risk situations. He also tried to restrain the arms race. If he took few initiatives in addressing social and racial problems, he did sustain the major innovations of the New Deal. If he tolerated unemployment of as much as 7 percent at times, inflation remained minimal during his two terms.

Eisenhower's farewell address to the American people showed his remarkable foresight in his own area of special expertise, the military. Like George Washington, Eisenhower couched his wisdom largely in the form of warnings: that America's "leadership and prestige depend, not merely upon our unmatched material strength, but on how we use our power in the interests of world peace and human betterment"; that the temptation to find easy answers should take into account "the need to maintain balance in and among national problems"; and above all that Americans "must avoid the impulse to live only for today, plundering, for our own ease and convenience, the precious resources of tomorrow."

As a soldier, Eisenhower highlighted, perhaps better than anyone else could have, the dangers of a military establishment in a time of peace. "In the councils of government we must guard against the acquisition of unwarranted influence, whether sought or unsought, by the military-industrial complex. The potential for the disastrous rise of misplaced power exists and will persist." Eisenhower confessed that his great disappointment was that he could only affirm that "war has been avoided," not that "a lasting peace is in sight."

MAKING CONNECTIONS

- The civil rights movement of the 1950s aimed to achieve the racial integration of public services and equal access to political rights. This struggle would continue into the 1960s and then move in several new directions. See Chapter 34.

- American involvement in Vietnam grew in the 1950s, but remained limited to an advisory role. Escalation to an active fighting role came under Lyndon Johnson in 1965, a topic covered in Chapter 34.

- Eisenhower's "hands-off" approach to the presidency was reminiscent of the Gilded-Age presidencies and those of the 1920s. See Chapters 18, 22, and 27.

FURTHER READING

Scholarship on the Eisenhower years is extensive. A carefully balanced overview of the period is Chester Pach, Jr., and Elmo Richardson's *The Presidency of Dwight D. Eisenhower* (1991). For the manner in which Eisenhower conducted foreign policy, see Robert A. Divine's *Eisenhower and the Cold War* (1981). Tom Wicker deems Eisenhower a better person than president in *Dwight D. Eisenhower* (2002).

For the buildup of American involvement in Indochina, consult Lloyd C. Gardner's *Approaching Vietnam: From World War II through Dien Bien Phu, 1941–1954* (1988) and David L. Anderson's *Trapped by Success: The Eisenhower Administration and Vietnam, 1953–1961* (1991). How the Eisenhower Doctrine came to be implemented is traced in Stephen Ambrose and Douglas Brinkley's *Rise to Globalism: American Foreign Policy Since 1938* (rev. ed., 1997).

The impact of the Supreme Court during the 1950s is the focus of Archibald Cox's *The Warren Court: Constitutional Decision as an Instrument of Reform* (1968). A masterful study of the important Warren Court decision on school desegregation is James T. Patterson's *Brown v. Board of Education* (2001).

For the story of the early civil rights movement, see Taylor Branch's *Parting the Waters: America in the King Years, 1954–1963* (1988), and Robert Weisbrot's *Freedom Bound: A History of America's Civil Rights Movement* (1990).

34   NEW FRONTIERS: POLITICS AND SOCIAL CHANGE IN THE 1960S

CHAPTER ORGANIZER

This chapter focuses on:

- Kennedy's New Frontier and Johnson's Great Society.

- the achievements of the civil rights movement and ensuing splinter movements.

- America's growing involvement in Vietnam and the rising opposition to it.

- Kennedy's efforts to combat communism in Cuba.

For those pundits who considered the social and political climate of the 1950s dull, the following decade would provide a striking contrast. The 1960s were years of extraordinary social turbulence and innovation in public affairs—as well as sudden tragedy and trauma. Many social ills that had been festering for decades suddenly forced their way onto the national agenda. At the same time, the deeply entrenched assumptions of cold war ideology led the country into the longest, most controversial, and least successful war in the nation's history.

THE NEW FRONTIER

KENNEDY VS. NIXON   In 1960, there was little awareness of such dramatic change on the horizon. The presidential election of that year pitted two candidates—Richard M. Nixon and John F. Kennedy—who seemed to symbolize the bland politics of the 1950s. Though better known than Kennedy because of his eight years as Eisenhower's vice-president, Nixon had also developed the reputation of a cunning chameleon, the "Tricky Dick" who concealed his duplicity behind a series of masks. "Nixon doesn't know who he is," Kennedy told an aide, "and so each time he makes a speech he has to decide which Nixon he is, and that will be very exhausting."

But Nixon could not be so easily dismissed. He possessed a shrewd intelligence and a compulsive love for politics, the more combative the better. Born in suburban Los Angeles in 1913, he grew up amid a working-class Quaker family struggling to make ends meet. In 1946, having completed law school and a wartime stint in the navy, Richard Nixon jumped into the political arena as a Republican and won election to Congress.

Nixon arrived in Washington eager to reverse the tide of New Deal liberalism. "I was elected to smash the labor bosses," he explained. Four years later he won election to the Senate. In his campaigns, Nixon unleashed scurrilous personal attacks on his opponents, employing half-truths, lies, and rumors, and he shrewdly manipulated and fed the growing anti-Communist hysteria. Yet Nixon became both a respected and effective member of Congress, and by 1950 he was the most requested Republican speaker in the country. The reward for his rapid rise to political stardom was the vice-presidential nomination in 1952, which led to successive terms as the partner of the popular Eisenhower.

In comparison to his Republican opponent, Kennedy was inexperienced. Despite an abundance of assets, including a record of heroism in World War II, a glamorous young wife, a bright, agile mind and Harvard education, a rich, powerful family, a handsome face, movie-star charisma, and robust outlook, the forty-three-year-old Kennedy had not distinguished himself in the House or Senate. His political rise owed not so much to his abilities or accomplishments as to the effective public relations campaign engineered by his ambitious father, Joseph Kennedy, who was a self-made tycoon.

John F. Kennedy's poise and precision in the debates with Richard Nixon impressed viewers and voters.

During his campaign for the Democratic nomination, Kennedy had shown that he had the energy to match his grace and ambition, even though he suffered from serious spinal problems, Addison's disease (a debilitating disorder of the adrenal glands), recurrent blood disorders, venereal disease, and fierce fevers. He took medicine daily, sometimes hourly. But like Franklin Roosevelt, he and his aides and family members successfully masked such physical ailments from the public.

By the time of the Democratic convention in 1960, Kennedy had traveled over 65,000 miles, visited twenty-five states, and made over 350 speeches. In his acceptance speech, he found the stirring, muscular rhetoric that would stamp the rest of his campaign and his presidency: "We stand today on the edge of a New Frontier—the frontier of unknown opportunities and perils—a frontier of unfulfilled hopes and threats." Kennedy and his staff quite consciously fastened upon the frontier metaphor as the label for their domestic program. As an avid student of American history, Kennedy knew that the frontier image possessed a special resonance for the American people. Americans had always been adventurers, eager to conquer and exploit new frontiers, and Kennedy promised to use his administration to continue the process.

Three events shaped the presidential campaign that fall. First, as the only Catholic to run for the presidency since Al Smith in 1928, Kennedy strove to dispel the impression that his religion was a major political liability. In a speech before the Houston Ministerial Association in 1960, he directly confronted the political implications of his Catholicism. In America, he told the Protestant clergy, "the separation of church and state is absolute," and "no Catholic prelate would tell the President—should he be a Catholic—how to act and no Protestant minister should tell his parishioners for whom to vote." The religious question thereafter drew little public attention; Kennedy's candor had neutralized it.

Second, Nixon violated one of the cardinal rules of politics when he agreed to debate his less prominent opponent on television. During the first of four debates, few significant policy differences surfaced, allowing viewers to shape their opinions more on matters of style. Some 70 million people watched this first-ever television debate, and they saw an obviously uncomfortable Nixon, still weak from a recent illness, perspiring heavily and sporting his perpetual five-o'clock shadow. He looked haggard, uneasy, and even sinister before the camera. Kennedy, on the other hand, projected a cool poise and offered crisp answers that made him seem equal, if not superior, in his fitness for the office. Kennedy's popularity immediately shot up in the polls. In the words of a bemused southern senator, Kennedy combined "the best qualities of Elvis Presley and Franklin D. Roosevelt."

Still, the momentum created by the first debate was not enough to ensure a Kennedy victory. The third key event in the campaign involved the civil rights issue. Democratic strategists knew that in order to offset the loss of southern conservatives suspicious of Kennedy's Catholicism and strong civil rights positions, they had to woo black voters. To do so they set up a special committee to increase minority voter registration and to attract the black vote.

Perhaps the most crucial incident of the campaign occurred when Martin Luther King, Jr., and some fifty demonstrators were arrested in Atlanta for "trespassing" in an all-white restaurant. Although the other demonstrators were soon released, King was sentenced to four months in prison, ostensibly because of an earlier traffic violation. Robert Kennedy, the candidate's younger brother and campaign manager, called the judge handling King's case, imploring him "that if he was a decent American, he would let King out of jail by sundown." King was soon released on bail, and the Kennedy campaign seized full advantage of the outcome, distributing some 2 million pamphlets in black neighborhoods extolling Kennedy's efforts on behalf of Dr. King.

When the votes were counted, Kennedy and his running mate, Lyndon B. Johnson of Texas, had won the closest presidential election since 1888. The winning margin was only 118,574 votes out of 68 million cast. Kennedy's wide lead in the electoral vote, 303 to 219, belied the paper-thin margin in several key states. Nixon had in fact carried more states than Kennedy, sweeping most of the West, and holding four of the six southern states Eisenhower had carried in 1956. Kennedy's majority was built out of victories in southern New England, the populous Middle Atlantic states, and key states in the South where black voters provided the critical margin of victory. Yet ominous rumblings of discontent appeared in the once-solid Democratic South, as all eight of Mississippi's electors and six of Alabama's eleven (as well as one elector

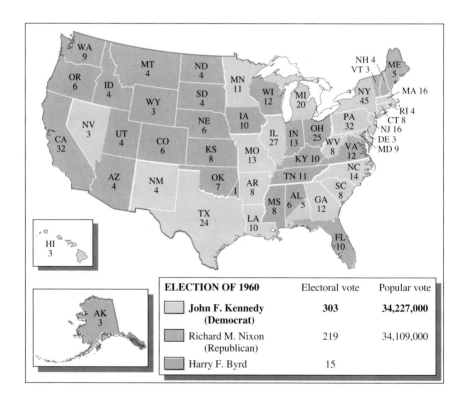

ELECTION OF 1960	Electoral vote	Popular vote
John F. Kennedy (Democrat)	**303**	**34,227,000**
Richard M. Nixon (Republican)	219	34,109,000
Harry F. Byrd	15	

from Oklahoma) defied the national ticket and voted for Virginia senator Harry Byrd, the arch-segregationist.

THE NEW ADMINISTRATION   John F. Kennedy was the youngest person ever elected president, and his cabinet appointments put an accent on youth. He was determined to attract the "best and the brightest" minds available, individuals who would inject a tough, pragmatic, and vigorous outlook into governmental affairs. Adlai Stevenson was favored by liberal Democrats for secretary of state, but Kennedy chose Dean Rusk, a career diplomat. Stevenson received the relatively minor post of ambassador to the United Nations. Robert S. McNamara, one of the "whiz kids" who had reorganized the Ford Motor Company, was asked to bring his managerial magic to bear on the Department of Defense. C. Douglas Dillon, a Republican banker, was made secretary of the treasury in an effort to reassure conservative business owners. When critics attacked the appointment of Kennedy's thirty-five-year-old brother, Robert, as attorney-general, the president quipped, "I don't see what's wrong with giving Bobby a little experience before he goes into law practice." McGeorge Bundy, whom Kennedy called "the second smartest man I know," was made special assistant for national security affairs, lending additional credence to the impression that foreign policy would remain under tight White House control.

The inaugural ceremonies set the tone of elegance and youthful vigor that would come to be called the "Kennedy style." Kennedy dazzled listeners with uplifting rhetoric. "Let the word go forth from this time and place," he proclaimed. "Let every nation know, whether it wishes us well or ill, that we shall pay any price, bear any burden, meet any hardship, support any friend, oppose any foe, to assure the survival and success of liberty. And so, my fellow Americans: ask not what your country can do for you—ask what you can do for your country." Spines tingled at the time; the glittering atmosphere and inspiring language of the inauguration seemed to herald an era of fresh promise and youthful energy.

THE KENNEDY RECORD   Despite his idealistic rhetoric, however, Kennedy had a difficult time launching his New Frontier domestic program. Elected by a razor-thin margin, he did not enjoy a popular mandate. Nor did he show much skill in shepherding legislation through a

Congress in the grip of a conservative southern coalition that blocked his efforts to increase federal aid to education, provide health insurance for the aged, and create a new Department of Urban Affairs. The Senate killed his initiatives on behalf of unemployed youth, migrant workers, and mass transit. When Kennedy finally came around to the advice of his advisers in 1963 and submitted a drastic tax cut, Congress blocked that as well.

Administration proposals, nevertheless, did win some notable victories in Congress. Those involving defense and foreign policy generally won favor; indeed, defense appropriations exceeded administration requests. On foreign aid there were some cuts, but Congress readily approved broad "Alliance for Progress" programs to help Latin America, and the celebrated Peace Corps, created in 1961 to supply volunteers to provide educational and technical services abroad. Kennedy's greatest legislative accomplishment, however, may have been the Trade Expansion Act of 1962, which eventually led to tariff cuts averaging 35 percent between the United States and the European Common Market.

In the field of domestic social legislation, the Kennedy administration scored a few more victories. They included a new Housing Act, which earmarked nearly $5 billion for urban renewal over four years; a raise in the minimum wage from $1 to $1.25 and its extension to more than 3 million additional workers; the Area Redevelopment Act of 1961, which provided nearly $400 million in loans and grants to "distressed areas;" an increase in Social Security benefits; and additional funds for sewage treatment plants. Kennedy also won support for an accelerated space program with the goal of landing on the moon before the end of the decade.

THE WARREN COURT   Under Chief Justice Earl Warren, the Supreme Court continued to be a decisive influence on American domestic life during the 1960s. The Court's decisions on civil liberties proved as controversial as its earlier decisions on civil rights. In 1962 the Court ruled that a school prayer adopted by the New York State Board of Regents violated the constitutional prohibition against an established religion. In *Gideon* v. *Wainwright* (1963) the Court required that every felony defendant be provided a lawyer regardless of the defendant's ability to pay. In 1964 the Court ruled in *Escobedo* v. *Illinois* that a person accused of a crime must also be allowed to consult a lawyer before being interrogated by police. Two years later, in *Miranda v. Arizona,* the Court issued perhaps its most bitterly criticized ruling when it ordered that an accused person in police custody must be informed of certain basic rights: the right to remain silent; the right to know that anything said can be used against the individual in court; and the right to have a defense attorney present during interrogation. In addition, the Court established rules for police to follow in informing suspects of their legal rights before questioning could begin.

EXPANSION OF THE CIVIL RIGHTS MOVEMENT

The most important development in American domestic life during the 1960s occurred in civil rights. John F. Kennedy entered the White House reluctant to challenge conservative southern Democrats on the race issue. He was never as personally committed to the cause of civil rights as his brother Robert, the attorney-general. Despite a few dramatic gestures of support toward black leaders, President Kennedy only belatedly grasped the moral and emotional significance of the most widespread reform movement of the decade. Like Franklin Roosevelt, he celebrated equality but did little to promote it. Eventually, however, his conscience was pricked by the grassroots civil rights movement led by Martin Luther King, Jr.

SIT-INS AND FREEDOM RIDERS   After the Montgomery bus boycott of 1955–1956, King's philosophy of "militant nonviolence" inspired others to challenge the deeply entrenched patterns of racial segregation in the South. At the same time, lawsuits to desegregate the schools got thousands of parents and young people involved. The momentum generated the first genuine mass movement in African-American history when four black college students sat down and demanded service at a "whites-only" Woolworth lunch counter in Greensboro, North Carolina, on February 1, 1960. Within a week, the "sit-in" movement had spread to six more towns in the state, and within two months, demonstrations had occurred in fifty-four cities in nine states.

In 1960 the student participants, black and white, formed the Student Nonviolent Coordinating Committee (SNCC), which worked

Sit-in at the Woolworth's Lunch Counter in Greensboro, North Carolina, *February 1, 1960. The four protesters, students at North Carolina A & T College, were* (from left) *Joseph McNeil, Franklin McCain, Billy Smith, and Clarence Henderson.*

with King's Southern Christian Leadership Conference (SCLC) to broaden the movement. The sit-ins became "kneel-ins" at churches and "wade-ins" at segregated public pools. Music provided a common source of inspiration and solace to the demonstrators. Drawing upon the tradition of slave spirituals, they developed freedom songs such as "Ain't Gonna Let That Sheriff Turn Me Around" and "We Shall Overcome."

Most of the protesters refused to retaliate, even when struck with clubs or poked with cattle prods. The conservative white editor of the *Richmond News Leader* conceded his admiration for their courage:

> Here were the colored students, in coats, white shirts, ties, and one of them was reading Goethe, and one was taking notes from a biology text. And here, on the sidewalk, was a gang of white boys come to heckle, a

ragtail rabble, slack-jawed, black-jacketed, grinning fit to kill, and some of them, God save the mark, were waving the proud and honored flag of the Southern States in the last war fought by gentlemen.

Words cannot do justice to the suffering, sacrifice, courage, and commitment of the young protesters. During the year after the Greensboro sit-ins, over 3,600 black and white activists spent time in jail. In many communities they were pelted with rocks, burned with cigarettes, and subjected to unending verbal abuse.

In 1961 the Congress of Racial Equality (CORE) sent a group of black and white "freedom riders" on buses to test a federal court ruling that had banned segregation on buses and trains and in terminals. In Alabama, mobs attacked the travelers with fists and pipes, burned one of the buses, and assaulted Justice Department observers, but the demonstrators persisted and drew national attention, generating new respect and support for their cause.

FEDERAL INTERVENTION   In 1962 Governor Ross Barnett of Mississippi, who believed that God made the Negro "different to punish him," defied a court order and refused to allow James H. Meredith, a black student, to enroll at the University of Mississippi. Attorney-General Robert Kennedy thereupon dispatched federal marshals to enforce the law. When the marshals were assaulted by a white mob, federal troops had to intervene, but only after two deaths and many injuries. Meredith was finally registered at "Ole Miss" a few days later.

In 1963 Martin Luther King launched a series of nonviolent demonstrations in Birmingham, Alabama, where Police Commissioner Eugene "Bull" Connor served as the perfect foil for King's tactic of nonviolent civil disobedience. Connor used attack dogs, tear gas, electric cattle prods, and fire hoses on the protesters while millions of outraged Americans watched the confrontations on television.

King, who was arrested and jailed during the demonstrations, wrote his "Letter from Birmingham City Jail," a stirring defense of the nonviolent strategy that became a classic of the civil rights movement. "One who breaks an unjust law," he stressed, "must do so openly, lovingly, and with a willingness to accept the penalty." He also signaled a shift in his strategy for social change. Heretofore, King had emphasized the need to educate southern whites about the injustice of segregation and other patterns of discrimination. Now he focused more on gaining federal enforcement and new legislation by provoking racists to display their violent hatreds in public. As King admitted in his "Letter," he sought through organized nonviolent protest to "create such a crisis and foster such a tension that a community which has constantly refused to negotiate is forced to confront the issue." This concept of civil disobedience outraged J. Edgar Hoover, the powerful head of the FBI, who labeled King "the most dangerous Negro of the future in this nation." He ordered agents to follow King, bugged his telephones and motel rooms, and circulated rumors intended to discredit King.

The sublime courage that King and many other protesters displayed in carrying out their program of nonviolent coercion helped mobilize national support for their integrationist objectives. (In 1964 King would be awarded the Nobel Peace Prize.) Nudged by his brother Robert, a man of conviction, compassion, and vision, President Kennedy finally decided that enforcement of existing statutes was not enough; new legislation was needed to deal with the race question. In 1963 he told the

Eugene "Bull" Connor's police unleash attack dogs on civil rights demonstrators in Birmingham, Alabama, May 1963.

nation that racial discrimination "has no place in American life or law." He then endorsed an ambitious civil rights bill intended to end discrimination in public facilities, desegregate the public schools, and protect black voters. But the bill was quickly blocked in Congress by southern conservatives who had become increasingly resistant to social change since mobilizing to thwart Roosevelt's New Deal in the late 1930s.

Throughout the Deep South, traditionalists remained steadfast in opposing integration. In the fall of 1963, Governor George Wallace dramatically stood in the doorway of a building at the University of Alabama to block the enrollment of several black students, but he stepped aside in the face of insistent federal marshals. That night President Kennedy spoke eloquently of the moral issue facing the nation: "If an American, because his skin is black, cannot enjoy the full and free life which all of us want, then who among us would be content to have the color of his skin changed and stand in his place? Who among us would be content with the counsels of patience and delay?" Later the same night, NAACP official Medgar Evers was shot to death as he returned to his home in Jackson, Mississippi.

The high point of the integrationist phase of the civil rights movement occurred on August 28, 1963, when over 200,000 blacks and whites marched down the Mall in Washington, D.C., toward the Lincoln Memorial singing "We Shall Overcome." The March on Washington was the largest civil rights demonstration in American history. Standing in front of Lincoln's statue, Martin Luther King, Jr. delivered one of the memorable public speeches of the century:

> I say to you today, my friends, that in spite of the difficulties and frustrations of the moment I still have a dream. It is a dream deeply rooted in the American dream.
>
> I have a dream that one day this nation will rise up and live out the true meaning of its creed: "We hold these truths to be self-evident; that all men are created equal."
>
> I have a dream that one day . . . the sons of former slaves and the sons of former slaveowners will be able to sit together at the table of brotherhood.

Such racial harmony had not yet arrived, however. Two weeks later a bomb exploded in a Birmingham church, killing four black girls who had arrived early for Sunday school. Yet King's dream—shared and promoted by thousands of other activists—survived. The intransigence

Protesters taking part in the March on Washington, on their way to the Lincoln Memorial to hear Martin Luther King, Jr.'s famous "I Have a Dream" speech, August 28, 1963.

and violence that civil rights workers encountered won converts to their cause all across the country. Moreover, corporate and civic leaders in large southern cities promoted civil rights advances in large part because the continuing protests threatened economic development. Atlanta, for example, described itself as "the city too busy to hate."

FOREIGN FRONTIERS

EARLY SETBACKS   John Kennedy's record in foreign relations, like that in domestic affairs, was mixed, but more spectacularly so. Although he had made the existence of a "missile gap" a major part of his campaign, he learned upon taking office that there was no "missile gap"—the United States remained far ahead of the Soviets in nuclear weaponry. Kennedy also discovered that there was in the works a secret CIA operation training 1,500 anti-Castro Cubans for an invasion of their homeland. The Joint Chiefs of Staff assured Kennedy that the plan was feasible in theory; analysts predicted that the invasion would inspire Cubans on the island to rebel against Castro.

In retrospect, it is clear that the scheme, poorly planned and poorly executed, had little chance of succeeding. When the invasion force landed at the Bay of Pigs in Cuba on April 17, 1961, it was brutally subdued in two days and more than 1,100 men were captured. A *New York Times* columnist lamented that the United States "looked like fools to our friends, rascals to our enemies, and incompetents to the rest." It was hardly an auspicious way for the new president to demonstrate his mastery of foreign policy.

Two months after the Bay of Pigs debacle, Kennedy met Soviet premier Nikita Khrushchev in Vienna, Austria. It was a tense confrontation during which Khrushchev browbeat the inexperienced Kennedy and threatened to limit Western access to Berlin, the divided city located deep within Communist East Germany. Kennedy was shaken by the aggressive Soviet stand. Upon his return home, he demonstrated

A West Berlin couple climbs up and looks over the newly constructed Berlin Wall to communicate with the woman's mother on the other side. The Berlin Wall both physically divided the city itself and served as a wedge between the United States and the Soviet Union.

American resolve by calling up Army Reserve and National Guard units. The Soviets responded by erecting the Berlin Wall, which cut off movement between East and West Berlin. Although no shooting incident triggered an accidental war, the Berlin Wall plugged the most accessible escape hatch for East Germans, showed Soviet willingness to challenge American resolve in Europe, and became another intractable barrier to the opening of new diplomatic frontiers.

THE CUBAN MISSILE CRISIS A year later Khrushchev and the Soviets posed another challenge, this time ninety miles off the coast of Florida. Kennedy's unwillingness to commit the forces necessary to overthrow Fidel Castro and his acquiescence to the erection of the Berlin Wall seemed to signify a failure of will, and the Soviets apparently reasoned that they could install their ballistic missiles in Cuba without American opposition. Their motives were to protect Cuba from another American-backed invasion, which Castro believed to be imminent, and to redress the strategic imbalance caused by the presence of American missiles in Turkey aimed at the Soviet Union. Khrushchev relished the idea of throwing "a hedgehog at Uncle Sam's pants."

American officials feared that Soviet missiles in Cuba would be placed in areas not covered by radar systems and, if launched, would arrive too quickly for warning. More important to Kennedy was the psychological effect of American acquiescence to a Soviet military presence on its doorstep. This might weaken the credibility of the American nuclear deterrent for Europeans and demoralize anti-Castro elements in Latin America. At the same time, the installation of Soviet missiles served Khrushchev's purpose of demonstrating his toughness to both Chinese and Soviet critics of his earlier advocacy of peaceful coexistence. But he misjudged the American response.

On October 14, 1962, American intelligence experts discovered that Soviet missile sites were under construction in Cuba. From the beginning, even though the Soviet actions violated no law or treaty, the administration decided that the weapons had to be removed; the only question was how. As the air force chief of staff told Kennedy, "you're in a pretty bad fix, Mr. President." In a series of secret meetings, the Executive Committee of the National Security Council narrowed the options to a choice between a "surgical" air strike and a naval blockade of Cuba. They opted for a blockade, which was carefully disguised by the

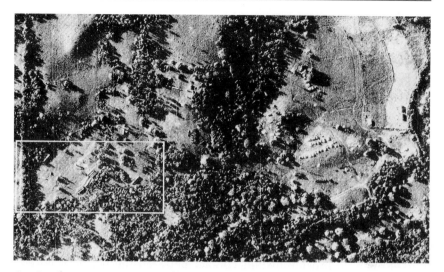

On October 14, 1962, a surveillance plane revealed both missile launchers and shelters in San Cristóbal, Cuba.

euphemism "quarantine," since a blockade was technically an act of war. A blockade offered the advantage of forcing the Soviets to shoot first, if it came to that, and left open the further options of stronger action. Monday, October 22, began one of the most anxious weeks in world history. On that day, the president announced to members of Congress and then to the public the discovery of the missile sites in Cuba; he also announced the naval quarantine. The United States and the Soviet Union now headed toward their closest encounter with nuclear war.

Tensions grew as Khrushchev blustered that Kennedy had pushed humankind "to the abyss of a world missile-nuclear war." Soviet ships, he declared, would ignore the quarantine. But on Wednesday, October 24, five Soviet ships, presumably with missiles aboard, stopped short of the quarantine line. Two days later an agent of the Soviet embassy privately approached an American television reporter with a proposal for an agreement: the Soviet Union would withdraw the missiles in return for a public pledge by the United States not to invade Cuba. The reporter was asked to relay the idea to the White House. Secretary of State Dean Rusk replied that the administration was interested, but told the newscaster: "Remember, when you report this, that eyeball to eyeball, they [the Soviets] blinked first."

That same evening Kennedy received two messages from Khrushchev, the first repeating the original offer and the second demanding in addition the removal of American missiles from Turkey. The two messages probably reflected divided counsels in the Kremlin. Ironically, Kennedy had already ordered removal of the outmoded missiles in Turkey, but he refused now to act under the gun. Instead he followed Robert Kennedy's suggestion that he respond favorably to the first letter and ignore the second. On Sunday, October 28, Khrushchev agreed to remove the missiles.

In the aftermath of the crisis, tension between the United States and the Soviet Union quickly subsided. Several symbolic steps helped to relax tensions: an agreement to sell the Soviet Union surplus American wheat, the installation of a "hot line" telephone between Washington and Moscow to provide instant contact between the heads of government, and the removal of obsolete American missiles from Turkey, Italy, and Britain. On June 10, 1963, the president announced that direct discussions with the Soviets would soon begin, and he called upon the nation to reexamine its attitude toward peace, the Soviet Union, and the cold war. Those discussions resulted in a treaty with the Soviet Union and Britain to stop nuclear testing in the atmosphere. The treaty, ratified in September 1963, did not provide for on-site inspection, nor did it ban underground testing, which continued, but it promised to end the dangerous pollution of the atmosphere with radioactivity. The treaty was an important symbolic and substantive move toward détente. As Kennedy put it: "A journey of a thousand miles begins with one step."

KENNEDY AND VIETNAM   As tensions with the Soviet Union were easing, a crisis was growing in Southeast Asia. Events there were moving toward what would become the greatest American foreign policy calamity of the century. The nation's costly involvement in Indochina left wounds in American institutions that have yet to heal. During John Kennedy's "thousand days" in office, the turmoil of Indochina never preoccupied public attention for any extended period, but it dominated international diplomatic debates from the time the administration entered office.

The landlocked kingdom of Laos, along with neighboring Cambodia, had been declared neutral in the Geneva Accords of 1954, but thereafter Laos had fallen into a complex struggle for power between the

Communist Pathet Lao insurgents and the Royal Laotian Army. There matters stood when Eisenhower left office and told Kennedy: "You might have to go in there and fight it out." The chairman of the Joint Chiefs of Staff argued in favor of a stand against the Pathet Lao, even if it meant direct American military intervention. After a lengthy consideration of alternatives, Kennedy and his advisers decided to favor a neutralist coalition government including Pathet Lao representatives that would preclude American military involvement in Laos, yet prevent a Pathet Lao victory. The Soviets, who were extending aid to the Pathet Lao, indicated a readiness to negotiate, and in 1961 talks began in Geneva. After more than a year of tangled negotiations, the three factions in Laos agreed to a neutral coalition. American and Soviet aid to the opposing parties was supposed to end, but both countries in fact continued covert operations, while North Vietnam kept open the Ho Chi Minh Trail through eastern Laos, over which it supplied its Viet Cong allies in South Vietnam.

There the situation worsened under the leadership of the Catholic premier Ngo Dinh Diem, despite encouraging reports from the commander of American military "advisers" in South Vietnam. At the time the problem was less the scattered Communist guerrilla attacks than Diem's failure to deliver promised social and economic reforms and his inability to rally popular support. His repressive tactics, directed not only against Communists but also against the Buddhist majority and other critics, played into the hands of his enemies. In 1961 White

Ngo Dinh Diem in 1962, celebrating the anniversary of Vietnamese independence.

House Assistant Walt Rostow and General Maxwell Taylor became the first in a long train of presidential emissaries to South Vietnam's capital, Saigon. Focusing on the military situation at the expense of the fragile nation's complex political culture, they proposed a major increase in the American military presence. Kennedy refused, but continued to dispatch more military "advisers" in the hope of stabilizing the situation: when he took office there had been 2,000 American troops in Vietnam; by the end of 1963 there were 16,000, none of whom had been officially committed to battle.

By 1963 sharply divergent reports were coming in from the South Vietnamese countryside. American military advisers, their eyes on the inflated "kill ratios" reported by the Army of the Republic of Vietnam (ARVN), drew optimistic conclusions. On-site political reporters, however, watching the reactions of the Vietnamese people, foresaw continued deterioration without the promised political and economic reforms. By midyear, growing Buddhist demonstrations made the discontent in South Vietnam more plainly visible. The spectacle of Buddhist monks setting themselves on fire in protest against government tyranny stunned Americans. By the fall of 1963, the Kennedy administration had decided that the autocratic Diem was a lost cause. When dissident generals proposed a coup d'état, U.S. ambassador Henry Cabot Lodge assured them that America would not stand in the way. On November 1 they seized the government and murdered Diem, though without explicit American approval. But the generals provided no more stability than earlier regimes, as successive coups set the country spinning from one military leader to another.

KENNEDY'S ASSASSINATION   By the fall of 1963, President Kennedy seemed to be facing up to the intractability of the situation in Vietnam. In September 1963 he declared of the South Vietnamese: "In the final analysis it's their war. They're the ones who have to win it or lose it. We can help them as advisers but they have to win it." The following month he announced the administration's intention to withdraw United States forces from South Vietnam by the end of 1965. What Kennedy would have done thereafter has remained a matter of endless controversy among historians, endless because it is unanswerable and unanswerable because on November 22, 1963, while visiting Dallas, Texas, Kennedy was shot in the neck and head by Lee Harvey Oswald.

Oswald's motives remain unknown. Although a blue-ribbon federal commission appointed by President Johnson and headed by Chief Justice Earl Warren concluded that Oswald acted alone, debate still swirls around various conspiracy theories. Kennedy's death and then the murder of Oswald by Jack Ruby, a Dallas nightclub owner, were shown over and over again on television, the medium that had so helped Kennedy's rise to the presidency and that now captured his death and the moving funeral at Arlington Cemetery. Kennedy's tragic death enshrined him in the public imagination as a martyred leader cut down in the prime of his life.

LYNDON JOHNSON AND THE GREAT SOCIETY

Texan Lyndon Johnson took the oath as president of the United States on board the plane that took John Kennedy's body back to Washington from Dallas. At age fifty-five he had spent twenty-six years on the Washington scene and had served nearly a decade as Democratic leader in the Senate, where he had displayed the greatest gift for compromise since Henry Clay.

Johnson brought to the White House a marked change of style from Kennedy. A self-made man who through gritty determination and shrewd manipulation had worked his way out of a hardscrabble rural Texas background to become one of Washington's most powerful figures, Johnson had none of the Kennedy elegance or charisma. He was a rough-hewn, gregarious, and domineering man who craved both political power and public affection. The first southern president since Woodrow Wilson, he harbored, like another southern president, Andrew Johnson, a sense of being the perpetual "outsider" despite his long experience with legislative power. And indeed he was so regarded by Kennedy "insiders."

Those who viewed Johnson as a stereotypical southern conservative failed to appreciate his long-standing admiration for Franklin Roosevelt, the depth of his concern for the poor, and his commitment to the cause of civil rights. In foreign affairs, however, he was, like Woodrow Wilson, a novice. Johnson wanted to be the greatest American president, the one who did the most good for the most people. And he would let nothing stand in his way. The grandiose Johnson ended up promising for

Kennedy's vice-president, Lyndon B. Johnson, takes the presidential oath as Air Force One *returns from Dallas with Jacqueline Kennedy* (right), *the presidential party, and the body of the assassinated president.*

more than he could accomplish, which raised false hopes and stoked fiery resentments.

POLITICS AND POVERTY   Domestic politics became Johnson's first priority as president. Amid the national grief after the assassination, he declared that Kennedy's cabinet and advisers would stay on and that his legislative program, stymied in several congressional committees, would be passed. Johnson loved the kind of political infighting and legislative detail that Kennedy had loathed. The logjam in the Congress that had blocked Kennedy's legislative efforts broke under Johnson's forceful leadership, and a torrent of legislation poured through.

Before the year 1963 was out Congress had approved a pending foreign aid bill and a plan to sell wheat to the Soviet Union. But America's commitment to foreign aid drew attention to its own people's needs. In 1964 the Council of Economic Advisers reported that 9.3 million American families, about 20 percent of the population, were living below the "poverty line" of $3,000 per year for a family of four. "Unfortunately, many Americans live on the outskirts of hope," Johnson told the Congress in his first State of the Union message, "some because of their poverty and some because of their color, and all too many because of both." At the top of his agenda he put the stalled measures for tax reduction and civil rights, then added to his "must" list a bold new idea that bore the LBJ brand: "This Administration today, here and now, declares unconditional war on poverty in America." The particulars of this "war on poverty" were to come later, the product of a task force already at work before Johnson took office.

Americans had rediscovered poverty in the early 1960s when the social critic Michael Harrington published a powerful exposé titled *The Other America* (1962). Harrington argued that more than 40 million people were mired in a "culture of poverty." Unlike the upwardly mobile immigrant poor at the turn of the century, these modern poor were impervious to hope. "To be impoverished," he asserted, "is to be an internal alien, to grow up in a culture that is radically different from the one that dominates the society."

President Kennedy read *The Other America* in 1963 and asked his advisers to investigate the problem and suggest solutions. Upon taking office, Lyndon Johnson announced that he wanted an antipoverty package that was "big and bold, that would hit the nation with real impact." Money for the program would come from the tax revenues generated by corporate profits that had resulted from the surge in capital investment and increased individual purchasing power made possible by the tax reduction of 1964, which had led to one of the longest sustained economic booms in American history.

The administration's "war on poverty" was embodied in an Economic Opportunity Bill that incorporated a wide range of programs: a Job Corps for inner-city youths aged sixteen to twenty-one, a Head Start

The Johnson Treatment. *Johnson used powerful body language and facial expressions to intimidate and manipulate anyone who dared to disagree with him.*

program for disadvantaged preschoolers, work-study jobs for college students, grants to farmers and rural businesses, loans to those willing to hire the chronically unemployed, the Volunteers in Service to America (VISTA, a "domestic Peace Corps"), and the Community Action Program, which would provide "maximum feasible participation" of the poor in directing neighborhood programs designed for their benefit. Speaking at Ann Arbor, Michigan, in 1964, Johnson called for a "Great Society" resting on "abundance and liberty for all. The Great Society demands an end to poverty and racial injustice, to which we are fully committed in our time."

THE 1964 ELECTION Johnson's well-intentioned but hastily conceived liberal social program provoked a Republican counterattack. For years conservatives had come to fear that the party had fallen into the hands of an "Eastern Establishment" that had given in to the same internationalism and big-government policies as liberal Democrats. Ever since 1940, so the theory went, the party had nominated "me-too" candidates who merely promised to run more efficiently the programs that Democrats designed. Offer the voters "a choice, not an echo," they reasoned, and a true conservative majority would assert itself.

By 1960 Arizona senator Barry Goldwater, a millionaire department-store magnate, had emerged as the leader of the Republican right. In his book *The Conscience of a Conservative* (1960), Goldwater proposed abolition of the income tax, sale of the Tennessee Valley Authority, and a drastic overhaul of Social Security. Almost from the time of Kennedy's victory in 1960 a movement to draft Goldwater began, mobilizing right-wing activists to capture party caucuses and contest primaries. In 1964 they took an early lead, and after sweeping the all-important California primary, Goldwater's forces controlled the Republican convention when it gathered in Los Angeles. "I would remind you," Goldwater told the delegates, "that extremism in the defense of liberty is no vice."

During the 1964 campaign, Goldwater displayed a gift for frightening voters. For example, he urged wholesale bombing of North Vietnam and left the impression of being trigger-happy. He savaged Johnson's war on poverty and the entire New Deal tradition. At times he was foolishly candid. In Tennessee he proposed the sale of the Tennessee Valley Authority; in St. Petersburg, Florida, a major retirement community, he questioned the value of Social Security. He also opposed the nuclear

Many voters feared that the Republican candidate for president in 1964, Arizona senator Barry Goldwater, was trigger-happy. In this cartoon he wields his book, The Conscience of a Conservative, *in one hand and a hydrogen bomb in the other.*

test ban and the Civil Rights Act. To Republican campaign buttons that claimed "In your heart, you know he's right," Democrats responded, "In your guts you know he's nuts."

Johnson, on the other hand, moved to the center. He appealed to the great consensus that spanned most of the political spectrum. He chose as his running mate Hubert Humphrey from Minnesota, a prominent liberal senator who had long promoted the cause of civil rights. In contrast to Goldwater's bellicose rhetoric on Vietnam, Johnson pledged: "We are not about to send American boys nine or ten thousand miles from home to do what Asian boys ought to be doing for themselves."

The result was a landslide. Johnson polled 61 percent of the total votes; Goldwater carried only Arizona and five states in the Deep South, where race remained the salient issue. Vermont went Democratic for the first time ever in a presidential election. Johnson won the electoral vote by a whopping 486 to 52. In the Senate the Democrats increased their majority by two (68 to 32) and in the House by thirty-seven (295 to 140). Johnson knew, however, that such a mandate could quickly erode. He shrewdly told aides, "every day I'm in office, I'm going to lose votes. I'm going to alienate somebody. . . . We've got to get this legislation fast. You've got to get it during my honeymoon." Goldwater's success in the Deep South also foreshadowed the shift in that traditionally Democratic region to the Republican party.

LANDMARK LEGISLATION   In 1965 Johnson flooded the new Congress with "Great Society" legislation that, he promised, would end poverty, revitalize the decaying central cities, provide every young American with the chance to attend college, protect the health of the elderly, enhance cultural life, clean up the air and water, and make the highways safer and prettier. The scope of Johnson's legislative program was unparalleled since Franklin Roosevelt's Hundred Days.

Priority went to federal health insurance and aid to education, proposals that had languished since President Truman advanced them in 1945. For twenty years the proposal for a comprehensive plan of medical insurance had been stalled by the steadfast opposition of the American Medical Association (AMA). But now that Johnson had the votes, the AMA joined Republicans in boarding the bandwagon for a bill serving those over age sixty-five. The AMA proposed, in addition to hospital insurance, a program for payment of doctor bills and drug costs, with the government footing half the premium. The act that finally emerged went well beyond the original program. It not only incorporated the new proposal into the Medicare program for the aged, but added another program, dubbed Medicaid, for federal grants to states that would help cover medical payments for the indigent. President Johnson signed the bill on July 30, 1965, in Independence, Missouri, with eighty-one-year-old Harry Truman looking on.

Five days after he submitted his Medicare program, Johnson sent to Congress his proposal for $1.5 billion in federal aid to elementary and secondary education. Such proposals had been ignored since the 1940s, blocked alternately by issues of segregation or separation of church and state. The first issue had been laid to rest, legally at least, by the Civil Rights Act of 1964. Now the Congress devised a means of extending aid to "poverty-impacted" school districts, regardless of their public or parochial character.

The momentum generated by the progress of these measures had already begun to carry others along, and the momentum continued through the following year. Before the Eighty-ninth Congress adjourned, it had established a record in the passage of landmark legislation unequaled since the time of the New Deal. Altogether the tide of Great Society legislation had carried 435 bills through the Congress. Among them was the Appalachian Regional Development Act of 1966, which provided $1 billion for programs in remote mountain areas that had long been pockets of desperate poverty. The Housing and Urban Development Act of 1965 provided aid for construction of 240,000 housing units and $3 billion for urban renewal. Funds for rent supplements for low-income families followed in 1966, and in that year a new Department of Housing and Urban Development appeared, headed by Robert C. Weaver, the first black cabinet member. Lyndon Johnson had, in the words of one Washington reporter, "brought to harvest a generation's backlog of ideas and social legislation."

THE IMMIGRATION ACT   Little noticed in the stream of legislation flowing from the Congress was a major new immigration bill that had originated in the Kennedy White House. President Johnson signed the Immigration Act of 1965 in a ceremony held on Liberty Island in New York Harbor. In his speech, he stressed that the new law would redress the wrong done to those "from southern and eastern Europe" and the "developing continents" of Asia, Africa, and Latin America. It did so by abolishing the discriminatory quotas based on national origins that had governed immigration policy since the 1920s. The new law treated all nationalities and races equally. In place of national quotas it created hemispheric ceilings on visas issued: 170,000 for persons from outside the Western Hemisphere, 120,000 for persons from within. It also stipulated that no more than 20,000 people could come from any one country each year. The new act allowed the entry of immediate family members of American residents without limit. Most of the annual visas were to be given on a first-come-first-served basis to "other relatives" of American residents, and only a small proportion (about 10 percent) were allocated to those with special talents or job skills.

During the 1960s, few western Europeans sought to emigrate to the United States; those living in Communist-controlled eastern Europe could not leave. But Asians and Latin Americans flocked to American consulates in search of visas. And within a few years the new arrivals in turn used the family-preference system to bring their family members as well. This so-called chain immigration quickly filled the annual quotas for nations such as the Philippines, Mexico, Korea, and the Dominican Republic. Hispanics and Asians became the largest contingent of new Americans.

ASSESSING THE GREAT SOCIETY   The Great Society programs included several genuine success stories. The Highway Safety Act and the Traffic Safety Act (1966) established safety standards for automobile manufacturers and highway design, and the scholarships provided for college students under the Higher Education Act (1965) were quite popular. Many Great Society initiatives aimed at improving the health, nutrition, and education of poor Americans, young and old, made some headway against these problems. So, too, did federal efforts to clean up air and water pollution. Several ambitious programs, however, were ill conceived, others were vastly underfunded, and many were mismanaged. Medicare, for example, removed any incentives for hospitals to control costs, and medical bills skyrocketed. Often funds appropriated for various programs never made it through the tangled bureaucracy to the needy. Widely publicized cases of welfare fraud became a powerful weapon in the hands of those who were opposed to liberal social programs. By 1966 middle-class resentment over the cost and waste of the Great Society programs helped to generate a conservative backlash.

FROM CIVIL RIGHTS TO BLACK POWER

CIVIL RIGHTS LEGISLATION   Among the successes of the Great Society were several landmark pieces of civil rights legislation. After Kennedy's death, President Johnson, who had maneuvered through the Senate the Civil Rights Acts of 1957 and 1960, called for passage of a new civil rights bill as a memorial to the fallen leader. With bipartisan support, he finally broke the Senate filibuster mounted by southern segregationists. On July 2 Johnson signed the Civil Rights Act of 1964, the most far-reaching civil rights measure ever enacted by the Congress. The act outlawed discrimination in hotels, restaurants, and other public accommodations. It required that literacy tests for voting be administered in writing, and defined as literate anybody who had finished the sixth grade. The attorney-general could now bring suits for school desegregation, relieving parents of a painful necessity. Federally assisted programs and private employers alike were required to eliminate discrimination. An Equal Employment Opportunity Commission (the old Fair Employment Practices Commission reborn) administered a ban on job discrimination by race, religion, national origin, or sex. After Johnson signed the Civil Rights Act, an aide told him it was "the greatest day of your presidency." Johnson said, "Yes, and it's the day we gave the South to the Republican party for the rest of our lifetimes."

Early in 1965, Martin Luther King, Jr., announced a drive to enroll the 3 million blacks in the South who had not registered to vote. In Selma, Alabama, civil rights protesters began a march to Montgomery, about fifty miles away, only to be violently dispersed by state troopers and a mounted posse. A federal judge agreed to allow the march, and President Johnson provided troops for protection. By March 25, when the demonstrators reached Montgomery, some 35,000 people were with them, and King delivered a rousing address from the steps of the state capitol.

Several days before the march, President Johnson went before Congress with a moving plea that reached its climax when he slowly intoned the words of the movement's hymn: "And we shall overcome." The resulting Voting Rights Act of 1965 was passed to ensure all citizens the right to vote. It authorized the attorney-general to dispatch federal examiners to register voters. In states or counties where fewer than half the adults had voted in 1964, the act suspended literacy tests and other devices commonly used to defraud citizens of the vote. By the end of the year, some 250,000 blacks were newly registered.

"BLACK POWER" Amid this success, however, the civil rights movement began to fragment. On August 11, 1965, less than a week after the passage of the Voting Rights Act, Watts, a predominantly black and poor community in Los Angeles, exploded in a frenzy of riots and looting. When the uprising ended, there were thirty-four dead, almost 4,000 rioters in jail, and property damage exceeding $35 million. Liberal commentators were stunned, as the riots occurred in the wake of the greatest legislative victories for black Americans since Reconstruction.

Chicago and Cleveland, along with forty other American cities, experienced similar racial riots in the summer of 1966. The following summer Newark and Detroit burst into flames. Detroit provided the most graphic example of urban violence, as tanks rolled through the streets and soldiers used machine guns to deal with snipers in the tenements.

In retrospect, it was predictable that the civil rights movement would shift its focus to the plight of urban blacks. By the middle 1960s, about 70 percent of America's black population lived in metropolitan areas, most of them in central-city ghettos that had been bypassed by the postwar prosperity. And again it seemed clear, in retrospect, that the nonviolent tactics that had worked in the rural South would not work in the northern cities. In the North the problems were *de facto* segregation resulting from residential patterns, not *de jure* segregation amenable to changes in law. Moreover, northern white ethnic groups did not have the cultural heritage that southern whites shared with blacks. "It may be," wrote a contributor to *Esquire*, "that looting, rioting and burning . . . are really nothing more than radical forms of urban renewal, a response not only to the frustrations of the ghetto but the collapse of all ordinary modes of change, as if a body despairing of the indifference of doctors sought to rip a cancer out of itself." A special Commission on Civil Disorders noted that, unlike earlier race riots, the urban upheavals of the middle 1960s were initiated by blacks themselves; earlier riots had been started by whites, which had then provoked black counterattacks. Now blacks visited violence and destruction on themselves in an effort to destroy what they could not stomach and what civil rights legislation seemed unable to change.

By 1966 "black power" had become the new rallying cry. Radical members of the SNCC had become estranged from Martin Luther King's theories of militant nonviolence. King's popularity led SNCC members to refer to him cynically as "de Lawd." When Stokely Carmichael, a twenty-five-year-old graduate of Howard University, became head of the SNCC in 1966, he made the separatist philosophy of black power the official objective of the organization and ousted whites from the organization. H. Rap Brown, who succeeded Carmichael as head of the SNCC in 1967, urged blacks to "get you some guns" and "kill the honkies." Carmichael, meanwhile, had moved on to the Black Panther party, a self-professed group of urban revolutionaries founded in Oakland, California, in 1966. Headed by Huey P. Newton and Eldridge Cleaver, the provocative, armed Black Panthers terrified the public, but eventually fragmented in spasms of violence.

The most articulate spokesman for black power was Malcolm X (formerly Malcolm Little, with the "X" denoting his lost African surname). Malcolm had risen from a ghetto childhood of narcotics and crime to become the chief disciple of Elijah Muhammad, the Black Muslim leader in the United States. "Yes, I'm an extremist," Malcolm acknowledged in 1964. "The black race in the United States is in extremely bad shape. You show me a black man who isn't an extremist and I'll show you one who needs psychiatric attention." By 1964 Malcolm had broken with Elijah Muhammad and founded his own organization committed to the establishment of alliances between African Americans and the nonwhite peoples of the world. But just after the publication of his *Autobiography* in 1965, Malcolm was gunned down in Harlem by assassins representing a rival faction of Black Muslims. With him went the most effective voice for urban black militancy since Marcus Garvey. What made the assassination of Malcolm X especially tragic was that he had just months before begun to abandon his strident antiwhite rhetoric and to preach a biracial message of social change.

Malcolm X, influential spokesman for the Black Muslim movement.

Although widely publicized and highly visible, the black power movement never attracted more than a small minority of African Americans. Only about 15 percent of blacks labeled themselves separatists. The preponderant majority continued to identify with the philosophy of nonviolent integration promoted by Martin Luther King, Jr., and organizations such as the NAACP. King dismissed black separatism and the promotion of violent social change. He reminded his followers that "we can't win violently."

The black power philosophy, despite its hyperbole, violence, and the small number of its adherents, had two positive effects upon the civil rights movement. First, it helped African Americans take greater pride in their racial heritage. As Malcolm X often pointed out, prolonged slavery and institutionalized racism had eroded the self-esteem of many blacks in the United States. "The worst crime the white man has committed," he declared, "has been to teach us to hate ourselves." He and others helped blacks appreciate their African roots and their American accomplishments. In fact, it was Malcolm X who insisted that blacks call themselves African Americans as a symbol of pride in their roots and as a spur to learn more about their history as a people. As the popular singer James Brown urged, "Say it loud—I'm black and I'm proud."

Second, the black power phenomenon forced King and other mainstream black leaders and organizations to launch a new stage in the civil rights movement to focus attention on the plight of poor inner-city blacks. Legal access to restaurants, schools, and other public accommodations, King pointed out, meant little to people mired in a culture of urban poverty. They needed jobs and decent housing as much as they needed legal rights. To this end, King began to emphasize the economic plight of the black urban underclass. The time had come for radical measures "to provide jobs and income for the poor." Yet as King and others sought to escalate the war on poverty at home, the war in Vietnam was consuming more and more of America's resources and energies.

THE TRAGEDY OF VIETNAM

As racial violence erupted in America's cities, the war in Vietnam reached new levels of intensity and destruction. In November 1963, when John Kennedy was assassinated, there were 16,000 American military "advisers" in South Vietnam. Lyndon Johnson inherited an American commitment to prevent a Communist takeover in Indochina as well as a reluctance on the part of American presidents to assume primary responsibility for fighting the Viet Cong (Communist-led guerrillas in South Vietnam) and their North Vietnamese allies. Beginning with Harry Truman, one president after another had done just enough to avoid being charged with having "lost" Vietnam to communism. Johnson initially sought to do the same, fearing that any other course of action would undermine his political influence and jeopardize his Great

Society programs in Congress. But this path took him and the United States inexorably deeper into an expanding military commitment in Southeast Asia.

During the presidential campaign of 1964, Johnson had opposed the use of American combat troops in Vietnam, "a raggedy-ass fourth-rate country" not worthy of American blood. "I just don't think it's worth fightin' for, and I don't think we can get out," he told an aide. "It's just the biggest damned mess." Yet Johnson's fear of appearing weak was stronger than his misgivings and forebodings. By the end of 1965, there were 184,000 American troops in Vietnam; in 1966 the troop level reached 385,000; and by 1969, the height of the American presence, 542,000. By the time the last American troops left in March 1973, some 58,000 Americans had died and another 300,000 had been wounded. The war had cost the American taxpayers $150 billion, generated economic dislocations that destroyed many Great Society programs, produced 570,000 draft offenders and 563,000 less-than-honorable military discharges, toppled Johnson's administration, and divided the country as no event in American history had since the Civil War.

ESCALATION   The official sanction for military "escalation" in Southeast Asia—a Defense Department term coined in the Vietnam era— was the Tonkin Gulf Resolution, voted by Congress on August 7, 1964. Johnson told a national television audience that two American destroyers, the U.S.S. *Maddox* and the *C. Turner Joy,* had been attacked by North Vietnamese vessels on August 2 and 4 in the Gulf of Tonkin off the coast of North Vietnam. Although Johnson described the attack as unprovoked, in truth the destroyers had been monitoring South Vietnamese attacks against two North Vietnamese islands—attacks planned by American advisers. Even though there was no tangible evidence of the attack on the American ships, the Tonkin Gulf Resolution authorized the president to "take all necessary measures to repel any armed attack against the forces of the United States and to prevent further aggression." Only Senator Wayne Morse of Oregon and Senator Ernest Gruening of Alaska voted against the resolution, which Johnson thereafter interpreted as equivalent to a congressional declaration of war.

Soon after his landslide victory over Goldwater in 1964, Johnson, while still plagued with private doubts, made the crucial decisions that

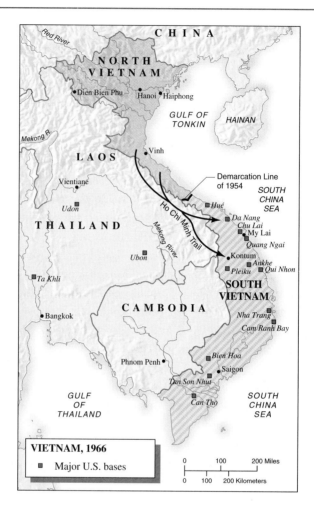

VIETNAM, 1966

■ Major U.S. bases

0   100   200 Miles

0   100   200 Kilometers

shaped American policy in Vietnam for the next four years. On February 5, 1965, the Viet Cong killed 8 and wounded 126 Americans at Pleiku. Further attacks on Americans later that week led Johnson to order operation "Rolling Thunder," the first sustained bombings of North Vietnam, which were intended to stop the flow of soldiers and supplies into the south. Six months later, a task force conducted an extensive study of the bombing's effects on the supplies pouring down the Ho Chi Minh Trail from North Vietnam through Laos into South Vietnam. It concluded that there was "no way" to stop the traffic.

In March 1965 the new American army commander in Vietnam, General William C. Westmoreland, greeted the first installment of combat troops. By the summer, American forces were engaged in "search-and-destroy" operations throughout South Vietnam. As combat operations increased, so did the mounting list of American casualties, announced each week on the nightly news along with the "body count" of alleged Viet Cong dead. "Westy's War," although fought with helicopter gunships, chemical defoliants, and napalm, became like the trench warfare of World War I—a war of attrition.

THE CONTEXT FOR POLICY   Lyndon Johnson's decision to "Americanize" the Vietnam War, so ill-starred in retrospect, was consistent with the foreign policy principles pursued by all American presidents after World War II. The version of the containment theory articulated in the Truman Doctrine, endorsed by Eisenhower and Dulles throughout the 1950s, and reaffirmed by Kennedy, pledged United States opposition to the advance of communism anywhere in the world. "Why are we in Vietnam?" Johnson asked rhetorically at Johns Hopkins University in 1965. "We are there because we have a promise to keep. . . . To leave Vietnam to its fate would shake the confidence of all these people in the value of American commitment." Secretary of State Dean Rusk repeated this rationale before countless congressional committees, warning that Thailand, Burma, and the rest of Southeast Asia would fall like dominoes to communism if American forces withdrew. Military intervention in Vietnam was thus a logical culmination of the assumptions that were widely shared by the foreign policy establishment and the leaders of both political parties since the early days of the cold war.

Johnson and his advisers presumed that American military involvement in Vietnam must not reach levels that would provoke the Chinese or Soviets into direct intervention. And this meant, in effect, that a complete military victory was never possible. The goal of the United States was not to win the war in any traditional sense, but to prevent the North Vietnamese and Viet Cong from winning and eventually force a negotiated settlement with the North Vietnamese. This meant that America would have to maintain a military presence as long as the enemy retained the will to fight.

As it turned out, American public support for the war eroded faster than the will of the North Vietnamese leaders to tolerate devastating casualties. Systematic opposition to the war on college campuses began

"How deep do you figure we'll get involved, sir!" *Although American soldiers were first sent to Vietnam as noncombatant advisers, they soon found themselves involved in a "quagmire" of actual fighting.*

in 1965 with "teach-ins" at the University of Michigan. The following year, Senator J. William Fulbright of Arkansas, chairman of the Senate Foreign Relations Committee, began congressional investigations into American policy in Vietnam. George Kennan, the founding father of the containment doctrine, told Senator Fulbright's committee that the doctrine was appropriate for Europe, but not for Southeast Asia. And a respected general testified that General Westmoreland's military strategy had no chance of achieving victory. By 1967 antiwar demonstrations in New York and at the Pentagon attracted massive support. Nightly television accounts of the fighting—Vietnam was the first war to receive extended television coverage, and hence has been dubbed "the living room war"—called into question the official optimism. By May 1967 even Secretary of Defense McNamara was wavering: "The picture of the world's greatest superpower killing or injuring 1,000 noncombatants a week, while trying to pound a tiny backward nation into submission on an issue whose merits are hotly disputed, is not a pretty one."

In a war of political will, North Vietnam had the advantage. Johnson and his advisers grievously underestimated the tenacity of the North Vietnamese commitment to unify Vietnam and expel American forces. While the United States fought a limited war for limited objectives, the Vietnamese Communists fought an all-out war for their very survival. Just as General Westmoreland was assuring Johnson and the American public that the American war effort in early 1968 was on the verge of gaining the upper hand, the Communists again displayed their cunning and tenacity.

THE TURNING POINT   On January 31, 1968, the first day of the Vietnamese New Year (Tet), the Viet Cong defied a holiday truce to launch assaults on American and South Vietnamese forces throughout South Vietnam. The old capital city of Hué fell to the Communists, and Viet Cong units temporarily occupied the grounds of the American embassy in Saigon. General Westmoreland proclaimed the Tet offensive a major defeat for the Viet Cong, and most students of military strategy later agreed with him. While Viet Cong casualties were enormous, however, the impact of the events on the American public was more telling. The scope and intensity of the Tet offensive contradicted upbeat claims by American commanders that the war on the ground was going well. *Time* and *Newsweek* magazines soon ran antiwar editorials urging American withdrawal. Polls showed that Lyndon Johnson's popularity had declined to 35 percent, lower than any president since Truman's darkest days. Civil rights leaders and social activists felt betrayed as they saw federal funds earmarked for the war on poverty siphoned off by the expanding war. In 1968 the United States was spending $322,000 on every

During the 1968 Tet offensive, Viet Cong units temporarily infiltrated the American embassy in Saigon. Here, American military police lead a captured Viet Cong guerrilla away from the embassy.

The Vietnam War sapped the spirit of Lyndon Johnson, who decided not to run for reelection in 1968.

Communist killed in Vietnam; the poverty programs at home received only $53 per person.

During 1968 Johnson grew increasingly embittered and isolated. He suffered from depression and bouts of paranoia. It had become painfully evident that the Vietnam War was a never-ending stalemate that was fragmenting the nation and undermining Johnson's Great Society programs. Secretary of Defense Clark Clifford reported to Johnson that a task force of prominent soldiers and civilians saw no prospect for a military victory. Senator Robert Kennedy was reportedly considering a run for the presidency in order to challenge Johnson's Vietnam policy. Senator Eugene McCarthy of Minnesota had already decided to oppose Johnson in the Democratic primaries. With antiwar students rallying to his candidacy, McCarthy polled 42 percent of the vote to Johnson's 48 percent in New Hampshire's March primary. It was a remarkable showing for a little-known senator. Each presidential primary now promised to become a referendum on Johnson's Vietnam policy. In Wisconsin, scene of the next primary, the president's political advisers forecast a humiliating defeat.

On March 31 Johnson appeared on national television to announce a limited halt to the bombing of North Vietnam and fresh initiatives for a negotiated cease-fire. Then he added a dramatic postscript: "I shall not seek, and I will not accept the nomination of my party for another term as your President." Although American troops would remain in Vietnam for five more years and the casualties would continue, the quest for military victory had ended. Now the question was how the most powerful nation in the world could extricate itself from Vietnam with a minimum of damage to its prestige.

Sixties Crescendo

A TRAUMATIC YEAR   Change moved at a fearful pace throughout the 1960s, but 1968 was a year of extreme turbulence even for that tumultuous decade. On April 4, only four days after Johnson's announced withdrawal from the presidential race, Martin Luther King, Jr., was gunned down while standing on the balcony of his motel in Memphis, Tennessee. The assassin, James Earl Ray, had expressed hostility toward blacks, but debate still continues over whether he was a pawn in an organized conspiracy. King's death set off an outpouring of grief among whites and blacks. It also ignited riots in over sixty American cities.

Two months later, on June 6, Robert Kennedy was shot in the head by a young Palestinian, Sirhan Sirhan, who resented Kennedy's strong support of Israel. Kennedy's death occurred at the end of the day on which he had convincingly defeated Eugene McCarthy in the California Democratic primary, thereby assuming leadership of the antiwar forces in the race for the nomination for president. Political reporter David Halberstam of the *New York Times* thought back to the assassinations of John Kennedy and Malcolm X, then the violent end of King, the most influential black leader of the twentieth century, and then Robert Kennedy, the heir to leadership of the Kennedy clan. "We could make a calendar of the decade," Halberstam wrote, "by marking where we were at the hours of those violent deaths."

CHICAGO AND MIAMI   In August 1968 Democratic delegates gathered inside the convention hall at Chicago to nominate for president Johnson's faithful vice-president Hubert Humphrey, while 24,000 police and National Guardsmen and a small army of television reporters stood watch over an eclectic gathering of protesters herded together miles away in a public park. Chicago mayor Richard Daley, who had given "shoot-to-kill" orders to police during the April riots protesting the King assassination, warned that he would not tolerate disruptions. Nonetheless, riots broke out in front of the Hilton Hotel and were televised nationwide. As police tear gas and billy clubs struck demonstrators, others chanted, "The whole world is watching."

The Democratic party liberal tradition was clearly in disarray, a fact that gave heart to the Republicans who gathered in Miami to nominate Richard Nixon. Only six years earlier, after he had lost the California

Richard Nixon (right) *and Spiro Agnew* (left), *victors in the 1968 election.*

gubernatorial race, Nixon had vowed never to run again for public office. But by 1968 he had become a spokesman for the values of "Middle America." Nixon and the Republicans offered a vision of stability and order that appealed to a majority of Americans—soon to be called "the silent majority."

George Wallace, the Democratic governor of Alabama who had made his reputation as a defender of segregation, ran as a third candidate in the campaign on the American Independent party ticket. Wallace moderated his position on the race issue, but appealed even more candidly than Nixon to voters' concerns about rioting antiwar protesters, the welfare system, and the growth of the federal government. Wallace's reactionary candidacy generated considerable appeal outside his native South, especially among white working-class communities, where resentment flourished against Lyndon Johnson's Great Society liberalism. Although never a possible winner, Wallace did pose the possibility of denying Humphrey or Nixon an electoral majority and thereby throwing the choice into the House of Representatives, which would have provided an appropriate climax to a chaotic year.

NIXON AGAIN   It did not happen that way. Nixon enjoyed an enormous lead in the polls, which narrowed as the election approached. Wallace's campaign was hurt by his outspoken running mate, retired air force general Curtis LeMay, who favored expanding the war in Vietnam and using nuclear weapons. In October 1968 Hubert Humphrey infuriated Johnson when he announced that, if elected, he would stop bombing North Vietnam "as an acceptable risk for peace."

Nixon and Governor Spiro Agnew of Maryland, his running mate, eked out a narrow victory by about 500,000 votes, a margin of about 1 percentage point. The electoral vote was more decisive, 301 to 191. George Wallace received 10 million votes, 13.5 percent of the total, for the best showing by a third-party candidate since Robert La Follette ran on the Progressive ticket in 1924. All but one of Wallace's 46 electoral votes were from the Deep South. Nixon swept all but four of the states west of the Mississippi. Humphrey's support came almost exclusively from the Northeast.

So at the end of a turbulent year near the end of a traumatic decade, political power passed peacefully to a president who was associated with the complacency of the 1950s. A nation that had seemed on the

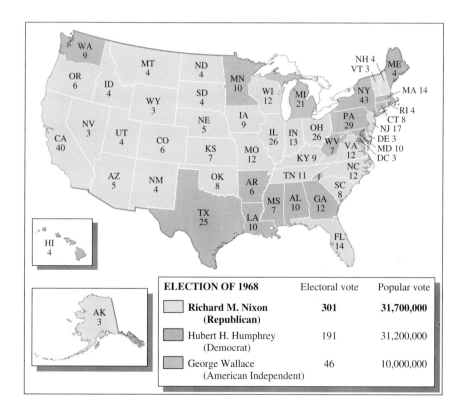

ELECTION OF 1968	Electoral vote	Popular vote
Richard M. Nixon (Republican)	**301**	**31,700,000**
Hubert H. Humphrey (Democrat)	191	31,200,000
George Wallace (American Independent)	46	10,000,000

verge of consuming itself in spasms of violence looked to Richard Nixon to provide what he had promised in the campaign: "peace with honor" in Vietnam and a middle ground on which a majority of Americans, silent or otherwise, could come together.

MAKING CONNECTIONS

- The reform movements of the 1960s galvanized the baby-boom generation into a new youth movement, described in the next chapter, that continued through the early 1970s.

- The conflict in Vietnam, America's longest war, would come to a bitter end for American forces, but the divisions it spawned would echo through the rest of the century.

- The Immigration Act of 1965 would have profound and unexpected consequences on American society: see Chapter 37.

- The success of the civil rights movement in the 1960s led to similar movements for women, gays, Native Americans, and Hispanics, as we will see in the next chapter.

FURTHER READING

A dispassionate analysis of Kennedy's life is Thomas C. Reeves's *A Question of Character: The Life of John F. Kennedy* (rev. ed., 1998). The best study of the Kennedy administration's domestic policies is Irving Bernstein's *Promises Kept: John F. Kennedy's New Frontier* (1991). For details on the assassination, see David W. Belin's *Final Disclosure: The Full Truth about the Assassination of President Kennedy* (1988).

The most comprehensive biography of LBJ is Robert Dallek's two-volume work, *Lone Star Rising: Lyndon Johnson and His Times, 1908–1960* (1991) and *Flawed Giant: Lyndon B. Johnson, 1960–1973* (1998).

Among the works that interpret liberal social policy during the 1960s, John Schwarz's *America's Hidden Success: A Reassessment of Twenty Years of Public Policy* (1983) offers a glowing endorsement of Democratic programs. For a contrasting perspective, see Charles Murray's *Losing Ground: American Social Policy, 1950–1980* (rev. ed., 1995).

On foreign policy, see *Kennedy's Quest for Victory: American Foreign Policy, 1961–1963* (1989), edited by Thomas G. Paterson. To learn more about Kennedy's problems in Cuba, see Mark White's *Missiles in Cuba: Kennedy, Krushchev, Castro and the 1962 Crisis* (1997).

American involvement in Vietnam has received voluminous treatment from all political perspectives. For an overview, see Larry Berman's *Planning a Tragedy: The Americanization of the War in Vietnam* (1982) and *Lyndon Johnson's War: The Road to Stalemate in Vietnam* (1989), as well as Stanley Karnow's *Vietnam: A History* (rev. ed., 1991). An excellent analysis of policy making concerning the Vietnam War is David M. Barrett's *Uncertain Warriors: Lyndon Johnson and His Vietnam Advisors* (1994).

Many scholars have dealt with various aspects of the civil rights movement and race relations of the 1960s. See especially Carl Brauer's *John F. Kennedy and the Second Reconstruction* (1977), David Garrow's *Bearing the Cross: Martin Luther King, Jr., and the Southern Christian Leadership Conference* (1986), Adam Fairclough's *To Redeem the Soul of America: The Southern Christian Leadership Conference and Martin Luther King, Jr.* (1987). William Chafe's *From Civilities to Civil Rights: Greensboro, North Carolina and the Black Struggle for Freedom* (1980) details the original sit-ins. An award-winning study of racial and economic inequality in a representative American city is Thomas J. Sugrue's *The Origins of the Urban Crisis: Race and Inequality in Postwar Detroit* (1996).

35 ✦ REBELLION AND REACTION IN THE 1960S AND 1970S

CHAPTER ORGANIZER

This chapter focuses on:

- rebellion and struggles for rights in the 1970s.

- ending the war in Vietnam.

- Watergate and Nixon's resignation.

- the Ford and Carter administrations.

*A*s Richard Nixon entered the White House, he faced a nation whose social fabric was in tatters. Everywhere, it seemed, traditional institutions and notions of authority were under attack. The turbulent events of 1968 revealed how deeply divided American society had become and how difficult a task Nixon faced in carrying out his pledge to restore social harmony. Yet the stability he promised proved to be elusive. His policies and his combative temperament served to heighten rather than reduce societal tensions. Those tensions reflected profound fissures in the postwar consensus promoted by Eisenhower and inherited by Kennedy and Johnson. Ironically, many of the same forces that had promoted the flush times of the

Eisenhower years helped generate the social upheavals of the 1960s and 1970s.

THE ROOTS OF REBELLION

YOUTH REVOLT   By the 1960s the "baby-boomers" were maturing. Now young adults, they differed from their elders in that they had experienced neither economic depression nor a major war. Record numbers of these young people were attending American colleges and universities during the 1960s: college enrollment quadrupled between 1945 and 1970. At the same time, many universities had become gigantic institutions dependent on research contracts from corporations and the federal government. As these "multiversities" grew more bureaucratic and hierarchical, they unknowingly invited resistance from a generation of students wary of involvement in what President Eisenhower had labeled the "military-industrial complex."

The Greensboro sit-ins in 1960 not only precipitated a decade of civil rights activism, they also signaled an end to the supposed apathy that had enveloped college campuses and social life during the 1950s. Although most immediately concerned with the rights and status of African Americans, the sit-ins, marches, protests, principles, and sacrifices associated with the civil rights movement provided the model and inspiration for other groups that demanded justice, freedom, and equality as well.

During 1960–1961 a small but significant number of white students joined African Americans in the sit-in movement. They and many others were also inspired by President Kennedy's direct appeals to their youthful idealism. Thousands enrolled in the Peace Corps and VISTA (Volunteers in Service to America, the domestic version of the Peace Corps), and others continued to participate in civil rights demonstrations. But as it became clear that politics was mixed with principle in the president's position on civil rights, and later, as criticism of escalating American involvement in Vietnam mounted, more and more young people grew disillusioned with the government and other institutional bastions of the status quo. There was a growing feeling among young people that something was fundamentally wrong, not just with the political system but with the entire structure of American life and values.

By the mid-1960s, a full-fledged youth revolt had broken out across the country. Rebellious students began to flow into two distinct, yet frequently overlapping, movements: the New Left and the counterculture.

THE NEW LEFT   The explicitly political strain of the youth revolt had its official origin when Tom Hayden and Al Haber, two University of Michigan students, formed the Students for a Democratic Society (SDS) in 1960. In 1962 Hayden and Haber convened a meeting of sixty activists at Port Huron, Michigan. After four days of intense discussion and a final all-night session, Hayden drafted what became known as the Port Huron Statement: "We are the people of this generation, bred in at least moderate comfort, housed in universities, looking uncomfortably to the world we inherit."

Hayden's manifesto focused on the absence of individual freedom in modern American life. The country, he insisted, was dominated by huge organizational structures—governments, corporations, unions, universities—all of which conspired to oppress and alienate the individual. Inspired by the example of black activism in the South, Hayden declared that students had the power to restore "participatory democracy" to American life by wresting "control of the educational process from the administrative bureaucracy" and then forging links with other dissident movements. He and others adopted the term "New Left" to distinguish their efforts at grassroots democracy from the Old Left of the 1930s that had espoused an orthodox Marxism and had embraced Stalinism.

In the fall of 1964 students at the University of California at Berkeley took Hayden's program to heart. Several of them had returned to the campus after spending the summer working with the SNCC voter registration project in Mississippi. Three volunteers had been killed, dozens shot, and nearly a thousand arrested. The Berkeley student activists returned to school with mixed emotions—exhilarated, frustrated, and embittered. When University Chancellor Clark Kerr announced that political demonstrations would no longer be allowed at the Telegraph Avenue street corner traditionally used for such activity, several hundred students staged a sit-in at the scene. Soon thereafter over 2,000 more joined in. After a tense thirty-two-hour standoff the administration relented. Student groups then formed the Free Speech Movement (FSM).

Led by Mario Savio, a philosophy major and compelling public speaker, the FSM initially protested on behalf of student rights. But it quickly escalated into a more general criticism of the modern university and what Savio called the "depersonalized, unresponsive bureaucracy" infecting American life. In 1964 Savio led hundreds of students into the administration building and organized a sit-in. In the early-morning hours 600 policemen, dispatched by the governor, arrested the protesters.

The program and tactics of the FSM and SDS soon spread to colleges throughout the country. Issues large and small became the subject of student protest: unpopular faculty tenure decisions, mandatory ROTC programs, dress codes, curfews, dormitory regulations, appearances by Johnson administration officials.

Escalating American involvement in Vietnam soon changed the student agenda. With the dramatic expansion of the military draft after 1965, millions of young American men faced the grim prospect of being drafted to fight in an increasingly unpopular Asian war. In fact, however, the Vietnam conflict, like virtually every other American war, was primarily a poor man's fight. Deferments enabled college students to postpone military service until they received their degree or reached the age of twenty-four; in 1965–1966 they made up only 2 percent of all military inductees. In 1966, however, the Selective Service System modified the provisions so even undergraduates were eligible for the draft.

As the war dragged on and opposition mounted, 200,000 young men simply refused to obey their draft notices, and some 4,000 of those served prison sentences. Another 56,000 men qualified for conscientious-objector status during the Vietnam War, compared with 7,600 during the Korean conflict. Still others left the country altogether—several thousand fled to Canada or Sweden—to avoid military service. The most popular way to avoid the draft was to flunk the physical examination. Whatever the preferred method, many students succeeded in avoiding military service. Of the 1,200 men in the Harvard class of 1970, only fifty-six served in the military, and just two of those went to Vietnam.

In the spring of 1967, 500,000 war protesters of all ages converged on Manhattan's Central Park, chanting "Hey, hey, LBJ, how many kids did you kill today?" Dozens ceremoniously burned their draft cards, and the so-called resistance phase of the antiwar movement was born. Thereafter a coalition of draft-resistance groups around the country sponsored draft-card-burning rallies and sit-ins that led to numerous arrests. Meanwhile, some SDS leaders were growing even more militant. Inspired by the rhetoric and revolutionary violence of black power spokesmen such as Stokely Carmichael, Rap Brown, and Huey Newton, Tom Hayden abandoned his earlier commitment to participatory democracy and passive civil disobedience. Rap Brown told the white radicals to remember the heritage of John Brown: "Take up a gun and go shoot the enemy." As the SDS became more militant, it grew more centralized and authoritarian. Capitalist imperialism replaced university bureaucracy as the primary foe.

Throughout 1967 and 1968, the antiwar movement grew more volatile at the same time that inner-city ghettos were seething with tension and exploding into flames. Frustration over patterns of discrimination in employment and housing and staggering rates of joblessness among inner-city black youth festered into violence. "There was a sense everywhere, in 1968," the journalist Garry Wills wrote, "that things were giving way. That man had not only lost control of his history, but might never regain it." At the end of March, Lyndon Johnson announced that he would not run for reelection, and in early April Martin Luther King, Jr., was murdered.

During that eventful spring, campus unrest enveloped the country. Over 200 major demonstrations took place. The turmoil reached a climax

Mark Rudd, leader of the SDS at Columbia University, talking to the media during student protests over various university policies, April 1968.

with the disruption of Columbia University. There Mark Rudd, leader of the SDS chapter, led a small cadre of radicals in occupying the president's office and classroom buildings. They also kidnapped a dean—all in protest of the university's insensitive decision to displace neighboring black housing in order to build a new gymnasium. During the next week, more buildings were occupied, faculty and administrative offices were ransacked, and classes were canceled. University officials finally called in the New York City police. In the process of arresting the protesters, the police injured a number of innocent bystanders. Their excessive force aroused the anger of many unaligned students, and they staged a strike that shut down the university for the remainder of the semester. The events at Columbia buoyed the militants. Similar clashes between students, administrators, and police occurred at Harvard, Cornell, and San Francisco State.

At the 1968 Democratic convention in Chicago, the polarization of American society reached a tragic and bizarre climax. Inside the tightly guarded convention hall, Democrats nominated Hubert Humphrey. Meanwhile, outside on Chicago's streets, the whole spectrum of antiwar dissenters was gathered, from the earnest supporters of Eugene McCarthy to the nihilistic Yippies, members of the new Youth International party. The Yippies were determined to provoke anarchy in the streets of Chicago. Abbie Hoffman, one of their leaders, explained that they were "revolutionary artists. Our conception of revolution is that it's fun." The Yippies distributed a leaflet at the convention calling for the immediate legalization of marijuana and all psychedelic drugs, the abolition of money, student-run schools, and free sex.

The outlandish behavior of the Yippies and the other demonstrators did not justify the unrestrained response of Mayor Richard J. Daley and his army of 12,000 police. As a horrified television audience watched, many of the police went berserk, clubbing and gassing demonstrators as well as bystanders caught up in the chaotic scene. The spectacle lasted three days and seriously damaged Humphrey's presidential candidacy. The Chicago riots also generated a wave of anger among many middle-class Americans, anger that Richard Nixon and the Republicans shrewdly exploited at their convention in Miami. At the same time, the riots helped to fragment the antiwar movement. Those groups committed to nonviolent protest, while castigating the reactionary policies of Mayor Daley and the police, also felt betrayed by the actions of the

The violence at the 1968 Democratic National Convention in Chicago seared the nation.

Yippies and other anarchistic militants.

In 1968 the SDS began to break up into rival factions, the most extreme of which was the Weathermen, a term derived from a Bob Dylan lyric: "You don't need a weatherman to know which way the wind blows." These hardened young activists embarked on a campaign of violence and disruption, firebombing university buildings and killing innocent people—as well as several of their own members. Government forces arrested most of the Weathermen and sent the rest underground. By 1971 the New Left was dead as a political movement. In large measure it had committed suicide by abandoning the democratic and pacifist principles that had originally inspired participants and given the movement moral legitimacy. The larger antiwar movement also began to fade. There would be a wave of student protests against the Nixon administration in 1970, but thereafter, campus unrest virtually disappeared.

If the social mood was changing during the Nixon years, still a large segment of the public continued the quest for personal fulfillment and social justice. The burgeoning environmental and consumer movements attested to the continuity of sixties idealism. A *New York Times* survey of college campuses in 1969 revealed that many students were transferring their attention from the antiwar movement to the environment. This ecological conscience would blossom in the 1970s into one of the most compelling items on the nation's social agenda.

THE COUNTERCULTURE The numbing events of 1968 led other disaffected activists away from radical politics altogether and toward another manifestation of the sixties youth revolt: the "counterculture."

Long hair, jeans, tie-dyed shirts, sandals, mind-altering drugs, rock music, and cooperative living arrangements were more important than revolutionary ideology to the "hippies," the direct descendants of the Beats of the 1950s. These advocates of the counterculture were, like their New Left peers, primarily affluent, well-educated young whites alienated by the Vietnam War, racism, political and parental demands, runaway technology, and a crass corporate mentality that equated the good life with material goods. In their view, a complacent materialism had settled over urban and suburban life. But they were uninterested in or disillusioned with organized political action. Instead they eagerly embraced the credo outlined by the zany Harvard professor Timothy Leary: "Tune in, turn on, drop out."

For some the counterculture entailed the study and practice of Oriental mysticism. For many it meant the daily use of hallucinogenic drugs. Collective living in urban enclaves such as San Francisco's Haight-Ashbury district, New York's East Village, or Atlanta's Fourteenth Street was the rage for a time among hippies, until conditions grew so crowded, violent, and depressing that residents migrated elsewhere. Rural communes also attracted bourgeois rebels. During the 1960s and early 1970s, thousands of young, inexperienced romantics flocked to the countryside, eager to be liberated from parental and institutional restraints, to live in harmony with nature, and to coexist in an atmosphere of love and openness.

But only a handful of these utopian homesteads survived more than a few months. Rooted in the pleasure principle, rustic hippies often produced more babies than bread. Initially intent upon rejecting conventional society, many found themselves utterly dependent on it, and they were soon panhandling on street corners or lined up at government offices, collecting welfare, unemployment compensation, and food stamps to help them survive the rigors of natural living.

Huge outdoor rock music concerts were also a popular source of community for hippies. The largest of these was the Woodstock Music Festival. In August 1969 some 500,000 young people converged on a 600-acre farm near the tiny rural town of Bethel, New York. The lineup of musicians was a powerful attraction. So too was the easy availability of drugs. For three days the assembled flower children reveled in good music, cheap marijuana, and free love. "Everyone swam nude in the lake," a journalist reported. The country had never "seen a society so free of repression."

The Woodstock Festival drew nearly a half million people to a farm in Bethel, New York. The concert was billed as three days of "peace, music, . . . and love."

But the carefree spirit of Woodstock was short-lived. When other promoters tried to repeat the scene four months later, this time at Altamont, California, the counterculture encountered the criminal culture. The Rolling Stones hired Hell's Angels motorcycle gang members to provide the "security" for their show. In the midst of Mick Jagger's performance of "Sympathy for the Devil," drunken white motorcyclists beat to death a black man wielding a knife in front of the stage. Three other spectators were accidentally killed that night; much of the vitality and innocence of the counterculture died with them.

After 1969 the hippie phenomenon began to wane. The counterculture had become counterproductive and had developed both faddish and fashionable overtones. Entrepreneurs were quick to see profits in protest. Retailers developed a banner business in faded blue jeans, surplus army jackets, beads, incense, and sandals. Health-food stores and "head" shops appeared in shopping malls alongside Neiman Marcus and Sears. Rock music groups, for all their lyrical protests against the capitalist "system," made millions from it. The search on the part of alienated youth for a better society and a good life was strewn with both comic and tragic aspects, and it reflected the deep social ills that had been allowed to fester throughout the post–World War II period.

FEMINISM The seductive ideal of liberation spawned during the sixties helped accelerate a powerful women's rights crusade. Like the New Left, the new feminism drew much of its inspiration and tactics from the civil rights movement. Its aim was to challenge the "cult of female domesticity" that had prevailed since the 1950s.

The mainstream of the women's movement was led by Betty Friedan. Her influential book, *The Feminine Mystique* (1963), launched the new phase of female protest on a national level. During the 1950s, Friedan, a Smith College graduate, raised three children in a New York suburb. Still

Betty Friedan, author of The Feminine Mystique.

politically active but now socially domestic, she mothered her children, pampered her husband, "read *Vogue* under the hair dryer," and occasionally did some freelance writing. In 1957 she conducted a poll of her fellow Smith alumnae and discovered that, despite all the rhetoric about the happy suburban housewife during the fifties, many were in fact miserable. This revelation led to more research, which culminated in the publication of *The Feminine Mystique*.

Women, Friedan wrote, had actually lost ground during the years after World War II, when many left wartime assembly lines and settled down in suburbia. A propaganda campaign engineered by advertisers and women's magazines encouraged them to do so by creating the "feminine mystique" of blissful domesticity. This notion that women were "gaily content in a world of bedroom, kitchen, sex, babies, and home" thus served to imprison women. In Friedan's view, the American middle-class home had become "a comfortable concentration camp" where women suffocated in an atmosphere of mindless materialism, daytime television, and neighborhood gossip.

The Feminine Mystique, an immediate best-seller, raised the consciousness of many women who had long suffered from a feeling of being trapped in a rut with no way out. Moreover, Friedan discovered that

In 1967 Syracuse University student Kathy Switzer challenged the Boston Marathon's men-only tradition. Officials tried to pull her from the course, but with the aid of fellow runners she completed the race. Women became official entrants in 1971.

there were far more women working outside the home than the pervasive "feminine mystique" suggested. Many of these working women were frustrated by the demands of holding "two full-time jobs instead of just one—underpaid clerical worker and unpaid housekeeper."

In 1966 Friedan and a small group of other spirited activists founded the National Organization for Women (NOW). Soon regarded as the NAACP of the women's movement, NOW grew rapidly. It initially sought to end discrimination in the workplace on the basis of sex, and went on to spearhead efforts to legalize abortion, and to obtain federal and state support for childcare centers.

In the early 1970s, Congress and the Supreme Court advanced the cause of sexual equality. Under Title IX of the Educational Amendments Act of 1972, colleges were required to institute "affirmative action" programs to ensure equal opportunities for women. In the same year Congress overwhelmingly approved the Equal Rights Amendment, which had been bottled up in a House committee for almost half a century. In 1973 the Supreme Court, in *Roe* v. *Wade,* struck down state laws forbidding abortions during the first three months of pregnancy. Meanwhile the educational bastions of male segregation, including Yale and Princeton, led a new movement for coeducation that swept the country. "If the 1960s belonged to blacks," said one feminist, "the next ten years are ours."

By the end of the 1970s, however, sharp disputes between moderate and radical feminists fractured the women's movement. The movement's failure to broaden its appeal much beyond the confines of the middle class also caused reform efforts to stagnate. The Equal Rights Amendment, which had once seemed a straightforward assertion of equal opportunity ("Equality of rights under the law shall not be denied or abridged by the United States or by any State on account of sex") and assured of ratification, was stymied in several state legislatures. Despite a congressional extension of the normal time allowed for ratification, by 1982 it had died, several states short of passage. And the very success of NOW's efforts to liberalize local and state abortion laws generated a powerful backlash, especially among Catholics and fundamentalist Protestants, who mounted a potent "right-to-life" crusade.

Yet the success of the women's movement endured long after the militant rhetoric had evaporated. Women's growing presence in the labor force assured them of a greater share of economic and political influence. By 1976, over half the married women in America and nine of ten women college graduates were employed outside the home, a development that one economist called "the single most outstanding phenomenon of this century." Many career women, however, did not regard themselves as "feminists"; they took jobs because they and their families needed the money to survive or to achieve higher levels of material comfort. Whatever the motives, traditional gender roles and childbearing practices were being changed to accommodate the two-career family and the sexual revolution.

THE SEXUAL REVOLUTION AND THE PILL   The feminist movement coincided with the so-called sexual revolution, a much-discussed loosening of traditional restrictions on social behavior. Young people opposed to the conflict in Vietnam chanted "Make Love, Not War." Other members of the counterculture promoted "free love" as an alternative to what they claimed was a repressive, materialistic capitalist society. Activists promoting more permissive sexual attitudes staged rallies, formed organizations, engaged in civil disobedience, filed suits against prevailing laws, and flouted convention.

The publicity given to the sexual revolution exaggerated its scope and depth, but the movement did help generate two major cultural changes: society became more tolerant of premarital sex and women became more sexually active. Between 1960 and 1975 the number of college women reporting having had sexual intercourse doubled, from 27 percent to 50 percent. What facilitated this change was a scientific breakthrough in contraception: the birth-control pill.

Approved by the Food and Drug Administration in 1960, the "pill," as it came to be known, blocked ovulation by releasing synthetic hormones into a woman's body. Initially, birth-control pills were available only to married couples, but such restrictions soon ended. Widespread access to the pill gave women a greater sense of sexual freedom than any previous contraceptive device. The pill promised to erase fear of pregnancy and to make contraception discreet and planned. Many women viewed the birth-control pill as a godsend. "When the pill came out, it was a savior," recalled Eleanor Smeal, president of the Fund for the Feminist Majority. "The whole country was waiting for it. I can't even describe to you how excited people were." By the end of 1961, some 408,000 American women were taking the pill. A year later the figure was 1,187,000, and by the end of 1963 it was 2,300,000 and still rising.

The pill quickly became America's most popular birth-control method. In 1960, the U.S. birth rate was 3.6 children per woman. By

In an effort to spread the word about birth-control options, Planned Parenthood displayed posters like this one in New York City buses, 1967.

1970 it had plummeted to 2.5 children, and since 1980 it has remained slightly below 2. Eight out of ten women have taken birth-control pills at some time in their lives. Clare Boothe Luce, the congresswoman, ambassador, journalist, and author, viewed the advent of the pill as a key element in the broader women's movement: "Modern woman is at last free as a man is free, to dispose of her own body, to earn her living, to pursue the improvement of her mind, to try a successful career."

HISPANIC RIGHTS   The activism that animated the student revolt, the civil rights movement, and the crusade for women's rights soon spread to various ethnic minority groups. The labor shortages during World War II led defense industries to offer Hispanic Americans their first significant access to industrial and skilled-labor jobs in the cities. And as was the case with African Americans, service in the military during the war years helped to heighten an American identity among Hispanic Americans and to excite their desire for equal rights and opportunities.

But equality was elusive. After World War II, Hispanic Americans still faced widespread discrimination in hiring, housing, and education. Poverty was widespread. In 1960, for example, the median income of a Mexican-American family was only 62 percent of the median income of a family in the general population. Hispanic-American activists during the 1950s and 1960s mirrored the efforts of black civil rights leaders such as Martin Luther King, Jr. They too denounced segregation, promoted efforts to improve the quality of public education, and struggled to increase Hispanic-American political influence and economic opportunities.

One of the most popular initiatives was the use of the term *Chicano* as an inclusive label for all Mexican immigrants, Spanish Americans in New Mexico, as well as old *Californios* (descendants of the inhabitants of California before it was seized by the United States, most of whom were Indians or of mixed ancestry), and *Tejanos* (descendants of the inhabitants of Texas before it became independent). The word *Chicano* was originally a Mexican slang term for a clumsy person. Over the years, Anglo Americans had fastened upon the term as a pejorative reference. Now *Chicano* took on a positive connotation. In southern California, students formed Young Chicanos for Community Action, a social service group designed to promote greater self-reliance and local involvement within Chicano neighborhoods. Wearing brown berets, the members protested the disproportionate number of Hispanics being killed in the Vietnam War and demanded improvements in their neighborhood schools.

Unlike their black counterparts, however, Chicano leaders faced an awkward dilemma: what should they do about the continuing stream of illegal Mexican aliens flowing across the border? Many Mexican Americans argued that their own hopes for economic advancement and social equality were put at risk by the influx of Mexican laborers willing to accept low-paying jobs. Mexican-American leaders thus helped to end the *bracero* program (which trucked in *braceros,* Mexican contract day laborers, at harvest time) in 1964 and formed the United Farm Workers (UFW) in 1962 (originally the National Farm Workers Association) to represent Mexican-American migrant workers.

The founder of the UFW was César Chavez. Born in Yuma, Arizona, in 1927 to Mexican immigrant parents, Chavez moved with his family to California in 1939. There they joined thousands of other migrant farm workers traversing the state, moving from job to job, living in tents, cars, or ramshackle cabins. In 1944, at age seventeen, Chavez joined the navy and served for two years in the Pacific. After the war he married and found work, first as a sharecropper raising strawberries and then as a migrant laborer in apricot orchards. In 1952 Chavez joined the Community Service Organization (CSO), a social service group that sought to educate and organize the migrant poor so that they could become more self-reliant. He founded new CSO chapters and was named general director in 1958.

Chavez left the organization in 1962 when it refused to back his proposal to establish a union for farm workers. Other CSO leaders believed that it was impossible to organize migrant workers into an effective union. They thought migrants were too mobile, too poor, too illiterate, too ethnically diverse, and too easily replaced by *braceros.* Moreover, farm workers did not enjoy protected status under the National Labor Relations Act of 1935 (the Wagner Act). Unlike industrial laborers, they were not guaranteed the right to organize or to receive a minimum wage. Nor did federal regulations govern the safety of their workplaces.

Despite such obstacles, Chavez resolved to organize the migrant farm workers. His fledgling Farm Workers Association gained national attention in 1965 when it joined a strike by Filipino farm workers against the corporate grape farmers in California's San Joaquin Valley. Chavez's personal charisma and Catholic piety, his insistence on nonviolent tactics

César Chavez (center) *with organizers of the grape boycott.*

and his reliance upon college student volunteers, his skillful alliance with organized labor and religious groups, all combined to attract media interest and popular support. Soon the UFW began organizing migrant workers in the lettuce fields of the Salinas Valley.

Still, the grape strike itself brought no tangible gains. So Chavez organized a nationwide consumer boycott of grapes. Contrary to Chavez's own principles and orders, some of the striking workers used violence to express their frustration at the recalcitrant growers. In an effort to break the impasse and defuse the tension among his followers, Chavez began a personal fast in 1968. He explained that "the truest act of courage, the strongest act of manliness, is to sacrifice ourselves for others in a totally nonviolent struggle for justice." After fasting for three weeks, he had lost thirty-five pounds, and doctors began to fear for his life. A week later he ended his fast by taking communion and breaking bread with Senator Robert F. Kennedy.

Two years later, in 1970, the grape strike and consumer boycott finally succeeded in bringing twenty-six grape growers to the bargaining table. They signed formal contracts recognizing the UFW, and soon migrant workers throughout the West were benefiting from Chavez's strenuous efforts on their behalf. Wages increased and working conditions improved. In 1975 the California state legislature passed a bill that required growers to bargain collectively with the elected representatives of the farm workers. As Robert Kennedy had observed, César Chavez was "one of the heroic figures of our time."

But the chief strength of the Hispanic movement lay less in the duplication of civil rights strategies than in the rapid growth of the Hispanic population. In 1960 Hispanics in the United States had numbered slightly more than 3 million; by 1970 they had increased to 9 million, and by 2000 they numbered over 35 million, making them the largest minority in America. By 1980, aspiring presidential candidates were openly courting the Hispanic vote, promising support for urban renewal projects in New York and amnesty programs for illegal immigrants in Texas, and delivering rousing anti-Castro speeches in Miami. The voting power of Hispanics and their concentration in states with key electoral votes has helped give the Hispanic point of view political clout.

NATIVE AMERICANS   American Indians—many of whom now called themselves Native Americans—also emerged as a new political force in the late 1960s. Two conditions combined to make Indian rights a priority: first, white Americans felt a deep and persistent sense of guilt for the destructive policies of their ancestors toward a people who had, after all, been here first; second, the plight of the Native American minority was more desperate than that of any other group in the country. Indian unemployment was ten times the national rate, life expectancy was twenty years lower than the national average, and the suicide rate was a whopping one hundred times higher than the rate for whites.

Although President Lyndon Johnson recognized the poverty of the Native Americans and attempted to target federal antipoverty program funds into the reservations, militants within the Indian community became impatient with the slow pace of change and organized protests and demonstrations against local, state, and federal agencies. In 1963 two Chippewas living in Minneapolis, George Mitchell and Dennis Banks, founded the American Indian Movement (AIM) to promote "red power." The leaders of AIM occupied Alcatraz Island in San Francisco Bay in 1969, claiming the site "by right of discovery." And in 1972, a sit-in at the Department of the Interior's Bureau of Indian Affairs (BIA) in

Washington attracted national attention to their cause. The BIA, then and since, has been widely viewed as the worst-managed federal agency. Instead of finding creative ways to promote tribal autonomy and economic self-sufficiency, the BIA was a classic example of government inefficiency and paternalism gone awry.

In 1973 AIM led two hundred Sioux in occupying the tiny village of Wounded Knee, South Dakota, the site where the U.S. 7th Cavalry had massacred a Sioux village in 1890. Provoked by the light sentences given a group of local whites who had killed a Sioux in 1972, the organizers also sought to draw attention to the plight of the Indians living on the reservation there. Half of the families were dependent on government welfare checks, alcoholism was rampant, and over 80 percent of the children had dropped out of school. After the Indian militants took eleven hostages, federal marshals and FBI agents surrounded the encampment. For ten weeks, the two sides engaged in a tense standoff. When AIM leaders tried to bring in food and supplies, a shoot-out resulted, and one Indian was killed and another wounded. Soon

Instigating a standoff with the FBI, members of AIM and local Oglala Sioux occupied the town of Wounded Knee, South Dakota, in an effort to direct attention to dependence on welfare, poor living conditions, and rampant alcoholism among Indians on reservations, March 1973.

thereafter, the tense confrontation ended with a government promise to reexamine Indian treaty rights.

Thereafter, Indian protesters discovered a more effective tactic than direct action and sit-ins. They went into federal courts armed with copies of old treaties and demanded that these become the basis for restitution. In Alaska, Maine, South Carolina, and Massachusetts they won significant settlements that provided legal recognition of their tribal rights and financial compensation at levels that upgraded the standard of living on several reservations.

GAY RIGHTS   The liberationist impulses of the sixties also encouraged homosexuals to organize and assert their own right to equal treatment and basic dignity. On June 17, 1969, New York City police raided the Stonewall Inn, a male gay bar in the heart of Greenwich Village. The patrons fought back and the struggle spilled into the streets. Hundreds of other gays and their supporters joined the fracas against the police. Rioting lasted throughout the weekend. When it ended, gays had forged a new sense of solidarity and a new organization called the Gay Liberation Front (GLF). "Gay is good for all of us," proclaimed one member of the GLF. "The artificial categories 'heterosexual' and 'homosexual' have been laid on us by a sexist society."

As news of the Stonewall riots spread across the country, the gay rights movement assumed national proportions. One of its main tactics was to encourage people to "come out" and make public their homosexuality. This was by no means an easy decision, for professing gays faced social ostracism, physical assaults, exclusion from the military and civil service, and discrimination in the workplace. Yet despite the risks, thousands of homosexuals did "come out." By 1973 almost 800 gay and lesbian organizations had been formed across the country, and every major city had a visible gay community and cultural life.

As was the case with the civil rights crusade and the women's movement, however, the campaign for gay rights soon suffered from internal divisions and a conservative backlash. Gay activists engaged in fractious disputes over tactics and objectives, and conservative moralists and Christian fundamentalists launched a nationwide counterattack against the gay community. By the end of the 1970s, the gay movement had lost its initial momentum and was struggling to salvage many of its hard-won gains.

NIXON AND VIETNAM

The numerous liberation movements of the 1960s fundamentally changed the tone and texture of American social life. By the early 1970s, however, the pendulum of national mood was swinging back. The election of Richard Nixon and Spiro Agnew in 1968 and the rise of George Wallace as a serious political force reflected the emergence of the "silent majority"—those predominantly white working-class and middle-class citizens who were determined to regain control of a society they feared had become awash in permissiveness, anarchy, and tyranny by the minority. Large as the gap was between the silent majority and the forces of dissent, both sides agreed that the Vietnam War remained the dominant event of the time. Until the war was ended and all American troops had returned home, the nation would find it difficult to achieve the equilibrium that the new president had promised.

GRADUAL WITHDRAWAL   During the campaign of 1968, Nixon had claimed to have a secret plan that would bring "peace with honor" in Vietnam. Peace, however, was long in coming and not very honorable. By the time a settlement was finally reached in 1973, another 20,000 Americans had died, the morale of the American army had been shattered, millions of Asians were killed or wounded, and fighting continued in Southeast Asia. In the end, Nixon's policy gained nothing he could not have accomplished in 1969.

The new Vietnam policy of the Nixon administration moved along three separate fronts. First, American negotiators in Paris demanded the withdrawal of Communist forces from South Vietnam and the preservation of the American-supported regime of President Nguyen Van Thieu. The North Vietnamese and Viet Cong negotiators insisted on the retention of a military presence in the south and the reunification of the Vietnamese people under a government dominated by the Communists. There was no common ground on which to come together. Hidden from public awareness and from America's South Vietnamese allies were secret meetings between Henry Kissinger, Nixon's national security adviser, and the North Vietnamese.

Second, Nixon tried to quell domestic unrest over the war. He reduced the number of American troops in Vietnam, justifying the reduction as the natural result of "Vietnamization"—the equipping and training of the

Even as the Nixon administration began a phased withdrawal of American troops from Vietnam, the war took a heavy toll on Vietnamese and Americans alike.

South Vietnamese to assume the burden of ground combat in place of Americans. From a peak of 560,000 in 1969, American combat troops were withdrawn at a steady pace that matched almost precisely the pace of the American buildup from 1965 to 1969. By 1973 only 50,000 American troops remained in Vietnam. In 1969 Nixon also established a draft lottery system that eliminated many inequities and clarified the likelihood of being drafted—only those nineteen-year-olds with low lottery numbers would have to go—and in 1973 he did away with the draft altogether by creating an all-volunteer military. Nixon was more successful in achieving the goal of reducing antiwar activity than at forcing concessions from the North Vietnamese in Paris.

Third, while reducing the number of American combat troops, Nixon and Henry Kissinger expanded the air war in an effort to persuade the enemy to come to terms. Heavy bombing of North Vietnam was part of what Nixon called his "madman theory." He wanted the North Vietnamese leaders to believe that he "might do *anything* to stop the war." In March 1969, American planes began a fourteen-month-long bombing campaign aimed at Communist sanctuaries in Cambodia. Congress did not learn of these secret raids until 1970, although the total tonnage of bombs dropped was four times that dropped on Japan during World War II. But Hanoi's leaders did not flinch. Then on April 30, 1970, Nixon announced what he called an "incursion" into "neutral" Cambodia by United States troops to "clean out" North Vietnamese staging areas. The head of Cambodia's government for two decades, Prince Norodom Sihanouk, had previously objected to such American raids into his country, but Sihanouk had been replaced in a coup by General Lon Nol earlier in the spring, clearing the way for the American invasion.

DIVISIONS AT HOME   America's slow withdrawal from Vietnam had a devastating effect on the military's morale and reputation. "No one wants to be the last grunt to die in this lousy war," said one soldier. Between 1969 and 1971, there were 730 reported "fragging" incidents, efforts by American troops to kill or injure their own officers, usually with fragmentation grenades. Drug abuse became a major problem. In 1971 four times as many American troops were hospitalized for drug abuse as for combat-related wounds.

Back on the home front, the public learned of previously suppressed events in Vietnam that caused even the staunchest supporters of the war to wince. Late in 1969 the story of the My Lai massacre broke in the press and plunged the country into two years of exposure to the gruesome tale of Lieutenant William Calley, who ordered the murder of over 200 civilians in My Lai village in 1968. Twenty-five army officers were charged with complicity in the massacre and subsequent cover-up, but only Calley was convicted; Nixon soon granted him parole.

The loudest public outcry against Nixon's Indochina policy occurred in the wake of the Cambodian "incursion." Campuses across the country exploded in what the president of Columbia University called "the most disastrous month of May in the history of American higher education." Student protests led to the closing of hundreds of colleges and universities. At Kent State University, the Ohio National Guard was called in to quell rioting in which the campus Reserve Officer Training Corps (ROTC) building was burned down by antiwar protesters. The poorly trained Guardsmen panicked and opened fire on the demonstrators, killing four student bystanders. Eleven days later, on May 15, Mississippi highway patrolmen riddled a dormitory at Jackson State College with bullets, killing two black students. Although an official investigation of the Kent State episode condemned the "casual and indiscriminate shooting," polls indicated that the American public supported the National Guard; students had "got what they were asking for." In New York City, antiwar demonstrators who gathered to protest the deaths at Kent State and the invasion of Cambodia were attacked by "hard-hat" construction workers, who forced the student protesters to disperse and then marched on City Hall to raise the flag that had been lowered to half staff in mourning for the Kent State victims.

The following year, in June 1971, the *New York Times* began publishing excerpts from *The History of the U.S. Decision Making Process in Vietnam,*

National Guardsmen shot and killed four student bystanders during antiwar demonstrations on the campus of Kent State University.

a secret Defense Department study commissioned by Robert McNamara before his resignation as secretary of defense in 1968. The so-called Pentagon Papers, leaked to the press by a former Defense Department official, Daniel Ellsberg, confirmed what many critics of the war had long suspected: Congress and the public had not received the full story on the Gulf of Tonkin incident of 1964, and contingency plans for American entry into the war were being drawn up while Johnson was promising the American people that combat troops would never be sent to Vietnam. Moreover, there was no plan for bringing the war to an end so long as the North Vietnamese persisted. Although the Pentagon Papers dealt with events only up to 1965, the Nixon administration attempted to block their publication, arguing that they endangered national security and that their publication would prolong the war. By a vote of 6 to 3, the Supreme Court ruled against the government. Newspapers throughout the country began publication the next day.

WAR WITHOUT END   The mounting social divisions at home and the approach of the 1972 presidential election combined to produce a shift in the American negotiating position in Paris. In the summer of 1972

Henry Kissinger again began meeting privately with Le Duc Tho, the North Vietnamese negotiator, and he now dropped his insistence on the removal of all North Vietnamese troops from the south before the withdrawal of the remaining American troops. On October 26, only a week before the American presidential election, Kissinger announced: "Peace is at hand." But this was a cynical ploy to win votes. Several days earlier, the Thieu regime in South Vietnam had rejected the Kissinger plan for a cease-fire, fearful that the presence of North Vietnamese troops in the south virtually guaranteed an eventual Communist victory. The Paris peace talks broke off on December 16, and two days later the re-elected Nixon ordered the saturation bombing of Hanoi and Haiphong, the two largest cities in North Vietnam. These so-called Christmas bombings, and the simultaneous mining of North Vietnamese harbors, aroused worldwide protest.

But the bombings also made the North Vietnamese more flexible at the negotiating table. The "Christmas bombings" stopped on December 29, and the resumption of talks in Paris soon followed. On January 27, 1973, the United States, North and South Vietnam, and the Viet Cong signed an "agreement on ending the war and restoring peace in Vietnam." While Nixon and Kissinger both claimed that the bombing had brought North Vietnam to its senses, in truth the North Vietnamese

The scramble to board evacuation helicopters on the roof of the American Embassy, Saigon, April 30, 1975.

never altered their basic stance; they kept 150,000 troops in the south and remained committed to the reunification of Vietnam under one government. What had changed since the previous fall was the willingness of the South Vietnamese to accept these terms, albeit reluctantly, on the basis of Nixon's promise that the United States would respond "with full force" to any violation of the agreement.

On March 29, 1973, the last American combat troops left Vietnam. On that same day, the last of several hundred American prisoners of war, most of them downed pilots, were released from Hanoi. Within a period of months, however, the cease-fire in Vietnam ended, the war between north and south resumed, and the military superiority of the Communist forces soon became evident. In Cambodia (renamed Kampuchea after it fell to the Communists) and Laos, where fighting had been more sporadic, Communist victory also seemed inevitable. In 1975 the North Vietnamese launched a full-scale armored invasion against the south, and South Vietnamese president Thieu appealed to Washington for assistance. Congress refused. The much-mentioned "peace with honor" had proved to be, in the words of one CIA official, only a "decent interval"—enough time for the United States to extricate itself from Vietnam before the collapse of the South Vietnamese government. On April 30, 1975, Americans watched on television as North Vietnamese tanks rolled into Saigon, soon to be renamed Ho Chi Minh City, and helicopters lifted the officials in the American embassy to ships waiting offshore. In those last desperate moments, terrified South Vietnamese fought to get on the helicopters as they took off.

The longest war in American history was finally over, leaving in its wake a bitter legacy. During the period of American involvement in the fighting, almost 2 million combatants and civilians were killed on both sides. North Vietnam absorbed incredible losses—some 600,000 soldiers and countless civilians killed. More than 58,000 Americans died in Vietnam, 300,000 were wounded, 2,500 were declared missing, almost 100,000 returned missing one or more limbs, and over 150,000 combat veterans suffered drug or alcohol addiction or severe psychological disorders. To be sure, most of the Vietnam veterans readjusted well to civilian life, but even they carried for years the stigma of a "lost war."

The "loss" of the war and revelations of American atrocities such as My Lai eroded respect for the military so thoroughly that many young Americans came to regard military service as corrupting and ignoble.

The war, described as a noble crusade on behalf of democratic ideals, instead suggested that democracy was not easily transferable to Third World regions that lacked any historical experience with liberal values and representative government. Fought to show the world that the United States would be steadfast in containing the spread of communism, instead the war sapped the national will and fragmented the national consensus that had governed foreign affairs since 1947. It also changed the balance of power in domestic politics. Not only did the war cause the downfall of Lyndon Johnson's presidency; it also created enduring fissures in the Democratic party. Said antiwar senator and 1972 Democratic presidential candidate George McGovern: "The Vietnam tragedy is at the root of the confusion and division of the Democratic party. It tore up our souls."

Little wonder that most people at war's end wanted to "put Vietnam behind us" and forget. Although subsequent debates over American foreign policy in the Middle East, Africa, and Latin America frequently referred to "the lessons of Vietnam," the phrase was used by different factions for diametrically opposed purposes, ranging from refusal to commit any American troops and resources in El Salvador and Nicaragua to an insistence on massive military commitments unfettered by any diplomatic restrictions that might preclude outright victory. "In the end, then," one journalist wrote concerning the Vietnam era, "there was no end at all."

NIXON AND MIDDLE AMERICA

Richard Nixon had been elected in 1968 as the representative of "Middle America," those middle-class citizens fed up with the liberal politics and promises of the 1960s. The Nixon cabinet and White House staff reflected their values. The chief figures were John Mitchell, the gruff attorney-general who had made his fortune as a municipal bond lawyer in Nixon's old firm; H. R. Haldeman and John Ehrlichman, advisers on domestic policy whose major experience before their association with the Nixon campaign had been in advertising; William Rogers, the secretary of state, an old-time Nixon friend whose control over foreign policy was quickly preempted by Henry Kissinger; and Melvin Laird, the secretary of defense, who also found his influence undercut by Kissinger's access to the White House. The cabinet was all white, all male, all Republican.

DOMESTIC AFFAIRS   Nixon sought to stop social-welfare programs in their tracks, but, like Eisenhower before him, he found it difficult to dismantle liberal programs. Despite the efforts of the Nixon administration, the civil rights legislation enacted during the Johnson years continued to take effect. "There are those who want instant integration and those who want segregation forever," said Nixon in 1969. "I believe we need to have a middle course between these extremes." In practice this "middle course" took the shape of a concerted effort in 1970 to block congressional renewal of the Voting Rights Act of 1965 and to delay implementation of court orders requiring the desegregation of school districts in Mississippi. Sixty-five lawyers in the Justice Department signed a letter of protest against the administration's stance. Congress then extended the Voting Rights Act over Nixon's veto. The Supreme Court, in the first decision made under the new chief justice, Warren Burger—a Nixon appointee—ordered the integration of the Mississippi public schools. In *Alexander v. Holmes County Board of Education* (1969), a unanimous Court ordered a quick end to segregation. During Nixon's first term and despite his wishes, more schools were desegregated than in all the Kennedy-Johnson years combined.

Nixon's attempts to block desegregation efforts in urban areas also failed. The Burger Court ruled unanimously in *Swann v. Charlotte-Mecklenburg Board of Education* (1971) that school systems must bus students out of their neighborhoods if necessary to achieve integration. Protest over desegregation now began to manifest itself more in the North than in the South, as white families in Boston, Denver, and other cities denounced the destruction of "the neighborhood school," and angry parents in Pontiac, Michigan, firebombed school buses.

Nixon asked Congress to impose a moratorium on all busing orders by the federal courts. The House of Representatives, equally attuned to voter outrage at busing to achieve racial integration, went along. But a Senate filibuster blocked the president's antibusing bill. Busing opponents won a limited victory when the Supreme Court ruled, in *Milliken v. Bradley* (1974), that desegregation plans in Detroit requiring the transfer of students from the inner city to the suburbs were unconstitutional. This landmark decision, along with the *Bakke v. Regents of the University of California* (1978) decision, which restricted the use of quotas to achieve racial balance, marked the transition of desegregation from an issue of simple justice to a more tangled thicket of conflicting group and individual rights.

Anti-busing demonstra-
tors congregate at the
State House in Boston
to protest forced inte-
gration of the school
system, May 1973.

Nixon invented several names for his domestic program. At one point it was called the "New Federalism," which would "start resources and power flowing back from Washington to the States and to the people." To that end, in 1972 he pushed through Congress a five-year revenue-sharing plan that would distribute $30 billion of federal revenues to the states for use as they saw fit. At another point Nixon called for a "New American Revolution" to revive traditional values. These catchphrases never caught on, as had the "New Frontier" or the "Great Society," because Nixon's domestic program was mostly defensive and negative.

Meanwhile, the Democratic Congress moved forward with new legislation: the right of eighteen-year-olds to vote in national elections (1970), and in all elections under the Twenty-sixth Amendment (1971); increases in Social Security benefits indexed to the inflation rate and a rise in food-stamp funding; the Occupational Safety and Health Act (1970); the Clean Air Act (1970); new bills to control water pollution (1970 and 1972); and the Federal Election Campaign Act (1972), which modified the rules of campaign finance. These measures accounted for a more rapid rise in spending on social programs than Johnson's Great Society programs had.

ECONOMIC MALAISE   The major domestic development during the Nixon years was a floundering economy. Overheated by the expense of the Vietnam War, the annual inflation rate began to rise in 1967, when it was 3 percent. By 1973 it was at 9 percent; a year later it was at 12 percent, and it remained in double digits for most of the 1970s. The Dow Jones average of major industrial stocks fell by 36 percent between 1968 and 1970, its steepest decline in more than thirty years. Meanwhile unemployment, at a low of 3.3 percent when Nixon took office, climbed to 6 percent by the end of 1970 and threatened to keep rising. Somehow the American economy was undergoing a recession and inflation at the same time. Economists coined the term "stagflation" to describe the syndrome that defied the orthodox laws of economics.

The economic malaise had at least three deep-rooted causes. First, the Johnson administration had attempted to pay for both the Great Society social-welfare programs and the war in Vietnam without a major tax increase, generating larger federal deficits, a major expansion of the money supply, and price inflation. Second, and more important, by the late 1960s, American goods faced stiff competition in international markets from West Germany, Japan, and other emerging industrial powers. No longer was American technological superiority unquestioned. Third, the American economy had depended heavily on cheap sources of energy; no nation was more dependent on the automobile and the automobile industry, and no nation was more careless in its use of fossil fuels in factories and homes.

Just as domestic petroleum reserves began to dwindle and dependence on foreign sources increased, the Organization of Petroleum Exporting Countries (OPEC) combined to use their oil as a political and economic weapon. In 1973, when the United States sent massive aid to Israel after a devastating Syrian-Egyptian attack during Yom Kippur, the holiest day in the Jewish calendar, OPEC announced that it would not sell oil to nations supporting Israel and that it was raising its prices by 400 percent. Motorists thereafter faced long lines at gas stations and factories cut production.

Another condition leading to stagflation was the flood of new workers —mainly baby-boomers and women—entering the labor market. From 1965 to 1980 the workforce grew by 40 percent, almost 30 million workers, a number greater than the total labor force of France or West Germany. The number of new jobs could not keep up, leaving many unemployed. At the same time, worker productivity declined, pushing up inflation in the face of rising demand.

Stagflation posed a new set of economic problems, but Nixon responded erratically and ineffectively, trying old remedies for a new

An Earth Day demonstration dramatizing the dangers of air pollution, April 1972.

problem. First, he tried to reduce the federal deficit by raising taxes and cutting the budget. When the Democratic Congress refused to cooperate with this approach, he encouraged the Federal Reserve Board to reduce the money supply by raising interest rates. The stock market immediately collapsed, and the economy plunged into the "Nixon recession."

A sense of desperation seized the White House. In 1969, when asked about government restrictions on wages and prices, Nixon had been unequivocal: "Controls. Oh, my God, no! . . . We'll never go to controls." But in 1971, he reversed himself. He froze all wages and prices for ninety days and announced that the United States would no longer convert dollars into gold for foreign banks. The dollar, its link to gold cut, now drifted lower on world currency exchanges. After ninety days, Nixon established mandatory guidelines for subsequent wage and price increases under the supervision of a federal agency. Still the economy floundered. By 1973 the wage and price guidelines were made voluntary, and therefore almost entirely ineffective.

ENVIRONMENTAL PROTECTION The widespread recognition that America faced limits to economic growth fueled broad support for environmental protection in the early 1970s. The realization that cities and industrial development were damaging the physical environment and altering the earth's ecology was not new: Rachel Carson's book *Silent Spring* (1962) had sounded the warning years earlier. But in Nixon's first term the Democratic-controlled Congress took concerted action, passing several acts to protect and clean up the environment. The administration also created by executive order the Environmental Protection Agency, a consolidation of existing agencies, to oversee federal guidelines for controlling air pollution, toxic wastes, and water quality.

The Arab oil boycott and the OPEC price increase led to an energy crisis in the United States. People began to realize that natural resources were not infinitely expendable. "Although it's positively un-American to think so," said one sociologist, "the environmental movement and energy shortage have forced us all to accept a sense of our limits, to lower our expectations, to seek prosperity through conservation rather than growth."

As stagflation persisted into the middle and late 1970s, corporate criticism that environmental regulations were cutting into jobs and profit margins began to sound more persuasive, especially when the staggering cost of cleaning up accumulated toxic wastes became known. "Why worry about the long run," said one unemployed steelworker in 1976, "when you're out of work right now." Polls showed that protection of the environment remained a high priority among a majority of Americans, but that few were willing to suffer a cutback in their standard of living to achieve that goal. "It was," bemoaned one journalist, "as if passengers knew they were boarding the *Titanic,* but preferred to jostle with one another for first class accommodations so they might enjoy as much of the voyage as possible."

NIXON TRIUMPHANT

Nixon was the first president since Eisenhower in 1957 to confront a Congress in which both houses were under the control of the opposition party. It followed that he focused his energies on foreign policy, where presidential initiatives were less encumbered and where he, in tandem with Kissinger, achieved several stunning breakthroughs. He also continued to support the American space program and the efforts to beat the Soviets to the moon. In July 1969 American astronaut Neil Armstrong became the first man to walk on the moon.

This achievement buoyed American spirits at a time when troops were mired in Vietnam, cities teemed with racial unrest, and the economy proved more sickly than Nixon could remedy. Similarly, Nixon's foreign

In July 1969, a program begun by President Kennedy reached its goal: putting a man on the moon.

policy successes gave Americans some measure of confidence in their government. His administration managed to diagnose and improve American relations with the major powers of the Communist world—China and the Soviet Union—and to shift fundamentally the pattern of the cold war.

CHINA   In 1971 Nixon's diplomatic adviser Henry Kissinger made a secret trip to Beijing (Peking) to explore the possibility of American recognition of Communist China. Since 1949, when Mao Tse-tung's revolutionary movement established control in China, the United States had refused to recognize Communist China, preferring to regard Chiang Kai-shek's exiled regime on Taiwan as the legitimate government of China. In one simple but stunning stroke, Nixon and Kissinger ended two decades of diplomatic isolation for the People's Republic of China and drove a wedge between the two chief bastions of communism in the world.

In 1972 Americans watched on television as their president visited famous Chinese landmarks, which had been invisible to Americans for over two decades, and drank toasts with Premier Chou En-lai and

With President Richard Nixon's visit to China in 1972, the United States formally recognized China's Communist government. In this photo, Nixon and Chinese premier Chou En-lai drink a toast.

Mao Tse-tung. The United States and China agreed to scientific and cultural exchanges, steps toward the resumption of trade, and the eventual reunification of Taiwan with the mainland. A year after the Nixon visit, "liaison offices" were established in Washington and Beijing (Peking) that served as unofficial embassies, and in 1979 diplomatic recognition was formalized. Richard Nixon, the former anti-Communist crusader who had condemned the State Department for "losing" China in 1949, had accomplished a diplomatic feat that his Democratic predecessors could not.

DÉTENTE   In truth, China welcomed the breakthrough in relations with the United States because its rivalry with the Soviet Union, with which it shared a long border, had become more bitter than its rivalry with the West. The Soviet leaders, troubled by the Sino-American agreements, were also anxious for an easing of tensions with the United States now that they had, as the result of a huge arms buildup following the Cuban missile crisis, achieved virtual parity with the United States in nuclear weapons. Once again President Nixon surprised the world, by announcing that he would visit Moscow in 1972 for discussions with Leonid Brezhnev, the Soviet premier. The high theater of the China visit was repeated in Moscow, with toasts and elegant dinners between world leaders who had previously regarded each other as incarnations of evil.

What became known as "détente" with the Soviets offered the promise of a more orderly and restrained competition between the two superpowers. Nixon and Brezhnev signed agreements reached at the Strategic Arms Limitation Talks (SALT), which negotiators had been working on since 1969. The SALT agreement did not end the arms race, but it did limit both the number of intercontinental ballistic missiles (ICBMs) and the construction of antiballistic missile systems (ABMSs). In effect, the Soviets were allowed to retain a greater number of missiles with greater destructive power, while the United States retained a lead in the total number of warheads. No limitations were placed on new weapons systems, though each side agreed to work toward a permanent freeze on all nuclear weapons. The Moscow summit also produced new trade agreements, including an arrangement whereby the United States sold almost one-quarter of its wheat crop to the Soviets at a favorable price. American farmers rejoiced, since the wheat deal assured them a high price for their crop, but domestic critics grumbled that the deal would raise food prices in the United States and rescue the Soviets from troublesome economic problems.

SHUTTLE DIPLOMACY   The Nixon-Kissinger initiatives in the Middle East were less dramatic and less conclusive than the agreements with China and the Soviet Union, but they did show that America recognized Arab power in the region and its own dependence on the oil from Islamic states fundamentally opposed to Israel. After the Six-Day War of 1967, in which Israeli forces routed the armies of Egypt, Syria, and Jordan, Israel seized territory from all three Arab nations. Moreover, the number of Palestinian refugees, many of them homeless since the creation of Israel in 1948, increased after the Israeli victory in 1967. When Israel recovered from the initial shock of the surprise Yom Kippur War of 1973, Kissinger negotiated a cease-fire and exerted pressure to prevent Israel from taking additional Arab territory. American reliance on Arab oil led to closer ties with Egypt and its president, Anwar el-Sadat, and more restrained support for Israel. In an attempt to broker a lasting settlement, Kissinger made numerous flights among the capitals of the Middle East. This "shuttle diplomacy" won acclaim from all sides, but he failed to find a comprehensive formula for peace in the troubled region and ignored the Palestinian problem. He did, however, lay groundwork for the subsequent accord between Israel and Egypt in 1977.

THE 1972 ELECTION   Nixon's foreign policy achievements allowed him to stage the presidential campaign of 1972 as a triumphal procession. The main threat to his reelection came from Alabama's Democratic governor George Wallace, who had the potential to deprive the Republicans of conservative votes and thereby throw the election to the Democrats or the Democratic-controlled Congress. On May 15, 1972, however, Wallace was shot and left paralyzed below the waist by a man eager to achieve a grisly brand of notoriety. Wallace was forced to withdraw from the campaign.

Meanwhile, the Democrats were further ensuring Nixon's victory by nominating Senator George S. McGovern of South Dakota, a steadfast liberal who embodied antiwar and social-welfare values associated with the turbulence of the 1960s. At the Democratic convention in Miami Beach, McGovern benefited from party reforms that increased the representation of women, blacks, and minorities. But such changes alienated party regulars. Mayor Richard Daley of Chicago was actually ousted from the convention, and the AFL-CIO refused to endorse the liberal Democratic candidate.

The campaign was an exercise in futility for McGovern, while Nixon made only a few formal political trips and cast himself in the role of "global peacekeeper." Nixon won the greatest victory of any Republican presidential candidate in history, capturing 520 electoral votes to only 17 for McGovern. The popular vote was equally decisive: 46 million to 28 million, a proportion of the total vote (60.8 percent) that was second only to Johnson's victory over Goldwater in 1964.

During the course of the campaign McGovern complained about the "dirty tricks" of the Nixon administration, most especially the curious incident in which a group of burglars was caught breaking into the Democratic National Committee headquarters in the Watergate apartment complex in Washington, D.C. McGovern's accusations seemed shrill and biased at the time, the lamentations of an obvious loser. Nixon and his staff made plans for "four more years" as the investigation of the fateful Watergate break-in proceeded apace.

WATERGATE

During the trial of the accused Watergate burglars, the relentless prodding of Judge John J. Sirica led one of the accused to tell the full story of the Nixon administration's complicity in the Watergate episode. James W. McCord, a former CIA agent and security chief for the Committee to

Re-elect the President (CREEP), was the first in a long line of informers in a melodrama that unfolded over the next two years. It ended in the first resignation of a president in American history, the conviction and imprisonment of twenty-five officials of the Nixon administration, including four cabinet members, and the most serious constitutional crisis since the impeachment trial of President Andrew Johnson.

UNCOVERING THE COVER-UP   The trail of evidence pursued first by Judge Sirica, then by a grand jury, and then by a Senate investigation committee headed by Senator Samuel J. Ervin, Jr., of North Carolina, led directly to the White House. There was never any evidence that Nixon ordered the break-in or that he was aware of plans to burglarize the Democratic National Committee. From the start, however, Nixon was personally involved in the cover-up of the incident. He used his presidential powers to discredit and block the investigation. And, most alarming, the Watergate burglary was merely one small part of a larger pattern of corruption and criminality sanctioned by the Nixon White House.

The White House had adopted illegal tactics in 1970 when the *New York Times* disclosed that the secret American bombings in Cambodia had been going on for years. Nixon had ordered illegal telephone taps on several journalists and government employees suspected of leaking the story. The covert activity against the press and critics of Nixon's Vietnam policies increased in 1971 during the crisis generated by the publication of the Pentagon Papers, when a team of burglars under the direction of White House adviser John Ehrlichman had broken into Daniel Ellsberg's psychiatrist's office in an effort to obtain damaging information on Ellsberg, the man who had given the Pentagon Papers to the press. By the spring of 1972, Ehrlichman commanded a team of "dirty tricksters" who performed various acts of sabotage against prospective Democratic candidates for the presidency, including falsely accusing Hubert Humphrey and Senator Henry Jackson of sexual improprieties, forging press releases, setting off stink bombs at Democratic rallies, and associating the opposition candidates with racist remarks. By the time of the Watergate break-in, the money to finance such "pranks" was being illegally collected through the Committee to Re-elect the President and placed under the control of the White House staff.

The cover-up began to unravel as various people, including John Dean, legal counsel to the president, began to cooperate with prosecutors. It unraveled further in 1973 when L. Patrick Gray, acting director of the FBI, resigned after confessing that he had confiscated and destroyed several incriminating documents. On April 30 Ehrlichman and Haldeman resigned, together with Attorney-General Richard Kleindienst. A few days later the president nervously assured the public in a television address, "I am not a crook." Then John Dean, whom Nixon had dismissed because of his cooperation with prosecutors, testified to the Ervin Committee that there had been a cover-up and that Nixon had approved it. In another "bombshell" disclosure, a White House aide told the committee that Nixon had installed a taping system in the White House and that many of the conversations about Watergate had been recorded.

A year-long battle for the "Nixon tapes" began. Harvard law professor Archibald Cox, who had been appointed as special prosecutor to handle the Watergate case, took the president to court in October 1973 in order to obtain the tapes. Nixon, pleading "executive privilege," refused to release the tapes and ordered Cox fired. In what became known as the "Saturday Night Massacre," Attorney-General Elliot Richardson and Deputy Attorney-General William Ruckelshaus resigned rather than execute the order. Solicitor-General Robert Bork finally fired Cox. Cox's replacement as special prosecutor, Leon Jaworski, proved no more pliable than Cox, and he also took the president to court. In March 1974 the Watergate grand jury indicted Ehrlichman, Haldeman, and Mitchell for obstruction of justice, and it named Nixon as an "unindicted co-conspirator."

On July 24, 1974, the Supreme Court ruled unanimously that the president must surrender the tapes. A few days later the House Judiciary Committee dramatically voted to recommend three articles of impeachment: obstruction of justice through the payment of "hush money" to witnesses and the withholding of evidence; abuse of power through using federal agencies to deprive citizens of their constitutional rights; and defiance of Congress by withholding the tapes. But before the House of Representatives could meet to vote on impeachment, Nixon handed over the complete set of White House tapes. No sooner were the tapes handed over than investigators learned that sections of certain recordings were missing, including eighteen minutes of a key conversation during which Nixon first mentioned the Watergate burglary. The president's loyal secretary tried to accept blame for the erasure, claiming she accidentally pushed the wrong button, but experts

Having resigned his office, Richard Nixon waves farewell outside the White House, August 9, 1974.

later concluded that the missing segments had been intentionally deleted. On August 9, 1974, fully aware that the evidence on the tapes implicated him in the cover-up, Richard Nixon resigned from office, the only president ever to do so.

EFFECTS OF WATERGATE   Vice-President Spiro Agnew did not succeed Nixon because he himself had been forced to resign in October 1973 for having accepted bribes from contractors before and during his term as vice-president. In a plea bargain with prosecutors he agreed to resign. The vice-president at the time of Nixon's resignation was Gerald Ford, the former House minority leader from Michigan whom Nixon had appointed, with the approval of Congress, under provisions of the Twenty-fifth Amendment. Ratified in 1967, the amendment provided for the appointment of a vice-president when the office became vacant. Ford insisted that he had no intention of pardoning Nixon, who was still liable for criminal prosecution. "I do not think the public would stand for it," said Ford. But a month after Nixon's resignation, the new president did issue the pardon, explaining that it was necessary to end the national obsession with the Watergate scandals. Many suspected that Nixon and Ford had made a deal, though there was no evidence to confirm the speculation. President Ford testified personally to a congressional committee: "There was no deal, period."

If there was a silver lining in the dark cloud of Watergate, it was the vigor and resiliency of the institutions that had brought a president down—the press, Congress, the courts, and an aroused public opinion. Congress responded to the Watergate revelations with several pieces of legislation designed to curb executive power. Already nervous about possible efforts to renew American military assistance to South Vietnam, the Democratic-led Congress passed the War Powers Act (1973), which required the president to inform Congress within forty-eight hours if U.S. troops were being deployed in combat abroad and to withdraw troops after sixty days unless Congress specifically approved their stay. In an effort to correct abuses of campaign funds, Congress enacted legislation in 1974 that set new ceilings on political contributions and expenditures. And in reaction to the Nixon claim of "executive privilege" as a means of withholding evidence, Congress strengthened the 1966 Freedom of Information Act to require prompt responses to requests for information from government files and to place on government agencies the burden of proof for classifying information as secret.

With Nixon's resignation, the nation had weathered a profound constitutional crisis, but the aftershock of the Watergate episode produced a deep sense of disillusionment with the so-called imperial presidency. Apart from Nixon's illegal actions, the scurrilous language used in the White House and made public on the tapes stripped away the veils of mystery surrounding national leaders and left even the die-hard defenders of presidential authority shocked at the crudity and duplicity of Nixon and his subordinates. Coming on the heels of the erosion of public confidence generated by the Vietnam War, the Watergate affair renewed public cynicism toward a government that had systematically lied to the people and violated their civil liberties. Said one bumper sticker of the day: "Don't vote. It only encourages them."

An Unelected President

During Richard Nixon's last year in office the Watergate crisis so dominated the Washington scene that major domestic and foreign problems received little executive attention. The perplexing combination of inflation and recession worsened, as did the oil crisis. At the same time, Henry Kissinger, who assumed control over the management of foreign policy, watched helplessly as the South Vietnamese forces began to crumble before North Vietnamese attacks, attempted with limited success to establish a framework for peace in the Middle East, and supported a CIA role in overthrowing Salvador Allende, the popularly elected Marxist president of Chile. Allende was subsequently murdered and replaced by General Augusto Pinochet, a military dictator supposedly friendly to the United States.

THE FORD YEARS   Gerald Ford inherited these simmering problems when he assumed office after Nixon's resignation. An amiable, honest man, Ford candidly admitted upon becoming vice-president, "I am a Ford, not a Lincoln." He enjoyed widespread popular support for only a short time. His pardon of Nixon on September 8, 1974, generated a storm of criticism. The *New York Times* called it "an unconscionable act."

As president, Gerald Ford soon adopted the posture he had developed as a conservative minority leader in the House: nay-saying leader of the opposition who believed that the federal government exercised too much power over domestic affairs. In his fifteen months as president, Ford vetoed thirty-nine bills, thereby outstripping Herbert Hoover's veto record in less than half the time. By resisting congressional pressure to reduce taxes and increase federal spending, he succeeded in plummeting the economy into the deepest recession since the Great Depression. Unemployment jumped to 9 percent in 1975, and the federal deficit hit a record the next year. Ford rejected wage and price controls to curb inflation, preferring voluntary restraints that he tried to bolster by passing out "WIN" buttons, symbolizing his campaign to "Whip Inflation Now." The WIN buttons instead became a national joke and a popular symbol of Ford's ineffectiveness in the fight against stagflation.

In foreign policy, Ford retained Henry Kissinger as secretary of state and attempted to pursue Nixon's goals of stability in the Middle East, rapprochement with China, and détente with the Soviet Union. Late in 1974, Ford met with Soviet leader Leonid Brezhnev at Vladivostok in Siberia and accepted the framework for another arms-control accord that was to serve as the basis for SALT II. Meanwhile Kissinger's tireless shuttling between Cairo and Tel Aviv produced an agreement: Israel promised to return to Egypt most of the Sinai territory captured in the 1967 war, and the two nations agreed to rely on negotiations rather than force to settle future disagreements. These limited but significant achievements should have enhanced Ford's image, but they were drowned in the sea of criticism and carping that followed the collapse of South Vietnam to Communists in May 1975.

Not only had a decade of American effort in Vietnam proved futile, but the Khmer Rouge, the Cambodian Communist movement, had also won a resounding victory, plunging that country into a bloodbath. Meanwhile, the OPEC oil cartel was threatening another worldwide boycott while other Third World nations denounced the United States as a depraved and declining imperialistic power. Ford lost his patience when he sent in the marines to rescue the crew of the American merchant ship *Mayaguez,* which had been captured by the Cambodian Communists. This vigorous move won popular acclaim until it was disclosed that the Cambodians had already agreed to release the captured Americans: the forty-one Americans killed in the operation had died for no purpose.

THE 1976 ELECTION   In the midst of such turmoil, the Democrats could hardly wait for the 1976 election. At the Republican convention Ford managed to fend off a powerful challenge for the nomination from the former California governor and Hollywood actor, Ronald Reagan, whose robust appearance belied his sixty-five years. The Democrats chose an obscure former naval officer and engineer turned peanut farmer who had served one term as governor of Georgia. Jimmy Carter campaigned harder than any of the other Democratic hopefuls; he capitalized on the post-Watergate cynicism by promising "I will never tell a lie to the American people" and by citing his inexperience in the byways of Washington politics as an asset. Facing the prospect of the first president from the Deep South since 1849, reporters marveled at a Baptist candidate who claimed to be "born again."

To the surprise of many pundits, the little-known Carter revived the New Deal coalition of southern whites, blacks, urban labor, and ethnic groups to win 41 million votes to Ford's 39 million, and a narrow electoral vote majority of 297 to 241. A heavy turnout of blacks in the South enabled Carter to sweep every state in the region except Virginia. Carter also benefited from the appeal of Walter F. Mondale, his liberal running mate and a favorite among blue-collar workers and the urban poor. Carter lost most of the trans-Mississippi West, but no other Democratic candidate had made much headway there since Harry Truman in 1948. The big story of the election was the low voter turnout. "Neither Ford nor Carter won as many votes as Mr. Nobody," said one reporter, commenting on the fact that almost half the eligible voters, apparently alienated by Watergate and the lackluster candidates, chose to sit out the election.

THE CARTER INTERREGNUM

POLICY STALEMATE   Once in office, Carter suffered the fate of all American presidents since Kennedy: after an initial honeymoon, during which Carter displayed folksy charm by walking down Pennsylvania Avenue after his inauguration rather than riding in a limousine, and wearing cardigan sweaters during televised "fireside chats," his popularity and political effectiveness waned. Soon *Newsweek* was referring to the "corn bread-and-cardigan atmospherics." The truth was that, like Ford before him, Carter faced an almost insurmountable set of domestic and international problems. He was expected to cure the economic recession and inflation at a time when all industrial economies were shaken by a shortage of energy and confidence. He was expected to reassert America's global power at a time of waning respect for America's

President Jimmy Carter and his wife, Rosalynn, forgo the traditional limousine and walk down Pennsylvania Avenue after the inauguration, January 20, 1977.

international authority. And he was expected to do this, as well as buoy the national spirit, through a set of political institutions in which many Americans had lost faith.

Yet, during the first two years of his term, Carter enjoyed several successes. His administration included more blacks and women than ever before. Carter created a federal task force to study the problem of Vietnam-era draft evaders and eventually offered amnesty to the thousands of young Americans who had fled the country rather than serve in Vietnam. He reformed the civil service to provide rewards for merit, and he created new cabinet-level Departments of Energy and Education. He also pushed several significant environmental initiatives through Congress, including a bill to establish controls over strip mining, a "superfund" of $1.6 billion to clean up chemical waste sites, and a proposal to protect over 100 million acres of Alaskan land from development.

But success was short-lived. Carter's political predicament surfaced in the protracted debate over energy policy. Carter had a distaste for stroking legislators or wheeling and dealing to get legislation through. The energy bill passed in 1978 was a gutted version of the original proposed by the administration, reflecting the power of both conservative and liberal special-interest lobbies. One Carter aide said that the energy bill looked like it had been "nibbled to death by ducks." The clumsy political maneuvers that plagued Carter and his inexperienced aides repeatedly frustrated efforts to remedy the energy crisis.

In the summer of 1979, when renewed violence in the Middle East produced a second fuel shortage in the United States, motorists were again forced to wait in long lines for limited supplies of gas that they regarded as excessively expensive. Opinion polls showed Carter with an approval rating of only 26 percent, lower than Nixon during the worst moments of the Watergate crisis. During July Carter called his advisers to an extraordinary retreat at Camp David, Maryland, and emerged ten days later proclaiming a need for "a rebirth of the American spirit." He also called for a "new and positive energy program." Congress, however, only partially funded the major feature of his new plan—a federal agency to encourage development of synthetic fuels.

Several of Carter's early foreign policy initiatives also got caught in political crossfires. Soon after his inauguration, Carter vowed that "the soul of our foreign policy" should be the defense of human rights abroad. This human rights campaign, however, provoked attack from two sides: those who feared it sacrificed a detached appraisal of national interest for high-level moralizing, and those who believed that human rights were important but that the administration was applying the standard inconsistently.

Similarly, Carter's successful negotiation of treaties to turn over control of the Panama Canal to the government of Panama generated intense criticism. Republican Ronald Reagan claimed that the Canal Zone was sovereign American soil purchased "fair and square" in Theodore Roosevelt's administration. (In the congressional debate one senator quipped, "We stole it fair and square, so why can't we keep it?") Carter argued that the limitations on American influence in Latin America, and the deep resentment toward American colonialism in Panama left the United States with no other choice. The Canal Zone would revert in stages to Panama by 1999. The Senate ratified the treaties by a paperthin margin (68 to 32, two votes more than the required two-thirds), but conservatives lambasted Carter for surrendering American authority in a strategically critical part of the world.

THE CAMP DAVID ACCORDS Carter's crowning foreign policy achievement, which even his most bitter critics applauded, was the arrangement of a peace agreement between Israel and Egypt. In 1977 Egyptian president Anwar el-Sadat flew to Tel Aviv at the invitation of Israeli prime minister Menachem Begin. Sadat's bold act, and his accompanying announcement that Egypt was now willing to recognize the legitimacy of the Israeli state, opened up diplomatic opportunities that Carter and Secretary of State Cyrus Vance quickly pursued.

In 1978 Carter invited Sadat and Begin to the presidential retreat at Camp David for two weeks of difficult negotiations. The first part of the eventual agreement called for Israel to return all land in the Sinai in exchange for Egyptian recognition of Israel's sovereignty. This agreement was successfully implemented in 1982 when the last Israeli settler vacated the Sinai. But the second part of the agreement, calling for Israel to negotiate with Sadat to resolve the Palestinian refugee dilemma, began to unravel soon after the Camp David summit.

By March 26, 1979, when Begin and Sadat returned to Washington to sign the formal treaty, Begin had already made clear his refusal to block new Israeli settlements on the West Bank of the Jordan River, which Sadat had regarded as a prospective homeland for the Palestinians.

Egyptian president Anwar Sadat (left), *Jimmy Carter* (center), *and Israeli prime minister Menachem Begin* (right) *at the announcement of the Camp David accords, September 1978.*

In the wake of the Camp David accords, most of the Arab nations condemned Sadat as a traitor to their Islamic cause. Still, Carter and Vance were responsible for a dramatic display of high-level diplomacy that, whatever its limitations, made an all-out war between Israel and the Arab world less likely in the foreseeable future.

MOUNTING TROUBLES   Carter's crowning failure, which even his most avid supporters acknowledged, was his management of the economy. In effect he inherited a bad situation and left it worse. Carter employed the same economic policies as Nixon and Ford to fight stagflation, but he reversed the order of the federal "cure," preferring first to fight unemployment with a tax cut and increased public spending. Unemployment declined slightly, from 8 to 7 percent in 1977, but inflation soared; at 5 percent when he took office, it reached 10 percent in 1978 and kept going. During one month in 1980 it measured at an annual rate of no less than 18 percent. Like previous presidents, Carter then reversed himself to fight the other side of the economic malaise. By midterm he was delaying tax reductions and vetoing government spending programs that he had proposed in his first year. The result, however, was the worst of both possible worlds: a deepened recession and runaway inflation averaging between 12 and 13 percent per year.

The signing of a controversial new Strategic Arms Limitation Treaty (SALT II) with the Soviets put Carter's leadership to the test just as the mounting economic problems made him the subject of biting editorial cartoons nationwide. Like SALT I, the new agreement did not do much to slow down the nuclear arms race. It placed a ceiling of 2,250 bombers and missiles on each side and set limits on the number of warheads and new weapons systems. To pacify his conservative critics, who charged that SALT II would give the Soviets a decided advantage in the number and destructive power of land-based missiles, Carter announced that the United States would build a new missile system, called the MX.

But the proposed SALT II treaty became moot in 1979 when the Soviet army invaded Afghanistan to rescue the faltering Communist government there, which was being challenged by Muslim rebels. Carter immediately shelved SALT II, suspended grain shipments to the Soviet Union, and began a campaign for an international boycott of the 1980 Olympics, which were to be held that summer in Moscow.

IRAN   Then came the Iranian crisis, a year-long cascade of unwelcome events that epitomized the inability of the United States to control world affairs. The crisis began with the fall of the shah of Iran in 1979. The revolutionaries who toppled the shah rallied around Ayatollah Ruhollah Khomeini, a Muslim religious leader who symbolized the Islamic values the shah had tried to replace with Western ways. Khomeini's hatred of the United States dated back to the CIA-sponsored overthrow of Iran's Mossadegh government in 1953. Nor did it help the American image that the CIA had trained SAVAK, the shah's ruthless secret police force. Late in 1979 the exiled shah was allowed to enter the United States in order to undergo treatment for cancer. A few days later, a frenzied mob stormed the American embassy in Teheran and seized the diplomats and staff inside. Khomeini endorsed the mob action and demanded the return of the shah along with all his wealth in exchange for the release of the fifty-three American hostages. In the meantime, the Iranian militants staged daily demonstrations for the benefit of worldwide news and television coverage in which the

Iranian militants stormed the U.S. Embassy in Teheran in 1979, taking fifty-three Americans hostage for over a year. Here one of the hostages (face covered) *is paraded before a camera.*

American flag and effigies of the American president were burned and otherwise desecrated.

Indignant Americans demanded a military response to such outrages, but Carter's range of options was limited. He appealed to the United Nations, protesting what was a clear violation of diplomatic immunity and international law. Khomeini scoffed at U.N. requests for the release of hostages. Carter then froze all Iranian assets in the United States and appealed to American allies for a trade embargo of Iran. The trade restrictions were only partially effective—even America's most loyal European allies did not want to lose their access to Iranian oil—so a frustrated and besieged Carter authorized a risky rescue attempt by American commandos in 1980. Secretary of State Cyrus Vance resigned in protest against the rescue attempt, and against Carter's sharp turn toward a more hawkish foreign policy. The commando raid was aborted because of helicopter failures, and ended with eight fatalities when another helicopter collided with a transport plane in the desert. Nightly television coverage of the taunting Iranian rebels generated widespread popular craving for action and a near obsession with the falling fortunes of the United States and the fate of the hostages. The end came after 444 days of captivity when Carter released several billion dollars of Iranian assets to ransom the kidnapped hostages.

The turbulent and often tragic events of the 1970s—the conquest of South Vietnam, the Watergate scandal and Nixon's resignation, the energy shortage and stagflation, the Iranian hostage episode—provoked among Americans what Carter labeled a "crisis of confidence." By 1980, American power and prestige seemed to be on the decline, the economy remained in a shambles, and the sexual revolution launched in the 1960s, with the questions it raised for the family and other basic social and political institutions, had sparked a backlash of resentment among "Middle America." With theatrical timing, Ronald Reagan emerged to tap the growing reservoir of public frustration and transform his political career into a crusade to make "America stand tall again." He told his supporters that there was "a hunger in this land for a spiritual revival, a return to a belief in moral absolutes." The United States, he declared, remained the "greatest country in the world. We have the talent, we have the drive, we have the imagination. Now all we need is the leadership."

MAKING CONNECTIONS

- Foreign affairs in the 1970s show the changing patterns of the cold war. The next chapter details the end of both the cold war and the Soviet Union.

- Presidents Nixon and Ford tried, with limited success, to decrease the power of the federal government over domestic affairs. President Reagan was much more successful at advancing the conservative agenda, a topic covered in the next chapter.

- The rebellion and turbulence of the 1960s and 1970s became less apparent in the following decade; as Chapter 37 shows, however, that turbulence reappeared, in a somewhat different form, in the 1990s.

FURTHER READING

An engaging overview of the cultural trends of the 1960s is Maurice Isserman and Michael Kazin's *America Divided: The Civil War of the 1960s* (2000). The New Left is assessed in Irwin Unger's *The Movement: A History of the American New Left 1959–1972* (1974). On the Students for a Democratic Society, see Kirkpatrick Sale's *SDS* (1973) and Allen J. Matusow's *The Unraveling of America: A History of Liberalism in the 1960s* (1984). Also useful is Todd Gitlin's *The Sixties: Years of Hope, Days of Rage* (rev. ed., 1993).

Two influential assessments of the counterculture by sympathetic commentators are Theodore Roszak's *The Making of a Counterculture: Reflections on the Technocratic Society and Its Youthful Opposition* (1969) and Charles Reich's *The Greening of America* (1970). A good scholarly analysis of the hippies that takes them seriously is Timothy Miller's *The Hippies and American Values* (1991).

The best study of the women's liberation movement is Ruth Rosen's *The World Split Open: How the Modern Women's Movement Changed America* (2001). The organizing efforts of César Chavez are detailed in Ronald Taylor's *Chavez and the Farm Workers* (1975). The struggles of Native Americans for recognition and power are sympathetically described in Stan Steiner's *The New Indians* (1968).

On Nixon, see Richard Reeves, *President Nixon* (2001). For a solid overview of the Watergate scandal, see Stanley Kutler's *The Wars of Watergate: The Last Crisis of Richard Nixon* (1990). For the way the Republicans handled foreign affairs, consult Tad Szulc's *The Illusion of Peace: Foreign Policy in the Nixon Years* (1978).

The loss of Vietnam and the end of American involvement are traced in Larry Berman's *No Peace, No Honor: Nixon, Kissinger, and Betrayal in Vietnam* (2001). William Shawcross's *Sideshow: Kissinger, Nixon, and the Destruction of Cambodia* (1978) deals with the broadening of the war, while Larry Berman's *Planning a Tragedy: The Americanization of the War in Vietnam* (1982) assesses the final impact of American involvement. The most comprehensive treatment of the antiwar movement in the United States is Tom Wells's *The War Within: America's Battle over Vietnam* (1994).

The best overview of the Carter administration is Burton I. Kaufman's *The Presidency of James Earl Carter, Jr.* (1993). A work more sympathetic to the Carter administration is John Dumbrell's *The Carter Presidency: A Re-Evaluation* (1993). Gaddis Smith's *Morality, Reason, and Power* (1986) provides an overview of American diplomacy in the Carter years. Background on how the Middle East came to dominate much of American policy is found in William B. Quandt's *Decade of Decisions: American Policy toward the Arab-Israeli Conflict, 1967–1976* (1977).

36 ~~ A CONSERVATIVE
INSURGENCY

CHAPTER ORGANIZER

This chapter focuses on:

- the demographic, social, and economic reasons for the rise of Ronald Reagan and Republican conservatism.

- changing relations with the Soviet Union, including the end of the cold war.

- the economic and social aspects of the 1980s.

- the cause and aftermath of the Gulf War.

President Jimmy Carter and his embattled Democratic administration hobbled through 1979. The economy remained sluggish, double-digit inflation continued unabated, and failed efforts to free the American hostages in Iran made the administration appear indecisive. Carter's inability to mobilize the nation behind his ill-fated energy program revealed mortal flaws in his reading of the public mood and his understanding of legislative politics.

While the lackluster Carter administration was foundering, Republican conservatives were forging a plan to win the White House in 1980 and to assault the "New Deal welfare state" mentality in Washington. Those plans centered on the popularity and charisma of Ronald Reagan, the Hollywood actor turned California governor and prominent political commentator. Reagan was not a deep thinker, but he was a superb analyst of the public mood, an unabashed patriot, and a committed champion of conservative principles. He was also charming and cheerful, a likable politician renowned for his relentless anecdotes. Where the dour Carter denounced the evils of free enterprise capitalism and tried to scold Americans into reviving long-forgotten virtues of frugality, a sunny Reagan promised a "revolution of ideas" designed to unleash the capitalist spirit, restore national pride, and regain international respect.

During the late 1970s, Reagan's simple message promoting a grassroots political revolution and a restoration of American pride and prosperity offered an uplifting alternative to Carter's strident moralism. Reagan wanted to increase military spending, dismantle the "bloated" federal bureaucracy, reduce taxes and regulations, and in general, undo the welfare state. He also wanted to affirm old-time morality by ending abortions and reinstituting school prayer. Reagan's appeal derived from his remarkable skills as a public speaker and his dogmatic commitment to a few overarching ideas and simple themes. As a true believer and an able compromiser, he combined the fervor of a revolutionary with the pragmatism of a diplomat.

Such attributes won Reagan two presidential terms in 1980 and 1984 and ensured the election of his successor, George Bush, in 1988. Just how revolutionary the Reagan era was remains a subject of intense partisan debate. What cannot be denied, however, is that Reagan's actions and beliefs set the tone for the decade's political and economic life.

THE REAGAN REVOLUTION

THE MAKING OF A PRESIDENT   Born in 1911, Ronald Reagan graduated from tiny Eureka College and then worked as a radio announcer and sportscaster before starting a movie career in Hollywood in 1937. As president of the Screen Actors Guild, Reagan was at first a liberal

President Ronald Reagan, "the Great Communicator."

and a New Dealer. But he bounced to the far right on the political spectrum during the 1950s. He campaigned for both Eisenhower (1952, 1956) and Nixon (1960), switched his registration to Republican in 1962, then achieved political stardom in 1964 when he delivered a rousing speech on national television on behalf of Barry Goldwater.

The Republican right found in Ronald Reagan a new idol whose appeal survived the defeat of Goldwater. Those who discounted Reagan as a minor actor and a mental midget underrated his many virtues, including the importance of his years in front of the camera. Politics had always been a performing art, the more so in an age of television, and few, if any, others in public life had Reagan's stage presence or extraordinary charm. Drawn by wealthy admirers into the campaign for governor of California in 1966, Reagan moderated his rawest rhetoric, and won the governorship by a landslide.

Reagan appealed especially to middle-class and lower-middle-class voters resentful of "high" taxes, welfare programs for the dependent, the "neurotic vulgarities" of university students running wild, crime in the streets, and challenges to traditional values in general. In the forefront of the counterculture, California was in the forefront of reaction against it as well.

By the eve of the 1980 election, Reagan had become the beneficiary of a development that made his conservative vision of America more than a harmless flirtation with nostalgia. The 1980 census revealed that the elderly proportion of the nation's population was increasing and moving to the "Sunbelt" states of the South and West. This dual development—an increase in the numbers of senior citizens and the steady transfer of population to conservative regions of the country where hostility to "big government" was endemic—meant that demographics were carrying the United States toward Reagan's conservative political philosophy.

THE MORAL MAJORITY   Reagan's presidential aspirations also bene-fited from a major revival of evangelical religion. No longer a local or provincial phenomenon, Christian evangelicals now owned their own television and radio stations and operated their own schools and univer-sities. A survey in 1977 revealed that more than 70 million Americans described themselves as born-again Christians.

The Reverend Jerry Falwell's "Moral Majority" (later renamed the Liberty Lobby) expressed the sentiments of the religious right wing: the economy should operate without "interference" by the government, which should be reduced in size; the Supreme Court decision in *Roe* v. *Wade* (1973) legalizing abortion should be reversed; Darwinian evolu-tion should be replaced in schoolbooks by the biblical story of creation; prayer should be allowed back in public schools; and Soviet expansion should be opposed as a form of pagan totalitarianism. The moralistic zeal and financial resources of the religious right made them formidable opponents of liberal political candidates and programs. By 1980 Fal-well's Moral Majority organization claimed over 4 million members. Its base of support was in the South and was strongest among Baptists, but its appeal extended across the country.

A curiosity of the 1980 campaign was that the religious right opposed Jimmy Carter, a self-professed born-again Christian, and supported Ronald Reagan, a man who was neither conspicuously pious nor even often in church. His divorce and remarriage, once an almost automatic disqualification for the presidency, got little mention. Nor did the fact that as governor he had signed one of the most permissive abortion laws in the country. That Ronald Reagan became the messiah of the religious right was a tribute both to the force of social issues and the candidate's political skills.

FEMINIST BACKLASH   Another factor contributing to the conserva-tive resurgence was a well-organized and well-financed backlash against the feminist movement. During the 1970s, women who opposed the social goals of feminism formed counter-organizations with names such as "Women Who Want to Be Women" and "Females Opposed to Equal-ity." Spearheading such efforts was Phyllis Schlafly, a right-wing Repub-lican activist from Illinois. She orchestrated the campaign to defeat the Equal Rights Amendment (ERA) and thereafter served as the galvanizing force behind a growing antifeminist movement. Schlafly characterized feminists as a "bunch of bitter women seeking a constitutional cure for their personal problems." She instead urged women to embrace their God-given roles as wives and mothers. Feminists, she charged, were "anti-family, anti-children, and pro-abortion."

Many of Schlafly's supporters in the anti-ERA campaign also participated in mushrooming anti-abortion or "pro-life" movement. By 1980 the National Right to Life committee, created by the National Conference of Catholic Bishops, boasted 11 million members representing all religious denominations. The intensity of their commitment made them a powerful political force in their own right, and the Reagan campaign was quick to highlight its own support for traditional "family values," gender roles, and the rights of the unborn. Such cultural issues helped convince many northern Democrats—mostly working-class Catholics—to support Reagan. Whites alienated by the increasingly liberal social agenda of the Democratic party became a crucial element in Reagan's electoral strategy.

THE 1980 ELECTION   By 1980 voters seemed eager to embrace Reagan's cheery promises of a new era of less government, lower taxes, renewed prosperity, waning inflation, and revived military strength and national pride. His "supply-side" economic proposals, soon dubbed "Reaganomics" by supporters and "voodoo economics" by critics, suggested that stagflation resulted from excessive taxes that weakened the incentive to work, save, and reinvest. The solution was to slash tax rates. For a long-suffering nation, it was, in theory, an alluring economic panacea.

Reagan was an adept campaigner who presented a consistent message to the voters: Carter and the Democrats, he insisted, believed that the United States had entered an era of permanent limits on economic growth and personal initiative. On the contrary, he asserted, the Republicans believed that America's greatest economic accomplishments were just around the corner. Reagan pledged that his recovery plans would restore prosperity and public confidence. He used folksy maxims and jokes to punctuate his themes. For instance, at one campaign stop he quipped: "A recession is when your neighbor loses his job. A depression is when you lose yours. A recovery is when Jimmy Carter loses his."

On election day Reagan swept to a decisive victory, with 489 electoral votes to 49 for Carter, who carried only six states. The popular vote was 44 million (51 percent) for Reagan to Carter's 35 million (41 percent), with 7 percent going to John Anderson, a moderate Republican who had bolted the party after Reagan's nomination and had run on an independent ticket.

More than a victory for the "new conservatism," the 1980 election reflected the triumph of what one political scientist called the "largest mass movement of our time"—nonvoting. Almost as striking as Reagan's one-sided victory was the fact that his vote total represented only 28 percent of the potential electorate. Only 53 percent of eligible voters cast ballots in the 1980 election; in western European countries such as France and Germany, voter participation hovered at 85 percent in national elections during the 1970s.

Where had all the voters gone? Analysts noted that most of the non-voters were working-class Democrats in the major urban centers. Voter turnout was lowest in poor inner-city neighborhoods. Turnout was highest, by contrast, in the affluent suburbs of large cities, areas where the Republican party was experiencing a dramatic surge in popularity. Such trends meant that American officeholders were being selected during

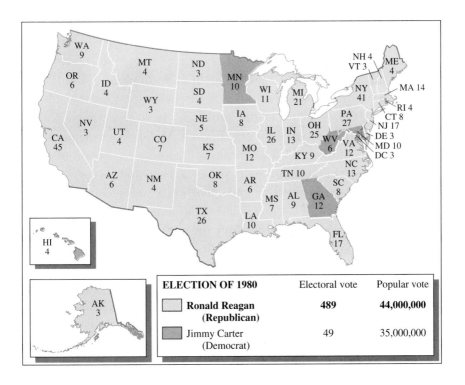

ELECTION OF 1980	Electoral vote	Popular vote
Ronald Reagan (Republican)	489	44,000,000
Jimmy Carter (Democrat)	49	35,000,000

the 1970s by an electorate increasingly dominated by middle- and upper-class voters.

Explanations for the high levels of voter apathy among working-class Americans vary. Some argue that they reflected the continuing sense of disillusionment with government itself, growing out of the Watergate affair. Another widespread perception influencing voting behavior was that the Democratic party had turned its back on its traditional blocs of support among common folk. Democratic leaders no longer spoke eloquently on behalf of those at the bottom of America's social scale. By embracing a fiscal conservatism indistinguishable from that of the Republicans, as Carter had done, Democrats lost their appeal among blue-collar workers and ghetto dwellers. And so the largest group of nonvoters in the 1980 election were former Democrats who had decided that neither party served their interests. When viewed in this light, Ronald Reagan's victory represented both a resounding victory for conservative Republicans and a self-inflicted defeat by a fractured Democratic party. Flush with a sense of power and destiny, Reagan headed toward Washington with a blueprint for dismantling the welfare state.

REAGAN'S FIRST TERM

REAGANOMICS   Ronald Reagan brought to Washington a simple conservative philosophy. "Government is not the solution to our problem," he insisted; "Government is the problem." Reagan credited Calvin Coolidge and his treasury secretary, Andrew Mellon, with demonstrating that by reducing taxes and easing government regulation of business, free-market capitalism would revive the economy. By cutting taxes and domestic federal spending and following a supply-side economic program, he claimed, a surging economy would produce *more* government revenues that would help reduce the budget deficit.

Early on, Reagan focused on dramatically increasing defense spending, sharply reducing social spending, and passing a sweeping tax reform proposal. Despite loud protests from liberal groups and politicians, Congress passed the entire Reagan economic package by the summer of 1981. Enough Democrats—mostly sympathetic southern conservatives dubbed "boll weevils"—supported the measures to pass them by overwhelming majorities. On August 1, 1981, Reagan signed the Economic

Recovery Tax Act, which cut personal income taxes by 25 percent, lowered the maximum rate from 70 to 50 percent for 1982, cut the capital gains tax by a third, and offered a broad array of other tax concessions.

The new legislation embodied an idea that went back to Alexander Hamilton, George Washington's treasury secretary: more money in the hands of the affluent would benefit society at large, since the wealthy would engage in productive investment. A closer parallel was Treasury Secretary Andrew Mellon's tax reduction program of the 1920s. The difference was that the Reagan tax cuts were accompanied by massive increases in defense spending that generated ever-mounting federal deficits. Reagan's advisers insisted that such unbalanced budgets were only temporary; once the new tax plan began to take effect, the economy would take off and government tax revenues would soar as personal incomes and corporate profits skyrocketed. But it did not work out that way. By the summer of 1983, a major economic recovery was underway, but the federal deficits grew ever larger, so much so that the president, who in 1980 had pledged to have a balanced federal budget by 1983, had in fact run up debts larger than those of all his predecessors combined.

BUDGET CUTS   In trying to slash expenditures, David Stockman, Reagan's budget director, pushed through $35 billion in budget cuts in educational and cultural programs, housing, food stamps, and school lunches in 1981. Reagan assured critics that despite these cuts he was committed to maintaining the "safety net" of government services for the "truly needy." This meant that aid would remain available only to those who could not work because of either disability or child-care responsibilities. New Deal welfare programs had had the same purpose, but the Roosevelt administration had also provided federal jobs for those who could work. This was not a part of "Reaganomics." Cuts in programs to the disadvantaged, when added to the sluggish economy, helped raise the percentage of persons living under the poverty level from 11.7 in 1979 to 15.3 in 1983.

While publicly proclaiming a great accomplishment in making such cuts in domestic spending, Reagan and his advisers knew privately that the figures were not adding up to those they had pledged. David Stockman realized that the cuts in domestic spending were far short of what would be needed to balance the budget in four years as Reagan had promised. He pleaded with Reagan to cut back on new defense

Demonstrators in Ohio rail against the effects of "Reaganomics," protesting the Reagan economic package that sacrificed funding in areas such as Social Security.

spending and to slow the proposed tax cuts, but the president refused. The result was a soaring budget deficit and the worst economic recession since the 1930s.

Bankers and investors feared that the rising government debt would send interest rates soaring, a fear expressed in sagging bond and stock markets. A business slump and rising unemployment continued through most of 1982. That same year the federal deficit doubled. Aides finally convinced Reagan that to reassure the public about deficits and the threat of inflation the government needed "revenue enhancements," a euphemism for tax increases. With Reagan's support, Congress passed a new tax bill in 1982 that would raise almost $100 billion.

During the midterm elections of 1982, Reagan rarely mentioned the new tax bill. Instead he focused his campaign speeches on the benefits of supply-side economics and rosy economic forecasts. He urged voters to "stay the course" and appealed for more time to let his economic program take effect. Meanwhile, the economic slump persisted through 1982, with unemployment standing at 10.4 percent, and the Republicans experienced moderate losses in the midterm elections.

CONFLICTS OF INTEREST   Like Harding and Coolidge in the 1920s, Reagan named people to government positions who were unsympathetic to the regulatory functions for which they were responsible. Interior Secretary James Watt, for example, castigated environmentalists for hindering the commercial use of timber and mineral resources. He was finally forced out of office by the uproar over an offensive joke he made.

The Reagan administration also paralleled the Harding administration by finding itself embroiled in charges of conflict of interest, ethical misconduct, and actual criminal behavior. Public outcry forced the administrator of the Environmental Protection Agency to resign for granting favors to industrial polluters.

Although some 200 Reagan appointees were accused of unethical or illegal activities, the president himself remained untouched by any hint of impropriety. His personal charisma and aloof managerial style helped shield him from the political fallout associated with the growing scandals and conflicts of interest among his aides and cronies. Public affection for him as a person remained his most enduring asset. This led one member of Congress to label the Reagan White House the "Teflon presidency," where the buck never stopped because the blame never stuck.

Organized labor suffered severe setbacks during the Reagan years. Presidential appointments to the National Labor Relations Board tended to favor management, and in 1981 Reagan fired members of the Professional Air Traffic Controllers (PATCO) who had participated in an illegal strike. Even more important, Reagan's smashing electoral victories in 1980 and 1984 broke the political power of the AFL-CIO. His criticism of unions seemed to reflect a general trend in public opinion. Although record numbers of new jobs were created during the 1980s, union membership steadily dropped. By 1987 unions represented only 17 percent of the nation's full-time workers, down from 24 percent in 1979.

Reagan also went on the offensive against feminism. He ardently opposed the Equal Rights Amendment, abortion on demand, and the legal guarantee of equal pay for jobs of comparable worth. He did name Sandra Day O'Connor as the first woman justice to the Supreme Court, but critics labeled it a token gesture rather than a reflection of any genuine commitment to gender equality.

Blacks and other minorities shared a similar aggravation at the administration's limited support for affirmative action programs in employment. Reagan cut funds for civil rights enforcement and the Equal

Employment Opportunity Commission, and he initially opposed renewal of the Voting Rights Act of 1965, but was overruled by Congress.

THE DEFENSE BUILDUP   Reagan's conduct of foreign policy reflected his belief that trouble in the world stemmed mainly from Moscow. He charged that the Soviets were "prepared to commit any crime, to lie, to cheat," and do anything necessary to promote world communism. Reagan and Secretary of Defense Caspar Weinberger embarked on a major buildup of nuclear and conventional weapons to close the gap that they claimed had developed between Soviet and American military forces.

In 1983 Reagan escalated the nuclear arms race by authorizing the Defense Department to develop a Strategic Defense Initiative (SDI). It involved a complex anti-missile defense system using super-secret laser and high-energy particles weapons to destroy enemy missiles in outer space well before they reached their targets. To Reagan the great appeal of this "Star Wars" program was the ability to destroy weapons rather than people, thereby freeing defense strategy from the concept of mutually assured destruction that had long governed Soviet and American attitudes toward nuclear war. Despite skepticism among the media and many scientists that such a "foolproof" celestial defense system could be built, it forced the Soviets to launch an expensive research and development program of their own to keep pace.

Reagan borrowed the rhetoric of Harry Truman, John Foster Dulles, and John F. Kennedy's inaugural to express American resolve in the face of "Communist aggression anywhere in the world." Détente deteriorated even further when the Soviets imposed martial law in Poland during the winter of 1981. The crackdown came after Polish workers, united under the banner of an independent union called Solidarity, challenged the Communist monopoly of power. As with Hungary in 1956 and Czechoslovakia in 1968, there was little the United States could do except register protest and impose economic sanctions against Poland's Communist government.

THE AMERICAS   Reagan's foremost international concern, however, was in Central America, where he detected the most serious Communist threat. The tiny nation of El Salvador, caught up since 1980 in a brutal struggle between Communist-supported revolutionaries and right-wing extremists, received American economic and military assistance. Reagan stopped short of sending American troops, but he did increase the number of military advisers and the amount of financial aid to the Salvadoran government. He also abandoned Carter's strident criticism of right-wing Salvadoran militants whose "death squads" engaged in systematic terror and murder. Critics argued that American involvement ensured that the revolutionary forces would emerge as the victorious representatives of Salvadoran nationalism by capitalizing on "anti-Yankee" sentiment. Supporters countered by warning that American failure to act would allow for a repeat of Communist victories in Nicaragua, and that Honduras, Guatemala, and then all of Central America would eventually enter the Communist camp. By 1984, however, the American-backed government of President José Napoleón Duarte brought a modicum of stability to El Salvador.

Even more troubling was the situation in Nicaragua. The State Department claimed that the Cuban-sponsored Sandinista government in Nicaragua, which had only recently taken control of the country after ousting a corrupt dictator, was funneling Soviet and Cuban arms to leftist

"Shhhh. It's top secret." *A comment on Reagan administration covert operations in Nicaragua.*

Salvadoran rebels. In response, the Reagan administration ordered the CIA to train and supply guerrilla bands of disgruntled Nicaraguans, tagged "Contras," who staged attacks on Sandinista bases and officials from sanctuaries in Honduras. In supporting these "freedom fighters," Reagan sought not only to impede the traffic in arms to Salvadoran rebels but also to overthrow the Communist Sandinistas.

Critics of Reagan's anti-Sandinista policy questioned the motives and ethics of the Contras, accusing them of being mostly right-wing fanatics who indiscriminately killed civilians as well as Sandinista soldiers. They also feared that the United States might eventually commit its own combat forces, thus threatening another Vietnam-like intervention. Reagan warned that if the Communists prevailed in Central America, "our credibility would collapse, our alliances would crumble, and the safety of our homeland would be jeopardized."

THE MIDDLE EAST   The Middle East remained a tinderbox of conflict. No peaceable end seemed possible for the prolonged, bloody Iran-Iraq war, entangled as it was with the passions of Islamic fundamentalism. In 1984 both sides began to attack tankers in the Persian Gulf, a major source of the world's oil. (The main international response was the sale of arms to both sides.) Nor was any settlement in sight for Afghanistan, where the Soviets had bogged down as badly as the Americans had in Vietnam.

American governments continued to see Israel as the strongest and most reliable ally in the region, all the while seeking to encourage moderate Arab groups. But the forces of moderation were dealt a blow during the mid-1970s when Lebanon, long an enclave of peace despite its ethnic complexity, collapsed into an anarchy of warring groups. The capital, Beirut, became a battleground for Sunni and Shi'ite Muslims, the Druze, the Palestine Liberation Organization (PLO), Arab Christians, Syrian invaders cast as peacekeepers, and Israelis responding to PLO attacks across the border.

In 1982 Israeli forces pushed the PLO out of southern Lebanon all the way north to Beirut and then the Israelis began heavy shelling of PLO strongholds in Beirut. The United States neither endorsed nor condemned the invasion, but sent a special ambassador to negotiate a settlement. Israeli troops moved into Beirut and looked the other way when Christian militiamen slaughtered Muslim women and children in

Palestinian refugee camps. French, Italian, and American forces then moved into Lebanon as "peacekeepers," but in such small numbers as to become only targets. Angry Muslims kept them under constant harassment. American warships and planes responded by shelling and bombing Muslim positions in the highlands behind Beirut, which only increased Muslim resentment. On October 23, 1983, an Islamic suicide bomber drove a truck laden with explosives into U.S. Marine headquarters at the Beirut airport; the explosion left 241 Americans dead. In early 1984, Reagan announced that the marines would be "redeployed" to warships offshore. The Israelis pulled back to southern Lebanon, while the Syrians remained in eastern Lebanon. And bloody anarchy remained a way of life in a formerly peaceful country.

GRENADA   Fortune, as it happened, presented Reagan the chance for an easy triumph closer to home, a "rescue mission" that eclipsed news of the debacle in Lebanon. On the tiny Caribbean island of Grenada, the smallest independent country in the Western Hemisphere, a leftist government had admitted Cuban workers to build a new airfield and signed military agreements with Communist countries. In 1983 an even more radical military council seized power.

Appeals from the governments of neighboring islands led Reagan to order 1,900 marines to invade the island, depose the new government, and evacuate a small group of American students at Grenada's medical school. The U.N. General Assembly condemned the action, and many Latin Americans saw it as a revival of gunboat diplomacy, but it was popular among Grenadans and their neighbors, and immensely popular in the United States. Although a lopsided affair, the action made Reagan look decisive, and it served as notice to Latin American revolutionaries that Reagan might use military force elsewhere in the region.

REAGAN'S SECOND TERM

By 1983, prosperity had returned, and the Reagan economic program seemed to be working as touted. Contradictory policies of fiscal stimulus (tax cuts and heavy expenditures for defense) and monetary restraint (high interest rates) brought at least in the short run an economic recovery without inflation. The gradual unraveling of the OPEC cartel and resultant decline in oil prices was the greatest stroke of luck for Reagan and the economy.

THE ELECTION OF 1984   Republican strategy for the presidential election was to take full credit for the economic recovery. Reagan had brought strength and vitality to the White House and the nation. The slogan at the Republican convention was "America is back." By contrast, the nominee of the Democrats, former vice-president Walter Mondale, never quite got his act together. Endorsed by the AFL-CIO, the National Organization for Women, and many blacks despite a serious challenge from Jesse Jackson, Mondale was tagged the candidate of the "special interests." He set a precedent by choosing as his running mate New York representative Geraldine Ferraro, but she was quickly placed on the defensive by the need to explain her spouse's complicated finances.

A fit of frankness in his acceptance speech further complicated Mondale's campaign. "Mr. Reagan will raise taxes, and so will I," he told the convention. "He won't tell you. I just did." Reagan responded by vowing never to approve a tax increase, and by chiding Mondale for his candid stand. Mondale never caught up. In the end, Reagan took 59 percent of the popular vote and lost only Minnesota and the District of Columbia. His coattails were not as strong, however. Republicans had a net gain of only fifteen seats in the House, and lost two in the Senate. Entering his second term, Reagan faced several political time bombs ticking away. They were planted around the world from Nicaragua to Afghanistan.

DOMESTIC CHALLENGES   Buoyed by his overwhelming victory, Reagan called for "a Second American Revolution of hope and opportunity." He dared Congress to raise taxes. His veto pen was ready: "Go ahead and make my day," he said in echo of a movie line. Through much of 1985 the president drummed up support for a tax simplification plan to eliminate loopholes and set only two or three brackets. It was a retreat from the principle of a progressive tax, which levied higher rates on high incomes, but that principle had long since been eroded by a variety of complex tax dodges within the reach mainly of the rich.

After vigorous debate that ran nearly two years, Congress passed, and in 1986 the president finally signed, a comprehensive Tax Reform Act. The new measure would reduce the number of tax brackets from fourteen to two and reduce rates from the maximum of 50 percent to 15 and 28 percent—the lowest since Coolidge. Tax shelters were also sharply limited.

ARMS CONTROL   Meanwhile Reagan, for all his talk about the Soviet Union being an "evil empire," seemed unwilling to be the first president since World War II to arrive at no agreement on arms reduction with the Soviets. In 1985, for the first time in six years, an American president met with the leader of the Soviet Union. After much preliminary maneuvering, Reagan and Mikhail Gorbachev, the recently elected Soviet president, met in Geneva on November 19 for a series of talks. They soon signed six agreements on cultural and scientific exchanges and other matters, but reached no agreements on arms limitations.

THE IRAN-CONTRA AFFAIR   During the fall of 1986, the Reagan administration suffered a double blow. In the midterm elections Democrats regained control of the Senate by 55 to 45. The Democrats picked up only six seats in the House, but they increased their already comfortable

Soviet premier Mikhail Gorbachev (left) *and U.S. president Ronald Reagan* (right) *during a light moment at the Geneva summit, November 1985.*

margin there to 259 to 176. For his last two years as president Reagan would face an opposition Congress.

What was worse, on election day reports surfaced that the United States had been secretly selling arms to Iran in hopes of securing the release of American hostages held in Lebanon by extremist groups sympathetic to Iran. Such actions contradicted Reagan's repeated public insistence that his administration would never negotiate with terrorists. The disclosures angered America's allies as well as many Americans who vividly remembered the 1979 Iranian takeover of their country's embassy in Teheran.

There was even more to the sordid story. Over the next several months, a series of revelations reminiscent of the Watergate affair disclosed a more complicated and even more incredible series of covert activities carried out by administration officials. At the center of the Iran-Contra affair was the much-decorated Marine lieutenant-colonel Oliver North. A swashbuckling aide to the National Security Council who specialized in counterterrorism, North had been running secret operations from the basement of the White House involving many governmental, private, and foreign individuals. His most farfetched scheme sought to use the profits gained from the secret sale of military supplies to Iran to subsidize the Contra rebels fighting in Nicaragua, at a time when Congress had voted to ban such aid.

Oliver North's activities, it turned out, had been approved by National Security Adviser Robert McFarlane, his successor Admiral John Poindexter, and CIA Director William Casey. Secretary of State George Shultz and Secretary of Defense Caspar Weinberger both criticized the arms sale to Iran, but their objections were ignored, and they were thereafter kept in the dark about what was going on. Later, on three occasions, Shultz threatened to resign over the continuing operation of the "pathetic" scheme. As information about the secret (and illegal) dealings surfaced in the press, McFarlane attempted suicide, Poindexter resigned, North was fired, and Casey, who denied any connection, left the CIA for health reasons. Casey died shortly thereafter from a brain tumor.

The White House, meanwhile, assumed a siege mentality as the president's popularity plummeted. Under increasing criticism, Reagan appointed both an independent counsel and a three-man commission, led by former Republican senator John Tower, to investigate the spreading scandal. The Tower Commission issued a devastating report early in 1987 that placed much of the responsibility for the bungled Iran-Contra affair on Reagan's loose management style. During the spring and summer of 1987, a joint House-Senate investigating committee began holding televised hearings into the Iran-Contra affair. The sessions dominated public attention for months and revealed a tangled web of inept financial and diplomatic transactions, the shredding of incriminating government documents, crass profiteering, and misguided patriotism.

The investigations of the independent counsel led to six indictments in 1988. A Washington jury found Oliver North guilty of three relatively minor charges but innocent of nine more serious counts, apparently reflecting the jury's reasoning that he acted as an agent of higher-ups. His conviction was later overturned on appeal. Of those involved in the affair, only John Poindexter got a jail sentence—six months for his conviction on five felony counts of obstructing justice and lying to Congress.

TURMOIL IN CENTRAL AMERICA The Iran-Contra affair showed the lengths to which members of the Reagan administration would go to support the rebels fighting the ruling Sandinistas in Nicaragua. Fearing heightened Soviet and American involvement in Central America, neighboring countries pressed during the mid-1980s for a negotiated settlement to the unrest in Nicaragua. In 1988 Daniel Ortega, the Nicaraguan president, pledged to negotiate directly with the Contra rebels. In the spring of 1988 these negotiations produced a cease-fire agreement, ending nearly seven years of fighting in Nicaragua. Secretary of State George Shultz called the pact an "important step forward," but the settlement surprised and disappointed hardliners within the Reagan administration who saw in it a Contra surrender. The Contra leaders themselves, aware of the eroding support for their cause in the United States Congress, saw the truce as their only chance for tangible concessions such as amnesty for political prisoners, the return of the Contras from exile, and "unrestricted freedom of expression."

Meanwhile, in neighboring El Salvador, the Reagan administration's attempt to shore up the centrist government of José Napoleón Duarte through economic and military aid suffered a body blow when the far-right ARENA party scored an upset victory at the polls during the spring of 1988.

DEBT AND THE PLUNGE IN THE STOCK MARKET   During the 1980s, debt, all kinds of debt—personal, corporate, and governmental—increased dramatically. Whereas in the 1960s Americans on average saved 10 percent of their income, in 1987 the figure was less than 4 percent. The Reagan budget deficits also reached record levels as legislators reluctant to offend constituents by raising taxes or cutting popular programs engaged in talk and symbolic action with a president ideologically resistant to taxes. The federal debt more than tripled from $908 billion in 1980 to $2.9 trillion at the end of the 1989 fiscal year.

Then, on October 19, 1987, the bill collector suddenly arrived at the nation's doorstep. On that "Black Monday," the stock market, already buffeted by sharp declines the previous week, experienced a tidal wave of selling reminiscent of the 1929 crash. The Dow Jones industrial average plummeted 508 points, or an astounding 22.6 percent. The market plunge nearly doubled the record 12.8 percent fall on October 28, 1929. Wall Street's selling frenzy reverberated throughout the capitalist world, sending stock prices plummeting in Tokyo, London, Paris, and Toronto.

What caused such a goring of the bull market? Some analysts argued that the runaway market of the 1980s had become artifically high, driven by excessive greed and hope rather than by the economy's actual

Despite the nation's prosperity and some efforts to build low-cost housing, the number of homeless people continued to increase during the 1980s.

performance. Others blamed new computerized trading programs that distorted market activity. But most agreed that the fundamental problem was the nation's spiraling indebtedness and chronically high trade deficits. Americans were consuming more than they were producing, importing the difference, and paying for imported goods with borrowed money and dollars whose value had sharply declined. Foreign investors had lost confidence in Reaganomics and were no longer willing to finance America's spending binge.

In the aftermath of the calamitous selling spree on Black Monday, few observers actually feared a depression of the magnitude of the 1930s; there were too many safeguards built into the system to allow that. But there was real concern of an impending recession, and this led business leaders and economists to attack the president for glossing over such a profound warning signal. Within a few weeks, Reagan agreed to work with Congress in developing a deficit reduction package, and for the first time indicated that he was willing to include increased taxes in such a package. But the eventual compromise plan was so modest that it did little to restore investor confidence. As one Republican senator lamented, "There is a total lack of courage among those of us in the Congress to do what we all know has to be done."

THE POOR, THE HOMELESS, AND AIDS VICTIMS   The 1980s were years of vivid contrast. Despite unprecedented prosperity, there were beggars in the streets and homeless people sleeping in doorways, in cardboard boxes, and on heat grates. A variety of causes led to the shortage of low-cost housing: government had given up on building public housing; urban renewal programs had demolished blighted areas but provided no housing for the displaced; and owners had abandoned unprofitable buildings in poor neighborhoods or converted them into expensive condominiums. The last was called "gentrification." New medications allowed for the deinstitutionalization of the mentally ill, but many of these individuals ended up on the streets when the promised community mental health services failed to materialize. By the summer of 1988, the *New York Times* estimated, more than 45 percent of the city's adult residents constituted an underclass totally outside the labor force for lack of skills, lack of motivation, drug use, and other problems.

Still another group of outcasts were those suffering from a new malady known as AIDS (acquired immune deficiency syndrome). At the

A quilt, commemorating the deaths of many thousands of Americans from AIDS, is stretched out and displayed before the White House in October 1988, so that friends and family can walk amidst the entire quilt and view the various sections up close.

beginning of the decade, public health officials had begun to report that gay men and intravenous drug users were especially at risk for this syndrome. Those infected with AIDS showed signs of fatigue, developed a strange combination of infections, and eventually died. People contracted the AIDS-causing virus (HIV) by coming into contact with the blood or body fluids of an infected person. One reason the Reagan administration showed little interest in AIDS was that it initially was viewed as a "gay" disease. Patrick Buchanan, the conservative spokesman who served as White House director of communications, said that homosexuals had "declared war on nature, and now nature is extracting an awful retribution."

By 2000, however, AIDS had claimed almost 300,000 American lives and was spreading among the larger population. Nearly a million Americans were estimated to be carrying the deadly HIV virus, and it had become the leading cause of death among men aged twenty-five to forty-four. The potential for exponential spread of HIV, owing to the very long incubation period before the onset of symptoms, provoked the surgeon general to launch a controversial public education program that included encouraging "safe sex" through the use of condoms. With no prospect for an early cure and with skyrocketing treatment costs, AIDS emerged as one of the nation's most horrifying and intractable problems.

A HISTORIC TREATY The main prospect for positive achievement before the end of Reagan's second term seemed to lie in arms-reduction agreements with the Soviet government. Under Mikhail Gorbachev, the Soviets pursued renewed détente in order to free their energies and financial resources to address pressing domestic problems. The logjam that had impeded arms negotiations suddenly broke in 1987, when Gorbachev announced that he was willing to deal separately on a medium-range missile treaty. After nine months of strenuous negotiations, Reagan and Gorbachev met amid much fanfare in Washington on December 9, 1987, and signed a treaty to eliminate intermediate-range (300–3,000 miles) nuclear forces (INF).

It was an epochal event, not only because it marked the first time that the two nations had agreed to destroy a whole class of weapons systems, but because it represented a key first step toward the eventual end of the arms race altogether. Under the terms of the treaty, the United States would destroy 859 missiles, and the Soviets would eliminate 1,752. On-site inspections by each side would verify compliance. Still, this winnowing would represent only 4 percent of the total nuclear missile count on both sides. Arms-control advocates thus looked toward a second and more comprehensive treaty dealing with long-range strategic missiles.

Gorbachev's successful efforts to liberalize Soviet domestic life and improve East-West foreign relations cheered Americans. The Soviets suddenly began stressing cooperation with the West in dealing with "hot spots" around the world. They urged the Palestine Liberation Organization to recognize Israel's right to exist and advocated a greater role for the U.N. in the volatile Persian Gulf. Perhaps the most dramatic symbol of a thawing cold war was the phased withdrawal of 115,000 Soviet troops from Afghanistan, which began in 1988.

THE REAGAN LEGACY Historians are just beginning to assess the legacy of the nation's fortieth president. Although Reagan had declared in 1981 his intention to "curb the size and influence of the federal establishment," the New Deal welfare state remained intact when Reagan left office. Neither the Social Security system nor Medicare nor other major welfare programs were dismantled or overhauled. And the federal agencies that Reagan threatened to abolish, such as the Department of Education, not only remained in place in 1989, their budgets grew. The federal budget as a percentage of the gross domestic product (GDP) was actually higher when Reagan left office than when he had entered. Moreover, he did not try to push through Congress the incendiary social issues championed by the religious right such as school prayer and a ban on abortions.

Yet Ronald Reagan nonetheless succeeded in redefining the national political agenda and accelerated the conservative insurgency that had been developing for over twenty years. Reagan's critics highlighted his lack of intellectual sophistication and his indifference to day-to-day administrative details. Yet he excelled as a leader because he was relentlessly optimistic about America's potential and unflinchingly committed to a philosophy of free enterprise, limited government, and strenuous anti-communism. His greatest successes were in renewing America's soaring sense of possibilities, bringing inflation under control, stimulating the longest sustained period of peacetime prosperity in history, negotiating the nuclear disarmament treaty, and helping to light the fuse of democratic freedom in eastern Europe. By redirecting the thrust of both domestic and foreign policy, he put the Democratic party on the defensive and forced conventional New Deal "liberalism" into a panicked retreat. The fact that Reagan's tax policies widened the gap between the rich and poor and created huge budget deficits for future presidents to confront did not diminish the popularity of the "Great Communicator."

THE 1988 ELECTION   In 1988, eight Democratic presidential candidates entered a wild scramble for their party's nomination. As the primary season progressed, however, it soon became a two-man race between Massachusetts governor Michael Dukakis and Jesse Jackson, the charismatic black civil rights activist who had been one of Martin Luther King, Jr.'s chief lieutenants. Dukakis eventually won out and managed a difficult reconciliation with the Jackson forces that left the Democrats unified and confident as the fall campaign began.

The Republicans nominated Reagan's two-term vice-president, George Bush, who after a bumpy start had easily cast aside his rivals in the primaries. As Reagan's handpicked heir, Bush claimed credit for the administration's successes, but like all dutiful vice-presidents, he also faced the challenge of asserting his own political identity. Although a veteran government official, having served as a Texas congressman, envoy to China, ambassador to the U.N., and head of the CIA, Bush projected none of Reagan's charisma or rhetorical skills. Cartoonists caricatured the patrician vice-president, the son of a rich Connecticut senator, as a well-heeled "wimp," and one Democrat described him as a man born "with a silver foot in his mouth." Early polls showed Dukakis with a wide lead.

Yet Bush delivered a forceful convention address that sharply enhanced his stature. Although pledging to continue the Reagan agenda, he also recognized that "things aren't perfect" in America, an admission his boss rarely acknowledged. Bush promised to use the White House to fight bigotry, illiteracy, and homelessness. Humane sympathies, he insisted, would guide his conservatism. "I want a kinder, gentler nation," Bush said softly in his acceptance speech. But the most memorable line was a defiant statement on taxes: "The Congress will push me to raise taxes, and I'll say no, and they'll push, and I'll say no, and they'll push again, and I'll say to them, 'Read my lips: no new taxes.'"

In a campaign given over to mudslinging, Bush and his aides attacked Dukakis as a camouflaged liberal in the mold of George McGovern, Jimmy Carter, and Walter Mondale. The Republican onslaught took its toll against the less organized, less focused Dukakis campaign. In the end, Dukakis took only ten states plus the District of Columbia, with clusters in the Northeast, Midwest, and Northwest. Bush carried the rest, with a margin of about 54 percent to 46 percent in the popular vote and 426 to 111 in the electoral college.

Generally speaking, the more affluent and better-educated voters preferred the Republican ticket. While Dukakis won the inner-city vote, garnering 86 percent of the black vote, Bush scored big in the suburbs

George Bush (right) *at the 1988 Republican National Convention with his newly chosen running mate, Dan Quayle, a former senator from Indiana.*

and in rural areas, especially in the once-Democratic South, where his margins of white voters ranged from a low of 63 percent in Florida to a high of 80 percent in Mississippi. More significant was Bush's success among blue-collar workers. He captured 46 percent of these typically Democratic voters.

Hidden among the election returns was a long-term trend that did not bode well for the American political system: voter turnout continued to decline. In the 1988 election, only 50 percent of the voting-age population cast ballots, the lowest in any presidential election since 1924. Voting was highest among affluent whites (52 percent), while 46 percent of eligible blacks and only 23 percent of eligible Hispanics turned out. But the most alarming statistic was that two-fifths of all the nonvoters were under thirty years of age. Apparently, many young adults no longer viewed the political process as significant enough to participate in.

THE BUSH ADMINISTRATION

George Bush viewed himself as a guardian president rather than an activist. Lacking Reagan's visionary outlook and his skill as a speaker, Bush was a pragmatist caretaker eager to avoid "stupid mistakes" and to find a way to get along with the Democratic majority in Congress. "We don't need to remake society," he announced. Bush sought to consolidate and nurture the programs that Reagan had put in place rather than launch his own array of new programs and policies.

DOMESTIC INITIATIVES   The Reagan administration left some issues that demanded immediate attention from the Bush White House. The biggest problem was the national debt, which stood at $2.6 trillion by the time Bush was elected, nearly three times its 1980 level. Bush's taboo on tax increases (meaning, mainly, income taxes) and his insistence upon lowering capital gains taxes—on profits from the sales of stocks and other property—made it more difficult to reduce the annual deficit or trim the long-term debt. By 1990 the country faced "a fiscal mess." Bipartisan budget talks between administration and congressional leaders spawned "rancorous partisanship [and] deep divisions within the two parties." Eventually, Bush decided "that both the size of

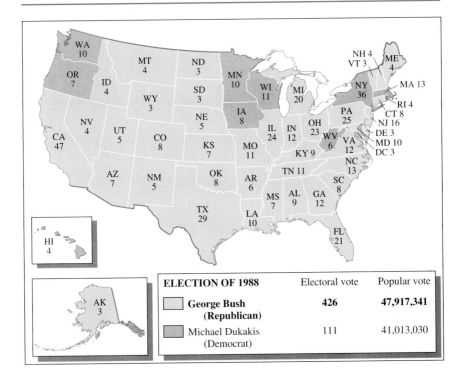

ELECTION OF 1988	Electoral vote	Popular vote
George Bush (Republican)	426	47,917,341
Michael Dukakis (Democrat)	111	41,013,030

the deficit problem and the need for a package that can be enacted" required a number of measures, including "tax revenue increases." Then he claimed that the Democrats had forced him to accept such language, a message that did not convey strong leadership. These elaborate partisan dances continued through the summer, until a budget plan was announced in September 1990. Through a combination of tax hikes and spending cuts, the measure promised to reduce the budget deficit by $43 billion in 1991 and by $331 billion in 1991–1995.

Another domestic initiative was President Bush's war on illegal drugs. During the 1980s, cocaine addiction spread through sizable segments of American society, luring not only those with money to spend but also those with little money to spare, who used the drug in its smokable form, known as crack. Bush vowed to make drug abuse his number-one domestic priority, and appointed William J. Bennett, former education secretary, as "drug czar," or head of a new Office of National Drug Control Policy, with cabinet status but no department. Total outlays in the war on drugs amounted to $8 billion in the 1990 fiscal year, although only $716 million represented new spending. The message, on this and on education, housing, and other social problems, was that more of the burden should fall on state and local authorities.

THE DEMOCRACY MOVEMENT ABROAD   Bush entered the White House with more foreign policy experience than most presidents, and he found the spotlight of the world stage more congenial than wrestling with the intractable problems of the inner cities, drug abuse, or the deficit. Within two years of his inauguration, George Bush would lead the United States into two wars, a record unequaled by any of his predecessors. Throughout most of 1989, however, he merely had to sit back and observe the dissolution of one totalitarian or authoritarian regime after another. For the first time in years, democracy was suddenly on the march in a sequence of mostly bloodless revolutions that surprised most of the world.

Although a democracy movement in China came to a tragic end in 1989 when government forces mounted a deadly assault on demonstrators in Beijing's (Peking's) Tiananmen Square, eastern Europe had an entirely different experience. With a rigid economic system failing to deliver the goods to the Soviet peoples, Mikhail Gorbachev responded with policies of "perestroika" (restructuring) and "glasnost" (openness), a loosening of central economic planning and censorship. His foreign policy sought rapprochement and trade with the West, and he aimed to relieve the Soviet economy of burdensome military costs.

Gorbachev also backed off from Soviet imperial ambitions. Early in 1989, Soviet troops left Afghanistan, after nine years of being bogged down in civil war there. Gorbachev then repudiated the "Brezhnev doctrine," which had asserted the right of the Soviet Union to intervene in the internal affairs of Communist countries. The days when Soviet tanks rolled through Warsaw and Prague were over, and hardline leaders in the East-bloc countries found themselves beset by demands for reform from their own peoples. With opposition strength building, the old regimes fell with surprisingly little bloodshed. Communist party rule ended first in Poland and Hungary, then in Czechoslovakia and Bulgaria. In Romania, the year of peaceful revolution ended in a bloodbath when the Romanian people joined the army in a bloody uprising against the brutal dictator Nicolae Ceauşescu. He and his wife were captured, tried, and then executed on Christmas Day. But lacking experienced opposition leaders, as did all the eastern European countries, the new government fell under the control of members of the old Communist establishment.

West Germans hacking away at the Berlin Wall on November 11, 1989, two days after all crossings between East and West Germany were opened.

The most spectacular event in the collapse of the Soviet empire in eastern Europe came on November 9, 1989, when the chief symbol of the cold war—the Berlin Wall—was torn down by Germans using small tools and even their hands. With the borders to the West now fully open, the Communist government of East Germany collapsed, a freely elected government came to power, and on October 3, 1990, the five states of East Germany were united with those of West Germany. The unified German nation remained in NATO, and the Warsaw Pact alliance was dissolved.

The reform impulse that Gorbachev helped unleash in the East-bloc countries began to career out of control within the Soviet Union itself. Gorbachev proved unusually adept at political restructuring, yielding the Communist monopoly of government but building a new presidential system that gave him, if anything, increased powers. His skills in the Byzantine politics of the Kremlin, though, did not extend to an antiquated economy that resisted change. The revival of old ethnic allegiances added to the instability. Although Russia proper included slightly over half the Soviet Union's population, it was only one of fifteen constituent republics, most of which began to seek autonomy, if not independence.

Gorbachev's popularity shrank in the Soviet Union as it grew abroad. It especially eroded among the Communist hardliners, who saw in his reforms the unraveling of their bureaucratic and political empire. Once the genie of freedom was released from the Communist lamp, however, it took on a momentum of its own. On August 18, 1991, a cabal of political and military leaders suddenly tried to seize the reins of power. They accosted Gorbachev at his vacation retreat in the Crimea and demanded that he sign a decree proclaiming a state of emergency and transferring his powers to them. He replied: "Go to hell," whereupon he was placed under house arrest.

The coup, however, was doomed from the start. Poorly planned and clumsily implemented, it lacked effective coordination. The plotters failed to arrest popular leaders such as Boris Yeltsin, the populist president of the Russian republic, they neglected to close the airports or cut off telephone and television communications, and they were opposed by key elements of the military and KGB (secret police). But most important, the plotters failed to recognize the strength of the democratic idealism unleashed by Gorbachev's reforms.

As the political drama unfolded in the Soviet Union, foreign leaders around the world spoke out against the coup. On August 20 President Bush, after a day of indecision, responded favorably to Yeltsin's request for support and convinced world leaders to join him in refusing to recognize the legitimacy of the new Soviet government. The next day word

A day after Gorbachev was placed under house arrest by Communists planning a coup, Russian Federation president Boris Yeltsin (with papers) makes a speech criticizing the plotters.

began to seep out that the plotters had given up and were fleeing. Several committed suicide, and a newly released Gorbachev ordered the others arrested. Yet things did not go back to the way they had been. Although Gorbachev reclaimed the title of president, he was forced to resign as head of the Communist party and admit that he had made a grave mistake in appointing the men who had turned against him. Boris Yeltsin emerged as the most popular political figure in the country.

What began as a reactionary coup turned into a powerful accelerant for stunning new changes in the Soviet Union, or the "Soviet Disunion," as one wag termed it. No sooner had the plotters been arrested than most of the fifteen republics proclaimed their independence, with the Baltic republics of Latvia, Lithuania, and Estonia regaining the status of independent nations. The Communist party apparatus was dismantled, prompting celebrating crowds to topple statues of Lenin and other Communist heroes.

A chastened Gorbachev could only acquiesce in the breakup of the Soviet empire. The man who had put reform into motion was now buffeted by the whirlwind of change. The systemic problems burdening the Soviet Union before the coup remained intractable. The economy was stagnant, food and coal shortages loomed on the horizon, and consumer goods remained scarce. The reformers had won, but they had yet to establish deep roots in a country with no democratic tradition. Leaping into the unknown, they faced years of hardship and uncertainty ahead.

The aborted coup also accelerated Soviet and American efforts to reduce the stockpiles of nuclear weapons. In late 1991 President Bush stunned the world by announcing that the United States would destroy all its tactical nuclear weapons on land and at sea in Europe and Asia, take its long-range bombers off twenty-four-hour alert status, and initiate discussions with the Soviet Union for the purpose of instituting sharp cuts in ICBMs (intercontinental ballistic missiles) with multiple warheads. Bush explained that the prospect of a Soviet invasion of western Europe was "no longer a realistic threat," and this provided an unprecedented opportunity for reducing the threat of nuclear holocaust. President Gorbachev responded by announcing reciprocal Soviet cutbacks.

PANAMA The end of the cold war did not spell the end of international tensions and conflict, however. Indeed, before the end of 1989, American troops were engaged in battle in Panama, where a petty tyrant provoked the first of America's military engagements under George Bush. In 1983 General Manuel Noriega had maneuvered himself into the leadership of the Panamanian Defense Forces—which made him head of government in fact if not in title. Earlier, as chief of intelligence, Noriega had developed a profitable business of supplying information on the region to the CIA, including during the period when Bush headed the agency. At the same time, he was developing avenues in the region for drug smuggling and gunrunning, laundering the money from these activities through Panamanian banks. For a time, American intelligence analysts looked the other way, regarding him as a useful contact, but eventually he became an embarrassment. In 1987 a rejected associate published charges of Noriega's drug activities and accused him further of rigged elections and political assassination.

In 1988 federal grand juries in Miami and Tampa, Florida, indicted Noriega and fifteen others on drug charges. The Panamanian president tried to fire Noriega, but the National Assembly ousted the president instead and named Noriega "maximum leader." It then proclaimed that Panama "is declared to be in a state of war" with the United States. The next day, December 16, 1989, four off-duty American servicemen were stopped at a roadblock, and as they tried to proceed, one marine was killed. President Bush thereupon ordered an invasion of Panama with the purpose of capturing Noriega for trial on the American indictments and installing a government headed by President Guillermo Endara.

The 12,000 American military personnel already in Panama were quickly joined by 12,000 more, and in the early morning of December 20, five military task forces struck at strategic targets in the country. Within hours, Noriega surrendered to American forces. Twenty-three American servicemen were killed in the action, and estimates of Panamanian casualties ranged up to 4,000, including many civilians caught in the crossfire. In April 1992 Noriega was convicted in the United States on eight counts of racketeering and drug distribution.

THE GULF WAR   Months after Panama had moved to the background of public attention, Saddam Hussein, dictator of Iraq, focused attention on the Middle East when his army suddenly invaded tiny Kuwait on August 2, 1990. Kuwait had raised its production of oil, contrary to agreements with the Organization of Petroleum Exporting Countries (OPEC). The resultant drop in oil prices offended the Iraqi regime, deep in debt and heavily dependent on oil revenues. Complaining of "economic aggression" against Iraq, he demanded that Kuwait reduce its oil production.

Saddam Hussein did not expect the sudden storm his invasion of Kuwait provoked. The U.N. Security Council quickly voted 14–0 to condemn the invasion and demand withdrawal. American secretary of state James Baker and Soviet foreign minister Eduard Shevardnadze issued a joint statement of condemnation. On August 6, the Security Council endorsed Resolution 661, an embargo on trade with Iraq, by a vote of 13–0, with Cuba and Yemen abstaining. Such unanimity, of course, would have been unlikely during the cold war era.

Bush condemned Iraq's "naked aggression" and dispatched planes and troops to Saudi Arabia on a "wholly defensive" mission—to protect Saudi Arabia. British forces soon joined in, as did Arab units from Egypt, Morocco, Syria, Oman, the United Arab Emirates, and Qatar. On August 22, Bush began to order the mobilization of American reserve forces for the operation, now dubbed "Desert Shield."

American soldiers adapting to the desert conditions during the Gulf War.

On November 8, Bush announced that he was doubling American forces in the Middle East from about 200,000 to 400,000, to build up "an adequate offensive military capability." Bush asserted that he already had authority to take such action under the Security Council resolutions. Congress erupted in debate, with many arguing that the embargo should have a chance to work, and that it would be ill advised to go to war without formal congressional support. Bush's position was strengthened on November 29 by U.N. Resolution 678, which authorized the use of force to dislodge Iraq from Kuwait, and set a deadline for Iraqi withdrawal of January 15, 1991.

A flurry of peace efforts sent diplomats scurrying all over, but without result. Iraq refused to yield. On January 10, Congress began to debate a resolution authorizing the use of U.S. armed forces. Senate Majority Leader George Mitchell warned, "A grave decision for war is being made prematurely. There has been no clear rationale, no convincing explanation for shifting American policy from one of sanctions to one of war." Others insisted on the need to present a united front behind the president. The outcome was uncertain to the end, but on January 12 the resolution for the use of force passed the House by 250–183, and the Senate by 52–47.

By January 1991, a twenty-eight-nation allied force was committed to Operation Desert Shield. Some nations sent only planes, ships, or support forces, but sixteen committed ground combat forces, ten of these Islamic countries. Desert Shield became Operation Desert Storm when the first cruise missiles began to hit Iraq on January 16.

With the allies in control of the air from the beginning, Saddam Hussein's only recourse was to fire off lumbering Soviet-made SCUD missiles, which he aimed into Israel with the hope of provoking Israeli retaliation and undermining the Arab coalition against him. But the resulting damage and casualties were light, and the Israelis showed remarkable restraint in the face of the continuing attacks. The Iraqis responded also with desperation moves, which did more damage to the environment than to enemy forces: releasing oil into the Persian Gulf from tankers and loading platforms in Kuwait and setting fire to Kuwaiti oil wells.

Saddam Hussein concentrated his forces in Kuwait and expected a landing on the coast and an allied attack northward into Kuwait. But the

Iraqis were outflanked when 200,000 allied troops, largely American, British, and French, turned up on the undefended Iraqi border with Saudi Arabia 100–200 miles to the west. The allied ground assault began on February 24 and lasted only four days. Iraqi soldiers surrendered by the thousands.

On February 28, six weeks after the fighting began, President Bush called for a cease-fire, the Iraqis accepted, and the shooting ended. There were 137 American fatalities. The lowest estimates of Iraqi fatalities, civilian and military, were around 100,000. The coalition forces occupied about one-fifth of Iraq. The Persian Gulf War, the "mother of all battles" in Saddam Hussein's words, had been intense and deadly and had left consequences to be played out far into the future. Despite all the destruction, Saddam Hussein remained in power.

The volatile Middle East, as it had for centuries, still resisted any quick fix, as it does today. After the Iraqi surrender, there was an understanding—details to be worked out—that the United States would maintain a military presence in the Persian Gulf. It was, ironically, an American missionary who said to one of the British planners carving up the former Ottoman territory after World War I: "You are flying in the face of four millenniums of history." The words retain their haunting quality.

MAKING CONNECTIONS

- Much of what happened in the 1980s, from economic and social policy to presidential leadership style, was reminiscent of the late nineteenth century as well as the 1920s and 1950s.

- Another parallel between the late nineteenth century and the 1980s was a rise in immigration and a change in immigration patterns. This is discussed in the next chapter.

- Chapter 37 shows how the economic and political conservatism of the 1980s became much more ideological in the early 1990s.

FURTHER READING

It is too early for a definitive scholarly analysis of the Reagan administration, but two brief accounts are David Mervin's *Ronald Reagan and the American Presidency* (1990) and Michael Schaller's *Reckoning with Reagan: America and Its President in the 1980s* (1992). More partisan is Steven Hayward's *The Age of Reagan: The Fall of the Old Liberal Order* (2001).

On Reaganomics, see David Stockman's *The Triumph of Politics: How the Reagan Revolution Failed* (1986) and Robert Lekachman's *Greed Is Not Enough: Reaganomics* (1982). On the issue of arms control, see Strobe Talbott's *Deadly Gambits: The Reagan Administration and the Stalemate in Nuclear Arms Control* (1984).

For Reagan's foreign policy in Central America, see James Chace's *Endless War: How We Got Involved in Central America and What Can Be Done* (1984) and Walter LaFeber's *Inevitable Revolutions: The United States in Central America* (2nd ed., 1993). Insider views of Reagan's foreign policy are offered in Alexander M. Haig, Jr.'s *Caveat: Realism, Reagan, and Foreign Policy* (1984) and Caspar W. Weinberger's *Fighting for Peace: Seven Critical Years in the Pentagon* (1990).

On Reagan's second term, see Jane Mayer and Doyle McManus's *Landslide: The Unmaking of the President, 1984–1988* (1988). For a masterful work on the Iran-Contra affair, see Theodore Draper's *A Very Thin Line: The Iran Contra Affair* (1991). Several collections of essays include varying assessments of the Reagan years. Among these are *The Reagan Revolution* (1988), edited by B. B. Kymlicka and Jean V. Matthews; *The Reagan Presidency: An Incomplete Revolution* (1990), edited by Dilys M. Hill, et al.; and *Looking Back on the Reagan Presidency* (1990), edited by Larry Berman.

On the 1988 campaign see Jack Germond and Jules Witcover's *Whose Broad Stripes and Bright Stars? The Trivial Pursuit of the Presidency, 1988* (1989) and Sidney Blumenthal's *Pledging Allegiance: The Last Campaign of the Cold War* (1990).

37 ⌒ TRIUMPH AND TRAGEDY: AMERICA AT THE TURN OF THE CENTURY

*T*he United States entered the final decade of the twentieth century triumphant. American vigilance in the cold war had led to the stunning collapse of the Soviet Union and the birth of democratic capitalism in eastern Europe. The United States was now the world's only superpower. By the mid-1990s the American economy would become the marvel of the world, as remarkable gains in productivity afforded by new technologies created the greatest period of prosperity in modern history. Yet no sooner did the century come to an end than America's comfortable sense of physical and material security was shattered by a terrorist assault that killed thousands, plummeted the economy into a steep recession, and called into question conventional notions of national security and personal safety. Insecurity and instability became the norm. As President George W. Bush observed in 2003, "This nation and our friends are all that stand between a world at peace, and a world of chaos and constant alarm." In two years, he went on to explain, "America has gone from a sense of invulnerability to an awareness of peril, from bitter division in small matters to calm unity in great causes. And we go forward with confidence, because this call of history has come to the right country." Bush claimed too much. There was less "calm unity" in the United States than he implied. It remained to be seen whether the nation was moving "forward with confidence" into the new century.

AMERICA'S CHANGING FACE

DEMOGRAPHIC SHIFTS   During the 1980s and 1990s, the nation's population grew by 20 percent, or some 50 million people, boosting the total to almost 275 million. The much-discussed baby-boom generation—the 43 million people born between 1946 and 1964—entered middle age. This generation's maturation and its preoccupation with practical concerns such as raising families, paying for college, and buying houses helped explain the surge of political conservatism during the 1980s. Surveys revealed that baby-boomers wanted stronger family and religious ties and a greater respect for authority. Yet having come to maturity during the turbulent sixties and early seventies, the baby-boomers also displayed more tolerance of social and cultural diversity than their parents.

During the last quarter of the twentieth century, the "Sunbelt" states of the South and West continued to lure residents from the Midwest and Northeast. Fully 90 percent of the nation's total population growth during the 1980s occurred in southern or western states. These population shifts forced a massive redistricting of the House of Representatives, with Florida, California, and Texas gaining seats, and states such as New York losing seats.

Americans at the end of the century tended to settle in large communities. This continuing move to the cities largely reflected trends in the job market, as the "postindustrial" economy continued to shift from manufacturing to professional service industries, particularly those specializing in telecommunications and information processing. By 2000 fewer than 2 million people out of a total population of 275 million worked on farms.

Women continued to enter the workforce in large numbers. In 1970, 38 percent of the workforce was female; in 2000 the figure was almost 50 percent. Women made up over a third of the new medical doctors (4 percent in 1970); 40 percent of new lawyers (8 percent in 1970); and 23 percent of new dentists (less than 1 percent in 1970).

The decline of the traditional family unit—two parents with children—continued. In 2000 only 65 percent of children lived with two parents, down from 85 percent in 1970. And more people were living alone than ever before, largely as a result of high divorce rates or a growing practice of delaying marriage until well into the twenties. The number of single mothers increased 35 percent during the decade. The rate was much higher for African Americans: in 2000 less than 32 percent of black children lived with both parents, down from 67 percent in 1960.

Young blacks burdened by the absence of one or both parents faced shrinking economic opportunities at the start of the twenty-first century. The urban poor were particularly victimized by high rates of crime and violence, with young black males suffering the most. In 2000 the leading cause of death among black males between the ages of fifteen and twenty-four was homicide. Over 25 percent of black males aged twenty to twenty-nine were in prison, on parole, or on probation, while only 4 percent were enrolled in college. Forty percent of black adult males were functionally illiterate.

THE NEW IMMIGRANTS   The racial and ethnic composition of the country also changed rapidly at the turn of the century. By 2000, the United States had more foreign-born and first-generation residents than ever before. Almost 30 percent of Americans claimed African, Asian, Hispanic, or American Indian ancestry. Blacks represented 13 percent of the total population, Hispanics 11 percent, Asians about 4 percent, and American Indians almost 1 percent. The rate of increase among those four groups was twice as fast as it had been during the 1970s.

Increased numbers of Chinese risked their money and their lives trying to gain entry into the United States. These illegal immigrants from China are trying to keep warm after being captured when the freighter carrying them to the United States ran aground in Rockaway, New York.

The primary cause of this dramatic change in the nation's ethnic mix was a surge of immigration. During the 1990s, legal immigration into the United States totaled over 10 million people, 40 percent higher than the previous decade and more than in any other decade. These figures do not include the hundreds of thousands of illegal aliens, mostly Mexicans and Haitians. In 2000 the United States welcomed more than twice as many immigrants as all other countries in the world combined.

For the first time in the nation's history, the majority of immigrants came not from Europe but from other parts of the world—Asia, Latin America, and Africa. Among the legal immigrants, Mexicans made up the largest share, averaging over 100,000 a year.

The wave of new immigration, younger, poorer, and less well-educated than the native population, brought rising conflict between old and new ethnicities. Critics charged that America was being "overrun" with foreigners; they questioned whether Hispanics and Asians could be "assimilated" into American culture. In 1994 a large majority of California voters approved Proposition 187, a controversial initiative that denied the state's estimated 4 million illegal immigrants access to public schools, nonemergency health care, and other social services. In 1998 California voters passed a referendum ending bilingual education.

The bitter irony of this new nativism was that it targeted recent immigrants for bringing with them to the United States virtues long prized by Americans—hope, energy, persistence, and an aggressive work ethic. Many new immigrants compiled an astonishing record of achievement, yet their very success contributed to the resentment they encountered from other groups.

THE COMPUTER REVOLUTION   Not only demographic shifts and immigration but also technological changes were transforming the nation. A surge in productivity and prosperity during the 1980s and 1990s resulted from a dramatic revolution in information technology. Cellular phones, laser printers, VCRs, fax machines, and personal computers became commonplace at work and in homes. The computer age had arrived.

The idea of a programmable machine that would rapidly perform mental tasks had been around since the eighteenth century, but it took the crisis atmosphere of World War II to gather the intellectual and financial resources needed to create such a "computer." A team of engineers at the University of Pennsylvania created ENIAC (Electronic Numerical Integrator and Computer), the first all-purpose, all-electronic digital computer. Unveiled in 1944, it could perform 5,000 operations per second. ENIAC took up 3,000 cubic feet of space and included 18,000 vacuum tubes (glass canisters designed to amplify electrical current), 70,000 resistors, 10,000 capacitors, and 6,000 switches.

During the 1950s and 1960s, corporations (such as International Business Machines—IBM) and government agencies transformed computers from mathematical calculators to electronic data-processing machines. The key development in facilitating such a transformation occurred in 1947 when three physicists at Bell Laboratories in central New Jersey invented the transistor (so named because it *transfers* electric current across a *resistor*, which is a conductor used to control voltage in an electrical circuit). Tiny transistors took the place of the glass vacuum tubes. The availability of transistors led to the development of hearing aids and portable radios.

The next major breakthrough was the invention in 1971 of the microprocessor—literally a computer on a silicon chip. The functions that had once been performed by computers taking up an entire room could now be performed by a microchip circuit the size of a postage stamp. Engineers soon incorporated microchips into television sets, wristwatches, automobiles, kitchen appliances, and spacecraft.

The invention of the microchip made possible the idea of a personal computer. In 1975, an engineer named Ed Roberts developed the first prototype of a "personal computer." The Altair 8800 was imperfect and cumbersome, with no display, no keyboard, and not enough memory to do anything useful. But its potential excited a Harvard sophomore named Bill Gates. He improved the software of the Altair 8800 and formed a new company called Microsoft to sell the new system. By 1977, Gates and others had helped to transform the personal computer from a hobby machine to a mass consumer product. In 1986 Gates became a billionaire at the age of thirty-one.

By the end of the 1980s, there were 60 million personal computers in the United States, and people began to talk about an "information superhighway," a worldwide network of linked computers and databases connected by fiber-optic lines that facilitated high-speed transmission.

Beginning with the cumbersome Electronic Numerical Integrator and Computer (ENIAC), pictured here in 1946, computer technology flourished with the development of personal computers in the 1980s and the creation of the Internet in the 1990s.

During the 1990s, the development of the Internet and electronic mail enabled anyone with a personal computer and modem the opportunity to travel on the information superhighway. Such advances helped to facilitate almost instantaneous communication across the continents. To the extent that computers had become essential tools for educational and economic success, however, they threatened to widen the gap between rich and poor. As always, it seems, technological progress has provided uneven benefits.

CULTURAL CONSERVATISM

Cultural conservatives helped elect Reagan and Bush in the 1980s, but they were disappointed in the results. Once in office, neither president had, in their eyes, adequately addressed their moral agenda, including a complete ban on abortions and the restoration of prayer in public schools. By the 1990s, a new generation of young conservative activists, mostly political independents or Republicans, began to emerge as a force to be reckoned with in national affairs. They were more ideological, more libertarian, more partisan, and more impatient than their predecessors.

ATTACKS ON LIBERALISM   The new breed of conservatives abhorred the excesses of cultural and political liberalism. They lamented the disappearance of basic forms of decency and propriety, and believed that fundamental liberties were at risk. They attacked affirmative action programs designed to redress historic injustices against women and minorities. During the 1990s, powerful groups inside and outside the Republican party mobilized to roll back government programs giving preferences to specified social groups. Prominent black conservatives supported such efforts, arguing that racially based preferences were demeaning and condescending remedies. They argued that preferential government treatment of African Americans raised doubts in the minds of both blacks and whites about the inherent worth of any black achievement.

THE RELIGIOUS RIGHT   Although quite diverse, cultural conservatives tended to be evangelical Christians or orthodox Catholics who joined together to exert increasing pressure on the political process. In

1989 the television evangelist Pat Robertson organized the Christian Coalition to replace Jerry Falwell's Moral Majority as the flagship organization of the resurgent religious right. The Christian Coalition encouraged religious conservatives to vote, run for public office, and support only those candidates who shared the organization's views.

With a well-organized grassroots movement in every state, the Christian Coalition chose the Republican party as the best vehicle for transforming its pro-family campaign into new public policies. It encouraged its supporters to withhold political support from any candidate who did not provide an ironclad promise to support the Coalition's school prayer, anti-abortion, anti–gay rights positions. In addition to promoting "traditional family values," it urged politicians to "radically downsize and delimit government."

As a centrist professional politician, George H. W. Bush initially tried to keep the cultural conservatives at arm's length, only to find himself the target—and victim—of their in-your-face attacks and take-no- prisoners tenacity. His Democratic successor, Bill Clinton, also underestimated the growing strength of organized groups such as the Christian Coalition. In the 1994 congressional elections, religious conservatives went to the polls in record numbers, and 70 percent of them voted Republican. A third of the voters identified themselves as "white, evangelical, born-again Christians." In many respects, they took control of the political and social agendas in the nineties. As one journalist acknowledged in 1995, "the religious right is moving toward center stage in American secular life."

BUSH TO CLINTON

For months after the Gulf War, George Bush seemed unbeatable. In the polls his approval rating rose to 91 percent. But the aftermath of Desert Storm was mixed, with Saddam Hussein's grip on Iraq still intact. Despite his image of strength abroad, the president began to look weak even on foreign policy. The Soviet Union meanwhile stumbled on to its surprising end. On December 25, 1991, the Soviet flag over the Kremlin was replaced by the flag of the Russian Federation. The cold war had ended with not just the collapse but the dismemberment of the Soviet Union into its fifteen constituent republics. As a result, the United States was now the world's only superpower.

"Containment" of the Soviet Union, the bedrock of American foreign policy for more than four decades, had lost its reason for being. Bush, the ultimate cold war careerist—ambassador to the U.N., envoy to China, head of the CIA, vice-president under Reagan—struggled to interpret the fluid new international scene. He spoke of a "New World Order" but never defined it. By his own admission he had trouble with the "vision thing." The international situation, in fact, did not lend itself to a simple vision—unless the answer was to drift into isolation, a great temptation, with foreign dangers seemingly lessened. By the end of 1991, Bush faced a challenge in the Republican primary from the television commentator and former White House aide Patrick Buchanan, who adopted the slogan "America First" and called on Bush to "bring home the boys." As the Gulf War victory euphoria wore off, a popular bumper sticker reflected the growing public frustration with the Bush administration: "Saddam Hussein still has his job. What about you?"

RECESSION AND DOWNSIZING   In November 1988, a few days after George Bush was elected president, a journalist observed that the most important issue to be addressed by the new administration was the nation's deepening financial debt. "It is the issue that probably will determine the fate of the President. Indeed, it could also be his ultimate undoing." It was an accurate prediction. For the Bush administration and for the nation, the most devastating development in the early nineties was a prolonged economic recession that began in 1990. The first economic setback in more than eight years, it grew into the longest, if not the deepest, since the Great Depression. During 1991, 25 million workers—about 20 percent of the labor force—were unemployed at some time.

What made this recession unusual was that its victims included large numbers of white-collar workers. In 1991, for instance, General Motors, Xerox, and IBM cut 100,000 salaried employees from their payrolls. In the corporate world, terms such as "restructuring" and "downsizing" ruled the day as companies began reducing personnel, switching employees to part-time status to reduce benefits, and finding other ways to cut labor costs.

At the same time, the country was experiencing a continuing imbalance in foreign trade, the lack of a plan for demobilization of the military-industrial complex after the cold war, and soaring expenditures on defense and social entitlement programs. During 1991 a $150 billion annual deficit had become a $450 billion shortfall.

A Senate committee analysis of the stagnant economy confirmed a chilling fact. Under the Bush administration "the average standard of living has actually declined." The euphoria over the Allied victory in the Gulf War quickly gave way to anxiety and resentment generated by the depressed economy. At the end of 1991, *Time* magazine declared that "no one, not even George Bush" could deny "that the economy was sputtering."

Whatever the reasons for recession, the cure remained elusive. Although the Federal Reserve Board began cutting interest rates, the economy remained in the doldrums through 1992. The Democratic Congress and the Republican president squabbled over legislation to promote economic recovery but little was done to prod new growth or to reduce the hemorrhaging deficits. With his domestic policies in disarray and his foreign policy abandoned, George Bush tried a clumsy balancing act in addressing the recession, on the one hand acknowledging that "people are hurting" while on the other urging Americans that "this is a good time to buy a car."

THE THOMAS HEARINGS AND THE WOMEN'S MOVEMENT Other developments affected the president's popularity, among them the retirement in 1991 of the first black Supreme Court justice, Thurgood Marshall, after twenty-four years on the bench. To succeed him Bush named Clarence Thomas, a black federal judge who had been raised in poverty in the segregated South. After graduating from Yale Law School, Thomas had worked as an aide to a Republican senator before serving as chairman of the Equal Employment Opportunity Commission (EEOC) from 1982 to 1990. Then, after sixteen months on the U.S. Court of Appeals, he was tapped for the Supreme Court.

Thomas's views delighted conservative senators. He questioned the wisdom of the minimum wage, school busing for desegregation, and affirmative action hiring programs, and he preached "black self-help," once declaring that all civil rights leaders ever did was "bitch, bitch, bitch, moan, and whine."

Such opinions promised trouble in the Democratic Senate, but the real explosion occurred when Anita Hill, a soft-spoken law professor at the University of Oklahoma, charged that Thomas had sexually harassed her when she worked for him at the EEOC. Pro-Thomas senators orchestrated an often savage and sometimes absurd cross-examination of Hill. Some accused her of mental instability. An indignant Thomas denied her charges and called the hearings a "high-tech lynching for uppity blacks." He implied that Hill had fabricated the charges at the behest of civil rights groups determined to thwart his confirmation.

The televised hearings revealed that either Hill or Thomas had lied, and the committee's tie vote reflected the doubt: seven to recommend confirmation and seven against. The full Senate then narrowly confirmed Thomas by a 52–48 margin.

The Thomas hearings sparked a new surge in the women's movement. Anita Hill's rough treatment at the hands of male senators revitalized feminism as an organized political movement. As early as 1975 Betty Friedan had broken away from the National Organization for Women (NOW), the organization she had started less than a decade before, claiming that its radical leaders had abandoned the core constituency of working women. By 1992 many claimed that NOW had reached a dead end. Columnist Sally Quinn charged that "many women have come to see the feminist movement as anti-male, anti-child, anti-family, anti-feminine. And therefore it has nothing to do with us."

In the ambiguous aftermath of the Thomas hearings, many women grew incensed at the treatment of Hill, and an unprecedented number of women ran for national and local offices in 1992. The Thomas confirmation struggle thus widened the gender gap for a Republican party already less popular with women than with men. As one political commentator put it: "The war with Anita Hill was not a war Bush needed."

REPUBLICAN TURMOIL   President Bush had already set a political trap for himself when he declared in his 1988 convention address: "Read my lips: no new taxes." Fourteen months into his term, he had decided that the deficit was a greater risk than violating his "no tax" pledge. After intense negotiations with congressional Democrats, Bush had announced that reducing the federal deficit required "tax revenue increases." Bush's backsliding set off a revolt among House Republicans, but a bipartisan majority (most Republicans opposing) finally approved a tax measure raising the top personal rate from 28 to 31 percent, disallowing certain deductions to the upper brackets, and raising various excises. Conservative Republicans would not let George Bush forget his abandoned pledge.

Social issues had been one of the adhesives in the Reagan coalition, keeping the focus away from divisive economic issues, but as hardships crowded in on the attention of blue-collar workers, the economy became the primary concern. Moreover, social issues strengthened the force of the new "Christian Right" and grated on traditional Republicans. At the 1992 convention Patrick Buchanan, who had won about a third of the votes in the Republican primaries, used the occasion for a defense of "family values." Pat Robertson, the television evangelist, insisted that the proposed Equal Rights Amendment represented "a socialist, anti-family, political movement that encourages women to leave their husbands, kill their children, practice witchcraft, destroy capitalism and become lesbians."

DEMOCRATIC RESURGENCE   In contrast to such strident rhetoric, the Democrats presented an image of centrist forces in control. For several years the Democratic Leadership Council (DLC), in which Arkansas governor William Jefferson Clinton figured prominently, had pushed the party to the center of the political spectrum. Clinton strove to move the Democrats closer to the mainstream of political opinion. A graduate of Georgetown University, he had won a Rhodes scholarship to Oxford, and then earned a law degree from Yale, where he met and married Hillary Rodham. By 1979, at age thirty-two, he was back in his native Arkansas as the youngest governor in the country. He served three more terms as governor and in the process emerged as a dynamic young leader committed to winning back the middle-class white voters who had voted Republican during the eighties. Democrats had grown so liberal, he argued, that they had alienated their key constituencies.

A self-described moderate, Clinton promised to cut the defense budget, provide tax relief for the middle class, and create a massive economic aid package for the former republics of the Soviet Union. He was less precise about how such initiatives would be funded. Handsome, witty, intelligent, and a compelling speaker, Clinton reminded many political observers of John F. Kennedy.

But underneath the veneer of Clinton's charisma were several flaws. He often seemed so determined to become president that he was willing to sacrifice consistency and principle. He made extensive use of polls to shape his stance on issues, pandered to special-interest groups, and flip-flopped on controversial issues, leading critics to label him "Slick Willie." Said one former opponent in Arkansas, "He'll be what people want him to be. He'll do or say what it will take to get elected." Even more enticing to the media and more embarrassing to Clinton were unending reports that he was a chronic adulterer and that he had manipulated the ROTC program during the Vietnam War to avoid the draft. Clinton's denials of both allegations could not dispel a lingering distrust of his personal character.

After a series of bruising party primaries, Clinton emerged as the front-runner by the time of the nominating convention in the summer of 1992. The Clinton forces dominated the convention, where Clinton chose Albert Gore, Jr., of Tennessee as his running mate. So the candidates were two southern Baptists from adjoining states.

Flushed with their convention victory, sporting a ten-point lead in the polls, the Clinton-Gore team stressed economic issues to win over working-class white and black voters. This strategy worked. Exit polls showed that the most important issue had been the economy. Clinton won with 370 electoral votes and about 43 percent of the vote; Bush had 168 electoral votes and 39 percent of the vote; and off-and-on independent candidate H. Ross Perot of Texas garnered 18 percent of the

Presidential candidate Bill Clinton and his running mate Al Gore brought youthful enthusiasm to the campaign trail in 1992.

popular vote but no electoral votes. A feisty billionaire, Perot found a big audience for his simplified explanations of public problems and his offers to just "get under the hood and fix them."

Domestic Policy in Clinton's First Term

Once faced with the realities of governing, Clinton alienated many who had voted for him when he reneged on several of his campaign promises. He abandoned his proposed middle-class tax cut in order to keep down the federal deficit. When his attempt to allow professed homosexuals in the military provoked strong opposition among military commanders and in Congress, he backed down nine days into office and later announced an ambiguous new policy concerning gays in the military that came to be known as "Don't ask, don't tell." In Clinton's first two weeks in office, his approval ratings dropped 20 percent.

THE ECONOMY Clinton entered office determined to reduce the federal deficit without damaging the economy. To this end, on February 17, he laid out a program of tax hikes and spending cuts. He proposed higher taxes for corporations and for individuals in higher tax brackets and called for an economic stimulus package for "investment" in public works (transportation, utilities, and the like) and in "human capital" (education, skills, health, and welfare). The Republican minority in the Senate used a filibuster to block the stimulus package, which they described as a "budget buster" that would fail to pep up the economy. The Democrats were unable to muster enough votes to cut off debate, and the stimulus package lay dead in the water. In response to Clinton's deficit reduction package of spending cuts and tax hikes on upper incomes, both Republicans and conservative Democrats who favored even deeper spending cuts opposed the package. The hotly contested bill finally passed by 218–216 in the House and 51–50 in the Senate, with Vice-President Gore breaking the tie.

Equally contested was the North American Free Trade Agreement (NAFTA), which the Bush administration had negotiated with Canada and Mexico. The debate over its approval revived old arguments on the tariff, pro and con. Clinton stuck with his party's tradition of low tariffs and urged approval of NAFTA, which would make North America the largest free trade area in the world. He and his supporters argued that tariff reductions would open up foreign markets to American industries. Opponents of the bill like wealthy gadfly Ross Perot and organized labor favored barriers against cheaper foreign products and believed that with NAFTA the country would hear a "giant sucking sound" of American jobs being drawn to Mexico. Yet Clinton prevailed with solid Republican support while losing a sizable minority of Democrats, mostly from the South, where textile mills feared the loss of business to "cheap-labor" countries.

HEALTH CARE REFORM   Clinton's major public policy initiative was a new federal health care plan. Government-subsidized health insurance was not a new idea. Other industrial countries had long ago started national health insurance programs, Germany as early as 1883, Britain in 1911. Off and on the idea had been a subject of political discussion in the United States throughout the twentieth century. Medicare, initiated in 1965, provided insurance for people sixty-five and older, and Medicaid supported state medical assistance for the indigent. These programs had grown enormously in the years since, as had business spending on private health insurance.

Sentiment for health care reform spread as annual medical costs approached the trillion-dollar mark, and some 39 million Americans went without insurance either by choice or out of necessity. The administration argued that universal medical insurance would reduce the overall costs of health care. Medicare covered older people, the most vulnerable to medical expenses, and the costs were soaring. Many of the working poor could not afford insurance, and many younger, healthier people took a chance on doing without. When they got in trouble, they reported to emergency rooms, which were reluctant to reject desperate people. As a result, those who could pay covered the others' costs in higher fees.

Universal medical coverage as proposed by Clinton would entitle every American and legal immigrant to health insurance. Government would subsidize all or part of the payments for small businesses and the poor, the latter from funds that formerly went to Medicaid, and would collect a "sin tax" on tobacco and perhaps on alcoholic beverages to pay for the program. Hillary Clinton chaired the health care plan task force and became the administration's lead witness on the plan before congressional committees. Throughout 1994, a comprehensive health insurance plan remained the centerpiece of the Clinton agenda.

The bill, however, aroused opposition from vested interests, especially the pharmaceutical and insurance industries. By the summer of 1994, the health insurance plan was pretty well doomed. Republican senators began a filibuster to prevent a vote on the bill. Lacking the votes to stop the filibuster, the Democrats acknowledged defeat and gave up the fight for universal medical coverage.

HANDGUNS AND THE CRIME BILL   During Clinton's first year in office, fear of violent crime prompted legislators to limit the availability of unregistered guns. In 1993, Congress passed the Brady Bill, which required a five-day wait to buy a handgun. Clinton called for passage of a crime bill in his State of the Union message. The bill had been passed in both houses in 1993, but when a conference committee reported back a compromise bill, a coalition of unlikely bedfellows—black Democrats who objected to expanding use of the death penalty, pro-gun Democrats who objected to a ban on assault weapons, and Republicans who dismissed crime-prevention programs as "pork" and who sought to embarrass the administration—joined together to oppose the legislation. After Congress voted 225–210 to postpone consideration of the bill, the Clinton administration pulled out all the stops to win its approval, and the new vote in the House in favor of the bill was 235–195. When the Senate passed the bill, people characterized it as one of Clinton's greatest victories. Ironically, however, it damaged the chances for health care legislation, as Clinton was preoccupied with the crime bill for ten days and used up much of his political leverage in the final moves to win its approval. This meant that there were fewer favors he could pull in to overcome the growing opposition to universal health care.

MISTRUST OF GOVERNMENT AND THE MILITIA MOVEMENT While Clinton sparred with Republicans in Washington, a burgeoning "militia" or "patriot" movement spread across the country in the 1990s. It represented the paranoid and populist strain in cultural politics. Convinced that the federal government was conspiring against individual liberties (especially the right to bear arms), thousands of mostly working-class folk joined well-armed militia organizations. Some militias harkened back to the origins of the Ku Klux Klan and fomented racial and ethnic hatred. Others aligned themselves with right-wing Christian groups, particularly the militant wing of the anti-abortion movement. In the Far West, several of the militias challenged the federal control of public lands, refused to pay taxes, and threatened to arrest and execute local government officials and judges.

In Waco, Texas, a confrontation between federal authorities and a militia group resulted in catastrophic consequences. Responding to reports and rumors about the stockpiling of weapons, child abuse, and the violation of immigration laws by the Branch Davidians, an apocalyptic sect headed by David Koresh, agents from the Treasury Department's Bureau of Alcohol, Tobacco, and Firearms (BATF) tried to serve a warrant on the sect on February 28, 1993. When the agents entered the sect's compound, they were met with gunfire. Four agents and two Branch Davidians were killed, and twenty or so people were injured. The next day, the FBI took over the siege of the compound, waging fruitless psychological warfare against the Branch Davidians. On April 19, the fifty-first day of the siege, FBI agents attacked the compound with armored vehicles and tear gas. Amid the commotion, the compound caught fire and quickly burned to the ground. At least seventy-seven people died in the inferno.

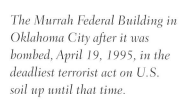

The Murrah Federal Building in Oklahoma City after it was bombed, April 19, 1995, in the deadliest terrorist act on U.S. soil up until that time.

On the second anniversary of the Waco incident, April 19, 1995, a massive truck bomb exploded in front of the federal office building in Oklahoma City, Oklahoma. The entire front portion of the nine-story building collapsed, killing 168 people, 19 of them children in a day-care center that was in the building. Six hundred others were injured. Within days, the FBI arrested Timothy McVeigh and Terry Nichols and charged them with the bombing. A third man pleaded guilty to separate charges of conspiring to produce explosives. All three men were militia members who hated the federal government and who had been incensed by the way the BATF and FBI had dealt with the Branch Davidians at Waco.

The Oklahoma City bombing shocked and saddened the nation. It brought to public attention the rise of right-wing militia groups and also revealed the depth of anti-government sentiment among such fringe groups.

REPUBLICAN INSURGENCY

During 1994, Clinton began to see his presidency unravel. Unable to get either health care reform or welfare reform bills through the Democratic Congress, and having failed to carry out his campaign pledge for middle-class tax relief, he and his party found themselves on the defensive.

In the midterm elections of 1994, the Democrats suffered a humbling defeat. It was the first election since 1952 in which Republicans captured both houses of Congress at the same time. In both, the majority was solid: 52–48 in the Senate, a majority that soon increased when two Democrats switched parties, and 230–204 in the House. Not a single Republican incumbent was defeated. Republicans also won a net gain of eleven governorships and fifteen state legislatures.

There could be little question that the election returns signaled a repudiation of Clinton and the Democratic Congress. Squabbling between the president and congressional Democrats did not help matters. Clinton's waffling on major issues began to convince many in his own party that he was a politician rather than a leader, someone who thrived as a campaigner but was bereft of genuine convictions. Said Democratic congressman David Obey: "I think most of us learned some time ago that if you don't like the president's position on a particular issue, you simply need to wait a few weeks." When Clinton joined the chorus of conservatives calling for a scaling back of affirmative action plans designed to remedy historic patterns of racial discrimination in hiring and the awarding of government contracts, liberals felt betrayed.

CONTRACT WITH AMERICA   A Georgian named Newton Leroy Gingrich led the Republican insurgency in Congress. In early 1995 he became the first Republican Speaker of the House in forty-two years. In the late 1980s he had launched a series of attacks on the ethics of the Democratic leadership in the House, ultimately leading to the resignation of both Democratic Speaker Jim Wright and Democratic whip Tony Coelho. Gingrich had also helped mobilize religious and social conservatives associated with the Christian Coalition.

In 1995 Gingrich assaulted the "welfare state" and sought to restore conservative values and principles. He was aided by the freshman Republicans, who came to Washington filled with ardor for Gingrich. Now the majority in the House, freshman Republicans promoted what Gingrich called the "Contract with America." The ten-point contract outlined an anti-big-government program with less regulation, less conservation, term limits for members of Congress, a line-item veto for the president, welfare reform, and a balanced-budget amendment.

By April 13, exactly 100 days after taking office, the Republicans had passed twenty-six bills growing out of the Contract with America, and had failed to pass only two: a proposal for an anti-missile ("Star Wars") defense system and term limits for Congress. Nonetheless, twenty-two of these bills did not become law. The four successful bills were: a law mandating that all laws applicable to ordinary Americans should also apply to members of Congress; a law in which Congress agreed to stop imposing mandated programs on local and state governments without footing the bill; a large defense spending bill, which Clinton reluctantly accepted, lest Republicans rebel on foreign policy; and a new crime bill providing for stiff penalties for child abuse and pornography. The line-item veto would not pass until a year later and soon thereafter it was rescinded.

Thereafter, the much ballyhooed GOP revolution and the "Contract with America" fizzled out. The revolution that Gingrich touted was far too ambitious to carry out in so limited a time, with so slim a majority, and with so little sense of crisis. What is more, many of the Republican freshmen were scornful of compromise and amateurs at the rules of order, and they limited the Speaker's room for maneuver. The Senate rejected many of the bills that had been passed in the House, as senators were less under Gingrich's spell and not party to the Contract with America anyway. And beyond them, a presidential veto stood in the path. Finally, President Clinton shrewdly moved to the political center and co-opted much of the Republican agenda. His distinctive strength—at least in the eyes of his supporters—resided in his agile responsiveness to changing public moods. To Clinton, the Republican victory in the 1994 congressional elections and in the passage of the Contract with America initiatives bore a simple message: he must recapture the political center by radically changing his agenda.

The Republicans' Contract with America succeeded in focusing public and presidential attention on basic questions of governmental philosophy. But Gingrich and other House Republican insurgents had overestimated the public's interest in dismantling the federal government and many of its social programs. By the end of 1995, Clinton's fortunes were back on the rise as the Gingrich revolution petered out, leaving Gingrich with a bag of unfilled promises and with low ratings in the polls. If the American people had voted a mandate for anything, it may have been a mandate for the status quo. Said one contrite Republican freshman in 1996: "We scared too many people in the last year talking with such revolutionary fervor. I think we showed more guts than brains sometimes."

LEGISLATIVE BREAKTHROUGH   In the late summer of 1996, as lawmakers were preparing to adjourn and participate in the presidential nominating conventions, the 104th Congress broke through its partisan gridlock and passed a flurry of important legislation that President Clinton quickly signed, including a bill increasing the minimum wage and a bill broadening public access to health insurance.

Even more significant was a comprehensive welfare reform measure that ended the federal government's open-ended guarantee of aid to the poor, a guarantee that had been in place since 1935. The Personal Responsibility and Work Opportunity Act turned over the major federal welfare programs to the states, which would receive federal grants to fund the programs. The bill also limited the amount of time a person could receive welfare benefits funded by federal money and required that at least half of a state's welfare recipients have jobs or be enrolled in job training programs by the year 2002.

Those states failing to meet the deadline would have their federal funds cut.

The Republican-sponsored welfare reform legislation passed the Senate by a vote of 74–24. It had the effect of cutting $56 billion over six years from Aid to Families with Dependent Children, food stamps, and other welfare programs, several of which dated back to Franklin Roosevelt's New Deal. In total budgets of about $1.5 trillion, that amounted to less than 1 percent.

Liberals charged that Clinton was abdicating Democratic social principles in order to gain reelection amid the conservative climate of the times. Clinton and his centrist advisers, however, dismissed such criticisms. With his reelection bid at stake, he was determined to live up to his 1992 campaign pledge to "end welfare as we know it." Clinton also knew that most voters in both parties were eager to see major cuts in federal entitlement programs.

THE 1996 CAMPAIGN   After clinching the Republican presidential nomination in 1996, Senate majority leader Bob Dole resigned his seat in order to devote his attention to defeating Bill Clinton. As the 1996

Former Republican Senate majority leader Bob Dole on the campaign trail.

presidential campaign unfolded, however, Clinton maintained a large lead in the polls. With a generally healthy economy and with no major foreign policy crises to confront, cultural and personal issues surged into prominence. Concern about Dole's age (seventy-three) and his acerbic manner, as well as rifts in the Republican party between economic and social conservatives over issues such as abortion and gun control, hampered Dole's efforts to generate widespread support.

On November 5 Clinton won again with an electoral vote of 379 to 159 and 49 percent of the popular vote. He lost Georgia, Colorado, and Montana, but added Arizona and Florida to his column. Dole received 41 percent and Ross Perot got 8 percent of the popular vote. The Republicans lost eight seats in the House, but suspicions of Democratic money scandals may have helped them hold a 227–207 edge over the Democrats in the House; in the Senate Republicans gained two seats for a 55–45 majority. The resulting deadlock reflected the conservative mood of the times.

ECONOMIC AND SOCIAL TRENDS OF THE 1990s

After the 1996 election, Clinton reshuffled his cabinet and other posts. Madeleine Albright, ambassador to the United Nations, became the first woman to head the State Department, and Senator William Cohen, a Republican from Maine, took over at the Defense Department. The overall direction of his changes was a move to the right. These changes reflected profound economic and social developments.

THE "NEW ECONOMY"   As the twentieth century came to a close, the United States benefited from a prolonged period of unprecedented prosperity. Buoyed by low inflation, high employment, declining federal budget deficits, dramatic improvements in productivity, the rapid "globalization" of economic life, and the firm and astute leadership of Federal Reserve Board chairman Alan Greenspan, American business and industry witnessed record profits.

The stock market soared during the late 1990s. In 1993 the Dow Jones industrial average hit 3,500. By 1996 it had topped 6,000. During 1998, it reached 9,000, defying the predictions of experts that the economy could not sustain such performance. In 1998 unemployment was only 4.3 percent, the lowest since 1970. Inflation was a measly 1.7 percent. People began to talk of a "new economy" that defied the boom-and-bust cycles of the previous hundred years. "It is possible," Greenspan suggested, "that we have moved 'beyond history.' "

In the 1990s, much of the surging economy resulted from "globalization." The "new" economy favored free markets on a world scale— markets without tariffs and other barriers to free trade. More and more gigantic corporations such as International Business Machines (IBM) or General Electric (GE) had become international in scope. This encouraged free trade agreements such as NAFTA as well as most-favored-nation treatment for China and other countries. American companies might then "outsource" much of their production to plants in countries with lower labor costs. This led to a decline of the labor union movement and to corporate moves toward "downsizing," which worked wonders with stock prices, whether or not it served business efficiency. Blue-collar labor lost ground to cheap foreign labor in assembly plants or "sweatshops" elsewhere in the world. Part-time labor became popular because employers could avoid paying for expensive benefits.

THE WHITE-COLLAR SWEATSHOP The "new economy" brought with it a frenetic work ethic for salaried executives. As the service and high-tech sectors of the economy continued to grow at the expense of the traditional manufacturing sector, the proportion of white-collar workers grew rapidly. Fueled by perennial improvements in productivity, the new American economy demanded more work and greater efficiency from salaried employees. Overwork became an epidemic during the 1990s. One writer coined the term "white-collar sweatshop" to describe the new phenomenon. On average, Americans at the end of the twentieth century worked 350 hours more per year than Europeans. The average workweek for professionals in the United States rose to forty-seven hours. Over 25 million Americans worked more than fifty hours per week, and another 11 million spent more than sixty hours on the job. As a bumper sticker proclaimed, "Sure, We Take Vacations. They're Called Lunch Breaks."

New technologies made work a round-the-clock activity during the go-go 1990s. Driven by demands for ever-increasing productivity, more and more people took laptops, beepers, Palm Pilots, and cell phones home at night and on vacation. Hurtling from meeting to meeting, project to project, cell phone to laptop, drained by long commutes and frequent travel, fast-track executives complained of fatigue and burnout. The American Medical Association reported that the average white-collar worker got sixty to ninety minutes less sleep than needed. Job dissatisfaction emerged as the surest predictor of heart trouble, and divorce rates among high-powered executives and professionals soared.

Some people, however, seemed to thrive amid the longer hours and constant pressure. A Gallup poll reported that 44 percent of Americans called themselves "workaholics." Some exhausted workers, however, sought to escape the "white-collar sweatshop." Some 20 percent of salaried employees during the 1990s exchanged fewer working hours for lower salaries.

RACE INITIATIVE   After the triumphs of the civil rights movement in the 1960s, the momentum for minority advancement had run out— except for gains in college admissions and employment under the rubric of "affirmative action." The conservative mood during the mid-1990s manifested itself in the Supreme Court. In 1995, the Court ruled against election districts redrawn to create black or Hispanic majorities, narrowed federal affirmative action programs, and limited the legal remedies for segregated public schools. All were decided by the same vote of 5–4 (Chief Justice Rehnquist, and Justices Kennedy, O'Connor, Scalia, and Thomas deciding against Justices Breyer, Ginsburg, Souter, and Stevens).

In one of the cases, *Adarand Constructors* v. *Peña* (1995), the Court assessed a program that gave some advantages to businesses owned by "disadvantaged" minorities. An Hispanic-owned firm had won a highway guard rail contract over a lower bid by a white-owned company. The white-owned company sued on the ground of "reverse discrimination." Writing for the majority, Justice O'Connor said that such programs had to be "narrowly tailored" to serve a "compelling national interest." O'Connor did not define what the Court meant by a "compelling national interest," but the implication of her language was clear: the Court had come to embrace the growing public suspicion of the value and legality of such race-based programs.

In 1996 two major new steps were taken against affirmative action in college admissions. In *Hopwood* v. *Texas* (1996), the Fifth Circuit Court ruled that considering race to achieve a diverse student body at the University of Texas was "not a compelling interest under the Fourteenth Amendment." Later that year, the state of California passed Proposition 209, an initiative that ruled out race, sex, ethnicity, or national origin as criteria for preferring any group. These rulings eviscerated affirmative action programs and drastically reduced black enrollments, something that caused second thoughts. In addition, the nation still did not address intractable problems that lay beyond civil rights, that is, problems of dependency—illiteracy, poverty, unemployment, urban decay, and slums.

THE SCANDAL MACHINE   Since before his first election in 1992, Bill Clinton had faced allegations of both sexual and financial scandal that grew into a relentless inquiry such as no previous president had ever before encountered. During his first term, Clinton was dogged by allegations of improper involvement in the Whitewater Development Company. In 1978, as governor of Arkansas, he had invested in a resort project on the White River in northern Arkansas. The project turned out to be a fraud and a failure, and the Clintons took a loss on their investment. An independent counsel investigated the allegations of improper Clinton involvement in Whitewater. While revealing that Hillary Clinton had handled some legal work for the Whitewater Development Company, the investigation did not uncover evidence that the Clintons were directly involved in the fraud.

In 1994, Kenneth Starr, a Republican, was appointed to serve as independent counsel in the Whitewater case. Although Starr had a reputation for fairness, many believed that his unwillingness to end the investigation and his former position in the Bush administration suggested a taint of partisanship. After nearly four years of expensive investigation, Starr found no criminal involvement by the Clintons, although a number of their close associates had been caught in the web and convicted of various charges, some related to Whitewater and some not.

By early 1998, some $50 million had been spent investigating Clinton and his administration. Besides Whitewater, these investigators looked into Paula Jones's allegations that Clinton had sexually harassed her while he was governor and she was a state employee in Arkansas. In the course of the investigation, it surfaced that the president may have had a sexual affair with a former White House intern, Monica Lewinsky, and may have pressed her to lie about it under oath. Polls suggested

The ongoing Whitewater investigation threatened to derail important initiatives as it occupied the attention of the president and Congress.

that a majority of the public did not care whether Clinton had had an affair with Lewinsky. This seemed to imply the public's contentment with the way things were going, especially the soaring economy.

But the tawdry scandal would not disappear. In August 1998, in the face of a possible subpoena from the independent counsel, President Clinton agreed to testify before the grand jury investigating the sexual allegations about him. He was the first president in history to do so. On August 17, with the nation anxiously awaiting the results, the federal grand jury watched on closed-circuit television while Clinton testified using a video hookup from the White House. During his six hours of closed-door testimony, the president recanted his earlier denials and acknowledged having had "inappropriate intimate physical contact" with White House intern Monica Lewinsky.

That evening Clinton delivered a four-minute televised address to the nation in which he admitted that he did have a "wrong" relationship with Lewinsky, but insisted he had done nothing illegal. "I know that my public comments and my silence about this matter gave a false impression. I misled people, including even my wife," Clinton said. "I deeply regret that."

Public reaction to Clinton's remarkable about-face was mixed. A majority of Americans expressed sympathy for the president because of his public humiliation and wanted the entire matter dropped. But polls also showed that Clinton's credibility had suffered a serious blow.

Meanwhile, Kenneth Starr continued his tenacious investigation. On September 9, 1998, he submitted to Congress a 445-page report and eighteen boxes of supporting material. The Starr Report found "substantial and creditable" evidence of presidential wrongdoing. Drawing upon such evidence, the Republican-controlled House Judiciary Committee voted 21 to 16 to recommend a full impeachment inquiry into perjury and obstruction of justice allegations against Clinton. On October 8, the House of Representatives voted 258 to 176 to begin a wide-ranging impeachment inquiry of President Clinton. Thirty-one Democrats joined Republicans in supporting the investigation.

On December 19, 1998, William Jefferson Clinton became the second president to be impeached by the House of Representatives. The House officially approved two articles of impeachment, charging Clinton with lying under oath to a federal grand jury and obstructing justice.

House Judiciary Committee representative Edward Pease puts his hands on his head during the vote to approve the third of four articles on the impeachment of President Clinton, December 1998.

The Senate trial of President Clinton began on January 7, 1999, with the swearing in of Chief Justice William Rehnquist to preside and the senators as jurors. Five weeks later, on February 12, the Senate acquitted Clinton. Rejecting the first charge of perjury, 10 Republicans and all 45 Democrats voted "not guilty." On the charge of obstruction of justice, the Senate split 50–50 (which meant acquittal, since 67 votes would have been needed to convict Clinton). In both instances, senators had a hard time interpreting Clinton's philandering as "high crimes and misdemeanors," the constitutional requirement for removal of a president. Clinton's supporters portrayed him as the victim of a puritanical special prosecutor and partisan conspiracy run amok. His critics lambasted him as a lecherous man without honor or integrity.

Both characterizations were incomplete. Politically astute, charismatic, and well-informed, Clinton had as much ability and potential as any president. Yet he was also shamelessly self-indulgent. The result was a scandalous presidency punctuated by dramatic achievements in welfare reform, economic growth, as well as foreign policy.

FOREIGN POLICY CHALLENGES   Like Woodrow Wilson, Lyndon Johnson, and Jimmy Carter before him, Clinton was a Democratic president who came into office determined to focus on the nation's domestic problems, only to find himself mired in foreign entanglements that had no easy resolution.

Clinton continued the Bush administration's intervention in Somalia, on the northeastern horn of Africa, where collapse of the government early in 1991 had left the country in anarchy, prey to tribal marauders. President Bush in 1992 had gained U.N. sanction for a military force led by American troops to relieve hunger and restore peace. In early 1993, U.S. troop levels peaked and began to shrink with the arrival of international forces. The Somalia operation proved successful at its primary mission, but it never solved the political problems that lay at the root of the starvation.

HAITI   The most successful departure in foreign policy for the Clinton administration during its first term came in Haiti. The island nation had emerged suddenly from a cycle of coups with a rebellion in the army rank and file and a democratic election in 1990, which brought to the top a popular priest, Jean-Bertrand Aristide. When a Haitian army general ousted Aristide, the United States immediately announced its intention to bring him back and welcomed the U.N. to the process.

With drawn-out negotiations leading nowhere, Clinton eventually moved in July 1994 to get a U.N. resolution authorizing force as a last resort. At this juncture, former president Jimmy Carter asked permission to negotiate. He went to Port-au-Prince and convinced the military leaders to quit by October 15. Aristide returned to Haiti and on March 31, 1995, the occupation was turned over to a U.N. force commanded by an American general.

THE MIDDLE EAST   Clinton also continued the Bush policy of sponsoring patient negotiations between Arabs and Israelis. A new development was the inclusion of the Palestine Liberation Organization (PLO) in the negotiations. In 1993 a draft agreement between Israel and the PLO resulted from secret talks between Israeli and Palestinian representatives in Oslo, Norway. This agreement provided for the restoration of Palestinian self-rule in the occupied Gaza Strip and in Jericho on the

President Clinton presides over the signing of the peace accord between Israel and the Palestinians with Israeli prime minister Yitzhak Rabin (left) *and PLO leader Yasir Arafat* (right), *September 1993.*

West Bank, in an exchange of land for peace as provided in U.N. Security Council resolutions. A formal signing occurred at the White House on September 13, 1993. With President Clinton presiding, Israeli prime minister Yitzhak Rabin and PLO leader Yasir Arafat exchanged handshakes, and their foreign ministers signed the agreement.

In the aftermath of this dramatic agreement, talks continued by fits and starts, interrupted by violent incidents provoked by extremist Jewish settlers and Palestinian factions. The Middle East peace process suffered a terrible blow in early November 1995 when Israeli prime minister Yitzhak Rabin was assassinated at a peace rally in Tel Aviv by an Israeli Jewish zealot who resented Rabin's efforts to negotiate with the Palestinians.

Some observers feared that the assassin had killed the peace process as well when seven months later conservative hard-liner Benjamin Netanyahu narrowly defeated the U.S.-backed Shimon Peres in the election for a new prime minister. Yet in October 1998, Clinton brought Arafat and Netanyahu together at a conference center in Wye Mills, Maryland, where they reached an agreement, the Wye River Accord. Under this agreement Israel would surrender land in return for security guarantees by the Palestinians. As hardliners attempted to derail the tenuous peace process, Netanyahu called elections early, and the Israeli public swept into power former general Ehud Barak, who promised to jump-start the peace process.

THE BALKANS   Clinton's foreign policy also addressed the transition in eastern Europe. With the collapse of Communist power, old ethnic and religious hatreds quickly resurfaced, often leading to violent clashes that were difficult to resolve quickly. When Yugoslavia imploded in 1991, fanatics and tyrants provoked ethnic conflict as four of its six republics seceded. Serb minorities, backed by Serbia itself, stirred up civil wars in Croatia and Bosnia. In Bosnia especially, the war involved "ethnic cleansing"—driving Muslims from their homes and towns. The United States faced sobering options: to ignore the butchery, to accept the refugees, to use American airpower, or to risk introducing ground troops. Clinton settled for dropping food and medical supplies to besieged Bosnians and sending planes to retaliate for attacks on places designated "safe havens" by the United Nations.

In 1995 American negotiators finally convinced the foreign ministers of Croatia, Bosnia, and Yugoslavia to agree to a comprehensive peace plan. Bosnia would remain a single nation but would be divided into two states: a Muslim-Croat federation controlling 51 percent of the territory and a Bosnian-Serb republic controlling the remaining 49 percent. Basic human rights would be restored and free elections held to appoint a parliament and joint presidency. To enforce the agreement, 60,000 NATO peacekeeping troops would be dispatched to Bosnia. A cease-fire went into effect in October 1995.

In 1998 the Balkan tinderbox flared up again, this time in the Yugoslav province of Kosovo. A rugged rural region the size of Connecticut, Kosovo has long been considered sacred ground to Christian Serbs. By 1989, however, over 90 percent of the 2 million Kosovars were ethnic Albanian Muslims. In that year, Yugoslav president Slobodan Milošević decided to reassert Serbian control over the province. He stripped Kosovo of its autonomy and established de facto martial law. When the Albanian Kosovars resisted and large numbers of Muslim men began to join the Kosovo Liberation Army, Serbian soldiers and state police ruthlessly suppressed them and launched another program of ethnic cleansing, burning Albanian villages, murdering males, raping females, and displacing hundreds of thousands of Muslim Albanian Kosovars.

On March 24, 1999, NATO, relying heavily upon American military resources and leadership, launched air strikes against Yugoslavia. "Ending this tragedy is a moral imperative," explained President Clinton. After seventy-two days of unrelenting bombardment, Slobodan Milošević sued for peace on NATO's terms. An agreement was reached on June 3, 1999. It was an unprecedented victory for air power and for NATO, which was celebrating its fiftieth birthday. Not a single allied pilot was killed in combat.

As the Albanian Kosovars started to return to Kosovo, however, large numbers of Serbs began to leave the province in fear of Muslim retribution, and some of them were killed. Members of the Kosovo Liberation Army stepped into the vacuum left by the departing Serbs and began to take control of the province.

THE ELECTION OF 2000

The election of 2000 revealed that American voters were split evenly along partisan lines. The two major-party candidates for president, Democratic vice-president Al Gore and Texas Republican governor

George W. Bush, the son of the former president, presented sharply contrasting views on the role of the federal government, tax cuts, and the best way to preserve Social Security and Medicare. Gore, a Tennessee native and Harvard graduate whose father had been a senator, favored an active federal government that would preserve Social Security and subsidize prescription-medicine expenses for the elderly. He criticized proposed Republican tax cuts for catering to the wealthy. An environmental activist, Gore reaffirmed his support for the Environmental Protection Agency and the Interior Department.

Bush, on the other hand, sought to transfer power from the federal government to the states, particularly regarding environmental and educational issues. He promoted more drilling for oil on federal lands, and he endorsed the use of vouchers (cash grants) to enable parents to send their children to private schools. In international affairs, Bush questioned the need to maintain American peacekeeping forces in Bosnia and the continuing expense of other global military commitments. By contrast, Gore promised to sustain America's military involvement and financial obligations around the world, favoring U.S. support for humanitarian and environmental concerns abroad.

Two independent candidates added zest to the campaign: conservative columnist Patrick Buchanan and liberal activist Ralph Nader. Buchanan focused his campaign on criticism of the North American Free Trade Agreement (NAFTA), while Nader concentrated on the corrupting effects of campaign finances.

In the end, the election was the one of the closest—and most controversial—in American history. The television networks initially reported that Gore had narrowly won the state of Florida and its decisive twenty-five electoral votes. Later in the evening, however, the networks reversed themselves and said that Florida was too close to call. In the chaotic early morning hours, the networks declared Bush the overall winner. Gore called Bush to concede, only to issue a retraction a short time later when the networks announced that Florida remained a toss-up. The final tally in Florida showed Bush with a razor-thin lead, but state law required a recount. For the first time in 125 years, the results of a presidential election remained in doubt for weeks after the voting.

As a painstaking hand count of presidential ballots proceeded in Florida, ugly disputes between the partisan camps erupted over misleading ballot designs and indeterminate punch-card votes. Days passed

A rally in Florida protesting the handling of ballots in the disputed 2000 election.

with no decision. Both parties pursued victory through legal maneuvers in the Florida courts and the U.S. Supreme Court; each side accused the other of trying to "steal" the election. The stalemated political drama continued for five weeks. Americans were by turn transfixed, appalled, and exhausted by the political wrangling among the courts, local electoral boards, and the partisans of both candidates. In the end, the Supreme Court on December 12, 2000, halted the statewide manual recounts in Florida. The case, known as *Bush v. Gore*, was quite controversial. A bare 5–4 majority ruled that any new recount would clash with existing Florida law.

Bush was deemed the winner in Florida by the slimmest of margins: 537 votes. Although Gore amassed a 540,000-vote lead nationwide, he lost the electoral college when he lost Florida. The 2000 election provided a revealing test of the resiliency of the American political system. The post-election drama was fractious and prolonged, but the general willingness of the public and the rival parties to seek a solution within the political system rather than outside it provided a valuable demonstration of the continuing vitality of America's constitutional tradition. The rule of law prevailed. Although Al Gore "strongly disagreed" with the Supreme Court's decision, he accepted it and asked that the nation rally around President-elect Bush and move forward: "Partisan rancor must be put aside."

Obscured by the riveting dispute over the presidential vote count in the 2000 election was the remarkable balance that had emerged in American politics. Not since the 1880s had the two major parties been so evenly divided. Republicans retained a slim lead in the voting for candidates in the House, 49.2 percent to 47.9 percent. The number of senators was split down the middle, 50–50. For all of the strident rhetoric in the campaign, both major-party presidential candidates, Bush and Gore, represented the moderate center of their parties when compared to the more ideological candidacies of Buchanan and Nader. Bush talked frequently about his commitment to "compassionate conservatism." Gore ran on a platform dedicated to "fiscal responsibility." Analysts stressed that cultural issues such as abortion and gun control, as well as the Clinton scandals, had become more important to many voters than economic concerns over taxes or defense spending. Differences in outlook between urban and rural voters, between cosmopolitan liberalism and heartland conservatism, were key indicators of voter preference. Some 71 percent of city residents voted for Gore, while only 26 percent chose Bush. Conversely, 59 percent of rural voters cast ballots for Bush, while only 37 percent opted for Gore. Gore won less than a third of votes in the South and lost his home state of Tennessee. Bush won the Mountain West and South while Gore dominated the Northeast, the West Coast, and the industrial Midwest. Women favored Gore over Bush by eleven percentage points, exactly the reverse of the male voters.

THE BUSH PRESIDENCY   George Walker Bush was the first president since John Quincy Adams to follow his father in the White House. He was also the fifth president to have been elected with fewer popular votes than his opponent. None of the others was reelected to a second term. During the 2000 election campaign, commentators criticized Bush's inexperience and lack of knowledge about world affairs. As president-elect, he addressed such concerns by appointing to his cabinet seasoned, highly respected public figures. His vice-president, Richard "Dick" Cheney, was a former congressman from Wyoming who had served as secretary of defense under the senior George Bush. Colin

Powell, the former army general and chairman of the Joint Chiefs of Staff, became the first African-American secretary of state. Donald Rumsfeld, former secretary of defense under Gerald Ford, returned to that position in the Bush administration. Bush named former Missouri senator John Ashcroft attorney-general.

Bush not only arrived in the White House amid the controversy of a disputed election; he also faced a sputtering economy and falling stock market. By the spring of 2000, the high-tech companies that had led the dizzying run-up on Wall Street during the 1990s had begun to stall. The claim that the "new economy" was somehow recession-proof turned out to be painfully naive. Greed fed by record profits and speculative excesses had led businesses, investors, and consumers to take dangerous risks; many leading corporate executives, it turned out, had engaged in unethical practices that undermined the economy. The Internet bubble burst in 2001. Stock values collapsed, sucking over $2 trillion from household wealth. Many of the dazzling new "dot-com" companies declared bankruptcy. Consumer confidence and capital investment plummeted with the stock market. By March 2001 the economy was in recession for the first time in over a decade. "These are times of shattered illusions," said economist Robert Samuelson. "The mythology of the 'New Economy' is receding before the reality of declining jobs and profits."

Bush's disputed election and the political balance in Congress did not prevent the new president from launching an ambitious legislative agenda. Confident that he could win over Democrats, he promised to provide "an explosion of legislation" within a few months of his inauguration. The top item on Bush's wish list was a $1.6 trillion tax cut intended to stimulate the sagging economy. "The people of America have been overcharged, and on their behalf I am here to ask for a refund," Bush said in presenting his proposal to Congress. The tax bill generated bitter debate in Congress, with Democrats arguing that the proposal heavily favored the rich and would squander the budget surplus. The Senate eventually trimmed the tax cut to $1.35 trillion over eleven years, and Bush signed it into law on June 7, 2001. White House celebrations of the tax-cut victory were deflated by the defection of Vermont senator James Jeffords, who changed his party affiliation from Republican to Independent—a major blow for the president, since it resulted in the Democrats gaining narrow control of the Senate, 50–49.

GLOBAL TERRORISM   With the collapse of the Soviet Union and the ending of the cold war, world politics grew ever more unstable during the 1990s. The basic premise of American foreign policy was "unipolar," to maintain the nation's "leadership" role in global affairs. As one Pentagon document declared, this required discouraging the "advanced industrial nations from challenging our leadership or . . . even aspiring to a larger regional or global role." Yet the very preponderance of American military power and economic influence created instability. A simmering mistrust of America's geopolitical dominance festered around the globe at the same time that traditional diplomatic relations were being fractured by growing competition among the world's major civilizations. Where ideologies such as capitalism and communism had earlier been the cause of conflict and tension in foreign relations, issues of religion, ethnicity, and clashing cultural values now divided peoples. "Most important," wrote Harvard University scholar Samuel Huntington, "the efforts of the West to promote its values of democracy and liberalism as universal values, to maintain its military predominance, and to advance its economic interests, engender countering responses from other civilizations."

As the twenty-first century unfolded, nations were no longer the sole actors on the stage of world politics. Instead, nebulous multinational groups inspired by religious fanaticism and anti-American rage began to use high-tech methods of terrorism to gain notoriety and exact vengeance. The very rootlessness of such zealots—their alienation from their native societies and ability to move around at will in order to infiltrate other countries and cultures—proved to be an ironic strength. Well-financed and well-armed terrorists flourished in the cracks of foundering nations such as Sudan, Somalia, Pakistan, Yemen, and Afghanistan. Throughout the 1990s, the United States fought a losing secret war against organized terrorism. The ineffectiveness of intelligence agencies in tracking the movements and intentions of militant extremists became tragically evident in 2001.

SEPTEMBER 11, 2001: A DAY OF INFAMY   At 8:45 A.M. on the morning of September 11, 2001, the world watched in horror as a hijacked commercial airliner slammed into the north tower of the World Trade Center in New York City. As people on the streets and in front of television screens watched the famous skyscraper burning, a second jumbo jet, traveling at 500 miles per hour, hit the south tower. The fuel-laden planes tore

gaping holes in the majestic buildings and turned them into infernos.
But worse was to come. The twin
towers, both 110 stories tall and filled
with thousands of employees, collapsed from the intense heat, one after the other. Surrounding buildings
also collapsed. The entire southern
end of Manhattan—"Ground Zero"—
became a hellish scene of twisted
steel, suffocating smoke, and wailing
sirens.

While the catastrophic drama in
New York was unfolding, a third hijacked plane crashed into the Pentagon in Washington, D.C. A fourth
airliner, probably headed for the
White House, missed its mark when
passengers—who had heard reports, via
cell phones, of the earlier hijackings—
assaulted the hijackers to prevent the
plane from being used as a weapon.

*Smoke pours out of the north tower
of the World Trade Center as the
south tower bursts into flames from
the impact of the second hijacked
airplane. About an hour later both
towers collapsed.*

During the struggle in the cockpit, the plane went out of control and
plummeted into the Pennsylvania countryside, killing all aboard.

The aerial jihad represented the most costly terrorist assault on the
United States in the nation's history. There were 266 passengers and
crew members aboard the crashed jets. More than 100 civilians and military personnel were killed at the Pentagon. The death toll at the World
Trade Center was over 2,800, many of them firefighters, police, and rescue workers. Hundreds of those killed were foreign nationals working in
the financial district; some eighty nations lost citizens in the attacks.
The terrorists also destroyed a powerful symbol of America: the tallest
buildings in the richest city in the most powerful nation on earth. The
World Trade Center towers were the central offices of global capitalism.

The terrorist attacks of September 11 created shock and chaos, grief
and anger. They also prompted an unprecedented display of national
unity and patriotism. People rushed to donate blood, food, and money.
Volunteers clogged military-recruiting centers. American flags were

everywhere in evidence. Citizens around the world held vigils at U.S. embassies. World leaders offered condolences and support. For the first time in its history, NATO invoked Article V of its charter, which states that an attack on any member will be considered an attack on all.

Within hours of the hijackings, officials identified the nineteen terrorists as members of Al Qaeda ("the base"), a well-financed worldwide network of Islamic extremists, led by a wealthy Saudi renegade, Osama bin Laden. Years before, bin Laden had declared holy war on America, Israel, and the Saudi monarchy. Bin Laden was linked to previous bombings of U.S. military barracks in Saudi Arabia, the U.S. embassies in Kenya and Tanzania, and the U.S.S. *Cole* at a port in Yemen, among others.

For several years, bin Laden had been using remote bases in war-torn Afghanistan as his personal refuge and terrorist training centers. Afghanistan's ruling Taliban regime collaborated with bin Laden's terrorist agenda. The Taliban was an ultraconservative Islamic faction that emerged in the mid-1990s following the forced withdrawal of Soviet troops from Afghanistan. Taliban leaders provided bin Laden with a safe haven in exchange for his financial and military support against the Northern Alliance, a coalition of rebel groups opposed to Taliban rule. Bin Laden sought to mobilize Muslim militants, energized by local causes, into a global army aimed at the West. As many as 20,000 militants from twenty different countries circulated through bin Laden's training camps. Most of the recruits received religious indoctrination and basic infantry training to prepare them to fight for the Taliban. A smaller group was selected by Al Qaeda for elite training to launch terrorist actions abroad. They learned how to organize secret cells around the world and engage in urban warfare, assassination, demolition, and sabotage.

BUSH DECLARES WAR ON TERRORISM The September 11 terrorist assault on America changed the course of a new presidency, a nation, and even the world. The economy, already in decline, went into free fall. Airlines laid off tens of thousands of employees. Insurance companies struggled to pay off an estimated $30 billion in claims resulting from the terrorist attacks. On Wall Street, markets plummeted in anticipation of a recession combined with a war against terrorism.

President Bush, who had never professed to know much about international relations or world affairs and had shown only disdain for Bill

Clinton's "multilateralism," suddenly was thrust onto center stage as commander-in-chief of a wounded nation eager for vengeful action. The new president, elected by the slimmest electoral margin since 1876, responded with unexpected poise, grit, and courage. He told the nation that the "deliberate and deadly attacks . . . were more than acts of terror. They were acts of war." In waging the "first war of the twenty-first century," the United States, he vowed, would use "all the tools and weapons at our disposal" to fight global terrorism. The crisis gave the untested, happy-go-lucky president a profound sense of purpose. "I will not yield. I will not rest. I will not relent in waging this struggle for freedom and security."

The Bush administration immediately forged an international coalition to fight terrorism worldwide. The coalition demanded that Afghanistan's Taliban government surrender the terrorists or risk military attack. In a televised address on September 20, Bush warned Americans that the war against terrorism would be a lengthy campaign, involving covert action as well as conventional military forces that would target not only terrorists but the groups and governments that abet them. "Every nation in every region," he said, "now has a decision to make: either you are with us or you are with the terrorists."

On October 7, after the Taliban defiantly refused to turn over bin Laden, the United States and its allies launched a ferocious military campaign—Operation Enduring Freedom—to find and punish terrorists or "those harboring terrorists." American and British cruise missiles and bombers destroyed Afghan military installations and Al Qaeda training camps. The coalition found key allies in neighboring Pakistan and in Afghanistan's Northern Alliance. American military commanders used new high-tech weapons—precision-guided bombs, spy satellites, and laser-targeting devices—that enabled U.S. forces to engage the enemy and occupy territory without risking soldiers.

The first major breakthrough of the military campaign came on November 9, when Northern Alliance fighters broke through Taliban defenses and seized the strategic city of Mazar-i-Sharif. The Alliance then advanced across northern Afghanistan. In the early hours of November 13, Alliance troops captured the Afghan capital of Kabul. Many residents viewed the American and Northern Alliance forces as liberators. They took to the streets in celebration, shaving off their beards and playing music, actions that had been banned under the repressive Taliban regime.

A young woman shows her face in public for the first time in five years after Northern Alliance troops capture Kabul, November 2001. The strict Sharia law enforced by the Taliban had required that Afghanistan's women be covered from head to foot.

On December 9, only two months after the American-led military campaign in Afghanistan had begun, the Taliban regime collapsed entirely. Thousands of Taliban soldiers had been killed while only a handful of American troops were lost, many of them in accidents rather than in combat. Al Qaeda fighters, once believed to number 3,000 in Afghanistan, were whittled down to less than 1,000. With the collapse of the Taliban, the war in Afghanistan devolved into a high-stakes manhunt. The Taliban leader, Mullah Muhammad Omar, remained at large, as did the elusive Osama bin Laden and an international network of terrorists operating in sixty countries. Destroying such a far-flung and elusive network would require the closing of bank accounts and safe houses, and the mass arrests of suspects.

In December 2001, Afghanistan's long-feuding factions, minus the Taliban, met in Bonn, Germany. They signed a U.N.-brokered peace agreement that created an interim government, led by Hamid Karzai, an exiled tribal leader who had re-entered the country in October to rally opposition to the Taliban. While the American-led coalition forces continued to track down Al Qaeda stragglers and search for bin Laden, the interim Afghan government faced the stern challenge of providing basic services and creating stability in a faction-ridden, war-torn country.

TERRORISM AT HOME   While the military campaign continued in Afghanistan, American government officials worried that terrorists might launch additional attacks in the United States with biological, chemical, or even nuclear weapons. To address the threat and to help restore public confidence, President Bush created a new federal agency, the Office of Homeland Security, and named Pennsylvania governor Tom Ridge as its first director. National Guard troops were dispatched to airports and public facilities around the country. Businesses, schools, hospitals, nuclear reactors, and public transportation systems tightened security. A new federal agency, the Transportation Security Administration, assumed responsibility for airport security. At the same time, President Bush and a supportive Congress created new legislation, known as the USA Patriot Act, which gave government agencies the right to eavesdrop on confidential conversations between prison inmates and their lawyers. It also permitted terrorist suspects to be tried in military courts. Such tribunals would have less stringent standards regarding the burden of proof than civilian courts: they could be held in secret; they allowed for the admission of hearsay and illegally obtained information as evidence; and they required only a two-thirds majority for conviction. Civil liberties groups voiced grave concerns that the measures jeopardized constitutional rights and protections. But the crisis atmosphere after September 11 caused most people to support such extraordinary steps.

No sooner had the Homeland Security agency been created than a new assault on American security occurred when anthrax-contaminated mail began to arrive at major newspapers and television networks. During October 2001, several people died from exposure to the powdery white spores. Congressional offices were closed after thirty employees tested positive for anthrax exposure from a letter sent to Tom Daschle, the Senate majority leader. A few days later, two Washington, D.C., postal workers died of anthrax inhalation. A New York hospital worker then became the first person not working in the media or the postal service to die of the virus.

Many Americans were seized with panic. Hoaxes and false alarms aggravated the fear and confusion. President Bush urged the public to remain calm amid the chaos, and public health officials were quick to minimize the anthrax threat. Within a few weeks the scare subsided, although no arrests were made.

MIDDLE EAST TURMOIL   The Middle East, long a tinderbox of tension, again exploded into violence in the new century. Seven years of relative calm ended when peace talks in Oslo, Norway, collapsed in 2000. Disputes over the fate of Jerusalem, the holy city claimed by Jews, Christians, and Muslims, undermined any new accords between the Israelis and Palestinians. Frustrated by the collapse of negotiations, Palestinians declared an *intifada,* or uprising, in October 2000. Street demonstrations in the West Bank and Gaza Strip soon gave way to an unrelenting series of suicide bombing attacks against Israeli soldiers and civilians. Israeli troops retaliated. Hundreds of casualties resulted, many of them children.

In February 2001, Israeli voters, themselves angry over the rising level of violence, elected Ariel Sharon, a militant conservative, as their new prime minister. Sharon vowed that that there would be no negotiating with the Palestinians as long as their *intifada* continued. Sharon's government responded to attacks with air strikes and armored assaults on Palestinian-controlled areas. Israeli agents also assassinated leaders of Hamas and Islamic Jihad, two Palestinian terrorist groups.

The new Bush administration initially withdrew from active involvement in Middle East diplomacy. But as the violence mounted, Secretary of State Colin Powell dispatched two envoys to the region at the end of 2001. Their diplomatic efforts, however, proved impotent. In December 2001, after a series of suicide attacks in Israel and attacks on Jewish settlers in the Gaza Strip and the West Bank, some of which were conducted by militia groups allied with Yasir Arafat, head of the Palestinian Authority, Prime Minister Sharon declared that Arafat was "irrelevant." The escalating violence in the Middle East threatened to unravel the fragile antiterrorism coalition that the Bush administration had organized.

THE BUSH DOCTRINE   In the fall of 2002 President Bush unveiled a new national security doctrine that marked a distinct shift from previous administrations. Containment and deterrence had been the guiding strategic concepts of the cold war years. Beginning with Harry Truman in 1947, American presidents had sought to "contain" communism and keep it from spreading by propping up nations around the borders of Soviet-controlled Europe. Likewise, American administrations had sought to "deter" the Soviets and Chinese Communists from overt military action by promising "massive retaliation." The threat of nuclear war and mutual destruction kept the major nations in check during the cold war era. In the war against terrorism, however, such cold war policies were bankrupt. Fanatics willing to become suicide bombers would not be deterred. The growing menace posed by "shadowy networks" of terrorist groups and unstable rogue nations with weapons of mass destruction, President Bush declared, required a new doctrine of preemptive military action. "If we wait for threats to fully materialize," he explained, "we will have waited too long. In the world we have entered, the only path to safety is the path of action. And this nation will act."

THE SECOND GULF WAR   During 2002 and 2003, Iraq emerged as the focus of the Bush administration's new policy of "preemptive" military action to prevent terrorism and destroy weapons of mass destruction. Following the Gulf War of 1991, U.N. inspectors were sent to Iraq to search for such biological and chemical weapons. Iraqi leader Saddam Hussein never accepted the legitimacy of such efforts, and in the fall of 1998 he ordered the U.N. inspectors to leave. Thereafter, American officials grew increasingly concerned about Iraq's possession of biological and chemical weapons and its support of global terrorism. In September

President George W. Bush addresses soldiers who were among the first to be deployed abroad after the September 11 terrorist attacks, July 2002.

2002 President Bush urged the U.N. to confront the "grave and gathering danger"posed by Hussein's dictatorial regime in Iraq. He warned that the United States would act alone if the U.N. did not respond. In October, Congress approved a resolution proposed by Bush authorizing him to use "all means that he determines to be appropriate, including force" to defend the United States against the threat posed by Iraq. On November 8, the U.N. Security Council passed Resolution 1441 ordering Iraq to disarm immediately or face "serious consequences." Faced with growing international pressure, Hussein grudgingly allowed U.N. weapons inspectors to return to Iraq "without conditions."

As the U.N. inspectors resumed their efforts, however, the Iraqi government continued its partial cooperation and stalling tactics. President Bush, insistent that "time is running out," gained the support of Great Britain and Spain in proposing a new U.N. resolution that would authorize military action to ensure that Iraq eliminated its weapons of mass destruction. "The United States," Bush insisted, "will not permit the world's most dangerous regimes to threaten us with the world's most destructive weapons."

During early 2003, American and British military forces began to assemble in the Persian Gulf. France, China, Germany, and Russia opposed the American-led effort to use military force against Iraq, arguing that the U.N. inspectors should be given more time to complete their task. Bush responded that more time for inspections would be like a "rerun of a bad movie."

During the early months of 2003, Secretary of State Colin Powell's efforts to marshal international support for the forceful American stance proved fruitless. On March 17, the United States, Great Britain, and Spain withdrew their proposed Security Council resolution, announcing that diplomatic efforts had failed. President Bush issued an ultimatum to Saddam Hussein: he and his sons must leave Iraq within 48 hours or face a U.S.-led invasion. Hussein refused. Two days later, on March 19, American and British forces supported by what George Bush called the "coalition of the willing," attacked Iraq.

The invasion of Iraq ignited intense criticism both at home and abroad. Massive demonstrations erupted around the world, especially in Arab countries and western Europe. What the Bush administration described as "preemptive" action to destroy Iraq's weapons of mass destruction and relieve the Iraqis of Saddam Hussein's brutal tyranny struck others as an imperialistic effort to control Iraqi oil and recreate an Arab country in its own image.

American military planners sought to remove Saddam Hussein's regime through a massive "shock and awe" bombing campaign followed closely by a fast-moving ground invasion. After two weeks of intense fighting, coalition forces occupied Baghdad and Basra, the two largest cities in Iraq. As the regime of Saddam Hussein crumbled, it remained to be seen whether the "preemptive action" strategy of the Bush administration was resulting in a more secure world. In the process of attacking a dangerous dictator the United States and Great Britain had further alienated many Arabs. Terrorism remained a constant global threat. In addition, the U.N. Security Council remained fractured by the dispute over Iraq and growing concerns among France, Germany, and Russia that the United States was developing hegemonic power.

The Bush Doctrine made sense to many Americans who were traumatized by the threat of global terrorism. But to many outside the United States it reinforced fears of American arrogance, interventionism, and unilateralism. As the French foreign minister explained, "We cannot accept either a politically unipolar world, nor a culturally uniform world, nor the unilateralism of a single hyperpower." The ultimate test of the Bush Doctrine would be whether the United States could convert its overwhelming global power into an international consensus for dealing with terrorism and the proliferation of weapons of mass destruction.

FURTHER READING

On George H. W. Bush's presidency, see Ryan J. Barilleaux and Mary E. Stuckey's *Leadership and the Bush Presidency: Prudence or Drift in an Era of Change* (1992), Charles Tiefer's *The Semi-Sovereign Presidency: The Bush Administration's Strategy for Governing without Congress* (1994). Among the journalistic accounts of the presidential election of 1992, the best narrative is Jack Germond and Jules Witcover's *Mad as Hell: Revolt at the Ballot Box, 1992* (1993). The best scholarly study is Theodore J. Lowi and Benjamin Ginsberg's *Democrats Return to Power: Politics and Policy in the Clinton Era* (1994).

Analysis of the Clinton years can be found in Joe Klein's *The Natural: The Misunderstood Presidency of Bill Clinton* (2002). Clinton's impeachment is assessed in Peter Baker's *The Breach: Inside the Impeachment and Trial of William Clinton* (2000).

On social and cultural problems and issues of the times, a good account is Haynes Johnson's *Divided We Fall: Gambling with History in the Nineties* (1994), based on street interviews around the country during 1992. Collections of magazine and newspaper articles are in John Leo's *Two Steps Ahead of the Thought Police* (1994), Molly Ivins's *Nothin' But Good Times Ahead* (1993), and George F. Will's *The Leveling Wind: Politics, the Culture, and Other News, 1990–1994* (1994). The onset and growth of the AIDS epidemic are traced in *And the Band Played On: Politics, People, and the AIDS Epidemic* (1987) by Randy Shilts.

Aspects of fundamentalist and apocalyptic movements are the subject of Paul L. Boyer's *When Time Shall Be No More: Prophecy and Belief in Modern American Culture* (1992), George M. Marsden's *Understanding Fundamentalism and Evangelicalism* (1991), and Ralph Reed's *Politically Incorrect: The Emerging Faith Factor in American Politics* (1994).

On the rising stress within the workplace, see Jill Fraser's *White-Collar Sweatshop: The Deterioration of Work and Its Reward in Corporate America* (2001). Aspects of corporate restructuring and downsizing are the subject of Bennett Harrison's *Lean and Mean: The Changing Landscape of Corporate Power in the Age of Flexibility* (1994). The story of the Whitewater affair is the subject of Martin L. Gross's *The Great Whitewater Fiasco: An American Tale of Money, Power, and Politics* (1994).

For further treatment of the end of the cold war, see Michael R. Beschloss's *At the Highest Levels: The Inside Story of the End of the Cold War* (1993) and Richard Crockatt's *The Fifty Years War: The United States and the Soviet Union in World Politics, 1941–1991* (1995). On the Persian Gulf conflict, see Lester H. Brune's *America and the Iraqi Crisis, 1990–1992: Origins and Aftermath* (1993).

The disputed 2000 presidential election is the focus of Jeffrey Toobin's *Too Close to Call: The Thirty-Six Day Battle to Decide the 2000 Election* (2002). On the attacks of September 11, 2001, and their aftermath, see *The Age of Terror and the World after September 11*, edited by Strobe Talbott and Nayan Chanda (2002).

GLOSSARY

Agricultural Adjustment Act (1933) New Deal legislation that established the Agricultural Adjustment Administration (AAA) to improve agricultural prices by limiting market supplies; declared unconstitutional in *United States* v. *Butler* (1936).

Alamo, Battle of the Siege in the Texas War for Independence, 1836, in which the San Antonio mission fell to the Mexicans, and Davy Crockett and Jim Bowie died.

Alexander **v.** *Holmes County Board of Education* (1969) Case fifteen years after the *Brown* decision in which the U.S. Supreme Court ordered an immediate end to segregation in public schools.

Alien and Sedition Acts (1798) Four measures passed during the undeclared war with France that limited the freedoms of speech and press and restricted the liberty of noncitizens.

America First Committee Largely midwestern isolationist organization supported by many prominent citizens, 1940–41.

American Anti-Slavery Society National abolitionist organization founded in 1833 by New York philanthropists Arthur and Lewis Tappan, propagandist Theodore Dwight Weld, and others.

American Colonization Society Organized in 1816 to encourage colonization of free blacks to Africa; West African nation of Liberia founded in 1822 to serve as a homeland for them.

American Federation of Labor Founded in 1881 as a federation of trade unions, the AFL under president Samuel Gompers successfully pushed for the eight-hour workday.

American Protective Association Nativist, anti-Catholic secret society founded in Iowa in 1887 and active until the end of the century.

American System Program of internal improvements and protective tariffs promoted by Speaker of the House Henry Clay in his presidential campaign of 1824; his proposals formed the core of Whig ideology in the 1830s and 1840s.

Antietam, Battle of (Battle of Sharpsburg) One of the bloodiest battles of the Civil War, fought to a standoff on September 17, 1862, in western Maryland.

Antifederalists Forerunners of Thomas Jefferson's Democratic-Republican party; opposed the Constitution as a limitation on individual and states' rights, which led to the addition of a Bill of Rights to the document.

Appomattox Court House, Virginia Site of the surrender of Confederate general Robert E. Lee to Union general Ulysses S. Grant on April 9, 1865, marking the end of the Civil War.

Army-McCarthy hearings Televised U.S. Senate hearings in 1954 on Senator Joseph McCarthy's charges of disloyalty in the Army; his tactics contributed to his censure by the Senate.

Atlanta Compromise Speech to the Cotton States and International Exposition in 1895 by educator Booker T. Washington, the leading black spokesman of the day; black scholar W. E. B. Du Bois gave the speech its derisive name and criticized Washington for encouraging blacks to accommodate segregation and disenfranchisement.

Atlantic Charter Issued August 12, 1941, following meetings in Newfoundland between President Franklin D. Roosevelt and British prime minister Winston Churchill, the charter signaled the allies' cooperation and stated their war aims.

Atomic Energy Commission Created in 1946 to supervise peacetime uses of atomic energy.

Axis powers In World War II, the nations of Germany, Italy, and Japan.

Aztec Mesoamerican people who were conquered by the Spanish under Hernando Cortés, 1519–28.

Baby boom Markedly higher birth rate in the years following World War II; led to the biggest demographic "bubble" in American history.

Bacon's Rebellion Unsuccessful 1676 revolt led by planter Nathaniel Bacon against Virginia governor William Berkeley's administration because it had failed to protect settlers from Indian raids.

Bakke v. *Board of Regents of California* (1978) Case in which the U.S. Supreme Court ruled against the California university system's use of racial quotas in admissions.

Balance of trade Ratio of imports to exports.

Bank of the United States Proposed by the first secretary of the treasury, Alexander Hamilton, the bank opened in 1791 and operated until 1811 to issue a uniform currency, make business loans, and collect tax monies. The Second Bank of the United States was chartered in 1816 but was not renewed by President Andrew Jackson twenty years later.

Barbary pirates Plundering pirates off the Mediterranean coast of Africa; President Thomas Jefferson's refusal to pay them tribute to protect American ships sparked an undeclared naval war with North African nations, 1801–1805.

Barbed wire First practical fencing material for the Great Plains was invented in 1873 and rapidly spelled the end of the open range.

Battle of the Currents Conflict in the late 1880s between inventors Thomas Edison and George Westinghouse over direct versus alternating electric current; Westinghouse's alternating current (AC), the winner, allowed electricity to travel over long distances.

Bay of Pigs Invasion Hoping to inspire a revolt against Fidel Castro, the CIA sent 1,500 Cuban exiles to invade their homeland on April 17, 1961, but the mission was a spectacular failure.

Bill of Rights First ten amendments to the U.S. Constitution, adopted in 1791 to guarantee individual rights and to help secure ratification of the Constitution by the states.

Black Codes (1865–66) Laws passed in southern states to restrict the rights of former slaves; to combat the codes, Congress passed the Civil Rights Act of 1866 and the Fourteenth Amendment and set up military governments in southern states that refused to ratify the amendment.

Black Power Post-1966 rallying cry of a more militant civil rights movement.

Bland-Allison Act (1878) Passed over President Rutherford B. Hayes's veto, the inflationary measure authorized the purchase each month of 2 to 4 million dollars' worth of silver for coinage.

"Bleeding" Kansas Violence between pro- and antislavery settlers in the Kansas Territory, 1856.

Bloody shirt, Waving the Republican references to Reconstruction-era violence in the South, used effectively in northern political campaigns against Democrats.

Bonus Expeditionary Force Thousands of World War I veterans, who insisted on immediate payment of their bonus certificates, marched on Washington in 1932; violence ensued when President Herbert Hoover ordered their tent villages cleared.

Boston Massacre Clash between British soldiers and a Boston mob, March 5, 1770, in which five colonists were killed.

Boston Tea Party On December 16, 1773, the Sons of Liberty, dressed as Indians, dumped hundreds of chests of tea into Boston harbor to protest the Tea Act of 1773, under which the British exported to the colonies millions of pounds of cheap—but still taxed—tea, thereby undercutting the price of smuggled tea and forcing payment of the tea duty.

Boxer Rebellion Chinese nationalist protest against Western commercial domination and cultural influence, 1900; a coalition of American, European, and Japanese forces put down the rebellion and reclaimed captured embassies in Peking (Beijing) within the year.

Brain trust Group of advisers—many of them academics—that Franklin D. Roosevelt assembled to recommend New Deal policies during the early months of his presidency.

Branch Davidians Religious cult that lived communally near Waco, Texas, and was involved in a fiery 1993 confrontation with federal authorities in which dozens of cult members died.

Brook Farm Transcendentalist commune in West Roxbury, Massachusetts, populated from 1841 to 1847 principally by writers (Nathaniel Hawthorne, for one) and other intellectuals.

***Brown v. Board of Education of Topeka* (1954)** U.S. Supreme Court decision that struck down racial segregation in public education and declared "separate but equal" unconstitutional.

Budget and Accounting Act of 1921 Created the Bureau of the Budget and the General Accounting Office.

Bull Run, Battles of (First and Second Manassas) First land engagement of the Civil War took place on July 21, 1861, at Manassas Junction, Virginia, at which surprised Union troops quickly retreated; one year later, on August 29–30, Confederates captured the federal supply depot and forced Union troops back to Washington.

Bunker Hill, Battle of First major battle of the Revolutionary War; it actually took place at nearby Breed's Hill, Massachusetts, on June 17, 1775.

"Burned-Over District" Area of western New York strongly influenced by the revivalist fervor of the Second Great Awakening; Disciples of Christ and Mormons are among the many sects that trace their roots to the phenomenon.

Burr conspiracy Scheme by Vice-President Aaron Burr to lead the secession of the Louisiana Territory from the United States; captured in 1807 and charged with treason, Burr was acquitted by the U.S. Supreme Court.

Bush v. *Gore* **(2000)** U.S. Supreme Court case that determined the winner of the disputed 2000 presidential election.

Calhoun Resolutions In making the proslavery response to the Wilmot Proviso, Senator John C. Calhoun argued that barring slavery in Mexican acquisitions would violate the Fifth Amendment to the Constitution by depriving slaveholding settlers of their property.

Calvinism Doctrine of predestination expounded by Swiss theologian John Calvin in 1536; influenced the Puritan, Presbyterian, German and Dutch Reformed, and Huguenot churches in the colonies.

Camp David Accords Peace agreement between Israeli prime minister Menachem Begin and Egyptian president Anwar Sadat, brokered by President Jimmy Carter in 1978.

Carpetbaggers Northern emigrants who participated in the Republican governments of the Reconstruction South.

Chancellorsville, Battle of Confederate general Robert E. Lee won his last major victory and General "Stonewall" Jackson died in this Civil War battle in northern Virginia on May 1–4, 1863.

Chattanooga, Battle of Union victory in eastern Tennessee on November 23–25, 1863; gave the North control of important rail lines and cleared the way for General William T. Sherman's march into Georgia.

Chinese Exclusion Act (1882) Halted Chinese immigration to the United States.

Civil Rights Act of 1866 Along with the Fourteenth Amendment, guaranteed the rights of citizenship to freedmen.

Civil Rights Act of 1957 First federal civil rights law since Reconstruction; established the Civil Rights Commission and the Civil Rights Division of the Department of Justice.

Civil Rights Act of 1964 Outlawed discrimination in public accommodations and employment.

Clipper ships Superior oceangoing sailing ships of the 1840s to 1860s that cut travel time in half; the clipper ship route around Cape Horn was the fastest way to travel between the coasts of the United States.

Closed shop Hiring requirement that all workers in a business must be union members.

Coercive Acts/Intolerable Acts (1774) Four parliamentary measures in reaction to the Boston Tea Party that forced payment for the tea, disallowed colonial trials of British soldiers, forced their quartering in private homes, and set up a military government.

Cold war Term for tensions, 1945–89, between the Soviet Union and the United States, the two major world powers after World War II.

Commonwealth v. Hunt (1842) Landmark ruling of the Massachusetts supreme court establishing the legality of labor unions.

Compromise of 1850 Complex compromise mediated by Senator Henry Clay that headed off southern secession over California statehood; to appease the South it included a stronger fugitive slave law and delayed determination of the slave status of the New Mexico and Utah territories.

Compromise of 1877 Deal made by a special congressional commission on March 2, 1877, to resolve the disputed presidential election of 1876; Republican Rutherford B. Hayes, who had lost the popular vote, was declared the winner in exchange for the withdrawal of federal troops from the South, marking the end of Reconstruction.

Congress of Industrial Organizations (CIO) Umbrella organization of semiskilled industrial unions, formed in 1935 as the Committee for Industrial Organization and renamed in 1938.

Congress of Racial Equality (CORE) Civil rights organization started in 1944 and best known for its "freedom rides," bus journeys challenging racial segregation in the South in 1961.

Conspicuous consumption Phrase referring to extravagant spending to raise social standing, coined by Thorstein Veblen in *The Theory of the Leisure Class* (1899).

Constitutional Convention Meeting in Philadelphia, May 25–September 17, 1787, of representatives from twelve colonies—excepting Rhode Island—to revise the existing Articles of Confederation; convention soon resolved to produce an entirely new constitution.

Containment General U.S. strategy in the cold war that called for containing Soviet expansion; originally devised in 1947 by U.S. diplomat George F. Kennan.

Continental Army Army authorized by the Continental Congress, 1775–84, to fight the British; commanded by General George Washington.

Continental Congress Representatives of a loose confederation of colonies met first in Philadelphia in 1774 to formulate actions against British policies; the Second Continental Congress (1775–89) conducted the war and adopted the Declaration of Independence and the Articles of Confederation.

Convict leasing System developed in the post–Civil War South that generated income for the states and satisfied planters' need for cheap labor by renting prisoners out; the convicts, however, were often treated poorly.

Copperheads Northerners opposed to the Civil War.

Coral Sea, Battle of the Fought on May 7–8, 1942, near the eastern coast of Australia, it was the first U.S. naval victory over Japan in World War II.

Cotton gin Invented by Eli Whitney in 1793, the machine separated cotton seed from cotton fiber, speeding cotton processing and making profitable the cultivation of the more hardy, but difficult to clean, short-staple cotton; led directly to the dramatic nineteenth-century expansion of slavery in the South.

Counterculture "Hippie" youth culture of the 1960s, which rejected the values of the dominant culture in favor of illicit drugs, communes, free sex, and rock music.

Court-packing plan President Franklin D. Roosevelt's failed 1937 attempt to increase the number of U.S. Supreme Court justices from nine to fifteen in order to save his Second New Deal programs from constitutional challenges.

Credit Mobilier scandal Millions of dollars in overcharges for building the Union Pacific Railroad were exposed; high officials of the Ulysses S. Grant administration were implicated but never charged.

Cuban missile crisis Caused when the United States discovered Soviet offensive missile sites in Cuba in October 1962; the U.S.-Soviet confrontation was the cold war's closest brush with nuclear war.

Crop-lien system Merchants extended credit to tenants based on their future crops, but high interest rates and the uncertainties of farming often led to inescapable debts (debt peonage).

D-Day June 6, 1944, when an Allied amphibious assault landed on the Normandy coast and established a foothold in Europe from which Hitler's defenses could not recover.

Dartmouth College v. *Woodward* (1819) U.S. Supreme Court upheld the original charter of the college against New Hampshire's attempt to alter the board of trustees; set precedent of support of contracts against state interference.

Declaration of Independence Document adopted on July 4, 1776, that made the break with Britain official; drafted by a committee of the Second Continental Congress including principal writer Thomas Jefferson.

Deism Enlightenment thought applied to religion; emphasized reason, morality, and natural law.

Department of Homeland Security Created to coordinate federal antiterrorist activity following the 2001 terrorist attacks on the World Trade Center and Pentagon.

Depression of 1893 Worst depression of the century, set off by a railroad failure, too much speculation on Wall Street, and low agricultural prices.

Dixiecrats Deep South delegates who walked out of the 1948 Democratic National Convention in protest of the party's support for civil rights legislation and later formed the States' Rights (Dixiecrat) party, which nominated Strom Thurmond of South Carolina for president.

Dominion of New England Consolidation into a single colony of the New England colonies—and later New York and New Jersey—by royal governor Edmund Andros in 1686; dominion reverted to individual colonial governments three years later.

Donner Party Forty-seven surviving members of a group of migrants to California were forced to resort to cannibalism to survive a brutal winter trapped in the Sierra Nevadas, 1846–47; highest death toll of any group traveling the Overland Trail.

Dred Scott v. Sandford (1857) U.S. Supreme Court decision in which Chief Justice Roger B. Taney ruled that slaves could not sue for freedom and that Congress could not prohibit slavery in the territories, on the grounds that such a prohibition would violate the Fifth Amendment rights of slaveholders.

Due-process clause Clause in the Fifth and the Fourteenth amendments to the U.S. Constitution guaranteeing that states could not "deprive any person of life, liberty, or property, without due process of law."

Dust Bowl Great Plains counties where millions of tons of topsoil were blown away from parched farmland in the 1930s; massive migration of farm families followed.

Eighteenth Amendment (1919) Prohibition amendment that made illegal the manufacture, sale, or transportation of alcoholic beverages.

Ellis Island Reception center in New York Harbor through which most European immigrants to America were processed from 1892 to 1954.

Emancipation Proclamation (1863) President Abraham Lincoln issued a preliminary proclamation on September 22, 1862, freeing the slaves in the Confederate states as of January 1, 1863, the date of the final proclamation.

Embargo Act of 1807 Attempt to exert economic pressure instead of waging war in reaction to continued British impressment of American sailors; smugglers easily circumvented the embargo, and it was repealed two years later.

Emergency Banking Relief Act (1933) First New Deal measure that provided for reopening the banks under strict conditions and took the United States off the gold standard.

Emergency Immigration Act of 1921 Limited U.S. immigration to 3 percent of each foreign-born nationality in the 1910 census; three years later Congress restricted immigration even further.

Encomienda System under which officers of the Spanish conquistadores gained ownership of Indian land.

ENIAC Electronic Numerical Integrator and Computer, built in 1944, the early, cumbersome ancestor of the modern computer.

Enlightenment Revolution in thought begun in the seventeenth century that emphasized reason and science over the authority of traditional religion.

Enola Gay American B-29 bomber that dropped the atomic bomb on Hiroshima, Japan, on August 6, 1945.

Environmental Protection Agency (EPA) Created in 1970 during the first administration of President Richard M. Nixon to oversee federal pollution control efforts.

Equal Rights Amendment Amendment to guarantee equal rights for women, introduced in 1923 but not passed by Congress until 1972; it failed to be ratified by the states.

Era of Good Feelings Contemporary characterization of the administration of popular Democratic-Republican president James Monroe, 1817–25.

Erie Canal Most important and profitable of the barge canals of the 1820s and 1830s; stretched from Buffalo to Albany, New York, connecting the Great Lakes to the East Coast and making New York City the nation's largest port.

Espionage and Sedition Acts (1917–18) Limited criticism of government leaders and policies by imposing fines and prison terms on those who acted out in opposition to the First World War; the most repressive measures passed up to that time.

Fair Deal Domestic reform proposals of the second Truman administration (1949–53); included civil rights legislation and repeal of the Taft-Hartley Act, but only extensions of some New Deal programs were enacted.

Fair Employment Practices Commission Created in 1941 by executive order, the FEPC sought to eliminate racial discrimination in jobs; it possessed little power but represented a step toward civil rights for African Americans.

Family and Medical Leave Act (1993) Allowed certain workers to take twelve weeks of unpaid leave each year for family health problems, including birth or adoption of a child.

Farmers' Alliance Two separate organizations (Northwestern and Southern) of the 1880s and 1890s that took the place of the Grange, worked for similar causes, and attracted landless, as well as landed, farmers to their membership.

Federal Trade Commission Act (1914) Established the Federal Trade Commission to enforce existing antitrust laws that prohibited business combinations in restraint of trade.

The Federalist Collection of eighty-five essays that appeared in the New York press in 1787–88 in support of the Constitution; written by Alexander Hamilton, James Madison, and John Jay but published under the pseudonym "Publius."

Federalist party One of the two first national political parties, it favored a strong central government.

Fence-Cutters' War Violent conflict in Texas, 1883–84, between large and small cattle ranchers over access to grazing land.

"Fifty-four forty or fight" Democratic campaign slogan in the presidential election of 1844, urging that the northern border of Oregon be fixed at 54°40′ north latitude.

Fletcher v. Peck (1810) U.S. Supreme Court decision in which Chief Justice John Marshall upheld the initial fraudulent sale contracts in the Yazoo Fraud cases; Congress paid $4.2 million to the original speculators in 1814.

Fort Laramie Treaty (1851) Restricted the Plains Indians from using the Overland Trail and permitted the building of government forts.

Fort McHenry Fort in Baltimore Harbor unsuccessfully bombarded by the British in September 1814; Francis Scott Key, a witness to the battle, was moved to write the words to "The Star-Spangled Banner."

Fort Sumter First battle of the Civil War, in which the federal fort in Charleston (South Carolina) Harbor was captured by the Confederates on April 14, 1861, after two days of shelling.

"Forty-niners" Speculators who went to northern California following the discovery of gold in 1848; the first of several years of large-scale migration was 1849.

Fourteen Points President Woodrow Wilson's 1918 plan for peace after World War I; at the Versailles peace conference, however, he failed to incorporate all of the points into the treaty.

Fourteenth Amendment (1868) Guaranteed rights of citizenship to former slaves, in words similar to those of the Civil Rights Act of 1866.

Franchise The right to vote.

"Free person of color" Negro or mulatto person not held in slavery; immediately before the Civil War, there were nearly a half million in the United States, split almost evenly between North and South.

Free Soil party Formed in 1848 to oppose slavery in the territory acquired in the Mexican War; nominated Martin Van Buren for president in 1848, but by 1854 most of the party's members had joined the Republican party.

Free Speech Movement Founded in 1964 at the University of California at Berkeley by student radicals protesting restrictions on their right to demonstrate.

Freedmen's Bureau Reconstruction agency established in 1865 to protect the legal rights of former slaves and to assist with their education, jobs, health care, and landowning.

French and Indian War Known in Europe as the Seven Years' War, the last (1755–63) of four colonial wars fought between England and France for control of North America east of the Mississippi River.

Fugitive Slave Act of 1850 Gave federal government authority in cases involving runaway slaves; so much more punitive and prejudiced in favor of slaveholders than the 1793 Fugitive Slave Act had been that Harriet Beecher Stowe was inspired to write *Uncle Tom's Cabin* in protest; the new law was part of the Compromise of 1850, included to appease the South over the admission of California as a free state.

Fundamentalism Anti-modernist Protestant movement started in the early twentieth century that proclaimed the literal truth of the Bible; the name came from *The Fundamentals*, published by conservative leaders.

Gadsden Purchase (1853) Thirty thousand square miles in present-day Arizona and New Mexico bought by Congress from Mexico primarily for the Southern Pacific Railroad's transcontinental route.

Gentlemen's Agreement (1907) United States would not exclude Japanese immigrants if Japan would voluntarily limit the number of immigrants coming to the United States.

Gettysburg, Battle of Fought in southern Pennsylvania, July 1–3, 1863; the Confederate defeat and the simultaneous loss at Vicksburg spelled the end of the South's chances in the Civil War.

Gibbons v. *Ogden* (1824) U.S. Supreme Court decision reinforcing the "commerce clause" (the federal government's right to regulate interstate commerce) of the Constitution; Chief Justice John Marshall ruled against the State of New York's granting of steamboat monopolies.

Gideon v. *Wainwright* (1963) U.S. Supreme Court decision guaranteeing legal counsel for indigent felony defendants.

The Gilded Age Mark Twain and Charles Dudley Warner's 1873 novel, the title of which became the popular name for the period from the end of the Civil War to the turn of the century.

Glass-Owen Federal Reserve Act (1913) Created a Federal Reserve System of regional banks and a Federal Reserve Board to stabilize the economy by regulating the supply of currency and controlling credit.

Glass-Steagall Act (Banking Act of 1933) Established the Federal Deposit Insurance Corporation and included banking reforms, some designed to control speculation. A banking act of the Hoover administration, passed in 1932 and also known as the Glass-Steagall Act, was designed to expand credit.

Good Neighbor Policy Proclaimed by President Franklin D. Roosevelt in his first inaugural address in 1933, it sought improved diplomatic relations between the United States and its Latin American neighbors.

Grandfather clause Loophole created by southern disfranchising legislatures of the 1890s for illiterate white males whose grandfathers had been eligible to vote in 1867.

Granger movement Political movement that grew out of the Patrons of Husbandry, an educational and social organization for farmers founded in 1867; the Grange had its greatest success in the Midwest of the 1870s, lobbying for government control of railroad and grain elevator rates and establishing farmers' cooperatives.

Great Awakening Fervent religious revival movement in the 1720s through the 1740s that was spread throughout the colonies by ministers like New England Congregationalist Jonathan Edwards and English revivalist George Whitefield.

Great Compromise (Connecticut Compromise) Mediated the differences between the New Jersey and Virginia delegations to the Constitutional Convention by providing for a bicameral legislature, the upper house of which would have equal representation and the lower house of which would be apportioned by population.

Great Depression Worst economic depression in American history; it was spurred by the stock market crash of 1929 and lasted until World War II.

Great Migration Large-scale migration of southern blacks during and after World War I to the North, where jobs had become available during the labor shortage of the war years.

Great Society Term coined by President Lyndon B. Johnson in his 1965 State of the Union address, in which he proposed legislation to address problems of voting rights, poverty, diseases, education, immigration, and the environment.

Greenback party Formed in 1876 in reaction to economic depression, the party favored issuance of unsecured paper money to help farmers repay debts; the movement for free coinage of silver took the place of the greenback movement by the 1880s.

Habeas corpus, Writ of An essential component of English common law and of the U.S. Constitution that guarantees that citizens may not be imprisoned without due process of law; literally means, "you must have the body."

Half-Breeds During the presidency of Rutherford B. Hayes, 1877–81, a moderate Republican party faction led by Senator James G. Blaine that favored some reforms of the civil service system and a restrained policy toward the defeated South.

Harlem Renaissance African-American literary and artistic movement of the 1920s and 1930s centered in New York City's Harlem district; writers Langston Hughes, Jean Toomer, Zora Neale Hurston, and Countee Cullen were among those active in the movement.

Harper's Ferry, Virginia Site of abolitionist John Brown's failed raid on the federal arsenal, October 16–17, 1859; he intended to arm the slaves, but ten of his compatriots were killed, and Brown became a martyr to his cause after his capture and execution.

Hartford Convention Meeting of New England Federalists on December 15, 1814, to protest the War of 1812; proposed seven constitutional amendments (limiting embargoes and changing requirements for officeholding, declaration of war, and admission of new states), but the war ended before Congress could respond.

Hawley-Smoot Tariff Act (1930) Raised tariffs to an unprecedented level and worsened the depression by raising prices and discouraging foreign trade.

Haymarket Affair Riot during an anarchist protest at Haymarket Square in Chicago on May 4, 1886, over violence during the McCormick Harvester Company strike; the deaths of eleven, including seven policemen, helped hasten the demise of the Knights of Labor, even though they were not responsible for the riot.

Hessians German soldiers, most from Hesse-Cassel principality (hence the name), paid to fight for the British in the Revolutionary War.

Holding company Investment company that holds controlling interest in the securities of other companies.

Homestead Act (1862) Authorized Congress to grant 160 acres of public land to a western settler, who had only to live on the land for five years to establish title.

Homestead Strike Violent strike at the Carnegie Steel Company near Pittsburgh in 1892 that culminated in the disintegration of the Amalgamated Association of Iron and Steel Workers, the first steelworkers' union.

House Un-American Activities Committee (HUAC) Formed in 1938 to investigate subversives in the government; best-known investigations were of Hollywood notables and of former State Department official Alger Hiss, who was accused in 1948 of espionage and Communist party membership.

Hundred Days Extraordinarily productive first three months of President Franklin D. Roosevelt's administration in which a special session of Congress enacted fifteen of his New Deal proposals.

Impeachment Bringing charges against a public official; for example, the House of Representatives can impeach a president for "treason, bribery, or other high crimes and misdemeanors" by majority vote, and after the trial the Senate can remove the president by a vote of two-thirds.

Implied powers Federal powers beyond those specifically enumerated in the U.S. Constitution; the Federalists argued that the "elastic clause" of Article I, Section 8, of the Constitution implicitly gave the federal government broad powers, while the Antifederalists held that the federal government's powers were explicitly limited by the Constitution.

"In God We Trust" Phrase placed on all new U.S. currency as of 1954.

Indentured servant Settler who signed on for a temporary period of servitude to a master in exchange for passage to the New World; Virginia and Pennsylvania were largely peopled in the seventeenth and eighteenth centuries by English indentured servants.

Independent Treasury Act (1840) Promoted by President Martin Van Buren, the measure sought to stabilize the economy by preventing state banks from printing unsecured paper currency and establishing an independent treasury based on specie.

Indian Peace Commission Established in 1867 to end the Indian wars in the West, the commission's solution was to contain the Indians in a system of reservations.

Indian Removal Act (1830) Signed by President Andrew Jackson, the law permitted the negotiation of treaties to obtain the Indians' lands in exchange for their relocation to what would become Oklahoma.

Industrial Workers of the World Radical union organized in Chicago in 1905 and nicknamed the Wobblies; its opposition to World War I led to its destruction by the federal government under the Espionage Act.

Internal improvements In the early national period the phrase referred to road building and the development of water transportation.

Interstate Commerce Commission Reacting to the U.S. Supreme Court's ruling in *Wabash Railroad v. Illinois* (1886), Congress established the ICC to curb abuses in the railroad industry by regulating rates.

Iran-Contra affair Scandal of the second Reagan administration involving sale of arms to Iran in partial exchange for release of hostages in Lebanon and use of the arms money to aid the Contras in Nicaragua, which had been expressly forbidden by Congress.

Iron Curtain Term coined by Winston Churchill to describe the cold war divide between western Europe and the Soviet Union's eastern European satellites.

Irreconcilables Group of isolationist U.S. senators who fought ratification of the Treaty of Versailles, 1919–20, because of their opposition to American membership in the League of Nations.

Jamestown, Virginia Site in 1607 of the first permanent English settlement in the New World.

Jay's Treaty Treaty with Britain negotiated in 1794 by Chief Justice John Jay; Britain agreed to vacate forts in the Northwest Territories, and festering disagreements (border with Canada, prewar debts, shipping claims) would be settled by commission.

Jim Crow Minstrel show character whose name became synonymous with post-Reconstruction laws revoking civil rights for freedmen and with racial segregation generally.

Judiciary Act of 1801 Enacted by the lame duck Congress to allow the Federalists, the losing party in the presidential election, to reorganize the judiciary and fill the open judgeships with Federalists.

Kansas-Nebraska Act (1854) Law sponsored by Illinois senator Stephen A. Douglas to allow settlers in newly organized territories north of the Missouri border to decide the slavery issue for themselves; fury over the resulting nullification of the Missouri Compromise of 1820 led to violence in Kansas and to the formation of the Republican party.

Kellogg-Briand Pact Representatives of sixty-two nations in 1928 signed the pact (also called the Pact of Paris) to outlaw war.

Kentucky and Virginia Resolutions (1798–99) Passed in response to the Alien and Sedition Acts, the resolutions advanced the state-compact theory that held states could nullify an act of Congress if they deemed it unconstitutional.

King William's War (War of the League of Augsburg) First (1689–97) of four colonial wars between England and France.

King's Mountain, Battle of Upcountry South Carolina irregulars defeated British troops under Patrick Ferguson on October 7, 1780, in what proved to be the turning point of the Revolutionary War in the South.

Knights of Labor Founded in 1869, the first national union picked up many members after the disastrous 1877 railroad strike but lasted, under the leadership of Terence V. Powderly, only into the 1890s; supplanted by the American Federation of Labor.

Know-Nothing (American) party Nativist, anti-Catholic third party organized in 1854 in reaction to large-scale German and Irish immigration; the party's only presidential candidate was Millard Fillmore in 1856.

Korean War Conflict touched off in 1950 when Communist North Korea invaded South Korea, which had been under U.S. control since the end of World War II; fighting largely by U.S. forces continued until 1953.

Ku Klux Klan Organized in Pulaski, Tennessee, in 1866 to terrorize former slaves who voted and held political offices during Reconstruction; a revived organization in the 1910s and 1920s stressed white, Anglo-Saxon, fundamentalist Protestant supremacy; the Klan revived a third time to fight the civil rights movement of the 1950s and 1960s in the South.

Land Ordinance of 1785 Directed surveying of the Northwest Territory into townships of thirty-six sections (square miles) each, the sale of the sixteenth section of which was to be used to finance public education.

League of Nations Organization of nations to mediate disputes and avoid war established after World War I as part of the Treaty of Versailles; President Woodrow Wilson's "Fourteen Points" speech to Congress in 1918 proposed the formation of the league.

Lecompton Constitution Controversial constitution drawn up in 1857 by proslavery Kansas delegates seeking statehood; rejected in 1858 by an overwhelmingly antislavery electorate.

Legal Tender Act (1862) Helped the U.S. government pay for the Civil War by authorizing the printing of paper currency.

Lend-Lease Act (1941) Permitted the United States to lend or lease arms and other supplies to the Allies, signifying increasing likelihood of American involvement in World War II.

Levittown Low-cost, mass-produced development of suburban tract housing built by William Levitt on Long Island in 1947.

Lexington and Concord, Battle of The first shots fired in the Revolutionary War, on April 19, 1775, near Boston; approximately 100 minutemen and 250 British soldiers were killed.

Leyte Gulf, Battle of Largest sea battle in history, fought on October 25, 1944, and won by the United States off the Philippine island of Leyte; Japanese losses were so great that they could not rebound.

Liberty party Abolitionist political party that nominated James G. Birney for president in 1840 and 1844; merged with the Free Soil party in 1848.

Lincoln-Douglas debates Series of senatorial campaign debates in 1858 focusing on the issue of slavery in the territories; held in Illinois between Republican Abraham Lincoln, who made a national reputation for himself, and incumbent Democratic senator Stephen A. Douglas, who managed to hold onto his seat.

Little Bighorn, Battle of Most famous battle of the Great Sioux War took place in 1876 in the Montana Territory; combined Sioux and Cheyenne warriors massacred a vastly outnumbered U.S. Cavalry commanded by Lieutenant Colonel George Armstrong Custer.

Lost Colony English expedition of 117 settlers, including Virginia Dare, the first English child born in the New World; colony disappeared from Roanoke Island in the Outer Banks sometime between 1587 and 1590.

Louisiana Purchase President Thomas Jefferson's 1803 purchase from France of the important port of New Orleans and 828,000 square miles west of the Mississippi River to the Rocky Mountains; it more than doubled the territory of the United States at a cost of only $15 million.

Lusitania British passenger liner sunk by a German U-boat, May 7, 1915, creating a diplomatic crisis and public outrage at the loss of 128 Americans (roughly 10 percent of the total aboard); Germany agreed to pay reparations, and the United States waited two more years to enter World War I.

Lyceum movement Founded in 1826, the movement promoted adult public education through lectures and performances.

Maize Indian corn, native to the New World.

Manhattan Project Secret American plan during World War II to develop an atomic bomb; J. Robert Oppenheimer led the team of physicists at Los Alamos, New Mexico.

Manifest Destiny Imperialist phrase first used in 1845 to urge annexation of Texas; used thereafter to encourage American settlement of European colonial and Indian lands in the Great Plains and Far West.

Marbury v. Madison (1803) First U.S. Supreme Court decision to declare a federal law—the Judiciary Act of 1801—unconstitutional; President John Adams's "midnight appointment" of Federalist judges prompted the suit.

March on Washington Civil rights demonstration on August 28, 1963, where the Reverend Martin Luther King, Jr., gave his "I Have a Dream" speech on the steps of the Lincoln Memorial.

Marshall Plan U.S. program for the reconstruction of post–World War II Europe through massive aid to former enemy nations as well as allies; proposed by General George C. Marshall in 1947.

Massive resistance In reaction to the *Brown* decision of 1954, U.S. senator Harry Byrd encouraged southern states to defy federally mandated school integration.

Maya Pre-Columbian society in Mesoamerica before about A.D. 900.

Mayflower Compact Signed in 1620 aboard the *Mayflower* before the Pilgrims landed at Plymouth, the document committed the group to majority-rule government; remained in effect until 1691.

Maysville Road Bill Federal funding for a Kentucky road, vetoed by President Andrew Jackson in 1830.

McCarran Internal Security Act (1950) Passed over President Harry S. Truman's veto, the law required registration of American Communist party members, denied them passports, and allowed them to be detained as suspected subversives.

McCulloch **v.** *Maryland* (1819) U.S. Supreme Court decision in which Chief Justice John Marshall, holding that Maryland could not tax the Second Bank of the United States, supported the authority of the federal government versus the states.

McNary-Haugen Bill Vetoed by President Calvin Coolidge in 1927 and 1928, the bill to aid farmers would have artificially raised agricultural prices by selling surpluses overseas for low prices and selling the reduced supply in the United States for higher prices.

Meat Inspection Act (1906) Passed largely in reaction to Upton Sinclair's *The Jungle,* the law set strict standards of cleanliness in the meat-packing industry.

Mercantilism Limitation and exploitation of colonial trade by an imperial power.

Mestizo Person of mixed Native American and European ancestry.

Mexican War Controversial war with Mexico for control of California and New Mexico, 1846–48; the Treaty of Guadalupe Hidalgo fixed the border at the Rio Grande and extended the United States to the Pacific coast, annexing more than a half-million square miles of potential slave territory.

Midway, Battle of Decisive American victory near Midway Island in the South Pacific on June 4, 1942; the Japanese navy never recovered its superiority over the U.S. navy.

Military Reconstruction Act (1867) Established military governments in ten Confederate states—excepting Tennessee—and required that the states ratify the Fourteenth Amendment and permit freedmen to vote.

Minstrel show Blackface vaudeville entertainment popular in the decades surrounding the Civil War.

Miranda v. Arizona **(1966)** U.S. Supreme Court decision required police to advise persons in custody of their rights to legal counsel and against self-incrimination.

Missouri Compromise Deal proposed by Kentucky senator Henry Clay to resolve the slave/free imbalance in Congress that would result from Missouri's admission as a slave state; in the compromise of March 20, 1820, Maine's admission as a free state offset Missouri, and slavery was prohibited in the remainder of the Louisiana Territory north of the southern border of Missouri.

Molly Maguires Secret organization of Irish coal miners that used violence to intimidate mine officials in the 1870s.

Monitor **and** *Merrimack* **Battle of the** First engagement between ironclad ships; fought at Hampton Roads, Virginia, on March 9, 1862.

Monroe Doctrine President James Monroe's declaration to Congress on December 2, 1823, that the American continents would be thenceforth closed to colonization but that the United States would honor existing colonies of European nations.

Moral Majority Televangelist Jerry Falwell's political lobbying organization, the name of which became synonymous with the religious right—conservative evangelical Protestants who helped ensure President Ronald Reagan's 1980 victory.

Mormons Founded in 1830 by Joseph Smith, the sect (officially, the Church of Jesus Christ of Latter-Day Saints) was a product of the intense revivalism of the "Burned-Over District" of New York; Smith's successor Brigham Young led 15,000 followers to Utah in 1847 to escape persecution.

Montgomery bus boycott Sparked by Rosa Parks's arrest on December 1, 1955, a successful year-long boycott protesting segregation on city buses; led by the Reverend Martin Luther King.

Muckrakers Writers who exposed corruption and abuses in politics, business, meat-packing, child labor, and more, primarily in the first decade of the twentieth century; their popular books and magazine articles spurred public interest in progressive reform.

Mugwumps Reform wing of the Republican party which supported Democrat Grover Cleveland for president in 1884 over Republican James G. Blaine, whose influence peddling had been revealed in the Mulligan letters of 1876.

Munn* v. *Illinois (1877) U.S. Supreme Court ruling that upheld a Granger law allowing the state to regulate grain elevators.

NAFTA Approved in 1993, the North American Free Trade Agreement with Canada and Mexico allowed goods to travel across their borders free of tariffs; critics argued that American workers would lose their jobs to cheaper Mexican labor.

National Aeronautics and Space Administration (NASA) In response to the Soviet Union's launching of *Sputnik*, Congress created this federal agency in 1957 to coordinate research and administer the space program.

National Association for the Advancement of Colored People (NAACP) Founded in 1910, this civil rights organization brought lawsuits against discriminatory practices and published *The Crisis*, a journal edited by African-American scholar W. E. B. Du Bois.

National Defense Education Act (1958) Passed in reaction to America's perceived inferiority in the space race, the appropriation encouraged education in science and modern languages through student loans, university research grants, and aid to public schools.

National Industrial Recovery Act (1933) Passed on the last of the Hundred Days, it created public-works jobs through the Federal Emergency Relief Administration and established a system of self-regulation for industry through the National Recovery Administration, which was ruled unconstitutional in 1935.

National Organization for Women Founded in 1966 by writer Betty Friedan and other feminists, NOW pushed for abortion rights and nondiscrimination in the workplace, but within a decade it became radicalized and lost much of its constituency.

National Road First federal interstate road, built between 1811 and 1838 and stretching from Cumberland, Maryland, to Vandalia, Illinois.

National Security Act (1947) Authorized the reorganization of government to coordinate military branches and security agencies; created the National Security Council, the Central Intelligence Agency, and the National Military Establishment (later renamed the Department of Defense).

National Youth Administration Created in 1935 as part of the Works Progress Administration, it employed millions of youths who had left school.

Nativism Anti-immigrant and anti-Catholic feeling in the 1830s through the 1850s; the largest group was New York's Order of the Star-Spangled Banner, which expanded into the American, or Know-Nothing, party in 1854.

Naval stores Tar, pitch, and turpentine made from pine resin and used in shipbuilding; an important industry in the southern colonies, especially North Carolina.

Navigation Acts Passed by the English Parliament to control colonial trade and bolster the mercantile system, 1650–1775; enforcement of the acts led to growing resentment by colonists.

Neutrality Acts Series of laws passed between 1935 and 1939 to keep the United States from becoming involved in war by prohibiting American trade and travel to warring nations.

New Deal Franklin D. Roosevelt's campaign promise, in his speech to the Democratic National Convention of 1932, to combat the Great Depression with a "new deal for the American people"; the phrase became a catchword for his ambitious plan of economic programs.

New England Anti-Slavery Society Abolitionist organization founded in 1832 by William Lloyd Garrison of Massachusetts, publisher of the *Liberator*.

New Freedom Democrat Woodrow Wilson's political slogan in the presidential campaign of 1912; Wilson wanted to improve the banking system, lower tariffs, and, by breaking up monopolies, give small businesses freedom to compete.

New Frontier John F. Kennedy's program, stymied by a Republican Congress and his abbreviated term; his successor Lyndon B. Johnson had greater success with many of the same concepts.

New Harmony Founded in Indiana by British industrialist Robert Owen in 1825, the short-lived New Harmony Community of Equality was one of the few nineteenth-century communal experiments not based on religious ideology.

New Left Radical youth protest movement of the 1960s, named by leader Tom Hayden to distinguish it from the Old (Marxist-Leninist) Left of the 1930s.

New Nationalism Platform of the Progressive party and slogan of former president Theodore Roosevelt in the presidential campaign of 1912; stressed government activism, including regulation of trusts, conservation, and recall of state court decisions that had nullified progressive programs.

New Orleans, Battle of Last battle of the War of 1812, fought on January 8, 1815, weeks after the peace treaty was signed but prior to its ratification; General Andrew Jackson led the victorious American troops.

New South *Atlanta Constitution* editor Henry W. Grady's 1886 term for the prosperous post–Civil War South he envisioned: democratic, industrial, urban, and free of nostalgia for the defeated plantation South.

Nineteenth Amendment (1920) Granted women the right to vote.

Nisei Japanese Americans; literally, "second generation."

Normalcy Word coined by future president Warren G. Harding as part of a 1920 campaign speech—"not nostrums, but normalcy"—signifying his awareness that the public was tired of progressivism, war, and sacrifice.

North Atlantic Treaty Organization (NATO) Defensive alliance founded in 1949 by ten western European nations, the United States, and Canada to deter Soviet expansion in Europe.

Northwest Ordinance of 1787 Created the Northwest Territory (area north of the Ohio River and west of Pennsylvania), established conditions for self-government and statehood, included a Bill of Rights, and permanently prohibited slavery.

Nullification Concept of invalidation of a federal law within the borders of a state; first expounded in the Kentucky and Virginia Resolutions (1798), cited by South Carolina in its Ordinance of Nullification (1832) of the Tariff of Abominations, used by southern states to explain their secession from the Union (1861), and cited again by southern states to oppose the *Brown* v. *Board of Education* decision (1954).

Nullification Proclamation President Andrew Jackson's strong criticism of South Carolina's Ordinance of Nullification (1832) as disunionist and potentially treasonous.

Office of Price Administration Created in 1941 to control wartime inflation and price fixing resulting from shortages of many consumer goods, the OPA imposed wage and price freezes and administered a rationing system.

Okies Displaced farm families from the Oklahoma dust bowl who migrated to California during the 1930s in search of jobs.

Old Southwest In the antebellum period, the states of Alabama, Mississippi, Louisiana, Texas, Arkansas, and parts of Tennessee, Kentucky, and Florida.

Oneida Community Utopian community founded in 1848; the Perfectionist religious group practiced universal marriage until leader John Humphrey Noyes, fearing prosecution, escaped to Canada in 1879.

OPEC Organization of Petroleum Exporting Countries.

Open Door Policy In hopes of protecting the Chinese market for U.S. exports, Secretary of State John Hay unilaterally announced in 1899 that Chinese trade would be open to all nations.

Operation Desert Storm Multinational allied force that defeated Iraq in the Gulf War of January 1991.

Operation Dixie CIO's largely ineffective post–World War II campaign to unionize southern workers.

Oregon fever Enthusiasm for emigration to the Oregon Country in the late 1830s and early 1840s.

Ostend Manifesto Memorandum written in 1854 from Ostend, Belgium, by the U.S. ministers to England, France, and Spain recommending purchase or seizure of Cuba in order to increase the United States' slaveholding territory.

Overland (Oregon) Trail Route of wagon trains bearing settlers from Independence, Missouri, to the Oregon Country in the 1840s through the 1860s.

Overseer Manager of slave labor on a plantation.

Panic of 1819 Financial collapse brought on by sharply falling cotton prices, declining demand for American exports, and reckless western land speculation.

Panic of 1837 Major economic depression lasting about six years; touched off by a British financial crisis and made worse by falling cotton prices, credit and currency problems, and speculation in land, canals, and railroads.

Panic of 1857 Economic depression lasting about two years and brought on by falling grain prices and a weak financial system; the South was largely protected by international demand for its cotton.

Panic of 1873 Severe six-year depression marked by bank failures and railroad and insurance bankruptcies.

Peace of Paris Signed on September 3, 1783, the treaty ending the Revolutionary War and recognizing American independence from Britain also established the border between Canada and the United States, fixed the western border at the Mississippi River, and ceded Florida to Spain.

Pendleton Civil Service Act (1883) Established the Civil Service Commission and marked the end of the spoils system.

Pentagon Papers Informal name for the Defense Department's secret history of the Vietnam conflict; leaked to the press by former official Daniel Ellsberg and published in the *New York Times* in 1971.

Pequot War Massacre in 1637 and subsequent dissolution of the Pequot Nation by Puritan settlers, who seized the Indians' lands.

Personal Responsibility and Work Opportunity Act (1996) Welfare reform measure that mandated state administration of federal aid to the poor.

Philippine Sea, Battle of the Costly Japanese defeat of June 19–20, 1944; led to the resignation of Premier Tojo and his cabinet.

Pilgrims Puritan Separatists who broke completely with the Church of England and sailed to the New World aboard the *Mayflower*, founding Plymouth Colony on Cape Cod in 1620.

Pinckney's Treaty Treaty with Spain negotiated by Thomas Pinckney in 1795; established United States boundaries at the Mississippi River and the thirty-first parallel and allowed open transportation on the Mississippi.

Planter In the antebellum South, the owner of a large farm worked by twenty or more slaves.

Platt Amendment (1901) Reserved the United States' right to intervene in Cuban affairs and forced newly independent Cuba to host American naval bases on the island.

Plessy v. *Ferguson* (1896) U.S. Supreme Court decision supporting the legality of Jim Crow laws that permitted or required "separate but equal" facilities for blacks and whites.

Poll tax Tax that must be paid in order to be eligible to vote; used as an effective means of disenfranchising black citizens after Reconstruction, since they often could not afford even a modest fee.

Popular sovereignty Allowed settlers in a disputed territory to decide the slavery issue for themselves.

Populist party Political success of Farmers' Alliance candidates encouraged the formation in 1892 of the National People's party (later renamed the Populist party); active until 1912, it advocated a variety of reform issues, including free coinage of silver, income tax, postal savings, regulation of railroads, and direct election of U.S. senators.

Pottawatomie Massacre Murder of five proslavery settlers in eastern Kansas led by abolitionist John Brown on May 24–25, 1856.

Potsdam Conference Last meeting of the major Allied powers, the conference took place outside Berlin from July 17 to August 2, 1945; United States president Harry Truman, Soviet dictator Joseph Stalin, and British prime minister Clement Atlee finalized plans begun at Yalta.

Proclamation of Amnesty and Reconstruction President Lincoln's plan for reconstruction, issued in 1863, allowed southern states to rejoin the Union if 10 percent of the 1860 electorate signed loyalty pledges, accepted emancipation, and had received presidential pardons.

Proclamation of 1763 Royal directive issued after the French and Indian War prohibiting settlement, surveys, and land grants west of the Appalachian Mountains; although it was soon overridden by treaties, colonists continued to harbor resentment.

Progressive party Created when former president Theodore Roosevelt broke away from the Republican party to run for president again in 1912; the party supported progressive reforms similar to the Democrats but stopped short of seeking to eliminate trusts.

Progressivism Broad-based reform movement, 1900–17, that sought governmental help in solving problems in many areas of American life, including education, public health, the economy, the environment, labor, transportation, and politics.

Protestant Reformation Reform movement that resulted in the establishment of Protestant denominations; begun by German monk Martin Luther when he posted his "Ninety-five Theses" (complaints of abuses in the Catholic church) in 1517.

Pullman Strike Strike against the Pullman Palace Car Company in the company town of Pullman, Illinois, on May 11, 1894, by the American Railway Union under Eugene V. Debs; the strike was crushed by court injunctions and federal troops two months later.

Pure Food and Drug Act (1906) First law to regulate manufacturing of food and medicines; prohibited dangerous additives and inaccurate labeling.

Puritans English religious group that sought to purify the Church of England; founded the Massachusetts Bay Colony under John Winthrop in 1630.

Quartering Act (1765) Parliamentary act requiring colonies to house and provision British troops.

Radical Republicans Senators and congressmen who, strictly identifying the Civil War with the abolitionist cause, sought swift emancipation of the slaves, punishment of the rebels, and tight controls over the former Confederate states after the war.

Railroad Strike of 1877 Violent but ultimately unsuccessful interstate strike, which resulted in extensive property damage and many deaths.

Reaganomics Popular name for President Ronald Reagan's philosophy of "supply side" economics, which combined tax cuts, less government spending, and a balanced budget with an unregulated marketplace.

Reconstruction Finance Corporation Federal program established in 1932 under President Herbert Hoover to loan money to banks and other institutions to help them avert bankruptcy.

Red Scare Fear among many Americans after World War I of Communists in particular and noncitizens in general, a reaction to the Russian Revolution, mail bombs, strikes, and riots.

Redcoats Nickname for British soldiers, after their red uniform jackets.

Redeemers/Bourbons Conservative white Democrats, many of whom had been planters or businessmen before the Civil War, who reclaimed control of the South following the end of Reconstruction.

Regulators Groups of backcountry Carolina settlers who protested colonial policies; North Carolina royal governor William Tryon retaliated at the Battle of Alamance on May 17, 1771.

Report on Manufactures First secretary of the treasury Alexander Hamilton's 1791 analysis that accurately foretold the future of American industry and proposed tariffs and subsidies to promote it.

Republican party Organized in 1854 by antislavery Whigs, Democrats, and Free Soilers in response to the passage of the Kansas-Nebraska Act; nominated John C. Frémont for president in 1856 and Abraham Lincoln in 1860.

Republicans Political faction that succeeded the Antifederalists after ratification of the Constitution; led by Thomas Jefferson and James Madison, it soon developed into the Democratic-Republican party.

Reservationists Group of U.S. senators led by Majority Leader Henry Cabot Lodge who would only agree to ratification of the Treaty of Versailles subject to certain reservations, most notably the removal of Article X of the League of Nations Covenant.

Revolution of 1800 First time that an American political party surrendered power to the opposition party; Jefferson, a Democratic-Republican, had defeated incumbent Adams, a Federalist, for president.

Right-to-work State laws enacted to prevent imposition of the closed shop; any worker, whether or not a union member, could be hired.

Roe v. Wade (1973) U.S. Supreme Court decision requiring states to permit first-trimester abortions.

Roosevelt Corollary (1904) President Theodore Roosevelt announced in what was essentially a corollary to the Monroe Doctrine that the United States could intervene militarily to prevent interference from European powers in the Western Hemisphere.

Romanticism Philosophical, literary, and artistic movement of the nineteenth century that was largely a reaction to the rationalism of the previous century; romantics valued emotion, mysticism, and individualism.

Rough Riders The 1st U.S. Volunteer Cavalry, led in battle in the Spanish-American War by Theodore Roosevelt; they were victorious in their only battle near Santiago, Cuba, and Roosevelt used the notoriety to aid his political career.

Santa Fe Trail Beginning in the 1820s, a major trade route from St. Louis, Missouri, to Santa Fe, New Mexico Territory.

Saratoga, Battle of Major defeat of British general John Burgoyne and more than 5,000 British troops at Saratoga, New York, on October 17, 1777.

Scalawags Southern white Republicans—some former Unionists—who served in Reconstruction governments.

Schenck v. *U.S.* (1919) U.S. Supreme Court decision upholding the wartime Espionage and Sedition Acts; in the opinion he wrote for the case, Justice Oliver Wendell Holmes set the now-familiar "clear and present danger" standard.

Scientific management Analysis of worker efficiency using measurements like "time and motion" studies to achieve greater productivity; introduced by Frederick Winslow Taylor in 1911.

Scottsboro case (1931) In overturning verdicts against nine black youths accused of raping two white women, the U.S. Supreme Court established precedents in *Powell* v. *Alabama* (1932), that adequate counsel must be appointed in capital cases, and in *Norris* v. *Alabama* (1935), that African Americans cannot be excluded from juries.

Second Great Awakening Religious revival movement of the early decades of the nineteenth century, in reaction to the growth of secularism and rationalist religion; began the predominance of the Baptist and Methodist churches.

Second Red Scare Post–World War II Red Scare focused on the fear of Communists in U.S. government positions; peaked during the Korean War and declined soon thereafter, when the U.S. Senate censured Joseph McCarthy, who had been a major instigator of the hysteria.

Seneca Falls Convention First women's rights meeting and the genesis of the women's suffrage movement; held in July 1848 in a church in Seneca Falls, New York, by Elizabeth Cady Stanton and Lucretia Coffin Mott.

"Separate but equal" Principle underlying legal racial segregation, which was upheld in *Plessy* v. *Ferguson* (1896) and struck down in *Brown* v. *Board of Education* (1954).

Servicemen's Readjustment Act (1944) The "GI Bill of Rights" provided money for education and other benefits to military personnel returning from World War II.

Settlement houses Product of the late nineteenth-century movement to offer a broad array of social services in urban immigrant neighborhoods; Chicago's Hull House was one of hundreds of settlement houses that operated by the early twentieth century.

Seventeenth Amendment (1913) Progressive reform that required U.S. senators to be elected directly by voters; previously, senators were chosen by state legislatures.

Seward's Folly Secretary of State William H. Seward's negotiation of the purchase of Alaska from Russia in 1867.

Shakers Founded by Mother Ann Lee Stanley in England, the United Society of Believers in Christ's Second Appearing settled in Watervliet, New York, in 1774 and subsequently established eighteen additional communes in the Northeast, Indiana, and Kentucky.

Sharecropping Type of farm tenancy that developed after the Civil War in which landless workers—often former slaves—farmed land in exchange for farm supplies and a share of the crop; differed from tenancy in that the terms were generally less favorable.

Shays's Rebellion Massachusetts farmer Daniel Shays and 1,200 compatriots, seeking debt relief through issuance of paper currency and lower taxes, stormed the federal arsenal at Springfield in the winter of 1787 but were quickly repulsed.

Sherman Anti-Trust Act (1890) First law to restrict monopolistic trusts and business combinations; extended by the Clayton Anti-Trust Act of 1914.

Sherman Silver Purchase Act (1890) In replacing and extending the provisions of the Bland-Allison Act of 1878, it increased the amount of silver periodically bought for coinage.

Shiloh, Battle of At the time it was fought (April 6–7, 1862), Shiloh, in western Tennessee, was the bloodiest battle in American history; afterward, General Ulysses S. Grant was temporarily removed from command.

Single tax Concept of taxing only landowners as a remedy for poverty, promulgated by Henry George in *Progress and Poverty* (1879).

Sixteenth Amendment (1913) Legalized the federal income tax.

Smith-Connally War Labor Disputes Act (1943) Outlawed labor strikes in wartime and allowed the president to take over industries threatened by labor disputes.

Smith* v. *Allwright (1944) U.S. Supreme Court decision that outlawed all-white Democratic party primaries in Texas.

Social Darwinism Application of Charles Darwin's theory of natural selection to society; used the concept of the "survival of the fittest" to justify class distinctions and to explain poverty.

Social gospel Preached by liberal Protestant clergymen in the late nineteenth and early twentieth centuries; advocated the application of Christian principles to social problems generated by industrialization.

Social Security Act (1935) Created the Social Security system with provisions for a retirement pension, unemployment insurance, disability insurance, and public assistance (welfare).

Sons of Liberty Secret organizations formed by Samuel Adams, John Hancock, and other radicals in response to the Stamp Act; they impeded British officials and planned such harassments as the Boston Tea Party.

South Carolina Exposition and Protest Written in 1828 by Vice-President John C. Calhoun of South Carolina to protest the so-called Tariff of Abominations, which seemed to favor northern industry; introduced the concept of state interposition and became the basis for South Carolina's Nullification Doctrine of 1833.

Southeast Asia Treaty Organization (SEATO) Pact among mostly western nations signed in 1954; designed to deter Communist expansion and cited as a justification for U.S. involvement in Vietnam.

Southern Christian Leadership Conference (SCLC) Civil rights organization founded in 1957 by the Reverend Martin Luther King, Jr., and other civil rights leaders.

Southern renaissance Literary movement of the 1920s and 1930s that included such writers as William Faulkner, Thomas Wolfe, and Robert Penn Warren.

Spanish flu Unprecedentedly lethal influenza epidemic of 1918 that killed more than 22 million people worldwide.

Spoils system The term—meaning the filling of federal government jobs with persons loyal to the party of the president—originated in Andrew Jackson's first term; the system was replaced in the Progressive Era by civil service.

Sputnik First artificial satellite to orbit the earth; launched October 4, 1957, by the Soviet Union.

Stalwarts Conservative Republican party faction during the presidency of Rutherford B. Hayes, 1877–81; led by Senator Roscoe B. Conkling of New York, Stalwarts opposed civil service reform and favored a third term for President Ulysses S. Grant.

Stamp Act (1765) Parliament required that revenue stamps be affixed to all colonial printed matter, documents, dice, and playing cards; the Stamp Act Congress met to formulate a response, and the act was repealed the following year.

Standard Oil Company Founded in 1870 by John D. Rockefeller in Cleveland, Ohio, it soon grew into the nation's first industry-dominating trust; the Sherman Anti-Trust Act (1890) was enacted in part to combat abuses by Standard Oil.

Staple crop Important cash crop, for example, cotton or tobacco.

Steamboats Paddlewheelers that could travel both up- and down-river in deep or shallow waters; they became commercially viable early in the nineteenth century and soon developed into America's first inland freight and passenger service network.

Stimson Doctrine In reaction to Japan's 1932 occupation of Manchuria, Secretary of State Henry Stimson declared that the United States would not recognize territories acquired by force.

Strategic Defense Initiative ("Star Wars") Defense Department's plan during the Reagan administration to build a system to destroy incoming missiles in space.

Student Non-violent Coordinating Committee Founded in 1960 to coordinate civil rights sit-ins and other forms of grassroots protest.

Students for a Democratic Society (SDS) Major organization of the New Left, founded at the University of Michigan in 1960 by Tom Hayden and Al Haber.

Sugar Act (Revenue Act of 1764) Parliament's tax on refined sugar and many other colonial products; the first tax designed solely to raise revenue for Britain.

Taft-Hartley Act (1947) Passed over President Harry Truman's veto, the law contained a number of provisions to control labor unions, including the banning of closed shops.

Tariff Federal tax on imported goods.

Tariff of Abominations (Tariff of 1828) Taxed imported goods at a very high rate; the South hated the tariff because it feared it would provoke Britain to reject American cotton.

Tariff of 1816 First true protective tariff, intended strictly to protect American goods against foreign competition.

Tax Reform Act (1986) Lowered federal income tax rates to 1920s levels and eliminated many loopholes.

Teapot Dome Harding administration scandal in which Secretary of the Interior Albert B. Fall profited from secret leasing to private oil companies of government oil reserves at Teapot Dome, Wyoming, and Elk Hills, California.

Tenancy Renting of farmland by workers who owned their own equipment; tenant farmers kept a larger percentage of the crop than did sharecroppers.

Tennessee Valley Authority Created in 1933 to control flooding in the Tennessee River Valley, provide work for the region's unemployed, and produce inexpensive electric power for the region.

Tenure of Office Act (1867) Required the president to obtain Senate approval to remove any official whose appointment had also required Senate approval; President Andrew Johnson's violation of the law by firing Secretary of War Edwin Stanton led to the Radical Republicans retaliating with Johnson's impeachment.

Tertium Quid Literally, the "third something": states' rights and strict constructionist Republicans under John Randolph who broke with President Thomas Jefferson but never managed to form a third political party.

Tet Offensive Surprise attack by the Viet Cong and North Vietnamese during the Vietnamese New Year of 1968; turned American public opinion strongly against the war in Vietnam.

Tippecanoe, Battle of On November 7, 1811, Indiana governor William Henry Harrison (later president) defeated the Shawnee Indians at the Tippecanoe River in northern Indiana; victory fomented war fever against the British, who were believed to be aiding the Indians.

Title IX Part of the Educational Amendments Act of 1972 that required colleges to engage in "affirmative action" for women.

Tonkin Gulf Resolution (1964) Passed by Congress in reaction to supposedly unprovoked attacks on American warships off the coast of North Vietnam; it gave the president unlimited authority to defend U.S. forces and members of SEATO.

Tories Term used by Patriots to refer to Loyalists, or colonists who supported the Crown after the Declaration of Independence.

Townshend Acts (1767) Parliamentary measures (named for the chancellor of the exchequer) that punished the New York Assembly for failing to house British soldiers, taxed tea and other commodities, and established a Board of Customs Commissioners and colonial vice-admiralty courts.

Trail of Tears Cherokees' own term for their forced march, 1838–39, from the southern Appalachians to Indian lands (later Oklahoma); of 15,000 forced to march, 4,000 died on the way.

Transcendentalism Philosophy of a small group of mid-nineteenth-century New England writers and thinkers, including Ralph Waldo Emerson, Henry David Thoreau, and Margaret Fuller; they stressed "plain living and high thinking."

Transcontinental railroad First line across the continent from Omaha, Nebraska, to Sacramento, California, established in 1869 with the linkage of the Union Pacific and Central Pacific railroads at Promontory, Utah.

Truman Doctrine President Harry S. Truman's program of post–World War II aid to European countries—particularly Greece and Turkey—in danger of being undermined by communism.

Trust Companies combined to control competition.

Twenty-first Amendment (1933) Repealed prohibition on the manufacture, sale, and transportation of alcoholic beverages, effectively nullifying the Eighteenth Amendment.

Twenty-second Amendment (1951) Limited presidents to two full terms of office or two terms plus two years of an assumed term; passed in reaction to President Franklin D. Roosevelt's unprecedented four elected terms.

Twenty-sixth Amendment (1971) Lowered the voting age from twenty-one to eighteen.

U.S.S. *Maine* Battleship that exploded in Havana Harbor on February 15, 1898, resulting in 266 deaths; the American public, assuming that the Spanish had mined the ship, clamored for war, and the Spanish-American War was declared two months later.

Uncle Tom's Cabin Harriet Beecher Stowe's 1852 antislavery novel popularized the abolitionist position.

Underground Railroad Operating in the decades before the Civil War, the "railroad" was a clandestine system of routes and safehouses through which slaves were led to freedom in the North.

Understanding clause Added to state constitutions in the late nineteenth century, it allowed illiterate whites to circumvent literacy tests for voting by demonstrating that they understood a passage in the Constitution; black citizens would be judged by white registrars to have failed.

Underwood-Simmons Tariff (1913) In addition to lowering and even eliminating some tariffs, it included provisions for the first federal income tax, made legal the same year by the ratification of the Sixteenth Amendment.

Unitarianism Late eighteenth-century liberal offshoot of the New England Congregationalist church; rejecting the Trinity, Unitarianism professed the oneness of God and the goodness of rational man.

United Farm Workers Union for the predominantly Mexican-American migrant laborers of the Southwest, organized by César Chavez in 1962.

United Nations Organization of nations to maintain world peace, established in 1945 and headquartered in New York.

Universal Negro Improvement Association Black nationalist movement active in the United States from 1916 to 1923, when its leader Marcus Garvey went to prison for mail fraud.

Universalism Similar to Unitarianism, but putting more stress on the importance of social action, Universalism also originated in Massachusetts in the late eighteenth century.

V-E Day May 8, 1945, the day World War II officially ended in Europe.

Vertical integration Company's avoidance of middlemen by producing its own supplies and providing for distribution of its product.

Veto President's constitutional power to reject legislation passed by Congress; a two-thirds vote in both houses of Congress can override a veto.

Vicksburg, Battle of The fall of Vicksburg, Mississippi, to General Ulysses S. Grant's army on July 4, 1863, after two months of siege was a turning point in the war because it gave the Union control of the Mississippi River.

Virginia and New Jersey Plans Differing opinions of delegations to the Constitutional Convention: New Jersey wanted one legislative body with equal representation for each state; Virginia's plan called for a strong central government and a two-house legislature apportioned by population.

Volstead Act (1919) Enforced the prohibition amendment, beginning January 1920.

Voting Rights Act of 1965 Passed in the wake of Martin Luther King's Selma to Montgomery March, it authorized federal protection of the right to vote and permitted federal enforcement of minority voting rights in individual counties, mostly in the South.

Wabash Railroad **v.** *Illinois* (1886) Reversing the U.S. Supreme Court's ruling in *Munn* v. *Illinois*, the decision disallowed state regulation of interstate commerce.

Wade-Davis Bill (1864) Radical Republicans' plan for reconstruction that required loyalty oaths, abolition of slavery, repudiation of war debts, and denial of political rights to high-ranking Confederate officials; President Lincoln refused to sign the bill.

Wagner Act (National Labor Relations Act of 1935) Established the National Labor Relations Board and facilitated unionization by regulating employment and bargaining practices.

War Industries Board Run by financier Bernard Baruch, the board planned production and allocation of war materiel, supervised purchasing, and fixed prices, 1917–19.

War of 1812 Fought with Britain, 1812–14, over lingering conflicts that included impressment of American sailors, interference with shipping, and collusion with Northwest Territory Indians; settled by the Treaty of Ghent in 1814.

War on Poverty Announced by President Lyndon B. Johnson in his 1964 State of the Union address; under the Economic Opportunity Bill signed later that year, Head Start, VISTA, and the Jobs Corps were created, and grants and loans were extended to students, farmers, and businesses in efforts to eliminate poverty.

War Production Board Created in 1942 to coordinate industrial efforts in World War II; similar to the War Industries Board in World War I.

War Relocation Camps Internment camps where Japanese Americans were held against their will from 1942 to 1945.

Warren Court The U.S. Supreme Court under Chief Justice Earl Warren, 1953–69, decided such landmark cases as *Brown v. Board of Education* (school desegregation), *Baker v. Carr* (legislative redistricting), and *Gideon v. Wainwright* and *Miranda v. Arizona* (rights of criminal defendants).

Washington Armaments Conference Leaders of nine world powers met in 1921–22 to discuss the naval race; resulting treaties limited to a specific ratio the carrier and battleship tonnage of each nation (Five-Power Naval Treaty), formally ratified the Open Door to China (Nine–Power Treaty), and agreed to respect each other's Pacific territories (Four-Power Treaty).

Watergate Washington office and apartment complex that lent its name to the 1972–74 scandal of the Nixon administration; when his knowledge of the break-in at the Watergate and subsequent coverup was revealed, Nixon resigned the presidency under threat of impeachment.

Webster-Ashburton Treaty Settlement in 1842 of U.S.-Canadian border disputes in Maine, New York, Vermont, and in the Wisconsin Territory (now northern Minnesota).

Webster-Hayne debate U.S. Senate debate of January 1830 between Daniel Webster of Massachusetts and Robert Hayne of South Carolina over nullification and states' rights.

Whig Party Founded in 1834 to unite factions opposed to President Andrew Jackson, the party favored federal responsibility for internal improvements; the party ceased to exist by the late 1850s, when party members divided over the slavery issue.

Whigs Another name for revolutionary Patriots.

Whiskey Rebellion Violent protest by western Pennsylvania farmers against the federal excise tax on corn whiskey, 1794.

Whitewater Development Corporation Failed Arkansas real estate investment that kept President Bill Clinton and his wife Hillary under investigation by Independent Counsel Kenneth Starr throughout the Clinton presidency; no charges were ever brought against either of the Clintons.

Wilderness, Battle of the Second battle fought in the thickly wooded Wilderness area near Chancellorsville, Virginia; in the battle of May 5–6, 1864, no clear victor emerged, but the battle served to deplete the Army of Northern Virginia.

Wilderness Road Originally an Indian path through the Cumberland Gap, it was used by over 300,000 settlers who migrated westward to Kentucky in the last quarter of the eighteenth century.

Wilmot Proviso Proposal to prohibit slavery in any land acquired in the Mexican War, but southern senators, led by John C. Calhoun of South Carolina, defeated the measure in 1846 and 1847.

Works Progress Administration (WPA) Part of the Second New Deal, it provided jobs for millions of the unemployed on construction and arts projects.

Wounded Knee, Battle of Last incident of the Indians Wars took place in 1890 in the Dakota Territory, where the U.S. Cavalry killed over 200 Sioux men, women, and children who were in the process of surrender.

Writs of assistance One of the colonies' main complaints against Britain, the writs allowed unlimited search warrants without cause to look for evidence of smuggling.

XYZ Affair French foreign minister Tallyrand's three anonymous agents demanded payments to stop French plundering of American ships in 1797; refusal to pay the bribe led to two years of sea war with France (1798–1800).

Yalta Conference Meeting of Franklin D. Roosevelt, Winston Churchill, and Joseph Stalin at a Crimean resort to discuss the postwar world on February 4–11, 1945; Soviet leader Joseph Stalin claimed large areas in eastern Europe for Soviet domination.

Yazoo Fraud Illegal sale of the Yazoo lands (much of present-day Alabama and Mississippi) by Georgia legislators; by 1802 it had become a tangle of conflicting claims that the U.S. Supreme Court settled in *Fletcher v. Peck* (1810).

Yellow journalism Sensationalism in newspaper publishing that reached a peak in the circulation war between Joseph Pulitzer's *New York World* and William Randolph Hearst's *New York Journal* in the 1890s; the papers' accounts of events in Havana Harbor in 1898 led directly to the Spanish-American War.

Yeoman farmers Small landowners (the majority of white families in the South) who farmed their own land and usually did not own slaves.

Yorktown, Battle of Last battle of the Revolutionary War; General Lord Charles Cornwallis along with over 7,000 British troops surrendered at Yorktown, Virginia, on October 17, 1781.

Zimmermann telegram From the German foreign secretary to the German minister in Mexico, February 1917, instructing him to offer to recover Texas, New Mexico, and Arizona for Mexico if it would fight the United States to divert attention from Germany in case of war.

APPENDIX

THE DECLARATION
OF INDEPENDENCE

WHEN IN THE COURSE OF HUMAN EVENTS, it becomes necessary for one people to dissolve the political bands which have connected them with another, and to assume the Powers of the earth, the separate and equal station to which the Laws of Nature and of Nature's God entitle them, a decent respect to the opinions of mankind requires that they should declare the causes which impel them to the separation.

We hold these truths to be self-evident, that all men are created equal, that they are endowed by their Creator with certain unalienable rights, that among these are Life, Liberty, and the pursuit of Happiness. That to secure these rights, Governments are instituted among Men, deriving their just powers from the consent of the governed. That whenever any Form of Government becomes destructive of these ends, it is the Right of the People to alter or to abolish it, and to institute new Government, laying its foundation on such principles and organizing its powers in such form, as to them shall seem most likely to effect their Safety and Happiness. Prudence, indeed, will dictate that Governments long established should not be changed for light and transient causes; and accordingly all experience hath shown, that mankind are more disposed to suffer, while evils are sufferable, than to right themselves by abolishing the forms to which they are accustomed. But when a long train of abuses and usurpations, pursuing invariably the same Object evinces a design to reduce them under absolute Despotism, it is their right, it is their duty, to throw off such Government, and to provide new Guards for their future security.—Such has been the patient sufferance of these Colonies; and such is now the necessity which constrains them to alter their former Systems of Government. The history of the present King of Great Britain is a history of repeated injuries and usurpations, all having in direct object the establishment of an absolute Tyranny over these States. To prove this, let Facts be submitted to a candid world.

He has refused his Assent to Laws, the most wholesome and necessary for the public good.

He has forbidden his Governors to pass Laws of immediate and pressing importance, unless suspended in their operation till his Assent should be obtained; and when so suspended, he has utterly neglected to attend to them.

He has refused to pass other Laws for the accommodation of large districts of people, unless those people would relinquish the right of Representation in the Legislature, a right inestimable to them and formidable to tyrants only.

He has called together legislative bodies at places unusual, uncomfortable, and distant from the depository of their public Records, for the sole purpose of fatiguing them into compliance with his measures.

He has dissolved Representative Houses repeatedly, for opposing with manly firmness his invasions on the rights of the people.

He has refused for a long time, after such dissolutions, to cause others to be elected; whereby the Legislative powers, incapable of Annihilation, have returned to the People at large for their exercise; the State remaining in the mean time exposed to all dangers of invasion from without, and convulsions within.

He has endeavoured to prevent the population of these States; for that purpose obstructing the Laws of Naturalization of Foreigners; refusing to pass others to encourage their migrations hither, and raising the conditions of new Appropriations of Lands.

He has obstructed the Administration of Justice, by refusing his Assent to Laws for establishing Judiciary powers.

He has made Judges dependent on his Will alone, for the tenure of their offices, and the amount and payment of their salaries.

He has erected a multitude of New Offices, and sent hither swarms of Officers to harass our People, and eat out their substance.

He has kept among us, in times of peace, Standing Armies without the Consent of our legislatures.

He has affected to render the Military independent of and superior to the Civil Power.

He has combined with others to subject us to a jurisdiction foreign to our constitution, and unacknowledged by our laws; giving his Assent to their Acts of pretended Legislation:

For quartering large bodies of armed troops among us:

For protecting them, by a mock Trial, from Punishment for any Murders which they should commit on the Inhabitants of these States:

For cutting off our Trade with all parts of the world:

For imposing taxes on us without our Consent:

For depriving us of many cases, of the benefits of Trial by jury:

For transporting us beyond Seas to be tried for pretended offences:

For abolishing the free System of English Laws in a neighbouring Province, establishing therein an Arbitrary government, and enlarging its Boundaries so as to render it at once an example and fit instrument for introducing the same absolute rule into these Colonies:

For taking away our Charters, abolishing our most valuable Laws, and altering fundamentally the Forms of our Governments:

For suspending our own Legislatures, and declaring themselves in vested with Power to legislate for us in all cases whatsoever.

He has abdicated Government here, by declaring us out of his Protection and waging War against us.

He has plundered our seas, ravaged our Coasts, burnt our towns, and destroyed the lives of our people.

He is at this time transporting large armies of foreign mercenaries to compleat the works of death, desolation, and tyranny, already begun with circumstances of Cruelty & perfidy scarcely paralleled in the most barbarous ages, and totally unworthy the Head of a civilized nation.

He has constrained our fellow Citizens taken Captive on the high Seas to bear Arms against their Country, to become the executioners of their friends and Brethren, or to fall themselves by their Hands.

He has excited domestic insurrections amongst us, and has endeavoured to bring on the inhabitants of our frontiers, the merciless Indian Savages, whose known rule of warfare, is an undistinguished destruction of all ages, sexes, and conditions.

In every stage of these Oppressions We have Petitioned for Redress in the most humble terms: Our repeated Petitions have been answered only by repeated injury. A Prince, whose character is thus marked by every act which may define a Tyrant, is unfit to be the ruler of a free people.

Nor have We been wanting in attention to our British brethren. We have warned them from time to time of attempts by their legislature to extend an unwarrantable jurisdiction over us. We have reminded them of the circumstances of our emigration and settlement here. We have appealed to their native justice and magnanimity, and we have conjured them by the ties of our common kindred to disavow these usurpations, which, would inevitably interrupt our connections and correspondence. They too must have been deaf to the voice of justice and of consanguinity. We must, therefore, acquiesce in the necessity, which denounces our Separation, and hold them, as we hold the rest of mankind, Enemies in War, in Peace Friends.

WE, THEREFORE, the Representatives of the UNITED STATES OF AMERICA, in General Congress, Assembled, appealing to the Supreme Judge of the world for the rectitude of our intentions, do, in the Name, and by Authority of the good People of these Colonies, solemnly publish and declare, That these United Colonies are, and of Right ought to be FREE AND INDEPENDENT STATES; that they are Absolved from all Allegiance to the British

Crown, and that all political connection between them and the State of Great Britain, is and ought to be totally dissolved; and that as Free and Independent States, they have full Power to levy War, conclude Peace, contract Alliances, establish Commerce, and to do all other Acts and Things which Independent States may of right do. And for the support of this Declaration, with a firm reliance on the Protection of Divine Providence, we mutually pledge to each other our Lives, our Fortunes, and our sacred Honor.

The foregoing Declaration was, by order of Congress, engrossed, and signed by the following members:

John Hancock

NEW HAMPSHIRE
Josiah Bartlett
William Whipple
Matthew Thornton

MASSACHUSETTS BAY
Samuel Adams
John Adams
Robert Treat Paine
Elbridge Gerry

RHODE ISLAND
Stephen Hopkins
William Ellery

CONNECTICUT
Roger Sherman
Samuel Huntington
William Williams
Oliver Wolcott

NEW YORK
William Floyd
Philip Livingston
Francis Lewis
Lewis Morris

NEW JERSEY
Richard Stockton
John Witherspoon
Francis Hopkinson
John Hart
Abraham Clark

PENNSYLVANIA
Robert Morris
Benjamin Rush
Benjamin Franklin
John Morton
George Clymer
James Smith
George Taylor
James Wilson
George Ross

DELAWARE
Caesar Rodney
George Read
Thomas M'Kean

MARYLAND
Samuel Chase
William Paca
Thomas Stone
Charles Carroll, of Carrollton

VIRGINIA
George Wythe
Richard Henry Lee
Thomas Jefferson
Benjamin Harrison
Thomas Nelson, Jr.
Francis Lightfoot Lee
Carter Braxton

NORTH CAROLINA
William Hooper
Joseph Hewes
John Penn

SOUTH CAROLINA
Edward Rutledge
Thomas Heyward, Jr.
Thomas Lynch, Jr.
Arthur Middleton

GEORGIA
Button Gwinnett
Lyman Hall
George Walton

Resolved, That copies of the Declaration be sent to the several assemblies, conventions, and committees, or councils of safety, and to the several commanding officers of the continental troops; that it be proclaimed in each of the United States, at the head of the army.

ARTICLES OF
CONFEDERATION

To all to whom these Presents shall come, we the undersigned Delegates of the States affixed to our Names send greeting.

Whereas the Delegates of the United States of America in Congress assembled did on the fifteenth day of November in the Year of our Lord One Thousand Seven Hundred and Seventy-seven, and in the Second Year of the Independence of America agree to certain articles of Confederation and perpetual Union between the States of Newhampshire, Massachusetts-bay, Rhodeisland and Providence Plantations, Connecticut, New York, New Jersey, Pennsylvania, Delaware, Maryland, Virginia, North-Carolina, South-Carolina and Georgia in the Words following, viz.

Articles of Confederation and perpetual Union between the States of Newhampshire, Massachusetts-bay, Rhodeisland and Providence Plantations, Connecticut, New-York, New-Jersey, Pennsylvania, Delaware, Maryland, Virginia, North-Carolina, South-Carolina and Georgia.

ARTICLE I. The stile of this confederacy shall be "The United States of America."

ARTICLE II. Each State retains its sovereignty, freedom and independence, and every power, jurisdiction and right, which is not by this confederation expressly delegated to the United States, in Congress assembled.

ARTICLE III. The said States hereby severally enter into a firm league of friendship with each other, for their common defence, the security of their liberties, and their mutual and general welfare, binding themselves to assist each other, against all force offered to, or attacks made upon them, or any of them, on account of religion, sovereignty, trade or any other pretence whatever.

ARTICLE IV. The better to secure and perpetuate mutual friendship and intercourse among the people of the different States in this Union, the free inhabitants of each of these States, paupers, vagabonds and fugitives from justice excepted, shall be entitled to all privileges and immunities of free citizens in the several States; and the people of each State shall have free ingress and regress to and from any other State, and shall enjoy therein all the privileges of trade and commerce, subject to the same duties, impositions and restrictions as the inhabitants thereof respectively, provided that such restrictions shall not extend so far as to prevent the removal of property imported into any State, to any other State of which the owner is an inhabitant; provided also that no imposition, duties or restriction shall be laid by any State, on the property of the United States, or either of them.

If any person guilty of, or charged with treason, felony, or other high misdemeanor in any State, shall flee from justice, and be found in any of the United States, he shall upon demand of the Governor or Executive power, of the State from which he fled, be delivered up and removed to the State having jurisdiction of his offence.

Full faith and credit shall be given in each of these States to the records, acts and judicial proceedings of the courts and magistrates of every other State.

ARTICLE V. For the more convenient management of the general interests of the United States, delegates shall be annually appointed in such manner as the legislature of each State shall direct, to meet in Congress on the first Monday in November, in every year, with a power reserved to each State, to recall its delegates, or any of them, at any time within the year, and to send others in their stead, for the remainder of the year.

No State shall be represented in Congress by less than two, nor by more than seven members; and no person shall be capable of being a delegate for more than three years in any term of six years; nor shall any person, being a delegate, be capable of holding any office under the United States, for which he, or another for his benefit receives any salary, fees or emolument of any kind.

Each State shall maintain its own delegates in a meeting of the States, and while they act as members of the committee of the States.

In determining questions in the United States, in Congress assembled, each State shall have one vote.

Freedom of speech and debate in Congress shall not be impeached or questioned in any court, or place out of Congress, and the members of Congress shall be protected in their persons from arrests and imprisonments, during the time of their going to and from, and attendance on Congress, except for treason, felony, or breach of the peace.

ARTICLE VI. No State without the consent of the United States in Congress assembled, shall send any embassy to, or receive any embassy from, or enter into any conference, agreement, alliance or treaty with any king, prince or state; nor shall any person holding any office of profit or trust under the United States, or any of them, accept of any present, emolument, office or title of any kind whatever from any king, prince or foreign state; nor shall the United States in Congress assembled, or any of them, grant any title of nobility.

No two or more States shall enter into any treaty, confederation or alliance whatever between them, without the consent of the United States in Congress assembled, specifying accurately the purposes for which the same is to be entered into, and how long it shall continue.

No State shall lay any imposts or duties, which may interfere with any stipulations in treaties, entered into by the United States in Congress assembled, with any king, prince or state, in pursuance of any treaties already proposed by Congress, to the courts of France and Spain.

No vessels of war shall be kept up in time of peace by any State, except such number only, as shall be deemed necessary by the United States in Congress assembled, for the defence of such State, or its trade; nor shall any body of forces be kept up by any State, in time of peace, except such number only, as in the judgment of the United States, in Congress assembled, shall be deemed requisite to garrison the forts necessary for the defence of such State; but every State shall always keep up a well regulated and disciplined militia, sufficiently armed and accoutred, and shall provide and constantly have ready for use, in public stores, a due number of field pieces and tents, and a proper quantity of arms, ammunition and camp equipage.

No State shall engage in any war without the consent of the United States in Congress assembled, unless such State be actually invaded by enemies, or shall have received certain advice of a resolution being formed by some nation of Indians to invade such State, and the danger is so imminent as not to admit of a delay, till the United States in Congress assembled can be consulted: nor shall any State grant commissions to any ships or vessels of war, nor letters of marque or reprisal, except it be after a declaration of war by the United States in Congress assembled, and then only against the kingdom or state and the subjects thereof, against which war has been so declared, and under such regulations as shall be established by the United States in Congress assembled, unless such State be infested by pirates, in which case vessels of war may be fitted out for that occasion, and kept so long as the danger shall continue, or until the United States in Congress assembled shall determine otherwise.

ARTICLE VII. When land-forces are raised by any State of the common defence, all officers of or under the rank of colonel, shall be appointed by the

Legislature of each State respectively by whom such forces shall be raised, or in such manner as such State shall direct, and all vacancies shall be filled up by the State which first made the appointment.

ARTICLE VIII. All charges of war, and all other expenses that shall be incurred for the common defence or general welfare, and allowed by the United States in Congress assembled, shall be defrayed out of a common treasury, which shall be supplied by the several States, in proportion to the value of all land within each State, granted to or surveyed for any person, as such land and the buildings and improvements thereon shall be estimated according to such mode as the United States in Congress assembled, shall from time to time direct and appoint.

The taxes for paying that proportion shall be laid and levied by the authority and direction of the Legislatures of the several States within the time agreed upon by the United States in Congress assembled.

ARTICLE IX. The United States in Congress assembled, shall have the sole and exclusive right and power of determining on peace and war, except in the cases mentioned in the sixth article—of sending and receiving ambassadors—entering into treaties and alliances, provided that no treaty of commerce shall be made whereby the legislative power of the respective States shall be restrained from imposing such imposts and duties on foreigners, as their own people are subjected to, or from prohibiting the exportation or importation of and species of goods or commodities whatsoever—of establishing rules for deciding in all cases, what captures on land or water shall be legal, and in what manner prizes taken by land or naval forces in the service of the United States shall be divided or appropriated—of granting letters of marque and reprisal in times of peace—appointing courts for the trial of piracies and felonies committed on the high seas and establishing courts for receiving and determining finally appeals in all cases of captures, provided that no member of Congress shall be appointed a judge of any of the said courts.

The United States in Congress assembled shall also be the last resort on appeal in all disputes and differences now subsisting or that hereafter may arise between two or more States concerning boundary, jurisdiction or any other cause whatever; which authority shall always be exercised in the manner following. Whenever the legislative or executive authority or lawful agent of any State in controversy with another shall present a petition to Congress, stating the matter in question and praying for a hearing, notice thereof shall be given by order of Congress to the legislative or executive authority of the other State in controversy, and a day assigned for the appearance of the parties by their lawful agents, who shall then be directed to appoint by joint consent, commissioners or judges to constitute a court for hearing and determining the matter in question: but if they cannot agree, Congress shall name three persons out of each of the United States, and from the list of such persons each party shall alternately strike out one, the petitioners beginning, until the number shall be reduced to thirteen; and from that number not less than seven, nor more than nine names as Congress shall direct, shall in the presence of Congress be drawn out by lot, and the persons whose names shall be so drawn or any five of them, shall be commissioners or judges, to hear and finally determine the controversy, so always as a major part of the judges who shall hear the cause shall agree in the determination: and if either party shall neglect to attend at the day appointed, without reasons, which Congress shall judge sufficient, or being present shall refuse to strike, the Congress shall proceed to nominate three persons out of each State, and the Secretary of Congress shall strike in behalf of such party absent or refusing; and the judgment and sentence of the court to be appointed, in the manner before prescribed, shall be final and conclusive; and if any of the parties shall refuse to submit to the authority of such court, or to appear or defend their claim or cause, the court shall nevertheless proceed to pronounce sentence, or judgment, which shall in like manner be final and decisive, the judgment or sentence and other proceedings being in either case transmitted to Congress, and lodged among the acts of Congress for the security of the parties concerned: provided that every commissioner, before he sits in judgment, shall take an oath to be administered by one of the judges of the supreme or superior court of the State where the case shall be tried, "well and truly to hear and determine the matter in question, according to the best of his judgment, without favour, affection or hope of reward:" provided also that no State shall be deprived of territory for the benefit of the United States.

All controversies concerning the private right of soil claimed under different grants of two or more States, whose jurisdiction as they may respect such lands, and the states which passed such grants are adjusted, the said grants or either of them being at the same time claimed to have originated antecedent to such settlement of jurisdiction, shall on the petition of either party to the Congress of the United States, be finally determined as near as may be in the same manner as is before prescribed for deciding disputes respecting territorial jurisdiction between different States.

The United States in Congress assembled shall also have the sole and exclusive right and power of regulating the alloy and value of coin struck by their own authority, or by that of the respective States—fixing the standard of weights and measures throughout the United States—regulating the trade and managing all affairs with the Indians, not members of any of the States, provided that the legislative right of any State within its own limits be not infringed or violated—establishing and regulating post-offices from one State to another, throughout all of the United States, and exacting such postage on the papers passing thro' the same as may be requisite to defray the expenses of the said office—appointing all officers of the land forces, in the service of the United States, excepting regimental officers—appointing all the officers of the naval forces, and commissioning all officers whatever in the service of the United States—making rules for the government and regulation of the said land and naval forces, and directing their operations.

The United States in Congress assembled shall have authority to appoint a committee, to sit in the recess of Congress, to be denominated "a Committee of the States," and to consist of one delegate from each State; and to appoint such other committees and civil officers as may be necessary for managing the general affairs of the United States under their direction—to appoint one of their number to preside, provided that no person be allowed to serve in the office of president more than one year in any term of three years; to ascertain the necessary sums of money to be raised for the service of the United States, and to appropriate and apply the same for defraying the public expenses—to borrow money, or emit bills on the credit of the United States, transmitting every half year to the respective States an account of the sums of money so borrowed or emitted,—to build and equip a navy—to agree upon the number of land forces, and to make requisitions from each State for its quota, in proportion to the number of white inhabitants in such State; which requisition shall be binding, and thereupon the Legislature of each State shall appoint the regimental officers, raise the men and cloath, arm and equip them in a soldier like manner, at the expense of the United States; and the officers and men so cloathed, armed and equipped shall march to the place appointed, and within the time agreed on by the United States in Congress assembled: but if the United States in Congress assembled shall, on consideration of circumstances judge proper that any State should not raise men, or should raise a smaller number of men than the quota thereof, such extra number shall be raised, officered, cloathed, armed and equipped in the same manner as the quota of such State, unless the legislature of such State shall judge that such extra number cannot be safely spared out of the same, in which case they shall raise officer, cloath, arm and equip as many of such extra number as they judge can be safely spared. And the officers and men so cloathed, armed and equipped, shall march to the place appointed, and within the time agreed on by the United States in Congress assembled.

The United States in Congress assembled shall never engage in a war, nor grant letters of marque and reprisal in time of peace, nor enter into any treaties or alliances, nor coin money, nor regulate the value thereof, nor ascertain the sums and expenses necessary for the defence and welfare of the United States, or any of them, nor emit bills, nor borrow money on the credit of the United

States, nor appropriate money, nor agree upon the number of vessels to be built or purchased, or the number of land or sea forces to be raised, nor appoint a commander in chief of the army or navy, unless nine States assent to the same: nor shall a question on any other point, except for adjourning from day to day be determined, unless by the votes of a majority of the United States in Congress assembled.

The Congress of the United States shall have power to adjourn to any time within the year, and to any place within the United States, so that no period of adjournment be for a longer duration than the space of six months, and shall publish the journal of their proceedings monthly, except such parts thereof relating to treaties, alliances or military operations, as in their judgment require secresy; and the yeas and nays of the delegates of each State on any question shall be entered on the Journal, when it is desired by any delegate; and the delegates of a State, or any of them, at his or their request shall be furnished with a transcript of the said journal, except such parts as are above excepted, to lay before the Legislatures of the several States.

ARTICLE X. The committee of the States, or any nine of them, shall be authorized to execute, in the recess of Congress, such of the powers of Congress as the United States in Congress assembled, by the consent of nine States, shall from time to time think expedient to vest them with; provided that no power be delegated to the said committee, for the exercise of which, by the articles of confederation, the voice of nine States in the Congress of the United States assembled is requisite.

ARTICLE XI. Canada acceding to this confederation, and joining in the measures of the United States, shall be admitted into, and entitled to all the advantages of this Union: but no other colony shall be admitted into the same, unless such admission be agreed to by nine States.

ARTICLE XII. All bills of credit emitted, monies borrowed and debts contracted by, or under the authority of Congress, before the assembling of the United States, in pursuance of the present confederation, shall be deemed and considered as a charge against the United States, for payment and satisfaction whereof the said United States, and the public faith are hereby solemnly pledged.

ARTICLE XIII. Every State shall abide by the determinations of the United States in Congress assembled, on all questions which by this confederation are submitted to them. And the articles of this confederation shall be inviolably observed by every State, and the Union shall be perpetual; nor shall any alteration at any time hereafter be made in any of them; unless such alteration be agreed to in a Congress of the United States, and be afterwards confirmed by the Legislatures of every State.

And whereas it has pleased the Great Governor of the world to incline the hearts of the Legislatures we respectively represent in Congress, to approve of, and to authorize us to ratify the said articles of confederation and perpetual union. Know ye that we the undersigned delegates, by virtue of the power and authority to us given for that purpose, do by these presents, in the name and in behalf of our respective constituents, fully and entirely ratify and confirm each and every of the said articles of confederation and perpetual union, and all and singular the matters and things therein contained: and we do further solemnly plight and engage the faith of our respective constituents, that they shall abide by the determinations of the United States in Congress assembled, on all questions, which by the said confederation are submitted to them. And that the articles thereof shall be inviolably observed by the States we respectively represent, and that the Union shall be perpetual.

In witness thereof we have hereunto set our hands in Congress. Done at Philadelphia in the State of Pennsylvania the ninth day of July in the year of our Lord one thousand seven hundred and seventy-eight, and in the third year of the independence of America.

THE CONSTITUTION OF
THE UNITED STATES

WE THE PEOPLE OF THE UNITED STATES, in order to form a more perfect Union, establish Justice, insure domestic Tranquility, provide for the common defence, promote the general Welfare, and secure the Blessings of Liberty to ourselves and our Posterity, do ordain and establish this Constitution for the United States of America.

ARTICLE. I.

Section. 1. All legislative Powers herein granted shall be vested in a Congress of the United States, which shall consist of a Senate and House of Representatives.

Section. 2. The House of Representatives shall be composed of Members chosen every second Year by the People of the several States, and the Electors in each State shall have the Qualifications requisite for Electors of the most numerous Branch of the State Legislature.

No Person shall be a Representative who shall not have attained to the Age of twenty five Years, and been seven Years a Citizen of the United States, and who shall not, when elected, be an Inhabitant of that State in which he shall be chosen.

Representatives and direct Taxes shall be apportioned among the several States which may be included within this Union, according to their respective Numbers, which shall be determined by adding to the whole Number of free Persons, including those bound to Service for a Term of Years, and excluding Indians not taxed, three fifths of all other Persons. The actual Enumeration shall be made within three Years after the first Meeting of the Congress of the United States, and within every subsequent Term of ten Years, in such Manner as they shall by Law direct. The Number of Representatives shall not exceed one for every thirty Thousand, but each State shall have at Least one Representative; and until such enumeration shall be made, the State of New Hampshire shall be entitled to chuse three, Massachusetts eight, Rhode-Island and

Providence Plantations one, Connecticut five, New-York six, New Jersey four, Pennsylvania eight, Delaware one, Maryland six, Virginia ten, North Carolina five, South Carolina five, and Georgia three.

When vacancies happen in the Representation from any state, the Executive Authority thereof shall issue Writs of Election to fill such Vacancies.

The House of Representatives shall chuse their Speaker and other Officers; and shall have the sole Power of Impeachment.

Section. 3. The Senate of the United States shall be composed of two Senators from each State, chosen by the legislature thereof, for six Years; and each Senator shall have one Vote.

Immediately after they shall be assembled in Consequence of the first Election, they shall be divided as equally as may be into three Classes. The Seats of the Senators of the first Class shall be vacated at the Expiration of the second Year, of the second Class at the Expiration of the fourth Year, and of the third Class at the Expiration of the sixth Year, so that one third maybe chosen every second Year; and if Vacancies happen by Resignation, or otherwise, during the Recess of the Legislature of any State, the Executive thereof may make temporary Appointments until the next Meeting of the Legislature, which shall then fill such Vacancies.

No Person shall be a Senator who shall not have attained to the Age of thirty Years, and been nine Years a Citizen of the United States, and who shall not, when elected, be an Inhabitant of that State for which he shall be chosen.

The Vice President of the United States shall be President of the Senate, but shall have no Vote, unless they be equally divided.

The Senate shall chuse their other Officers, and also a President pro tempore, in the Absence of the Vice President, or when he shall exercise the Office of President of the United States.

The Senate shall have the sole Power to try all Impeachments. When sitting for that Purpose, they shall be on Oath or Affirmation. When the President of the United States is tried, the Chief Justice shall preside: And no Person shall be convicted without the Concurrence of two thirds of the Members present.

Judgment in Cases of Impeachment shall not extend further than to removal from Office, and disqualification to hold and enjoy any Office of honor, Trust or Profit under the United States: but the Party convicted shall nevertheless be liable and subject to Indictment, Trial, Judgment and Punishment, according to Law.

Section. 4. The Times, Places and Manner of holding Elections for Senators and Representatives, shall be prescribed in each State by the Legislature thereof; but the Congress may at any time by Law make or alter such Regulations, except as to the Places of chusing Senators.

The Congress shall assemble at least once in every Year, and such Meeting shall be on the first Monday in December, unless they shall by Law appoint a different Day.

Section. 5. Each House shall be the Judge of the Elections, Returns and Qualifications of its own Members, and a Majority of each shall constitute a Quorum to do Business; but a smaller Number may adjourn from day to day, and may be authorized to compel the Attendance of absent Members, in such Manner, and under such Penalties as each House may provide.

Each House may determine the Rules of its Proceedings, punish its Members for disorderly Behaviour, and, with the Concurrence of two thirds, expel a Member.

Each House shall keep a Journal of its Proceedings, and from time to time publish the same, excepting such Parts as may in their Judgment require Secrecy; and the Yeas and Nays of the Members of either House on any question shall, at the Desire of one fifth of those Present, be entered on the Journal.

Neither House, during the Session of Congress, shall, without the Consent of the other, adjourn for more than three days, not to any other Place than that in which the two Houses shall be sitting.

Section. 6. The Senators and Representatives shall receive a Compensation for their Services, to be ascertained by Law, and paid out of the Treasury of the United States. They shall in all Cases, except Treason, Felony and Breach of the Peace, be privileged from Arrest during their Attendance at the Session of their respective Houses, and in going to and returning from the same; and for any Speech or Debate in either House, they shall not be questioned in any other Place.

No Senator or Representative shall, during the Time for which he was elected, be appointed to any civil Office under the Authority of the United States, which shall have been created, or the Emoluments whereof shall have been encreased during such time; and no Person holding any Office under the United States, shall be a Member of either House during his Continuance in Office.

Section. 7. All Bills for raising Revenue shall originate in the House of Representatives; but the Senate may propose or concur with Amendments as on other Bills.

Every Bill which shall have passed the House of Representatives and the Senate shall, before it become a Law, be presented to the President of the United States; If he approve he shall sign it, but if not he shall return it, with his Objections to that House in which it shall have originated, who shall enter the Objections at large on their Journal, and proceed to reconsider it. If after such Reconsideration two thirds of that House shall agree to pass the Bill, it shall be sent, together with the Objections, to the other House, by which it shall likewise be reconsidered, and if approved by two thirds of that House, it shall become a Law. But in all such Cases the Votes of both Houses shall be determined by yeas and Nays, and the Names of the Persons voting for and against the Bill shall be entered on the Journal of each House respectively. If any Bill shall not be returned by the President within ten Days (Sundays excepted) after it shall have been presented to him, the Same shall be a Law, in like Manner as if he had signed it, unless the Congress by their Adjournment prevent its Return, in which Case it shall not be a Law.

Every Order, Resolution, or Vote to which the Concurrence of the Senate and House of Representatives may be necessary (except on a question of Adjournment) shall be presented to the President of the United States; and before the Same shall take Effect, shall be approved by him, or being disapproved by him, shall be repassed by two thirds of the Senate and House of Representatives, according to the Rules and Limitations prescribed in the Case of a Bill.

Section. 8. The Congress shall have Power To lay and collect Taxes, Duties, Imposts and Excises, to pay the Debts and provide for the common Defence and general Welfare of the United States; but all Duties, Imposts and Excises shall be uniform throughout the United States;

To borrow Money on the credit of the United States;

To regulate Commerce with foreign Nations, and among the several States, and with the Indian Tribes;

To establish an uniform Rule of Naturalization, and uniform Laws on the subject of Bankruptcies throughout the United States;

To coin Money, regulate the Value thereof, and of foreign Coin, and fix the Standard of Weights and Measures;

To provide for the Punishment of counterfeiting the Securities and current Coin of the United States;

To establish Post Offices and Post Roads;

To promote the Progress of Science and useful Arts, by securing for limited Times to Authors and Inventors the exclusive Right to their respective Writings and Discoveries;

To constitute Tribunals inferior to the supreme Court;

To define and punish Piracies and Felonies committed on the high Seas, and Offences against the Law of Nations;

To declare War, grant Letters of Marque and Reprisal, and make Rules concerning Captures on land and Water;

To raise and support Armies, but no Appropriation of Money to that Use shall be for a longer Term than two Years;

To provide and maintain a Navy;

To make Rules for the Government and Regulation of the land and naval Forces;

To provide for calling forth the Militia to execute the Laws of the Union, suppress Insurrections and repel Invasions;

To provide for organizing, arming, and disciplining, the Militia, and for governing such Part of them as may be employed in the Service of the United States, reserving to the States respectively, the Appointment of the Officers, and the Authority of training the Militia according to the discipline prescribed by Congress.

To exercise exclusive Legislation in all Cases whatsoever, over such District (not exceeding ten Miles square) as may, by Cession of Particular States, and the Acceptance of Congress, become the Seat of the Government of the United States, and to exercise like Authority over all Places purchased by the Consent of the Legislature of the State in which the Same shall be, for the Erection of Forts, Magazines, Arsenals, dock-Yards, and other needful Buildings;—And

To make all Laws which shall be necessary and proper for carrying into Execution the foregoing Powers, and all other Powers vested by this Constitution in the Government of the United States, or in any Department or Officer thereof.

Section. 9. The Migration or Importation of such Persons as any of the States now existing shall think proper to admit, shall not be prohibited by the Congress prior to the Year one thousand eight hundred and eight, but a Tax or duty may be imposed on such Importation, not exceeding ten dollars for each Person.

The Privilege of the Writ of Habeas Corpus shall not be suspended, unless when in Cases of Rebellion or Invasion the public Safety may require it.

No Bill of Attainder or ex post facto Law shall be passed.

No Capitation, or other direct, Tax shall be laid, unless in Proportion to the Census or Enumeration herein before directed to be taken.

No Tax or Duty shall be laid on Articles exported from any State.

No Preference shall be given by any Regulation of Commerce or Revenue to the Ports of one State over those of another: nor shall Vessels bound to, or from, one State, be obliged to enter, clear, or pay Duties in another.

No Money shall be drawn from the Treasury, but in Consequence of Appropriations made by Law; and a regular Statement and Account of the Receipts and Expenditures of all public Money shall be published from time to time.

No Title of Nobility shall be granted by the United States: And no Person holding any Office of Profit or trust under them, shall, without the Consent of the Congress, accept of any present, Emolument, Office, or Title, of any kind whatever, from any King, Prince, or foreign State.

Section 10. No State shall enter into any Treaty, Alliance, or Confederation; grant Letters of Marque and Reprisal; coin Money; emit Bills of Credit; make any Thing but gold and silver Coin a Tender in Payment of Debts; pass any Bill of Attainder, ex post facto Law, or Law impairing the Obligation of Contracts, or grant any Title of Nobility.

No State shall, without the Consent of the Congress, lay any Imposts or Duties on Imports or Exports, except what may be absolutely necessary for executing its inspection Laws: and the net Produce of all Duties and Imposts, laid by any State on Imports or Exports, shall be for the Use of the Treasury of the United States; and all such Laws shall be subject to the Revision and Controul of the Congress.

No State shall, without the Consent of Congress, lay any Duty of Tonnage, keep Troops, or Ships of War in time of Peace, enter into any Agreement or Compact with another State, or with a foreign Power, or engage in War, unless actually invaded, or in such imminent Danger as will not admit of delay.

ARTICLE. II.

Section. 1. The executive Power shall be vested in a President of the United States of America. He shall hold his Office during the term of four Years, and, together with the Vice President, chosen for the same Term, be elected, as follows:

Each State shall appoint, in such Manner as the Legislature thereof may direct, a Number of Electors, equal to the whole Number of Senators and Representatives to which the State may be entitled in the Congress: but no Senator or Representative, or Person holding an Office of Trust or Profit under the United States, shall be appointed an Elector.

The Electors shall meet in their respective States, and vote by Ballot for two Persons, of whom one at least shall not be an Inhabitant of the same State with themselves. And they shall make a List of all the Persons voted for, and of the Number of Votes for each; which List they shall sign and certify, and transmit sealed to the Seat of the Government of the United States, directed to the President of the Senate. The President of the Senate shall, in the Presence of the Senate and House of Representatives, open all the Certificates, and the Votes shall then be counted. The Person having the greatest Number of Votes shall be the President, if such Number be a Majority of the whole Number of Electors appointed; and if there be more than one who have such Majority, and have an equal Number of Votes, then the House of Representatives shall immediately chuse by Ballot one of them for President; and if no Person have a Majority, then from the five highest on the List the said House shall in like Manner chuse the President. But in chusing the President, the Votes shall be taken by States, the Representation from each State having one Vote; A quorum for this Purpose shall consist of a Member or Members from two thirds of the States, and a Majority of all the States shall be necessary to a Choice. In every Case, after the Choice of the President, the Person having the greatest

Number of Votes of the Electors shall be the Vice President. But if there should remain two or more who have equal Votes, the Senate shall chuse from them by Ballot the Vice President.

The Congress may determine the Time of chusing the Electors, and the Day on which they shall give their Votes; which Day shall be the same throughout the United States.

No Person except a natural born Citizen, or a Citizen of the United States, at the time of the Adoption of this Constitution, shall be eligible to the Office of President; neither shall any Person be eligible to that Office who shall not have attained to the Age of thirty five Years, and been fourteen Years a Resident within the United States.

In Case of the Removal of the President from Office, or of his Death, Resignation, or Inability to discharge the Powers and Duties of the said Office, the Same shall devolve on the Vice President, and the Congress may by Law provide for the Case of Removal, Death, Resignation or Inability, both of the President and Vice President, declaring what Officer shall then act as President, and such Officer shall act accordingly, until the Disability be removed, or a President shall be elected.

The President shall, at stated Times, receive for his Services, a Compensation, which shall neither be encreased or diminished during the Period for which he shall have been elected, and he shall not receive within that Period any other Emolument from the United States, or any of them.

Before he enters on the Execution of his Office, he shall take the following Oath or Affirmation:—"I do solemnly swear (or affirm) that I will faithfully execute the Office of President of the United States, and will to the best of my Ability, preserve, protect and defend the Constitution of the United States."

Section. 2. The President shall be Commander in Chief of the Army and Navy of the United States, and of the Militia of the several States, when called into the actual Service of the United States; he may require the Opinion, in writing, of the principal Officer in each of the executive Departments, upon any Subject relating to the Duties of their respective Offices, and he shall have Power to grant Reprieves and Pardons for Offences against the United States, except in Cases of Impeachment.

He shall have Power, by and with the Advice and Consent of the Senate, to make Treaties, provided two thirds of the Senators present concur; and he shall nominate, and by and with the Advice and Consent of the Senate, shall appoint Ambassadors, other public Ministers and Consuls, Judges of the supreme Court, and all other Officers of the United States, whose Appointments are not herein otherwise provided for, and which shall be established by Law; but the Congress may by Law vest the Appointment of such inferior Officers, as they think proper, in the President alone, in the Courts of Law, or in the Heads of Departments.

The President shall have Power to fill up all Vacancies that may happen during the Recess of the Senate, by granting Commissions which shall expire at the End of their next Session.

Section. 3. He shall from time to time give to the Congress Information of the State of the Union, and recommend to their Consideration such Measures as he shall judge necessary and expedient; he may, on extraordinary Occasions, convene both Houses, or either of them, and in Case of Disagreement between them, with Respect to the Time of Adjournment, he may adjourn them to such Time as he shall think proper; he shall receive Ambassadors and other public Ministers; he shall take Care that the Laws be faithfully executed, and shall Commission all the Officers of the United States.

Section. 4. The President, Vice President and all civil Officers of the United States, shall be removed from Office on Impeachment for, and Conviction of, Treason, Bribery, or other high Crimes and Misdemeanors.

ARTICLE. III.

Section. 1. The judicial Power of the United States, shall be vested in one supreme Court, and in such inferior Courts as the Congress may from time to time ordain and establish. The Judges, both of the supreme and inferior Courts, shall hold their Offices during good Behavior, and shall, at stated Times, receive for their Services, a Compensation, which shall not be diminished during their Continuance in Office.

Section. 2. The judicial Power shall extend to all Cases, in Law and Equity, arising under this Constitution, the Laws of the United States, and Treaties made, or which shall be made, under their Authority;—to all Cases affecting Ambassadors, other public Ministers and Consuls;—to all Cases of admiralty and maritime Jurisdiction;—the Controversies to which the United States shall be a Party;—to Controversies between two or more States;—between a State and Citizens of another State;—between Citizens of different States;—between Citizens of the same State claiming Lands under Grants of different States, and between a State, or the Citizens thereof, and foreign States, Citizens or Subjects.

In all cases affecting Ambassadors, other public Ministers and Consuls, and those in which a State shall be Party, the supreme Court shall have original Jurisdiction. In all the other Cases before mentioned, the supreme Court shall have appellate Jurisdiction, both as to Law and Fact, with such Exceptions, and under such Regulations as the Congress shall make.

The Trial of all Crimes, except in Cases of Impeachment, shall be by Jury; and such Trial shall be held in the State where the said Crimes shall have been committed; but when not committed within any State, the Trial shall be at such Place or Places as the Congress may by Law have directed.

Section. 3. Treason against the United States, shall consist only in levying War against them, or in adhering to their Enemies, giving them Aid and Comfort. No Person shall be convicted of Treason unless on the Testimony of two Witnesses to the same overt Act, or on Confession in open Court.

The Congress shall have Power to declare the Punishment of Treason, but no Attainder of Treason shall work Corruption of Blood, or Forfeiture except during the Life of the Person attainted.

ARTICLE. IV.

Section. 1. Full Faith and Credit shall be given in each State to the public Acts, Records, and judicial Proceedings of every other State. And the Congress may by general Laws prescribe the Manner in which such Acts, Records and Proceedings shall be proved, and the Effect thereof.

Section. 2. The Citizens of each State shall be entitled to all Privileges and Immunities of Citizens in the several States.

A Person charged in any State with Treason, Felony, or other Crime, who shall flee from Justice, and be found in another State, shall on Demand of the executive Authority of the State from which he fled, be delivered up, to be removed to the State having Jurisdiction of the Crime.

No Person held to Service or Labour in one State, under the Laws thereof, escaping into another, shall, in Consequence of any Law or Regulation therein, be discharged from such Service or Labour, but shall be delivered up on Claim of the Party to whom such Service or Labour may be due.

Section. 3. New States may be admitted by the Congress into this Union; but no new State shall be formed or erected within the Jurisdiction of any other State; nor any State be formed by the Junction of two or more States, or Parts of States, without the consent of the Legislatures of the States concerned as well as of the Congress.

The Congress shall have Power to dispose of and make all needful Rules and Regulations respecting the Territory or other Property belonging to the United States; and nothing in this Constitution shall be so construed as to Prejudice any Claims of the United States, or of any particular States.

Section. 4. The United States shall guarantee to every State in this Union a Republican Form of Government, and shall protect each of them against Invasion; and on Application of the Legislature, or of the Executive (when the Legislature cannot be convened) against domestic Violence.

ARTICLE. V.

The Congress, whenever two thirds of both Houses shall deem it necessary, shall propose Amendments to this Constitution, or, on the Application of the Legislatures of two thirds of the several States, shall call a Convention for proposing Amendments, which, in either Case, shall be valid to all Intents and Purposes, as Part of this Constitution, when ratified by the Legislatures of three fourths of the several States, or by Conventions in three fourths thereof, as the one or the other Mode of Ratification may be proposed by the Congress; Provided that no Amendment which may be made prior to the Year One thousand eight hundred and eight shall in any Manner affect the first and fourth Clauses in the Ninth Section of the first Article; and that no State, without its Consent, shall be deprived of its equal Suffrage in the Senate.

ARTICLE. VI.

All Debts contracted and Engagements entered into, before the Adoption of this Constitution, shall be as valid against the United States under this Constitution, as under the Confederation.

This Constitution, and the Laws of the United States which shall be made in Pursuance thereof; and all Treaties made, or which shall be made, under the Authority of the United States, shall be the supreme Law of the Land; and the Judges in every State shall be bound thereby, any Thing in the Constitution or Laws of any State to the Contrary notwithstanding.

The Senators and Representatives before mentioned, and the Members of the several State Legislatures, and all executive and judicial Officers, both of the United States and of the several States, shall be bound by Oath or Affirmation, to support this Constitution; but no religious Test shall ever be required as a Qualification to any Office or public Trust under the United States.

ARTICLE. VII.

The Ratification of the Conventions of nine States, shall be sufficient for the Establishment of this Constitution between the States so ratifying the Same.

Done in Convention by the Unanimous Consent of the States present the Seventeenth Day of September in the Year of our Lord one thousand seven hundred and Eighty seven and of the Independence of the United States of America the Twelfth. In witness thereof We have hereunto subscribed our Names,

G°. WASHINGTON—Presd^t.
and deputy from Virginia.

New Hampshire	{ John Langdon Nicholas Gilman		Delaware	{ Geo: Read Gunning Bedford jun John Dickinson Richard Bassett Jaco: Broom
Massachusetts	{ Nathaniel Gorham Rufus King			
Connecticut	{ Wm Saml Johnson Roger Sherman		Maryland	{ James McHenry Dan of St Thos Jenifer Danl Carroll
New York: . . .	Alexander Hamilton		Virginia	{ John Blair— James Madison Jr.
New Jersey	{ Wil: Livingston David A. Brearley. Wm Paterson. Jona: Dayton		North Carolina	{ Wm Blount Richd Dobbs Spaight. Hu Williamson
Pennsylvania	{ B Franklin Thomas Mifflin Robt Morris Geo. Clymer Thos FitzSimons Jared Ingersoll James Wilson Gouv Morris		South Carolina	{ J. Rutledge Charles Cotesworth Pinckney Charles Pinckney Pierce Butler.
			Georgia	{ William Few Abr Baldwin

AMENDMENTS TO THE CONSTITUTION

ARTICLES IN ADDITION TO, and Amendment of the Constitution of the United States of America, proposed by Congress, and ratified by the Legislatures of the several States, pursuant to the fifth Article of the original Constitution.

AMENDMENT I.

Congress shall make no law respecting an establishment of religion, or prohibiting the free exercise thereof; or abridging the freedom of speech, or of the press; or the right of the people peaceably to assemble, and to petition the Government for a redress of grievances.

Amendment II.

A well regulated Militia, being necessary to the security of a free State, the right of the people to keep and bear Arms, shall not be infringed.

Amendment III.

No Soldier shall, in time of peace be quartered in any house, without the consent of the Owner, nor in time of war, but in a manner to be prescribed by law.

Amendment IV.

The right of the people to be secure in their persons, houses, papers, and effects, against unreasonable searches and seizures, shall not be violated, and no Warrants shall issue, but upon probable cause, supported by Oath or affirmation, and particularly describing the place to be searched, and the persons or things to be seized.

Amendment V.

No person shall be held to answer for a capital, or otherwise infamous crime, unless on a presentment or indictment of a Grand Jury, except in cases arising in the land or naval forces, or in the Militia, when in actual service in time of War or public danger; nor shall any person be subject for the same offence to be twice put in jeopardy of life or limb; nor shall be compelled in any criminal case to be a witness against himself, nor be deprived of life, liberty, or property, without due process of law; nor shall private property be taken for public use, without just compensation.

Amendment VI.

In all criminal prosecutions, the accused shall enjoy the right to a speedy and public trial, by an impartial jury of the State and district wherein the crime shall have been committed, which district shall have been previously ascertained by law, and to be informed of the nature and cause of the accusation; to be confronted with the witnesses against him; to have compulsory process for obtaining witnesses in his favor, and to have the Assistance of Counsel for his defence.

AMENDMENT VII.

In Suits at common law, where the value in controversy shall exceed twenty dollars, the right of trial by jury shall be preserved, and no fact tried by a jury, shall be otherwise re-examined in any Court of the United States, than according to the rules of the common law.

AMENDMENT VIII.

Excessive bail shall not be required, nor excessive fines imposed, nor cruel and unusual punishments inflicted.

AMENDMENT IX.

The enumeration in the Constitution, of certain rights, shall not be construed to deny or disparage others retained by the people.

AMENDMENT X.

The powers not delegated to the United States by the Constitution, nor prohibited by it to the States, are reserved to the States respectively, or to the people. [The first ten amendments went into effect December 15, 1791.]

AMENDMENT XI.

The Judicial power of the United States shall not be construed to extend to any suit in law or equity, commenced or prosecuted against one of the United States by Citizens of another State, or by Citizens or Subjects of any Foreign State. [January 8, 1798.]

AMENDMENT XII.

The Electors shall meet in their respective states, and vote by ballot for President and Vice-President, one of whom, at least, shall not be an inhabitant of the same state with themselves; they shall name in their ballots the person voted for as President, and in distinct ballots the person voted for as Vice-President, and they shall make distinct lists of all persons voted for as President, and of all persons voted for as Vice President, and of the number of votes for each, which lists they shall sign and certify, and transmit sealed to the seat of the government of the United States, directed to the President of the Senate;—The President of the Senate shall, in the presence of the Senate and House of Representatives, open all the certificates and the votes shall then be counted;—The person having the greatest number of votes for President, shall be the President, if such number be a majority of the whole number of Electors appointed; and if no person have such majority, then from the persons having the highest numbers not exceeding three on the list of those voted for as President, the House of Representatives shall choose immediately, by ballot, the President. But in choosing the President, the votes shall be taken by states, the representation from each state having one vote; a quorum for this purpose shall consist of a member or members from two-thirds of the states, and a majority of all the states shall be necessary to a choice. And if the House of Representatives shall not choose a President whenever the right of choice shall devolve upon them, before the fourth day of March next following, then the Vice-President shall act as President, as in the case of the death or other constitutional disability of the President.—The person having the greatest number of votes as Vice-President, shall be the Vice-President, if such number be a majority of the whole number of Electors appointed, and if no person have a majority, then from the two highest numbers on the list, the Senate shall choose the Vice-President; a quorum for the purpose shall consist of two-thirds of the whole number of Senators, and a majority of the whole number shall be necessary to a choice. But no person constitutionally ineligible to the office of President shall be eligible to that of Vice-President of the United States. [September 25, 1804.]

AMENDMENT XIII.

Section 1. Neither slavery nor involuntary servitude, except as a punishment for crime whereof the party shall have been duly convicted, shall exist within the United States, or any place subject to their jurisdiction.

Section 2. Congress shall have power to enforce this article by appropriate legislation. [December 18, 1865.]

Amendment XIV.

Section 1. All persons born or naturalized in the United States, and subject to the jurisdiction thereof, are citizens of the United States and of the State wherein they reside. No State shall make or enforce any law which shall abridge the privileges or immunities of citizens of the United States; nor shall any State deprive any person of life, liberty, or property, without due process of law; nor deny to any person within its jurisdiction the equal protection of the laws.

Section 2. Representatives shall be apportioned among the several States according to their respective numbers, counting the whole number of persons in each State, excluding Indians not taxed. But when the right to vote at any election for the choice of electors for President and Vice President of the United States, Representatives in Congress, the Executive and Judicial officers of a State, or the members of the Legislature thereof, is denied to any of the male inhabitants of such State, being twenty-one years of age, and citizens of the United States, or in any way abridged, except for participation in rebellion, or other crime, the basis of representation therein shall be reduced in the proportion which the number of such male citizens shall bear to the whole number of male citizens twenty-one years of age in such State.

Section 3. No person shall be a Senator or Representative in Congress, or elector of President and Vice President, or hold any office, civil or military, under the United States, or under any State, who, having previously taken an oath, as a member of Congress, or as an officer of the United States, or as a member of any State legislature, or as an executive or judicial officer of any State, to support the Constitution of the United States, shall have engaged in insurrection or rebellion against the same, or given aid or comfort to the enemies thereof. But Congress may by a vote of two-thirds of each House, remove such disability.

Section 4. The validity of the public debt of the United States, authorized by law, including debts incurred for payment of pensions and bounties for services in suppressing insurrection or rebellion, shall not be questioned. But neither the United States nor any State shall assume or pay any debt or obligation incurred in aid of insurrection or rebellion against the United States, or any claim for the loss or emancipation of any slave; but all such debts, obligations and claims shall be held illegal and void.

Section 5. The Congress shall have power to enforce, by appropriate legislation, the provisions of this article. [July 28, 1868.]

Amendment XV.

Section 1. The right of citizens of the United States to vote shall not be denied or abridged by the United States or by any State on account of race, color, or previous condition of servitude—

Section 2. The Congress shall have power to enforce this article by appropriate legislation.—[March 30, 1870.]

Amendment XVI.

The Congress shall have power to lay and collect taxes on incomes, from whatever source derived, without apportionment among the several States, and without regard to any census or enumeration. [February 25, 1913.]

Amendment XVII.

The Senate of the United States shall be composed of two senators from each State, elected by the people thereof, for six years; and each Senator shall have one vote. The electors in each State shall have the qualifications requisite for electors of the most numerous branch of the State legislature.

When vacancies happen in the representation of any State in the Senate, the executive authority of such State shall issue writs of election to fill such vacancies: *Provided,* That the legislature of any State may empower the executive thereof to make temporary appointments until the people fill the vacancies by election as the legislature may direct.

This amendment shall not be so construed as to affect the election or term of any senator chosen before it becomes valid as part of the Constitution. [May 31, 1913.]

Amendment XVIII.

After one year from the ratification of this article, the manufacture, sale, or transportation of intoxicating liquors within, the importation thereof into, or the exportation thereof from the United States and all territory subject to the jurisdiction thereof for beverage purposes is hereby prohibited.

The Congress and the several States shall have concurrent power to enforce this article by appropriate legislation.

This article shall be inoperative unless it shall have been ratified as an amendment to the Constitution by the legislatures of the several States, as provided in the Constitution, within seven years from the date of the submission thereof to the States by Congress. [January 29, 1919.]

AMENDMENT XIX.

The right of citizens of the United States to vote shall not be denied or abridged by the United States or by any State on account of sex.

The Congress shall have power by appropriate legislation to enforce the provisions of this article. [August 26, 1920.]

AMENDMENT XX.

Section 1. The terms of the President and Vice-President shall end at noon on the twentieth day of January, and the terms of Senators and Representatives at noon on the third day of January, of the years in which such terms would have ended if this article had not been ratified; and the terms of their successors shall then begin.

Section 2. The Congress shall assemble at least once in every year, and such meeting shall begin at noon on the third day of January, unless they shall by law appoint a different day.

Section 3. If, at the time fixed for the beginning of the term of the President, the President-elect shall have died, the Vice-President-elect shall become President. If a President shall not have been chosen before the time fixed for the beginning of his term, or if the President-elect shall have failed to qualify, then the Vice-President-elect shall act as President until a President shall have qualified; and the Congress may by law provide for the case wherein neither a President-elect nor a Vice-President-elect shall have qualified, declaring who shall then act as President, or the manner in which one who is to act shall be selected, and such person shall act accordingly until a President or Vice-President shall have qualified.

Section 4. The Congress may by law provide for the case of the death of any of the persons from whom the House of Representatives may choose a President whenever the right of choice shall have devolved upon them, and for the case of the death of any of the persons from whom the Senate may choose a Vice-President whenever the right of choice shall have devolved upon them.

Section 5. Sections 1 and 2 shall take effect on the 15th day of October following the ratification of this article.

Section 6. This article shall be inoperative unless it shall have been ratified as an amendment to the Constitution by the legislatures of three-fourths of the several States within seven years from the date of its submission. [February 6, 1933.]

AMENDMENT XXI.

Section 1. The eighteenth article of amendment to the Constitution of the United States is hereby repealed.

Section 2. The transportation or importation into any State, Territory or possession of the United States for delivery or use therein of intoxicating liquors, in violation of the laws thereof, is hereby prohibited.

Section 3. This article shall be inoperative unless it shall have been ratified as an amendment to the Constitution by convention in the several States, as provided in the Constitution, within seven years from the date of the submission thereof to the States by the Congress. [December 5, 1933.]

AMENDMENT XXII.

Section 1. No person shall be elected to the office of the President more than twice, and no person who has held the office of President, or acted as President, for more than two years of a term to which some other person was elected President shall be elected to the office of the President more than once. But this Article shall not apply to any person holding the office of President when this Article was proposed by the Congress, and shall not prevent any person who may be holding the office of President, or acting as President, during the term within which this Article becomes operative from holding the office of President or acting as President during the remainder of such term.

Section 2. This article shall be inoperative unless it shall have been ratified as an amendment to the Constitution by the legislatures of three-fourths of the several states within seven years from the date of its submission to the States by the Congress. [February 27, 1951.]

AMENDMENT XXIII.

Section 1. The District constituting the seat of government of the United States shall appoint in such manner as the Congress may direct:

A number of electors of President and Vice-President equal to the whole number of Senators and Representatives in Congress to which the District would be entitled if it were a State, but in no event more than the least populous State; they shall be in addition to those appointed by the States, but they shall be considered, for the purposes of the election of President and Vice-President, to be electors appointed by a State; and they shall meet in the District and perform such duties as provided by the twelfth article of amendment.

Section 2. The Congress shall have the power to enforce this article by appropriate legislation. [March 29, 1961.]

AMENDMENT XXIV.

Section 1. The right of citizens of the United States to vote in any primary or other election for President or Vice President, for electors for President or Vice President, or for Senator or Representative in Congress, shall not be denied or abridged by the United States or any State by reason of failure to pay any poll tax or other tax.

Section 2. The Congress shall have power to enforce this article by appropriate legislation. [January 23, 1964.]

AMENDMENT XXV.

Section 1. In case of the removal of the President from office or of his death or resignation, the Vice President shall become President.

Section 2. Whenever there is a vacancy in the office of Vice President, the President shall nominate a Vice President who shall take office upon confirmation by a majority vote of both Houses of Congress.

Section 3. Whenever the President transmits to the President pro tempore of the Senate and the Speaker of the House of Representatives his written declaration that he is unable to discharge the powers and duties of his office, and until he transmits to them a written declaration to the contrary, such powers and duties shall be discharged by the Vice President as Acting President.

Section 4. Whenever the Vice President and a majority of either the principal officers of the executive departments or of such other body as Congress may by law provide, transmit to the President pro tempore of the Senate and the Speaker of the House of Representatives their written declaration that the President is unable to discharge the powers and duties of his office, the Vice President shall immediately assume the powers and duties of the office as Acting President.

Thereafter, when the President transmits to the President pro tempore of the Senate and the Speaker of the House of Representatives his written declaration that no inability exists, he shall resume the powers and duties of his office unless the Vice President and a majority of either the principal officers of the executive departments or of such other body as Congress may by law provide, transmit within four days to the President pro tempore of the Senate and the Speaker of the House of Representatives their written declaration that the President is unable to discharge the powers and duties of his office. Thereupon Congress shall decide the issue, assembling within forty-eight hours for that purpose if not in session. If the Congress, within twenty-one days after receipt of the latter written declaration, or, if Congress is not in session, within twenty-one days after Congress is required to assemble, determines by two-thirds vote of both Houses that the President is unable to discharge the powers and duties of his office, the Vice President shall continue to discharge the same as Acting President; otherwise, the President shall resume the powers and duties of his office. [February 10, 1967.]

Amendment XXVI.

Section 1. The right of citizens of the United States, who are eighteen years of age or older, to vote shall not be denied or abridged by the United States or by any State on account of age.

Section 2. The Congress shall have power to enforce this article by appropriate legislation [June 30, 1971.]

Amendment XXVII.

No law, varying the compensation for the services of the Senators and Representatives shall take effect, until an election of Representatives shall have intervened. [May 8, 1992.]

PRESIDENTIAL ELECTIONS

Year	Number of States	Candidates	Parties	Popular Vote	% of Popular Vote	Electoral Vote	% Voter Participation
1789	11	**GEORGE WASHINGTON**	No party designations			69	
		John Adams				34	
		Other candidates				35	
1792	15	**GEORGE WASHINGTON**	No party designations			132	
		John Adams				77	
		George Clinton				50	
		Other candidates				5	
1796	16	**JOHN ADAMS**	Federalist			71	
		Thomas Jefferson	Democratic-Republican			68	
		Thomas Pinckney	Federalist			59	
		Aaron Burr	Democratic-Republican			30	
		Other candidates				48	
1800	16	**THOMAS JEFFERSON**	Democratic-Republican			73	
		Aaron Burr	Democratic-Republican			73	
		John Adams	Federalist			65	
		Charles C. Pinckney	Federalist			64	
		John Jay	Federalist			1	
1804	17	**THOMAS JEFFERSON**	Democratic-Republican			162	
		Charles C. Pinckney	Federalist			14	

Year	Number of States	Candidates	Parties	Popular Vote	% of Popular Vote	Electoral Vote	% Voter Participation
1808	17	**JAMES MADISON**	Democratic-Republican			122	
		Charles C. Pinckney	Federalist			47	
		George Clinton	Democratic-Republican			6	
1812	18	**JAMES MADISON**	Democratic-Republican			128	
		DeWitt Clinton	Federalist			89	
1816	19	**JAMES MONROE**	Democratic-Republican			183	
		Rufus King	Federalist			34	
1820	24	**JAMES MONROE**	Democratic-Republican			231	
		John Quincy Adams	Independent			1	
1824	24	**JOHN QUINCY ADAMS**	Democratic-Republican	108,740	30.5	84	26.9
		Andrew Jackson	Democratic-Republican	153,544	43.1	99	
		Henry Clay	Democratic-Republican	47,136	13.2	37	
		William H. Crawford	Democratic-Republican	46,618	13.1	41	
1828	24	**ANDREW JACKSON**	Democratic	647,286	56.0	178	57.6
		John Quincy Adams	National-Republican	508,064	44.0	83	

Year	Number of States	Candidates	Parties	Popular Vote	% of Popular Vote	Electoral Vote	% Voter Participation
1832	24	**ANDREW JACKSON**	Democratic	688,242	54.5	219	55.4
		Henry Clay	National-Republican	473,462	37.5	49	
		William Wirt	Anti-Masonic	101,051	8.0	7	
		John Floyd	Democratic			11	
1836	26	**MARTIN VAN BUREN**	Democratic	765,483	50.9	170	57.8
		William H. Harrison	Whig			73	
		Hugh L. White	Whig	739,795	49.1	26	
		Daniel Webster	Whig			14	
		W. P. Mangum	Whig			11	
1840	26	**WILLIAM H. HARRISON**	Whig	1,274,624	53.1	234	80.2
		Martin Van Buren	Democratic	1,127,781	46.9	60	
1844	26	**JAMES K. POLK**	Democratic	1,338,464	49.6	170	78.9
		Henry Clay	Whig	1,300,097	48.1	105	
		James G. Birney	Liberty	62,300	2.3		
1848	30	**ZACHARY TAYLOR**	Whig	1,360,967	47.4	163	72.7
		Lewis Cass	Democratic	1,222,342	42.5	127	
		Martin Van Buren	Free Soil	291,263	10.1		
1852	31	**FRANKLIN PIERCE**	Democratic	1,601,117	50.9	254	69.6
		Winfield Scott	Whig	1,385,453	44.1	42	
		John P. Hale	Free Soil	155,825	5.0		
1856	31	**JAMES BUCHANAN**	Democratic	1,832,955	45.3	174	78.9
		John C. Frémont	Republican	1,339,932	33.1	114	
		Millard Fillmore	American	871,731	21.6	8	

Year	Number of States	Candidates	Parties	Popular Vote	% of Popular Vote	Electoral Vote	% Voter Participation
1860	33	**ABRAHAM LINCOLN**	Republican	1,865,593	39.8	180	81.2
		Stephen A. Douglas	Democratic	1,382,713	29.5	12	
		John C. Breckinridge	Democratic	848,356	18.1	72	
		John Bell	Constitutional Union	592,906	12.6	39	
1864	36	**ABRAHAM LINCOLN**	Republican	2,206,938	55.0	212	73.8
		George B. McClellan	Democratic	1,803,787	45.0	21	
1868	37	**ULYSSES S. GRANT**	Republican	3,013,421	52.7	214	78.1
		Horatio Seymour	Democratic	2,706,829	47.3	80	
1872	37	**ULYSSES S. GRANT**	Republican	3,596,745	55.6	286	71.3
		Horace Greeley	Democratic	2,843,446	43.9	66	
1876	38	**RUTHERFORD B. HAYES**	Republican	4,036,572	48.0	185	81.8
		Samuel J. Tilden	Democratic	4,284,020	51.0	184	
1880	38	**JAMES A. GARFIELD**	Republican	4,453,295	48.5	214	79.4
		Winfield S. Hancock	Democratic	4,414,082	48.1	155	
		James B. Weaver	Greenback-Labor	308,578	3.4		
1884	38	**GROVER CLEVELAND**	Democratic	4,879,507	48.5	219	77.5
		James G. Blaine	Republican	4,850,293	48.2	182	
		Benjamin F. Butler	Greenback-Labor	175,370	1.8		
		John P. St. John	Prohibition	150,369	1.5		
1888	38	**BENJAMIN HARRISON**	Republican	5,477,129	47.9	233	79.3
		Grover Cleveland	Democratic	5,537,857	48.6	168	
		Clinton B. Fisk	Prohibition	249,506	2.2		
		Anson J. Streeter	Union Labor	146,935	1.3		

Year	Number of States	Candidates	Parties	Popular Vote	% of Popular Vote	Electoral Vote	% Voter Participation
1892	44	**GROVER CLEVELAND**	Democratic	5,555,426	46.1	277	74.7
		Benjamin Harrison	Republican	5,182,690	43.0	145	
		James B. Weaver	People's	1,029,846	8.5	22	
		John Bidwell	Prohibition	264,133	2.2		
1896	45	**WILLIAM McKINLEY**	Republican	7,102,246	51.1	271	79.3
		William J. Bryan	Democratic	6,492,559	47.7	176	
1900	45	**WILLIAM McKINLEY**	Republican	7,218,491	51.7	292	73.2
		William J. Bryan	Democratic; Populist	6,356,734	45.5	155	
		John C. Wooley	Prohibition	208,914	1.5		
1904	45	**THEODORE ROOSEVELT**	Republican	7,628,461	57.4	336	65.2
		Alton B. Parker	Democratic	5,084,223	37.6	140	
		Eugene V. Debs	Socialist	402,283	3.0		
		Silas C. Swallow	Prohibition	258,536	1.9		
1908	46	**WILLIAM H. TAFT**	Republican	7,675,320	51.6	321	65.4
		William J. Bryan	Democratic	6,412,294	43.1	162	
		Eugene V. Debs	Socialist	420,793	2.8		
		Eugene W. Chafin	Prohibition	253,840	1.7		
1912	48	**WOODROW WILSON**	Democratic	6,296,547	41.9	435	58.8
		Theodore Roosevelt	Progressive	4,118,571	27.4	88	
		William H. Taft	Republican	3,486,720	23.2	8	
		Eugene V. Debs	Socialist	900,672	6.0		
		Eugene W. Chafin	Prohibition	206,275	1.4		

Year	Number of States	Candidates	Parties	Popular Vote	% of Popular Vote	Electoral Vote	% Voter Participation
1916	48	**WOODROW WILSON**	Democratic	9,127,695	49.4	277	61.6
		Charles E. Hughes	Republican	8,533,507	46.2	254	
		A. L. Benson	Socialist	585,113	3.2		
		J. Frank Hanly	Prohibition	220,506	1.2		
1920	48	**WARREN G. HARDING**	Republican	16,143,407	60.4	404	49.2
		James M. Cox	Democratic	9,130,328	34.2	127	
		Eugene V. Debs	Socialist	919,799	3.4		
		P. P. Christensen	Farmer-Labor	265,411	1.0		
1924	48	**CALVIN COOLIDGE**	Republican	15,718,211	54.0	382	48.9
		John W. Davis	Democratic	8,385,283	28.8	136	
		Robert M. La Follette	Progressive	4,831,289	16.6	13	
1928	48	**HERBERT C. HOOVER**	Republican	21,391,993	58.2	444	56.9
		Alfred E. Smith	Democratic	15,016,169	40.9	87	
1932	48	**FRANKLIN D. ROOSEVELT**	Democratic	22,809,638	57.4	472	56.9
		Herbert C. Hoover	Republican	15,758,901	39.7	59	
		Norman Thomas	Socialist	881,951	2.2		
1936	48	**FRANKLIN D. ROOSEVELT**	Democratic	27,752,869	60.8	523	61.0
		Alfred M. Landon	Republican	16,674,665	36.5	8	
		William Lemke	Union	882,479	1.9		
1940	48	**FRANKLIN D. ROOSEVELT**	Democratic	27,307,819	54.8	449	62.5
		Wendell L. Willkie	Republican	22,321,018	44.8	82	
1944	48	**FRANKLIN D. ROOSEVELT**	Democratic	25,606,585	53.5	432	55.9
		Thomas E. Dewey	Republican	22,014,745	46.0	99	

Year	Number of States	Candidates	Parties	Popular Vote	% of Popular Vote	Electoral Vote	% Voter Participation
1948	48	HARRY S. TRUMAN	Democratic	24,179,345	49.6	303	53.0
		Thomas E. Dewey	Republican	21,991,291	45.1	189	
		J. Strom Thurmond	States' Rights	1,176,125	2.4	39	
		Henry A. Wallace	Progressive	1,157,326	2.4		
1952	48	DWIGHT D. EISENHOWER	Republican	33,936,234	55.1	442	63.3
		Adlai E. Stevenson	Democratic	27,314,992	44.4	89	
1956	48	DWIGHT D. EISENHOWER	Republican	35,590,472	57.6	457	60.6
		Adlai E. Stevenson	Democratic	26,022,752	42.1	73	
1960	50	JOHN F. KENNEDY	Democratic	34,226,731	49.7	303	62.8
		Richard M. Nixon	Republican	34,108,157	49.5	219	
1964	50	LYNDON B. JOHNSON	Democratic	43,129,566	61.1	486	61.9
		Barry M. Goldwater	Republican	27,178,188	38.5	52	
1968	50	RICHARD M. NIXON	Republican	31,785,480	43.4	301	60.9
		Hubert H. Humphrey	Democratic	31,275,166	42.7	191	
		George C. Wallace	American Independent	9,906,473	13.5	46	
1972	50	RICHARD M. NIXON	Republican	47,169,911	60.7	520	55.2
		George S. McGovern	Democratic	29,170,383	37.5	17	
		John G. Schmitz	American	1,099,482	1.4		

Year	States	Candidates	Parties	Popular Vote	% Popular Vote	Electoral Vote	% Voter Participation
1976	50	**JIMMY CARTER**	Democratic	40,830,763	50.1	297	53.5
		Gerald R. Ford	Republican	39,147,793	48.0	240	
1980	50	**RONALD REAGAN**	Republican	43,901,812	50.7	489	52.6
		Jimmy Carter	Democratic	35,483,820	41.0	49	
		John B. Anderson	Independent	5,719,437	6.6		
		Ed Clark	Libertarian	921,188	1.1		
1984	50	**RONALD REAGAN**	Republican	54,451,521	58.8	525	53.1
		Walter F. Mondale	Democratic	37,565,334	40.6	13	
1988	50	**GEORGE H. W. BUSH**	Republican	47,917,341	53.4	426	50.1
		Michael Dukakis	Democratic	41,013,030	45.6	111	
1992	50	**BILL CLINTON**	Democratic	44,908,254	43.0	370	55.0
		George H. W. Bush	Republican	39,102,343	37.4	168	
		H. Ross Perot	Independent	19,741,065	18.9		
1996	50	**BILL CLINTON**	Democratic	47,401,185	49.0	379	49.0
		Bob Dole	Republican	39,197,469	41.0	159	
		H. Ross Perot	Independent	8,085,295	8.0		
2000	50	**GEORGE W. BUSH**	Republican	50,455,156	47.9	271	50.4
		Al Gore	Democrat	50,997,335	48.4	266	
		Ralph Nader	Green	2,882,897	2.7		

Candidates receiving less than 1 percent of the popular vote have been omitted. Thus the percentage of popular vote given for any election year may not total 100 percent.

Before the passage of the Twelfth Amendment in 1804, the electoral college voted for two presidential candidates; the runner-up became vice-president.

ADMISSION OF STATES

Order of Admission	State	Date of Admission	Order of Admission	State	Date of Admission
1	Delaware	December 7, 1787	26	Michigan	January 26, 1837
2	Pennsylvania	December 12, 1787	27	Florida	March 3, 1845
3	New Jersey	December 18, 1787	28	Texas	December 29, 1845
4	Georgia	January 2, 1788	29	Iowa	December 28, 1846
5	Connecticut	January 9, 1788	30	Wisconsin	May 29, 1848
6	Massachusetts	February 7, 1788	31	California	September 9, 1850
7	Maryland	April 28, 1788	32	Minnesota	May 11, 1858
8	South Carolina	May 23, 1788	33	Oregon	February 14, 1859
9	New Hampshire	June 21, 1788	34	Kansas	January 29, 1861
10	Virginia	June 25, 1788	35	West Virginia	June 30, 1863
11	New York	July 26, 1788	36	Nevada	October 31, 1864
12	North Carolina	November 21, 1789	37	Nebraska	March 1, 1867
13	Rhode Island	May 29, 1790	38	Colorado	August 1, 1876
14	Vermont	March 4, 1791	39	North Dakota	November 2, 1889
15	Kentucky	June 1, 1792	40	South Dakota	November 2, 1889
16	Tennessee	June 1, 1796	41	Montana	November 8, 1889
17	Ohio	March 1, 1803	42	Washington	November 11, 1889
18	Louisiana	April 30, 1812	43	Idaho	July 3, 1890
19	Indiana	December 11, 1816	44	Wyoming	July 10, 1890
20	Mississippi	December 10, 1817	45	Utah	January 4, 1896
21	Illinois	December 3, 1818	46	Oklahoma	November 16, 1907
22	Alabama	December 14, 1819	47	New Mexico	January 6, 1912
23	Maine	March 15, 1820	48	Arizona	February 14, 1912
24	Missouri	August 10, 1821	49	Alaska	January 3, 1959
25	Arkansas	June 15, 1836	50	Hawaii	August 21, 1959

POPULATION OF THE UNITED STATES

Year	Number of States	Population	% Increase	Population per Square Mile
1790	13	3,929,214		4.5
1800	16	5,308,483	35.1	6.1
1810	17	7,239,881	36.4	4.3
1820	23	9,638,453	33.1	5.5
1830	24	12,866,020	33.5	7.4
1840	26	17,069,453	32.7	9.8
1850	31	23,191,876	35.9	7.9
1860	33	31,443,321	35.6	10.6
1870	37	39,818,449	26.6	13.4
1880	38	50,155,783	26.0	16.9
1890	44	62,947,714	25.5	21.1
1900	45	75,994,575	20.7	25.6
1910	46	91,972,266	21.0	31.0
1920	48	105,710,620	14.9	35.6
1930	48	122,775,046	16.1	41.2
1940	48	131,669,275	7.2	44.2
1950	48	150,697,361	14.5	50.7
1960	50	179,323,175	19.0	50.6
1970	50	203,235,298	13.3	57.5
1980	50	226,504,825	11.4	64.0
1985	50	237,839,000	5.0	67.2
1990	50	250,122,000	5.2	70.6
1995	50	263,411,707	5.3	74.4
2000	50	281,421,906	6.8	77.0

IMMIGRATION TO THE UNITED STATES, FISCAL YEARS 1820–1998

Year	Number	Year	Number	Year	Number	Year	Number
1820–1989	55,457,531	1871–80	2,812,191	1921–30	4,107,209	1971–80	4,493,314
1820	8,385	1871	321,350	1921	805,228	1971	370,478
1821–30	143,439	1872	404,806	1922	309,556	1972	384,685
1821	9,127	1873	459,803	1923	522,919	1973	400,063
1822	6,911	1874	313,339	1924	706,896	1974	394,861
1823	6,354	1875	227,498	1925	294,314	1975	386,914
1824	7,912	1876	169,986	1926	304,488	1976	399,613
1825	10,199	1877	141,857	1927	335,175	1976	103,676
1826	10,837	1878	138,469	1928	307,255	1977	462,315
1827	18,875	1879	177,826	1929	279,678	1978	601,442
1828	27,382	1880	457,257	1930	241,700	1979	460,348
1829	22,520	1881–90	5,246,613	1931–40	528,431	1980	530,639
1830	23,322	1881	669,431	1931	97,139	1981–90	7,338,062
1831–40	599,125	1882	788,992	1932	35,576	1981	596,600
1831	22,633	1883	603,322	1933	23,068	1982	594,131
1832	60,482	1884	518,592	1934	29,470	1983	559,763
1833	58,640	1885	395,346	1935	34,956	1984	543,903
1834	65,365	1886	334,203	1936	36,329	1985	570,009
1835	45,374	1887	490,109	1937	50,244	1986	601,708
1836	76,242	1888	546,889	1938	67,895	1987	601,516
1837	79,340	1889	444,427	1939	82,998	1988	643,025
1838	38,914	1890	455,302	1940	70,756	1989	1,090,924
1839	68,069	1891–1900	3,687,564	1941–50	1,035,039	1990	1,536,483
1840	84,066	1891	560,319	1941	51,776		
1841–50	1,713,251	1892	579,663	1942	28,781		
1841	80,289	1893	439,730	1943	23,725		
1842	104,565	1894	285,631	1944	28,551		
		1895	258,536	1945	38,119		
		1896	343,267	1946	108,721		

Year	Number	Year	Number	Year	Number	Year	Number
1843	52,496	1897	230,832	1947	147,292	**1991–98**	**7,605,068**
1844	78,615	1898	229,299	1948	170,570	1991	1,827,167
1845	114,371	1899	311,715	1949	188,317	1992	973,977
1846	154,416	1900	448,572	1950	249,187	1993	904,292
1847	234,968					1994	804,416
1848	226,527	**1901–10**	**8,795,386**	**1951–60**	**2,515,479**	1995	720,461
1849	297,024	1901	487,918	1951	205,717	1996	915,900
1850	369,980	1902	648,743	1952	265,520	1997	798,378
		1903	857,046	1953	170,434	1998	660,477
1851–60	**2,598,214**	1904	812,870	1954	208,177		
1851	379,466	1905	1,026,499	1955	237,790		
1852	371,603	1906	1,100,735	1956	321,625		
1853	368,645	1907	1,285,349	1957	326,867		
1854	427,833	1908	782,870	1958	253,265		
1855	200,877	1909	751,786	1959	260,686		
1856	200,436	1910	1,041,570	1960	265,398		
1857	251,306						
1858	123,126	**1911–20**	**5,735,811**	**1961–70**	**3,321,677**		
1859	121,282	1911	878,587	1961	271,344		
1860	153,640	1912	838,172	1962	283,763		
		1913	1,197,892	1963	306,260		
1861–70	**2,314,824**	1914	1,218,480	1964	292,248		
1861	91,918	1915	326,700	1965	296,697		
1862	91,985	1916	298,826	1966	323,040		
1863	176,282	1917	295,403	1967	361,972		
1864	193,418	1918	110,618	1968	454,448		
1865	248,120	1919	141,132	1969	358,579		
1866	318,568	1920	430,001	1970	373,326		
1867	315,722						
1868	138,840						
1869	352,768						
1870	387,203						

Source: U.S. Immigration and Naturalization Service, 1999.

IMMIGRATION BY REGION AND SELECTED COUNTRY OF LAST RESIDENCE, FISCAL YEARS 1820–1999

Region and Country of Last Residence[1]	1820	1821–30	1831–40	1841–50	1851–60	1861–70	1871–80	1881–90
All countries	8,385	143,439	599,125	1,713,251	2,598,214	2,314,824	2,812,191	5,246,613
Europe	7,690	98,797	495,681	1,597,442	2,452,577	2,065,141	2,271,925	4,735,484
Austria-Hungary	—[2]	—[2]	—[2]	—[2]	—[2]	7,800	72,969	353,719
Austria	—[2]	—[2]	—[2]	—[2]	—[2]	484[3]	63,009	226,038
Hungary	—[2]	—[2]	—[2]	—[2]	—[2]	7,124[3]	9,960	127,681
Belgium	1	27	22	5,074	4,738	6,734	7,221	20,177
Czechoslovakia	—[4]	—[4]	—[4]	—[4]	—[4]	—[4]	—[4]	—[4]
Denmark	20	169	1,063	539	3,749	17,094	31,771	88,132
France	371	8,497	45,575	77,262	76,358	35,986	72,206	50,464
Germany	968	6,761	152,454	434,626	951,667	787,468	718,182	1,452,970
Greece	—	20	49	16	31	72	210	2,308
Ireland[5]	3,614	50,724	207,381	780,719	914,119	435,778	436,871	655,482
Italy	30	409	2,253	1,870	9,231	11,725	55,759	307,309
Netherlands	49	1,078	1,412	8,251	10,789	9,102	16,541	53,701
Norway-Sweden	3	91	1,201	13,903	20,931	109,298	211,245	568,362
Norway	—[6]	—[6]	—[6]	—[6]	—[6]	—[6]	95,323	176,586
Sweden	—[6]	—[6]	—[6]	—[6]	—[6]	—[6]	115,922	391,776
Poland	5	16	369	105	1,164	2,027	12,970	51,806
Portugal	35	145	829	550	1,055	2,658	14,082	16,978
Romania	—[7]	—[7]	—[7]	—[7]	—	—	11	6,348
Soviet Union	14	75	277	551	457	2,512	39,284	213,282
Spain	139	2,477	2,125	2,209	9,298	6,697	5,266	4,419
Switzerland	31	3,226	4,821	4,644	25,011	23,286	28,293	81,988
United Kingdom[5,8]	2,410	25,079	75,810	267,044	423,974	606,896	548,043	807,357
Yugoslavia	—[9]	—[9]	—[9]	—[9]	—[9]	—[9]	—[9]	—[9]
Other Europe	—	3	40	79	5	8	1,001	682

Asia	6	30	55	141	41,538	64,759	124,160	69,942
China[10]	1	2	8	35	41,397	64,301	123,201	61,711
Hong Kong	—[11]	—[11]	—[11]	—[11]	—[11]	—[11]	—[11]	—[11]
India	1	8	39	36	43	69	163	269
Iran	—[12]	—[12]	—[12]	—[12]	—[12]	—[12]	—[12]	—[12]
Israel	—[13]	—[13]	—[13]	—[13]	—[13]	—[13]	—[13]	—[13]
Japan	—[14]	—[14]	—[14]	—[14]	—[14]	186	149	2,270
Korea	—[15]	—[15]	—[15]	—[15]	—[15]	—[15]	—[15]	—[15]
Philippines	—[16]	—[16]	—[16]	—[16]	—[16]	—[16]	—[16]	—[16]
Turkey	1	20	7	59	83	131	404	3,782
Vietnam	—[11]	—[11]	—[11]	—[11]	—[11]	—[11]	—[11]	—[11]
Other Asia	3	—	1	11	15	72	243	1,910
America	387	11,564	33,424	62,469	74,720	166,607	404,044	426,967
Canada & Newfoundland[17,18]	209	2,277	13,624	41,723	59,309	153,878	383,640	393,304
Mexico[18]	1	4,817	6,599	3,271	3,078	2,191	5,162	191,319
Caribbean	164	3,834	12,301	13,528	10,660	9,046	13,957	29,042
Cuba	—[12]	—[12]	—[12]	—[12]	—[12]	—[12]	—[12]	—[12]
Dominican Republic	—[20]	—[20]	—[20]	—[20]	—[20]	—[20]	—[20]	—[20]
Haiti	—[20]	—[20]	—[20]	—[20]	—[20]	—[20]	—[20]	—[20]
Jamaica	—[21]	—[21]	—[21]	—[21]	—[21]	—[21]	—[21]	—[21]
Other Caribbean	164	3,834	12,301	13,528	10,660	9,046	13,957	29,042
Central America	2	105	44	368	449	95	157	404
El Salvador	—[20]	—[20]	—[20]	—[20]	—[20]	—[20]	—[20]	—[20]
Other Central America	2	105	44	368	449	95	157	404
South America	11	531	856	3,579	1,224	1,397	1,128	2,304
Argentina	—[20]	—[20]	—[20]	—[20]	—[20]	—[20]	—[20]	—[20]
Colombia	—[20]	—[20]	—[20]	—[20]	—[20]	—[20]	—[20]	—[20]
Ecuador	—[20]	—[20]	—[20]	—[20]	—[20]	—[20]	—[20]	—[20]
Other South America	11	531	856	3,579	1,224	1,397	1,128	2,304
Other America	11	531	856	3,579	1,224	1,397	1,128	2,304
Africa	1	16	54	55	210	312	358	857
Oceania	1	2	9	29	158	214	10,914	12,574
Not specified[22]	300	33,030	69,902	53,115	29,011	17,791	790	789

Region and Country of Last Residence[1]	1891–1900	1901–10	1911–20	1921–30	1931–40	1941–50	1951–60	1961–70
All countries	3,687,564	8,795,386	5,735,811	4,107,209	528,431	1,035,039	2,515,479	3,321,677
Europe	3,555,352	8,056,040	4,321,887	2,463,194	347,566	621,147	1,325,727	1,123,492
Austria-Hungary	592,707[23]	2,145,266[23]	896,342[23]	63,548	11,424	28,329	103,743	26,022
Austria	234,081[3]	668,209[3]	453,649	32,868	3,563[24]	24,860[24]	67,106	20,621
Hungary	181,288[3]	808,511[3]	442,693	30,680	7,861	3,469	36,637	5,401
Belgium	18,167	41,635	33,746	15,846	4,817	12,189	18,575	9,192
Czechoslovakia	—[4]	—[4]	3,426[4]	102,194	14,393	8,347	918	3,273
Denmark	50,231	65,285	41,983	32,430	2,559	5,393	10,984	9,201
France	30,770	73,379	61,897	49,610	12,623	38,809	51,121	45,237
Germany	505,152[23]	341,498[23]	143,945[23]	412,202	114,058[24]	226,578[24]	477,765	190,796
Greece	15,979	167,519	184,201	51,084	9,119	8,973	47,608	85,969
Ireland[5]	388,416	339,065	146,181	211,234	10,973	19,789	48,362	32,966
Italy	651,893	2,045,877	1,109,524	455,315	68,028	57,661	185,491	214,111
Netherlands	26,758	48,262	43,718	26,948	7,150	14,860	52,277	30,606
Norway-Sweden	321,281	440,039	161,469	165,780	8,700	20,765	44,632	32,600
Norway	95,015	190,505	66,395	68,531	4,740	10,100	22,935	15,484
Sweden	226,266	249,534	95,074	97,249	3,960	10,665	21,697	17,116
Poland	96,720[23]	—[23]	4,813[23]	227,734	17,026	7,571	9,985	53,539
Portugal	27,508	69,149	89,732	29,994	3,329	7,423	19,588	76,065
Romania	12,750	53,008	13,311	67,646	3,871	1,076	1,039	2,531
Soviet Union	505,290[23]	1,597,306[23]	921,201[23]	61,742	1,370	571	671	2,465
Spain	8,731	27,935	68,611	28,958	3,258	2,898	7,894	44,659
Switzerland	31,179	34,922	23,091	29,676	5,512	10,547	17,675	18,453
United Kingdom[5,8]	271,538	525,950	341,408	339,570	31,572	139,306	202,824	213,822
Yugoslavia	—[9]	—[9]	1,888[9]	49,064	5,835	1,576	8,225	20,381
Other Europe	282	39,945	31,400	42,619	11,949	8,486	16,350	11,604

Asia	74,862	323,543	247,236	112,059	16,595	37,028	153,249	427,642
China[10]	14,799	20,605	21,278	29,907	4,928	16,709	9,657	34,764
Hong Kong	—[11]	—[11]	—[11]	—[11]	—[11]	—[11]	15,541[11]	75,007
India	68	4,713	2,082	1,886	496	1,761	1,973	27,189
Iran	—[12]	—[12]	—[12]	241[12]	195	1,380	3,388	10,339
Israel	—[13]	—[13]	—[13]	—[13]	—[13]	476[13]	25,476	29,602
Japan	25,942	129,797	83,837	33,462	1,948	1,555	46,250	39,988
Korea	—[15]	—[15]	—[15]	—[15]	—[15]	107[15]	6,231	34,526
Philippines	—[16]	—[16]	—[16]	—[16]	528[16]	4,691	19,307	98,376
Turkey	30,425	157,369	134,066	33,824	1,065	798	3,519	10,142
Vietnam	—[11]	—[11]	—[11]	—[11]	—[11]	—[11]	335[11]	4,340
Other Asia	3,628	11,059	5,973	12,739	7,435	9,551	21,572	63,369
America	38,972	361,888	1,143,671	1,516,716	160,037	354,804	996,944	1,716,374
Canada & Newfoundland[17,18]	3,311	179,226	742,185	924,515	108,527	171,718	377,952	413,310
Mexico[18]	971[19]	49,642	219,004	459,287	22,319	60,589	299,811	453,937
Caribbean	33,066	107,548	123,424	74,899	15,502	49,725	123,091	470,213
Cuba	—[12]	—[12]	—[12]	15,901[12]	9,571	26,313	78,948	208,536
Dominican Republic	—[20]	—[20]	—[20]	—[20]	1,150[20]	5,627	9,897	93,292
Haiti	—[20]	—[20]	—[20]	—[20]	191[20]	911	4,442	34,499
Jamaica	—[21]	—[21]	—[21]	—[21]	—[21]	—[21]	8,869[21]	74,906
Other Caribbean	33,066	107,548	123,424	58,998	4,590	16,874	20,935[21]	58,980
Central America	549	8,192	17,159	15,769	5,861	21,665	44,751	101,330
El Salvador	—[20]	—[20]	—[20]	—[20]	673[20]	5,132	5,895	14,992
Other Central America	549	8,192	17,159	15,769	5,188	16,533	38,856	86,338
South America	1,075	17,280	41,899	42,215	7,803	21,831	91,628	257,954
Argentina	—[20]	—[20]	—[20]	—[20]	1,349[20]	3,338	19,486	49,721
Colombia	—[20]	—[20]	—[20]	—[20]	1,223[20]	3,858	18,048	72,028
Ecuador	—[20]	—[20]	—[20]	—[20]	337[20]	2,417	9,841	36,780
Other South America	1,075	17,280	41,899	42,215	4,894	12,218	44,253	99,425
Other America	—[22]	—[22]	—[22]	31[22]	25	29,276	59,711	19,630
Africa	350	7,368	8,443	6,286	1,750	7,367	14,092	28,954
Oceania	3,965	13,024	13,427	8,726	2,483	14,551	12,976	25,122
Not specified[22]	14,063	33,523[25]	1,147	228	—	142	12,491	93

Region and Country of Last Residence[1]	1971–80	1981–89	1990–99	1994	1995	1996	1997	1998[26]	1999	Total 179 Years 1820–1999
All countries	4,493,314	5,801,579	9,781,496	804,368	720,401	915,847	798,339	654,420	646,539	65,239,029
Europe	800,368	637,524	1,291,299	160,916	128,185	147,581	119,871	90,793	92,672	38,268,333
Austria-Hungary	16,028	20,152	N/A	N/A	N/A	N/A	N/A	N/A	N/A	4,338,049
Austria	9,478	14,566	5,094	499	518	554	487	291	231	1,830,266
Hungary	6,550	5,586	11,003	880	900	1,183	949	809	698	1,677,804
Belgium	5,329	6,239	5,783	516	569	651	554	421	428	215,512
Czechoslovakia[27]	6,023	6,649	7,597	642	599	561	395	342	319	152,820
Czech Republic	N/A	N/A	723	11	72	165	186	144	145	723
Slovak Republic	N/A	N/A	3,010	221	503	663	629	491	493	3,010
Denmark	4,439	4,696	5,785	606	551	608	429	457	368	375,523
France	25,069	28,088	26,879	2,715	2,505	3,079	2,568	2,352	2,209	812,201
Germany	74,414	79,809	60,082	6,992	6,237	6,748	5,723	5,472	5,201	7,131,395
Germany, East	N/A	N/A	105	N/A	N/A	N/A	N/A	N/A	N/A	105
Germany, West	N/A	N/A	7,338	N/A	N/A	N/A	N/A	N/A	N/A	7,338
Greece	92,369	34,490	15,403	1,440	1,309	1,452	1,049	863	727	715,420
Ireland	11,490	22,229	67,975	17,256	5,315	1,731	1,001	944	812	4,738,368
Italy	129,368	51,008	23,365	2,305	2,231	2,501	1,982	1,831	1,530	5,380,227
Netherlands	10,492	10,723	12,334	1,239	1,196	1,423	1,059	917	777	385,051
Norway-Sweden	10,472	13,252	15,720	1,599	1,396	1,729	1,330	1,121	1,130	2,099,489
Norway	3,941	3,612	4,618	459	420	478	372	298	308	805,290
Sweden	6,531	9,640	11,102	1,140	976	1,251	958	823	822	1,294,199
Poland	37,234	64,888	180,035	28,048	13,824	15,772	12,038	8,469	8,798	768,007
Portugal	101,710	36,365	25,428	2,169	2,615	2,984	1,665	1,536	1,071	522,623
Romania	12,393	27,361	55,303	3,444	4,871	5,801	5,545	5,112	5,686	256,648
Russia	N/A	N/A	110,921	15,249	14,560	19,668	16,632	11,529	12,347	110,921
Soviet Union[28]	38,961	42,898	126,115	6,954	6,784	3,513	2,944	6,336	5,058	3,555,042
Former Soviet Republics[29]	N/A	N/A	255,552	42,981	34,838	41,769	31,269	14,044	18,614	255,552
Spain	39,141	17,689	14,310	1,418	1,321	1,659	1,241	1,043	874	296,714
Switzerland	8,235	7,561	8,840	877	881	1,006	1,063	828	649	366,991
United Kingdom	137,374	140,119	138,380	16,326	12,427	13,624	10,708	9,018	7,690	5,238,476
Yugoslavia[28]	30,540	15,984	25,923	2,038	2,907	3,605	2,793	2,408	1,897	159,416

Former Yugoslavian States	61,389	8,494	7,954	10,688	11,777	8,242	3,338	61,389	N/A	N/A
Other Europe	1,003,225	62,380	59,808	84,548	105,406	89,446	94,794	822,161	7,324	9,287
Asia	8,662,661	199,411	219,696	265,810	307,807	267,931	292,589	2,965,360	2,416,278	1,588,178
China, People's Republic	1,284,473	32,204	36,884	41,147	41,728	35,463	53,985	410,736	306,108	124,326
Hong Kong	365,879	4,917	5,275	5,577	7,824	7,249	7,731	78,016	83,848	113,467
India	798,832	30,237	36,482	38,071	44,859	34,748	34,921	371,925	221,977	164,134
Iran	291,001	7,203	7,883	9,642	11,084	9,201	11,422	129,055	101,267	45,136
Israel	165,448	1,858	1,991	2,448	3,126	2,523	3,425	33,814	38,367	37,713
Japan	515,925	4,217	5,138	5,097	6,011	4,837	6,093	60,112	40,654	49,775
Korea	799,078	12,840	14,268	14,239	18,185	16,047	16,011	187,794	302,782	267,638
Philippines	1,482,209	31,026	34,466	49,117	55,876	50,984	53,535	526,835	477,485	354,987
Taiwan	112,464	6,714	7,097	6,745	13,401	9,377	10,032	112,464	N/A	N/A
Turkey	435,300	2,219	2,682	3,145	3,657	2,947	1,840	26,178	20,028	13,399
Vietnam	886,695	20,393	17,649	38,519	42,067	41,752	41,345	443,173	266,027	172,820
Other Asia	1,709,524	71,065	73,743	84,127	95,310	77,529	62,663	769,425	557,735	244,783
Africa	675,497	36,700	40,660	47,791	52,889	42,456	26,712	374,149	144,096	80,779
Oceania	246,858	3,676	3,935	4,344	5,309	4,695	4,592	49,040	38,401	41,242
America	6,546,533	271,336	252,965	307,449	340,487	231,466	272,178	4,529,512	2,564,698	1,982,735
Canada	142,435	8,864	10,190	11,609	15,825	12,932	16,068	138,165	132,296	169,939
Mexico	5,965,056	147,573	131,575	146,865	163,572	89,932	111,398	2,756,513	975,657	640,294
Caribbean	3,613,779	71,683	75,521	105,299	116,801	96,788	104,804	1,023,237	759,416	741,126
Cuba	909,949	14,132	17,375	33,587	26,466	17,937	14,727	170,675	135,142	264,563
Dominican Republic	833,598	17,864	20,387	27,053	39,604	38,512	51,189	365,598	209,899	148,135
Haiti	394,613	16,532	13,449	15,057	18,386	14,021	13,333	179,725	118,510	56,335
Jamaica	588,385	14,733	15,146	17,840	19,089	16,398	14,349	182,552	184,481	137,577
Other Caribbean	887,234	8,422	9,164	11,762	13,256	9,920	11,206	124,687	111,384	134,216
Central America	1,284,982	43,216	35,679	43,676	44,259	31,814	39,908	611,597	321,845	134,640
El Salvador	470,055	14,606	14,590	17,969	17,903	11,744	17,644	274,989	133,938	34,436
Other Central America	384,427	28,610	21,089	25,707	26,386	20,070	22,264	336,608	187,907	100,204
South America	1,733,132	41,585	45,394	52,877	61,769	45,666	47,377	569,650	375,026	295,741
Argentina	152,596	1,393	1,511	1,964	2,456	1,762	2,318	27,431	21,374	29,897
Colombia	412,255	9,966	11,836	13,004	14,283	10,838	10,847	140,685	99,066	77,347
Ecuador	224,497	8,904	6,852	7,780	8,321	6,397	5,906	81,204	43,841	50,077
Other South America	943,784	21,322	25,195	30,129	36,709	26,669	28,306	320,330	210,745	138,420
Other America	110,721	29	31	39	53	60	48	595	458	995
Unknown or not reported	269,495	1,159	977	197	5	2	4	2,486	N/A	N/A

Source: U.S. Immigration and Naturalization Service, 1999.

[1]Data for years prior to 1906 relate to country whence alien came; data from 1906–79 and 1984–89 are for country of last permanent residence; and data for 1980–99 refer to country of birth. Because of changes in boundaries, changes in lists of countries, and lack of data for specified countries for various periods, data for certain countries, especially for the total period 1820–1999, are not comparable throughout. Data for specified countries are included with countries to which they belonged prior to World War I.

[2]Data for Austria and Hungary not reported until 1861.

[3]Data for Austria and Hungary not reported separately for all years during the period.

[4]No data available for Czechoslovakia until 1920.

[5]Prior to 1926, data for Northern Ireland included in Ireland.

[6]Data for Norway and Sweden not reported separately until 1871.

[7]No data available for Romania until 1880.

[8]Since 1925, data for United Kingdom refer to England, Scotland, Wales, and Northern Ireland.

[9]In 1920, a separate enumeration was made for the Kingdom of Serbs, Croats, and Slovenes. Since 1922, the Serb, Croat, and Slovene Kingdom recorded as Yugoslavia.

[10]Beginning in 1957, China includes Taiwan.

[11]Data not reported separately until 1952.

[12]Data not reported separately until 1925.

[13]Data not reported separately until 1949.

[14]No data available for Japan until 1861.

[15]Data not reported separately until 1948.

[16]Prior to 1934, Philippines recorded as insular travel.

[17]Prior to 1920, Canada and Newfoundland recorded as British North America. From 1820 to 1898, figures include all British North America possessions.

[18]Land arrivals not completely enumerated until 1908.

[19]No data available for Mexico from 1886 to 1893.

[20]Data not reported separately until 1932.

[21]Data for Jamaica not collected until 1953. In prior years, consolidated under British West Indies, which is included in "Other Caribbean."

[22]Included in countries "Not specified" until 1925.

[23]From 1899 to 1919, data for Poland included in Austria-Hungary, Germany, and the Soviet Union.

[24]From 1938 to 1945, data for Austria included in Germany.

[25]Includes 32,897 persons returning in 1906 to their homes in the United States.

[26]Data for fiscal year 1998 have been revised due to changes in the count for asylees and cancellation of removal. The previously reported total was 660,477.

[27]Prior to 1993, data include independent republics; beginning in 1993, data are for unknown republic only.

[28]Prior to 1992, data include independent republic; beginning in 1992, data are for Yugoslavia only.

[29]Prior to 1992, data include previously independent republics only; beginning in 1992, data are for all former republics except Russia.

— represents zero.

NOTE: From 1820 to 1867, figures represent alien passengers arrived at seaports; from 1868 to 1891 and 1895 to 1897, immigrant aliens arrived; from 1892 to 1894 and 1898 to 1989, immigrant aliens admitted for permanent residence. From 1892 to 1903, aliens entering by cabin class were not counted as immigrants. Land arrivals were not completely enumerated until 1908. For this table, fiscal year 1843 covers 9 months ending September 1843; fiscal years 1832 and 1850 cover 15 months ending December 31 of the respective years; and fiscal year 1868 covers 6 months ending June 30, 1868.

PRESIDENTS, VICE-PRESIDENTS,
AND SECRETARIES OF STATE

	President	*Vice-President*	*Secretary of State*
1.	George Washington, Federalist 1789	John Adams, Federalist 1789	Thomas Jefferson 1789 Edmund Randolph 1794 Timothy Pickering 1795
2.	John Adams, Federalist 1797	Thomas Jefferson, Dem.-Rep. 1797	Timothy Pickering 1797 John Marshall 1800
3.	Thomas Jefferson, Dem.-Rep. 1801	Aaron Burr, Dem.-Rep. 1801 George Clinton, Dem.-Rep. 1805	James Madison 1801
4.	James Madison, Dem.-Rep. 1809	George Clinton, Dem.-Rep. 1809 Elbridge Gerry, Dem.-Rep. 1813	Robert Smith 1809 James Monroe 1811
5.	James Monroe, Dem.-Rep. 1817	Daniel D. Tompkins, Dem.-Rep. 1817	John Q. Adams 1817
6.	John Quincy Adams, Dem.-Rep. 1825	John C. Calhoun, Dem.-Rep. 1825	Henry Clay 1825
7.	Andrew Jackson, Democratic 1829	John C. Calhoun, Democratic 1829 Martin Van Buren, Democratic 1833	Martin Van Buren 1829 Edward Livingston 1831 Louis McLane 1833 John Forsyth 1834
8.	Martin Van Buren, Democratic 1837	Richard M. Johnson, Democratic 1837	John Forsyth 1837
9.	William H. Harrison, Whig 1841	John Tyler, Whig 1841	Daniel Webster 1841

	President	Vice-President	Secretary of State
10.	John Tyler, Whig and Democratic 1841	None	Daniel Webster 1841 Hugh S. Legaré 1843 Abel P. Upshur 1843 John C. Calhoun 1844
11.	James K. Polk, Democratic 1845	George M. Dallas, Democratic 1845	James Buchanan 1845
12.	Zachary Taylor, Whig 1849	Millard Fillmore, Whig 1848	John M. Clayton 1849
13.	Millard Fillmore, Whig 1850	None	Daniel Webster 1850 Edward Everett 1852
14.	Franklin Pierce, Democratic 1853	William R. King, Democratic 1853	William L. Marcy 1853
15.	James Buchanan, Democratic 1857	John C. Breckinridge, Democratic 1857	Lewis Cass 1857 Jeremiah S. Black 1860
16.	Abraham Lincoln, Republican 1861	Hannibal Hamlin, Republican 1861 Andrew Johnson, Unionist 1865	William H. Seward 1861
17.	Andrew Johnson, Unionist 1865	None	William H. Seward 1865
18.	Ulysses S. Grant, Republican 1869	Schuyler Colfax, Republican 1869 Henry Wilson, Republican 1873	Elihu B. Washburne 1869 Hamilton Fish 1869
19.	Rutherford B. Hayes, Republican 1877	William A. Wheeler, Republican 1877	William M. Evarts 1877

	President	Vice-President	Secretary of State
20.	James A. Garfield, Republican 1881	Chester A. Arthur, Republican 1881	James G. Blaine 1881
21.	Chester A. Arthur, Republican 1881	None	Frederick T. Frelinghuysen 1881
22.	Grover Cleveland, Democratic 1885	Thomas A. Hendricks, Democratic 1885	Thomas F. Bayard 1885
23.	Benjamin Harrison, Republican 1889	Levi P. Morton, Republican 1889	James G. Blaine 1889 John W. Foster 1892
24.	Grover Cleveland, Democratic 1893	Adlai E. Stevenson, Democratic 1893	Walter Q. Gresham 1893 Richard Olney 1895
25.	William McKinley, Republican 1897	Garret A. Hobart, Republican 1897 Theodore Roosevelt, Republican 1901	John Sherman 1897 William R. Day 1898 John Hay 1898
26.	Theodore Roosevelt, Republican 1901	Charles Fairbanks, Republican 1905	John Hay 1901 Elihu Root 1905 Robert Bacon 1909
27.	William H. Taft, Republican 1909	James S. Sherman, Republican 1909	Philander C. Knox 1909
28.	Woodrow Wilson, Democratic 1913	Thomas R. Marshall, Democratic 1913	William J. Bryan 1913 Robert Lansing 1915 Bainbridge Colby 1920
29.	Warren G. Harding, Republican 1921	Calvin Coolidge, Republican 1921	Charles E. Hughes 1921
30.	Calvin Coolidge, Republican 1923	Charles G. Dawes, Republican 1925	Charles E. Hughes 1923 Frank B. Kellogg 1925

	President	Vice-President	Secretary of State
31.	Herbert Hoover, Republican 1929	Charles Curtis, Republican 1929	Henry L. Stimson 1929
32.	Franklin D. Roosevelt, Democratic 1933	John Nance Garner, Democratic 1933 Henry A. Wallace, Democratic 1941 Harry S. Truman, Democratic 1945	Cordell Hull 1933 Edward R. Stettinius, Jr. 1944
33.	Harry S. Truman, Democratic 1945	Alben W. Barkley, Democratic 1949	Edward R. Stettinius, Jr. 1945 James F. Byrnes 1945 George C. Marshall 1947 Dean G. Acheson 1949
34.	Dwight D. Eisenhower, Republican 1953	Richard M. Nixon, Republican 1953	John F. Dulles 1953 Christian A. Herter 1959
35.	John F. Kennedy, Democratic 1961	Lyndon B. Johnson, Democratic 1961	Dean Rusk 1961
36.	Lyndon B. Johnson, Democratic 1963	Hubert H. Humphrey, Democratic 1965	Dean Rusk 1963
37.	Richard M. Nixon, Republican 1969	Spiro T. Agnew, Republican 1969 Gerald R. Ford, Republican 1973	William P. Rogers 1969 Henry Kissinger 1973
38.	Gerald R. Ford, Republican 1974	Nelson Rockefeller, Republican 1974	Henry Kissinger 1974
39.	Jimmy Carter, Democratic 1977	Walter Mondale, Democratic 1977	Cyrus Vance 1977 Edmund Muskie 1980

	President	*Vice-President*	*Secretary of State*
40.	Ronald Reagan, Republican 1981	George H. W. Bush, Republican 1981	Alexander Haig 1981 George Schultz 1982
41.	George H. W. Bush, Republican 1989	J. Danforth Quayle, Republican 1989	James A. Baker 1989 Lawrence Eagleburger 1992
42.	William J. Clinton, Democrat 1993	Albert Gore, Jr., Democrat 1993	Warren Christopher 1993 Madeleine Albright 1997
43.	George W. Bush, Republican 2001	Richard B. Cheney, Republican 2001	Colin L. Powell 2001

CREDITS

CHAPTER 18: p. 715, Library of Congress; **p. 717,** Library of Congress; **p. 718,** Library of Congress/Corbis; **p. 721,** © Corbis; **p. 723,** Library of Congress; **p. 725,** Harper's Weekly; **p. 726,** Library of Congress; **p. 728,** Library of Congress; **p. 733,** U.S. Signal Corps photo no. 111-B-4371 (Brady Collection) in the National Archives; **p. 736,** The Granger Collection, New York; **p. 739,** Corbis-Bettman; **p. 741,** National Archives; **p. 743,** Library of Congress; **p. 747,** Library of Congress; **p. 750,** Library of Congress.

CHAPTER 19: p. 764, Rare Book, Manuscript, & Special Collections Library, Duke University; **p. 770,** The Granger Collection, New York; **p. 773,** The Warder Collection; **p. 775,** Special Collections Research Center, The University of Chicago Library; **p. 777,** Library of Congress; **p. 778,** The Warder Collection; **p. 780,** Library of Congress; **p. 782,** © Corbis; **p. 788,** Princeton University Press; **p. 789,** The Smithsonian Institution; **p. 792,** © Corbis; **p. 794,** National Archives; **p. 798,** Western History Collections, University of Oklahoma Libraries.

CHAPTER 20: p. 804, Amon Carter Museum, Fort Worth, Texas; **p. 806,** Union Pacific Museum Collection; **p. 809,** © Collection of the New-York Historical Society; **p. 810,** National Archives; **p. 812,** The Granger Collection, New York; **p. 813,** Courtesy of American Petroleum Institute Historical Photo Collection; **p. 815,** The Warder Collection; **p. 816,** Carnegie Library, Pittsburgh; **p. 817,** Keystone-Mast Collection (WX 13101). UCR/California Museum of Photography. University of California, Riverside; **p. 818,** The Pierpont Morgan Library. Reprinted with permission of Joanna T. Steichen; **p. 819,** Carnegie Library, Pittsburgh; **p. 820,** Courtesy of Sears, Roebuck and Co.; **p. 823,** © Bettmann/Corbis; **p. 828,** The American Catholic History Research Center and University Archives at The Catholic University of America; **p. 831,** © Bettmann/Corbis; **p. 832,** © Museum of the City of New York/Corbis; **p. 834,** Library of Congress; **p. 835,** © Bettmann/Corbis; **p. 838,** Collection of The Archives of Labor and Urban Affairs, University Archives, Wayne State University.

CHAPTER 21: **p. 846,** Culver Pictures; **p. 849,** Museum of the City of New York; **p. 851,** The New York Public Library, Astor, Lenox and Tilden Foundations; **p. 853,** Library of Congress; **p. 856,** Courtesy Denver Public Library, Western History Collection; **p. 858,** Library of Congress; **p. 861,** Brown Brothers; **p. 862,** Old York Library; **p. 864,** The Granger Collection, New York; **p. 868,** Library of Congress; **p. 870,** © Corbis; **p. 872,** Mount Holyoke College Library; **p. 874,** Negative No. 326662, Courtesy Department of Library Services, American Museum of Natural History; **p. 876,** Courtesy of the Brown University Library; **p. 877,** National Library of Medicine; **p. 878,** Mansell/TIME Inc; **p. 882,** The Salvation Army; **p. 884,** Jane Addams Memorial Collection, Special Collections, The University Library, The University of Illinois at Chicago; **p. 885,** The Granger Collection, New York.

CHAPTER 22: **p. 896,** Library of Congress; **p. 900,** © Bettmann/Corbis; **p. 902,** The Warder Collection; **p. 903,** The Warder Collection; **p. 906,** UPI/Corbis-Bettman; **p. 909,** The Warder Collection; **p. 913,** Corbis-Bettman; **p. 916,** Wooten Studios; **p. 918,** Kansas State Historical Society, Topeka, Kansas; **p. 920,** Nebraska State Historical Society; **p. 924,** Library of Congress.

CHAPTER 23: **p. 937,** © Bettmann/Corbis; **p. 939,** Public Archives of Hawaii; **p. 940,** Brown Brothers; **p. 942,** Library of Congress; **p. 948,** Library of Congress; **p. 951,** National Archives; **p. 955,** © Bettmann/Corbis; **p. 958,** Drake, in the *New York Times*; **p. 962,** © Bettmann/Corbis; **p. 964,** Library of Congress.

CHAPTER 24: **p. 971,** Valdis Kupris; **p. 973,** Library of Congress; **p. 975,** © Corbis; **p. 977** *(top)* © Collection of the New-York Historical Society, and *(bottom)* Library of Congress; **p. 980,** © Bettmann/Corbis; **p. 983,** Library of Congress; **p. 984,** © Corbis; **p. 986,** Library of Congress; **p. 990,** Library of Congress; **p. 992,** Library of Congress; **p. 998,** The Warder Collection.

CHAPTER 25: **p. 1009,** Corbis-Bettman; **p. 1013,** The Warder Collection; **p. 1016,** *New York Times*; **p. 1018,** Princeton University Libraries; **p. 1021,** UPI/Corbis-Bettman; **p. 1024,** © Swim Ink/Corbis; **p. 1027,** © Bettmann/Corbis; **p. 1030,** © Corbis; **p. 1033,** National Archives; **p. 1034,** National Archives; **p. 1035,** The Warder Collection; **p. 1037,** Mary Evans Picture Library; **p. 1040,** Ding Darling Foundation; **p. 1044,** © Bettmann/Corbis; **p. 1045,** Chicago Historical Society.

CHAPTER 26: **p. 1051,** Ben Shahn, *Bartolomeo Vanzetti and Nicola Sacco,* from the Sacco-Vanzetti series of twenty-three paintings. Tempera on paper over composition board, 10.5 x 14.5". Collection, The Museum of Modern Art, New York. Gift of Abby Aldrich Rockefeller; **p. 1053,** UPI/Corbis-Bettman; **p. 1055,** Corbis-Bettman; **p. 1057,** © Bettmann/Corbis; **p. 1060,** Ramsey Archive; **p. 1062,** © Corbis; **p. 1064,** © Bettmann/Corbis; **p. 1066,** Hulton/Archive by Getty Images; **p. 1069,**

INDEX

Page numbers in *italics* refer to illustrations.

Douglass, Frederick, 717
downsizing, 1475, 1489
draft:
in Vietnam War, 1385, 1402, 1424
in World War I, 1024, 1029
in World War II, 1194
Dreiser, Theodore, 879
drugs:
George H. W. Bush's policy on, 1457–58
illegal, 1387, 1389, 1403, 1452, 1457–58, 1462
patent medicines, 982
Duarte, José Napoleón, 1443, 1449
Dubinsky, David, 1153
Du Bois, W. E. B., 777–78, 778, 1069–71
"due-process clause," 728–29, 888, 915
Dukakis, Michael, 1454–56, 1457
Duke, James Buchanan "Buck," 763–64
Duke, Washington, 763
Dulles, John Foster, 1312, 1315–17, 1316, 1319, 1320, 1322, 1323, 1325, 1327, 1442
dust bowl, 1129, 1135–36, 1140
Dutch East Indies, 1184, 1186, 1187, 1192, 1317
Dylan, Bob, 1388
Dynamic Sociology (Ward), 876

Earhart, Amelia, 1094
East St. Louis, Ill., race riot in (1917), 1026
Economic Cooperation Administration (ECA), 1255
Economic Opportunity Bill (1964), 1361–62
Economic Recovery Tax Act (1981), 1438–39
economics, 881
Keynesian, 1155, 1156
Reaganomics, 1436, 1438–40, 1440
Veblen on, 881
economy:
agriculture and, 913–14
airplanes and automobiles in, 1093–96
Carter and, 1426–27, 1432
Civil War influence on, 803
Clinton and, 1488–89
in early twenty-first century, 1501
entrepreneurs in, 812–21
exploitation, imperialism and, 934, 935
Ford and, 1421
George H. W. Bush and, 1475–76, 1478
George W. Bush and, 1501
globalization in, 1489
Hayes's views on, 898–99
investment bankers in, 818–19
and laissez-faire policies, 887–89
in late nineteenth century, 802–12
in late twentieth century, 1467–68
in 1920s, 1085–86, 1089, 1090–1103, 1105–6
Nixon and, 1409–11

"postindustrial," 1469
Reagan and, 1436, 1438–40, 1440, 1445–46, 1451
rise of consumer goods in, 1090–1103
sea power in, 935–36
September 11, 2001 attacks and, 1504
social criticism and, 880–81
in South, 762–65, 767–68
of Soviet Union, 1459, 1461
stock market and, 1106–8, 1450–51, 1488–89
trusts in, 814–15, 909–10, 978–81, 980, 989, 994, 998–1000
white-collar sweat shop and, 1489–90
after World War I, 1044–45
in World War I, 1025
after World War II, 1238, 1244–46, 1279–80
in World War II, 1194–97, 1198–99, 1234
see also agriculture, farmers; banking industry; corporations, business; currency; debt; Depression, Great; industry; manufactures; tariffs and duties; trade and commerce; *specific panics and depressions*
Economy Act (1933), 1122–23
Edison, Thomas, 811–12
Edison General Electric Company, 812
education:
affirmative action in, 1392, 1490
of African Americans, 738, 742, 767, 768, 769, 778, 1281–82
agricultural, 1002
of Asian Americans, 963–64
bilingual, 1471
busing and, 1409, 1476
Dewey's views on, 877
evolution in, 1054
Farmers' Alliances and, 917
federal aid to, 714
GI Bill of Rights and, 1280–82
Great Society and, 1364, 1366
immigration and, 1470–71
in nineteenth century, 738, 742, 843, 869–72
parochial, 895, 911
professional schools, 873
public schools, 869
in Reconstruction, 738, 742
school prayer and, 1346, 1473
secondary schools, 869
segregation and desegregation in, 963–64, 1259, 1281, 1332–34, 1347, 1349, 1366–67, 1408, 1490
in South, 767, 768, 769
space program and, 1328
vocational training, 870, 1002
vouchers and, 1498
women and, 871
see also colleges and universities

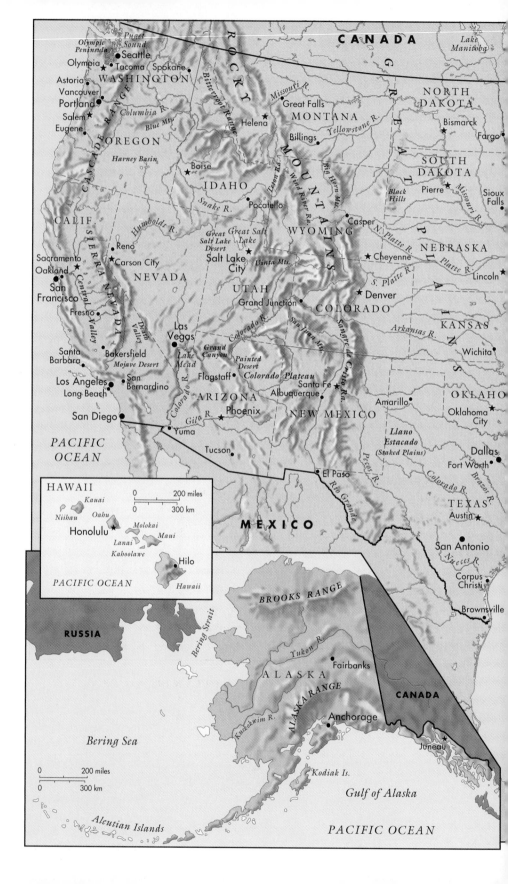

CANADA

Lake
Manitoba

Olympic
Peninsula
Puget
Sound
Seattle
Olympia
Tacoma Spokane
WASHINGTON
Astoria
Vancouver
Portland
Salem
Columbia R.
Blue Mts.
Eugene
OREGON

NORTH
DAKOTA
Bismarck
Fargo

Missouri R.
Great Falls
Helena
MONTANA
Billings
Yellowstone R.

SOUTH
DAKOTA
Pierre
Missouri R.
Sioux
Falls

Boise
IDAHO
Snake R.
Pocatello

Bitterroot Range

Lemhi Rge.
Wind River Rge.
Big Horn Mts.
WYOMING
Casper
Black
Hills

Reno
Sacramento
Oakland
Carson City
Humboldt R.
NEVADA

Great
Salt Lake
Desert
Great Salt
Lake
Salt Lake
City
Uinta Mts.
UTAH

N. Platte R.
Cheyenne
NEBRASKA
Lincoln

S. Platte R.
Platte R.

San
Francisco
Fresno
CENTRAL VALLEY
SIERRA NEVADA
Death
Valley

Grand Junction
Denver
COLORADO

Arkansas R.
KANSAS
Wichita

CALIF.

Las
Vegas
Colorado R.
San Juan Mts.
Sangre de Cristo Ra.

Santa
Barbara
Bakersfield
Mojave Desert
San
Bernardino
Los Angeles
Long Beach
Lake
Mead
Grand
Canyon
Flagstaff
Painted
Desert
Colorado Plateau
Santa Fe
Albuquerque
Amarillo
OKLAHOMA
Oklahoma
City

San Diego
Colorado R.
Yuma
Gila R.
Phoenix
ARIZONA
NEW MEXICO

PACIFIC
OCEAN
Tucson
Llano
Estacado
(Staked Plains)
Dallas
Fort Worth

El Paso
Pecos R.
Colorado R.
Brazos R.

Rio Grande
MEXICO
TEXAS
Austin

San Antonio
Nueces R.
Corpus
Christi
Brownsville

RUSSIA
Bering Strait

BROOKS RANGE

Yukon R.
ALASKA
Fairbanks
ALASKA RANGE
Kuskokwim R.
Anchorage

CANADA

Juneau

Bering Sea

0   200 miles
0   300 km

Kodiak Is.
Gulf of Alaska

Aleutian Islands
PACIFIC OCEAN

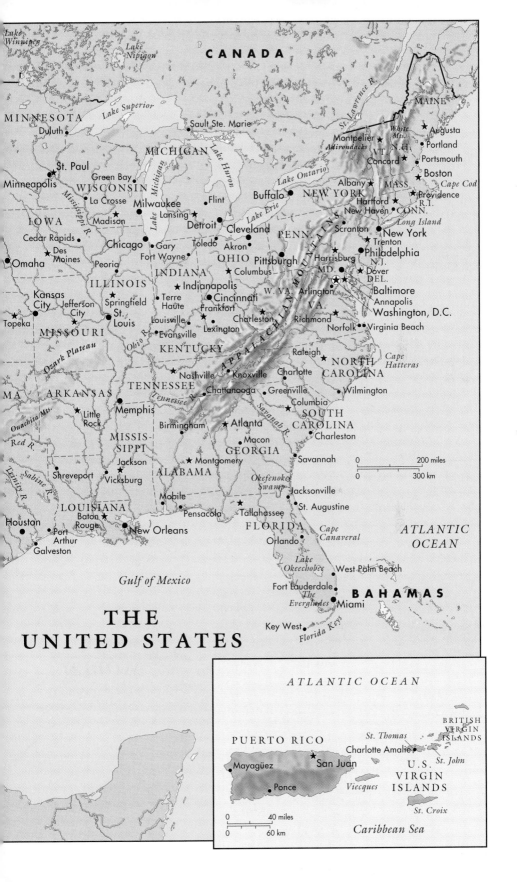

THE
UNITED STATES

CANADA

Lake Winnipeg

Lake Nipigon

Lake Superior

MINNESOTA
Duluth •

Sault Ste. Marie •

MICHIGAN

Lake Huron

MAINE

St. Lawrence R.

White Mts. ★ Augusta

Montpelier ★ Portland
Adirondacks • VT. N.H.
Concord ★ Portsmouth

St. Paul •
Minneapolis •

Green Bay •
WISCONSIN
La Crosse •   Milwaukee •
Madison •

Lake Michigan
Flint •
Lansing •
Detroit •

Cleveland •
Lake Ontario

Albany ★   MASS. • Boston
Cape Cod

NEW YORK
Hartford ★ • Providence
New Haven • CONN.   R.I.
Long Island
New York ★

Buffalo •
Lake Erie
Akron •

IOWA
Cedar Rapids •
Des
Moines •
Omaha •

Mississippi R.

Chicago • Gary •
Fort Wayne •

Peoria •

ILLINOIS

Toledo •
INDIANA
Indianapolis ★

PENN.
Pittsburgh •
Columbus ★
OHIO

Scranton •
Trenton ★
Philadelphia ★
N.J.
Harrisburg ★ Dover ★
MD. • DEL.

Kansas
City •   Jefferson
City ★ Springfield ★
St.
Louis •

Topeka ★

MISSOURI

Terre
Haute •
Frankfort ★

W. VA.
Cincinnati •
Louisville •   Lexington •
Charleston ★
Richmond ★
VA.

Arlington •
Baltimore
Annapolis ★
Washington, D.C.

Norfolk • • Virginia Beach

Ozark Plateau

Ohio R.
Evansville •
KENTUCKY

Raleigh ★
NORTH
CAROLINA
Cape Hatteras

MA.
ARKANSAS
Ouachita Mts.
Red R.

Little
Rock ★

Memphis •

Nashville ★
Chattanooga •
Tennessee R.

Knoxville •
Charlotte •

Greenville •
Columbia ★

Wilmington •

Sabine R.
Trinity R.

MISSIS-
SIPPI
Jackson ★
Vicksburg •

Birmingham •
ALABAMA

Atlanta ★
Macon •
GEORGIA

SOUTH
CAROLINA
Charleston •

0 ____ 200 miles
0 ____ 300 km

Shreveport •

LOUISIANA
Baton ★
Rouge
New Orleans •

Mobile •
Pensacola •
Montgomery ★

Tallahassee ★
Okefenokee Swamp

Savannah •

Jacksonville •
St. Augustine •

Houston •
Port
Arthur •
Galveston •

Gulf of Mexico

FLORIDA
Orlando •
Cape Canaveral

ATLANTIC
OCEAN

Lake Okeechobee
West Palm Beach •
Fort Lauderdale •
The Everglades
Miami •

BAHAMAS

Key West •
Florida Keys

ATLANTIC OCEAN

BRITISH
VIRGIN
ISLANDS

PUERTO RICO
St. Thomas •
Charlotte Amalie •
St. John •

Mayagüez •
San Juan ★
U.S.
VIRGIN
ISLANDS

Ponce •
Vieccues

St. Croix •

0 ____ 40 miles
0 ____ 60 km

Caribbean Sea

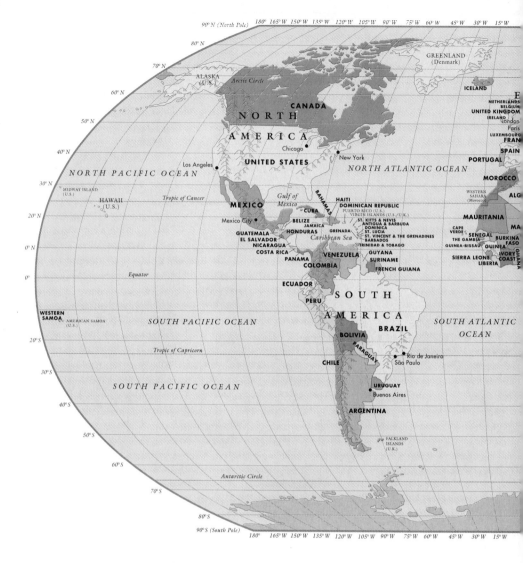

THE WORLD

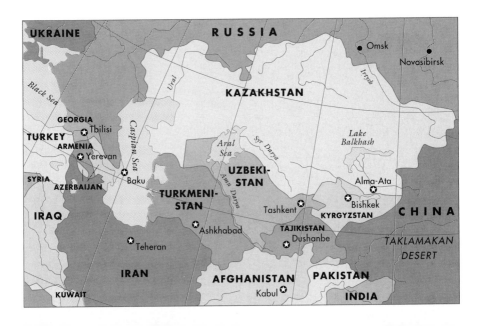